THE ARDENNES

The Official History of
The Battle Of The Bulge

by Hugh M. Cole

Red and Black Publishers, St Petersburg, Florida

Originally published by Office Of The Chief Of Military History, Department Of The
Army, Washington, D.C., 1965

Library of Congress Cataloging-in-Publication Data

Cole, Hugh M. (Hugh Marshall)
  The Ardennes : the official history of the Battle of the Bulge / by Hugh M. Cole.
    p. cm.
  "Originally published by Office of the Chief of Military History, Department of the
Army, Washington, D.C., 1965"--T.p. verso.
  ISBN 978-1-61001-015-3
1. Ardennes, Battle of the, 1944-1945. 2. World War, 1939-1945--Campaigns--
Belgium. 3. World War, 1939-1945--Campaigns--Luxembourg. I. Title.
  D756.5.A7C65 2011
  940.54'219348--dc22

                              2011008546

Red and Black Publishers, PO Box 7542, St Petersburg, Florida, 33734
Contact us at: info@RedandBlackPublishers.com
         Printed and manufactured in the United States of America

Contents

Chapter I. The Origins

On Saturday, 16 September 1944, the daily Fuehrer Conference convened in the Wolf's Lair, Hitler's East Prussian headquarters. No special word had come in from the battle fronts and the briefing soon ended, the conference disbanding to make way for a session between Hitler and members of what had become his household military staff. Wilhelm Keitel and Alfred Jodl were in this second conference. So was Heinz Guderian, who as acting chief of staff for OKL held direct military responsibility for the conduct of operations on the Russian front.

Herman Goering was absent. From this fact stems the limited knowledge available of the initial appearance of the idea which would be translated into historical fact as the Ardennes counteroffensive or Battle of the Bulge. Goering and the Luftwaffe were represented by Werner Kreipe, chief of staff for OKL. Perhaps Kreipe had been instructed by Goering to report fully on all that Hitler might say; perhaps Kreipe was a habitual diary-keeper. In any case he had consistently violated the Fuehrer ordinance that no notes of the daily conferences should be retained except the official transcript made by Hitler's own stenographic staff.

Trenchant, almost cryptic, Kreipe's notes outline the scene. Jodl, representing OKW and thus the headquarters responsible for managing the war on the Western Front, began the briefing. In a quiet voice and with the usual adroit use of phrases designed to lessen the impact of information which the Fuehrer might find distasteful, Jodl reviewed the relative strength of the opposing forces. The Western Allies possessed 96 divisions at or near the front; these were faced by 55 German divisions. An estimated 10 Allied divisions were en route from the United Kingdom to the battle zone. Allied airborne units still remained in England (some of these would make a dramatic appearance the very next day at Arnhem and Nijmegen). Jodl added a few words about shortages on the German side, shortages in tanks, heavy weapons, and ammunition. This was a persistent and unpopular topic; Jodl must have slid quickly to the next item—a report on the German forces withdrawing from southern and southwestern France.

Suddenly Hitler cut Jodl short. There ensued a few minutes of strained silence. Then Hitler spoke, his words recalled as faithfully as may be by the listening OKL chief of staff. "I have just made a momentous decision. I shall go over to the counterattack, that is to say"—and he pointed to the map unrolled on the desk before him—"here, out of the Ardennes, with the objective—Antwerp." While his audience sat in stunned silence, the Fuehrer began to outline his plan.

Historical hindsight may give the impression that only a leader finally bereft of sanity could, in mid-September of 1944, believe Germany physically capable of delivering one more powerful and telling blow. Politically the Third Reich stood deserted and friendless. Fascist Italy and the once powerful Axis were finished. Japan had politely suggested that Germany should start peace negotiations with the Soviets. In southern Europe, as the month of August closed, the Rumanians and Bulgarians had hastened to switch sides and join the victorious Russians. Finland had broken with Germany on 2 September. Hungary and the ephemeral Croat "state" continued in dubious battle beside Germany, held in place by German divisions in the line and German garrisons in their respective capitals. But the twenty nominal Hungarian divisions and an equivalent number of Croatian brigades were in effect canceled by the two Rumanian armies which had joined the Russians.

The defection of Rumanian, Bulgarian, and Finnish forces was far less important than the terrific losses suffered by the German armies themselves in the summer of 1944. On the Eastern and Western Fronts the combined German losses during June, July, and August had totaled at least 1,200,000 dead, wounded, and missing. The rapid Allied advances in the west had cooped up an additional 230,000 troops in positions from which they would emerge only to surrender. Losses in matériel were in keeping with those in fighting manpower.

Room for maneuver had been whittled away at a fantastically rapid rate. On the Eastern Front the Soviet summer offensive had carried to the borders of East Prussia, across the Vistula at a number of points, and up to the northern Carpathians. Only a small slice of Rumania was left to German troops. By mid-September the German occupation forces in southern Greece and the Greek islands (except Crete) already were withdrawing as the German grasp on the Balkans weakened.

On the Western Front the Americans had, in the second week of September, put troops on the soil of the Third Reich, in the Aachen sector, while the British had entered Holland. The German armies in the west faced a containing Allied front reaching from the Swiss border to the North Sea. On 14 September the newly appointed German commander in the west, Generalfeldmarschall Gerd von Rundstedt, acknowledged that the "Battle for the West Wall" had begun.

On the Italian front Generalfeldmarschall Albert Kesselring's two armies retained position astride the Apennines and, from the Gothic Line, defended northern Italy. Here, of all the active fronts, the German forces faced the enemy on something like equal terms—except in the air. Nonetheless the Allies were dangerously close to the southern entrances to the Po Valley.

In the far north the defection of Finland had introduced a bizarre operational situation. In northern Finland and on the Murmansk front nine German divisions held what earlier had been the left wing of the 700-mile Finno-German front. Now the Finns no longer were allies, but neither were they ready to turn their arms against Generaloberst Dr. Lothar Rendulic and his nine German divisions. The Soviets likewise showed no great interest in conducting a full-scale campaign in the subarctic. With Finland out of the war, however, the German troops had no worthwhile mission remaining except to stand guard over the Petsamo nickel mines. Only a month after Mannerheim took Finland out of the war, Hitler would order the evacuation of that country and of northern Norway.

Political and military reverses so severe as those sustained by the Third Reich in the summer of 1944 necessarily implied severe economic losses to a state and a war machine fed and grown strong on the proceeds of conquest. Rumanian oil, Finnish and Norwegian nickel, copper, and molybdenum, Swedish high-grade iron ore, Russian manganese, French bauxite, Yugoslavian copper, and Spanish mercury were either lost to the enemy or denied by the neutrals who saw the tide of war turning against a once powerful customer.

Hitler's Perspective September 1944

In retrospect, the German position after the summer reverses of 1944 seemed indeed hopeless and the only rational release a quick peace on the best possible terms. But the contemporary scene as viewed from Hitler's headquarters in September 1944, while hardly roseate, even to the Fuehrer, was not an unrelieved picture of despair and gloom. In the west what had been an Allied advance of astounding speed had decelerated as rapidly, the long Allied supply lines, reaching clear back to the English Channel and the Côte d'Azur, acting as a tether which could be stretched only so far. The famous West Wall fortifications (almost dismantled in the years since 1940) had not yet been heavily engaged by the attacker, while to the rear lay the great moat which historically had separated the German people from their enemies—the Rhine. On the Eastern Front the seasonal surge of battle was beginning to ebb, the Soviet summer offensive seemed to have run its course, and despite continuing battle on the flanks the center had relapsed into an uneasy calm.

Even the overwhelming superiority which the Western Allies possessed in the air had failed thus far to bring the Third Reich groveling to its knees as so many proponents of the air arm had predicted. In September the British and Americans could mount a daily bomber attack of over 5,000 planes, but the German will to resist and the means of resistance, so far as then could be measured, remained quite sufficient for a continuation of the war. Great, gaping wounds, where the Allied bombers had struck, disfigured most of the larger German cities west of the Elbe, but German discipline and a reasonably efficient warning and shelter system had reduced the daily loss of life to what the German people themselves would reckon as "acceptable." If anything, the lesson of London was being repeated, the noncombatant will to resist hardening under the continuous blows from the air and forged still harder by the Allied announcements of an unconditional surrender policy.

The material means available to the armed forces of the Third Reich appeared relatively unaffected by the ceaseless hammering from the air. It is true that the German war economy was not geared to meet a long-drawn war of attrition. But Reich Minister Albert Speer and his cohorts had been given over two years to rationalize, reorganize, disperse, and expand the German economy before the intense Allied air efforts of 1944. So successful was Speer's program and so industrious were the labors of the home front that the race between Allied destruction and German construction (or reconstruction) was being run neck and neck in the third quarter of 1944, the period, that is, during which Hitler instituted the far-reaching military plans eventuating in the Ardennes counteroffensive.

The ball-bearing and aircraft industries, major Allied air targets during the first half of 1944, had taken heavy punishment but had come back with amazing speed. By September bearing production was very nearly what it had been just before the dubious honor of nomination as top-priority target for the Allied bombing effort. The production of single-engine fighters had risen from 1,016 in February to a high point of 3,031 such aircraft in September. The Allied strategic attack leveled at the synthetic oil industry, however, showed more immediate results, as reflected in the charts which Speer put before Hitler. For aviation gasoline, motor gasoline, and diesel oil, the production curve dipped sharply downward and lingered far below monthly consumption figures despite the radical drop in fuel consumption in the summer of 1944. Ammunition production likewise had declined markedly under the air campaign against the synthetic oil industry, in this case the synthetic nitrogen procedures. In September the German armed forces were firing some 70,000 tons of explosives, while production amounted to only half that figure. Shells and casings were still unaffected except for special items which required the ferroalloys hitherto procured from the Soviet Union, France, and the Balkans.

Although in the later summer of 1944 the Allied air forces turned their bombs against German armored vehicle production (an appetizing target because of the limited number of final assembly plants), an average of 1,500 tanks and assault guns were being shipped to the battle front every thirty days. During the first ten months of 1944 the Army Ordnance Directorate accepted 45,917 trucks, but truck losses during the same period numbered 117,719. The German automotive industry had pushed the production of trucks up to an average of 9,000 per month, but in September production began to drop off, a not too important recession in view of the looming motor fuel crisis. The German railway system had been under sporadic air attacks for years but was still viable. Troops could be shuttled from one fighting front to another with only very moderate and occasional delays; raw materials and finished military goods had little waste time in rail transport. In mid-August the weekly car loadings by the Reichsbahn hit a top figure of 899,091 cars.

In September Hitler had no reason to doubt, if he bothered to contemplate the transport needed for a great counteroffensive, that the rich and flexible German railroad and canal complex would prove sufficient to the task ahead and could successfully resist even a coordinated and systematic air attack—as yet, of course, untried.

In German war production the third quarter of 1944 witnessed an interesting conjuncture, one readily susceptible to misinterpretation by Hitler and Speer or by Allied airmen and intelligence. On the one hand German production was, with the major exceptions of the oil and aircraft industries, at the peak output of the war; on the other hand the Allied air effort against the German means of war making was approaching a peak in terms of tons of bombs and the number of planes which could be launched against the Third Reich. But without the means of predicting what damage the Allied air effort could and would inflict if extrapolated three or six months into the future, and certainly without any advisers willing so to predict, Hitler might reason that German production and transport, if wisely husbanded and rigidly controlled, could support a major attack before the close of 1944. Indeed, only a fortnight prior to the briefing of 16 September Minister Speer had assured Hitler that German war stocks could be expected to last through 1945. Similarly, in the headquarters of the Western Allies it was easy and natural to assume the thousands of tons of bombs dropped on Germany must inevitably have weakened the vital sections of the German war economy to a point where collapse was imminent and likely to come before the end of 1944.

Hitler's optimism and miscalculation, then, resulted in the belief that Germany had the material means to launch and maintain a great counteroffensive, a belief nurtured by many of his trusted aides. Conversely, the miscalculation of the Western Allies as to the destruction wrought by their bombers contributed greatly to the pervasive optimism which would make it difficult, if not impossible, for Allied commanders and intelligence agencies to believe or perceive that Germany still retained the material muscle for a mighty blow.

Assuming that the Third Reich possessed the material means for a quick transition from the defensive to the offensive, could Hitler and his entourage rely on the morale of the German nation and its fighting forces in this sixth year of the war? The five years which had elapsed since the invasion of Poland had taken heavy toll of the best physical specimens of the Reich. The irreplaceable loss in military manpower (the dead, missing, those demobilized because of disability or because of extreme family hardship) amounted to 3,266,686 men and 92,811 officers as of 1 September 1944. Even without an accurate measure of the cumulative losses suffered by the civilian population, or of the dwellings destroyed, it is evident that the German home front was suffering directly and heavily from enemy action, despite the fact that the Americans and British were unable to get together on an air campaign designed to destroy the will of the German nation. Treason (as the Nazis saw it) had reared its ugly head in the abortive Putsch of July 1944, and the skeins of this plot against the person of the Fuehrer still were unraveling in the torture chambers of the Gestapo.

Had the Nazi Reich reached a point in its career like that which German history recorded in the collapse of the German Empire during the last months of the 1914-1918 struggle? Hitler, always prompt to parade his personal experiences as a Frontsoldat in the Great War and to quote this period of his life as testimony refuting opinions offered by his generals, was keenly aware of the moral disintegration of the German people and the armies in 1918. Nazi propaganda had made the "stab in the back" (the theory that Germany had not been defeated in 1918 on the battlefield but had collapsed as a result of treason and weakness on the home front) an article of German faith, with the Fuehrer its leading proponent. Whatever soul-searching Hitler may have experienced privately as a result of the attempt on his life and the precipitate retreats of his armies, there is no outward evidence that he saw in these events any kinship to those of 1918.

He had great faith in the German people and in their devotion to himself as Leader, a faith both mystic and cynical. The noise of street demonstrations directed against himself or his regime had not once, during the years of war, assailed his ears. German troops had won great victories in the past, why should they not triumph again? The great defeats had been, so Hitler's intuition told him, the fruit of treason among high officers or, at the least, the result of insufficient devotion to National Socialism in the hearts and minds of the defeated commanders and the once powerful General Staff. The assassination attempt, as seen through Hitler's own eyes, was proof positive that the suspicions which he had long entertained vis-à-vis the Army General Staff were correct. Now, he believed, this malignant growth could be cut away; exposure showed that it had no deep roots and had not contaminated either the fighting troops or the rank and file of the German people.

Despite the heavy losses suffered by the Wehrmacht in the past five years, Hitler was certain that replacements could be found and new divisions created. His intuition told him that too many officers and men had gravitated into headquarters staffs, administrative and security services. He was enraged by the growing disparity in the troop lists between "ration strength" and "combat strength" and, as a military dictator, expected that the issuance of threatening orders and the appointment of the brutal Heinrich Himmler as chief of the Replacement Army would eventually reverse this trend. At the beginning of September Hitler was impatiently stamping the ground and waiting for the new battalions to spring forth. The months of July and August had produced eighteen new divisions, ten panzer brigades and nearly a hundred separate infantry battalions. Now twenty-five new divisions, about a thousand artillery pieces, and a score of general headquarters brigades of various types were demanded for delivery in October and November.

How had Germany solved the manpower problem? From a population of some eighty million, in the Greater Reich, the Wehrmacht carried a total of 10,165,303 officers and men on its rosters at the beginning of September 1944. What part of this total was paper strength is impossible to say; certainly the personnel systems in the German armed forces had not been able to keep an accurate accounting of the tremendous losses suffered in the summer of 1944. Nonetheless, this was the strength figuratively paraded before Hitler by his adjutants. The number of units in the Wehrmacht order of battle was impressive (despite such wholesale losses as the twenty-seven divisions engulfed during the Russian summer offensive against Army Group Center). The collective German ground forces at the beginning of September 1944 numbered 327 divisions and brigades, of which 31 divisions and 13 brigades were armored. Again it must be noted that many of these units no longer in truth had the combat strength of either division or brigade (some had only their headquarters staff), but again, in Hitler's eyes, this order of battle represented fighting units capable of employment. Such contradiction as came from the generals commanding the paper-thin formations, some of whom privately regarded the once formidable Wehrmacht as a "paper tiger," would be brushed angrily aside as evidence of incompetence, defeatism — or treason.

But the maintenance of this formidable array of divisions and brigades reflected the very real military potential of the Greater Reich, not yet fully exploited even at the end of five years of what had been called total war. As in 1915 the Germans had found that in a long conflict the hospitals provided a constant flow of replacements, and that this source could be utilized very effectively by the simple expedient of progressively lowering the physical standards required for front-line duty. In addition, each year brought a new class to the colors as German youth matured. This source could be further exploited by lowering the age limit at one end of the conscription spectrum while increasing it at the other. In 1944, for example, the age limit for "volunteers" for the ranks was dropped to sixteen years and party pressure applied conducive to volunteering. At the same time the older conscription classes were combed through and, in 1944, registration was carried back to include males born in 1884.

Another and extremely important manpower acquisition, made for the first time on any scale in the late summer of 1944, came from the Navy and Air Force. Neither of these establishments remained in any position, at this stage of the war, to justify the relatively large numbers still carried on their rosters. While it is true that transferring air force ground crews to rifle companies would not change the numerical strength of the armed forces by jot or tittle, such practice would produce new infantry or armored divisions bearing new and, in most cases, high numbers.

In spite of party propaganda that the Third Reich was full mobilized behind the Fuehrer and notwithstanding the constant and slavish mouthing of the phrase "total war," Germany had not in five years of struggle completely utilized its manpower — and equally important, womanpower—in prosecuting the war. Approximately four million public servants and individuals deferred from military service for other reasons constituted a reserve as yet hardly touched. And, despite claims to the contrary, no thorough or rational scheme had been adopted to comb all able-bodied men out of the factories and from the fields for service in uniform. In five years only a million German men and women had been mobilized for the labor force. Indeed, it may be concluded that the bulk of industrial and agrarian replacements for men drafted into the armed services was supplied by some seven million foreign workers and prisoners of war slaving for the conqueror.

Hitler hoped to lay his hands on those of his faithful followers who thus far had escaped the rigors of the soldier life by enfolding themselves in the uniform of the party functionary. The task of defining the nonessential and making the new order palatable was given to Reich Minister Joseph Goebbels, who on 24 August 1944 announced the new mobilization scheme: schools and theaters to be closed down, a 60-hour week to be introduced and holidays temporarily abolished, most types of publications to be suspended (with the notable exception of "standard political works," *Mein Kampf*, for one), small shops of many types to be closed, the staffs of governmental bureaus to be denuded, and similar belt tightening. By 1 September this drastic comb-out was in full swing and accompanied within the uniformed forces by measures designed to reduce the headquarters staffs and shake loose the "rear area swine," in the Fuehrer's contemptuous phrase.

This new flow of manpower would give Hitler the comforting illusion of combat strength, an illusion risen from his indulgence in what may be identified to the American reader as "the numbers racket." Dozens of German officers who at one time or another had reason to observe the Fuehrer at work have commented on his obsession with numbers and his implicit faith in statistics no matter how murky the sources from which they came or how misleading when translated into fact. So Hitler had insisted on the creation of new formations with new numbers attached thereto, rather than bringing back to full combat strength those units which had been bled white in battle. Thus the German order of battle distended in the autumn of 1944, bloated by new units while the strength of the German ground forces declined. In the same manner Hitler accepted the monthly production goals set for the armored vehicle producers by Speer's staff as being identical with the number of tanks and assault guns which in fact would reach the front lines. Bemused by numbers on paper and surrounded by a staff which had little or no combat experience and by now was perfectly housebroken—never introducing unpleasant questions as to what these numbers really meant—Hitler still saw himself as the Feldherr, with the men and the tanks and the guns required to wrest the initiative from the encircling enemy.

Chapter II. Planning The Counteroffensive

How the Plan Was Born

The plan for the Ardennes counteroffensive was born in the mind and will of Hitler the Feldherr. Its conception and growth from ovum are worthy of study by the historian and the student of the military art as a prime example of the role which may be played by the single man and the single mind in the conduct of modern war and the direction of an army numbered in the millions.

Such was the military, political, economic, and moral position of the Third Reich in the autumn of 1944 that a leader who lacked all of the facts and who by nature clung to a mystic confidence in his star might rationally conclude that defeat could be postponed and perhaps even avoided by some decisive stroke. To this configuration of circumstances must be added Hitler's implicit faith in his own military genius, a faith to all appearance unshaken by defeat and treason, a faith that accepted the possibility, even the probability, that the course of conflict might be reversed by a military stroke of genius.

There was, after all, a prototype in German history which showed how the genius and the will of the Feldherr might wrest victory from certain defeat. Behind the desk in Hitler's study hung a portrait of Frederick the Great. This man, of all the great military leaders in world history, was Hitler's ideal. The axioms given by Frederick to his generals were on the tip of Hitler's tongue, ever ready to refute the pessimist or generalize away a sticky fact. When his generals protested the inability of soldier flesh and blood to meet further demands, Hitler simply referred to the harsh demands made of his grenadiers by Frederick. When the cruelties of the military punitive code were increased to the point that even the stomachs of Prussian officers rebelled, Hitler paraded the brutal code of Frederick's army before them. Even the oath taken by SS officer candidates was based on the Frederician oath to the flag.

An omnivorous reader of military history, Hitler was fond of relating episodes therefrom as evidence of his catholic military knowledge or as footnotes proving the soundness of a decision. In a very human way he selected those historical examples which seemed to support his own views. Napoleon, before the invasion of Russia, had forbidden any reference to the ill-fated campaign of Charles XII of Sweden because "the circumstances were altered." Hitler in turn had brushed aside the fate of both these predecessors, in planning his Russian campaign, because they had lacked tanks and planes. In 1944, however, Hitler's mind turned to his example, Frederick II, and found encouragement and support. Frederick, at the commencement of the Seven Years War, had faced superior forces converging on his kingdom from all points of the compass. At Rossbach and Leuthen he had taken great risk but had defeated armies twice the strength of his own. By defeating his enemies in detail, Frederick had been able to hang on until the great alliance formed against Prussia had split as the result of an unpredictable historical accident.

Three things seemed crystal clear to Hitler as explanation for Frederick's final victory over his great enemies: victory on the battlefield, and not defeat, was the necessary preliminary to successful diplomatic negotiations and a peace settlement; the enemy coalition had failed to present a solid front when single members had suffered defeat; finally, Prussia had held on until, as Hitler paraphrased Frederick's own words, "one of [the] damned enemies gets too tired to fight any more." If Hitler needed moral support in his decision to prepare for the counteroffensive at a time when Germany still was reeling from enemy blows, it is very probable that he found this in the experience and ultimate triumph of Frederick called the Great.

Although the first announcement of the projected counteroffensive in the Ardennes was made by Hitler in the meeting on 16 September, the idea had been forming for some weeks in the Fuehrer's mind. Many of the details in this development can never be known. The initial thought processes were buried with Hitler; his closest associates soon followed him to the grave, leaving only the barest information. The general outlines of the manner in which the plan took form can be discerned, however, of course with a gap here and there and a necessary slurring over exact dates.

The first and very faint glimmerings of the idea that a counteroffensive must be launched in the west are found in a long tirade made by Hitler before Generaloberst Alfred Jodl and a few other officers on 31 July 1944. At this moment Hitler's eyes are fixed on the Western Front where the Allies, held fast for several weeks in the Normandy hedgerows, have finally broken through the containing German forces in the neighborhood of Avranches. Still physically shaken by the bomb blast which so nearly had cut short his career, the Fuehrer raves and rambles, boasts, threatens, and complains. As he meanders through the "conference," really a solo performance, one idea reappears again and again: the final decision must come in the west and if necessary the other fronts must suffer so that a concentrated, major effort can be made there. No definite plans can be made as yet, says Hitler, but he himself will accept the responsibility for planning and for command; the latter he will exercise from a headquarters someplace in the Black Forest or the Vosges. To guarantee secrecy, nobody will be allowed to inform the Commander in Chief West or his staff of these far-reaching plans; the WFSt, that is, Jodl, must form a small operational staff to aid the Fuehrer by furnishing any needed data.

Hitler's arrogation to himself of all command and decision vis-à-vis some major and concerted effort in the west was no more than an embittered restatement, with the assassination attempt in mind, of a fact which had been stuffed down the throats of the General Staff and the famous field commanders since the first gross defeat in Russia and had been underlined in blood by the executions following the Putsch of 20 July. The decision to give priority to the Western Front, if one can take Hitler at his own word and waive a possible emotional reaction to the sudden Allied plunge through the German line at the base of the Cotentin peninsula, is something new and worthy of notice.

The strategic and operational problem posed by a war in which Germany had to fight an enemy in the east while at the same time opposing an enemy in the west was at least as old as the unification of Germany. The problem of a war on two fronts had been analyzed and solutions had been proposed by the great German military thinkers, among these Moltke the Elder, Schlieffen, and Ludendorff, whose written works, so Hitler boasted, were more familiar to him than to those of his entourage who wore the red stripe of the General Staff. Moltke and Schlieffen, traveling by the theoretical route, had arrived at the conclusion that Germany lacked the strength to conduct successful offensive operations simultaneously in the east and west. Ludendorff (Hitler's quondam colleague in the comic opera Beer Hall Putsch) had seen this theory put to the test and proven in the 1914-1918 war. Hitler had been forced to learn the same lesson the hard way in the summer of 1944.

A fanatical believer in the Clausewitzian doctrine of the offensive as the purest and only decisive form of war, Hitler only had to decide whether his projected counteroffensive should be made in the east or the west. In contrast to the situation that had existed in the German High Command of World War I, there was no sharp cleavage between "Easterners" and "Westerners" with the two groups struggling to gain control of the Army High Command and so dictate a favored strategy. It is true that OKH (personified at this moment by Guderian) had direct responsibility for the war on the Eastern Front and quite naturally believed that victory or defeat would be decided there. On the other hand, OKW, with its chiefs Keitel and Jodl close to the seat of power, saw the Western Front as the paramount theater of operations. Again, this was a natural result of the direct responsibility assigned this headquarters for the conduct of all operations outside of the Eastern Front. Hitler, however, had long since ceased to be influenced by his generals save in very minor matters. Nor is there any indication that Keitel or Jodl exercised any influence in turning the Fuehrer's attention to the west.

There is no simple or single explanation for Hitler's choice of the Western Front as the scene of the great German counterstroke. The problem was complex; so were Hitler's mental processes. Some part of his reasoning breaks through in his conferences, speeches, and orders, but much is left to be inferred.

As early as 1939 Hitler had gone on record as to the absolute necessity of protecting the Ruhr industrial area, the heart of the entire war-making machine. In November 1943, on the heels of Eastern Front reverses and before the Western Allies had set foot in strength across the Channel, Hitler repeated his fears for the Ruhr, "but now while the danger in the East remained it was outweighed by the threat from the West where enemy success would strike immediately at the heart of the German war economy." Even after the disastrous impact of the 1944 Soviet summer offensive he clung to the belief that the Ruhr factories were more important to Germany than the loss of territory in the east. He seems to have felt that the war production in Silesia was far out of Soviet reach: in any case Silesia produced less than the Ruhr. Then too, in the summer and early autumn of 1944 the Allied air attacks against the Ruhr had failed to deliver any succession of knockout blows, nor was the very real vulnerability of this area yet apparent.

Politically, if Hitler hoped to lead from strength and parlay a military victory into a diplomatic coup, the monolithic USSR was a less susceptible object than the coalition of powers in the west. Whereas Nazi propagandists breathed hatred of the Soviet, the tone toward England and the United States more often was that of contempt and derision, as befitted the "decadent democracies." Hitler seems to have partaken of this view, and in any case he believed that the Allies might easily split asunder if one of them was jolted hard enough. The inability of the western leaders to hold their people together in the face of defeat was an oft-expressed and cardinal axiom of the German Fuehrer, despite the example of the United Kingdom to the contrary.

From one point of view the decision for the west was the result of progressive elimination as to the other fronts. In no way could victory in Italy or Finland change the course of the war. Russia likewise offered no hope for any decisive victory with the forces which Germany might expect to gather in 1944. The campaigns in the east had finally convinced Hitler, or so it would appear, that the vast distances in the east and the seemingly inexhaustible flow of Soviet divisions created a military problem whose solution lay beyond the capabilities of the Third Reich as long as the latter was involved in a multifront war. To put it another way, what Germany now needed was a quick victory capable of bearing immediate diplomatic fruit. Between 22 June 1941 and 1 November 1942 the German armies in the USSR had swept up 5,150,000 prisoners of war (setting aside the Russians killed or severely wounded) but still had failed to bore in deep enough to deliver a paralyzing blow. A quick and decisive success in the second half of 1944 against 555 Soviet units of division size was out of the question, even though Hitler would rave about the "Russian bluff" and deride the estimates prepared by his Intelligence, Fremde Heere Ost.

Still other factors were involved in Hitler's decision. For one thing the Allied breakout in Normandy was a more pressing danger to the Third Reich than the Soviet advance in the east. Intuitively, perhaps, Hitler followed Schlieffen in viewing an enemy on the Rhine as more dangerous than an enemy in East Prussia. If this was Hitler's view, then the Allied dash across France in the weeks following would give all the verification required. Whether at this particular time Hitler saw the German West Wall as the best available springboard for a counteroffensive is uncertain. But it is quite clear that the possession of a seemingly solid base for such an operation figured largely in the ensuing development of a Western Front attack.

After the announcement of the west as the crucial front, in the 31 July conference, Hitler seemingly turned his attention, plus such reserves as were available, to the east. Perhaps this was only a passing aberration, perhaps Hitler had been moved by choler in July and now was in the grip of indecision. Events on both fronts, however, were moving so rapidly that a final decision would have to be made. The death of Generalfeldmarschall Guenther von Kluge, Commander in Chief West, seems to have triggered the next step toward irrevocable commitment. Coincident with the appointment of Model to replace the suicide, Hitler met with a few of his immediate staff on 19 August to consider the situation in France. During this conference he instructed Walter Buhle, chief of the Army Staff at OKW, and Speer, the minister in charge of military production and distribution, to prepare large allotments of men and materiel for shipment to the Western Front. At the same time Hitler informed the conferees that he proposed to take the initiative at the beginning of November when the Allied air forces would be unable to fly. By 19 August, it would appear, Hitler had made up his mind: an attack would be made, it would be made on the Western Front, and the target date would be early November.

The remaining days of August were a nightmare for the German divisions in the west and for the German field commanders. Shattered into bits and pieces by the weight of Allied guns and armor, hunted and hounded along the roads by the unopposed Allied air forces, captured and killed in droves, the German forces in France were thoroughly beaten. All requests for permission to withdraw to more defensible positions were rejected in peremptory fashion by Hitler's headquarters, with the cold rejoinder "stand and hold" or "fight to the last man." In most cases these orders were read on the run by the retreating divisions.

At the beginning of September Generalfeldmarschall Walter Model was "put in the big picture" by the Fuehrer. Hitler gave as his "intention" for the future conduct of operations that the retreating German armies must hold forward of the West Wall, thus allowing time needed to repair these defenses. In general the holding position indicated by Hitler ran from the Dutch coast, through northern Belgium, along the forward edge of the West Wall in the sector between Aachen and the Moselle River, then via the western borders of Alsace and Lorraine to some indefinite connection with the Swiss frontier. Here, for the first time on the Western Front, Hitler relaxed his seemingly pigheaded views on the unyielding defense and permitted, even enjoined, a withdrawal. This permission, however, was given for a very definite purpose: to permit the reorganization of Germany's defense at or forward of the West Wall, the outer limit of Greater Germany.

Despite the debacle in France, Hitler professed himself as unworried and even sanguine. On the first day of September, Rundstedt was recalled to the position of

Commander in Chief West which he had been forced to relinquish at the end of June under Hitler's snide solicitude for his "health." The new commander was told that the enemy in the west would shortly be brought to a halt by logistic failures (in this forecast the Fuehrer's intuition served him well) and that the giant steps being taken toward Germany were the work of isolated "armored spearheads" which had outrun the main Allied forces and now could be snipped off by local counterattacks, whereupon the front would stabilize. Since the U. S. Third Army under Lt. Gen. George S. Patton, Jr., was advancing with its right flank open (contact with the U.S. Seventh Army driving north from the Mediterranean had not as yet been made), Hitler ordered Rundstedt to counterattack against this exposed flank and cut the advanced American armor by seizing Reims. For this unenviable task the Fifth Panzer Army, at the moment little more than an army headquarters and a few army troops, would be beefed up and handed over to the new commander in chief.

The thrust to Reims was not intended as the grand-scale effort to regain the initiative which by this time was fully rooted in Hitler's mind. The Fifth Panzer Army was to counterattack, that is, to be committed with limited forces for the attainment of a limited object. The scheme visualized for November, no matter how vague its shape in the first week of September, was that of a counteroffensive, or a major commitment of men and matériel designed to wrest the initiative from the enemy in pursuance of a major strategic victory.

The counterattack was made, but not as planned and not toward Reims. The base for the proposed operation, west of the Moselle River, was lost to the Americans before the attack could be launched. A watered-down variant on the east side of the Moselle was set in motion on 18 September, with Luneville as the first objective; it degenerated into a series of small, piecemeal attacks of only momentary significance. This, the single major effort to win time and space by counterattack and so give breathing space to the Reich and footing for a counteroffensive, must be written a complete failure. Nonetheless, by the second week of September there were encouraging evidences all along the Western Front that the battered German troops were beginning to get a toehold here and there, and that the enemy who had run so fast and so far was not holding the pace. Except for a handful of bunkers and pillboxes the battle front was in process of stabilizing forward of the West Wall. Meanwhile German efforts to reactivate and rearm these fortifications were in full swing.

Despite the somber and often despairing reports prepared by Model and his successor, Rundstedt, during late August and early September, Hitler and his intimate staff in the East Prussian headquarters continued to give thought to a decisive attack in the west. About 6 September, Jodl gave the Fuehrer an evaluation of the situation inherited by Rundstedt. The task at hand was to withdraw as many troops from the line as possible, refit and re-form units. On the scale required, this work could not be completed before the first day of November. Since he was probably listening to a clearer phrasing of his own cloudy concept, Hitler agreed, but with the proviso that the battle front must be kept as far to the west as possible. The reason, expressed apparently for the first time, was that the Allied air effort had to be kept at a distance from the Rhine bridges or the consequences might be disastrous. Did Hitler fear that fighter-bombers operating from fields in France or Belgium might leave the Rhine crossing complex stricken and incapable of supporting the line of communications to the armies then on the left bank of the Rhine? Or did he foresee that the Rhine bridges would be systematically hammered in an effort to strangle the German bid for the initiative when the day for the counteroffensive came?

As a target date, 1 November now seemed firm. Hitler had tossed it out in an off-the-cuff gesture; Jodl had evaluated it in terms of the military situation as seen in the remote Wolf's Lair; and in his first report after assuming command, Rundstedt unwittingly added his blessing by estimating that the West Wall defenses would be refurbished and manned sometime around 20 October. The Commander in Chief West, be it noted, was not yet privy to any attack plans except those for the Fifth Panzer Army.

Since Hitler was convinced that his western armies would hold before or at the West Wall position, and by intuition or self-hypnosis he held to this conviction, the next step was to amass the forces needed to issue offensively from the West Wall base of operations. During July and August eighteen new divisions had been organized, fifteen of which were sent to the Eastern Front, one to Norway, and only two to the Western Front. A further Hitler order on 2 September commanded the creation of an "operational reserve" numbering twenty-five new divisions. This order lay behind the comb-out program entrusted to Goebbels and definitely was in preparation for a western counteroffensive. Early in August the Western Front had been given priority on tanks coming off the assembly line; this now was made a permanent proviso and extended to cover all new artillery and assault gun production.

Further additions to the contemplated reserve would have to come from other theaters of war. On 4 September OKW ordered a general movement of artillery units in the Balkans back to the Western Front. The southeastern theater now was bereft of much of its early significance and the German forces therein stood to lose most of their heavy equipment in the event of a Soviet drive into the Balkans. The northern theater likewise was a potential source of reinforcements, particularly following the defection of Finland in early September and the collapse of a homogeneous front. These "side shows" could be levied upon for the western counteroffensive, and even the sore-beset German armies in the east, or so Hitler reasoned, could contribute armored divisions to the west. But in the main, the plan still evolving within the closed confines of the Wolf's Lair turned on the withdrawal and rehabilitation of units which had taken part in the battle for France. As a first step the SS panzer divisions in the west were ordered out of the line (13 September) and turned over to a new army headquarters, that of the Sixth Panzer Army.

Having nominated a headquarters to control the reconstitution of units specifically named for participation in an attack to be made in the west, the logical next step in development of the plan came in Hitler's announcement on 16 September: the attack would be delivered in the Ardennes and Antwerp would be the objective.

Why the Ardennes? To answer this question in a simple and direct manner is merely to say that the Ardennes would be the scene of a great winter battle because the Fuehrer had placed his finger on a map and made a pronouncement. This simplified version was agreed to in the months after the war by all of those major German military figures in Hitler's entourage who survived the last battles and the final Gotterdammerung purges. It is possible, however, that Hitler had discussed the operational concept of a counteroffensive through the Ardennes with Jodl—and before the 16 September edict. The relationship between these two men has bearing on the entire "prehistory" of the Ardennes campaign. It is analyzed by the headquarters diary-keeper and historian, Maj. Percy E. Schramm, as follows:

"The function of Genobst Jodl in the Fuehrer's headquarters consisted of preparing—on the general staff level—the decisions the Fuehrer made in his capacity of C-in-C of the Wehrmacht. Jodl also was responsible for their execution. But these were not his only duties. Whenever the Fuehrer conceived a new military plan it was Jodl with whom the idea was discussed and closely examined. It was again Jodl who obtained the information necessary to transmute a vague idea into a workable plan. It was also he who raised objections and suggestions which had been voiced by the immediately subordinate commands. These facts were so little known to the outside world that the public scarcely knew Jodl, and that within the Wehrmacht—even among those in leading positions—he was mostly considered only as an executive tool, by some people even as too willing a tool. The view was widely held that the Fuehrer did not accept any opinion other than his own. It was not recognized that, although Hitler in the final analysis might only follow his own trend of thought, he acquired the inner assurance necessary for his actions by constantly discussing his intentions within the confines of his inner circle. For this reason, the Chief of the Wehrmacht Operations Staff (Jodl) was an extremely important figure in all strategic decisions. In his relationship to the Fuehrer, his functions were not merely executive, but involved a very complex process of giving and taking, altering and retrenching, warning and stimulating."

The evidence is clear that Jodl and a few of his juniors from the Wehrmacht Operations Staff did examine the Ardennes concept very closely in the period from 25 September, when Hitler gave the first order to start detailed planning, to 11 October, when Jodl submitted the initial operations plan. Other but less certain evidence indicates that those present in the select conference on 16 September were taken by surprise when Hitler made his announcement. Jodl definitely ascribes the selection of the Ardennes to Hitler and Hitler alone, but at the time Jodl expressed this view he was about to be tried before an international tribunal on the charge of preparing aggressive war. Even so, the "argument from silence"—the fact that there is no evidence of other thought on the Ardennes as the point of concentration prior to Hitler's statement on 16 September—has some validity.

The most impressive argument for ascribing sole authorship of the Ardennes idea to Hitler is found in the simple fact that every major military decision in the German High Command for months past had been made by the Fuehrer, and that these Hitler decisions were made in detail, never in principle alone.

The major reasons for Hitler's selection of the Ardennes were stated by himself, although never in a single tabulation on a single occasion nor with any ordering of importance:

The enemy front in the Ardennes sector was very thinly manned.

A blow here would strike the seam between the British and Americans and lead to political as well as military disharmony between the Allies. Furthermore an entrance along this seam would isolate the British 21 Army Group and allow the encirclement and destruction of the British and Canadians before the American leadership (particularly the political leadership) could react.

The distance from the jump-off line to a solid strategic objective (Antwerp) was not too great and could be covered quickly, even in bad weather.

The configuration of the Ardennes area was such that the ground for maneuver was limited and so would require the use of relatively few divisions. The terrain to the east of the breakthrough sector selected was very heavily wooded and offered cover against Allied air observation and attack during the build-up for the assault.

An attack to regain the initiative in this particular area would erase the enemy ground threat to the Ruhr.

Although Hitler never referred directly to the lightning thrust made in 1940 through the Ardennes as being in any sense a prototype for the operation in the same area four and a half years later, there is indication of a more than casual connection between the two campaigns in Hitler's own thinking. For example, during the 16 September expose he set the attainment of "another Dunkirk" as his goal. Then, as detailed planning began, Hitler turned again and again to make operational proposals which had more than chance similarity to those he had made before the 1940 offensive. When, in September 1939, Hitler had announced his intention to attack in the west, the top-ranking officers of the German armed forces had to a man shown their disfavor for this daring concept. Despite this opposition Hitler had gone ahead and personally selected the general area for the initial penetration, although perhaps with considerable stimulation from Generalfeldmarschall Fritz Erich von Manstein. The lightning campaign through the Netherlands, Belgium, and France had been the first great victory won by Hitler's intuition and the Fuehrerprinzip over the German General Staff, establishing a trend which had led almost inevitably to the virtual dictatorship in military command exercised by the Fuehrer in 1944. Also, the contempt for Allied generalship which Hitler continually expressed can be regarded as more than bombast. He would be prone to believe that the Western Allies had learned nothing from the experience of 1940, that the conservative military tradition which had deemed the Ardennes as impossible for armor was still in the saddle, and that what German arms had accomplished in 1940 might be their portion a second time. Two of the factors which had entered into the plans for the 1940 offensive still obtained: a very thin enemy line and the need for protecting the Ruhr. The German attack could no longer be supported by an air force which outweighed the opposition, but this would be true wherever the attack was delivered. Weather had favored movement through the Ardennes defiles in the spring of 1940. This could hardly be expected in the month of November, but there is no indication that Hitler gave any thought to the relation of weather and terrain as this might affect ground operations in the Ardennes. He tended to look at the sky rather than the ground, as the Luftwaffe deteriorated, and bad weather — bad flying weather — was his desire. In sum, Hitler's selection of the Ardennes may have been motivated in large part by the hope that the clock could be turned back to the glorious days of 1940.

Chapter III. Troops and Terrain

The Order of the Battle

During the long-drawn debate over the extent of the counteroffensive, the objective, and the attack form to be employed, the order of battle for Wacht am Rhein took form. This also led to differences of opinion and interpretation. How should the armies be aligned? What forces, missions, and zones should be assigned to each particular army? How many divisions, armored and infantry, would be available for use in the attack? The answers to these and like questions turned on the "Solution" adopted and the maneuver employed but will be set forth independently in an attempt to bring some order out of the confused interplay between Hitler, Jodl, Rundstedt, and Model.

When the representatives of OB WEST and Army Group B first heard of the Defensive Battle in the West, the Fuehrer had given Model, as the commander directly charged with the operation, three armies: the Fifth and Sixth Panzer Armies and the Seventh Army. Subsequently Hitler added the Fifteenth Army for a special role, although it would appear that he did not intend to take the Fifteenth away from Army Group Student until after the battle was joined. At the time Westphal and Krebs rejoined their respective headquarters they were in possession of a rather general plan of maneuver and a list of divisions numbering 29. Hitler had personally promised 30 divisions, of which 12 were to be armored. From this point forward there would be a constant question posed in each draft plan: how many divisions and which divisions? By 1 November, as planning progressed, the Hitler-Jodl estimate of the divisions which could be employed rose to 39, of which 13 would be armored. On the other hand the estimates fed into the successive OB WEST planning papers revolved between 29 and 31 divisions, with 12 armored divisions as a constant. It is the one extra panzer unit found in the OKW order of battle which furnishes the key to the conundrum as to the number of divisions. This unit, the 21st Panzer Division, belonged to Army Group G and was committed as a roving halfback, stiffening those parts of the line where attacks by the Third and Seventh U.S. Armies threatened to penetrate. Rundstedt knew that the 21st simply could not be stripped from the German south flank, already precariously thin. His list of "available" divisions, therefore did not name those divisions already fully committed in sectors where the Allied threat loomed large. Be it noted, then, that the Hitler-Jodl listing of available divisions did not contain a single new formation (from the Eastern Front or Italy for example) but simply reckoned on withdrawing more divisions from other sectors of the Western Front and throwing them into the counteroffensive force.

Fancy footwork in extending the length of the order of battle at OKW had a direct correlation with the alignment of forces laid down in Hitler's letter of instructions on 1 November. In this the Sixth Panzer Army would be deployed on the right or north flank of the attack formation and would make the main effort. In the center would be the Fifth Panzer Army; on the left the Seventh Army. This disposition was "unalterable." The decision to let the Sixth Panzer Army gather the largest sheaf of laurel leaves, if any, was politically inspired. Its commander, Sepp Dietrich, was high in the party and the panzer divisions assigned for the attack were SS divisions. Hitler's letter on 1 November calls Dietrich's command the Sixth SS Panzer Army, a Freudian slip, for this army did not officially bear the title SS and would not for some time to come. The question at issue, however, was the location of the Sixth Panzer Army. Rundstedt wanted the main effort to be launched in the center and so wished to reverse the position of the two panzer armies in the final deployment. But this was only one of several points at which the deployment outlined by OB WEST in the Martin plan (as finally agreed to by Model) differed from that given by Hitler's 1 November letter of instructions.

The Hitler-Jodl plan provided for an attack to be carried by the three armies of Army Group B advancing abreast. Plan Martin placed the Seventh Army to the left and rear of the two assault armies with its northern corps advancing behind the southern wing of the attack. Correspondingly, the Hitler-Jodl attack issued from an attack front sixty-five miles wide; the Martin attack took off from a forty-mile-wide base. In the first case the southern terminus of the penetration would be Grevenmacher; in Martin this terminus was set at Dasburg. Where the Hitler-Jodl attack moved straight through the Belgian Ardennes, that outlined in Martin skimmed the northern edge of the Ardennes. Of the thirteen panzer divisions listed by Hitler and Jodl, only four would be thrown into the first wave with six following in the second wave. The remaining three were to be held out for later employment in the holding attacks planned for Army Group Student. In Martin, contrariwise, Rundstedt put all of the panzer divisions he counted as available (twelve in number) in the first attack wave. As to reserves, the Hitler-Jodl order of battle counted four divisions in this category but provided for their commitment as the third wave of the attack. Rundstedt, far more concerned than OKW with the potential weakness of the southern flank, would assemble the three divisions of his reserve along the southern boundary of the expanding salient.

When, on 10 November, Hitler signed the operation directive Wacht am Rhein, it became clear that Rundstedt's Plan Martin had been sunk without trace. This was nowhere more evident than in the order of battle. The revised Hitler-Jodl list gave an impressive total of 4 armies (the Fifteenth had been added), 11 army corps, and 38 divisions (15 motorized and mechanized and 23 infantry), plus 9 Volks artillery corps and 7 Volks Werfer brigades. By what sleight of hand had Jodl and the WFSt been able to raise divisions for the counteroffensive which the Western Front commanders could not see? The answer is found in a combination of self-mesmerism at Hitler's headquarters and a kind of double entry order of battle. The assignment of the Fifteenth Army, fighting in the Aachen battle, theoretically added six divisions to the attacking force. The Fifteenth Army, however, was not to be employed until the Allies had reacted in force to the German attack, and in any case could not be expected to launch a large-scale attack until the Allied front east of Aachen had been drastically denuded of troops. Furthermore, the actual count of divisions in the Fifteenth Army was deceptive. Two of the divisions (the 49th Infantry and 246th Volks Grenadier) had been merged, the 49th being deactivated. This merger had been reported to the WFSt but the 49th continued on the Hitler-Jodl list. Another organization listed, the 89th Infantry Division, amounted to the strength of a single rifle battalion. Both OB WEST and Army Group B had asked for its disbandment, but this request was refused at the Fuehrer level.

An error of potentially greater import existed in the listing of three panzer-type divisions supposedly to come from other sectors of the Western Front. Rundstedt's protest against the nomination of the 21st Panzer Division as "available" has already been noted. Also tied down by the Allied attacks on the Army Group G front was the 17th SS Panzer Grenadier Division. In addition, the 10th SS Panzer Division, involved in the fight east of Aachen, had a very limited combat capability. But when Model attempted to replace this formation with a green parachute division, OKW turned down the relief because the second division was ticketed for Wacht am Rhein. In effect the felony was compounded insofar as the three panzer-type divisions were concerned. Not only was it very unlikely that they could be taken out of sectors where they already were hotly engaged, but each was so weakened by constant fighting—the 21st Panzer Division and 17th SS Panzer Grenadier Division had been in line without a break since the Allied invasion of Normandy—that the two together no longer had the combat value of a single full division.

The chain of events leading to the issuance of the questionable Hitler-Jodl order of battle was vicious in its working—but the sequence was not ended. Hitler had determined on a military solution in which the means were not adequate to the end desired. His commanders at first had attempted to bring the objective into some proper relation to the available means. As a retort to these efforts, Jodl and the WFSt had supported the Fuehrer scheme by an inflated listing of additional available divisions. The higher field commanders then bowed to the inevitable, although they personally were aware that the troop list attached to the final operation directive of 10 November was probably phony, or at least highly suspect. The troop list thereafter would be duplicated in army group, army, corps, and division orders and plans. Commanders and staffs in lower echelons could have little or no knowledge of the questionable basis of the troop list. Each time the list was reproduced it became more of a solid fact. When a corps commander was informed that he would be given one of the divisions whose availability originally had been questioned by Rundstedt or Model, he accepted this as a fact and made his plans accordingly. This was true at the army level—and eventually even at the headquarters of Army Group B. Constant repetition would turn a hypothesis, mendacious by origin, into a military "fact." There is a lesson here for those who may be called upon to plan large-scale military operations in the future.

The Allies Return to the Attack

Rundstedt's immediate reaction to the outline Fuehrer plan brought back to the OB WEST headquarters by his chief of staff on 24 October had been a caveat: the entire project for a German counteroffensive would have to be abandoned if the Western Allies launched any large-scale attack. Rundstedt was not simply being cagey. He was worried by the general quiet which had fallen over the Western Front following the American penetration of the West Wall outworks at Aachen. He anticipated that the Allies would make new attacks in the Aachen and Metz sectors as soon as their divisions were refitted and resupplied. The C-in-C West especially feared a thrust from the Aachen salient to the Ruhr and had so advised Hitler, asking as was his wont for reserves. Rundstedt's request for nine fresh divisions lay unanswered in the files of OKW until Westphal finally brought the news that OB WEST would not be given the nine divisions requested but instead would have to take nine divisions out of the line in the west and prepare them for use in the great counteroffensive. To make matters very much worse, OB WEST would lose two-thirds of its armored and mechanized troops during the rehabilitation period. After the meeting with Model at Fichtenhain, Rundstedt once again asked for additional divisions to meet the impending Allied attack and repeated the warning that an Allied offensive would cancel the German plans. This time (3 November) he specified the areas where the attack would be made: it would be a double thrust, one arm advancing from the Aachen front in the direction of Cologne, the other striking from the Metz sector toward Saarbrucken. Hitler's reply, telegraphed two days later, was unsympathetic. Rundstedt must hold with those divisions he had in the line. Divisions listed for Wacht am Rhein could be committed only if they became involved in a fight while assembling in their future attack positions, although an exception could be made in the event of Allied airborne landings. Otherwise the commitment of any Wacht am Rhein formation must have the express permission of the Fuehrer.

Rundstedt's prediction of things to come was made good when the US Third Army opened a two-corps attack on 8 November. Within twenty-four hours Hitler was in touch with OB WEST, reminding Rundstedt that he must keep his hands off the Wacht am Rhein divisions even if this meant giving ground all along the line. As a reassuring note OKW expressed the hope that the Allied attack would burn up divisions which might otherwise face the German counteroffensive.

Now the C-in-C West was responsible for two types of Wacht am Rhein divisions, those in the line which he must relieve for rest and refitting, and those which had been organized or rehabilitated in the Reserve Army and dispatched to Rundstedt's command. The weight of armor in the American attack east of Metz and the possibility that this thrust would rupture the German south wing at the joint between the First and Nineteenth Armies, impelled Rundstedt to cling to those tanks which were on the Army Group G front. This he did in flat disobedience of direct orders from OKW. He went a step further on 21 November and ordered the Panzer Lehr Division out of its assembly area and into a counterattack designed to block the American XV Corps, whose drive toward the Saverne Gap threatened to separate the First and Nineteenth Armies. OKW ultimately agreed to this use of Panzer Lehr, but then called off the counterattack on 25 November. The responsible Western Front commanders simply stalled the relief of the Panzer Lehr until it was clear that the division had suffered too much damage to allow any further hope of success.

The upshot of the Allied offensive in Lorraine was that two panzer-type divisions scheduled for Wacht am Rhein became irretrievably embroiled in the losing battle being waged by Army Group G, while the elite Panzer Lehr Division limped back to its assembly area much reduced in strength and with badly shaken morale. None of the infantry divisions engaged in the battles east of Metz were scheduled for employment in the Ardennes, but the redeployment in the south of two divisions from the Eifel sector necessitated the premature commitment of two Volks Grenadier divisions from the Replacement Army as their relief. In addition the American attack in Lorraine would cost the Hitler offensive an entire Volks artillery corps, two panzer brigades, and two heavy antitank battalions.

The Third Battle of Aachen, begun on 16 November, was even more threatening in the eyes of OB WEST than the Allied drive in Lorraine. Within twenty-four hours the situation was so desperate that Model threw in his only tactical reserve, the XLVIII Panzer Corps. As the German casualties mounted on the Army Group B front, Rundstedt began to bleed his north wing, taking one division after another from Army Group Student. By 20 November the prospect of an Allied breakthrough loomed so large that the C-in-C West asked OKW for the four reserve SS panzer divisions which were being readied to carry the main Ardennes attack by the Sixth Panzer Army. His request was denied. There ensued a tactical merry-go-round catching up divisions all the way from the Netherlands to Strasbourg. Rundstedt would bring in one of the divisions which had been kept on ice for the coming offensive, relieve a battered division in the line, then in a few days shuffle the relieving division back to a reserve position close behind the line—sometimes with OKW approval, but more often without. Meanwhile the German artillery was working desperately to take the place of tactical air support—so marked by its absence. As early as the third day of the attack the light and medium howitzers bolstering the Army Group B positions were dipping into the special ammunition stocks which had been reserved by the Fuehrer for the Ardennes battle and which bore his imprint, Fuehrer Reserve. At the close of the first week of fighting in the Aachen area the German casualties there had risen to 12,000. Replacements who had been sent forward to reflesh the divisions being reorganized for Wacht am Rhein found themselves filling the gaping ranks of formations in the line. By the first week of December the Aachen battle had resulted in the direct commitment or a cessation of training and rehabilitation in the case of five panzer-type and seven infantry divisions. An additional six Volks artillery corps had been tossed into the fray but, made up of over-age reservists, they probably profited by this enforced training period.

It is hardly surprising that the impact of the attacks around Aachen and Metz should have further shaken Rundstedt's and Model's already wavering belief in the possibility of any large measure of success for the Ardennes counteroffensive. Model reacted more strongly than Rundstedt, the latter fatigued by the constant tug of war with OKW and more and more adopting the resignation of the aged. When Model again took up the cudgels for the Small Solution, stressing the paucity of forces left for the counteroffensive, he sounded a prophetic warning: "Should the attack be stopped at the Meuse due to the lack of reserves the only result will be a bulge in the line and not the destruction of sizable enemy forces.... The widely stretched flanks, especially in the south, will only invite enemy counteractions." Hitler answered by assuring OB WEST that "the number of units originally projected will be made available." This was on 27 November. The initial target date for Wacht am Rhein had come and gone; the Allied November offensive had been a spoiling attack in the true sense of the term, albeit unwittingly so.

The German attack in the west launched on 10 May 1940, in so many respects the prototype for the 1944 counteroffensive in the Ardennes, had been postponed some sixteen times. The period of planning and preparation had covered six and a half months. In '40, however, there was no pressing reason to disturb the quiet of the "phony war," nor was the Third Reich seriously threatened on the ground or in the air. The summer disasters in 1944, on the contrary, demanded immediate action to recoup German losses and stave off an immediate threat. There is no question that Hitler's selection of the target date for the start of the offensive, 25 November 1944, was made with every intention that the operation should begin in fact before the end of November. Furthermore, Rundstedt and Model had accepted this date without official question, despite the fact that it would leave them only one month in which to make ready. Rundstedt, however, had added a cautionary note by reminding OKW that the actual attack date would depend upon the arrival of the panzer divisions in their forward assembly positions and the completion of ammunition and fuel stockpiling in the concentration area.

There is some evidence that the Fuehrer had chosen November not only for its promise of poor flying weather but also because he hoped to win a victory in the west and release divisions to the Eastern Front before the beginning of the annual Soviet winter offensive. If so, this second desideratum was not considered of really vital importance as planning progressed. The operation directive of 10 November in which Hitler ordered that the concentration period be ended by the 27th clearly referred to the weather and even included provisions for a stop-order to arrest the concentration in mid-flight should the weather suddenly turn fair. The concentration for Wacht am Rhein, already in progress when the US Third Army reopened large-scale fighting on the Western Front, continued at a wobbly pace during the second and third weeks of November. Eventually the impossibility of relieving the attack divisions as scheduled and the delays wrought by the temporary commitment of units like the Panzer Lehr became so obvious as to brook no denial — even by Hitler. His postponement of the attack cannot be pinpointed, but the word probably came sometime after 23 November. On that date Model reported that of the armor slated for Wacht am Rhein only the four SS panzer divisions and the 2d Panzer Division had escaped premature commitment in the battles then raging. In Model's opinion — mark the date — the other divisions could not be readied before 15 December.

The Terrain

The area through which Hitler chose to launch his counteroffensive was, with the exception of the Vosges, the most difficult terrain on the entire line of the Western Front. It consists of two major parts, the Eifel and the Ardennes. Although the whole is strewn with the relics of castles and fortified churches, there had been little military history enacted within this area before 1914. A straight line between Paris and Berlin will bisect the Eifel and Ardennes, but the movement of armies during the centuries normally had followed the easier roads going around this area: in the north via Liège-Maubeuge or the Flanders plains in the south via the Metz gateway. On occasion the Ardennes and Eifel had been used by large forces for movement without fighting, battle being joined at the natural defense lines of the Meuse River west of the Ardennes, or the Rhine River east of the Eifel.

In 1914, as part of the Schlieffen Plan, three of the Imperial German armies marched from the Eifel through the Ardennes. Schlieffen had predicted that the French would react to the pressure of the heavy German right wing as it swung through northern Belgium by counterattacking into the flank via southeastern Belgium. It was an integral part of the famous plan, therefore, that the German right wing would be covered by an extension through southern Belgium and Luxembourg, and that the Ardennes massif would be used, if needed, as a bastion from which the French flanking attack would be repelled. A portion of the Second and all of the Third and Fourth German Armies did advance through southern Belgium and Luxembourg, the march through the main portion of the Ardennes being covered by the rapid movement of Richthofen's I Cavalry Corps. French reaction was slow and the tiny Belgian Army had been drawn away to defend Liège and Brussels. As a result the Germans marched across the main body of the Ardennes mass without a fight, the ultimate meeting engagements with the French on 22 August taking place in the densely wooded but less rugged segment of the Ardennes (sometimes called the Forest of Ardennes) close to the Belgian-French border in the neighborhood of Neufchâteau and Virton.

In 1940 the Ardennes once again was invaded and crossed by German troops, the jangle of Richthofen's squadrons giving way to the roar and grind of Kleist's tanks. This time, at Hitler's insistence, the German maneuver departed from the classic concept of Schlieffen, the weight of the German attack being thrown south of Liège rather than north, while a narrow thrust replaced the bludgeon strokes of a massive wheeling movement. This main effort toward a decisive breakthrough was launched through a narrow corridor marked approximately by Bastogne in the north and Arlon in the south; but the bulk of three German armies debouched from the Eifel and marched across the Ardennes. As in 1914 the crossing of the Ardennes massif was little more than a route march, impeded ever so slightly by brave but tragic and futile attempts at resistance by the Belgian Chasseurs Ardennais. Without detracting from the courage of these few Belgians it is fair to say that the Germans did not have to fight before they reached the Meuse River, and even there they experienced little opposition. The German advance through southern Belgium and Luxembourg in 1914 had demonstrated that a huge modern force could be concentrated via rail in the abrupt, broken country of the Eifel, and from thence be moved afoot or ahorse through the worst of the Ardennes mass.

The events of 1940 proved that mechanized forces could move speedily through the Ardennes, and more, that not only was Hitler correct in his insistence on the use of large mechanized forces in the Ardennes, but that the professionals in OKH who had opposed him were wrong. In 1944, as a result, it was known that the terrain in the Eifel and Ardennes was not so bad but that it could be quickly negotiated by modern mechanized armies under conditions of good weather and little or no enemy resistance. What history could not demonstrate, for the lessons were lacking, was whether modern, mechanized armies could attack through the Ardennes and speedily overcome a combination of stubborn enemy defense, difficult ground, and poor weather. Terrain, then, would play a peculiarly important role in the development of the 1944 counteroffensive.

Although the Ardennes has given its name to the campaign under study, this area should be lumped with that of the Eifel, the composite of the tablelands to the east which sheltered the German concentration during the late autumn of 1944. These two areas are extensions of the Westerwald, blending almost insensibly into each other and sharing many of the same characteristics. The Eifel is the complex of hill ranges — they can hardly be called mountains — lying between the Rhine, the Moselle, and the Roer Rivers, mostly in Germany. Only the two westernmost of the Eifel highlands or ranges need be mentioned here. East of St. Vith and just inside the German border is the Schnee Eifel, a high tree-covered ridge or hogback. It extends from the northeast to the southwest, a characteristic thrust line in the entire area, and in 1944 was crested on much of its length by the West Wall fortifications. East of Liège is the Hohes Venn, a long table-land topped with lakes and marshes. The Hohes Venn is larger than the Schnee Eifel. Its northeast-southwest course is defined by a line through Malmédy and Monschau on the German face and by a line through Eupen and Spa on the Belgian. In the northeast the Hohes Venn is prolonged by the Hürtgen Forest. As the Schnee Eifel forms a barrier covering St. Vith on the east, so the Hohes Venn is a large outer bastion for Liège. Although the Hohes Venn is geologically a part of the Eifel it is somewhat removed from the other parts of the complex and represents the gradual and sometimes indefinable blending of the Eifel and Ardennes.

The Eifel is thickly covered with forests and provides good cover from air observation even in the fall and winter. The area has no large towns but rather is marked by numerous small villages, requiring extensive dispersion for any large forces billeted here. The road net is adequate for a large military concentration. The rail net is extensive, having been engineered and expanded before 1914 for the quick deployment of troops west of the Rhine. The railroads feed into the Eifel from Koblenz, Cologne, and the lesser Rhine bridgeheads between these two. The main rail line, however, does not cross the Eifel but follows the Moselle valley on the southern fringe of the Eifel. Rail and road systems throughout the Eifel are marked by meandering courses and numerous bridge crossings thrown over rivers and deep ravines.

The Ardennes, like the Eifel, is not a single and well-defined bloc. The general area may be defined as a wedge with the point between Aachen and Düren. The northern edge is a diagonal: Aachen, Liège, Maubeuge, Landrecis. The southern edge (much debated by geologists) is a more pronounced diagonal running from Aachen southwest to Arlon. The base, formed by the Forêt des Ardennes or French Ardennes, roughly coincides with the Franco-Belgian frontier and the Semois River. The Ardennes has three recognized subdepartments: the High Ardennes in the south, the Famenne Depression in the middle, and the Low Ardennes in the north. The Low Ardennes tends to be open and rolling, but includes two plateaus: that of Herve, between Liège and Aachen, and Condroz, between the lower Ourthe and the Meuse in the vicinity of Dinant. This sector is more readily traversed than is the High Ardennes, but it is relatively narrow, maneuver is constricted by the flanking line of the Meuse River, and entrance from the east presupposes that the invader has possession of Aachen and the roads circling north or south of the Hohes Venn.

The Famenne Depression is only a thin sliver of the Ardennes wedge. The Famenne is free from tree cover except for the characteristic buttes which dot the depression. Scooped out of the Ardennes massif, this long, narrow depression originates at the upper Ourthe and extends westward through Marche and Rochefort. It reaches the Meuse between Givet and Dinant, offering a good crossing site which often has been employed by European armies operating on the Meuse. But an invader from the German frontier must traverse much difficult terrain before debouching into this "march through" depression.

The High Ardennes is often called the "True Ardennes." It is not properly mountainous, nor yet a forest; rather it is a wide plateau or high plain out of which rise elevations in the form of ridges or higher plateaus erupting from the main mass. These elevations generally are unrelated to one another and combine with large forests to form isolated and independent compartments in which tactical domination of one hill mass seldom provides domination of another. The mass structure extends on a northeast-southwest axis, forming a watershed which drains away to the Meuse in the north and the Moselle in the southeast. Perhaps a third of the area is covered with forest, much of which is coniferous. This timber, however, is scattered all over the High Ardennes and presents a patchwork picture rather than a series of large forested preserves. The main mass is cut in zigzag patterns by winding, deeply eroded rivers and streams, some flowing parallel to the higher ridges, others crossing so as to chop the ridges and the welts on the plateau into separate sections. In some places the watercourses run through narrow, almost canyonlike depressions with steep walls rising from a hundred to three hundred feet. Even the wider valleys are narrow when compared with the western European norm.

The road net in 1944 was far richer than the population and the economic activity of the Ardennes would seem to warrant. This was not the result of military planning, as in the case of the Eifel rail lines, but rather of Belgian and Luxemburgian recognition of the value of automobile tourism just prior to World War II. All of the main roads had hard surfaces, generally of macadam. Although the road builders tried to follow the more level stretches of the ridge lines or wider valley floors, in many cases the roads twisted sharply and turned on steep grades down into a deep ravine and out again on the opposite side. The bridges were normally built of stone. There were ten all-weather roads crossing from the German frontier into Belgium and Luxembourg in the sector between Monschau and Wasserbillig, but there was not a single main highway traversing the Ardennes in a straight east-west direction.

There are no cities in the Ardennes, unless the capital of Luxembourg and Arlon are included in this area. The largest villages had, in 1944, populations of 2,500 to 4,000. The normal settlement in the Ardennes was the small village with stone houses and very narrow, winding streets. These villages often constricted the through road to single-lane traffic. Another military feature was the lone farmstead or inn which gave its name to the crossroads at which it stood.

The fact that most of the High Ardennes lies inside Belgium leads to some confusion, since one of the administrative subdivisions of that kingdom is named "Ardennes" but is not exactly conterminous with the geographical area. Luxembourg, into which the Ardennes extends, is divided in two parts, roughly along a line from

Attert on the west to a point midway between Vianden and Diekirch on the eastern boundary. The northern half generally is considered an extension of the High Ardennes (although one may find as many definitions of the south edge of the Ardennes as there are writers touching the subject); in any case it shares the same physical properties. The southern half of Luxembourg, known appropriately as the "Good Land," is less high, has more open space, and its valleys normally can be traveled. A single river, the Alzette, bisects this part of Luxembourg in a north-south course which takes it through the capital city. But the eastern approach to the Good Land erases much of its military attractiveness. Between Sierck and Wasserbillig the Moselle River forms the boundary between Luxembourg and Germany. In this sector the left or Luxembourg bank of the river is especially difficult even by comparison with the normal terrain obstacles encountered in the High Ardennes. Farther north, where the Sauer River continues the boundary, the river valley is somewhat less formidable but is backed up by a broken, gorge-riven area in the neighborhood of Echternach known as the "Luxembourg Switzerland."

It is natural, with the Ardennes mass forming a northeast-southwest divide between the tributaries of the Meuse and the Moselle and with rugged geological patterns twisting and turning these tributaries, that the military hydrography of the Ardennes should be important. The prolongation of the Ardennes in northern Luxembourg is dissected by four rivers. On the eastern frontier the Our River continues the boundary trace begun by the Moselle and the Sauer. In the interior the Wiltz, the Clerf, and the Sure divide the country into water-bound compartments. Their valleys are long and narrow, so narrow and tortuous that they cannot be followed by roads. They are further complicated by "cups" scoured out of the side walls and by cross ravines, deep and narrow.

In the Ardennes north of Luxembourg it is possible to cross from Germany into Belgium without traversing a major stream. About twenty miles west of the frontier, however, comes the first of the rivers descending from the High Ardennes into the Meuse; these are the Amblève and the Salm which serve as flankers for the swamp-encrusted tableland of the Hohes Venn and must be crossed in any movement west from St. Vith, Malmédy, or Spa. Next comes the longest of these rivers, the Ourthe, which is the most severe military obstacle east of the Meuse. It originates west of Bastogne as a small creek, then meanders north until it meets the Meuse at Liège. At Ortheuville the Ourthe begins to cut through a narrow and winding defile with steep, rocky sides fringed by pine trees. Just north of La Roche the Ourthe leaves its tortuous canyons and enters the Famenne Depression. That part of the course between Ortheuville and La Roche permits no road adjacent to the river bed; all approaches to the east-west crossing sites are difficult. Just east of the defile through which flows the middle Ourthe lies the Plateau Des Tailles, which rises to over 1,800 feet at the Baraque de Fraiture. Two rivers are found between the Ourthe and the Meuse: the Lesse and L'Homme, whose confluence is near Rochefort. Neither of these rivers is too difficult of negotiation, but the main westward crossing for movement toward Dinant and the Meuse centers at Rochefort. At the very edge of the Ardennes in the southwest is the Semois River, which wends its way westward from Arlon to the Meuse. The Semois is deeply sunk through much of its course, flowing between steep walls which descend directly to the water's edge and so deny space for road or rail on the valley bottom Although the rivers of the Eifel, as distinct from those of the Ardennes, would have no tactical significance in the battle of the Ardennes, they were to be of very considerable logistic, or what the Germans style "operational," importance. The northernmost, the Ahr, follows an oblique course northeast until it enters the Rhine at Sinzig. From the Schnee Eifel comes the Kyll, bending southward to meet the Moselle not far from Trier. Paralleling the Kyll in the west is the Prüm River. It is the last stream of any importance before the German frontier is reached. Like the Kyll its sources are in the heights of the Schnee Eifel. The beautiful Moselle attracts numerous small tributaries rushing down from the Eifel, but only the Moselle itself deserves attention. Alternating between scenes of towering rocks and meadow passages, the German Moselle winds and turns capriciously from its entrance on German soil, past Trier and a host of little villages whose names are known to all lovers of the vine, until finally it rushes past the "German Corner" at Koblenz and into the Rhine. Just as the Moselle vineyards of renown alternate from one bank to the other, so the railroad line and the highway crisscross the river throughout its middle reaches; but rail and road come to a focal point only a few kilometers from the Luxembourg frontier at the old Roman city of Trier.

Throughout this whole area military routes of movement, regardless of the weather, are synonymous with the road system. The roads of the Ardennes proliferate in accordance with the geological compartments incised in the high plateau by rivers and streams as they recede downward. The main roads tend to follow a north-south axis, although one, from Luxembourg to Namur, cuts across the grain of the main mass in a southeast-northwest direction. In the northeast the chief road centers are Monschau, Malmédy, and St. Vith. The southeastern nodal points are Ettelbruck, Mersch, and, of course, Luxembourg. To the northwest Bastogne, Marche, and Rochefort are the paramount links in the road system. Arlon, Neufchâteau, and Libramont, in the southwest, complete this picture. The Eifel is rimmed by a main road system which hugs the west bank of the Rhine between Bonn and Koblenz then follows the Moselle River until it breaks away cross-country via Wittlich to reach Trier. The circuit is completed by a road which goes north from Trier through Bitburg, Prüm, and Euskirchen, finally bifurcating to reach the Rhine at Bonn and at Cologne. Inside of this circuit the chief communications centers are Mayen, Daun, Kochem, and, attached to the outer ring, Wittlich.

The character of the Eifel-Ardennes terrain dictates three major bases of operations for an attack from the German frontier. In the north the Aachen sector is one such base. The direction of attack here would be through the Low Ardennes via Eupen, Verviers, Marche, and Rochefort to the Meuse at Givet. The next base, to the south, lies between Monschau and the Losheim Gap. The westward thrust from this base must go over and between Malmédy and St. Vith. The broadest base of operations is in the south between Prüm and Trier. In this case the attack must be made against the grain of the Ardennes mass except for a penetration from Trier to the French frontier at Virton or Longwy which may bypass the more rugged country to the north by movement through the Good Land of southern Luxembourg. This last route, however, is by far the longest for any attack aimed at reaching the Meuse River.

The geography of the Ardennes leads inevitably to the channelization of large troop movements east to west, will tend to force larger units to "pile up" on each other, and restricts freedom of maneuver once the direction of attack and order of battle are fixed. To a marked degree the military problem posed by the terrain is that of movement control rather than maneuver in the classic sense. For the smaller tactical units, the chopped-up nature of the ground plus the peculiar timber formations in which dense wood lots are interspersed with natural or manmade clearings, indicates the development of a series of small, semi-independent engagements once the larger battle is joined. Movement cross-country is limited, even in good weather; movement along the narrow valley floors may be blocked there or in the villages at points of descent and ascent. The backbone of the ridges sometimes offers good observation in the immediate area for detecting movement on the roads which climb the hills and plateaus. Locally, however, the gunner or fighter pilot will find many blind spots formed by the thick tree cover or the deep draws and ravines; the ability of high-angle fire to beat reverse slopes, which really are sheer, steep walls, is limited.

What the German planners saw in 1944 was this: the Ardennes could be traversed by large forces even when these were heavily mechanized. An attack from east to west across the massif would encounter initially the greatest obstacles of terrain, but these obstacles would decrease in number as an advance neared the Meuse. In 1914 and 1940 the German armies moving across the Ardennes had no reason to anticipate strong opposition on the ground until the Meuse had been reached and the tortuous defiles left behind. In 1940 the only German concern had been that the French air force would catch the armored columns at the crossings of the Sauer and Our Rivers. In both these earlier campaigns the Germans had thrown a protective screen clear to the Meuse within twenty-four hours after the advance began; the initial objectives of these screening movements have more than historic significance: Bastogne, St. Vith, Arlon, Malmédy, La Roche, and the bridges over the Ourthe River.

The ground offered the defender three natural defense positions east of the Meuse, although none of these constituted an impassable barrier to the attacker: (1) a covering line echeloned to the southeast between Liège and the Moselle, this pegged on the Hohes Venn, the rugged zone around Malmédy and St. Vith, and the boxed-in course of the Our and Sauer Rivers; (2) the Ourthe River line; and (3) an intermediate position, shorter in length, based on the plateau at Bastogne and extending along a chain of ridges to Neufchâteau.

There remains a word to be said about the climate of the Ardennes and Eifel. This is mountainous country, with much rainfall, deep snows in winter, and raw, harsh winds sweeping across the plateaus. The heaviest rains come in November and December. The mists are frequent and heavy, lasting well into late morning before they break. Precise predictions by the military meteorologist, however, are difficult because the Ardennes lies directly on the boundary between the northwestern and central European climatic regions and thus is affected by the conjuncture of weather moving east from the British Isles and the Atlantic with that moving westward out of Russia. At Stavelot freezing weather averages 112 days a year, at Bastogne 145 days. The structure of the soil will permit tank movement when the ground is frozen, but turns readily to a clayey mire in time of rain. Snowfall often attains a depth of ten to twelve inches in a 24-hour period. Snow lingers for a long time in the Ardennes but— and this is important in recounting the events of 1944—the deep snows come late.

Chapter IV. Preparations

Deception and Camouflage

Hitler's selection of the Ardennes as the sector in which the western counteroffensive would be launched was based in the main on the obvious advantage of attacking the Allies where they were weakest. Even so, although the Western Allies could not be strong everywhere along the line from Switzerland to the North Sea, they did outnumber the Germans in men, tanks, guns, and planes, they were possessed of greater facility for rapid movement of large forces, and they—not the Germans—had the strategic initiative. At the first word of German preparations in the Eifel and Ardennes the Allies could terminate one or both of their major offensives and divert large forces into the threatened area.

The accepted strategic gambit, practiced with great success by German commanders in the west during World War I, would be to deliver a series of large-scale attacks in sectors well removed from the area from which the main counteroffensive was to be launched. But the divisions and the logistic support for such diversionary attacks did not exist. The German armies in the west could not uncover the enemy's jaw by a blow in Holland or a kidney punch in Alsace; instead they had to rely on the adroit misdirection practiced by the conjurer, turning Allied eyes away from the Eifel long enough to complete the massive preparations therein.

The German military profession had a record of some notable achievements in the attainment of strategic surprise. The Ludendorff March offensive in 1918 had been a brilliant example—indeed a model—of a great offensive whose preparation had completely escaped detection. The meticulous detail employed by Ludendorff's planners had achieved such success that the 1918 plans for the cover and movement of artillery simply were copied in the artillery build-up for the Ardennes. The German offensive in 1940 likewise had been a marked example of strategic surprise, despite the forced landing on Belgian soil of a German plane carrying two liaison officers who had been entrusted with the attack plan. The chief security tenets adopted in preparation for the 1940 attack had been personally dictated by Hitler, and the first formal security order issued by OKW in preparation for the Ardennes counteroffensive was a restatement of the Fuehrer Directive of 11 January 1940. (This time, however, liaison officers party to the plan were expressly forbidden to travel by plane.) Subsequent security measures would reflect or rephrase those which had been so successful in 1940.

Probably the Fuehrer's personal influence was felt most directly in limiting the circle of those privy to the plan during its conception and initial implementation. Hitler, the highest authority in the German armed forces, personally named the officers who were to be admitted to the great secret; furthermore, he possessed the power to exact the death penalty for violations of security, a power he could be expected to exercise on the slightest provocation and without regard to the rank or prestige of the offender. Even the well-disciplined, high-ranking officers of the Wehrmacht seem to have been apprehensive of the personal risks which each encountered the moment he was admitted to the plan. So strict was the limitation of knowledge that in those headquarters charged with the command of the counteroffensive, OB WEST and Army Group B, the only officers brought into the planning phase were Rundstedt and Model, plus the chief of staff, the G-3, the quartermaster officer, and one aide in each of their respective staffs. In OB WEST, for example, the daily and most secret war diary contained no reference to the counteroffensive; instead a separate war diary was maintained, without benefit of secretary or stenographer, by the few officers working on the plan. The exchange of information between the responsible headquarters was carried by liaison officers whose every movement was watched by military and Gestapo security agents. All teletype and telephone lines were monitored the clock around and the officers in the know were so informed. Hitler had a mania for "oaths." Everyone admitted to the plan took not one but ofttimes several oaths to maintain secrecy, signing at least one statement which accepted the death penalty for any personal breach of security. Later, division and corps commanders would be compelled to take an oath that during the advance they would not trespass in the attack zone assigned neighboring units. The death penalty attached to this as well.

Although the immediate planning staffs could be drastically limited, it was obvious that some hundreds of officers would have to be involved in the actual handling of troops and supplies during the concentration period, that is from about 10 November, when the major reshuffling of headquarters and larger troop units would commence, until the date selected for the jump-off in the Ardennes. The German system of staff work, based on the rigid allocation of authority and unquestioning obedience to orders, was well designed to cope with this situation. Furthermore, the Allied attacks in November were launched on such a scale and achieved such success as to give real meaning to the Hitler-inspired cover plan, The Defensive Battle in the West. Until the very last hours before the counteroffensive the Western Front German commanders accepted as gospel the idea that the massing of matériel and the progressive withdrawal of divisions from the line was intended to provide fresh troops for the defense of the Ruhr and the Palatinate. Indeed the field commanders were much perplexed in the last days before the Ardennes counteroffensive by reason of what they regarded as the high command's capriciousness and folly in refusing to throw its reserves into the defensive battles then reaching a climax in the Aachen and Saverne Gap sectors.

The cover and deception plan, personally devised by Hitler, turned on a half-truth. A part of the strategic concentration would be made in the Rheydt-Jülich-Cologne area east of Aachen. Here the preparations for the counteroffensive would be paraded before the Allies. To the south, at the entry to the chosen path of attack, the Eifel concentration was to be accomplished under conditions of greatest secrecy behind the thin line manned by the weak Seventh Army. Then, at the last moment, the troops from the northern concentration area would slip south to join the main buildup in the Eifel. The cover plan, as propagated through the German commands on the Western Front and retailed to the Allies by neutrals and double-agents, had this scenario: Germany feared that the U.S. First and Ninth Armies would achieve a real breakthrough and drive to the Rhine in the sector between Cologne and Bonn; in preparation for this untoward event the Fuehrer was amassing a major counterattack force northwest of Cologne; a secondary and relatively small force of burned-out divisions was being gathered in the Eifel to contain the right flank of the expected Allied penetration.

The main actor in this play was the Sixth Panzer Army. Ostensibly its headquarters remained northwest of Cologne. Four of the armored divisions actually assigned to this headquarters also assembled in this area. The intensification of rail and road traffic which began here about mid-November was only partly concealed. Much movement was made in daylight. A program of road repair and civilian evacuation was begun with little attempt at camouflage. Radio traffic was increased commensurate with the troop concentration. Additional antiaircraft battalions came into the area and with them special allotments of ammunition to produce a thickening of fire which the Allied air forces could not possibly fail to notice. To emphasize further still what was transpiring here in the north, a ghost army was brought into being on 20 November; this, the Twenty-Fifth, supposedly had an order of battle of ten divisions including some of the panzer divisions which in fact belonged to the Sixth Panzer Army.

In contrast to this northern concentration, that in the Eifel was the product of secrecy carried to the limit. The Eifel terrain was well adapted to concealment. Thick forest cover cloaked its slopes, its valleys and plateaus. Small villages, singly not worthy of aerial investigation but in sum capable of harboring large forces, offered excellent dispersal. Camouflage had become second nature with the German soldier in the west—indeed since Normandy the art of camouflage had become the science of survival, and the Eifel made this task relatively easy. Strict traffic regulation confined all rail movements and road marches to hours of darkness. Special security detachments prowled the Eifel, and woe to the commander who allowed a vehicle park to grow beyond normal size. A radio blackout was thrown over the concentration area except for those units actually facing the enemy in the covering positions. No artillery registration was permitted except by guns in the line, and even they were limited to a few rounds per day. Reconnaissance was confined to a handful of higher officers; combat patrolling on the Ardennes front was almost entirely limited to nighttime search for American patrols.

There were a few potential weaknesses in the screen thrown around and over the Eifel. At one time the Allies had flown night reconnaissance missions across the Eifel, using flares for photography. Even Rundstedt was worried lest a repetition of these missions disclose the German secret. Next was the problem of deserters. A quiet sector, particularly in an area as rugged as the Ardennes and Eifel, offered numerous chances for a malcontent to slip over to the enemy. The so-called Volksdeutsch (Alsatians, Transylvanians, and the like) had the worst record in this regard; these were combed out of all forward units and would not rejoin their outfits until the battle began. Hitler himself required a special daily report from OB WEST listing all known deserters for the 24-hour period. As it turned out the number of deserters was surprisingly small, only five on the Western Front during the first twelve days of December.

There remained the problem of widening and improving miles of road in the Eifel without attracting undue enemy attention. Furthermore the roadblocks and barriers thrown up as part of the West Wall defenses had to be removed in those sectors where the initial armored penetration would be made. Such activity hardly could be concealed. The answer was to undertake road construction in both the northern and southern areas of concentration, tying this to the cover plan.

German discipline and experience, backed and enforced by all the security paraphernalia of a police state, might be able to divert enemy attention to the north and prepare a real strategic surprise in the Eifel. In the long run success or failure would turn on Allied activity in the air. Could the preparations for the counteroffensive be completed before enemy planes spotted the Eifel concentration of troops and vehicles?

The Western Front in Early December

The Allied attacks in November had as their objective the decisive defeat of the enemy west of the Rhine and the seizure of a foothold on the east bank of that river. By the end of November, the US First and Ninth Armies, charged with the main effort, had made some gains in the direction of Bonn and Cologne. The 21 Army Group, in the north, had crossed the Waal River, the left arm of the lower Rhine. The US Third Army had put troops on the Saar River. Farther to the south the US Seventh

Army had captured Strasbourg and reached the Rhine. The 1st French Army, on the extreme south flank, meanwhile had liberated Belfort and entrapped sizable German forces in the Colmar pocket. Although Allied losses had been high, those inflicted on the enemy had been even greater, probably on the order of two or three to one. But the Allies had failed to achieve their main strategic goals: they had not decisively defeated the German armies west of the Rhine, nor had they crossed the river.

On 7 December General Dwight D. Eisenhower, Air Chief Marshal Sir Arthur W. Tedder, Field Marshal Sir Bernard L. Montgomery, and Lt. Gen. Omar N. Bradley met at Maastricht to lay plans for future operations. There was general agreement that the Allies should launch an all-out offensive on the Western Front early in 1945 but considerable variance between the views of Eisenhower and Montgomery as to the future scheme of maneuver and disposition of forces. Montgomery held, as he had since September, for a single strong thrust across the Rhine north of the Ruhr and the restriction of all other operations to containing actions by limited forces. Eisenhower agreed with the proposal for a main attack north of the Ruhr by Montgomery's 21 Army Group and was prepared to give the field marshal the US Ninth Army. But he was unwilling to abandon his oft-expressed concept of the one-two punch with Patton's Third Army swinging a secondary blow toward the Frankfurt Gate.

After the Maastricht meeting, Eisenhower set plans in motion to continue pressure on the enemy and chew up as many German divisions as possible before the main offensive in the north. To accomplish this the Supreme Commander gave permission for the Third Army to mount an offensive along the Saar front on 19 December and directed Lt. Gen. Jacob L. Devers, the 6th Army Group commander, to support the drive with elements of the Seventh Army. In the meantime these two armies continued heavy local attacks, Patton driving on Saarlautern while Lt. Gen Alexander M. Patch's Seventh Army turned north into the Saverne Gap.

At the opposite end of the long Allied line, Montgomery gave orders in early December for the British Second Army to "tidy up" the 21 Army Group position on the Meuse with an attack calculated to erase the Heinsberg salient. This operation was flooded out, however, and on 16 December advance parties were moving north as the first step in a major shift to the left preparatory to the attack toward Krefeld and the Ruhr, now tentatively scheduled for the second week in January. South of 21 Army Group Lt. Gen. William H. Simpson's US Ninth Army liquidated the remaining enemy forces in the Jülich sector and by 14 December had closed along the Roer River. Lt. Gen. Courtney H. Hodges' First Army, to the right of the Ninth, also had reached the Roer, after the bloody Hürtgen battle, but could not risk a crossing attack while the Germans held the Urft-Roer dams. A series of air attacks was launched early in December to breach the dams and remove the threat of enemy-controlled floods, but with so little success that the deal passed to the First Army. Bradley ordered Hodges to seize the Schwammenauel and the Urftalsperre, the key points in the Roer valley system of dams, and on 13 December the First Army commander put the V Corps, his center, into an attack toward the dams. His northernmost corps, VII Corps, was assigned a support role in this attack and would attain its limited objectives by 16 December.

The mission and deployment of Maj. Gen. Leonard T. Gerow's V Corps late had a direct effect in determining the initial American reaction to the German attack. Gerow had four infantry divisions, two armored combat commands, and a cavalry group at his disposal. A new division, the 78th, was deployed in the corps center on a front extending from Lammersdorf to Monschau. On the left, the 8th Infantry Division fronted along the Kyll River line. The right wing was held by the 99th Infantry Division, whose positions reached from Monschau to the V–VIII Corps boundary in the Buchholz Forest northwest of the Losheim Gap. The first phase of the V Corps attack was to be carried by the 78th and 2d Infantry Divisions, the latter coming up from an assembly area at Camp Elsenborn and passing through the 99th Division left. The 8th and 99th would confine their efforts initially to demonstrations and line-straightening. The first day of the attack went as planned, but on 14 December the enemy stiffened and on the 15th counterattacked; the 78th Division became involved in a rough battle at Rollesbroich and Kesternich, while the 2d bogged down in a slow-moving fight for individual pillboxes in the Monschau Forest. This was the situation when the enemy onslaught hit the 9th Division and its VIII Corps neighbors on the morning of 16 December.

Maj. Gen. Troy H. Middleton's VIII Corps on First Army's right flank had no part in the Allied attacks of early December. Two of Middleton's infantry divisions were weary and casualty-ridden from the intense fighting of the November push to the Roer. The third was newly arrived from the United States. The corps mission, then, was to train, rest, re-equip, and observe the enemy. Nonetheless this was no Blighty, a haven for second-rate troops and bumbling commanders. The 28th Infantry Division (Maj. Gen. Norman D. Cota) and the 4th Infantry Division (Maj. Gen. Raymond O. Barton) had distinguished themselves in the bloody battles of the Hürtgen Forest. The veterans of this fight were well equipped to train and hearten the replacements for some 9,000 battle casualties the two divisions had sustained. General Middleton himself had a fine combat record reaching from World War I through Sicily, Normandy, and Brittany. Deliberate and calm but tenacious, he was regarded by Bradley and Patton as one of the best tacticians in the US Army.

As the result of the relief of the 83d Infantry Division, en route to the VII Corps, the deployment of the VIII Corps (as it would meet the German attack) took final form on the 13th. The 4th Infantry Division abutted on the Third Army at the Luxembourg-French frontier and followed the Moselle and Sauer Rivers, marking the German border, as far north as Bollendorf. A combat command of the 9th Armored Division, as yet inexperienced, had taken over a narrow sector to the left of the 4th on 10 December. The second combat command of this division, earlier comprising the corps reserve, was assigned to V Corps and started its march north on 13 December. The veteran 28th Infantry Division held the corps center, fronting on the Our River. The newly arrived and green 106th Infantry Division had completed the relief of the 2d Infantry Division in the Schnee Eifel sector on 12 December. Here the German West Wall turned northeastward following the Schnee Eifel crest. In the Losheim Gap, at the northern terminus of the Schnee Eifel, a light task force of the 14th Cavalry Group maintained a screening position between the 106th and 99th Infantry Divisions. It should be noted that this was the seam between the VIII and V Corps.

Although the VIII Corps forward area possessed many terrain features favoring the defender, notably the Schnee Eifel on the left wing and the river sequence fronting the corps center and right, there were numerous points of entry for an attack moving east to west. The three infantry divisions under Middleton's command were responsible for a front of about eighty-five miles, a distance approximately three times that normally assigned an equivalent defending force by US service school teaching and tactical doctrine. On the morning of 16 December the total assigned strength of the VIII Corps was 68,822 officers and men. Immediately after the Battle of the Bulge, the tag "a calculated risk" would be applied to the attenuated VIII Corps front as it existed on 16 December. Middleton was well aware of the risk—indeed he had made this clear in discussions with his superiors. Somewhat after the event General Eisenhower wrote General of the Army George C. Marshall (on 10 January 1945) that in early November he and Bradley had discussed the possibility of a German counteroffensive in the Ardennes but had agreed that such a move would be unprofitable to the enemy. The line of reasoning, as set before Marshall, was this: the "Volkssturm" would be no good in offensive operations, winter in the Ardennes would render continuous logistic support impossible, and Allied strength was so great that the Germans could not push far enough to reach really vital objectives.

Whatever thought may have been given to the Ardennes, the Allies were on the offensive and preparing for yet greater offensive operations well to the north and the south of the VIII Corps sector. Losses during November had been high and the reserve of new divisions in the United States was running low (in the United Kingdom such a reserve no longer existed). The old military axiom that the line cannot be strong everywhere applied with full force to the Allied positions reaching from Switzerland to the North Sea. Almost automatically Allied strength would concentrate in those areas where the offensive was the order of the day and where decision might be reached. The Ardennes sector seemed no special risk, it had been quiet for weeks, it offered—or so it seemed—no terrain attraction for the enemy, and there was no recognizable indication that enemy forces opposite the VIII Corps and 99th Infantry Division outnumbered those deployed on the friendly side of the line. If there was a "calculated risk," therefore, it was no more precise or specific than that taken wittingly by any commander who thins his front to mount an attack while knowing that he has over-all superiority and the ability to retain the initiative.

The Intelligence Failure

In the years that have passed since the close of World War II the Ardennes has ranked close to Pearl Harbor as an episode inviting public polemic, personal vituperation, and *ex parte* vindication. Sentences, phrases, and punctuation marks from American intelligence documents of pre-Ardennes origin have been twisted and turned, quoted in and out of context, "interpreted" and misinterpreted, in arduous efforts to fix blame and secure absolution. There no longer is point to such intensely personal examination of the failure by American and Allied intelligence to give warning of the Ardennes counteroffensive preparations. The failure was general and cannot be attributed to any person or group of persons. The intelligence story on the eve of the Ardennes is not germane in terms of personal opinions or the men who held them. What counts are the views held at the various American headquarters and the gist of enemy information which reached those headquarters.

In mid-September the Western Allies had felt imminent victory in their hands. Flushed with their own dazzling successes and heartened by news of the bloody defeats which the Soviet armies were administering to the Germans on the Eastern Front, the Allies saw the Wehrmacht collapsing and the Third Reich tottering to its knees. The pervasive optimism dissipated as the surprisingly revitalized German armies stood their ground in defense of the West Wall, but it never completely disappeared. When the Allied attack began to roll again in late November and early December, some of this earlier optimism reappeared. A 12th Army Group intelligence summary issued on 12 December echoes the prevailing tone: "It is now certain that attrition is steadily sapping the strength of German forces on the Western Front and that the crust of defenses is thinner, more brittle and more vulnerable than it appears on our G-2 maps or to the troops in the line." This optimism, particularly when heightened by reports that the enemy no longer had fuel for tanks and planes, conditioned all estimates of the enemy's plans and capabilities. It may be phrased this way: the enemy can still do something but he can't do much; he lacks the men, the planes, the tanks, the fuel, and the ammunition.

Another aspect of Allied thinking would contribute to the general misconception of German capabilities and intentions. The return of Field Marshal von Rundstedt to command in the west had been marked with much interest by Allied intelligence staffs. Accepted in military circles as one of the best soldiers in the world, Rundstedt's reputation, even among his opponents, rose to new stature as the result of the stubborn German defense in the autumn of 1944. Here, then, was a commander who could be expected to act and react according to the rational and accepted canons of the military art. He would husband his dwindling resources, at an appropriate time he would counterattack in accordance with available means, and ultimately he would fall back to the Rhine for the major defensive battle. Had Rundstedt actually commanded in the west, as the Allies believed, this analysis would have been correct. (Rundstedt's effort to delimit the scope of the Ardennes counteroffensive in order to achieve a reasonable symbiosis between the means and the end proves the point.)

But Hitler alone commanded. Intuition, not conventional professional judgment, would determine German action. Unaware of the true nature of the German decision-making process in the west, the Allied commanders and staffs awaited an enemy reaction which would be rational and therefore predictable. If the thought ever occurred to an Allied intelligence officer that Germany would gamble on one last great effort west of the Rhine, staking everything on a single throw of the dice, this idea disappeared in the aura of high professional military competence which attached to Rundstedt. In a way this may have been the field marshal's greatest personal contribution to the Ardennes counteroffensive.

It is impossible to determine the extent to which the Hitler cover plan deceived the Allies into accepting the area north of the Ardennes as the focal point for the anticipated German reaction. Here the Allies were making their greatest effort and it was natural to assume that the German reserves remaining would be committed to meet this effort. Even the US Third Army, far to the south, relaxed its normally parochial view of the front and predicted that the Sixth Panzer Army would be employed in a spoiling attack in the Aachen-Düren sector. Here, too, lay the direct route to the Ruhr. It long had been an article of faith in Allied strategy that Germany would make its greatest efforts in defense of what Eisenhower had called the two hearts of Germany: the Ruhr, the industrial heart, and Berlin, the political heart. Furthermore, the area between the Roer and Rhine Rivers represented good tank-going for the Allied armored divisions. Duly impressed with their own armored successes, the Allies expected that the enemy would throw his reserve armor into battle here in an attempt to prevent a repetition of the August tank race across France. Perhaps German deception did make some confirmatory contribution, but regardless of this Allied eyes were fixed immovably on the front north of the Ardennes.

One item would cause Allied intelligence some concern, although it seems that this concern was more academic than real. Where was Rundstedt's armored counterattack reserve, the Sixth Panzer Army? Allied situation maps of early December still carried the headquarters of this army in the vicinity of Cologne, and assigned four or five uncommitted panzer divisions as available to this command. But the actual location of the Sixth Panzer Army was a matter of debate. The 12th

Army Group thought that it might be concentrated around Bielefeld, northeast of Cologne. The US First Army placed it rather indefinitely between the Roer and the Rhine. The US Third Army plumped for a location between Düsseldorf and Cologne. The US Ninth Army apparently did not care to enter this guessing game. SHAEF intelligence summed up the matter nicely in the report of 10 December: "There is no further news of Sixth SS Panzer Army beyond vague rumours."

There was general agreement that Rundstedt's armored reserve would be thrown against the First and Ninth Armies in an effort to blunt their drive in the Roer area, although the severe German reverses sustained in the south during the second week of December led to some thought that divisions might be stripped from the Sixth Panzer reserve to shore up the defenses of the Palatinate. The two US armies carrying the attack in the north were agreed that the Sixth Panzer Army would be committed after their attack had crossed the Roer River. The 12th Army Group expected the same timing and anticipated the German reaction would come as a coordinated counterattack. There was less Allied interest in the Fifth Panzer Army than in the Sixth. The former had been sorely handled in the fight on the Roer front and the appearance of the Fifteenth Army in this sector, identified in the second week of December, led to the assumption that the Fifth and its most badly battered divisions had been withdrawn for rest and necessary overhaul. On 12 December the 12th Army Group reported the Fifth as assembling its weary divisions between Cologne and Koblenz.

American intelligence summaries, periodic reports, and briefings, for the month prior to the 16 December assault, gave only fragmentary and skeletal information on the enemy opposite the VIII Corps. German planners had predicted that the American high commanders would accept the theory that the rugged terrain in this area, particularly in poor weather, effectively precluded large scale mechanized operations. Perhaps there was some subconscious assumption by American staffs that the Ardennes was so nearly impassable as to be ruled out of consideration. But there were more tangible reasons for the scant attention accorded this sector. It had been a quiet sector of the Western Front since the Allied dash across France had halted in September. The German divisions identified here as fairly permanent residents were battle weary, understrength, and obviously in need of rest and refitting. At various times fresh divisions had appeared opposite the VIII Corps, but their stay had been brief. By December it had become axiomatic, insofar as US intelligence was concerned, that any new division identified on the VIII Corps front was no more than a bird of passage en route to the north or the south. As a result the Ardennes assumed a kind of neutral hue in American eyes. Important happenings, it seemed, transpired north of the Ardennes and south of the Ardennes, but never at the division point itself. This mental set offers a partial explanation of why the 99th Division in the V Corps zone identified only three of the twelve German divisions assembling to its front, while the VIII Corps identified only four out of ten divisions before 16 December.

Was there any warning note sounded for the VIII Corps and its troops in the line during the days just prior to the German onslaught? With the advantage of hindsight, seven items can be discerned in the corps reports for the period 13-15 December which might have given the alarm. Two divisions, the 28th and 106th, sent in reports of increased vehicular activity on the nights before the attack. The 28th discounted its own report by noting that this was the normal accompaniment of an enemy frontline relief and that the same thing had happened when a German unit had pulled out three weeks before. The 106th was a green division and unlikely to know what weight could be attached legitimately to such activity. In fact one regimental commander rebuked his S-2 for reporting this noise as "enemy movement." A third incident occurred on 14 December when a woman escapee reported to the 28th Infantry Division commander that the woods near Bitburg were jammed with German equipment. Her answers to questions posed by the division G-2 apparently were impressive enough to gain the attention of the VIII Corps G-2 who ordered that she be taken to the First Army headquarters. The woman arrived there on 16 December.

The four remaining incidents attach to the capture of German prisoners on 15 December, two each by the 4th and 106th Infantry Divisions. The time of capture is important: two at 1830, one at 1930, and one at an unspecified time thereafter. All four claimed that fresh troops were arriving in the line, that a big attack was in the offing, that it might come on the 16th or 17th but certainly would be made before Christmas. Two of the prisoners were deserters; they themselves did not take the reported attack too seriously since, as they told their captors, all this had been promised German troops before. The other two were wounded. One seems to have made some impression on the interrogators, but since he was under the influence of morphine his captors decided that further questioning would be necessary.

Of the seven incidents which in retrospect may be considered signposts pointing to an impending attack on the VIII Corps front, only four were reported to the corps headquarters. Three of the four prisoners seemed to be parroting wild and baseless rumors of a sort which was fairly common, and these three were bundled into prisoner of war cages without further ado. The incidents reported to the VIII Corps were forwarded to the First Army and duly noted by that headquarters on 14 and 15 December. Only one incident was deemed worthy of 12th Army Group attention. This, one of the reports of extraordinary traffic, was mentioned in the commanding general's briefing as confirmation of the predicted relief of the 326th Infantry Division. This briefing began at 0915 on 16 December.

Perhaps the appearance of these seven indicators might have been treated in combination to uncover the German preparations and allow the VIII Corps at least a minimum tactical preparation for the attack. Whether any commander would have been justified in making major alterations in his troop disposition on the basis of this intelligence alone is highly questionable. One might more reasonably conclude that the American acquisition of only this limited and suspect information was a tribute to the security measures enacted by the enemy.

What of air intelligence, the source of Rundstedt's greatest worry? Bad weather during the first half of December did reduce the number of Allied reconnaissance sorties flown east of the First Army front but by no means produced the kind of blackout for which the enemy hoped. In the month prior to the Ardennes attack the 67th Tactical Reconnaissance Group (IX Tactical Air Command), supporting the First Army, flew 361 missions of which 242 were judged successful. From the 10th through the 15th of December the group flew 71 missions with varying degrees of success; for example, on 14 December planes flown over Trier by the 30th Photo Reconnaissance Squadron reported the weather clear, but two hours later a second mission ran into haze and was able to see very little. Only one day, 13 December, in the five critical days before the attack found all US air reconnaissance grounded.

The pilots belonging to the 67th Group and the 10th Photo Reconnaissance Group, the latter attached to the Third Army's old partner, the XIX TAC, actually constructed an imposing picture of German buildup west of the Rhine in the month preceding the

Ardennes counteroffensive. In the last week of November the number of enemy columns on the roads showed a marked increase. On 30 November US reconnaissance planes reported a drastic heightening of rail activity west of the Rhine and this was confirmed by the fighter-bombers flying "armed-recce." Special indications of forthcoming attack were numerous: a large number of hospital trains on the west bank of the Rhine, several groups of flatcars carrying Tiger tanks, and fifty searchlights in one location. Lights representing large-scale night movements were consistently reported, although the two available night fighter squadrons were so badly understrength (averaging no more than ten P-61's operational) that their contribution perforce was limited.

The intelligence problem presented by the US air effort was not that of a paucity of information but rather one of interpretation. Both the Allied ground and air headquarters expected the enemy to reinforce those sectors to the north and south of the Ardennes where the First and Third US Armies were attacking. The main special indicators of coming attack were identified in transit areas on the routes to the Roer and the Saar. The trainloads of Tiger tanks, for example, were seen on the Euskirchen rail lines. This line ran northwest to Düren and the Roer, but a branch line led south to the Eifel. The reports of searchlights, turned in on the night of 6-7 December, came from the vicinity of Kaiserslautern, opposite the Third Army. Kaiserslautern, however, was only a few miles by rail from Trier, one of the chief unloading yards opposite the VIII Corps. There was considerable information, then, of the enemy's growing strength west of the Rhine. But the interpretation of his intentions was precisely what he desired: reinforcement of the Sixth Panzer Army counterattack reserve on the Roer front and piecemeal movement to shore up the divisions being battered by the Third and Seventh Armies.

Was there any special attempt at air reconnaissance over the Eifel? A large number of missions were flown here in November, that is, before the final assembly for attack began. During the first half of December the 67th Group rather consistently included Eifel targets in its daily mission orders; however, these missions were given low priority and often were scratched. In the critical period (10 through 15 December) the 67th flew only three missions directly opposite the VIII Corps, on 14 December over Trier. Numerous requests for air reconnaissance were made during this time by the VIII Corps divisions, but even when accepted by higher ground echelons and forwarded to air headquarters these missions retained so low a priority, when contrasted with the demands from the Roer and Saar fronts, as to fall at the bottom of the missions list. In sum, it can be said that the reconnaissance flown over the Eifel between 16 November and 15 December gave much information on enemy activity, but that this was interpreted as routine troop movement through the Eifel waystation en route to the north and the south. Thus, the SHAEF intelligence summary of 10 December gives air reports of "continuing troop movements towards the Eifel sector" and concludes that "the procession is not yet ended."

Could the proper combination of air and ground intelligence have weakened the Allied fixation on the Roer and Saar sectors? Perhaps, but this is extremely hypothetical. One thing seems clear. Although the ground headquarters were charged with the final analysis of photos and pilot reports secured by the air, there was little cooperation and liaison between the air and ground headquarters as to the initial interpretation placed by the air forces on the data gathered through aerial reconnaissance. The official US Army Air Forces account of this episode states the case justly: "Perhaps the chief fault was one of organization, for there seems to have been a twilight zone between air and ground headquarters in which the responsibility had not been sufficiently pinned down."

On 15 December the Allied air commanders' conference at SHAEF convened to review the big picture. Here the SHAEF G-3 told the assembled airmen that the Roer dam operations had failed to provoke a move by the main enemy armored reserve; as for the VIII Corps front, "nothing to report." Then the A-2 rose to sketch the activities of the Luftwaffe: it had continued the movement westward, closer to the battlefield, which had been noted in recent days, but all this was "defensive" only.

The prelude to the Ardennes counteroffensive of 16 December can only be reckoned as a gross failure by Allied ground and air intelligence. One of the greatest skills in the practice of the military art is the avoidance of the natural tendency to overrate or underestimate the enemy. Here, the enemy capability for reacting other than to direct Allied pressure had been sadly underestimated. Americans and British had looked in a mirror for the enemy and seen there only the reflection of their own intentions.

The German Concentration

Hitler's operation directive of 10 November set 27 November as the date for completion of the huge concentration preliminary to the Ardennes counteroffensive, with a target date two days earlier for the attack by the divisions in the initial thrust. But his commanders in the west, better versed in logistics, recognized from the first that the attack could not be made before the very last of the month. The Allied attacks in the Aachen and Metz sectors made further postponement unavoidable, pinning German divisions to the front long beyond their planned date of relief and bringing others back into the line when refitting had only just begun. Inside the Greater Reich the Replacement Army, charged with creating and training new Volks Grenadier divisions for the offensive, proved Hitler's optimism ill-founded. The task of building new divisions from air force troops, sailors, and the products of Goebbel's raid on the remaining civilian population was immense, the timing necessarily slow. In early December, when Hitler's target date had come and gone, another factor intervened to cause delay. The preliminary movement of armored divisions and vehicular columns had burned up far more fuel than German quartermasters had reckoned. The attack would have to be delayed until the diminished fuel tanks west of the Rhine could be replenished.

The concentration period, therefore, would run until 16 December but even these added days gave all too short a time for such a formidable array of preparations. The original plans called for the movement and assembly of 4 armies, 11 corps, 38 divisions, 9 Volks artillery corps, and 7 Volks Werfer brigades, plus service and support troops. By the beginning of December OKW's inflated order of battle had been reduced to about 30 divisions (the Fifteenth Army now was deleted from the initial attack order, although still envisioned as the subsidiary attack force), but the logistics problem remained of staggering proportions.

The area in which the Army Group B would concentrate its forces, equipment, and supplies was delimited on the south by the Moselle River and had as its base the Rhine crossings stretching from Düsseldorf to Koblenz. On the north there were actually two limits. That farthest north ran from the Rhine west on the axis München-Gladbach and Roermond. South of this line Allied intelligence officers watched, as they were intended to watch, the daylight, only half-disguised, movement of German troops and supplies. Farther south a second and true limit defined the main concentration area. Here the line extended from Bonn, through Euskirchen, to the front north of Monschau. The trick, then, would be to effect a large and secret concentration south of this second line while at the same time preparing to sideslip the forces from the north into this sector in the last hours before the attack.

The first problem of organization was that of rail transport. Troops, tanks, and guns had to be brought from East Prussia, Poland, Austria, the Netherlands, Denmark, and Norway. Fuel and ammunition had to be hauled across the exposed Rhine bridges and unloaded quickly and quietly at the Eifel dumps. A number of divisions, in particular those assigned to the Sixth Panzer Army, would have to be shuttled from the battle front back across the Rhine to training and refitting areas, then be moved across the Rhine again and into the concentration zone.

Probably no railway system in the world was better able to handle this tremendous task than the Reichsbahn (the German State Railroads). It had been modernized on the eve of the war, was a model of efficient management, and, through a program of systematic looting, had more than replaced the rolling stock lost to air attack. The cars and the locomotives in large freight yards, as many American soldiers will remember, read like a European railroad gazetteer. Militarization of the German railroads was complete. The German Army had been the first in history to employ railroads for a great strategic concentration, and the successes of 1870 had led to a tradition in General Staff thought and training which looked to the rail system as the primary means of strategic concentration. The rail lines along the Rhine and west of the river had been located in accordance with military desires. The Eifel branches had been constructed in preparation for the First World War, then had been reinforced for the campaign of 1940. But there was more than the tradition of the great General Staff to dictate this reliance on rail: Hitler's scheme for a military superhighway system, the Reichsautobahnen, had been cut short by the war; the Allied attacks against motor fuel production had depleted German stocks, although hardly to the extent that Allied intelligence estimated in the autumn of 1944.

The major threat, of course, was the overwhelming superiority of the Allied air forces and their ability, no longer effectively challenged by the Luftwaffe, to look and to strike almost at will. German railway preparations, as a result, had to take count of three dangers: Allied air reconnaissance over the Eifel and its rail approaches, bombing attacks to knock out the Rhine rail bridges, and rail-cutting attacks stepped up to the point where repair efforts could no longer hold the pace. In the short run, decisions on the form of the air war reached in the higher Allied councils during the autumn of 1944 made the German task much easier; in the long run, these same decisions contributed to the final failure of the Ardennes counteroffensive.

British and American air leaders had found themselves consistently at loggerheads on the issue of transportation versus oil targets. The American view was that the German rail system constituted too complex a target to be demolished in any reasonable time, but that enemy oil production was so highly concentrated (particularly in the synthetic oil plants) as to permit a killing blow in the time and with the effort available. Before 16 December the American view held first priority. Indeed, during the month of October second place was accorded to attacks—subsequently judged as "rather inconclusive"—against ordnance depots, tank assembly plants, and motor vehicle production. Eventually, at the close of October, the British succeeded in raising the priority on rail attacks, although this remained second to those on oil. November was the big month for attacks against the latter, the

Allied strategic air forces dropping 37,096 tons aimed at German oil production. In the second half of the month, however, the rail campaign stepped up; the Eighth Air Force and the RAF actually delivered more bombs against rail than against oil targets. The Rhine bridges presented a special problem. In November the SHAEF G-2 asked that the air mount a campaign to cut these bridges, but on this the American and British air commanders were in accord. The great Rhine bridges, heavily guarded by flak, were tough targets for the bombing techniques then current and the Allied air forces succeeded in staving off this demand.

German records, fairly full for the final quarter of 1944, give this picture of the effects of Allied air attacks. The Reichsbahn moved troop strength by rail equivalent to sixty-six divisions before the attack. Forces equivalent to seven divisions were moved by road Twenty-seven of the division-size rail movements were affected in some way by air attack, in most cases before they actually entered the buildup zone. Delays normally were no longer than one or two days, although from 10 December on some divisions were forced to march an extra fifty to sixty miles on foot. A number of units lost essential organic equipment during these attacks, the deprivation inevitably inhibiting their later performance. Very noticeable effects of Allied air efforts came on 10 and 11 December. On the first day a noon attack over the Koblenz rail yards left more than a hundred bomb craters. Nonetheless, the yards were in full operation twenty-four hours later. The main double-track line supporting the Sixth Panzer Army assembly (Cologne-Euskirchen) was hit so severely as to stop all rail traffic on 11 December; but the line was running again on the 12th. Two Rhine rail bridges took hits in November and four were under repair as the result of attacks during October. In all cases at least one rail line per bridge remained operable. An Allied plane hit one bridge with one bomb during the first half of December. Supply shipments generally went unscathed in the actual concentration area. About five hundred trains were employed to effect this buildup, of which air attack in October and November destroyed only fifteen carloads.

In sum, the greatest menace to the German rail concentration came from attacks by bombers and fighter-bombers against railroad tracks, stations, and yards. Hardly a day passed without one or more breaks somewhere in the system at and west of the Rhine. During the first two weeks of December the Allied air attacks inflicted 125 breaks on the rails feeding the Western Front, 60 of which were in the concentration area. German engineers, still working on November cuts, repaired 150 breaks of which 100 were in the concentration area. There was, then, an uneasy equilibrium between Allied air attacks and the German rail repair capability. Be it remembered, however, that the Allied air campaign against the Reichsbahn thus far was dispersed and a matter of second priority.

If nuclear weapons do not succeed in entirely removing rail transport from the logistic systems of future war, the German handling of the Ardennes buildup will stand as a military model. As a part of military history, the story of this German success, achieved despite Allied dominance in the air, merits some attention. One of Hitler's first concerns, following the fateful decision to gamble everything on a single stroke in the west, was to assure himself that the Rhine bridges would be secure and that the Reichsbahn could bear the weight he intended to impose upon it. Sometime during September—an exact date is lacking—the OKH Chief of Transportation, General der Infanterie Rudolf Gercke, was admitted to the tiny circle of those entrusted with the Ardennes plans. His initial task was to deal with the Rhine River crossing sites; this was the priority through September and October. First the pillars and piers supporting the Rhine bridges were reinforced so that a lucky hit could not send an entire bridge into the Rhine waters. Next, a number of ferries were modified to carry trains and a few highway bridges were strengthened for track-laying in the event that the regular railroad bridges failed. Special heavy spans of military bridging were floated into waiting positions along the banks. (At one time plans were made to expand two mining tunnels which ran under the Rhine so that troops could be marched from one side to the other.) Ruhr industry contributed large stocks of steel girders and plates; these stocks were then distributed for quick repair jobs at the main rail bridges. Early in October reinforcement was introduced on a number of bridges to permit the passage of trains carrying the 70-ton King Tiger tanks. By early December eight railway bridges were ready immediately behind the assembly area, plus an equal number of highway bridges and twelve Rhine ferries capable of handling locomotives. An additional four rail bridges, lower down on the Rhine, were scheduled for use if needed.

The Allied decision to forgo any intensive attacks against the Rhine crossings gave this segment of the German rail system relative immunity during the buildup The actual trackage and the freight yards, particularly those west of the Rhine, had no such immunity and would come under increasing attack in late November just when the concentration was swinging into full stride. Almost completely bereft of any friendly air cover, how did the Germans keep their rail transport functioning? Recall that the Wehrmacht had been forced to perfect the art of camouflage, that the traditionally severe German discipline functioned nowhere better than in the rigorous control of troop movement, and that the Reichsbahn was an integral member of the body military.

The first measure adopted to protect military trains from Allied observation and attack aimed at the utmost use of darkness and bad flying weather. All rail movement west of the line Bremen-Kassel-Ulm, a distance of 150-200 miles from the fighting front, was confined to those times when air reconnaissance would be stymied. A few exceptions, for purposes of deception, were permitted in the Aachen area. Control was decentralized and even the smaller rail stations were tied in to the main German weather service so as to wring the most mileage out of any local change in the weather. Supply trains were organized east of the Rhine and there allocated a particular line and army. Every effort was made to load down the branch lines, particularly when it became apparent that the Allies tended to concentrate on the main lines.

Train movement was very carefully controlled. The thick forests of the Eifel, plus an unusual number of rail tunnels near the chief supply dumps, gave considerable chance of concealment. Wherever possible the run was made to the unloading point and back to the west bank of the Rhine in one night. On double-tracked lines the movement was restricted to one-way traffic, then reversed. A host of small stations were given extra siding so that trains could be stationed serially all along the line and unloaded simultaneously. This system also permitted quick distribution to the many small, concealed dumps. Earlier it had been discovered that engine crews often were killed by Allied strafing while the locomotive remained intact. Special light armor plate therefore was introduced on all cabs. Also, it had been noticed that fighter-bomber pilots tended to work on a train at relatively high altitudes when subjected to antiaircraft fire. All trains, then, would carry a section of light flak. So successful were these measures that a number of divisions actually detrained at railheads only eight to twenty miles behind the front.

There were four main double-track lines running into the Eifel. From 4 September to 10 December all were under the control of the Seventh Army, but on 10 December the two panzer armies moved in to take command of their own sectors. In the north, two lines, Cologne-Düren and Bonn-Euskirchen, handled the bulk of Sixth Panzer Army traffic. The Ahr River line, fed mainly by the Remagen bridge, supported the Fifth Panzer Army. The Moselle line, following the old Napoleonic "cannon road," handled the Seventh Army trains plus some traffic for the Fifth. Although less rich in rail than areas to the north and south, the Eifel possessed a substantial, crisscross net of feeder lines. There was one main lateral line quite close to the front, that via Euskirchen-Kall-Ehrang-Trier. Until 16 December the main troop detraining points were Schleiden, Stadtkyll, Prüm, Niederweiss, the west station at Trier, and Konz. In addition there were four chief areas for unloading supplies: Rheinbach, Mechernich, Muesch (near Ahrdorf), and Kall.

The amount of ammunition and POL required to support the attack imposed a severe load not only upon the dwindling German war economy but on the Eifel rail system as well. Hitler had allocated one hundred trains of ammunition to nourish the counteroffensive, this coming from the special Fuehrer Reserve. Over and above this special reserve, Generalmajor Alfred Toppe, the Oberquartermeister, figured on scraping together four units of what in German practice was considered a basic load. Of these units, one was allocated for the artillery barrage preparatory to the attack, one half would be used in breaking through the enemy main line of resistance, and one and a half would be fired to keep the offensive rolling. Toppe had planned to have two basic loads of ammunition in the hands of troops when the attack commenced and did deliver the loads as scheduled. However, he had not counted on the Allied attacks, furnishing only enough extra ammunition for the normal day-to-day battle in the west. By the second week of December the two basic loads had been whittled down to one and a half. Even so, on the last day reported—13 December—Army Group B had 15,099 tons of ammunition in its dumps. The heavy concentration of antiaircraft artillery scheduled to support the attack was better off than the ground gunners: the III Flak Corps, with 66 heavy and 74 medium and light batteries, had 7 basic loads of ammunition. In net, the Army Group B logisticians estimated the attack would average a daily ammunition consumption of about 1,200 tons. Needless to say this figure was based on a fast-moving exploitation once the breakthrough was accomplished.

Motor fuel, a notorious logistic problem in German armies at this stage of the war, was the greatest headache in the Western Front headquarters, particularly in the last days before the attack. The journals of OB WEST are jammed during this period with messages attempting to trace promised trainloads of POL. By 16 December, however, the quartermaster and rail systems had combined to put the promised 4,680,000 gallons in the hands of OB WEST, although perhaps half of this was in dumps back at the Rhine.

During the period 9 September-15 December the Seventh Army, or main, concentration area received 1,502 troop trains and approximately 500 supply trains, most of which were earmarked for the counteroffensive. The Eifel rail net in this time unloaded 144,735 tons of supplies. At some point the Eifel rail system would be saturated; this point was reached on 17 December when OB WEST was forced to detrain its incoming reserve divisions on the west bank of the Rhine, a factor of some significance in the ensuing history of the Ardennes battle.

With the Allies hammering at the Roer, pushing along the Saar, and converging on the Saverne Gap, the Ardennes target date—25 November—passed into discard. On that day Hitler reviewed the situation with his household military staff. The enemy offensive, said he, had fulfilled the major prerequisites for a successful German attack. The Allies had taken heavy losses and had been forced to deploy their reserves close behind the attack front or feed them into the line. Now, more than ever, the Fuehrer was convinced of the Big Solution's feasibility. From somewhere in lower echelons the idea had been broached that the Meuse crossing sites should be seized on the first day. This brought hearty concurrence. Advance battalions should try for the Meuse bridges in the early morning (Hitler probably referred here to the end of the first 24-hour period). Again Hitler stressed the need for penetrations on narrow fronts, but once the breakthrough was accomplished he foresaw considerable maneuver as the two panzer armies hit the Meuse. To ensure flexibility in the choice of bridgeheads, he extended the Sixth Panzer Army zone (on the right) to include the crossings at Huy, while the Fifth Panzer Army southern boundary moved down to Givet. It may be that in this same briefing the Fuehrer set a new D-day. In any case Jodl visited Rundstedt on 26 November and delivered the news that Null Tag (D-day) would be 10 December. This date finally was scrapped because the fuel dumps were not full and a number of the assault divisions were still en route to the concentration zone. On the 11th Hitler approved further postponement until 0530 on 15 December, then on 19 December altered the attack order to read the 16th, with the usual proviso that if good flying weather intervened the whole operation would stop dead in its tracks.

The rail movement of the initial attack divisions had nearly ended by 11 December, although the transport of the second phase formations, belonging to the OKW reserve, still had a few days to go. The Seventh Army, quondam caretaker on the Ardennes front, had most of its divisions in the line but in the nights just before the attack would have to shift some of these southward into the final assembly area designated for the Seventh on the attack left wing. The Fifth Panzer Army, slated to make the attack in the center, had begun its concentration in the Remagen-Mayen area of the Eifel as early as 26 November, but some of its armor was coming from as far north as München-Gladbach—one attack division, the 116th Panzer, would not complete detraining until 16 December. The Sixth Panzer Army, which in Hitler's mind and in OKW plans represented the main effort and whose four SS panzer divisions were expected to pace the entire counteroffensive, by 6 December had closed its armor in a zone stretching from west of Cologne to southwest of Bonn. The question remained whether the Sixth infantry divisions, some of which were in the Roer battle line, could be pried loose and moved south in time for H-hour. The Fifteenth Army, once intended to cover the north flank of the Sixth Panzer Army advance, had its hands full on the Roer front. Here there was no immediate assembly problem, although the army would have to plug the gaps left as divisions pulled out for the Ardennes. Ultimately, however, the Fifteenth might be reinforced from the OKW reserve and join the attack. If the Fifteenth Army is excluded the German attack front extended for 143 kilometers (89 miles). The main armored concentration, however, would take place on a frontage of 97 kilometers (6 miles).

The timetable for final assembly in attack positions required three days, or better, three nights, since nearly all movement would be confined to hours of darkness. To prevent premature disclosure by some unit wandering into the assembly area, all formations except those already deployed on the original Seventh Army front or immediately behind it were banned from crossing the Army Group B base line, twelve miles behind the front, until the final assembly was ordered by Hitler. Once across the base line every movement had to follow rigid timing. For further control the infantry and armored divisions were each assigned two sectors for assembly. Infantry Area I was marked by a restraining line six miles from the front; Area II extended forward to points about two and a half to three miles from the front. Armor Area I actually was east of the base line which served as the forward restraining line; Area II was defined by a line six to ten miles from the front. The armored divisions, of course, would be strung out over greater distances than given here but their assault echelons would be fitted inside the two armored areas.

Timing was defined by coded days from the alphabet. Since O-Tag or D-day was in fact 16 December the calendar dates can be given for what in the plan was merely an undated sequence of events. On K-Tag (12 December) troops were alerted for movement. As yet they had no knowledge of the offensive; they would receive this information the night before the attack jumped off. By L-Tag (13 December) all units were supposed to have their forward detachments up to the base line; most of them did. During the night of 13 December the clockwork march to the final attack positions began. Those infantry divisions not already in place moved to the forward restraining line of their Area I. This also was the night for the guns and howitzers belonging to army and VAK batteries to move. Using horses from the neighboring infantry artillery regiments, and liberally employing straw to muffle the wheels (just as had been done in 1918), the batteries were dragged into positions about five miles to the rear of the ultimate firing emplacements. The rocket projectors, easier to camouflage, were hidden immediately behind their firing positions.

On the night of the 14th the infantry divisions not already in place marched quietly into Area II. Motorized artillery went to assigned firing positions while low-flying German planes zoomed noisily over the American listening posts, or it was dragged forward by horses. The rocket projector crews dug their pieces into the pits from which the preparation for the attack would be fired. The tracked elements of the panzer division assault groups churned into Armor Area II over roads which only two days earlier had been iced completely and along which treacherous stretches remained. Wheeled units moved up to the Area I restraining line. This armored movement in the dark of night was difficult indeed, but to avoid entanglement each panzer division had been given a road of its own and in no cases did the distance traveled during the two nights total more than fifty miles; for most it was less. On the night of 15 December all formations marched to the line of departure or to forward combat positions. It would appear that nearly all units were in place an hour or two before H-hour, 0530 on the morning of 6 December.

Although the troops knew nothing of their mission until the night of the 15th, save what they could surmise, the commanders had been given the picture in time to do some individual planning. By the end of the first week in December all corps and division commanders knew what was expected of them. Most of the division staffs seem to have been briefed on 10 December. Hitler received the commanders entrusted with the attack in two groups on the nights of 11 and 12 December. Most of the visitors seem to have been more impressed by the Fuehrer's obvious physical deterioration and the grim mien of the SS guards than by Hitler's rambling recital of his deeds for Germany which constituted this last "briefing."

The forces assembled for the counteroffensive were the product of an almost psychotic drive by Hitler to put every last man, gun, and tank that could be stripped from some part of the declining German war establishment into the attack. Thirteen infantry and seven armored divisions were ready for the initial assault. Five divisions from the OKW reserve were on alert or actually en route to form the second wave, plus one armored and one mechanized brigade at reinforced strength. Approximately five additional divisions were listed in the OKW reserve, but their availability was highly dubious. Some 1,900 artillery pieces — including rocket projectors — were ready to support the attack. The seven armored divisions in the initial echelon had about 970 tanks and armored assault guns. The armored and mechanized elements of the immediate OKW reserve had another 450 to swell the armored attack. If and when the Fifteenth Army joined in, the total force could be counted as twenty-nine infantry and twelve armored divisions.

These divisions and heavy weapons might or might not suffice for the task at hand, but the total represented the best that the Wehrmacht could do. Of the armored complement on the Western Front—2,567 tanks and assault guns—Army Group B and OKW reserve had been given 2,168. About a third of this latter total would have to be left for the time being with the Fifteenth Army to shore up the right-wing defenses in the Roer sector. Some four hundred tanks and assault guns were all that remained to German divisions on the rest of the long Western Front. The hard-pressed armies on the Eastern Front likewise had been denied the armored matériel to replace their heavy autumn losses. At the beginning of December the Eastern Front total in operational tanks and assault guns was roughly 1,500. Despite Hitler's personal emphasis on the power of the artillery arm and the very substantial number of tubes allocated for the offensive, the greatest portion of OB WEST artillery had to be left for corseting where armor and infantry had been pulled out, and, because of the scarcity of prime movers, a large number of batteries scheduled for the attack never got forward at all. The artillery flak and rocket projector support for the entire Western Front actually numbered 7,822 pieces on 16 December.

As proof that the Western Front's armored strength in December 1944 equaled that of the halcyon days at the beginning of the war, Hitler's personal staff compiled a special report which showed that 2,594 tanks had taken part in the victorious 1940 campaign in the west. Nobody, it would appear, cared to look at comparative figures of air strengths in previous campaigns. In the Polish campaign some 50 German divisions had been given direct support by 1,800 first-line aircraft. The Balkan campaign had seen 1,000 aircraft supporting 17 divisions. The victorious advance into the Soviet Union had brought 123 divisions into the line, with 2,500 first-line attack planes in the air. Now, for the 25 divisions certain to be committed in the Ardennes, Goering could promise only a thousand planes. By this time Hitler was chary of Luftwaffe promises and watered down this figure to 800-900 planes when he presented it to OB WEST. Hitler's estimate would be met—but only for one day and that when the ground battle already had been decided.

In December 1944, Germany was fighting a "poor man's war" on the ground as in the air. This must be remembered when assessing the actual military potential of the divisions arrayed for the western offensive. Motor transport was in sorry shape; the best-equipped divisions had about 80 percent of their vehicular tables of equipment, but many had only half the amount specified in the tables. One of the best mechanized divisions had sixty different types of automotive transport. Spare parts, a necessity in rough terrain and poor weather, hardly existed. There was only a handful of prime movers and heavy tank retrievers. Signal equipment was antiquated, worn-out, and sparse; the same held for engineer tools and vehicles. Antitank guns were scarce, the heavy losses in this weapon sustained in the summer and autumn disasters having never been made good. The German infantryman would have to defend himself against the enemy tank with bravery and the bazooka, or so the field service regulations read.

German military poverty was nowhere more apparent than in the stocks of ammunition and POL which had been laboriously amassed to support the attack. The Sixth Panzer Army artillery commander, for example, had pleaded for twelve to fifteen units of artillery ammunition for the first ten days of operations. On 16 December there were only one and a half units with the Army Group B guns and only two additional units in prospect. Although OB WEST appears to have estimated a daily POL consumption of 260,000 gallons per day for the Ardennes force, a number of the higher German quartermasters predicted that Army Group B would burn four times that amount on each day of the operation. The armored divisions had in their vehicles and trains enough fuel for perhaps go to 100 miles of normal cruising, but battle in the Ardennes could hardly be considered normal travel. Though it is a commonplace that commanders and supply officers at the tactical level always want more shells and gasoline than they probably can use, there is no question but that the Ardennes counteroffensive began on a logistical shoestring.

On 15 December the intelligence staff at Rundstedt's headquarters took one last look at the opposite side of the hill. In the days just previous there seems to have been a growing uneasiness that the Allies had recognized the impending attack and begun redeployment to meet it. Probably this was no more than a nervous reaction to the continued postponement of D-day, for on the 15th the picture was rosy. The US 4th, 28th, 106th, and 99th Infantry Divisions and their respective boundaries remained unaltered. The enemy "lack of interest" in this sector was "underlined" by the paucity of aerial reconnaissance. The only new American division to arrive on the Western Front, the 75th, had been identified the day before in the Roer sector. For several days it had been recognized that the US 12th Army Group lacked "large operational reserves." Agents working in France had reported on 7 December that the 82d and 101st Airborne Divisions were assembled at Mourmelon preparing for another airborne operation. These two divisions appeared to be the only US forces uncommitted. The "rubber duck" operation on the VIII Corps front in which Special Troops from the 12th Army Group simulated an additional division had been reflected for some days on German situation maps by a question mark. On the 15th, however, OB WEST was satisfied that no new division existed and the question mark disappeared.

The 4th and 28th Infantry Divisions were known to be exhausted and it was doubted that they were up to strength. There appeared to be relatively little armor opposite the three assault armies, probably no more than 370 tanks at the maximum. Although restrictions on patrolling had limited any recent information on exact tactical locations, there existed a complete file carefully built up since September. New arrivals on the Ardennes front had tended to occupy the same positions as their predecessors, and on this habit the Germans counted. The three communications intelligence companies operating under Army Group B were pleased to report that American carelessness in the use of radio and commercial telephone nets was up to par and that no reinforcements were en route to the Ardennes.

Across the line intelligence staffs were equally placid—although with less reason. The 12th Army Group G-2 situation map of 15 December showed no changes. For the sector from the Moselle to Monschau only five German divisions appeared, with a sixth apparently withdrawing from the Eifel. The Sixth Panzer Army symbol still crowded the dot on the map representing Cologne. All panzer divisions except the 9th SS and the 12th SS, which bore question marks, remained in locations north of the Eifel.

In the German camp there was one last hitch. On 15 December Model asked Rundstedt to postpone the attack, but the latter ruled that O-Tag would be as scheduled and so informed Fuehrer headquarters. At 1530 an officer named Waizenegger telephoned from OKW to give Hitler's confirmation of Rundstedt's decision; the liaison officers waiting with Rundstedt's staff departed for their commands at once, bearing the attack orders. And at midnight on the 15th the officer keeping the OB WEST War Diary made the last entry of that date: "Tomorrow brings the beginning of a new chapter in the Campaign In the West."

Chapter V. The Sixth Panzer Army Attack

On the night of 15 December German company commanders gave their men the watchword which had come from the Fuehrer himself: "Forward to and over the Meuse!" The objective was Antwerp. Hitler's concept of the Big Solution had prevailed; the enemy was not to be beaten east of the Meuse but encircled by a turning movement beyond that river. The main effort would be made by Dietrich's Sixth Panzer Army on the north wing, with orders to cross the Meuse on both sides of Liège, wheel north, and strike for the Albert Canal, fanning out the while to form a front extending from Maastricht to Antwerp. Meanwhile the infantry divisions to the rear of the armored columns would form the north shoulder of the initial advance and a subsequent blocking position east of the Meuse along the Vesdre River. Eventually, or so Hitler intended, the Fifteenth Army would advance to take a station protecting the Sixth Panzer Army right and rear.

Manteuffel's Fifth Panzer Army, initially acting as the center, had the mission of crossing the Meuse to the south of the Sixth, but because the river angled away to the southwest, might be expected to cross a few hours later than its armored partner on the right. Once across the Meuse, Manteuffel had the mission of preventing an Allied counterattack against Dietrich's left and rear by holding the line Antwerp-Brussels-Namur-Dinant. The left wing of the counteroffensive, composed of infantry and mechanized divisions belonging to Brandenberger's Seventh Army, had orders to push to the Meuse, unwinding a cordon of infantry and artillery facing south and southwest, thereafter anchoring the southern German flank on the angle formed by the Semois and the Meuse. Also, the Fuehrer had expressed the wish that the first segment of the Seventh Army cordon be pushed as far south as Luxembourg City if possible.

What course operations were to take once Antwerp was captured is none too clear. Indeed no detailed plans existed for this phase. There are numerous indications that the field commanders did not view the Big Solution too seriously but fixed their eyes on the seizure of the Meuse bridgeheads rather than on the capture of Antwerp. Probably Hitler had good reason for the final admonition, on 15 December, that the attack was not to begin the northward wheel until the Meuse was crossed.

Dietrich's Sixth Panzer Army, selected to make the main effort, had a distinct political complexion. Its armored divisions all belonged to the Waffen SS, its commander was an old party member, and when regular Wehrmacht officers were assigned to help in the attack preparations they were transferred to the SS rolls. Hitler's early plans speak of the Sixth SS Panzer Army, although on 16 December the army still did not bear the SS appellation in any official way, and it is clear that the Sixth was accorded the responsibility and honor of the main effort simply because Hitler felt he could depend on the SS.

Josef "Sepp" Dietrich had the appropriate political qualifications to ensure Hitler's trust but, on his military record, hardly those meriting command of the main striking force in the great counteroffensive. By profession a butcher, Dietrich had learned something of the soldier's trade in World War I, rising to the rank of sergeant, a rank which attached to him perpetually in the minds of the aristocratic members of the German General Staff. He had accompanied Hitler on the march to the Feldherrnhalle in 1923 and by 1940 had risen to command the Adolf Hitler Division, raised from Hitler's bodyguard regiment, in the western campaign. After gaining considerable reputation in Russia, Dietrich was brought to the west in 1944 and there commanded a corps in the great tank battles at Caen. He managed to hang onto his reputation during the subsequent retreats and finally was selected personally by Hitler to command the Sixth Panzer Army. Uncouth, despised by most of the higher officer class, and with no great intelligence, Dietrich had a deserved reputation for bravery and was known as a tenacious and driving division and corps commander. Whether he could command an army remained to be proven. The attack front assigned the Sixth Panzer Army, Monschau to Krewinkel, was narrower than that of its southern partner because terrain in this sector was poor at the breakthrough points and would not offer cross-country tank going until the Hohes Venn was passed. The initial assault wave consisted of one armored and one infantry corps. On the south flank the I SS Panzer Corps (Generalleutnant der Waffen-SS Hermann Priess) had two armored divisions, the 1st SS Panzer and the 12th SS Panzer, plus three infantry divisions, the 3d Parachute, the 12th Volks Grenadier and the 277th Volks Grenadier. On the north flank the LXVII Corps (General der Infanterie Otto Hitzfeld) had only two infantry divisions, the 326th and 246th Volks Grenadier. The doctrinal question as to whether tanks or infantry should take the lead, still moot in German military thinking after all the years of war, had been raised when Dietrich proposed to make the initial breakthrough with his two tank divisions. He was overruled by Model, however, and the three infantry divisions were given the mission of punching a hole on either side of Udenbreth. Thereafter the infantry was to swing aside, moving northwest to block the three roads which led south from Verviers and onto the route the armor would be taking in its dash for Liège. Hitzfeld's corps had a less ambitious program: to attack on either side of Monschau, get across the Mützenich-Elsenborn road, then turn north and west to establish a hard flank on the line Simmerath-Eupen-Limburg. All five of the Sixth Panzer Army infantry divisions ultimately would wind up, or so the plan read, forming a shoulder on an east-west line from Rotgen (north of Monschau) to Liège. Under this flank cover the armored divisions of the I SS Panzer Corps would roll west, followed by the second armored wave, the II SS Panzer Corps (General der Waffen-SS Willi Bittrich) composed of the 2d and 9th SS Panzer Divisions.

Dietrich's staff had selected five roads to carry the westward advance, the armor being assigned priority rights on the four southernmost. Actually it was expected that the 1st SS and 12th SS Panzer Divisions would use only one road each. (These two routes ran through the 99th Infantry Division sector.) Although the planning principle as regards the armored divisions was to hold the reins loose and let them run as far and as fast as they could, the Sixth Panzer did have a timetable: one day for penetration and breakout, one day to get the armor over the Hohes Venn, the Meuse to be reached by the evening of the third day, and crossings to be secured by the fourth.

This army was relatively well equipped and trained. Most of its armor had been out of combat for some time and the horde of replacements had some degree of training in night movement and fighting. The 1st and 2d SS had not been loaded with Luftwaffe and over-age replacements as had the other divisions. The artillery complement of the Sixth Panzer Army was very heavy, albeit limited in mobility by the paucity of self-propelled battalions. The four armored divisions had about 500 tanks and armored assault guns, including 90 Tigers (Mark VI). Lacking were two things which would markedly affect the operations of the Sixth Panzer Army once battle was joined. There were few trained engineer companies and these had little power equipment. The infantry lacked their full complement of assault guns, a weapon on which the German rifle platoon had learned to lean in the assault; only the 3d Parachute was fully armed with this critical infantry weapon.

The 99th Division Sector

The southern portion of the V Corps front was occupied by the 99th Infantry Division (Maj. Gen. Walter E. Lauer), which had arrived on the Continent in November 1944 and been placed in this defensive sector to acquire experience. The 99th Division front (left to right) extended from Monschau and Höfen to the railroad just north of Lanzerath, a distance of about nineteen miles. To the east lay the Germans in the West Wall pillbox line. The frontage assigned an untried division at first thought seems excessive, but the V Corps commander wished to free as much of his striking power as possible for use in the scheduled attack to seize the Roer dams; furthermore the nature of the terrain appeared little likely to attract a major German attack.

In the extreme northern portion of the sector, around Höfen, the ground was studded with open hills, to the east of which lay a section of the Monschau Forest. Only a short distance to the south of Höfen the lines of the 99th entered this forest, continuing to run through a long timber belt until the boundary between the V and VII Corps was reached at the Losheim Gap. The thick woods in the sector were tangled with rock gorges, little streams, and sharp hills. The division supply lines began as fairly substantial all-weather roads, then dwindled, as they approached the forward positions, to muddy ruts following the firebreaks and logging trails. Except for the open area in the neighborhood of Höfen, visibility was limited and fields of fire restricted. Any clearing operation in the deep woods would only give away the American positions. Although terrain seemed equally difficult for offense or defense, this balance would exist only so long as the defender could retain control over his units in the woods and provide some sort of cordon to check infiltration. The nature of the ground and the length of the front made such a cordon impossible; the 99th could maintain no more than a series of strongpoints, with unoccupied and undefended gaps between.

Three roads were of primary importance in and east of the division area. In the north a main paved road led from Höfen through the Monschau Forest, then divided as it emerged on the eastern edge (this fork beyond the forest would have some tactical importance.) A second road ran laterally behind the division center and right wing, leaving the Höfen road at the tiny village of Wahlerscheid, continuing south through the twin hamlets of Rocherath and Krinkelt, then intersecting a main eastwest road at Büllingen. This paved highway entered the division zone from the east at Losheimergraben and ran west to Malmédy by way of Büllingen and Butgenbach. As a result, despite the poverty of roads inside the forest belt where the forward positions of the 99th Division lay, the division sector could be entered from the east along roads tapping either flank.

From 8 December on, the 99th Division had been preparing for its first commitment in a large-scale operation, repairing roads, laying additional telephone wire, and shifting its guns for the V Corps attack toward the Roer dams. In addition a new supply road was constructed from the Krinkelt area to the sector held by the 395th Infantry. The 2d Infantry Division was to pass through the 99th, then the latter would attack to cover the southern flank of the 2d Division advance. As scheduled, the 2d Division passed through the 99th Division on 13 December, beginning its attack on a narrow front toward Dreiborn, located on the northern fork of the Höfen road beyond the Monschau Forest.

The dispositions of the 99th Division were these: On the north flank the 3d Battalion, 395th Infantry, occupied the Höfen area, with the 38th Cavalry Squadron on the left and the 99th Reconnaissance Troop on the right. The ground here was open and rolling, the 3d Battalion well dug in and possessed of good fields of fire. Next in line to the south, the 2d Division was making its attack on a thrust line running northeastward, its supply route following the section of the Höfen road which ran through the forest to the fork. The remaining two battalions of the 395th resumed the 99th Division front, succeeded to the south, in turn, by the 393d Infantry and the 394th. Conforming to the wooded contour, the elements of the 99th Division south of the 2d Division attacking column occupied a slight salient bellying out from the flanks.

Two battalions of the 99th Division (the 1st and 2d of the 395th) took part in the attack begun on 13 December, although other elements of the division put on demonstrations to create some diversion to their immediate front. The 2d Battalion, 395th, on the right of the 2d Division jumped off in deep snow and bitter cold in an attack intended to swing north, wedge through the West Wall bunker line, and seize Harperscheid on the southern fork of the road beyond the forest. The advance on the 13th went well; then, as the attack hit the German bunkers and enemy guns and mortars ranged in, the pace began to slow. By 16 December, however, several important positions were in American hands and it seemed that a breakthrough was in the making despite bad weather, poor visibility, and difficult terrain.

The German troops manning the West Wall positions in front of the 2d and 99th Divisions had been identified prior to the 13 December attack as coming from the 277th Volks Grenadier Division and the 294th Regiment of the 18th Volks Grenadier Division. An additional unit was identified on the second day of the offensive when prisoners were taken who carried the pay books of the 326th Volks Grenadier Division. Although this was the only indication of any German reinforcement, American commanders and intelligence officers anticipated that a counterattack shortly would be made against the shoulders of the 2d Division corridor held by the 99th, but that this would be limited in nature and probably no more than regimental in strength. The immediate and natural reaction, therefore, to the German attack launched against the 99th Division on the morning of the fourth day of the V Corps offensive (16 December) was that this was no more than the anticipated riposte.

To the south of the 393d Infantry, the 394th (Col. Don Riley) held a defensive sector marking the right flank terminus for both the 99th Division and V Corps. The 6,500-yard front ran along the International Highway from a point west of Neuhof, in enemy hands, south to Losheimergraben. Nearly the entire line lay inside the forest belt. On the right a two-mile gap existed between the regiment and the forward locations of the 14th Cavalry Group. To patrol this gap the regimental I and R Platoon held an outpost on the high ground slightly northwest of Lanzerath and overlooking the road from that village. Thence hourly jeep patrols worked across the gap to meet patrols dispatched by the cavalry on the other side of the corps boundary. Acutely aware of the sensitive nature of this southern flank, General Lauer had stationed his division reserve (3d Battalion of the 394th) near the Buchholz railroad station in echelon behind the right of the two battalions in the line. The fateful position of the 394th would bring against it the main effort of the I SS Panzer Corps and, indeed, that of the Sixth Panzer Army. Two roads ran obliquely through the regimental area. One, a main road, intersected the north-south International Highway (and the forward line held by the 394th) at Losheimergraben and continued northwestward through Büllingen and Butgenbach to Malmédy. The other, a secondary road but generally passable in winter, branched from the International Highway north of Lanzerath, and curved west through Buchholz, Honsfeld, Schoppen, and Faymonville, roughly paralleling the main road to the north.

Of the five westward roads assigned the I SS Panzer Corps the two above were most important. The main road to Büllingen and Malmédy would be called "C" on the German maps; the secondary road would be named "D." These two roads had been selected as routes for the main armored columns, first for the panzer elements of the I SS Panzer Corps, then to carry the tank groups of the II SS Panzer Corps composing the second wave of the Sixth Panzer Army's attack. But since the commitment of armored spearheads during the battle to break through the American main line of resistance had been ruled out, the initial German attempt to effect a penetration would turn on the efforts of the three infantry divisions loaned the I SS Panzer Corps for this purpose only. The 277th Volks Grenadier Division, aligned opposite the American 393d Infantry, had a mission which would turn its attack north of the axis selected for the armored advance. Nonetheless, success or failure by the 277th would determine the extent to which the tank routes might be menaced by American intervention from the north. The twin towns, Rocherath-Krinkelt, for example, commanded the road which cut across—and thus could be used to block—the Büllingen road, route C.

The two infantry divisions composing the I SS Panzer Corps center and south wing were directly charged with opening the chief armored routes. The 12th Volks Grenadier Division, regarded by the Sixth Army staff as the best of the infantry divisions, had as its axis of attack the Büllingen road (route C); its immediate objective was the crossroads point of departure for the westward highway at Losheimergraben and the opening beyond the thick Gerolstein Forest section of the woods belt. The ultimate objective for the 12th Division attack was the attainment of a line at Nidrum and Weywertz, eight air-line miles beyond the American front, at which point the division was to face north as part of the infantry cordon covering the Sixth Panzer Army flank. The 3d Parachute Division, forming the left wing in the initial disposition for the attack, had a zone of advance roughly following the southern shoulder of the Honsfeld or D route. The area selected for the breakthrough attempt comprised the north half of the U.S. 14th Cavalry Group sector and took in most of the gap between the cavalry and the 99th Division. In the first hours of the advance, then, the 3d Parachute Division would be striking against the 14th Cavalry Group in the Krewinkel-Berterath area. But the final objective of the 3d Parachute attack was ten miles to the northwest, the line Schoppen-Eibertingen on route D. The 3d Parachute axis thus extended through the right of the 99th Division.

The decision as to exactly when the two panzer divisions would be committed in exploitation of the penetrations achieved by the infantry was a matter to be decided by the commanders of the Sixth Panzer Army and Army Group B as the attack developed. Armored infantry kampfgruppen from the 12th SS Panzer Division and 1st SS Panzer Division were assembled close behind the infantry divisions, in part as reinforcements for the breakthrough forces, in part because none of the Volks Grenadier units were used to close cooperation with armor.

Considerable reshuffling had been needed in the nights prior to 16 December to bring the I SS Panzer Corps toward its line of departure and to feed the infantry into the West Wall positions formerly occupied by the 277th Division. All this was completed by 0400 on the morning set for the attack (except for the reconnaissance battalion which failed to arrive in the 3d Parachute Division lines), and the bulk of the two artillery corps and two Volks Werfer brigades furnishing the artillery reinforcement was in position. None of the three army assault gun battalions, one for each attacking division, had yet appeared. The German artillery, from the 75-mm. infantry accompanying howitzers up to the 210-mm. heavy battalions, were deployed in three groupments, by weight and range, charged respectively with direct support of the attacking infantry, counterbattery, and long-distance fire for destruction.

The first thunderclap of the massed German guns and Werfers at 0530 on 16 December was heard by outposts of the 394th Infantry as "outgoing mail," fire from friendly guns, but in a matter of minutes the entire regimental area was aware that something most unusual had occurred. Intelligence reports had located only two horse-drawn artillery pieces opposite one of the American line battalions; after a bombardment of an hour and five minutes the battalion executive officer reported, "They sure worked those horses to death." But until the German infantry were actually sighted moving through the trees, the American reaction to the searchlights and exploding shells was that the enemy simply was feinting in answer to the 2d and 99th attack up north. In common with the rest of the 99th the line troops of the 394th had profited by the earlier quiet on this front to improve their positions by log roofing; so casualties during the early morning barrage were few.

The German infantry delayed in following up the artillery preparation, which ended about 0700. On this part of the forest front the enemy line of departure was inside the woods. The problem, then, was to get the attack rolling through the undergrowth, American barbed wire, and mine fields immediately to the German front. The groping nature of the attack was enhanced by the heavy mist hanging low in the forest.

The 2d Battalion, on the north flank, was more directly exposed since a road led into the woods position from Neuhof. At this point, close to the regimental boundary, the battle was carried by a fusilier company attached to the 990th Regiment of the 277th Volks Grenadier Division. The fusiliers succeeded in reaching the 2d Battalion lines about 0800 but were driven off by small arms fire and artillery.

In midafternoon the 12th SS Panzer Division, waiting for the infantry to open the road to the International Highway, apparently loaned a few tanks to carry the fusiliers into the attack. Behind a smoke screen the tanks rolled out of Neuhof. An American sergeant spotted this move and with a sound-powered telephone brought friendly artillery into play. High explosive stopped the tanks in their tracks. A few infantrymen got through to the forest positions occupied by the 2d Battalion. There an unknown BAR man atop a log hut "raised hell with the Krauts" and the attack petered out. The 2d Battalion, during this day, never was really pressed. The chief enemy thrusts had gone to the north, where the right flank of the 393d Infantry was hit hard by the 277th Division, and to the south, against the center and refused right flank of the 394th. No word of events elsewhere on the 394th front reached the 2d Battalion command post, but the appearance of German infantry in the woods along the northern regimental boundary gave a clue to the penetration developing there, and the left company of the 2d Battalion was pulled back somewhat as flank protection.

The initial enemy action along the 394th Infantry center and south flank was intended to punch holes through which the panzer columns might debouch onto the Büllingen and Honsfeld roads. The prominent terrain feature, in the first hours of the fight, was a branch railroad line which crossed the frontier just north of Losheim and then twined back and forth, over and under the Büllingen-Malmédy highway westward. During the autumn retreat the Germans themselves had destroyed the bridge which carried the Büllingen road over the railroad tracks north of Losheim. To the west the highway overpass on the Lanzerath-Losheimergraben section of the International Highway had also been demolished. The crossroads at Losheimergraben would have to be taken if the German tanks were to have quick and easy access to the Büllingen road, but the approach to Losheimergraben, whether from Losheim or Lanzerath, was denied to all but infantry until such time as the railroad track could be captured and the highway overpasses restored.

The line of track also indicated the axis for the advance of the left wing of the 12th Volks Grenadier Division and, across the lines, marked a general boundary between the 1st and 3d Battalions of the 394th Infantry. When the barrage lifted, about 0700, the assault regiments of the 12th Division already were moving toward the American positions. The 48th Grenadier Regiment, in the north, headed through the woods for the Losheimergraben crossroads. Fallen trees, barbed wire, and mines, compounded with an almost complete ignorance of the forest trails, slowed this advance. The attack on the left, by the 27th Fuesilier Regiment, had easier going, with much open country and a series of draws leading directly to the track and the American positions.

The 3d Battalion (Maj. Norman A. Moore), to the south and west of the 1st Battalion position at Losheimergraben, first encountered the enemy. About 0745 L Company, at the Buchholz station, had taken advantage of the lull in the shelling and was just lining up for breakfast when figures were seen approaching through the fog, marching along the track in a column of two's. First thought to be friendly troops, the Germans were almost at the station before recognition brought on a fusillade of American bullets. The enemy scattered for the boxcars outside the station or sought shelter in ditches along the right of way and a close-quarters firefight began. A 3-inch tank destroyer systematically worked over the cars, while the American mortar crews raked the area beside the track. A few Germans reached the roundhouse near the station, but Sgt. Savino Travalini, leader of the antitank platoon, went forward with a bazooka, fired in enough rounds to flush the fusiliers, then cut them down with his rifle as they broke into the open. (Sergeant Travalini was awarded a battlefield commission as second lieutenant.) K Company, ordered up to reinforce the outnumbered defenders at the station, arrived in time to take a hand in the affray. By noon the Germans had been repelled, leaving behind about seventy-five dead; L Company had suffered twenty-five or thirty casualties.

As a result of the stubborn stand at the station, some of the assault platoons of the 27th Fuesilier Regiment circled back to the northeast and onto the left of the 1st Battalion (Lt Col. Robert H. Douglas). Here one of the battalion antitank guns stopped the lead German tank and the supporting fusiliers were driven back by 81-mm. mortar fire thickened by an artillery barrage. The major threat in the Losheimergraben sector came shortly after noon when the 48th Grenadier Regiment finally completed its tortuous approach through the woods, mines, and wire, and struck between B and C Companies. B Company lost some sixty men and was forced back about 400 yards; then, with the help of the attached heavy machine gun platoon, it stiffened and held. During the fight Sgt. Eddie Dolenc moved his machine gun forward to a shell hole which gave a better field of fire. When last seen Sergeant Dolenc still was firing, a heap of gray-coated bodies lying in front of the shell hole. The C Company outposts were driven in, but two platoons held their original positions throughout the day. Company A beat off the German infantry assault when this struck its forward platoon; then the battalion mortar platoon, raising its tubes to an 89-degree angle, rained shells on the assault group, leaving some eighty grenadiers dead or wounded.

The early morning attack against the right flank of the 394th had given alarming indication that the very tenuous connection with the 14th Cavalry Group had been severed and that the southern flank of the 99th Division was exposed to some depth. The only connecting link, the 30-man I and R Platoon of the 394th, northwest of Lanzerath, had lost physical contact early in the day both with the cavalry and with its own regiment. Radio communication with the isolated platoon continued for some time, and at 1140 word was relayed to the 99th Division command post that the cavalry was pulling out of Lanzerath—confirmation, if such were needed, of the German breakthrough on the right of the 99th. Belatedly, the 106th Infantry Division reported at 1315 that it could no longer maintain contact at the interdivision boundary. Less than an hour later the radio connection with the I and R Platoon failed. By this time observers had seen strong German forces pouring west through the Lanzerath area. (These were from the 3d Parachute Division.) General Lauer's plans for using the 3d Battalion, 394th Infantry, as a counterattack force were no longer feasible. The 3d Battalion, itself under attack, could not be committed elsewhere as a unit and reverted to its parent regiment. Not long after the final report from the I and R Platoon, the 3d Battalion was faced to the southwest in positions along the railroad.

A check made after dark showed a discouraging situation in the 394th sector. It was true that the 2d Battalion, in the north, had not been much affected by the day's events—but German troops were moving deeper on the left and right of the battalion. In the Losheimergraben area the 1st Battalion had re-formed in a thin and precarious line; the crossroads still were denied the enemy. But B Company had only twenty men available for combat, while the enemy settled down in the deserted American foxholes only a matter of yards away. Four platoons had been taken from the 3d Battalion to reinforce the 1st, leaving the former with no more than a hundred men along the railroad line. Farther to the west, however, about 125 men of the 3d

Battalion who had been on leave at the rest center in Honsfeld formed a provisional unit, extending somewhat the precarious 394th flank position.

Some help was on the way. General Lauer had asked the 2d Division for a rifle battalion to man a position which the 99th had prepared before the attack as a division backstop between Mürringen and Hünningen. At 1600 Colonel Riley was told that the 394th would be reinforced by the 1st Battalion, 23d Infantry, of the 2d Division. During the night this fresh rifle battalion, and a company each of tanks and tank destroyers, under the command of Lt. Col. John M. Hightower, moved from Elsenborn to take up positions south and southeast of Hünningen. Before sunrise, 17 December, these reinforcements were in place.

During the night of 16-17 December the entire infantry reserve in the 99th Division zone had been committed in the line or close behind it, this backup consisting of the local reserves of the 99th and the entire 23d Infantry, which had been left at Elsenborn while its sister regiments took part in the 2d Division attack to break out in the Wahlerscheid sector. The 3d Battalion of the 23d had set up a defensive position on a ridge northeast of Rocherath, prepared to support the 393d Infantry. The 2d Battalion had assembled in the late afternoon of the 16th approximately a mile and a quarter north of Rocherath. The 1st Battalion would be at Hünningen. Troops of the 2d Division had continued the attack on 16 December, but during the afternoon Maj. Gen. Walter M. Robertson made plans for a withdrawal, if necessary, from the Wahlerscheid sector.

As early as 1100 word of the German attacks on the V Corps front had produced results at the command post of the northern neighbor, the VII Corps. The 26th Infantry of the uncommitted 1st Infantry Division, then placed on a 6-hour alert, finally entrucked at midnight and started the move south to Camp Elsenborn. The transfer of this regimental combat team to the V Corps would have a most important effect on the ensuing American defense.

The First Attacks in the Monschau-Höfen Sector Are Repulsed, 16 December

The village of Höfen, the anchor point for the northern flank of the 99th Division, had considerable importance in the attack plans of the German Sixth Panzer Army. Located on high ground, Höfen overlooked the road center at Monschau, just to the north, and thus barred entry to the road to Eupen — at the moment the headquarters of the V Corps.

For some reason Field Marshal Model wished to save the German town of Monschau from destruction and had forbidden the use of artillery there. The plan handed General Hitzfeld for the employment of his LXVII Corps (Corps Monschau) called for an attack to the north and south of Monschau that was intended to put two divisions astride the Monschau-Eupen road in position to check any American reinforcements attempting a move to the south. The right division of the Corps Monschau, the 326th Volks Grenadier Division, had been ordered to put all three regiments in the initial attack: one to swing north of Monschau and seize the village of Mützenich on the Eupen road; one to crack the American line south of Monschau, then drive northwest to the high ground on the road just beyond Mützenich; the third to join the 246th Volks Grenadier Division drive through Höfen and Kalterherberg, the latter astride the main road from Monschau south to Butgenbach. If all went according to plan, the 326th and 246th would continue northwestward along the Eupen road until they reached the Vesdre River at the outskirts of Eupen. The force available to Hitzfeld on the morning of 16 December for use in the Monschau-Höfen sector was considerably weaker than the 2-division attack planned by the Sixth Panzer Army. In the two nights before the attack the 326th Volks Grenadier Division had moved into the West Wall fortifications facing Monschau and Höfen. The American attack against the 277th Volks Grenadier Division at Kesternich, however, siphoned off one battalion to reinforce the latter division; in addition one battalion failed to arrive in line by the morning of 16 December. Worse, the 246th Volks Grenadier Division, supposed to come south from the Jülich sector, had been held there by American attacks. Hitzfeld was thus left with only a few indifferent fortress troops on the south flank of the 326th Division. The total assault strength in the Höfen-Monschau area, as a result, was between three and four battalions. Nonetheless, Hitzfeld and the 326th commander Generalmajor Erwin Kaschner, could count on a heavy weight of artillery fire to give momentum to the attack. Two artillery corps (possibly totaling ten battalions) were in position to give fire either north or south of the no-fire zone at Monschau, plus one or two Volks Werfer brigades—a considerable groupment for the support of a division attack at this stage of the war.

The American strength in the Höfen-Monschau sector consisted of one rifle battalion and a reconnaissance squadron: the 3d Battalion, 395th Infantry, under Lt. Col. McClernand Butler, in Höfen, and the 38th Cavalry Reconnaissance Squadron (Lt. Col. Robert E. O'Brien) outposting Monschau and deployed to the north along the railroad track between Mützenich and Konzen station. The infantry at Höfen lay in a foxhole line along a thousand-yard front on the eastern side of the village, backed up by dug-out support positions on which the battalion had labored for some six weeks. Two nights prior to the German offensive, Company A of the 612th Tank Destroyer Battalion towed its 3-inch guns into the Höfen sector for the purpose of getting good firing positions against the village of Rohren, northeast of Höfen, which lay in the path of the 2d Infantry Division attack. The appearance of the guns, sited well forward and swathed in sheets for protective coloration in the falling snow, gave a lift to the infantry, who as yet had to fight their first battle.

The 38th Cavalry Squadron was aligned from Monschau north to Konzen station, holding a continuous position with fifty dismounted machine guns dug in behind mines, barbed wire, and trip flares covering the approaches from the east. The right flank of the squadron, outposting Monschau, was at some disadvantage because of the deep, rocky draws leading into and past the town. But to the north the terrain was less cut up and offered good fields of fire for the American weapons posted on the slopes west of the railroad track. In addition to the assault gun troop in Mützenich, the squadron was reinforced by a platoon of selfpropelled tank destroyers from the 893d Tank Destroyer Battalion, which was stationed behind the left flank to cover a secondary road which entered the American position, and the 62d Armored Field Artillery Battalion. On the whole the defense in the Monschau-Höfen area was well set when the battalions of the 326th Volks Grenadier Division moved forward to their attack positions on the morning of 16 December. The German guns and Werfers opened a very heavy barrage at 0525, rolling over the forward lines, then back to the west along the Eupen road, shelling the American artillery positions and cutting telephone wires. Neither the infantry nor cavalry (gone well to ground) suffered much from this fire, heavy though it was; but many buildings were set afire in Höfen and some were beaten to the ground. Monschau, as directed by Model, escaped this artillery pounding. In twenty minutes or so the German fire died away and off to the east the glow of searchlights rose as artificial moonlight. About 0600 the German grenadiers came walking out of the haze in front of the 3d Battalion. The wire to the

American guns was out and during the initial onslaught even radio failed to reach the gunners. The riflemen and tank destroyer gunners, however, had the German infantry in their sights, without cover and at a murderously easy range.

The result was fantastic. Yet the grenadiers who lived long enough came right up to the firing line—in three verified instances the bodies of Germans shot at close range toppled into the foxholes from which the bullets came. A few got through and into the village. Assault companies of the 1st Battalion, 751st Regiment, and the 1st Battalion, 753d Regiment, had made this attack. But the support companies of the two battalions were blocked out by an intense concentration of well-aimed 81-mm. mortar fire from the American heavy weapons company, this curtain strengthened within an hour by the supporting howitzer battalion. By 0745 the attack was finished, and in another hour some thirty or forty Germans who had reached the nearest houses were rounded up. Reports of the German dead "counted" in front of Höfen vary from seventy-five to two hundred. The casualties suffered by the 3d Battalion in this first action were extraordinarily light: four killed, seven wounded, and four missing.

At Monschau the 1st Battalion of the 752d Regiment carried the attack, apparently aimed at cutting between the Monschau and Höfen defenses. As the German shellfire lessened, about 0600, the cavalry outposts heard troops moving along the Rohren road which entered Monschau from the southeast. The grenadiers were allowed to approach the barbed wire at the roadblock, then illuminating mortar shell was fired over the Germans and the cavalry opened up with every weapon at hand—the light tanks doing heavy damage with 37-mm. canister. Beaten back in this first assault, the German battalion tried again at daylight, this time attempting to filter into town along a draw a little farther to the north. This move was checked quickly. No further attack was essayed at Monschau and a half-hearted attempt at Höfen, toward noon, was handily repelled. As it was, the 326th Volks Grenadier Division lost one-fifth of the troops put into these attacks.

To the south of Höfen and Monschau in the 2d Division and 395th Infantry zones, 16 December passed with the initiative still in American hands. The German attacks delivered north and south of the corridor through which the Americans were pushing had no immediate repercussion, not even in the 395th Infantry sector. The Sixth Panzer Army drive to make a penetration between Hollerath and Krewinkel with the 1st SS Panzer Corps, therefore, had no contact with the Monschau Corps in the north, nor was such contact intended in the early stages of the move west. The German command would pay scant attention to the small American salient projecting between the LX VII Corps and the 1st SS Panzer Corps, counting on the hard-pressed 272d Volks Grenadier Division to hold in the Wahlerscheid-Simmerath sector so long as needed.

The German Effort Continues, 17-18 December

Although hard hit and in serious trouble at the end of the first day, particularly on the right flank as General Lauer saw it, the inexperienced 99th Division had acquitted itself in a manner calculated to win the reluctant admiration of the enemy. German losses had been high. Where the American lines had been penetrated, in the 393d and 394th sectors, the defenders simply had been overwhelmed by superior numbers of the enemy who had been able to work close in through the dense woods. Most important of all, the stanch defense of Losheimergraben had denied the waiting tank columns of the I SS Panzer Corps direct and easy entrance to the main Büllingen-Malmédy road.

The initial German failure to wedge an opening for armor through the 99th, for failure it must be reckoned, was very nearly balanced by the clear breakthrough achieved in the 14th Cavalry Group sector. The 3d Parachute Division, carrying the left wing of the I SS Panzer Corps forward, had followed the retreating cavalry through Manderfeld, swung north, and by dusk had troops in Lanzerath—only two kilometers from the 3d Battalion, 394th, position at Buchholz.

The 12th SS Panzer Division could not yet reach the Büllingen road. The 1st SS Panzer Division stood ready and waiting to exploit the opening made by the 3d Parachute Division by an advance via Lanzerath onto the Honsfeld road. During the early evening the advance kampfgruppe of the 1st SS Panzer Division, a task force built around the 1st SS Panzer Regiment (Obersturmbannfuehrer Joachim Peiper), rolled northwest to Lanzerath. At midnight—an exceptionally dark night—German tanks and infantry struck suddenly at Buchholz. The two platoons of Company K, left there when the 3d Battalion stripped its lines to reinforce the Losheimergraben defenders, were engulfed. One man, the company radio operator, escaped. Hidden in the cellar of the old battalion command post near the railroad station, he reported the German search on the floor above, then the presence of tanks outside the building with swastikas painted on their sides. His almost hourly reports, relayed through the 1st Battalion, kept the division headquarters informed of the German movements. About 0500 on 17 December the main German column began its march through Buchholz. Still at his post, the radio operator counted thirty tanks, twenty-eight half-tracks filled with German infantry, and long columns of foot troops marching by the roadside. All of the armored task force of the 1st SS Panzer Division and a considerable part of the 3d Parachute Division were moving toward Honsfeld.

Honsfeld, well in the rear area of the 99th, was occupied by a variety of troops. The provisional unit raised at the division rest camp seems to have been deployed around the town. Two platoons of the 801st Tank Destroyer Battalion had been sent in by General Lauer to hold the road, and during the night a few towed guns from the 612th Tank Destroyer Battalion were added to the defenses. Honsfeld was in the V Corps antiaircraft defense belt and two battalions of 90-mm. antiaircraft guns had been sited thereabout. In addition, Troop A, 32d Cavalry Reconnaissance Squadron, had arrived in Honsfeld late in the evening.

The stream of American traffic moving into the village during the night probably explains the ease with which the Honsfeld garrison was routed. The leading German tanks simply joined this traffic, and, calmly led by a man signaling with a flashlight, rolled down the village streets. With German troops pouring in from all sides the Americans offered no concrete resistance. Though some made a fight of it, most engaged in a wild scramble to get out of town. Some of the tank destroyers were overrun by infantry attack through the dark. Guns and vehicles, jammed on the exit roads, were abandoned; but many of the Americans, minus their equipment, escaped.

The predawn seizure of Honsfeld opened D route to the spearhead column of the 1st SS Panzer Division. Reconnaissance, however, showed that the next section of this route, between Honsfeld and Schoppen, was in very poor condition. Since the 12th SS Panzer Division had not yet reached C route, the main Büllingen-Malmédy road, Peiper's kampfgruppe now turned north in the direction of Büllingen with the intention of continuing the westward drive on pavement. At 0100 on 17 December the 24th Engineer Battalion had been attached to the 99th Division and ordered to Büllingen, there to prepare positions covering the entrances from the south and southeast. Twice during the dark hours the engineers beat back German infantry attacks; then, a little after 0700, enemy tanks hove into sight. Falling back to the shelter of the buildings, the 254th did what it could to fend off the tanks. Here, in the town, a reconnaissance platoon of the 644th Tank Destroyer Battalion had just arrived with orders to establish contact with the enemy column, but only one section managed to evade the panzers. The rest of the platoon were killed or captured. Upon receipt of orders from the division, the engineers, who had clung stubbornly to houses in the west edge, withdrew and dug in on higher ground 1,000 yards to the northwest so as to block the road to Butgenbach. There the two companies of the 254th still intact were joined by men hastily assembled from the 99th Division headquarters, the antiaircraft artillery units in the vicinity, and four guns from the 612th Tank Destroyer Battalion.

To the surprise of the Americans gathered along this last thin line the Germans did not pursue the attack. By 1030 a long line of tanks and vehicles were seen streaming through Büllingen, but they were moving toward the southwest! Later, the 99th Division commander would comment that "the enemy had the key to success within his hands, but did not know it." And so it must have seemed to the Americans on 17 December when a sharp northward thrust from Büllingen would have met little opposition and probably would have entrapped both the 99th and 2d Divisions.

In fact, Peiper's column had simply made a detour north through Büllingen and, having avoided a bad stretch of road, now circled back to its prescribed route.

American ground observers, on the 17th, attributed the change in direction to intervention by friendly fighter-bombers, whose attack, so it appeared, "diverted" the German column to the southwest. Two squadrons of the 366th Fighter Group, called into the area to aid the 99th Division, made two attacks during the morning. The 389th Squadron struck one section of the German column, which promptly scattered into nearby woods, and claimed a kill of thirty tanks and motor vehicles. It is doubtful that the Germans were crippled to any such extent—certainly the move west was little delayed—but the American troops must have been greatly heartened. The 390th Squadron, directed onto the column now estimated to be two hundred vehicles or more, was intercepted by a squadron of Me-109's which dropped out of the clouds over Büllingen. The Americans accounted for seven German aircraft, but had to jettison most of their bombs.

Losheimergraben Is Lost

The lack of highway bridges over the railroad south of Losheimergraben had turned the first day's battle for the Losheimergraben crossroads into an infantry fight in the surrounding woods. Both sides had sustained heavy losses. The 48th Grenadier Regiment had pushed the 1st Battalion of the 394th back, but had failed to break through to the tiny collection of customs buildings and houses at the crossroads. By daylight on 17 December the Americans held a fairly continuous but thinly manned front with the 1st Battalion around Losheimergraben, part of the 3d Battalion west of the village, and the 1st Battalion of the 23d Infantry holding the exposed right-flank position in Hünningen.

The 12th Volks Grenadier Division, under pressure from higher headquarters to take Losheimergraben, continued the attack with both its forward regiments, now considerably weakened. While the 27th Fuesilier Regiment moved to flank Losheimergraben on the west, the 48th Grenadier Regiment continued its costly frontal attack. The flanking attack was successful: at least a battalion of the 27th drove through a gap between the 1st and 3d Battalions. By 1100 the German infantry were able to bring the Losheim-Büllingen road under small arms fire and the noose was tightening on the Losheimergraben defenders. The frontal attack, at the latter point, was resumed before dawn by enemy patrols trying to find a way around the American firing line in the woods.

In a foxhole line 200 yards southeast of Losheimergraben, 1st Lt. Dewey Plankers had organized about fifty men. This small force—men from Companies B and C, jeep drivers, and the crew of a defunct antiaircraft gun—beat back all of the German patrols. But the game was nearly up. The enemy Pioneers finally threw a bridge over the railroad at the demolished overpass on the Losheim road, and at about 1100 three panzers, supported by a rifle company, appeared in the woods in front of Plankers' position. Lacking ammunition and weapons (twenty of the tiny force were armed only with pistols), Plankers ordered his men back to the customs buildings at the crossroads and radioed for help. Carbines, rifles, and ammunition, loaded on the only available jeep (the chaplain's), were delivered under fire to the American "blockhouses." The German tankers, unwilling to chance bazooka fire at close range, held aloof from the hamlet and waited for the German gunners and some Me-109's to finish the job. The garrison held on in the basements until the tanks finally moved in at dusk. Lieutenant Plankers had been informed in the course of the afternoon that neighboring troops were under orders to withdraw. He took the men he had left, now only about twenty, and broke through the Germans, rejoining what was left of the 394th Infantry at Mürringen late in the evening.

Even before the German penetration at the Losheimergraben angle, the 394th stood in danger of being cut off and destroyed piecemeal by the enemy infiltrating from the east and south. As part of a withdrawal plan put in effect during the afternoon for the entire division, General Lauer ordered the 394th to withdraw to a second defensive position at Mürringen, about four kilometers in the rear of the regiment's eastern front.

The 2d Battalion, holding the north flank, was under pressure from both right and left. At dawn of 17 December, the enemy had attacked along the Neuhof road with tanks in the van. Company E, directly in the path, used its bazookas with such good effect that three panzers were crippled. Excellent artillery support and fine shooting by the battalion mortars helped discourage any further frontal assault. Infiltration on the flanks, however, had placed the 2d Battalion in serious plight when, at 1400, the order came to withdraw west and tie in with the 3d Battalion. Leaving a small covering force behind, the 2d Battalion started on foot through the woods, carrying its heavy weapons over the rugged and snow-covered trails. The Germans also were moving through the forest, and the battalion was unable to turn toward the 3d as ordered. Withdrawing deeper into the forest the battalion bivouacked in the sector known as the Honsfelder Wald. The covering force, however, made its way to Mürringen, where it was set to defend the regimental command post.

The 1st Battalion, in the Losheimergraben sector, had been so splintered by incessant German attack that its withdrawal was a piecemeal affair. Isolated groups fought or dodged their way west. Two hundred and sixty officers and men made it. Two platoons from Company K which had been attached to the 1st Battalion did not receive word of the withdrawal and held on under heavy shelling until ammunition was nearly spent. It took these men twenty-four hours to wade back through the snow to the regimental lines. What was left of the 3d Battalion also fell back toward

Mürringen, harassed by groups of the enemy en route and uncertain as to what would be found at Mürringen.

The survivors of the 394th Infantry now assembling at Mürringen were given a brief breathing spell while the enemy concentrated on the 1st Battalion, 23d Infantry, defending the Hünningen positions 1,500 meters to the south. The 12th Volks Grenadier Division attack finally had broken through the American line but now was definitely behind schedule. The 48th Regiment, having been much reduced in strength in the fight around Losheimergraben, re-formed on the high ground between the forest edge and Mürringen. The north flank of the regiment lay exposed to counterattack, for the 277th Volks Grenadier Division on the right had been checked in its attempt to take the twin villages, Krinkelt-Rocherath. The fight now devolved on the 27th Regiment, which was ordered to take Hünningen before an attempt to roll up the American south flank.

Colonel Hightower's 1st Battalion was in a difficult and exposed position at Hünningen. His main strength, deployed to counter German pressure from the Buchholz-Honsfeld area, faced south and southeast, but the German columns taking the Honsfeld-Büllingen detour were moving toward the northwest and thus behind the Hünningen defenders. Whether any part of this latter enemy force would turn against the rear of the 1st Battalion was the question.

Through the morning the 1st Battalion watched through breaks in the fog as tanks and vehicles rolled toward Büllingen. Visibility, poor as it was, made artillery adjustment on the road difficult and ineffective. Shortly after noon about 120 men who had been cut off from the 2d and 254th Engineer Battalions arrived at Hightower's command post and were dispatched to form a roadblock against a possible attack from Büllingen. Somewhat earlier twelve Mark IV tanks had appeared south of Hünningen — perhaps by design, perhaps by accident. Assembled at the wood's edge some 800 yards from the American foxhole line, the panzers may have been seeking haven from the American fighter-bombers then working over the road. In any case they were shooting-gallery targets. One of the towed 3-inch guns which the 801st Tank Destroyer Battalion had withdrawn during the early morning debacle at Honsfeld knocked out four of the panzers in six shots. The rest withdrew in haste.

At 1600 the enemy made his first definite assault, preceded by six minutes of furious shelling. When the artillery ceased, German infantry were seen coming forward through a neck of woods pointing toward the southeastern edge of Hünningen. A forward observer with Company B, facing the woods, climbed into the church steeple and brought down shellfire which kept pace with the attackers until they were within a hundred yards of the American foxholes. A number of the enemy did break through, but the assault evaporated when nearly fifty were killed by four men manning automatic weapons from a platoon command post just in the rear of the firing line. The commander of the 27th Regiment sent forward seven "distinct attacking waves" in the course of the afternoon and early evening. In one assault the Germans captured two heavy machine guns and turned them on Company A, but a light machine gun section wiped out the German crews. At no time, despite numerous penetrations in the 1st Battalion line, was the enemy able to get Hünningen into his hands. Late in the afternoon an indistinct radio message was picked up by the 1st Battalion, 23d Infantry. It appeared that the battalion now was attached to the 9th Infantry (2d Division), to the north, and that orders were to pull out of Hünningen.

Up to this point, the 394th Infantry was still in Mürringen, gathering its companies and platoons as they straggled in. Furthermore the 1st Battalion was in a firefight with an enemy only a few score yards distant in the darkness. Colonel Hightower, therefore, tried by radio to apprise the 9th Infantry of his predicament and the importance of holding until the 394th could reorganize. At 2330 Colonel Hirschfelder, the 9th Infantry commander, reached Hightower by radio, told him that Hightower's battalion and the 394th Infantry were almost surrounded and that, if the battalion expected to withdraw, it must move at once. Colonel Hightower again explained his situation, said that in his opinion he could not pull out unless and until the 394th withdrew, but that he would discuss the situation with the commander of the 394th. Hirschfelder agreed and told Hightower to use his own judgment.

At Mürringen Colonel Riley's 394th had not been hard pressed although the German artillery had shown no favoritism and hammered Mürringen and Hünningen equally. The groups filtering back to Mürringen, however, generally had very little ammunition left, even though many detachments came back with all their heavy weapons. If the 394th was to make a stand at Mürringen it would have to be resupplied. At first Colonel Riley hoped to get ammunition by air, for it appeared that the German drive in the Krinkelt area to the north shortly would cut the last remaining supply road. This was a vain hope, for aerial supply missions in December were far too chancy. The alternative solution was for the 394th to withdraw north to Krinkelt, using the one route still open.

The German Attack Toward Rocherath and Krinkelt, 16-17 December

The 393d Infantry (Lt. Col. Jean D. Scott) had taken no part in the V Corps offensive of 13 December except to put on a "demonstration" in front of the West Wall positions. The regiment, minus its 2d Battalion (attached to the 395th Infantry), was deployed along the German frontier, a line generally defined by the eastern edge of the long forest belt in which the bulk of the 99th Division was stationed and the International Highway. The width of the front, held by the 3d Battalion on the left and the 1st Battalion on the right, was about 5,500 yards. Outposts on the regimental left lay only a few score yards from the West Wall bunkers, but the right was more than half a mile from the German lines. About four miles by trail behind the 393d, the twin villages of Rocherath and Krinkelt lay astride the main north-south road through the division area. In front of the 393d, across the frontier, were entrances to the two forest roads which ran through the regimental sector, one in the north at Hollerath, the second in the south at Udenbreth. Both villages were in enemy hands. At the western edge of the woods the roads converged, funneling along a single track into Rocherath-Krinkelt. The twin villages, therefore, had a tactical importance of the first order. Through them passed the main line of communications in the 2d Division corridor, and from them ran the supply route to the 393d Infantry and the 395th.

In the West Wall bunkers facing the 393d lay the 277th Volks Grenadier Division (Col. Hans Viebig). Reconstructed in Hungary from the remnants of an infantry division of the same number which had escaped from the Falaise pocket, the 277th arrived in the west during early November. In the days before the counteroffensive the division screened the entire front behind which the I SS Panzer Corps was assembling, but on the evening of 15 December, while two new infantry divisions moved into the line, the 277th assembled on the north flank of the corps zone between Hollerath and Udenbreth. One reinforced battalion, on the far southern flank of the original sector, was unable to reach the division line of departure in time to join the attack.

The I SS Panzer Corps commander had decided to put the weight of his armored thrust to the south and thus avoid entanglement with the American force which, it was thought, could be gathered quickly on the Elsenborn ridge in the northern sector of the zone of advance. But the Elsenborn area had to be neutralized, if for no other reason than to erase the American artillery groupment located there. The 277th Volks Grenadier Division had the task of making the penetration on the right wing of the corps and driving obliquely northwest to take the Elsenborn ridge. As finally prescribed by the corps commander, the phases of the attack planned for the 277th were these: to break through the American line and open the forest roads to Rocherath and Krinkelt; capture these twin villages; seize the Elsenborn area and block any American advance from Verviers. The division commander had received this mission with qualms, pointing out that the wooded and broken terrain favored the Americans and that without sufficient rifle strength for a quick breakthrough, success in the attack could only be won by very strong artillery support. But his orders stood. On the night of 15-16 December the 989th Regiment assembled near Hollerath, its objective Rocherath. To the south the 990th occupied the West Wall pillboxes near Udenbreth, poised for an attack to seize Krinkelt.

The artillery, Werfer, and mortar fire crashing into the American positions on the morning of 16 December gave the attacking German infantry the start the 277th commander had requested. The concentration thoroughly wrecked the American telephone lines which had been carefully strung from battalion to company command posts; in some cases radio communication failed at the same time. This preparatory bombardment continued until 0700.

The north wing of the 393d, held by the 3d Battalion (Lt. Col. Jack G. Allen), lay in the woods close to the German pillboxes from which the assault wave of the 989th, guided by searchlights beamed on the American positions, moved in on the Americans before they had recovered from the shelling. In the first rush all of Company K, save one platoon, were killed or captured. By 0855, when telephone lines were restored and the first word of the 3d Battalion's plight reached the regimental command post, the enemy had advanced nearly three-quarters of a mile beyond the American lines along the forest road from Hollerath. Colonel Allen stripped the reserve platoons from the balance of the 3d Battalion line in a futile attempt to block the onrush, but by 0930 the Germans had reached the battalion command post, around which Allen ordered Companies I and L to gather.

At this point the 81-mm. mortar crews laid down such a successful defensive barrage (firing over 1,200 rounds in the course of the fight) that the attackers swerved from this area of danger and continued to the west. By nightfall the forward companies of the 989th were at the Jansbach creek, halfway through the forest, but had been slowed down by troops switched from the left wing of the 3d Battalion and had lost many prisoners to the Americans. The 3d Battalion radio had functioned badly during the fight and contact with the 370th Field Artillery Battalion, supporting the 3d, was not established till the close of day. Despite the penetration between the 3d and 1st Battalions and the large number of enemy now to the rear and across the battalion supply road, Colonel Allen reported that the 3d could hold on during the night. His supply road had been cut in midafternoon, but Company I of the 394th had fought its way in with a supply of ammunition.

On the south the 1st Battalion (Maj. Matthew L. Legler) likewise had been outnumbered and hard hit. Here the 990th Regiment had assembled in Udenbreth during the dark hours and, when the barrage fire lifted at 0700, began an advance toward the 1st Battalion. The German assault companies, however, failed to get across the half mile of open ground before dawn and were checked short of the woods by mortar and machine gun fire. The commander of the 277th Volks Grenadier Division at once decided to throw in his reserve, the 991st Regiment, to spring the 990th loose. Sheer weight of numbers now carried the German attack across the open space and into the woods—but with high casualties amongst the riflemen and the officers and noncoms herding the assault waves forward. By 0830 the Germans had nearly surrounded Company C, on the 1st Battalion right. An hour later, the 991st Regiment, attacking southwest from Ramscheid, knocked out the light machine guns and mortars in the Company B sector (on the left) with bazooka fire and captured or killed all but one platoon. Company A (Capt. Joseph Jameson), which had been in reserve, counterattacked in support of what was left of Company B and by noon had dug in on a line only 300 yards behind the original line. Here Company A held for the rest of the day against repeated enemy attacks and constant artillery fire, with what the regimental after-action report characterized as "heroic action on the part of all men." In this fight friendly artillery played an important role. The surviving Company B platoon had retained an observation post overlooking the treeless draw along which reinforcements moved from Udenbreth and despite the German fire a telephone wire was run forward to this command post. The American gunners quickly made this avenue suicidal; through the afternoon cries from the wounded Germans lying in the draw floated back to the American line.

Company C on the 1st Battalion right had slowly succumbed to the weight of numbers; by 1015 two of its platoons had been engulfed. There was little that the regiment could do in response to Major Legler's plea for assistance, but at 1030 the mine-laying platoon from the regimental antitank company arrived to give a hand. This small detachment (26 riflemen plus 13 runners and cooks), led by Lt. Harry Parker, made a bayonet charge to reach the remaining Company C platoon and set up a new line of defense on the battalion right flank. A gap still remained between the battalion and the 394th Infantry farther south.

By the end of the day the 393d Infantry had restored a front facing the enemy. But the new line could hardly be called solid, the rifle strength remaining was too slim for that. The 1st Battalion had lost over half of its effective strength; the 3d Battalion had its right bent back for several hundred yards and had lost nearly three hundred men. The enemy wandered almost at will through the woods, firing into foxholes, shooting off flares, and calling out in English to trap the unwary. But even with the German strength apparent on all sides, the American situation seemed to be improving. Reinforcements, requested by General Lauer, had arrived from the 2d Division during the late afternoon, the supply roads might be restored to traffic when daylight came again, and the losses inflicted on the attacker were obvious and heartening.

The breakthrough on the south flank of the 99th Division, during 17 December, was paralleled that day by a strong German armored thrust into the division center. The 393d, whose left battalion had been driven back into the deep woods during the first day's attack, was under orders to counterattack and restore its original line. The 3d Battalion was close to being surrounded, and in order to recover its eastern position at the wood line it would have to reopen the battalion supply road. At 0800 Colonel Allen's tired and weakened battalion attacked to the west and drove the enemy off the road, but when the eastward counterattack started it collided with a battalion of German infantry. For half an hour Germans and Americans fought for a hundred-yard-wide strip of the woods. Then, about 0800, the German armor took a hand.

The failure by the 277th Volks Grenadier Division to clear the woods and reach Krinkelt-Rocherath on 16 December had led to some change of plan. The right flank, roughly opposite the 3d Battalion sector, was reinforced by switching the 990th Regiment to the north to follow the 989th Regiment. More important, the 12th SS Panzer Division (which now had come up on the left of the 277th) parceled out some of its tanks to give weight to the infantry attack by the right wing of the 277th Volks Grenadier Division.

The first tank entered the forest road from Hollerath, rolled to within machine gun range of the Americans, stopped, then for twenty minutes methodically spewed bullet fire. Attempts to get a hit by artillery fire were futile, although the American shelling momentarily dispersed the accompanying infantry and permitted a bazooka team to wreck one track. But even when crippled the single tank succeeded in immobilizing the American infantry. Four more enemy tanks appeared. One was knocked out by a bazooka round, but the rest worked forward along the network of firebreaks and trails. The combination of tanks and numerous infantry now threatened to erase the entire 3d Battalion position. Ammunition had run low and the 3d Battalion casualties could not be evacuated.

About 1030 Colonel Scott ordered the 3d Battalion, 393d Infantry, as well as its southern neighbor (the 1st), to remove to new positions about one and a half miles east of Rocherath. This would be done by withdrawing the 3d Battalion through the 3d Battalion, 23d Infantry (the reinforcements sent by Robertson), which had dug in some thousand yards to its rear. All the vehicles available to the forward troops were filled with wounded. Fifteen wounded men, most too badly hurt to be moved, were left behind, together with the 3d Battalion surgeon, Capt. Frederick J. McIntyre, and some enlisted aid men. By noon the entire battalion had pulled out (disengaging without much difficulty); it passed through the 3d Battalion, 23d Infantry, and two hours later was on the new position. Allen's battalion had fought almost continuously since the early morning of the 16th; then at full strength, it now was reduced to 475 men and all but two machine guns were gone.

The 1st Battalion of the 393d Infantry had not been hard pressed during the morning of 17 December because the German forces in its area had been content to move through the gap on the right, between the 393d and 394th. Ordered to withdraw about 1100, the battalion was in position alongside the 3d Battalion, 23d Infantry, by 1400, the two now forming a narrow front east of the twin villages.

The 3d Battalion, 23d Infantry (Lt. Col. Paul V. Tuttle, Jr.), had been rushed to the western edge of the woods on the afternoon of the 16th for use as a counterattack force. The hard-hitting German attack against the 3d Battalion, 393d, on the following morning so drastically changed the situation that Colonel Tuttle's orders were altered to: "hold at all costs." His battalion was none too well prepared for such defense, having arrived with no mines and very little ammunition. Trucks bringing ammunition forward found the road between Büllingen and Krinkelt barred by the enemy and never reached the battalion.

Shortly after the troops from the 393d passed through the battalion, Company I, on the open left flank, heard the clanking of tank treads. A few minutes later German tanks with marching infantry clustered around them struck the left platoon of Company I, rolling forward till their machine guns enfiladed the foxholes in which the American infantry crouched. Company I held until its ammunition was nearly gone, then tried to withdraw to a nearby firebreak but went to pieces under fire raking it from all directions. Company K, in line to the south, next was hit. The company started an orderly withdrawal, except for the left platoon which had lost its leader and never got the order to pull back. This platoon stayed in its foxholes until the tanks had ground past, then rose to engage the German infantry. The platoon was wiped out.

A medium tank platoon from the 741st Tank Battalion, loaned by Robertson, had arrived in the 3d Battalion area during the night. Lt. Victor L. Miller, the platoon leader, took two tanks to cover a forest crossroads near the Company K position. In a duel at close quarters the American tanks destroyed two panzers, but in turn were knocked out and Lieutenant Miller was killed.

Parts of Company K held stubbornly together, fighting from tree to tree, withdrawing slowly westward. For courage in this fight, Pfc. Jose M. Lopez, machine gunner, was awarded the Medal of Honor. This rear guard action, for the company was covering what was left of the battalion, went on until twilight. Then, as the survivors started to cross an open field, they were bracketed by artillery and Werfer fire and scattered. (Later the battalion would be given the Distinguished Unit Citation.) Company L, on the inner flank, had been given time for an orderly retreat; eighty or ninety men reached Krinkelt.

The 3d Battalion of the 393d had barely started to dig in behind the 3d Battalion, 23d Infantry, when the first stragglers came back with word of the German assault. Colonel Allen moved his spent battalion to a hastily organized position 500 yards to the northwest and prepared to make another stand. The main force of the German attack, however, had angled away while rolling over the flank of the forward battalion. About this time the 3d Battalion, 393d, met a patrol from the 1st Battalion, 9th Infantry, which had been rushed to the Rocherath area to cover the 2d Division withdrawal south from Wahlerscheid, and the two battalions joined forces.

The retreat of the 3d Battalion, 23d Infantry, left its right-flank neighbor, the 1st Battalion, 393d Infantry, completely isolated. Telephone lines long since had been destroyed, and radio communication had failed. In late afternoon Major Legler decided to withdraw but hearing that the 2d Battalion of the 394th was to tie in on his right reversed his decision. About dark, however, the Germans struck in force and the rifle companies pulled back closer together. Because the battalion supply road was already in German hands, Legler and his men struck out across country on the morning of the 18th, taking a few vehicles and those of the wounded who could be moved. The main body reached Wirzfeld but the rear guard became separated, finally joining other Americans in the fight raging around Krinkelt. The 1st Battalion by this time numbered around two hundred men.

The 395th Infantry Conforms to the Withdrawal

The 395th Infantry, which had supported the 2d Infantry Division attack in the Wahlerscheid sector, was little affected on the 16th and the morning of the 17th by the German power drive against the rest of the 99th Division. Information reaching the 395th command post was sparse and contradictory; both the 2d Division and the 395th still assumed that the battle raging to the south was an answer to the American threat at Wahlerscheid, where the 2d Division had made a sizable dent in the West Wall by evening of 16 December.

All this time a chain reaction was moving slowly from the menaced southern flank of the 99th northward. It reached the 395th before noon on 17 December with word that the 324th Engineer Battalion, stationed between that regiment and the 393d, was moving back to the west. Actually the engineers had not yet withdrawn but had moved to make contact with and cover the exposed flank of the 395th, this apparently on General Lauer's orders while the 395th was taking orders from Robertson. The withdrawal of the 2d Infantry Division to the Rocherath area resulted in the attachment of the 395th (reinforced by the 2d Battalion of the 393d) to General Robertson's division. Now the battalions were ordered to blow up all of the pillboxes taken in the advance. Finally, at 1600, Col. Alexander J. Mackenzie received a retirement order given by General Lauer or General Robertson, which one is uncertain. The plan was this. The two battalions of the 395th and the attached battalion from the 393d would fall back toward the regimental command post at Rocherath. From this point the regiment would deploy to cover the road leading out of Rocherath to the north and northeast, the road which the 2d Infantry Division was using in its march south from the Wahlerscheid battlefield.

The 1st Battalion reached Rocherath and on General Robertson's orders entrenched on both sides of the road north of the village. Heavy weapons were dragged through the deep mud and were placed to cover the road. The other two battalions dug in along a perimeter which faced east from Rocherath and the Wahlerscheid road. So emplaced, the 395th waited for the enemy to come pouring through the woods onto the 2d Division route of withdrawal.

On the opposite side of the 2d Division corridor, in the Höfen area, the enemy made no serious move on 17 December to repeat the disastrous attack of the previous day. The immediate objective of the 326th Volks Grenadier Division remained the high ground northwest of Monschau near Mützenich. General Kaschner apparently decided on 17 December to make his bid for a breakthrough directly in this sector and to abandon momentarily the attempt to force a penetration between Monschau and Höfen.

About 0400 on 17 December the 38th Cavalry Squadron outposts north of Monschau heard enemy troops moving along the draw running west from Menzerath. Quick and accurate response by American batteries ended this move. Three hours later the German batteries opened up, shelling the thin line of troopers deployed along the railroad cut north of Monschau. When the guns and Werfers ceased, a wave of German infantry headed for the railroad tracks. They were checked by machine gun fire, but more Germans appeared, extending the assault front from the north edge of Monschau to the hill beyond Mützenich. American firepower— artillery, tank destroyers, tank guns, and the numerous machine guns—stopped the first attack. But by 0900 the enemy had succeeded in gathering a battalion on the north flank, poised against the Troop B front 3,400 yards along the railroad line east of Mützenich Hill. In short rushes the enemy filtered into the Troop B area. Even the Luftwaffe took a hand; at least two squadrons made strafing runs over the cavalry positions. Although some Germans broke through the thin cavalry line, a sharp shelling administered by the 62d Field Artillery Battalion stopped the main support troops short of the railroad. More Germans could be seen assembling in Imgenbroich, but friendly aircraft were on the way to help the cavalry. Gunners from the 62d marked the village with red smoke and the fighter-bombers went in bombing and strafing. This ended the daylight phase of the fray. Company A of the 47th Infantry, which regiment was en route to the sector from Eupen, had appeared in time to help hunt down the Germans who had got through the cavalry line. Despite prisoner reports that the 326th would throw in a regimental attack during the afternoon, quiet reigned. The 47th Infantry arrived at Mützenich and bivouacked astride the Eupen road—the immediate threat was ended. The 38th Squadron could report a count of two hundred German dead in front of its lines. The 326th Volks Grenadier Division was finding its position at the pivot of the Sixth Panzer Army offensive a costly one.

The 2d Division Gives Up the Wahlerscheid Attack

On the night of 16-17 December the enemy counterattacked at Wahlerscheid. Actually the number of enemy troops available for use against the 2d Division was very small, too few for any telling maneuver out of the West Wall position. The bulk of the 272d Volks Grenadier Division, holding the sector, had been thrown in to stop the American 78th Division farther north. The 326th Volks Grenadier Division was already engaged in a costly attempt to penetrate the American lines at Monschau and Höfen. As a result the defense at the Wahlerscheid road junction had been conducted on a catch-as-catch-can basis by troops farmed out for brief periods prior to commitment in the counteroffensive. On 15 December, for example, elements of the 990th Regiment (277th Volks Grenadier Division) were relieved by a reinforced battalion of the 751st Regiment (326th Volks Grenadier Division), which, during the night of 15-16 December, was in the process of being relieved by the Replacement Battalion of the 326th. By coincidence the 2d Division attack on the night prior to the 16th engaged and detained troops which both the 277th and 326th expected to use elsewhere on the first day of the counteroffensive.

On the afternoon of 16 December Maj. Gen. Leonard T. Gerow, commanding the V Corps, concluded from the fragmentary reports coming out of the main battle area that the 2d Infantry Division might soon find itself in a difficult situation. He asked the First Army commander, General Hodges, for permission to call off the attack at Wahlerscheid and move the 2d Division to the natural defensive line offered by the ridge running north and south of Elsenborn. This was refused. Late in the evening the deputy corps commander (Maj. Gen. Clarence R. Huebner) cautioned General Robertson to keep the unengaged troops of his division in hand for a quick change of plan, despite the order to continue the attack. By this time the three battalions of the 9th Infantry and two of the 38th were committed. On the morning of the counteroffensive's second day, with the American position in the 99th Division and VIII Corps sector rapidly deteriorating, Gerow renewed his request. The First Army commander was unwilling to give orders for a withdrawal but authorized the V Corps commander to act as he saw fit. Gerow phoned Robertson; it was now about 0730.

For the first time the 2d Division commander learned that the enemy had broken through the 99th and that his own division was in danger of being cut off. Gerow's order was to set up a defensive position on the Elsenborn ridge—but first the 2d Division had to withdraw from the exposed Wahlerscheid sector. The immediate task confronting Robertson was that of gathering what troops he could to defend the single road back through Krinkelt-Rocherath to Wirtzfeld, while at the same time holding open the one-track road between Wirtzfeld and Elsenborn. Two-thirds of his reserve, the 23d Infantry, would be attached to the 99th Division. The rifle strength of the two regiments around Wahlerscheid had been reduced by nearly 1,200 men. The 1st Battalion of the 9th Infantry, for example, had begun the Wahlerscheid attack on 13 December with 35 officers and 678 men; on the morning of 17 December the active roster was 22 officers and 387 men. All of the original company commanders and most of the platoon leaders were casualties. Fortunately, the tank and tank destroyer strength attached to support the 2d Division attack had been held in reserve well to the south in order to prevent a jam on the single communicating road during the infantry phase of the operation and so constituted a readily available reserve. But the appearance of German armor early on 17 December would force some piecemeal distribution to meet this threat.

Even before the withdrawal order reached the 2d Division command post at Wirtzfeld on the morning of the 17th, German tanks had been spotted moving on Büllingen, the main division supply point. General Robertson ordered the headquarters commandant to prepare a defense at the division command post (a few hundred yards north of Büllingen) and sent his only free rifle battalion, the 2d of the 23d Infantry, south from the Rocherath area. After the capture of Büllingen the German column turned away to the southwest, but a reconnaissance party composed of a tank platoon and a few riflemen in half-tracks continued in the direction of Wirtzfeld. They had been anticipated by only a few minutes with the arrival of a self-propelled gun platoon from C Company of the 644th Tank Destroyer Battalion. When the Germans reached the ridge south of Wirtzfeld they were momentarily profiled against the skyline. Two of the American tank destroyers and a 57-mm. gun accounted for three of the panzers and a half-track. For the time being the threat to the southern terminus of the 2d Division line of withdrawal was ended. The 2d Battalion, 23d Infantry, and additional tank destroyers from the 644th soon arrived and deployed in the deep snow south of Wirtzfeld on the slope facing Büllingen, there to watch the 1st SS Panzer Regiment as it filed southwest.

The 394th Infantry Abandons the Mürringen Position

East of German-held Büllingen the American troops in Mürringen faced encirclement, occupying as they did a precarious and jutting angle between the defense forming on the evening of 17 December around the twin villages and the southern shoulder bracing at Butgenbach. The sole road remaining for withdrawal to the Elsenborn assembly area ran back through Krinkelt, the southernmost of the twin villages, whose tenure by friendly troops was none too certain on the night of the 17th. The chances for a successful withdrawal from Mürringen were dwindling by the hour.

The 37 1st Field Artillery Battalion which had been firing in support of the 394th from battery positions close by, was out of ammunition. Colonel Riley, the regimental commander, reported this to General Lauer at 0115 on the 18th, adding that he recommended "withdrawal." The division commander at once sent a radio message back: "Withdraw arty. Your order. Your time." Apparently Lauer expected that the 394th Infantry and Hightower's battalion from the 23d Infantry would send off the guns and then consolidate with the Krinkelt defenders. About this time Hightower arrived at Riley's command post and told him of his conversation with Colonel Hirschfelder. Hightower had just talked with one of his ambulance drivers who had come back from Wirtzfeld via the road through Krinkelt and said he could guide the vehicles out. Colonel Riley now decided to evade the closing jaws of the German trap by moving out through Krinkelt and retiring if possible, to Elsenborn. The ambulance driver would join the head of the column and Hightower's trucks would fall in behind the vehicles of the 394th.

Shortly after midnight the remnants of the 394th Infantry at Mürringen formed in two columns, one composed of foot troops, the other made up of the remaining vehicles. Colonel Riley started the motor column, which included Hightower's vehicles, along the road toward Krinkelt at 0215, a road beaten by hostile shellfire. Near Krinkelt, whence came the sound of heavy firing, the column halted while scouts moved toward the houses at the edge of the village. Here German tanks were seen, and so orders were passed along to abandon the vehicles and move west on foot to Elsenborn. The infantry column started a quarter of an hour after the vehicles, marching quietly toward Krinkelt along a tree-covered draw, carrying only helmets, overcoats, rifles, and ammunition. Debouching onto the road south of Krinkelt, the infantry found it lined with deserted trucks and jeeps. After some indecision the infantry manned a few of the empty vehicles—by this time it had been ascertained that the 2d Infantry Division had at least partial control of Krinkelt—and edged their way through the village and out the Wirtzfeld road. Most of the men from Mürringen reached Elsenborn during the 18th. The 371st Field Artillery Battalion, which had displaced closer to Krinkelt during the night, failed to get its heavy equipment out of the snow when a second move was ordered at daylight, and all but five howitzers were abandoned.

There remains to account for the 394th's 2d Battalion, which had been cut off from the regiment while in the Honsfelder Wald, and the 1st Battalion of the 23d, attached to the 394th and holding Hünningen, the southernmost position left to the 2d and 99th Divisions. In the Honsfelder Wald the 2d Battalion of the 394th met the 1st Battalion of the 393d; both were out of communication with their parent regiments and neither knew the location of neighboring units. Jointly deciding to withdraw further to the west, the two units began their march at daylight on the 18th. Diverted by the sound of intense firing in the direction of Krinkelt, they marched toward Mürringen.

Almost in the shadow of the houses the force got a hostile reception: the Germans had moved in on the heels of the 394th. At this critical juncture radio contact was made with a friendly unit, probably the 2d Division, and in answer to the plea for help American shells began exploding in the village. Between the confusion and the morning fog, the Americans were able to break away, turning this time toward Wirtzfeld. They carried as many of their wounded as they could, but some of the wounded had to be left behind in the care of two aid men. En route to Wirtzfeld the group suddenly was brought under fire by the 2d Division artillery, a number of casualties resulting. At this point the men nearly panicked, but order was restored while a squad leader raced ahead to a friendly outpost and stopped the shelling. Most of the weary, hungry troops reached Elsenborn during the early hours of 19 December. Capt. Robert McGee, S-3 of the 2d Battalion, 394th, had brought out about 570 officers and men. The 1st Battalion, 393d, which had been badly hurt in the first two days of the fight, was less fortunate. Fewer than 300 of its officers and men were left.

The 1st Battalion, 23d Infantry, at Hünningen, it will be recalled, had received radio orders late on the 17th which put it under the command of the 9th Infantry. Colonel Hightower's battalion was closely engaged, for the Germans had filtered through at a number of points, and when the order came to withdraw from the village the battalion had to fight its way free. Company B, most exposed, was under assault even as the withdrawal began. A platoon leader was wounded in front of the foxhole line; two aid men tried to reach him and were killed. A third reached the side of the fallen officer, then both were killed. The 3d Platoon, whose radio was gone, had no word as to the time when the battalion was pulling back. Runners who tried to reach the platoon were killed or captured, and this part of Company B was lost. Most of the badly depleted 1st Battalion withdrew in accordance with an earlier plan along a secondary road via Mürringen which had been scouted by the battalion medical officer, the vehicles following the 394th and the men on foot marching cross-country to Wirtzfeld.

Chapter VI. The German Northern Shoulder Is Jammed

The 2d Division Withdraws

General Robertson's plan for moving his 2d Division south was to "skin the cat," pulling the most advanced battalions in the Wahlerscheid sector back through the others. In addition to the main supply road, a part of the division could use the secondary route running more or less parallel to the Wahlerscheid road until the two met at a fork about a mile north of Rocherath. The 395th Infantry was in the woods east of the northernmost section of the 2d Division withdrawal route and would provide cover for the first stage of the tricky move parallel to and close behind the rapidly deteriorating front. Then too the enemy at the Wahlerscheid road junction seemed hardly strong or aggressive enough to make even a daylight disengagement difficult.

The danger zone would be the twin villages. Roads from the east led into Rocherath and Krinkelt. And, to the east, as information from the 99th Division rifle battalions warned, the Germans had made a deep penetration and were liable at any moment to come bursting out of the forest. Rocherath and Krinkelt had to be held if the 2d Division was to reach the Elsenborn position intact and with its heavy weapons and vehicles. The 99th Division had long since thrown its last reserve into the battle; therefore the 2d Division (with the attached 395th) alone had to provide for the defense of this endangered sector of the corridor south.

The 2d Division commander assigned responsibility to his officers as follows. Col. Chester J. Hirschfelder, commanding the 9th Infantry, was charged with the actual withdrawal from Wahlerscheid. The assistant division commander, Col. John H. Stokes, Jr., took over the defense of Rocherath. Col. Philip D. Ginder, assigned to the division as a spare regimental commander, was given the task of establishing a blocking position southeast of Wirtzfeld—the village at which the 2d Division would have to turn toward Elsenborn. General Robertson himself would spend the crucial hours of the 17th working up and down the Rocherath road, gathering additional troops where he could, intervening to change the disposition of battalions and even companies as the complexion of the battle altered.

The men turning south were concerned with a fight for their lives. Some units of the division would be able to occupy their assigned positions and entrench before the enemy struck. Others would have to attack in order to take their designated place in the new line of resistance. Meanwhile the rumor that American prisoners were being butchered in cold blood by SS troops was spreading like wildfire through the 2d Division, a partial explanation of the bitter fight finally made at the twin villages.

Robertson's order, "withdraw at once," reached the 9th Infantry a little after 1000. By 1100 the 2d Battalion had assembled and started south, with the 3d and 1st Battalions forming in that order to complete the column. The withdrawal from the front lines, shielded by a heavy barrage laid on the West Wall positions, was accomplished readily but of course took much time. The 1st Battalion, bringing up the rear of the 9th Infantry column, did not set out until 1415.

Before the five battalions at Wahlerscheid commenced to disengage, General Robertson marched his only reserve, the 3d Battalion of the 38th Infantry, south through Rocherath and Krinkelt. At this time in the morning the imminent German threat was in the area north of Büllingen. For this reason Robertson placed the 3d Battalion at the southern edge of Krinkelt, where, by 1130, it was entrenched. One rifle company, plus the antitank and service companies, took positions around Rocherath guarding the roads entering the village from the north and east.

The redeployment of the 2d Division had a double aim: securing a firm hold on Wirtzfeld, essential to the control of the road net in the final phase of the move to Elsenborn, and defending Krinkelt and Rocherath until such time as both the 2d and 99th Divisions could be withdrawn to the Elsenborn ridge. The 9th Infantry, leading the move, was to concentrate the bulk of its troops around Wirtzfeld; the 38th, to build up a defensive line at Krinkelt-Rocherath as its battalions arrived. Before dark the 2d Battalion of the 9th Infantry had traversed the seven and a half miles of congested and shell-torn road, deploying south of Wirtzfeld in line with the 2d Battalion of the 23d Infantry. The 3d Battalion, next in the 9th Infantry column, arrived after dark and dug in between the two battalions already south of Wirtzfeld. En route the 2d Division commander had detached Company K and sent it posthaste to the line forming northeast of Rocherath and to the rear of the fragmented 3d Battalion, 393d. Through the afternoon the prospect of a large-scale German armored attack from Büllingen had loomed large in the calculations of both General Robertson and General Lauer. Fortunately the attack failed to come.

In the late afternoon two rifle battalions were on their way to Krinkelt and Rocherath: the 1st Battalion of the 9th Infantry (Lt. Col. William D. McKinley) cleared the Wahlerscheid area at 1415; the 1st Battalion of the 38th Infantry (Lt. Col. Frank T. Mildren) started on its way at 1530. The road south was now under German shellfire, going was slow, and only a short span of daylight remained The danger involved in the movement across the front multiplied with each hour, for the 99th Division center, east of the twin villages, was collapsing. On the road General Robertson met Colonel McKinley and told him that he had just come from the command post of the 395th Infantry where he had learned that the Germans had broken through the 393d. Robertson had split the preceding battalion of the 9th Infantry to send a rifle company and part of the headquarters company to bar the main road from the forest into Rocherath. Now he ordered McKinley to rush his battalion to Rocherath and hold the woods road "until ordered to withdraw." At dusk the 1st Battalion was in position, deployed on a slight rise overlooking a shallow depression from which a gradual ascent led into the forest.

A thick fog lay close to the snow-covered ground. Around was a scene of wild confusion, stragglers with and without arms hurrying along the road and across the fields, the sound and flash of gunfire coming from the woods to the east. Company K, now attached to the 1st Battalion, already was north of the road, backed up by three guns from the 644th Tank Destroyer Battalion. Company C closed beside K; Company B dug in at the road; Company A lay to the south. The battalion had not picked up its mines during the disengagement, but was able to get a few from the tank destroyers for use at the road. There were fifteen extra bazookas on the ammunition vehicles, and these were handed to riflemen earlier trained by McKinley as bazooka men. Forward observers from the 15th Field Artillery Battalion hurriedly set up their communications. In the woods, less than a thousand yards away, firing continued as darkness closed over the American position.

Friendly infantry and tanks were known to be coming west. About 1930 three tanks and a platoon or so of infantry came through Company B. They had passed on toward Rocherath before anyone realized that this was the first of the enemy. Half an hour later more tanks came clanking along the road, the dark shapes of infantrymen following. This time Company B took no chances. The first two German tanks struck the American mines. Then two more tried to swing off the road, only to be knocked out by bazooka fire. By this time the Germans were milling about, apparently completely surprised, while the 15th Field Artillery Battalion added to the confusion by beating the road close to the 1st Battalion foxholes. It took the enemy an hour or so to reorganize. Then five or six German tanks attacked in line, rolling to within a couple of hundred yards of the foxhole line where they halted and fired for nearly half an hour. Next the accompanying infantry rushed in, but were cut down by the heavy machine guns on the final protective line. Finally the enemy tankers and riflemen got together in an assault that broke through.

The 1st Battalion refused to panic and set to work with bazookas against the flanks of the blinded tanks. One of the panzers was crippled, but the crew compartment proved impervious to bazooka rounds (perhaps this was a Tiger). So Cpl. Charles Roberts (Company D) and Sgt. Otis Bone (Company B) drained some gasoline from an abandoned vehicle, doused the tank, and lit the whole with thermite grenades. When German tanks moved into the Company A area, American artillery responded to the urgent call for help and within three minutes dropped in a concentration that stopped the assault. Meanwhile the American gunners, firing from new emplacements near Camp Elsenborn, had effectively checked further troop moves on the road from the forest, seven battalions finally joining in the shoot. By midnight all was quiet in front of the 1st Battalion except for the distant crash of friendly artillery—around the foxholes the silence was "frightening." Stubborn determination, mines, machine guns, and bazookas had checked this first series of assaults, but the battalion commander would credit the gunners at Elsenborn with saving his battalion.

It will be recalled that the 1st Battalion of the 38th Infantry had started south shortly after the departure of the last troops of the 9th Infantry. The actual withdrawal was screened by the 2d Battalion of the 38th, the final covering force of the 2d Division, and was aided by fire and smoke laid down by the 37th Field Artillery Battalion, 81-mm. and 4.2-inch mortars. On the road the regimental executive officer met Colonel Mildren and explained the 1st Battalion mission: to go into the line forming at the twin villages on the left of the 3d Battalion, 38th Infantry, east and northeast of Krinkelt. Mildren learned in addition that the battalion probably would have to fight its way to the assigned position, a jarring note that pleased none this close to nightfall.

About a thousand yards north of Rocherath the battalion column came to a crossroads which had been picked as a profitable target for the enemy artillery and Werfers. Company A at the head of the column passed safely, but the rest came into a gantlet of the most severe shelling the veteran battalion ever had encountered. Company C, third in the serial, suffered most and became badly disorganized. German tanks were near the crossroads and might have cut into the American infantry had not T/4 Truman Kimbro placed mines across the eastern entry. Kimbro was killed, after having been hit innumerable times. He was awarded the Medal of Honor posthumously.

The leading company, now alone, entered Rocherath at dusk but found no guides and marched on through the next village until met by bullet fire. Twice the company doubled back on its trail until finally found by the battalion executive and directed to the proper position. Company B arriving about 2130, moved in on the left of Company A but was still on the surface (not having had time to entrench) when German tanks and infantry struck from the northeast at Krinkelt. Company A, well dug in and with all its weapons emplaced, let the tanks roll past and then took on the infantry. Its neighbor, Company B, exposed and without its supporting weapons, was riddled, only one platoon managing to escape. The Company B survivors, joined by what was left of Company C, fell back to the regimental command post in Rocherath and joined the antitank company in the street fight raging there.

Back at Krinkelt three German tanks with infantry clinging to their decks got into the eastern streets: with this foothold won more Germans appeared as the night went on. The fight for Krinkelt surged back and forth, building to building, hedgerow to hedgerow. Men on both sides were captured and recaptured as the tide of battle turned. A German attempt to seize the heavy-walled church on the northern edge of the village was beaten off by the reconnaissance company of the 644th Tank Destroyer Battalion, which had lost a platoon at Büllingen during the morning. The communications officer of the 1st Battalion, 38th Infantry, 1st Lt. Jesse Morrow, knocked out a tank with only a rifle grenade. (Morrow later was awarded the DSC.) The situation in Krinkelt was further confused by retreating troops from the 99th Division, intermixed as they were with the infiltrating enemy. One German, using a captured American to give the password, got past two outposts, but a sentry finally killed both men. At midnight a column of 99th Infantry vehicles started pouring through the town and continued the rest of the night.

At Rocherath, the Germans who had so boldly entered the village earlier in the evening destroyed three American tanks as these inched their way out of the village to help Company K of the 38th Infantry. Here too the fight was bitter and confused. At one time a battalion commander of the 38th was reported to have men from sixteen different companies fighting under his command. By midnight, however, the enemy tanks behind the American lines had been accounted for and the German infantrymen captured or killed.

When the wild night of fighting drew to a close, the Americans still were in control of the two villages and the near sector of the Wahlerscheid withdrawal route. The rear guard 2d Battalion of the 38th had made a highly successful withdrawal and was assembled a half mile north of Rocherath. The 395th Infantry had moved back as ordered and, thus far in good shape, held the left flank of the 2d Division northeast of Rocherath astride the two approaches to the fork above the village. (It had left the 324th Engineer Battalion isolated on Rath Hill, however, and when the engineers started west on the morning of the 18th they came under fire from both the 395th and the enemy.) Straggler lines were operating around the twin villages and a start was being made at regrouping the strays and tying together the bits and pieces of the American line. Wirtzfeld, the one good escape hatch to Elsenborn, was ready for a defense in force. The 2d Division artillery and its reinforcing battalions had displaced to the Elsenborn ridge in positions within range of the entire front. General Robertson's 2d Division and attached troops had carried through a highly complex maneuver in the face of the enemy, disengaging in a fortified zone, withdrawing across a crumbling front, then wheeling from column to secure and organize a defensive line in the dark and under attack. Having completed this mission, the 2d

Division was under orders to hold in place while the remnants of the 99th Division right wing passed through to Elsenborn; then it was to break away and re-form for the defense of the Elsenborn ridge.

The appearance of the 2d Infantry Division at the twin villages probably came as a complete surprise to the German command. German intelligence had failed completely as regards the location of this division and believed that it was in reserve at Elsenborn. Peculiarly enough, the fact that the 2d was attacking through the 99th positions never was reported to the Sixth Panzer Army headquarters. Dietrich expected, therefore, to break through the 99th and meet the 2d somewhere to the rear or possibly to the right rear of the 99th. This may explain the German failure to attempt an end run and drive for Elsenborn.

The 1st Infantry Division Sends Reinforcements to Butgenbach

The advance guard of the 1st SS Panzer Division had reached Büllingen on the early morning of 17 December, by its presence threatening the open right flank and the rear of the 99th Division. Although the German armored column veered southwest, under the eyes of the astonished Americans, the presence of the enemy this deep within the bare south flank was a cause of grave concern to General Lauer and later to General Robertson. Through the morning only a handful of engineers and headquarters personnel, backed up with single tank destroyer and antiaircraft pieces, stood in the way of a German dash north across the American rear. But the 1st SS Panzer, intent on objectives far to the west, failed to make this play. A platoon of Mark IV tanks did scout the Butgenbach road but withdrew when three were destroyed by the few guns of Company B, 612th Tank Destroyer Battalion, which Capt. John J. Kennedy had emplaced near Dom Butgenbach.

Reinforcements from the 1st Infantry Division, as promised by the VII Corps, arrived at Camp Elsenborn about 0900, reported to the 99th Division, and were dispatched at once toward Butgenbach. This village lay on high ground belonging to the vital Elsenborn ridge and would be the point of entry for any German thrust on the road net north of Büllingen.

The 26th Infantry (Col. John F. R. Seitz), which had been transferred to V Corps control the previous midnight, was the only unit thus far sent south by the 1st Division. At Elsenborn, after General Lauer had given a quick resume of the situation, the regimental executive officer, then in command, put the 2d Battalion in the lead, sending it south to occupy two hills midway between Butgenbach and Büllingen which overlooked the main road connecting the two villages. By dusk the 2d Battalion (Lt. Col. Derrill M. Daniel) was deployed on the high ground near the tiny hamlet of Dom Butgenbach, dug in along the reverse slopes on a 2,100 yard front. Both flanks were wide open. The enemy, however, failed to react forcefully to the American move, although a 2d Battalion patrol found that the Germans still were in Büllingen. The 26th Infantry ultimately would be hit and hit hard, but not until the German plans for shattering the eastern front of the 99th and 2d Divisions had failed. The night of 17 December passed uneventfully except for the booming of the guns of the 33d Field Artillery Battalion and 413th Antiaircraft Gun Battalion firing from their positions with the 26th Infantry against the hostile traffic streaming through Büllingen.

Early the following morning small enemy detachments appeared in the Dom Butgenbach area but showed no inclination to close with the Americans. The 26th Infantry had been busy during the night completing its deployment: the 3d Battalion now was dug in west of Wirtzfeld on the left of the 2d Battalion, which retained the responsibility for blocking the Büllingen-Butgenbach road; the 1st Battalion was in reserve around Butgenbach; and considerable artillery and tank destroyer strength reinforced the command. In anticipation of an all-out German attack at this critical section of the American front, the V Corps truckhead at Butgenbach was closed and all rations and gasoline were evacuated. Farther to the west, where no defense had yet formed, the Robertville ammunition supply point, holding six thousand tons, suspended operations and moved to the rear. But through the 18th the enemy showed no sign of any earnest intent in front of the 26th Infantry.

The Defense of the Twin Villages, 18 December
The German attempt to take Krinkelt and Rocherath during the night of 17-18 December had not been well coordinated, carried out as it was by the advance guards of two divisions attacking piecemeal in the dark over unknown terrain against resistance which was completely surprising. By the morning of 18 December, however, the enemy strength had increased substantially despite the miserable state of the woods roads leading to the twin villages. The 989th Regiment of the 277th Volks Grenadier Division (probably reinforced by a third battalion) had reached Rocherath. The 12th SS Panzer Division, whose tanks and armored infantry carriers made extremely slow progress on the muddy secondary roads quickly chewed up by churning tracks—was able by dawn to assemble the 25th Panzer Grenadier Regiment, an assault gun battalion, and one full tank battalion east of the villages. During the 18th this force was strengthened by one more tank battalion, the final armored commitment being about equally divided between Panther tanks and the heavy Tigers.

The American strength at Krinkelt and Rocherath was substantial and by daylight on 18 December was assuming a cohesive defensive pattern as the battalions reorganized after the race south and the confused night battle. Most of the 38th Infantry (Col. Francis H. Boos) was in and around the two villages, plus about a battalion and a half of the 9th Infantry and a few platoons of the 23d Infantry (Col. Jay B. Loveless). Although these 2d Division troops had gaping ranks, so had their opponents. Fortunately in view of the number of tanks ready in the German camp, the American infantry had the means of antitank defense at hand; the 741st Tank Battalion, 644th Tank Destroyer Battalion, a company of the 612th Tank Destroyer Battalion, and a few guns from the 801st Tank Destroyer Battalion. On Elsenborn ridge, but well within supporting range, lay the 2d Division artillery (which had displaced after firing from extreme forward positions), the bulk of the 99th Division artillery, and some corps field artillery battalions. The flanks of the 2d Division position at the villages were more or less covered by elements of the 9th and 23d Infantry in Wirtzfeld, to the southwest, and the battalions of the 393d deployed in blocking positions to hold the road net north of Rocherath. As yet, however, there was no homogeneous line sealing the 2d Division front, and the men and vehicles of the 99th Division still passing through to the west complicated the problem of coordinating the defense and artillery fire.

An ominous quiet prevailed around Rocherath during the early, dark hours of 18 December, but just before first light the enemy resumed the assault, this time employing his tanks and infantry in ordered company. The 1st Battalion of the 9th Infantry, deployed east of the village along the road from the woods, took the first blow. Apparently a company of tanks had been brought close to the American line during the night battle, and these now attacked with more than a battalion of infantry. While the batteries on Elsenborn ridge furiously shelled the road, a confused fight spread all along the foxhole line. The morning fog was heavy, visibility almost nil. The American infantry let the tanks roll past, then tailed them with bazookas or turned to meet the oncoming infantry at close quarters with grenades, and even bayonets or knives. This first assault was beaten off, while a number of the German tanks were crippled or destroyed by bazooka teams stalking successfully under cover of the fog.

When the fog lifted about 0830, three German tanks rolled right along the foxhole line firing their machine guns while the German infantry rushed forward. Lt. Stephen P. Truppner of Company A radioed that his company had been overrun and asked for artillery to fire on his own position. For thirty minutes an American battalion shelled this area. Only twelve men escaped. Company K, which had been attached to the battalion the day before, likewise was engulfed. Capt. Jack J. Garvey, sending a last message from the cellar of the house which was his command post, refused to leave because he could not get his company out. Ten men and one officer escaped. On the left Companies B and C were able to hold their ground; a few from Company B broke and ran but were sent back by the battalion commander.

The German wave carried tanks and infantry inside Rocherath, the fight eddying from house to house, wall to wall, along streets and down narrow alleys. Tanks fought tanks; men were captured, then captured again. Meanwhile, Colonel Boos did what he could to form some defense behind what was left of the 1st Battalion of the 9th. He radioed Colonel McKinley that as soon as the 2d Battalion of the 38th could swing into position, a matter of an hour or more, the 1st Battalion should withdraw. With his remaining two companies transfixed by direct tank fire and surrounded by German infantry, McKinley replied that no withdrawal was possible unless friendly tanks or tank destroyers arrived. "Miraculously, " as the 1st Battalion later reported, a platoon of Sherman tanks came into view. This was a part of A company, 741st Tank Battalion, which had been patrolling the Wahlerscheid road. When the platoon commander was asked if he wanted to do some fighting the reply was profanely affirmative. First the tanks joined the infantry in a counterattack to reach the positions which had been held by Companies A and K. Two of the three German tanks which had been harassing the battalion were destroyed by the Shermans, but no contact was made with the lost companies. A second counterattack by the tank platoon covered the 1st Battalion withdrawal, but the last riflemen out had the Germans yelling at their heels.

The shattered battalion withdrew through the 2d Battalion of the 38th, fell back to Rocherath, and then marched to Krinkelt, where it billeted in a deserted hotel. Approximately 240 officers and men were left of the original battalion and its attached units. In addition to the nearly total loss of Companies A and K, all of the Company M machine gunners attached to the 1st Battalion were missing in action. Of the group that had been rushed in the previous evening from Headquarters Company, 3d Battalion, only thirteen were left. It seems probable that the entire 989th Regiment had been employed in wresting the road to Rocherath from the stubborn 1st Battalion; the fight had gone on for nearly six hours and had given the 38th Infantry time to regroup to meet the enemy drive. Colonel Boos gratefully acknowledged that this gallant stand had saved his regiment.

The 3d Battalion of the 393d, after hard fighting on the 17th, had withdrawn northeast of Rocherath and tied in sketchily on the left of the 1st Battalion, 9th Infantry.

Colonel Allen's battalion was about half strength and had lost all of its machine guns, mortars, and antitank guns. The furious morning attack against the 1st Battalion, with a tank platoon in the lead, also struck the 3d Battalion. Unable to combat the tanks, although one was hit by a bazooka round, the battalion fell back a thousand yards to the northwest. Good radio communication with the 395th allowed its cannon company to take a hand, effectively covering the retirement and discouraging close pursuit. About noon Allen's men were ordered to Wirtzfeld, then on to the line forming at Elsenborn.

Although enemy tanks and foot troops had penetrated as far as the 38th command post inside Rocherath, they were successfully hunted out during the morning. The Germans continued to hammer along the forest road, striving to win free entrance to the village, but they found the 2d Battalion of the 38th (Lt. Col. Jack K. Norris), now standing in the way, a tough opponent. The most successful assault of the afternoon forced the 2d Battalion to retire "one hedgerow."

The battle for Krinkelt, if it can be separated from that raging around Rocherath, commenced sometime before dawn when five tanks and a body of infantry moved cautiously up to the eastern edge of the village. When the enemy tankers halted to confer with their infantry escort, Company L, 23d Infantry, which had been placed in the line after its retreat from the woods the evening before, killed some forty of the Germans and the panzers decamped. A brief period of quiet followed and during this lull the foot detachment of the 394th from Mürringen passed through the American lines en route to Wirtzfeld and Elsenborn. By 0830, however, the fight for Krinkelt was on in earnest. A number of attacks were checked by shellfire before they could make much headway. Nonetheless, a tank platoon penetrated as far as the 1st Battalion, 38th Infantry, command post before it was destroyed, and a few German tanks got as far as the road south to Wirtzfeld. In this quarter, as at Rocherath, the American tanks, tank destroyers, and bazooka teams left the German tanks smoking and broken.

During the night of 18 December, the 2d Division still held the twin villages while the last organized units of the 99th Division moved west on their way to Elsenborn. In the dark, German bazooka teams crept along walls and hedgerows seeking the hiding places of the American tanks and tank destroyers which had done so much to foil the armored attacks during the day. The panzers again made forays into the villages, made their kills, and in turn were destroyed.

Although the American hold in this sector remained firm, some of the confusion and loss of control normally inherent in a tactical situation like that faced by the 2d and 99th Divisions was beginning to tell. Orders from the 99th Division had been addressed to the 394th Infantry, at 0808, stressing that the regiment was not to withdraw to Elsenborn but instead should take position south of Krinkelt beside the 38th Infantry. The main body of the 394th already had passed through Krinkelt by that hour and probably never received the order until it arrived at Elsenborn.

Confused communications also had an impact in the area held by the 395th Infantry on the north flank. General Robertson, about 0200 on the morning of the 18th, had radioed the 395th Infantry to maintain contact with the 38th but to prepare for a move to Elsenborn. Thus far the enemy had made no move to strike the 395th positions in force. A radio message reached the 395th command post about 1600 ordering the regiment to withdraw to Elsenborn. The move began while Colonel Mackenzie went on to the 99th Division headquarters at Elsenborn to report. Here he was informed that no such order had been sent (it had been sent but was garbled) and General Lauer told him that his battalions must be sent back to their positions at once. Mackenzie was able to reach two battalions on the road and turn them back, but the 1st Battalion, 395th, had arrived in Elsenborn before word could reach it. The countermarch was made successfully and the old positions reoccupied at 0500 on 19 December. Information that the 395th had left, denuding the north flank, reached the 38th Infantry commander during the night and caused much concern.

But the 990th Volks Grenadier Regiment, at the forest edge east of the 395th positions, either had failed to notice the withdrawal or had been unwilling to make a move with darkness settling.

The Last Attack at Höfen Fails, 18 December

Ten miles by road north of Krinkelt and Rocherath the 3d Battalion, 395th Infantry, fought an isolated but important engagement on 18 December. Having failed the day before to breach the American cavalry line at Monschau, the 326th Volks Grenadier Division turned again toward Höfen where it had encountered such a sharp reverse on the first day of the German counteroffensive. The 2d Battalion of the 753d Regiment finally had rejoined the division; so General Kaschner put this regiment in the van, nourishing his assault waves with companies of the remaining two regiments as the fight developed. Some three hours before daybreak the German assault detachments moved forward from the hills surrounding Höfen to make a first test of the American defenses at the northern edge of the village. Well prepared for such an onslaught, concentrated artillery and mortar fire blanketed the ground over which the grenadiers had to advance. Despite heavy casualties from this fire the enemy broke through to the village. There followed a confused battle, but when day broke the last Germans were being routed from the houses.

The first daylight assault came about 0900, preceded by a barrage of artillery, rocket, and mortar fire. Advancing through a thick haze, ten tanks, seven armored cars, and an infantry battalion made for the village. Once more the defensive gun concentrations made great play in the gray ranks. The 3-inch tank destroyers of the 612th Tank Destroyer Battalion, although frozen in place, held the German fighting vehicles at bay—even with the limited traverse. As before, some of the attackers broke through. Colonel Butler phoned the forward observer of the 196th Field Artillery Battalion, whose little party was fighting off Germans around its observation post (a three-story brick building right in the forward line), and asked for three five-minute concentrations on his own positions. The shells came in promptly. As the fire finally lifted Butler sent his reserve, a single platoon of I Company, into the counterattack. Picking up strength at the foxhole line, the Americans drove the remaining foe back in the direction of Rohren. The German tanks, whose appearance had caused the 3d Battalion to request help "at once," took a singularly small part in the fray, retiring behind a ridge which gave shelter against direct antitank fire. It must be said that the German grenadiers were of sterner stuff. The American main line of resistance was not completely re-established until 1230. When night came the Germans tried once again but to no avail.

Thus ended the enemy plan to carry the northern pivot of the Sixth Panzer Army offensive as far forward as Eupen. Kaschner had planned to shift his attack later in the day toward Monschau, but this attack never was made. The bloody failure at Höfen gives a more than adequate explanation. German dead literally were piled in front of the 3d Battalion. The disparity in losses suffered by the combatants is amazing. The German dead counted in and around Höfen numbered 554; prisoners numbered 53. The American casualties were five killed and seven wounded. From this time on the 326th Volks Grenadier Division abandoned all but minor action in this sector, finally turning south to take a secondary role in the ensuing battle at the Elsenborn ridge. Höfen and Monschau remained in American hands through the rest of the Ardennes Campaign.

The 2d Division Withdraws to the Elsenborn Line, 19 December

At 1800 on 18 December the V Corps commander attached General Lauer's 99th Division to Robertson's 2d Division. General Gerow's instructions, given Robertson late on 17 December for a defense of the Rocherath-Krinkelt-Wirtzfeld line until such time as the isolated American troops to the east could be withdrawn, finally were fulfilled on the night of 18-19 December when the remnants of the 1st Battalion of the 393d and the 2d Battalion of the 394th came back through the 2d Division lines. These were the last organized units to find their way to safety, although small groups and individual stragglers would appear at the Elsenborn rallying point for some days to come. Then, despite the fact that the 2d Division was hard pressed, Robertson made good on his promise to the corps commander that he would release the 99th Division elements which had been placed in the 2d Division line and send them to Elsenborn for reorganization within their own division. The tactical problem remaining was to disengage the 2d Division and its attached troops, particularly those in the twin villages, while at the same time establishing a new and solid defense along the Elsenborn ridge.

The failure to break through at the twin villages on 18 December and so open the way south to the main armored route via Büllingen had repercussions all through the successive layers of German command on the Western Front. Realizing that the road system and the terrain in front of the Sixth Panzer Army presented more difficulties than those confronting the Fifth, it had been agreed to narrow the Sixth Panzer Army zone of attack and in effect ram through the American front by placing two panzer corps in column. The southern wing of the 1st SS Panzer Corps, in the Sixth Panzer Army van, had speedily punched a hole between the 106th and 99th American divisions and by 18 December the leading tank columns of the 1st SS Panzer Division were deep in the American rear areas. The northern wing, however, had made very slow progress and thus far had failed to shake any tanks loose in a dash forward on the northern routes chosen for armored penetration. Peremptory telephone messages from the headquarters of OB WEST harassed Dietrich, the Sixth Panzer Army commander, all during the 18th and were repeated—doubtless by progressively sharpening voices—all the way to the Krinkelt-Rocherath front. But exhortation had been fruitless.

Although Dietrich continued to needle his subordinates to get the right wing of the army rolling forward, he also sought to remedy the situation by changing the I SS Panzer Corps tactics. Dietrich suggested to General Priess that the 12th SS Panzer Division disengage, swing south, bypass Butgenbach, and get back onto the main route some place west of the thorny American position The I SS Panzer Corps commander and his staff politely rejected this idea on the grounds that the byroads were impassable and that Krinkelt, Rocherath, and Butgenbach must be cleared to open the better road net. Eventually Dietrich prevailed—or some compromise was reached—for late on 18 December armored elements of the 12th SS Panzer Division began to withdraw from the twin villages, while the 3d Panzer Grenadier Division, which had been scheduled for the fight at Monschau, marched west from reserve to take over the battle with the 2d Division.

The German plans for 19 December were these: the 277th Volks Grenadier Division and advancing troops of the 3d Panzer Grenadier Division were to continue the attack at Krinkelt and Rocherath; the 89th Regiment, 12 Volks Grenadier Division, which had come up from reserve and initiated an attack from Mürringen against Krinkelt the day before, was to maintain pressure in this sector. Meanwhile, the 12th SS Panzer Division was to complete its withdrawal from the twin villages and move as quickly as the poor roads would allow to join a kampfgruppe of the 12 Volks Grenadier Division in a thrust against the American flank position at Butgenbach. The direction of the German main effort, as a result, would shift, substituting an armored thrust against the flank for the battering-ram frontal attack against the now well-developed defenses in the area of Krinkelt-Rocherath. Fresh German infantry were en route to the twin villages, and some reinforcements would be employed there on the 19th, but the attack would lack the armored weight whose momentum had carried earlier assault waves into the heart of the American positions.

At dawn, on 19 December, and blanketed in thick fog, the German grenadiers advanced on Krinkelt and Rocherath. The batteries back on Elsenborn ridge once again laid down a defensive barrage, ending the attack before it could make any headway. Another advance, rolling forward under an incoming fog about 1000, placed enemy snipers and machine gunners close to the American positions. Shortly after noon a few German tanks churned toward the villages and unloaded machine gunners to work the weapons on derelict tanks which had been abandoned close to the American foxhole line. Apparently the enemy infantry were edging in as close as they could in preparation for a final night assault. Headlong assault tactics were no longer in evidence, however. In the meantime the defenders picked up the sounds of extensive vehicular movement (representing the departing elements of the 12th SS Panzer Division), and a platoon of tanks appeared northeast of Rocherath but quickly retired when artillery concentrations and direct fire were brought to bear.

Inside the twin villages' perimeter the defenders were aware that a phase of the battle was ending. Colonel Stokes, the assistant division commander, was preparing plans for withdrawal to the Elsenborn lines. Colonel Boos had the 38th Infantry and its attached troops at work quietly destroying the weapons and equipment, German and American, which could not be evacuated. Finally, at 1345, the withdrawal order was issued, to be put in effect beginning at 1730. The 395th Infantry was to retire from its lines north of the villages and move cross-country (by a single boggy trail) west to Elsenborn. The 38th Infantry and its attached units, more closely engaged and in actual physical contact with the enemy, would break away from the villages, fall back west through Wirtzfeld, then move along the temporary road which the 2d Division engineers had constructed between Wirtzfeld and Berg. Once the 38th had cleared through the Wirtzfeld position, now held by elements of the 9th Infantry and a battalion of the 23d, it would occupy a new defensive line west and northwest of Wirtzfeld, while the 9th Infantry in turn evacuated that village.

Company officers commanding troops facing the enemy had been carefully briefed to avoid the word "withdrawal" in final instructions to their men. This was to be "a move to new positions"; all were to walk, not run. Col. Leland W. Skaggs' 741st Tank Battalion, tank destroyers from the 644th Tank Destroyer Battalion, and the 2d Division engineers would form a covering force in the villages, laying mines and beating off any attempt at "pursuit." Disengagement was made from left to right, "stripping" the 2d Division line from Rocherath to Wirtzfeld. First, the 2d Battalion of the 38th Infantry pulled out of the north edge of Rocherath; the 1st Battalion, deployed in both villages, followed; the 3d Battalion tacked on at Krinkelt. A half hour later, just as the Germans moved into Rocherath, Company C of the 644th and Company B of the 741st hauled out, the tanks carrying the engineers. The move through Wirtzfeld, now in flames, brought the 38th under German guns and resulted in some casualties and confusion, but at 0200 on 20 December the rear guard tank platoon left Wirtzfeld and half an hour later the 9th Infantry passed through the new lines occupied by the 38th Infantry a thousand yards west of the village.

The four-day battle which had pitted the 2d Infantry Division and the 99th Infantry Division against the spearheads of the Sixth Panzer Army had cost both sides heavily in men and materiel. But in the balance sheet for this desperate initial phase of the German counteroffensive, where lives weighed less than hours won or lost, the reckoning was favorable to the Americans. What the fruitless bid for a quick decision had cost the Germans in terms of dead and wounded has no accounting. The losses of the untried 99th Division, fighting its first major action under circumstances far more difficult than was the lot of most American infantry divisions in the European Theater of Operations, have been compiled only as a total for the whole month of December. A careful check shows that the 99th had few casualties prior to 16 December or after 19 December; nine-tenths or more of the following list, therefore, represents the cost of four days of battle: 14 officers and men killed in action; 53 officers and 1,341 men missing in action; 51 officers and 864 men wounded in action. About 600 officers and men passed through the division clearing station before 20 December as nonbattle casualties; half were trench foot cases.

The veteran 2d Division had taken considerable punishment from exposure and battle loss beginning on 13 December with the start of the Wahlerscheid operation. It is impossible to determine the ratio between the casualties suffered in the first four days of attack and those of the final three days of defense. Indeed no total is available for the 2d Division during these important seven days. The 23d Infantry, in reserve before 16 December and then committed by battalion, sustained these battle losses: 1st Battalion, 10 officers and 221 men; 2d Battalion, 1 officer and 100 men; 3d Battalion, 10 officers and 341 men. The 9th Infantry, which was engaged both at Wahlerscheid and the twin villages, lists 47 officers and men killed, 425 wounded, and 192 missing. The regiment likewise had lost nearly 600 officers and men as nonbattle casualties (trench foot, respiratory diseases induced by exposure, fatigue, and related causes), a figure which tells something of the cost of lengthy battle in snow, damp, and mud, but also reflects the high incidence of nonbattle cases in a veteran unit whose ranks are filled with troops previously wounded or hospitalized — often more than once. The bitter character of the initial twenty-four hours of the 2d Division fight to occupy and hold Krinkelt and Rocherath, after the march south, is mirrored in the battle losses taken by the 38th Infantry in that critical period: 389 officers and men were missing (many of them killed in action but not so counted since the Americans subsequently lost the battleground); 50 wounded were evacuated; and 11 were counted as killed in action. In the three days at the twin villages the 38th Infantry suffered 625 casualties.

The defense of Krinkelt and Rocherath, so successful that by the second day many officers and men believed that the sector could be held against all attack, is a story of determination and skilled leadership in a veteran command. But more than that, the American battle here exemplifies a high order of coordination and cooperation (typed though these terms have become) between the ground arms.

Although the infantry almost single-handedly secured the ground and held it for the first few hours, the main German assaults were met and checked by infantry, tanks, tank destroyers, and artillery. The men of the 2d Division had on call and within range ample artillery support. Communications between the firing battalions on Elsenborn ridge and the rifle companies in buildings and foxholes functioned when needed—although the losses suffered among the artillery forward observers were unusually high. Artillery throughout this fight offered the first line of antitank defense, immobilizing many panzers before they reached the foxhole line, leaving them with broken tracks and sprocket wheels like crippled geese in front of the hunter. The 155-mm. batteries were best at this work. The accuracy and weight of the defensive concentrations laid on from Elsenborn ridge must also be accounted one of the main reasons the American infantry were not completely overrun during the night assaults of the 17th and 18th. One battalion of the 2d Division artillery (the 38th Field Artillery) fired more than 5,000 rounds on the 18th. But men counted as much as weight of metal. Of the 48 forward observers working with the 15th Field Artillery Battalion, 32 were evacuated for wounds or exposure in six days of battle.

Although an experienced outfit, the 2d Infantry Division made its first fight against a large force of tanks in the action at Krinkelt-Rocherath. In the early evening of 18 December General Robertson telephoned his assistant division commander: "This is a tank battle—if there are any tank replacements we could use them as crews are pretty tired. We could use the tanks mounting a 90m. [gun]." Robertson's wish for an American tank with adequate armament to cope with the German Panthers and Tigers was being echoed and would be echoed—prayerfully and profanely— wherever the enemy panzer divisions appeared out of the Ardennes hills and forests. What the 2d Division actually had was a little less than a battalion of Sherman tanks mounting the standard 75mm. Gun, a tank weapon already proven unequal to a duel with Panther or Tiger in head-to-head encounter. It must be said, however, that the 2d Division tank support came from a seasoned armored outfit—the 741st Tank Battalion—which had landed at OMAHA Beach on 6 June and had been almost constantly in action since. Unable to engage the 12th SS Panthers and the GHQ Tigers on equal terms in the open field, the Shermans were parceled out in and around the villages in two's and three's. Hidden by walls, houses, and hedgerows, or making sudden forays into the open, the American tankers stalked the heavier, better armed panzers, maneuvering under cover for a clear shot at flank or tail, or lying quietly in a lane until a Panther or Tiger crossed the sights.

Since most of the enemy tanks entered the villages in the dark or in the fog, the defenders generally fought on distinctly advantageous terms and at ranges where—if the heavy frontal protection of the German tank could be avoided—a kill was certain. The 741st knocked out an estimated 27 tanks (nearly all of which actually were examined) and lost 11 Shermans. Even disabled tanks, immobilized inside the American lines, continued to have a hand in the fight. Two crippled Shermans parked in a Rocherath lane accounted for five Tigers which incautiously came by broadside. On the second night the German tanks entered the villages prepared to ferret out the American armor. Each assault tank was accompanied by foot soldiers armed with bazookas, fires were started to light dark streets and alleys, and many of the Germans boldly used their searchlights. These tactics failed; illumination served the waiting American tanks as well as the enemy. German bazooka teams did succeed in knocking out a pair of Shermans but generally found the American infantry, dismounted tankers, and tank destroyer crewmen, waiting to erase the walking infantry screens.

The American tank destroyers shared honors with the tanks in this battle, but as it often happened in the Ardennes the fight had to be carried by the self-propelled guns, the towed guns serving mostly as convenient targets for the enemy. The 644th Tank Destroyer Battalion (minus one company) employed its self-propelled 3-inch guns with such effect as to destroy 17 tanks, disable 3, and knock out 2 German assault guns. Two guns of the battalion were damaged beyond recovery. Most of these kills were made in or near the villages against enemy tanks which had halted and were not firing, at ranges from 25 to 1,000 yards. In some instances one round of high-velocity, armor-piercing ammunition was sufficient to set a Panther aflame; generally two or three rounds with base detonating fuzes were needed and, as the Sherman tanks had found, direct hits on the German frontal armor or mantlet had the unpleasant habit of glancing off.

The experience of the 801st Tank Destroyer Battalion, a towed outfit, was markedly different. Emplaced close to the infantry line, its 3-inch guns were brought under intense shelling and could be moved only at night. During attack, bogged in mud and unable to shift firing positions, the towed tank destroyers quickly fell prey to direct fire or infantry assault. Between 17 and 19 December the 801st lost 17 guns and 16 half-tracks. Indeed, the greatest combat value of the towed battalion came from the mines carried on the half-tracks (which were used with effect by adjacent riflemen) and the employment of the gun crews as infantry. On the afternoon of 18 December, with guns and vehicles gone, the bulk of the battalion was ordered to Elsenborn. Even so there were a few instances when the towed guns were able to fight and make kills under favorable circumstances. One gun from the 801st had been placed to cover a straggler line in the vicinity of Hünningen and here, deep inside the American position, surprised and knocked out four Mark IV's before it was destroyed.

The infantry antitank weapons employed in the defense of Krinkelt-Rocherath varied considerably in effectiveness. The 57-mm. battalion antitank guns — and their crews — simply were tank fodder. The mobility of this towed piece, which had been a feature of the gun on design boards and in proving ground tests, failed in the mud at the forward positions. Only a very lucky shot could damage a Panther or Tiger, and at the close of this operation both the 2d and 99th Divisions recommended the abolition of the 57-mm. as an infantry antitank gun. The rifle battalions which were hurried south from Wahlerscheid on 17 December had left their mines in the forest or with the battalion trains. Even the few antitank mines on hand could not be put to proper use during the first night engagement when stragglers and vehicular columns were pouring along the same routes the enemy armor was using. In the first contact at the crossroads east of Rocherath the German tanks were halted by a hasty mine field, but the rifle company made its most effective use of this defense by laying mines to protect the rear of the American position after the tanks had rolled by. The bazooka in the hands of the defending infantry proved extremely useful. During the dark hours, bazooka teams were able to work close to their prey under the cover provided by walls, houses and hedgerows. But, as in the case of the tank destroyers, most hits were scored against tanks which had paused or been stranded by the detonation of mines and high-explosive shellfire. In the various melees at the villages the German tank crews seldom escaped no matter what weapon was used against them. Most crewmen were burned as the tank blew up or they were cut down by bullet fire at close range. The 2d Division, like most veteran divisions, had armed itself beyond the limits of approved tables of equipment. Nearly every rifle platoon, as a result, had at least two bazookas, so that team play to distract and then destroy the target tank was feasible.

Although fought mostly as a series of close quarter actions, the infantry battle in this sector saw little American use of the bayonet. Small arms and light machine guns took over where the friendly artillery left off, followed by grenades and rifle butts when the enemy closed. The problem of illuminating the scene of battle was partially solved by burning buildings and tanks. Illuminating shells fired by the 60-mm. mortars had some local usefulness, but the precise coordination between infantry and artillery required for the effective use of star shell never was achieved in this battle.

On 19 December German General Staff officers from the high headquarters of WFSt and OB WEST appeared in the battle zone to peer over the shoulders of the combat commanders and diagnose the irritating failure to achieve a complete breakthrough. The conclusions they reported (which obviously took no official account of stubborn American resistance) were as follows. The check sustained in this sector could not be attributed to intervention by Allied air, an interesting reflection of the importance which Allied air-ground cooperation had assumed in German tactical thought by the end of 1944. The road net opened by the advance on 16 December had not been put in good repair. This the observers attributed to a breakdown of the paramilitary Todt Organization, whose labor groups were charged with the mission. Since the whole concept of the Todt Organization reached high into the realm of Nazi politics and personalities, this open animadversion is surprising and undoubtedly caused some consternation. The chief source of failure, said the General Staff observers, was the inadequate training of the troops who had been used in the attack. The conclusion reached as to the future conduct of operations on the Sixth Panzer Army front was simple enough and in accordance with established German doctrine: more maneuver room must be secured so that the attack could "unfold"; the entire Elsenborn area, therefore, must be won and at once. The right wing must be brought abreast of the 1st SS Panzer Division, at this moment twenty miles to the west of Stoumont.

This new plan, probably only a reflection of conclusions already reached in the higher echelons, actually had gone into effect on 19 December when German tanks and infantry made the first serious attempt to drive northwest from Büllingen, shoulder the Americans out of the Butgenbach position, and open the Büllingen-Malmédy highway.

The Enemy Tries the Western Flank, 19-23 December

In Butgenbach, forty-five hundred yards straight west of the 2d Division anchor point at Wirtzfeld, the 26th Infantry of the 1st Division covered the 2d Division's flank and rear. The area between the two villages was neutralized, insofar as any enemy operation was concerned, by a large lake and a series of streams. To build a defense in depth along the Büllingen-Butgenbach section of the Malmédy road and secure a place on high ground, the 2d Battalion had pushed forward to a ridge near Dom Butgenbach, a hamlet astride the highway. When the enemy failed to follow up his earlier sorties from Büllingen, American patrols scouted on the 18th in the direction of that village and established that it still belonged to the Germans.

The 26th Infantry held a none too favorable position. It was separated from its own division and could expect little help from the 99th, under which it had occupied

Butgenbach, or from the 2d Division. Isolated action as a regimental combat team, however, was not unknown in the regiment's history, for it had been so committed in North Africa during the Kasserine fight and at Barrafranca in Sicily. Although the lake reservoir gave some protection on the left flank the position held by the forward battalion, the 2d, protruded beyond this cover. The regimental right flank was bare—at least no infantry had been brought in to solidify this section of the line—and in theory the 26th Infantry was responsible for the defense of the four miles to the west between Butgenbach and the town of Weismes.

Colonel Daniel's 2d Battalion, sticking out like a sore thumb ahead of the rest of the regiment, had arrived from the north in a depleted state, a condition endemic throughout the 26th as a result of the very heavy losses sustained during the 1st Division attack toward the Roer River early in December. There, on the fringe of the Hürtgen Forest, Companies E and F had been virtually annihilated, Company G shattered. Now the 2d Battalion rifle companies were nine-tenths replacements and numbered not more than a hundred men apiece. All told there were only seven officers in the battalion who had been on the roster at the beginning of December. Two of the heavy machine gun platoons were manned by inexperienced gunners. There was a shortage of BAR's and grenade launchers. Fortunately, however, the 2d Battalion had been given ample time to prepare for defense. The rifle platoons had dug deep, covering the holes with logs and sandbags; wire was in to the 33d Field Artillery Battalion, emplaced to give support; and the artillery observers were dug in well forward.

During the night of 18-19 December the I SS Panzer Corps gathered in Büllingen the advance striking force designed for the attack against Butgenbach. It appears too that the forward command post of the 12th SS Panzer Division opened in Büllingen to direct the coming fight. At least one battalion of the 25th SS Panzer Grenadier Regiment had arrived, plus a few tanks. The bulk of the division kampfgruppe which had fought at the twin villages was coming up by way of Losheimergraben. The tanks had an especially hard time on the road, which had been reduced to a river of mud (German officers later reported tanks along the route which had churned down nearly to their decks). In addition to the advance detachment and reconnaissance units of the 12th SS Panzer Division, the Büllingen force was swelled during the night by the 27th Fuesilier Regiment and 12th Fuesilier Battalion, both of the 12 Volks Grenadier Division, but the ranks of the latter units had been severely reduced during the fight for Losheimergraben.

About 0225 on the 19th some twenty truckloads of German infantry dismounted just west of Büllingen, deployed behind a dozen tanks, and moved against the 2d Battalion. The 33d Field Artillery Battalion opened up at once with illuminating shell, then poured in white phosphorus and high explosive. Some could reach the American line; others were discouraged by bazooka and battalion antitank gunfire. Three tanks, however, kept on along the road leading into Dom Butgenbach until the 155-mm. howitzers of the 5th Field Artillery Battalion began to lob HE uncomfortably close. Possibly crippled by concussion, the tanks were abandoned but the crews got away.

The next German attack, at 1010, consisted of attempts in company strength to find weak points in the 1,800-yard line occupied by the 2d Battalion. One of these, against Company G, was broken up by shells fired in by four battalions of field artillery. A Panther and an armored scout car got through. Then a 57-mm. antitank gun crew crippled both, but the scout car got off one round that killed the crew,

Cpl. Hale Williams and Pvt. Richard Wollenberg. However, the armored threat was ended at this point. On the east flank two of the battalion's antitank guns got the two leading tanks, and machine gun and mortar fire drove off the accompanying infantry. This action ended the first German attempt at cracking the Butgenbach block. The next would wait upon the assembly of the troops and vehicles slowly gathering at Büllingen, where the II SS Panzer Corps had taken over direction of the battle.

On 18 and 19 December the 3d Parachute Division, which had been following in the wake of the 1st SS Panzer Division westward, began to concentrate south of Weismes. It may be that the 3d Parachute Division thus far had received no orders as to the projected widening of the Sixth Panzer Army corridor of advance and was content with holding a blocking position along the German flank as originally planned. As it was, American reinforcements arrived in the Weismes area on 19 December before the enemy struck.

The 16th Infantry (Col. Frederick W. Gibb) was the second regimental combat team of the 1st Division to take its place in the barrier being erected on the northern shoulder of the expanding German salient. The 2d Battalion, leading the south-moving column, was well set in Weismes when, in the late afternoon of 19 December, the 3d Parachute Division commenced desultory jabs at the village. At the same time the balance of the 16th Infantry detrucked and swelled out the Weismes front, making contact to the west with troops of the veteran 30th Infantry Division which had just come into the Malmédy sector. By the evening of 19 December, then, the 1st Infantry Division had neighbors on either flank and its 26th Infantry, although still out in front, could concentrate on the enemy force building up at Büllingen.

During the night of 19-20 December the advance kampfgruppe of the 12th SS Panzer Division and the bulk of one regiment from the 12 Volks Grenadier Division completed their assembly. About 0600 twenty German tanks and a rifle battalion converged on Dom Butgenbach in the early morning fog and mist from south and east. The front lit up as the American mortars and artillery shot illuminating shell over the roads leading to the village. Concentration after concentration then plunged down, three battalions of field artillery and a 90-mm. battery of antiaircraft artillery firing as fast as the pieces could be worked. The enemy infantry, punished by this fire and the stream of bullets from the American foxhole line wavered, but a handful of tanks rolled off the roads and into Dom Butgenbach. (They had shot down three bazooka teams and a Company H machine gun section.) Here, in the dark, battalion antitank guns placed to defend the 2d Battalion command post went to work firing pointblank at the exhaust flashes as the German vehicles passed. Two enemy tanks were holed and the rest fled the village, although the antitank gun crews suffered at the hands of the German bazooka teams that had filtered in with the tanks.

A second try came just before dawn, this time straight down the road from Büllingen. Ten German tanks in single file were sighted as they came over a slight ridge to the front of Company F. Two tank destroyers and three antitank guns drove the tanks off or at least caused them to turn west in search of a weaker spot in the 2d Battalion defenses. In the next thrust a platoon of Company G was badly cut up before friendly artillery finally checked the attack. Fifteen minutes later, apparently still seeking a hole, the Germans hit Company E, next in line to the west. The 60-mm. mortars illuminated the ground in front of the company at just the right moment and two of three tanks heading the assault were knocked out by bazooka and 57-mm. fire from the flank. The third tank commander stuck his head out of the escape hatch to take a look around and was promptly pistoled by an American corporal. By this time shellfire had scattered the German infantry. Nor did the enemy make another try until dusk, and then only with combat patrols.

The hardest blows dealt the 2d Battalion defenders at Dom Butgenbach came on 21 December. After repeated pleas from the 12th SS Panzer the guns and Werfers which had been used at Krinkelt-Rocherath were committed, and the entire 25th Panzer Grenadier Regiment was also made available, as well as one battalion or more of the 12th SS Panzer Regiment. About three hours before dawn guns, mortars, tanks, and Werfers began pounding the American foxhole line, which was outlined by a double row of trees, and the few houses in Dom Butgenbach. This fire continued unremittingly until the first light in the east, inflicting many casualties, destroying weapons by direct hits, and tearing large gaps in the main line of resistance. American counterbattery fire was intense but failed to still the enemy shelling. Now, as the Germans crossed the fields in assault formation, the American forward observers called for a defensive barrage to box their own front lines. At least ten field artillery battalions ultimately joined the fight (for this batteries of the 2d and 99th Divisions were tied into the 1st Division fire control system) and succeeded in discouraging the German infantry.

Some panzers and assault guns did make their way through the storm of exploding shells and against the 2d Battalion right. During the previous night two platoons of the regimental antitank company had taken station here right on the foxhole line and surprised the panzers with fire at no more than 100 yards. Two or three kills were inflicted by the 1st Platoon, but other tanks quickly shot down the 57-mm. crews and then overran the guns of the 2d Platoon. At this segment of the 2d Battalion main line of resistance the foxhole line followed a long hedgerow. Having broken through and destroyed the American antitank guns, the German tankers drove along the hedgerows searching out the automatic weapons which earlier had helped check the infantry assault. Undefended against moving steel, the BAR and machine gun crews were wiped out.

Through this gaping hole on the 2d Battalion right more tanks appeared as the morning progressed and moved down the slope toward Dom Butgenbach. A self-propelled tank destroyer belonging to the 634th Tank Destroyer Battalion accounted for seven tanks in succession as these, in column, hove in sight over the ridge line. Two Sherman tanks, lying close to a barn, got two of the Germans before they, in turn, were knocked out. Three of the enemy reached the cluster of buildings and fired pointblank into the houses and barns Colonel Daniel and the 2d Battalion command post group were defending. Every device was used to reach the tanks but with no success until, finding it warm, two made a break for the open and were stopped by a section of 90-mm. tank destroyers which had just come up. The last tank was flushed out from behind a barn by 81-mm. mortar fire but got away.

The battalion mortars had played an important role all along the line (one section firing 70 rounds before its position was blasted by close range tank fire), and so had every American weapon that could be brought to bear. But in late afternoon, when the German assault was dwindling, the 2d Battalion commander paid the infantryman's heartfelt compliment to the guns. "The artillery did a great job. I don't know where they got the ammo or when they took time out to flush the guns but we wouldn't be here now if it wasn't for them.... A hundred [Germans] ... came at one platoon and not one of them got through." The regimental cannon company, the 1st Division Artillery, the 406th Field Artillery Group, and reinforcing batteries from the 2d and 99th Divisions fired over ten thousand rounds in support of the Dom

Butgenbach defenders during an eight-hour shoot on the 21st, plastering enemy assembly areas and the road net and plowing up the fields across which the German attack came. For one period of three hours all communication between the hard-pressed rifle battalion and the artillery broke under German fire, but the American shells continued to arrive with devastating effect. A patrol sent into the woods from which had come the final assault against the riddled battalion flank reported a count of three hundred dead enemy infantry—the reason, perhaps, why the tanks that penetrated to the 2d Battalion command post came alone. At any rate the 12 Volks Grenadier Division had had enough. The division commander told his superiors that no more attacks could be made unless a promised assault gun battalion arrived to ramrod the infantry. The total German casualty list must have been high, and after these three days of battle heavy inroads had been made in the tank strength of the 12th SS Panzer Regiment. The 2d Battalion, understrength when it arrived to face the Germans, had been reduced by perhaps one quarter. Indeed, in midafternoon of the 21st, the battalion commander had planned withdrawing a thousand yards to the rear to compensate for the dwindling strength in the firing line. But when the 2d reorganized that evening its position was somewhat strengthened. Company C, with extra bazookas, had come up to man the denuded right flank, the 1st Engineer Combat Battalion laid a hasty field of about a thousand mines in front of the lines, and the regiment had attached the 4.2-inch mortars of the 2d Division chemical battalion to Daniel's command.

Meanwhile the enemy regrouped to continue the attack with new forces. The armored infantry reserve of the 12th SS Panzer Division, the 26th Panzer Grenadier Regiment, finally had negotiated the poor roads and traffic jams along the German line of communications and arrived in Büllingen, ready for its first commitment in the offensive. Shortly after day broke on 22 December patrols from the 26th commenced to probe at the 2d Battalion lines. The fresh enemy regiment, however, set out to vary the unsuccessful headlong tactics previously employed by striking at the flanks of the Dom Butgenbach position. The first assault, shortly before 1000, carried an undetermined number of panzer grenadiers through a gap between Companies A and K, on the right of the 2d Battalion. Here there were about twenty Mark V's and tank destroyers, but the 90-mm. tank destroyers from the 613th Tank Destroyer Battalion rushed in on the flank and stopped the enemy. The continued threat, though serious, was countered by shifting local reserves from the 18th and 26th to close the gap, and by the end of the day the situation was well in hand. Again the American gunners had taken over a large share of the burden, firing over 300 missions. The cooperation between the artillery and infantry arms, it must be said, was reciprocal. The fact that the 26th Infantry had continued to hold its position on ground overlooking the German routes west had allowed the observers a grandstand seat and had caused the German columns taking the 1st SS Panzer Division detour through Schoppen to run a gantlet of accurate and continuous fire.

The successful withdrawal from the Krinkelt-Rocherath sector to the more favorable terrain of the Elsenborn ridge had resulted, by 20 December, in a fairly homogeneous and well-constructed defense with the 2d Division on the right and the 99th Division on the left. On the morning of this same day the 9th Infantry Division took over the Monschau-Höfen sector (its 47th Infantry had moved earlier into supporting position west of these two towns) and so covered the northern flank of the 99th.

The German attempt to crack the newly formed north-south line was handled in catch-as-catch-can and piecemeal fashion, for the primary mission was the flanking maneuver in the Butgenbach area. The 3d Panzer Grenadier Division, which had relieved the 12th SS Panzer Division at the twin villages, went to work at once against the 99th Division portion of the Elsenborn line although the bulk of its rifle strength was not yet in hand. On the morning of 20 December German tanks and infantry made the first of three assaults. But the 99th, on a forward slope with perfect visibility and good fields of fire, checked this and the subsequent attempts with heavy losses to the attacker. On the following day, the 3d Panzer Grenadier was caught by artillery fire just as its assault waves were forming. Confused and disorganized, the German infantry were unable to make another bid.

Farther north, on 22 December, the 277th Volks Grenadier Division returned to the fray after licking the wounds it had suffered at Krinkelt-Rocherath and adding some companies of the 29th Panzer Grenadier Regiment (3d Panzer Grenadier Division). Early in the morning two companies from the 277th made a sharp attack to gain the high ground east of Kalterherberg occupied by the 99th Reconnaissance Troop. No friendly artillery was ranged in and the German infantry marched through a minefield, crossed a stream under direct bullet fire, and drove through the extended cavalry line. Two of the cavalry platoons were encircled and the attack carried for a thousand yards before Company E of the 47th Infantry and the remaining troopers were able to halt it. Apparently intent on driving as deeply to the American rear as possible, the grenadiers gave the encircled platoons a breathing spell and with nightfall the Americans succeeded in escaping. The fight spread to the 39th Infantry during the afternoon when small groups of the enemy began to infiltrate. Reinforcements brought forward under a smoke screen nourished the German assault, which by nightfall had won a foothold inside the American main line of resistance.

During the night of 22 December an artillery bombardment prepared the way for German infiltration elsewhere on the 9th Division front. But when day broke the Americans drove the enemy back after a series of short firefights and restored the line in its entirety. The 277th Volks Grenadier Division no longer possessed the strength to make a real effort against the north wing of the Elsenborn line. The 326th Volks Grenadier Division, its northern neighbor, had given no hand in this fight—not surprising in view of the punishment taken at Höfen and Monschau. Both divisions now fell out of the drive to widen the way west. The surest signal of the failure on the right wing of the Sixth Panzer Army was the ignominious end of the attack in the Butgenbach sector. On the morning of 23 December the 18th Infantry barred the gap which had opened the day before on the right of the 26th Infantry—and the 12th SS Panzer Division threw in the sponge.

Maj. Gen. Leonard T. Gerow's V Corps now had four infantry divisions, the 9th, 99th, 2d, and 1st, standing firmly on well-organized ground from Monschau to Weismes. The barrier so presented would restrict and straitjacket the northern shoulder of the German salient, at this moment still expanding to the west. The question remained as to whether, at a later date, the Sixth Panzer Army would or could shake this shoulder free. As it stood, the 1st and 9th Divisions were given time to concentrate and regroup their hastily committed regiments, while the 2d and 99th set about the business of acquiring replacements for lost men and weapons, gaining a breather after days of savage and costly conflict. On the enemy side the LXVII Corps took over control of the line Monschau-Weismes with the 3d Panzer Grenadier, 12th Volks Grenadier, 3d Parachute, 277th, and 326th.

The American troops who had jammed the right shoulder of the Sixth Panzer Army knew they had made a fight of it. They could hardly know that they had knocked a part of Hitler's personal operations plan into a cocked hat. The elite SS panzer formations on which the Fuehrer so relied would continue to play a major role in the Ardennes counteroffensive but no longer would be charged with the main effort; this had passed on 20 December to Manteuffel and the Fifth Panzer Army. And if, as Manteuffel later suggested, the Fuehrer wanted to see an SS and a regular panzer army competing, it could be said that he had his answer.

Chapter VII. Breakthrough at the Schnee Eifel

Introductory Note

The story of the 106th Infantry Division and the attached 14th Cavalry Group is tragic. It is also highly controversial. Since the major part of the division was eliminated from combined operations with other American forces on the second day of the German counteroffensive, information from contemporary records is scanty and, as to particulars, often completely lacking. The historian, as a result, must tread warily through the maze of recrimination and highly personalized recollection which surrounds this story. It should not be concluded that reminiscence by those caught up in this disaster is consciously tendentious. But the officers and men of the 106th Division who so narrowly escaped the German trap or who spent months in German prisons would be less than human if they did not seek to discover the cause of this debacle in either human error or frailty. Since the author has been forced to depend in so great degree on the human memory, unaided or unchallenged by the written record, the scholar's old rule "one witness, no witness" has been generally applied. Even so, some relaxation of the rule is necessary if a sustained and sequential narrative is to be presented. Fortunately, the picture as seen from the German side of the Schnee Eifel is fairly complete and can be applied as a corrective in most of the major areas of controversy and contradiction.

Dispositions of the 106th Infantry Division

From the Eifel plateau protrude three distinct ridges or ranges, the central being called the Schnee Eifel. This middle ridge, so important in the action that developed in the 106th Division sector, inclines northeast-southwest. At the western foot of the Schnee Eifel there runs a long narrow valley incised in the high plain, the so-called Losheim Gap. On the western side of the gap the Our River meanders along, and beyond the river to the west the plateau appears once more in heavily wooded form. The Losheim Gap is no pleasant, pastoral valley but is cluttered by abrupt hills, some bare, others covered by fir trees and thick undergrowth. Most of the little villages here are found in the draws and potholes which further scoop out the main valley. The Losheim Gap was occupied on 16 December by a reinforced squadron of the 14th Cavalry Group.

The fate of the 106th Infantry Division and the 14th Cavalry Group was bound together on that day by official orders attaching the cavalry to the infantry, by circumstances of terrain, and by the German plan of attack. To the left of the cavalry group ran the boundary between the VIII Corps and V Corps, its northern neighbor being the 99th Infantry Division To the right of the 106th lay the 28th Division, constituting the center of General Middleton's corps. The 106th itself occupied the central and southern sections of the heavily forested Schnee Eifel.

American successes some weeks earlier had driven the enemy from a part of the West Wall positions along the Schnee Eifel, creating a salient which jutted deep into the German lines. Although such a salient was exposed, the possession of at least a wedge in the West Wall seemed to compensate for the risk involved. It should be noticed that the Schnee Eifel range is terminated in the south by a cross corridor, running against the usual north to south grain of the Eifel plateau. This is the valley of the Alf, a small creek which makes a long horseshoe bend around the Schnee Eifel east to the village of Pronsfeld.

Three main roads run through this area. From the crossroads village of Hallschlag the northernmost descends into the Our valley, crossing and recrossing the river until it reaches St. Vith. The center road, secondary in construction, traverses the Loshen Gap from Roth southwestward. The southernmost road follows the valley of the Alf from Prüm, but eventually turns through Winterspelt toward the northwest and St. Vith. Thus two main roads, of macadam construction and some twenty-two feet wide, ran through the American positions directly to St. Vith. These roads were characteristic of the eastern Ardennes, winding, with many blind turns, squeezing through narrow village streets, dipping abruptly, and rising suddenly across the ravines. But each of the roads to St. Vith circles around the Schnee Eifel at one of its termini.

The width of the sector held by the 106th Infantry Division and the attached 14th Cavalry Group was approximately eighteen air-line miles. When traced on the ground, the line these forces were responsible for defending was actually more than twenty-one miles in length. The 14th Cavalry Group (Col. Mark Devine) was charged with a 9,000-yard front in the 106th Division sector along the line Lanzerath-Krewinkel-Roth-Kobscheid. This disposition placed the cavalry to the north of the Schnee Eifel and across the northeastern entrance to the Losheim Gap. The section of the West Wall which barred egress from the gap lay beyond the cavalry positions.

The dispositions of the 106th Infantry Division (Maj. Gen. Alan W. Jones) followed an irregular line which in general trended from northeast to southwest. The 422d Infantry (Col. George L. Descheneaux, Jr.) occupied the forward positions of the West Wall on the crest and western slopes of the midsection of the Schnee Eifel. This regiment and the cavalry, therefore, combined as defenders of a salient protruding beyond the neighbors to the north and south. The line occupied by the 423d Infantry (Col. Charles C. Cavender) continued briefly on the Schnee Eifel, then as this range dropped away swung back into the western portion of the Alf valley. Thence followed a gap screened by the division reconnaissance troop. The 424th Infantry (Col. Alexander D. Reid) continued the bend to the west at Grosslangenfeld and joined the 28th Infantry Division, at least by periodic patrols, north of Lützkampen.

On 19 October the 18th Cavalry Reconnaissance Squadron had taken over the positions in the Losheim Gap from another cavalry squadron attached to the 2d Infantry Division with instructions to occupy the infantry positions then existing. The 14th Cavalry Group took over the sector on 11 December, using the 18th and a company of 3-inch towed tank destroyers much as they had been deployed earlier. The ground occupied by the cavalry was relatively flat here at the mouth of the gap, although broken by streams and knotted by hills as is common on the Ardennes plateau. In contrast to the ridge lines the floor of the gap had a few trees. The infantry positions inherited by the cavalry were in the little villages, most of which had been built in depressions offering some protection against the raw winds which sweep the Ardennes. There were eight garrison points; a homogeneous defense line, of course, was out of the question. In addition, there existed substantial gaps on both flanks of the cavalry. In the north the gap between the 14th Cavalry Group and the 99th Infantry Division was approximately two miles across. A small party from the attached tank destroyer outfit (Company A, 820th Tank Destroyer Battalion) patrolled this opening at two-hour intervals in conjunction with an I and R Platoon from the 99th Division. There was an unoccupied strip between the right of the cavalry and the left of the 422d Infantry about one and a half miles across; the responsibility for patrolling here was given to the infantry.

At best the cavalry positions could only be described as small islands of resistance, manned usually in platoon strength and depending on automatic weapons dismounted from the cavalry vehicles or on the towed 3-inch guns of the tank destroyer company. Some barbed wire had been strung around the garrison villages. Minefields, both German and American, were known to be in the area, but neither the 14th Cavalry Group nor the 2d Infantry Division before it could chart their location. On 14 December Colonel Devine had asked corps for engineers and more mines.

Contrary to the doctrine and training of mechanized cavalry, the 14th Cavalry Group was committed to a positional defense. Since the cavalry squadron does not have the staying power for defense in depth, and since the width of this front made an interlocking linear defense impossible, the 14th — if hit hard — was at best capable only of delaying action. Lacking the freedom of maneuver usually accorded cavalry, the 14th Cavalry Group would have little hope of winning time by counterattack. The 32d Cavalry Reconnaissance Squadron, refitting near Vielsalm, Belgium, was available on short notice to reinforce the rest of the cavalry group; its officers had reconnoitered forward positions and telephone wire had been laid in at a few points. There seems to have been no specific plan for the employment of the 32d Squadron. Colonel Devine and his staff, during the few days available, had worked out a general defensive plan giving specific routes of withdrawal and successive defense lines. Apparently this plan was finished on the night of 15 December but was never circulated.

The staff of the cavalry group was evidently familiar with the defensive plan worked out earlier by the 2d Division which, in the Losheim area, called for an initial withdrawal to the Manderfeld ridge and an American counterattack by forces taken from the Schnee Eifel. During the brief attachment of the 14th Cavalry Group to the 106th Division no comparable plan to support the forces on the low ground in the gap by withdrawing troops from the more readily defended line on the Schnee Eifel was ever issued, although Colonel Devine had made several trips to the 106th on this matter. The 2d Division also had an artillery plan which provided for approximately 200 prearranged concentrations to be fired on call in the gap. There is no evidence that this plan was taken over by the 106th Division artillery (which would have had to shift its battalions), but the cavalry did have one battalion of 105-mm. howitzers, the 275th Armored (Lt. Col. Roy Udell Clay), in support about two and a half miles west of Manderfeld.

Much of the subsequent story of events in the Losheim Gap and the Schnee Eifel turns on the relations between the 106th Division and the 14th Cavalry Group. The brief span of their acquaintance is therefore pertinent. On 20 October the 106th

Division shipped from the United States. On 11 December it assumed its first combat role, taking over the quiet sector on the left of the VIII Corps where the veteran 2d Infantry Division had been resting. The relief was completed a day later. The 18th Cavalry Squadron had been in the gap positions since 19 October, less B Troop which was deployed on the south flank of the 2d Division and which remained in that area when the 106th arrived. General Robertson, the 2d Division commander, had long regarded the single cavalry squadron as insufficient to cover the Losheim Gap and had centered his sole divisional reserve, a reinforced infantry battalion, in the vicinity of Auw so as to support either the cavalry or infantry. Robertson's recommendations finally were noticed and on 11 December the 106th Division had attached to it a full cavalry reconnaissance group instead of only the one squadron. But time to organize the defense of the individual sectors of the 106th Division, much less to coordinate overall defensive plans and preparations, was short.

The 106th Infantry Division had been activated in March 1943. Early in 1944 the division took part in the Tennessee maneuvers, but its training program (as in the case of many new divisions) was more or less vitiated when some 60 percent of the enlisted strength was drained off to meet the heavy demands for trained infantry before and after D-day. When the 106th Division relieved the 2d Division on 11-12 December, freeing the latter for use in the proposed V Corps attack to seize the Roer River dams, it moved into well-prepared positions and a fairly quiet front. The veteran 2d Division had protected its frontline units against the bitter Ardennes weather with log dugouts for the rifle and weapon squads. Stoves were in the squad huts and the kitchen ranges were up front in covered dugouts. Heavy weapons were exchanged, the 106th taking over the .50-caliber machine guns, mortars, and other weapons where they had been emplaced in order to conceal the relief from the enemy. The extensive communications net prepared by the 2d Division, with wire to almost every squad and outpost, was left to the 106th, but unlike its predecessor the 106th had few sound-powered telephones.

Before his departure the 2d Division commander handed over his defensive scheme and briefed the incoming commander and staff. Because General Robertson had looked upon the Losheim Gap as particularly sensitive, the 2d Division defensive and counterattack plans laid special emphasis on support for troops in that sector. In brief, the 2d Division planned to pull the forces in the gap back to the Manderfeld ridge while the two regimental combat teams on the Schnee Eifel would withdraw west to a shortened line along the Auw-Bleialf ridge road, thus freeing one combat team for counterattack in the north. Local counterattack plans prepared by regiments and battalions likewise were handed over. From 12 through 15 December the 106th Division commander and staff reconnoitered the new area; then, after a conference with the VIII Corps commander, they began study on detailed recommendations for a more adequate defense. These were never completed or submitted although General Jones did make oral requests to alter his deployment.

In the circumstances then existing, adequate measures to cope with the problem of such an extended front would have required one of two things: substantial reinforcement or withdrawal to a shorter line. Some five weeks earlier General Middleton had acted to reduce the Schnee Eifel salient by withdrawing the 23d Infantry (2d Division) from its forward positions in the West Wall. It was into this new westward sector on the right flank of the salient that the 424th Infantry moved—even so, the regiment took over a front of nearly six miles. Middleton was under compulsion from higher headquarters to retain the Schnee Eifel salient and the existing dispositions of the two regiments therein. There were plans afoot for an attack toward Bonn, as part of the forthcoming Allied offensive, and the gap in the West Wall represented by this salient would be extremely useful in any sortie against Bonn.

Besides the 14th Cavalry Group the 106th Division possessed the conventional attached units: a tank destroyer battalion (the 820th) and an antiaircraft battalion (the 634th Automatic Weapons). In addition to the 275th Armored Field Artillery Battalion, supporting the cavalry, eight battalions of corps artillery were in position to reinforce the 106th Division artillery by fire when called. These battalions represented the bulk of the VIII Corps artillery.

The road net within the division area and to its front was limited and in poor condition, but this was an endemic condition in the Ardennes, particularly during winter months. The macadam stretches required constant mending and the dirt roads quickly sank away where not shored up with logs and stone. But though transit by heavy vehicular columns was difficult it was by no means impossible—as the event proved. Four avenues of penetration were open to a road-bound enemy. All four would be used. Following from north to south, they were: (1) Hallschlag, southwest through Manderfeld (the 14th Cavalry Group command post) and Schönberg (at this point crossing the Our River), thence to St. Vith; (2) a secondary road from Roth, west through Auw, then to Schönberg or Bleialf; (3) Prüm (a large German communications center) northwest to Bleialf and on to Schönberg; (4) Pronsfeld, directly northwest through Habscheid and Winterspelt to the Our River bridges at Steinebrück, then on to St. Vith. These roads, following the natural channels around and west of the Schnee Eifel, extend across the Our River by way of bridges at Andler, Schönberg, and Steinebrück. St. Vith is the funnel through which the roads coming from the Our pass to the west.

The degree to which the green 106th Division had been acclimatized to its new surroundings by the morning of 16 December is impossible to determine. The arduous truck journey across France and Belgium, through bitter cold and clinging damp, must have been dispiriting to untried troops. The frontline shelters in which the veterans of the 2d Infantry Division had made themselves relatively comfortable probably did little more than take the raw edge off the miserable weather prevalent when the 106th marched to the bunkers, foxholes, and dugouts. By 15 December a number of trench foot cases already had occurred, particularly in the 422d Infantry, which had been the last regiment to draw overshoes.

The extent to which the division was armed to defend itself is also a matter of debate. All units had the normal basic load of ammunition on hand, although there seems to have been a shortage of carbine and bazooka rounds. The nearest ammunition supply point was at Noville, over forty miles southwest of St. Vith, making resupply slow and difficult. Jones had requested antitank mines but these were not delivered in time. A thin, linear defense such as that inherited in the Schnee Eifel required an extraordinary number of automatic weapons. Although by this time the veteran ETO divisions were carrying BAR's and light machine guns far in excess of authorized allowances, the 106th Division possessed only the regulation number and type of issue weapons—fewer than were needed to organize a twenty-one mile front. On the whole, however, the 106th seems to have entered the line with a high state of morale; had it not exchanged the tedium of training and "show-down" inspections for the excitement of an active theater of operations where victory was always the American portion?

Enemy Preparations for Another Cannae

Late in November 1944 General Lucht, commander of the LXVI Corps, was called to the headquarters of the Fifth Panzer Army. Here Manteuffel told him of the coming offensive in the Ardennes and said that his corps would form the army right wing. The corps' mission, in brief, would be to bypass the Schnee Eifel on either side, seize the road net at St. Vith, and thrust in columnar formation to and across the Meuse River. Lucht would be given only two infantry divisions, one of which, the 18th Volks Grenadier Division, was holding the section of the West Wall along the northern reaches of the Schnee Eifel. The second division, unnamed, would not be designated or available until shortly before the attack. The LXVI Corps commander apparently was not unduly concerned by the lack of weight allotted; after all, the main army effort turned on its two panzer corps. But like all veteran German field commanders on the Western Front, Lucht was vitally concerned with the problem of air support. The first question he put to Manteuffel phrased this concern. Manteuffel parried with the stock answer: OKW had promised adequate air support; but in any case it was hoped that bad flying weather during December would drastically curtail the enemy effectiveness in the air.

About 1 December the commander of the 18th Volks Grenadier Division, Generalmajor Hoffmann-Schonborn, was let in on the closely guarded secret, joining Lucht and his chief of staff at the planning table. The Luftwaffe could furnish no terrain photos, but detailed maps and terrain appreciations for this area were on file. The final terrain estimate concluded that the sector north of the Schnee Eifel offered fewer natural obstacles than that to the south. Furthermore, the Losheim Gap appeared to have the weakest defending force. The Our River was an obstacle, but known crossing sites existed at Andler, Schönberg, and Steinebrück. St. Vith was nearly equidistant from the planned attack positions north or south of the Schnee Eifel, twelve to fourteen straightline miles.

The final plan of maneuver, largely dictated by Manteuffel, made the 18th Volks Grenadier Division responsible for a concentric attack moving north and south of the Schnee Eifel. The division would place its strongest kampfgruppe in the north, however, and make the main corps effort there. Lucht reasoned that the 18th knew the ground and would make the quickest progress; but he also wished to retain close control over the drive when it reached St. Vith, and such control could best be exercised by a single command. Furthermore the second division would have no time to learn the ground and, set to make a single envelopment in the southern part of the corps sector, would face extensive field fortifications on broken, wooded terrain. The fact that Lucht did not expect the thin American line to his front to offer strong resistance may be one of the reasons he risked splitting the 18th Volks Grenadier Division, rather than committing one division at each end of the Schnee Eifel. Since none of the German planners expected an American counterthrust across the Schnee Eifel range, a very small force from the 18th Volks Grenadier Replacement Battalion was reckoned a sufficient screen on the heights. The corps lacked a tank battalion and was assigned an assault gun brigade in its place. The corps artillery was deemed too weak to engage the Americans in a counterbattery duel at the outset of the attack, and in addition the Germans hoped to make early and deep penetrations by surprise; concerted artillery preparations prior to H-hour, then, were ruled out. Neither Fifth Panzer Army nor LXVI Corps seems to have fixed a definite timetable; the 18th Volks Grenadier Division is said not to have expected to reach St. Vith earlier than 18 December.

Both the divisions which subsequently took part in the Schnee Eifel operation were newly organized and inexperienced. The 18th had been formed during September on the ruins of the 18th Air Force Field Division, earlier destroyed in the Mons pocket. Reconstructed from Luftwaffe and Navy units, plus a strong admixture of Volksdeutsche and workers drawn in by the new draft laws, the 18th lacked trained noncoms and officers. But the unit was more fortunate than many another in that its occupation of the northern sector in the Schnee Eifel did not bring on many losses prior to the counteroffensive and permitted its troops to be rotated through training areas in the rear.

The division commander seems to have sold General Lucht on the idea of making the main thrust toward St. Vith from north of the Schnee Eifel—although both were certain that the double envelopment envisaged would cut off a very large American force. The right attack group was heavily weighted, consisting of two regiments, most of the division artillery, and the assault gun brigade. In reserve, for exploitation of any success on the right wing, was a mobile battalion, made up of the division tank destroyer battalion, a reconnaissance company, and an engineer company. The main breakthrough was to be attempted in the vicinity of Roth. The left attack group, one regiment and a battalion of self-propelled artillery, was directed to make its penetration through Bleialf, where the Americans probably would be encountered in force. Nevertheless, this kampfgruppe had the mission of seizing the Schönberg bridge. The division replacement battalion, two hundred strong, would be left to man the division center along the Schnee Eifel. Early in December the 62d Volks Grenadier Division, Lucht's second division, detrained at Prüm, but did not go immediately into the forward corps sector. The 62d bore the number of an infantry division which had been destroyed on the Eastern Front, but it had been rebuilt from the ground up. Never before in action, the 62d was commanded by a general who likewise lacked combat experience, Generalmajor Frederich Kittel. The division was at full strength for its class: like the 18th it numbered three regiments of two-battalion strength. Equipment was new and complete. The mission now handed the newly arrived division was to effect a breakthrough on the left of the 18th Volks Grenadier Division in the Grosslangenfeld-Heckhuscheid sector, advance northwest on a broad front (clearing the Pronsfeld-St. Vith road), and seize the Our River crossings at Steinebrück. The 62nd Volks Grenadier Division was to leave to its northern neighbor the task of capturing St. Vith, but was expected to block the western and southern exits.

The LXVI Corps staff was acutely conscious that the American observation posts on the Schnee Eifel overlooked the German positions. Everything possible was done to avoid exciting American suspicion or arousing American interest. All patrolling was banned from 10 December on, but the arrival of the 106th Division (which the Germans immediately spotted as new and inexperienced) led to a limited relaxation of this order. Patrols working at night about 12 or 13 December did discover something of interest—but in the 14th Cavalry Group sector. Here it was found that the two thousand yards separating Roth and Weckerath (on the south flank of the cavalry position) was unoccupied, and that the two villages were weakly held. Plans were made at once to exploit this weak spot—an explanation, perhaps, of the decision to make the main penetration by the northern attack group in the Roth area.

From 5 to 12 December the German artillery moved forward to carefully camouflaged positions from which the attack could be supported. The artillery regiment of the 18th Volks Grenadier Division occupied old emplacements in the West

Wall area behind the corps right flank. Corps artillery formed a groupment southwest of Prüm to give general support to the southern attack group of the 18th and the green 62d. On the north wing the assault gun brigade would have to move to its attack positions through the West Wall antitank line. Because demolition might alert the Americans, underpinning for inclined ramps was built over the dragon's teeth during the nights before the attack. All that remained was to fasten on the planking (and this job was later done, the assault guns climbing over with ease). Meanwhile a special field artillery observation battalion was at work, spotting the American gun positions and reporting minor changes in the opposing battery alignment. The LXVI Corps staff, it may be added, were very much concerned over the artillery weight known to be available to the American defenders in the zone of projected advance.

On the night of 14 December it seemed for a moment that all the careful precautions the LXVI Corps had taken to mask its intentions might go for naught. The 2d Panzer Division tanks, which had detrained at Stadtkyll, moved along the roads behind the corps' left flank en route to the south. Through the clear, cold air the noise of tracks and motors could be heard for miles. But much to General Lucht's relief no American reconnaissance planes appeared the following day. Apparently the secret preparations for attack still were secret.

The 18th Volks Grenadier Division sector narrowed somewhat on 15 December when the northern neighbor, I SS Panzer Corps, extended its left wing to include Neuhof and Ormont; the division sector at the commencement of the attack now would be about ten miles wide. The night of 15 December was frosty and clear, offering good visibility for the last moves to the line of departure. On the right the forty guns of the assault gun brigade took station near the dragon's teeth. On the left the two assault regiments of the 62d Volks Grenadier Division moved for the first time into the positions held earlier by the 26th Volks Grenadier Division. Also for the first time, the assault company commanders heard officially of the great counteroffensive and were given instructions as to their own particular roles.

With assembly completed, the juxtaposition of German and American formations on the morning of 16 December was as follows. The boundary between the Fifth and Sixth Panzer Armies bisected the 14th Cavalry Group area by an extension south of Krewinkel and Manderfeld. North of the line elements of the 3d Parachute Division, reinforced by tanks, faced two platoons of Troop C, 18th Cavalry Squadron, two reconnaissance platoons and one gun company of the 820th Tank Destroyer Battalion, plus the squadron and group headquarters at Manderfeld. South of the boundary the 294th and 295th Regiments of the 18th Volks Grenadier Division, forty assault guns, and a reinforced tank destroyer battalion faced Troop A and one platoon of Troop C, 18th Cavalry Squadron. On no other part of the American front would the enemy so outnumber the defenders at the start of the Ardennes counteroffensive.

On the Schnee Eifel the 422d Infantry, composing the left wing of the 106th Division, had only minute screening elements opposite. The 423d Infantry, with one flank on the Schnee Eifel range and the other in the Bleialf depression, was in the path of the 293d Regiment (18th Volks Grenadier Division). The 424th Infantry, in positions running to the southwest, stood opposite the 62d Volks Grenadier Division. In the event that the neighboring corps south of the LXVI made progress, one of its regiments, the 60th Regiment (116th Panzer Division), would be brought against the right flank of the 424th Infantry.

The compilation of opposing forces, above, will show that the odds against the defender in the Schnee Eifel area were not inordinate—except in the cavalry sector.

The Germans would have to make the utmost use of surprise, concentration of effort, and ground favorable to attack, if they were to achieve any large measure of success. Fully aware that the American line had numerous weak spots and that no substantial reserves were near, General Lucht and his division commanders saw three factors that might limit success: the weakness of the 18th Volks Grenadier Division center, enemy superiority in the artillery arm, and strong intervention by unfriendly air. All evidence of the play of these factors, particularly the last two, would be carefully observed as D-day came.

Although the LXVI advance on 16 December was planned and effected as the co-ordinated effort of two divisions, the story must begin with the 18th Volks Grenadier Division attack. This in turn will follow the German scheme of maneuver, the right wing first, then the left. The fight in the zone of the 424th Infantry quickly becomes an independent action and will be so considered.

The Attack in the Losheim Gap

The shock companies of the 18th began to move toward the American cavalry positions about 0400 on 16 December. An hour later the main strength of the two attacking regiments followed, the 294th advancing toward Weckerath and the Our valley, the 294th heading for Roth and Kobscheid. Supporting artillery, mortars, and Werfers opened fire over the heads of the German infantry shortly after 0830. (Actually the first concentrations to arouse the Americans were fired as part of the Sixth Panzer Army artillery preparation prior to H-hour and landed in the northern part of the 14th Cavalry zone). Roth and Kobscheid, closest to the enemy jump-off positions, received only one battery salvo; apparently the German infantry were already around the villages. When day broke, cloudy and drizzling, the assault force moving between Weckerath and Roth was well on its way to the commanding crossroads village of Auw. Visibility was so poor, the American village positions so dispersed, that the cavalrymen for some time did not detect nor engage the infantry moving past. (The Germans, having received no fire, first suspected that the main American line had been moved back to the Our River.) Furthermore, predawn attacks on Roth and Kobscheid had occupied the attention of the troopers. At Roth a company of grenadiers was checked by shellfire. The attackers at Kobscheid actually got inside the cavalry defense, but nearly forty were captured.

Before dawn none of the village garrisons in the southern sector had been seriously menaced. The effects of the enemy penetrations, however, became apparent soon after daylight. At 0830 a message from Roth reported that the Germans were inside the village, that a tank seventy-five yards from the command post was "belting us with direct fire." Light tanks, dispatched from Manderfeld, hurried to give aid but were stopped cold by fire from Auw, some 3,500 yards to the west, which was occupied by the Germans. Nothing more was heard from Roth. The remainder of Troop A, in Kobscheid, also was cut off; by 0900 the attackers had established a hold inside the village. Weckerath, which lay to one side of the German advance on Auw, was hit by elements of the 294th. Here the 3d Platoon of Troop C was located east of the village in a small patch of woods on the road to Krewinkel, well dug in and protected by barbed wire on all sides. The first German assault was checked by mortars and machine guns, reinforced by accurate artillery fire. Two enemy companies, however, swept around the wood and converged on the village, where some twenty men of Troop C headquarters held them at bay with bullet fire. A platoon of American light tanks arrived from Manderfeld shortly after 0930, appearing just in time to engage groups of enemy infantry infiltrating the eastern edge of the village. At 1100 observers at Weckerath saw an enemy column moving from Roth in the direction of Auw. They counted fifteen "tanks"—probably a battalion of assault guns—and at least one battalion of foot troops, marching intermixed with the assault guns. Artillery fire was directed onto the column, with but little effect. The Germans pressed on to the west. In the northern sector of the 14th Cavalry Group fortune had treated the defenders with mixed favor during the morning. The German force committed here consisted of a reinforced regiment of the 3d Parachute Division (it will be recalled that the boundary between the Fifth and Sixth Panzer Armies ran just south of Krewinkel and Manderfeld) attacking initially without the support of heavy weapons. The 3d Parachute Division axis cut straight through the northern cavalry sector, then angled northwest in the direction of Faymonville, the division advancing as the left flank of the I SS Panzer Corps. At Krewinkel, the most advanced American post in the area, the 2d Platoon of Troop C and a reconnaissance platoon of Company A, 820th Tank Destroyer Battalion, occupied a position from which excellent observation and fields of fire covered all approaches to the village from the east. An hour before dawn a German shock company boldly approached the village in column of fours. The troopers held their fire until the enemy infantry were within twenty yards of the outer strands of wire, then cut loose. The column disintegrated, but the assault was quickly resumed in more open order and shortly the Germans were in the village streets. At one point half the village was in German hands, but eventually the defenders got the upper hand and the enemy withdrew.

One of the last to leave shouted in English, "Take a ten minute break. We'll be back." An exasperated trooper hastened to assure him profanely, "we'll still be here." With the full morning light the enemy returned, as promised, after his artillery had tried unsuccessfully to jar the Americans loose. Head-on assault from the east by fresh troops made no progress. By noon, but two of the defenders had been wounded. The troopers estimated that the German dead now totaled 375—doubtless an exaggerated figure but still an indication of the costliness of the German tactics. At the neighboring village of Afst, the 1st Platoon of Troop C was similarly attacked. The platoon beat off two enemy companies, with heavy loss to the Germans.

The American left wing was composed of Company A and two reconnaissance platoons of the 820th Tank Destroyer Battalion, occupying the villages of Berterath, Merlscheid, and Lanzerath. The 3-inch towed guns, sited to cover the roads and eastern approaches, had no protection whatever. The gun sections were unable to put up more than short resistance to the German infantry, nor could most of the pieces be hooked up and towed out with the enemy already in the position. Here as elsewhere during the Ardennes fighting the towed tank destroyer lacked the maneuverability to deal with infiltration or to displace when in danger. Three tank destroyers were pulled back toward Manderfeld and better firing positions; the rest, with one exception, were destroyed on orders. Most of the company reached the cavalry group headquarters at Manderfeld and continued the fight as infantry.

Colonel Devine and the staffs of the 14th Cavalry Group and 18th Cavalry Squadron had been alerted by the first shells of the opening predawn concentration dropping on Manderfeld. Telephone wires went out during the barrage, and radio communication was made difficult by the cacophony of phonograph records introduced by the Germans along the American wavelengths. About 0600 the 14th Cavalry Group executive officer talked by phone to the 106th Division command post and asked for wire teams to restore the lines. Whether he asked for permission to move up the 32d Cavalry Squadron is uncertain. In any event the orders from the division were to alert the reserve squadron, but not to move it. At 0640 another call from Manderfeld reached the command post at St. Vith, this time with a request to move the 32d forward to a position halfway between the division and group command posts. Twenty-five minutes later the G-3 journal of the 106th Division records a telephone order to the cavalry: "Move 32 Cavalry Squadron as soon as you like." This squadron had been resting and refitting, indeed some of its vehicles were partially disassembled when the alert order arrived. About 0930 the squadron was on the road, minus Company F, which took another hour and a half to ready its light tanks for movement.

Colonel Devine, realizing that the forward platoons of the 18th Cavalry Squadron were in danger of destruction and could make no more futile efforts, cut off and isolated as they were, planned to make a stand along the Manderfeld ridge. This ridge line was some 3,000 yards in the rear of the original cavalry line and about twice that distance from the West Wall positions out of which the German attack had erupted. Devine intended to defend along the ridge with the 32d Squadron and thus cover the withdrawal of his forward troops. Shortly after 1100 the fresh squadron reached Manderfeld, Troop E moving its assault guns into previously reconnoitered positions at Manderfeld, Troop C deploying northwest of the town to cover the road from Lanzerath, and two dismounted platoons of Troop A digging in southwest of Manderfeld. While this area defense was forming Troop B took stations near Andler; at this village, just west of the German spearhead in Auw, the Our bridge remained an intact and important prize. The remainder of Troop A was dispatched to Holzheim, there to cover the group's left and rear.

Shortly before the arrival of the 32d Cavalry Squadron, Devine had asked General Jones to make a counterattack north from the 106th Division area. He was told that no infantry support could be given "at this time." When Devine answered that he would have to withdraw in the south to a line from Manderfeld through Verschneid, Jones made no comment. Thus far, it must be said, there was little or no inclination at the 106th Division headquarters to regard the situation in the cavalry sector as unduly serious. Devine's final comment during this telephone conversation—that he intended to counterattack with the 32d Cavalry Squadron on its arrival and attempt to restore the Krewinkel-Roth-Kobscheid line—may have helped confirm the somewhat optimistic view held at the division headquarters.

At noon Colonel Devine finally issued withdrawal orders to the 18th Cavalry Squadron. Troop C alone was able to comply. The 3d Platoon, which had held its own in the fight east of Weckerath, mounted two armored cars and a few jeeps, then made its way with guns blazing into the village. Here the command post group and light tanks joined, the column moving west along roads lined with German riflemen, but this was no headlong dash because cold motors and congealed transmission grease slowed the column to fifteen miles per hour. Meanwhile the village it had just left was blasted by a terrific shelling—apparently the Germans had been preparing for a final assault. The garrisons at Krewinkel and Afst moved back at 1240 without incident. As Krewinkel was lost to view the troopers could see German infantry swarming in from the east. When Troop C and the light tanks reached Manderfeld, the assault gun troop, which had been deployed along the ridge north and south of the town, poured direct fire on the enemy now streaming southwest through the draws at the source of the Our River. The morning fog had lifted and the gunners were able to inflict considerable damage with their 75-mm. howitzers.

The story of the garrisons in Roth and Kobscheid is difficult to reconstruct, although the troopers held on for some hours after being surrounded. In the early part of the fight, forward observers in Kobscheid were in contact with the 275th Armored Field Artillery Battalion; this artillery support unquestionably was of signal aid to the troopers, as were the quad mounts of the 413th Antiaircraft Battalion which were sent to help the Roth defenders. About 1100 the Roth command post radioed Kobscheid that the troops of the 106th Division farther south were moving back, that the Roth garrison would try to withdraw, and that the Kobscheid group should do likewise. Apparently the German grip on Roth was too firm; sometime during the afternoon the troopers there surrendered. Kobscheid held out until about 1630. Then, as dusk settled sixty-one men led by 1st Lt. Lorenz Herdrick started through the snow cross-country in a westerly direction. They returned to the American lines at St. Vith on 19 December.

Early in the afternoon it was apparent to the force at Manderfeld that the Germans were pushing west around both flanks. A patrol sent in the direction of Auw reported that the entrance to the Our valley was wide open, contact with the 99th Division in the north had been lost, and the 106th Division reported that it lacked the troops to counterattack toward the cavalry. Colonel Devine therefore organized a task force about 1400 to retake the ground around Lanzerath and thus cover his northern flank. The task force, commanded by Maj. J. L. Mayes, consisted of Troop C and the assault gun troop of the 18th Cavalry Squadron. Moving north the task force reached a road junction 1,600 yards north of Manderfeld, where it was beset from three sides by infantry and self-propelled guns. The cavalry self-propelled howitzers were able to maneuver and do considerable execution in this close-range firefight, but the counterattack was checked. By this time the situation on the opposite flank was precarious; the Germans already had passed through Wischeid, southwest of Manderfeld, and were moving toward the Our bridge at Andler.

Shortly after four o'clock the 14th Cavalry Group executive officer telephoned the 106Th Division command post and asked permission to withdraw to the line Andler-Holzheim, a position represented by a series of ridges covered on the east by a tributary of the Our. The division headquarters authorized the withdrawal. Devine ordered Task Force Mayes to fight a delaying action southwest along the road from Losheim, while the Manderfeld defenders withdrew to the west. This movement was carried through successfully, the 32d Cavalry howitzers on the Manderfeld ridge ably supporting the task force. The last troops left Manderfeld about 1700, setting the town afire in an attempt to destroy records of value to the enemy.

Troops E and C of the 18th reached Holzheim at twilight, joining Troop A of the 32d which already was in position as the anchor of the 14th Cavalry north flank. Troop B of the 32d had remained at Andler since its morning arrival; it now screened the southern flank with reconnaissance teams pushing out on the roads to south, east, and north. The light tank company of the 32d Squadron was disposed to the southwest of the cavalry line at Heuem, covering the road from Schönberg to St. Vith and worrying about the absence of communications. The remainder of the 32d Squadron was at Herresbach and that of the 18th Squadron near Wereth, both villages behind the Holzheim-Andler line. By early evening the 14th Cavalry Group was in its defensive positions, except for such regrouping as would be needed to sort out elements of the two squadrons. Its supporting artillery battalion (the 275th) was in the process of moving to new positions near St. Vith. As yet there were no signs of an enemy pursuit. The forward artillery observers were active "along the deserted front" until 1900 but found nothing to report. Contact with the Germans had been lost.

The German attack in the Losheim Gap during 16 December had gone according to schedule. The northern arm of the 18th Volks Grenadier Division envelopment had penetrated as far as Auw and overrun most of the American artillery positions. As daylight ended the 294th Regiment assembled around Auw and the 295th regrouped in the Roth-Kobscheid area, both awaiting the arrival of their heavy weapons. Now General Lucht told the division commander to call forward his armored mobile battalion and send it to join the 294th and elements of the assault gun brigade the next morning in a drive on Andler. In the north the 3d Parachute Division continued its advance during the night, marching through the rough, heavily forested area northwest of Manderfeld and Lanzerath. Along the roads to the east the armored formations of the 1st SS Panzer Division toiled forward in the dark, ready to push through the opening between the American 99th Division and the 14th Cavalry Group. As things stood, therefore, the 14th Cavalry was deployed in the gap which was opening as the 18th Volks Grenadier Division continued westward and the 3d Parachute Division angled toward the northwest. The cavalry flanks, however, rested on roads which would be essential to the enemy — roads along which the German armor was moving for commitment on the second day of the offensive. In the meantime the 14th Cavalry Group commander had gone to St. Vith to explain to the 106th Division staff his situation and the arrangements he had made. General Jones, busy with plans for a counterattack by armored reinforcements which the corps commander had promised for the next morning, had no comment to offer and merely asked Colonel Devine to wait at the command post.

The Attack Hits the 106th Division

The 14th Cavalry Group withdrawal to the Holzheim-Andler line in the late afternoon of 16 December had no practical adverse effect on its southern neighbor, the 422d Infantry. By this time the enemy thrust had driven so deep and with such force between the cavalry and the 422d that the northern flank of the 106th Infantry Division was exposed regardless of movements undertaken by the cavalry. Ominous events had transpired in the zone of the 106th.

Seven of the nine rifle battalions under General Jones' command were in the line on the morning of 16 December. The 2d Battalion, 423d Infantry, was in division reserve near Born, 5,000 yards north of St. Vith. The 1st Battalion, 424th Infantry, was located at Steinebrück on the road to Winterspelt and also was in division reserve. The 422d Infantry had its three battalions in the West Wall positions on the Schnee Eifel, defending a front of eight to nine thousand yards. Attached was Company A, 81st Engineer Combat Battalion; direct support was given by the 589th Field Artillery Battalion whose batteries were emplaced southwest of Auw. Located west of Auw were the 155-mm. howitzers of the 592d Field Artillery Battalion. The regimental command post was in the crossroads village of Schlausenbach, with the cannon company to the west on Hill 612. All of these locations lay in the northern section of the regimental area not far from the 14th Cavalry Group boundary. A company of engineers occupied Auw, the most important road center in the 422d sector. The forward positions of the 422d in the West Wall were based on a series of heavily wooded ridges running north and south. However a number of ravines, densely screened by trees, led directly back into the regimental area; one such ran straight down to Schlausenbach.

The 423d Infantry—in the division center—was deployed on a curving line a little more than 8,000 yards long, with one battalion in the West Wall, the other bending around the southern nose of the Schnee Eifel and back to the west. A gap existed between the rifle battalion positions and the village of Bleialf. The regimental right wing was fleshed out by a provisional battalion (the antitank company, one platoon of the cannon company, a rifle platoon, and Troop B, 18th Cavalry Squadron). This scratch force, acting as riflemen, was reinforced by Company C, 820th Tank Destroyer Battalion. The 590th Field Artillery Battalion supported the regiment from positions northwest of Oberlascheid, and the regimental cannon company was close to that village.

The 424th Infantry held a six-mile line angled slightly from the Ihren Creek southwestward to the vicinity of Grosskampenberg. The gap between it and the 423d, a distance of 4,000 yards, was screened thinly by the 106th Reconnaissance Troop and the cannon company. The 591st Field Artillery Battalion was situated behind the regimental center with two battalions forward and one in the rear to cover any displacement.

During the evening of 15 December enemy aircraft droned through the air over the 106th Division lines attempting to divert attention from the noise created by the German ground columns moving forward to the line of departure. Their efforts were wasted. The vehicular activity behind the German front was heard and duly recorded, but it caused no alarm. Enemy patrols also were unusually active during the night—except at the Schnee Eifel positions of the 422d Infantry which did not figure in the German attack plans. Again there was no particular reaction among the Americans. No one anticipated a German attack, although with the advantage of hindsight all these warning signs and others would be resurrected and given an importance never accorded them on the night of 15 December.

At 0530, 16 December, the guns, Werfers, and mortars of the LXVI Corps opened fire, marking the commencement of the advance against the 106th Division. The artillery available to the LXVI was limited, by comparison with most other parts of the front, but was well served by its forward observers and did much damage to telephone wire, ammunition dumps, and other supply points. The first word from a specific target reached the division headquarters at St. Vith about 0550, a report that the 423d Antitank Company had been shelled since 0530. The 423d Infantry was in fact bearing the brunt of the enemy barrage and most of its telephone lines to the forward units went out in the first few minutes. Within the hour messages from the 28th Division and the 99th Division told of heavy shelling to the south and the north of the 106th. But the German assault troops who had been moving forward in the darkness onto the 106th Positions since 0500 were not immediately detected. German pressure would first be felt in these areas within the regimental sectors: the Heckhuscheid and Winterspelt areas (424th Infantry); the Bleialf area (423d Infantry); and on the Auw-Schönberg road (422d Infantry). In the last case, the northern assault wing of the 18th Volks Grenadier Division concentric attack would strike the American cavalry before turning on the north flank of the 106th Division.

At dusk on 15 December the 62d Volks Grenadier Division, forming the left of the LXVI Corps, had come into the lines opposite the left and center of the 424th Infantry. This new division would have no opportunity to reconnoiter the broken and heavily wooded ground over which it was to advance the next morning—a fact which had direct bearing on the subsequent story of the 424th Infantry — but its scheme of maneuver had been given detailed study. The attack would open with two regiments abreast attempting a breakthrough on a wide front. The main effort would be made in the vicinity of Winterspelt, breaching the American switch line southeast of that village and thus gaining entrance to the main macadam road to St. Vith. Once in position astride the road, the mobile reserve of the 62d would be committed for the penetration, while the two regiments extended their hold on either side of the road. On the left, therefore, the 183d Regiment had as its objective the northern side of the plateau on which lay the village of Heckhuscheid. Possession of this high ground was deemed essential to the German plan. On the right the 190th Regiment aimed at the wooded heights at Eigelscheid around which twisted the road to Winterspelt, two thousand yards westward.

The 3d Battalion of the 424th Infantry received the first German blow in its positions north of Heckhuscheid. After a 20-minute concentration of artillery and mortar fire a shock company of the 183d drove in on Companies K and L about 0645. Although the defenders got word back to their own artillery, when daylight came the enemy had penetrated well into the position. The 3d Battalion, however, was on ground which favored the defender and not unduly extended. The most serious threat developed to the north on the weak flank screening the switch position. Here the regimental cannon company (Capt. Joseph Freesland), armed only with rifles and machine guns, was deployed at the Weissenhof crossroads blocking the main road to Winterspelt. Guided by flashlights and flares the Germans made their attack in column, advancing erect, shouting and screaming. The cannoneers, nothing daunted, did well in their infantry role, holding for several hours against assault from front and flank. Colonel Reid, the regimental commander, ordered his 1st Battalion, in reserve at Steinebrück, to the support of the threatened north flank. Company C arrived to reinforce the cannon company and the rest of the reserve battalion hurriedly established defensive positions to the rear at Winterspelt.

In the 3d Battalion zone Company I came in to help restore the line. A series of counterattacks, well supported by fire from the 591st Field Artillery Battalion, erased the dents in the American position, and a sortie led by the battalion S-3, Capt. Lee Berwick, entered Heckhuscheid and took 107 prisoners. A four-man patrol from Company K rounded up another forty prisoners in the woods nearby. By noon the 424th had driven the enemy back along the whole of its front.

Coincidentally and without realizing what had been accomplished, the southern elements of the 424th put a crimp in the plans of the Germans attacking to outflank the neighboring 112th Infantry. Men of the 2d Battalion, supported by the 3d Platoon of Company B, 820th Tank Destroyer Battalion, caught the assault company leading the 60th Panzer Grenadier Regiment attack in a wood west of Grosskampenberg. German reports say that the company was "nearly destroyed." This sharp setback so discouraged the 116th Panzer Division commander that before the day ended he switched the 60th Panzer Grenadier Regiment to the south. Although this attempt to drive a wedge between the 112th and 424th was not renewed, the latter was able to give its neighbors a helping hand later in the day. During the afternoon a gunner from the tank destroyer platoon, Pfc. Paul C. Rosenthal, sighted five German tanks and a truck moving north of Lützkampen. Firing his 3-inch gun at 2,000 yards range he destroyed all, tanks and truck; he had used only eighteen rounds of high-explosive and armor-piercing-capped ammunition.

About noon a report reached the 62d Volks Grenadier Division command post that troops of the 190th Regiment (the Germans who had broken through north of the cannon company positions) were on high ground north of Eigelscheid overlooking the road to Winterspelt. General Kittel ordered his mobile battalion up from the 164th Regiment reserve at Pronsfeld and into the attack along the Winterspelt road. This battalion, "mobile" in the sense that it was mounted on bicycles and reinforced by a company of self-propelled assault guns, was forced to stick to the macadam road. As a result it came up against the American cannon company at the Weissenhof crossroads. Outnumbered and in danger of encirclement the cannoneers and their rifle support from Company C made a deliberate and fighting withdrawal toward Winterspelt, platoon by platoon. When the 2d Platoon was ordered back, its commander (Lt. Crawford Wheeler) stayed behind with a bazooka to meet the leading assault gun and was killed by pointblank fire.

By dark the German mobile battalion and infantry from the 190th Regiment were closing in on Winterspelt, where the 1st Battalion and remnants of the cannon company stood ready to meet them. The fight raged through the evening and by midnight at least a company of Germans was inside the village, with more coming in by the hour. In the 3d Battalion sector the enemy had got nowhere with his frontal attacks around Heckhuscheid, the village remaining under American control at the close of the day. Casualties in the 62d Volks Grenadier Division had been substantial, particularly, as might be expected in the case of a green division in its first attack, among the officers. Losses in the 424th had not been high. But the position of the regiment on the night of the 16th was potentially a serious one—despite the rough body check given the enemy. The battalion and regimental reserves all had been committed, the 591st Field Artillery Battalion had fired nearly all its ammunition (over 2,600 rounds), and the enemy had made a dent toward Winterspelt. Contact with the 112th Infantry, on the south flank, had been lost. But fortunately the enemy had given over the idea of a penetration here.

The intense fire laid on the 423d Infantry on the morning of 16 December had disrupted telephone lines, but the radio net seems to have functioned well. By 0600 the regimental commander had word that his antitank company was under small arms fire at Bleialf, the key to the southern route around the Schnee Eifel and the Alf Creek depression. Along this depression extended the 423d's weak wing, echeloned to the right and rear of the two rifle battalions, one on the Schnee Eifel and one curving along the southern nose of the range. The heterogeneous units screening along the wing had been grouped as a provisional battalion, but they formed no cohesive front and were charged with defending the least defensible ground on the regimental front. When shock troops of the 293d Regiment (18th Volks Grenadier Division) struck the antitank company in Bleialf, one group filtered into the village and another, marching along the railroad, cut between Bleialf and Troop B (18th Cavalry Squadron), blocking out the latter and destroying the right platoon of the antitank company.

Although radio reception was poor in this area the commander of the 423d Infantry and the regimental executive (Lt. Col. Frederick W. Nagle) were able to alert and move reserves promptly, but Colonel Cavender's request for the release of his 2d Battalion, then in division reserve, was refused. About 0920 the service company and cannon company were at Bleialf, where they found most of the village held by the Germans. Later Company B, 81st Engineer Combat Battalion, and the headquarters company were thrown into the fight. By 1500 these units had ejected the enemy from

Bleialf after a series of hand-to-hand fights in the streets and houses. The cavalry troop on the extreme regimental right remained cut off from the friendly troops to the north. Finally getting permission by radio to withdraw, the troopers pulled back in the early afternoon to Winterscheid, 2,500 yards southwest of Bleialf. While the enemy was attacking around Bleialf, a few small patrols tried to get into the positions of the 1st and 3d Battalions to the north—but no real attack was attempted during the 16th.

The 293d had failed to carry out its part as the southern jaw of the 18th Volks Grenadier Division pincers, for without Bleialf the road to Steinebrück was barred. The Americans had recovered their balance quickly after the initial shock at Bleialf. The battalions on the Schnee Eifel had brought the German flank under accurate and punishing fire at the first light of day, interdicting all reinforcement by the heavy weapons needed to reduce the village. On the whole the situation in the 423d sector seemed satisfactory, although two items remained for a final accounting. The southern flank of the regiment now was in the air, and its 2d Battalion, as division reserve, had been sent forward to aid the endangered 422d Infantry on the north.

High on the center of the Schnee Eifel the 422d Infantry missed the first rude shock of a predawn attack. Although it was no part of the German plan to engage the 422d by frontal assault, the enemy penetration between Roth and Weckerath, during the dark hours, quickly brought the assault troops of the 294th Regiment down the road to Auw and onto the American regiment's flank and rear. Company A of the 81st Engineer Combat Battalion was billeted at Auw, and despite the enemy shelling in the early morning the engineers had turned out as usual to work on the roads. As the enemy approached Auw the bulk of the company hurried back to the village, set up their machine guns, and engaged the German column. This column (at least a battalion of the 294th) was reinforced by self-propelled guns, which shelled the engineers out of their positions. When the 1st Platoon, the last to leave, finally essayed a dash from the village to the protection of a nearby wood lot, Cpl. Edward S. Withee remained behind to cover his comrades, with only his submachine gun as a weapon against the enemy armor. By this time the American batteries southwest of the village were blasting the Germans there, for a time halting further advance. At daylight small groups began pressure against the forward battalions of the 422d, but this seems to have been no more than an attempt to fix American attention to the front. Company L, however, had to be rushed to the defense of the regimental command post at Schlausenbach.

About noon the enemy in Auw became active, moving south against the artillery groupment composed of the 589th Field Artillery Battalion (astride the Auw-Bleialf road) and the 592d, a 155-mm. howitzer battalion, close by. The German 294th was acting under orders to clear the way into the Our valley, but to do so it had to neutralize or destroy the American artillery, whose positions had been plotted earlier by the corps observation battalion. Stealing forward by squads and platoons, the grenadiers brought the battery positions under crossfire from their machine pistols while mortar crews and gunners worked to knock out the American field pieces.

Colonel Descheneaux, intent on easing the increasing pressure, dispatched a task force about 1300 to recapture Auw and cut off the enemy to the south. This counterattack, employing Company L, the cannon company, and part of the antitank company, was based on a plan taken over from the 2d Infantry Division. The task force started its advance in the midst of a sudden snowstorm, made contact with the Germans near Auw, then suddenly received orders to return to the regimental command post at Schlausenbach, which was now threatened by infantry advancing along the draw from the east. Even while the task force was approaching Auw the enemy had stepped up the drive to overrun the artillery, sending assault guns in to do the job. But the American cannoneers stayed with their howitzers, firing with the shortest fuze possible, while others of the artillery worked their way to within bazooka range of enemy assault guns. The attack was stopped, after three assault guns had been knocked out. The Germans returned to the softening-up process and waited for night to fall; artillery and mortar fire accounted for 36 men in Battery A of the 592d in the late afternoon.

When day closed, the attempt to destroy the artillery was resumed, flares and searchlights marking the German movements. Earlier, General Jones had taken steps to block the gap between the 14th Cavalry Group and the 422d, ordering his reserve, the 2d Battalion, 423d Infantry (Lt. Col. Joseph F. Puett), to move through St. Vith to Schönberg. By 1730 Puett's battalion had detrucked and set up defenses to cover the road net at the latter point. Three hours later General Jones telephoned Colonel Puett, ordering an immediate attack to cover the open left flank of the 422d and permit the two hard-pressed artillery battalions to displace southward. Apparently General Jones intended that the battalion should turn north to Andler and push aside the enemy along the Auw-Andler-Schönberg road. Puett, however, got on the wrong road and turned south, leaving the northern approach to Schönberg open. (About the same time, the cavalry troop at Andler pulled out.) Ultimately the 2d Battalion found its way through the dark across country and reached the 89th Field Artillery Battalion. Meanwhile the 422d commander had swung his left battalion (the 2d) around to face north, expecting to link up with the reserve battalion.

This, then, was the situation. The 106th Division had lost relatively little ground during the daylight hours of the 16th. Still, the enemy had succeeded in creating a shallow salient in the Winterspelt sector, had penetrated between the 424th and 423d, and had uncovered the left flank and rear of the 422d Infantry. Through the night of 16-17 December, therefore, the German LXVI Corps continued to push its tired infantry into these sectors, while fresh troops moved up with heavy weapons and motor vehicles for commitment on the morrow. There was no longer any doubt as to the German maneuver. The intelligence section of the 106th Division staff analyzed the enemy plan correctly in its report on the night of 16 December. "The enemy is capable of pinching off the Schnee Eifel area by employing one VG Division plus armor from the 14th Cavalry Group sector and one VG Division plus armor from the 423d Infantry sector at any time." This estimate hardly is vitiated by the fact that only one German division, the 18th Volks Grenadier, formed the pincers poised to grip the 106th Division. After all, the entire 62d Volks Grenadier Division stood poised to break through in the Winterspelt area and to strengthen or lengthen the southern jaw of the pincers.

General Lucht, leading the LXVI Corps, could look with some complacency at the events of this first day, even though his left wing had failed to break through the American main line of resistance. Not a single one of the much feared Jabo's had appeared in the sky, the superior weight of metal available to the American artillery had not been utilized in the early and crucial hours of the assault, and the defenders on the Schnee Eifel had made not a single move to threaten the weak and grossly extended center of the 18th Volks Grenadier Division. This inactivity by the 106th Division on the first day, combined with the failure to counterattack against the weak center on the Schnee Eifel or the flanks of the German salients, was inexplicable to the

German commanders but also a matter of relief. Lucht anticipated that the Americans would counterattack on 17 December but that their reaction would come too late and the encirclements would be completed according to plan. His own plans for the second day were simple. On the right the mobile battalion of the 18th Volks Grenadier Division was already moving on Andler en route to seize the Schönberg bridge and the road to St. Vith. The left kampfgruppe of the 18th also would make way for a mobile thrust. Finally, the 62d Volks Grenadier Division had orders to break loose at Heckhuscheid and drive for the Our valley "at all costs."

By the night of 16 December General Jones had committed all the reserves available to the 106th Division except a battalion of engineers at St. Vith. But reinforcements, hastily gathered by the VIII Corps, First Army, and 12th Army Group, were on the way. When the 2d Infantry Division turned over its area to the 106th it had taken its armored support, Combat Command B, 9th Armored Division, north to the V Corps sector. Replacement was made by the 9th Armored's Combat Command R, which assembled at Trois Vierges—some twenty road miles south of St. Vith—in position to reinforce the 106th if need should arise. This small armored group represented the only mobile counterattack force available in the VIII Corps. The extent of the German threat on 16 December, slowly comprehended though it was, obviously required more drastic countermeasures than the limited resources of the VIII Corps could provide. At 1025, therefore, the First Army released CCB, 9th Armored, to the VIII Corps, thus permitting Middleton to move his armored reserve as a backstop for the 28th Division. CCB, 9th Armored (Brig. Gen. William M. Hoge), was assembled around Faymonville, about 12 miles north of St. Vith, awaiting orders to reinforce the 2d Infantry Division attack toward the Roer River dams.

The attachment of CCB to the 106th Division, as ordered by Middleton, was logical; Hoge's troops would be returning to old and familiar terrain. During the day CCB remained at Faymonville "attached in place," as the military verbalism runs. The 106th Division commander could not move CCB without corps approval and was not too concerned with the enemy advance in his northern sector. He made no move to put CCB on the road, merely ordering a platoon of its tank destroyers to St. Vith. Shortly after dark General Hoge and his staff arrived at St. Vith to confer with General Jones. There a plan was made for CCB to counterattack and retake Schönberg. This plan shortly was discarded for during the evening the corps commander telephoned Jones that he now could have additional armored help, that CCB, 7th Armored Division, was on its way from the Ninth Army and would reach St. Vith by 0700 the next morning.

As events would show, this estimate of the 7th Armored combat command's availability was far too sanguine. Why it was made is not clear. Lt. Col. W. M. Slayden of the VIII Corps staff was with General Jones at the time of this call. He later said that he should have warned Jones that the corps commander was "over optimistic" because he knew that the combat command was so far distant. In any case, Jones decided at midnight that the 7th Armored combat command should make the counterattack on the north flank and that Hoge's command should march at once to a position near Steinebrück, there ready to attack toward Winterspelt where incoming reports showed a rapidly deteriorating situation. It would appear that this decision to employ CCB, 9th Armored, on the south flank reflected either General Middleton's intention to restore the connection between the 106th and 28th Divisions or a direct order from the corps to that effect. Also, the corps commander did not want to pass both armored commands through St. Vith. Subsequently, however, both commands did move through the city.

The 424th Infantry and CCB, 9th Armored

On the morning of 17 December the precarious situation of the 424th Infantry gave Colonel Reid reason to fear encirclement. His extended left flank was in the air. Because communications had failed, Reid did not know that his right flank was still covered by the 112th Infantry. In any case, the enemy in this sector had brought up tanks and was attacking in considerable force. The 424th had its back to the Our River and if the enemy seized the bridge at Steinebrück and spread along the far bank it would be hard put to withdraw westward. Communications with the division command post at St. Vith was limited to the exchange of liaison officers traveling along a road now being shelled by the German guns.

Through the early, dark hours of the 17th the enemy laid mortar and artillery fire on the frontline positions of the 424th. Opposite the right battalion, which thus far had held its ground, German patrols wormed forward to cut the barbed wire and lob hand grenades toward the American foxholes. An hour or so before dawn the German searchlights flickered on, followed by a storm of shells from guns and Werfers. The fusillade actually was directed against the juncture between the 424th and 112th, but Company G, 424th, came under this fire and suffered many dead as day came and the pounding continued. The main German thrust, however, was made farther north, at Winterspelt. A company or more of the 62d Volks Grenadier Division had taken possession of the eastern half of the village during the night and at daybreak reinforcements finally drove the 1st Battalion from Winterspelt.

Even so, the 424th still blocked the road to the Our River and Steinebrück. To speed up the attack, the German corps commander, General Lucht, himself hurried to Winterspelt to get the 62d moving toward the Our. Apparently the 62d had become somewhat disorganized, its losses had been high, and its left regiment had made little headway in the Heckhuscheid sector. Furthermore, the division on its left, which had been pushing toward the south flank of the 424th, now pulled out and left the 62d to go it alone, seriously hampering Lucht's ability to exploit the dent hammered into the American lines at Winterspelt. But the right regiment of the 62d advanced almost unopposed north of Winterspelt while the division center, now composed of the 2d Battalion, 164th Regiment, reinforced by assault guns and engineers, Continued beyond Winterspelt to occupy the saddle which overlooked the approaches to Steinebrück. The left wing of the 424th was pushed out of the way, folding back toward the south and west, but finally was pegged down by a scratch task force led by 1st Lt. Jarrett M. Huddleston, Jr. To hold this flank and extend it as the enemy moved into the gap, Colonel Reid kept adding whatever troops he could find to this junior officer's command. Steinebrück bridge remained in American hands.

General Hoge's CCB, 9th Armored Division, diverted to the Winterspelt area on the night of the 16th, arrived in St. Vith before dawn on the 17th and received its final orders. The armored infantry (27th Armored Infantry Battalion) would move at once to seize the series of hills near Winterspelt; the tanks (14th Tank Battalion) would assemble west of the Our River and thence be committed as the situation unrolled. About this time the 106th Division commander borrowed a platoon of the 811th Tank Destroyer Battalion from CCB, sending it to Schönberg to relieve the forward command post of the 106th (the platoon did reach the 423d Infantry). The situation in front of St. Vith was changing so rapidly that a platoon of the reconnaissance troop leading CCB had to be sent to defend the road out of St. Vith to the east, while a company of tanks and another of tank destroyers were diverted to screen the entry of the 7th Armored Division.

Word that Winterspelt was no longer in friendly hands reached CCB just as its two leading rifle companies started moving to the Our. By 0930 one company was across the river and had run into German infantry dug in along the high ground overlooking the village of Elcherath, fifteen hundred yards from Steinebrück. The terrain and general uncertainty as to the enemy strength and dispositions dictated a coordinated attack. By noon the 16th Armored Field Artillery Battalion was in position west of the river to support the attack. At this time General Hoge had in hand three companies of armored infantry and the 14th Tank Battalion, a force deemed sufficient to drive the Germans back from Elcherath. But the enemy also was bringing up reinforcements, for at noon an American spotter plane reported a column of vehicles entering Winterspelt (perhaps this was the 2d Battalion of the 164th Regiment).

Two companies of the 27th Armored Infantry Battalion (Lt. Col. George W. Seeley) advanced to clear the hills flanking Elcherath while Company B moved along the main road. Threshed by small arms fire from the grenadiers on the wooded slopes Company B suffered about forty casualties, but the surprise appearance of a tank platoon shook the enemy infantry somewhat. About ninety Germans, hands high, came forward to surrender. A little after 1500 General Hoge ordered his infantry to halt and dig in; he had decided to throw in the less vulnerable tank battalion and thrust for the high ground east of Winterspelt. The 14th Tank Battalion was on its way to the Steinebrück bridge when the assistant division commander of the 106th arrived with word from General Jones that Hoge might make the attack if he wished, but that CCB must withdraw behind the Our that night. Since there was little or no point to further effort in the direction of Winterspelt, Hoge told his infantry to dig in and wait for nightfall, then withdrew the tanks to their assembly area.

In the early afternoon Colonel Reid had gathered the staff of the 424th to review the regimental position. Nothing was known of friendly units to the right and left; no information was getting through from the division headquarters; the enemy appeared to be working his way around the left flank of the 424th and had penetrated into the regimental service area. If a withdrawal was to be made starting in the early evening, preparations would have to begin at once. Reid decided to hold where he was for he had no orders releasing his regiment from the "hold at all costs" mission. Finally, at 1730, the regimental liaison officer arrived with orders from Jones that the 424th should withdraw immediately. During the night of 17-18 December both CCB, 9th Armored, and the 424th Infantry made a successful move across the river, although in the hurried withdrawal the latter was forced to leave much equipment behind. The line now occupied by these two units stretched a distance of seven thousand yards, from Weppler (northeast of Steinebrück) south to Burg Reuland.

The intervention of the 9th Armored combat command had not achieved the results which had been hoped for, but had contributed indirectly to the successful withdrawal of the 424th Infantry and had delayed the drive by the 62d Volks Grenadier Division toward the Our crossings—and St. Vith. The German division commander later wrote of the "serious crisis" caused by the American counterattacks around Elcherath. The heavy concentration of American artillery supporting CCB also gave the Germans pause. It seems probable that the failure of the 183d Regiment to make any headway against the American right wing in the Heckhuscheid sector on 16 and 17 December was largely caused by the sharp tactics in progressive displacement and the excellent defensive fires of the 591st Field Artillery Battalion (Lt. Col. Phillip F. Hoover) and its reinforcing battalions from the corps artillery. The 8-inch howitzers of the 578th Field Artillery Battalion, for example, fired 108 tons of shells between the beginning of the German attack and 1030 on 17 December against the enemy attack positions opposite the 424th Infantry. But only in the Heckhuscheid-Winterspelt sector had the prearranged and sizable groupment of VIII Corps artillery behind the corps left wing played any decisive role on 16 and 17 December.

Cannae in the Schnee Eifel

During a telephone conversation early in the evening of 16 December the corps commander had apprised General Jones of his concern over the security of the 422d and 423d Regiments. General Middleton stressed the importance of retaining the Schnee Eifel position but told Jones that it was untenable unless the north flank could be "heavily protected." Later, when reports coming into the corps headquarters at Bastogne indicated that enemy pressure along the corps front was not only continuing but increasing, Middleton got a call from Jones in which the 106th commander made a tentative suggestion to pull the two regiments back to less exposed positions. Middleton answered in the sense of the time-honored Army rule of decision by "the man on the ground" and left the phone expecting Jones to withdraw. Perhaps General Jones's opinion was altered by the knowledge that armored support was on its way, perhaps by the VIII Corps order, received somewhat later, that no troops were to be withdrawn unless their positions became completely untenable. (However, the "hold at all costs" line drawn to accompany this order was fixed as the west bank of the Our and all nine rifle battalions of the 106th Division were east of that river.) Perhaps Jones felt that the corps commander was passing the buck and would leave him in the lurch if a withdrawal order was issued. In any case Jones decided not to withdraw the two regiments.

The fateful day for the 106th Division would be 17 December. On both sides of the battle line reinforcements were moving, the Germans to close the trap on the Schnee Eifel troops, the Americans to wedge its jaws apart. The battle had continued all through the night of 16-17 December, with results whose impact would be fully appreciated only after daylight on the 17th.

Colonel Devine, the 14th Cavalry group commander, left the 106th Division command post about 0800 on the morning of 17 December, still, insofar as it can be ascertained, without instructions. The previous evening V Corps had asked VIII Corps to re-establish contact between the 99th Division and the 14th Cavalry. This call had been routed to Colonel Devine, at St. Vith, who spoke on the phone to the 99th Division headquarters and agreed to regain contact at Wereth. The conversation took place about 2130. But in the ensuing hours the situation of Devine's command had altered radically.

It will be recalled that the 14th Cavalry Group had withdrawn to the Holzheim-Andler line, breaking contact with the enemy. About 1830 on 16 December the units of the 18th Reconnaissance Squadron which had moved to Holzheim on the left of the line withdrew to Wereth, farther west, with the consent of the group commander. This move left Troop A of the 32d by itself at Holzheim. The troop commander was concerned with his exposed left flank and requested permission to move to Honsfeld, in the 99th Division zone, somewhat over two miles to the north. Group headquarters was loath to approve such a move and asked for a report by liaison officer. Finally the commander of Troop A decided to act on his own initiative; the troop reached

Honsfeld at 2100 and was incorporated in the defense of that village. Its subsequent story belongs with that of the 99th Division.

During the evening German troops had been reported on the road south of Holzheim. The executive officer of the 32d Squadron received this report at Herresbach, where the squadron headquarters and Troops E and C were assembled. Although no Germans had yet appeared, the executive officer was apprehensive lest Herresbach become a cul-de-sac. The road southeast to Andler might be ambushed. The poor secondary road northwest to Wereth was blocked by fallen trees, probably felled by the Belgians. Reconnaissance showed one way out of the village, a poor dirt trail, which led westward for about four miles. It was decided that this trail would be used if the elements in Herresbach had to withdraw any farther.

As a result of the reshuffling during the night the cavalry position extended obliquely southeast from Wereth through Herresbach to Andler. Troop B at Andler, then, lay close to the enemy, directly astride the main approach to Schönberg and St. Vith. At daybreak two of the troop's reconnaissance teams—about twenty men— were suddenly engulfed by Tiger tanks and infantry. This apparition was the 506th Panzer Battalion which had been thrown in by the Sixth Panzer Army to reinforce its advance toward Vielsalm, and which had detoured south of the inter-army boundary in search of a passable road. Contact was momentary. Troop B hastily withdrew south to Schönberg while the Tigers went lumbering off to the northwest. Now that Andler was in enemy hands the 32d Cavalry Squadron at Herresbach was isolated. The squadron executive officer requested permission to withdraw via the woods trail, which had been surveyed earlier, and the 14th Cavalry Group commander—who had arrived at his command post in Meyerode—gave consent. About 0830 the 32d Squadron and the numerous strays and stragglers who had congregated in Herresbach began the difficult move. All vehicles finally emerged from the woods and joined group headquarters at Meyerode.

Thus far only Troop B had actually seen and engaged the Germans. Troop B was hit again at Schönberg, this time by elements of the 294th Regiment led in person by the 18th Volks Grenadier Division commander, and headed west along the St. Vith road, looking for a defile or cut which would afford an effective delaying position. The abandonment of Schönberg proved to be decisive. The northern kampfgruppe of the 18th Volks Grenadier Division would shortly be joined by the southern, which had just broken through the American lines at Bleialf, thus closing the trap on the American forces within the triangle Auw-Schönberg-Bleialf.

Troop B finally reached a favorable point at a sharp bend in the road near Heuem, about 2,000 yards west of Schönberg. Here, while other American troops streamed through from the east, the cavalry deployed its six armored cars and ten machine gun and mortar jeeps. When the first German vehicle, a tank or assault gun, rounded the bend two of the armored cars opened up with 37-mm. guns which did no damage but induced it to withdraw. Then, for nearly two hours, the troopers' light machine guns and mortars repelled every attempt that the advance guard of the 294th made to move forward. Finally at 100 the 14th Cavalry Group sent radio orders for Troop B to withdraw through St. Vith and rejoin the 32d Squadron northeast of that city. This move was part of a general withdrawal which Colonel Devine had ordered on his own initiative after scouts sent out by the 18th Squadron at Wereth reported seeing German troops to the west (probably the advance guard of the 3d Parachute Division moving in the direction of Malmédy).

By noontime, or shortly thereafter, the 32d Squadron was in position at Wallerode and the 18th Squadron was on the high ground at Born, northwest of Wallerode On the whole this represented a favorable defensive line and placed the group in position to block the main road from Büllingen in the north to St. Vith. Colonel Devine informed the headquarters at St. Vith that he had withdrawn to a "final delaying position," and sent an overlay to the 106th command post showing the new position. Furthermore, Devine advised that he would "have [a] counterattack force available your orders." It seems that General Jones did not question this latest retrograde movement, for it was reported to the VIII Corps forthwith and without comment. At 1220 the G-3 journal of the 106th Division records a telephone message from the 14th Cavalry Group asking for "the general plan" (this was an hour after the withdrawal message arrived at St. Vith). The reply was "stay on the line where you are. I am coming to you."

Although the 106th Division had not ordered the group to withdraw in the first instance to the Wallerode-Born position, a cavalry screen in this area would be very useful as outpost cover for the 7th Armored Division elements still moving south to St. Vith. Certainly a roadblock here to the north of the city was essential.

But once more the group commander gave the order to withdraw, this about 1530. There never has been a clear explanation for this order; the group had no contact with the enemy and had reported the Wallerode-Born line as a "final delaying position." A liaison officer from the 106th Division was at the group command post, but it is impossible to say whether Colonel Devine received any definite order to hold this position. Liaison officers carried the new orders to the two squadrons: the 18th to occupy the village of Recht and the 32d to deploy along the Recht River astride the St. Vith-Vielsalm road. Again there was confusion, either in the orders issued or their execution. Instead of moving back by separate roads both squadrons moved onto the main highway leading west from St. Vith to Vielsalm. Darkness found the group caught up in the traffic jam, three columns wide, crawling slowly out of or into St. Vith.

Before dawn, on 17 December, the enemy renewed his attack to envelop the major part of the 106th Division. At 0725 a radio message from the 423d Infantry reported that the Germans had overrun Bleialf and requested the division to send help at once to prevent a thrust in force to the north. In the 14th Cavalry Group sector, the enemy was in Andler and driving toward Schönberg. Finally, at 0905, the news reached the 106th Division command post in St. Vith that the enemy forces striking north from Bleialf had pushed the 423d Infantry back to the northeast and had joined hands with the forces at Schönberg. The German plan of envelopment had succeeded—the 422d and 423d Regiments were encircled. The only question remaining was whether the two units could break out or be released by an American counterthrust from the west. The answer lies in the state and dispositions of the trapped regiments.

The 2d Battalion, 423d, committed the previous evening, had organized a defensive position astride the Auw-Bleialf road close behind the beleaguered 589th Field Artillery Battalion. Most of the 589th reached the infantry lines, but Battery C had become mired in an area which was under constant fire and toward dawn the bogged howitzers were destroyed where they lay. The medium pieces of the 592d Field Artillery Battalion had been less close-pressed by the German infantry; during the early morning of 17 December the battalion, with only one howitzer missing, withdrew to St. Vith. The two remaining batteries of the 589th were less fortunate.

While en route to St. Vith the column was surprised on the road about a mile south of Schönberg; three of the remaining pieces were lost there (two had been lost at firing positions). The three howitzers left to the battalion were emplaced in support of the hasty defenses being reared around St. Vith. The 590th Field Artillery Battalion, having moved north from the 423d Infantry zone during the night, also was en route to the west when suddenly its escape was blocked by the tanks which had struck the 589th. Reconnaissance showed that the other exit routes were held by the enemy or were mired to the extent of being impassable. The battalion therefore rejoined the forces in the pocket and took up firing positions in the Halenfelder Wald. This one battalion of the division artillery could be of little help, for its service battery, sent west for ammunition, would be unable to return.

While the artillery was attempting escape, with varying degrees of success, the 2d Battalion, 423d, repelled two enemy attempts to advance south of Auw. Meanwhile patrols had discovered some German troops at Laudesfeld, about a thousand yards west of the battalion positions. The 2d Battalion commander, now out of contact with the command post at St. Vith, decided to fall back and defend Schönberg. When the battalion finally turned to follow the artillery out of the trap, it found the way effectively blocked by German tanks. Although the battalion antitank guns did well in the unequal contest with the panzers—destroying three at one point—neither they nor the attached platoon of tank destroyers could hope to force the entry to the Schönberg road. Puett's battalion could now move only in one direction to the east. At noontime the 2d Battalion joined the 423d Infantry near Radscheid. Communication with the division having failed, Puett placed himself and his battalion at the disposal of the commander of the 423d and was ordered into the perimeter defense slowly forming.

It is probable that both the 423d and 422d were aware of their plight by 0900; at least radio reports of the unsuccessful attempt by the 590th to run the Schönberg gantlet had been received. The 106th Division took cognizance of the situation in which the regiments now found themselves by a radio order sent out at 0945: "Withdraw from present positions if they become untenable." The message added that the division expected to clear out the area "west of you" with reinforcements during the afternoon. This communication, unfortunately, was delayed in transit. Actually neither regiment made any move except to bring some troops out of the Schnee Eifel and sketch in perimeter defenses. The only contact between the 422d and 423d was by radio and patrols. During the afternoon the enemy constricted their hold, albeit loosely by deployment along the Bleialf-Auw road, but on the whole the Americans were left to their own devices while German infantry guns, and vehicles poured past on their way to the west.

The early morning breakthrough in the Bleialf sector, necessary to the German encirclement of the Schnee Eifel forces, had been accomplished by the southern jaw of the German vise only after strong exhortation and admonition of the 293d Regiment by its parent division and corps. At the close of 16 December the provisional battalion of the 423d Infantry still held Bleialf, from which the enemy had been ejected earlier in the day. During the night the 293d Regiment re-formed for the attack, urged on by its higher headquarters, and at 0530 the next morning struck Bleialf in force. Within an hour the attackers had driven the provisional battalion from the village (the Germans later reported a stiff fight) and were on the march north to Schönberg. Nothing stood in the way, although the enemy vanguard ran into the American artillery withdrawal and was slightly delayed, and about 0900 the leading troops of the 293d met their division commander and his battalion from the 294th near Schönberg.

Most of the Bleialf garrison succeeded in joining the two rifle battalions of the 423d. But on the extreme right flank of the regiment, south of Bleialf, elements of Company B, 81st Engineer Battalion, were overrun and Troop B, 18th Cavalry Squadron, was left isolated. Unable to reach the 423d, the troop was given permission to try the Schönberg exit. About dark Troop B started north, followed by a part of the 106th Reconnaissance Troop which had become separated from the 424th Infantry. Keeping to the west of the enemy-occupied Bleialf-Schönberg road, the cavalry column reached the edge of Schönberg. (By this time the situation was so confused that a Volkswagen full of grenadiers moved into the column just ahead of an armored car—whose gunner promptly destroyed the intruding vehicle and its occupants.)

Because Schönberg was known to be in German hands, the 3d Platoon moved in to determine the situation. The platoon had crossed the Our bridge and was at the north end of the village when there appeared a column of American trucks, but filled with Germans carrying arms. The three armored cars, forming the point of the platoon, wheeled over to the side of the road and raced toward the head of the column, firing their machine guns and 37-mm. cannon as they passed the yelling Germans. Suddenly a Mark IV tank slipped out of a side road. Only one of the American armored cars got away. When informed by radio of this engagement the 423d Infantry instructed Troop B to "make your own decision." Unsuccessful in finding any passable secondary road, the troopers destroyed their vehicles and broke up into small groups for the journey toward St. Vith. Hiding by day and traveling by night some fifty reached the St. Vith lines. The 106th Reconnaissance Troop had become completely disorganized while following Troop B, and one platoon was left in Grosslangenfeld with neither orders nor word of the withdrawal. Most of the officers and men surrendered the next morning without a fight. When darkness came on 17 December, some eight or nine thousand Americans were effectively bottled up west of the Schnee Eifel. Their story henceforth has little connection with events outside the pocket. In addition to the 422d and 423d Infantry Regiments the list of attached and supporting units that were severed from the main thread of American operations included all or part of the following: 589th Field Artillery Battalion, 590th Field Artillery Battalion Company B, 81st Engineer Battalion Battery D, 634th Antiaircraft Automatic Weapons Battalion Company C, 820th Tank Destroyer Battalion Company B, 331st Medical Battalion 106th Reconnaissance Troop Troop B, 18th Cavalry Reconnaissance Squadron.

The 422d Infantry on that night was forming a perimeter defense, its center south of Schlausenbach. To the southwest the 423d Infantry was assuming a similar stance on the high ground around Oberlascheid and Buchet. At the moment there was no shortage of rifle ammunition, there was a basic load for the mortars (but the 590th Field Artillery Battalion had only about 300 rounds for its 105-mm. howitzers), approximately one day's extra K rations were at hand, and surgical supplies were very short. Most of the regimental vehicles had been saved—although the service company of the 422d had been cut off near Auw and some kitchen trucks had been lost. Casualties were not high in either regiment; the 422d, for example, reported only forty wounded for evacuation.

Both regimental commanders had been assured by radio that reinforcements from the west would attempt to break through sometime after daylight on 18 December and, further, that supplies would be dropped by air. A division order to withdraw to the Our River, sent out at 1445, was followed six hours later by the question: "When do you plan to move?" These orders, relayed through the artillery radio net, took a long time and much repetition before they could reach the entrapped regiments. The initial order to withdraw to the Our River line was not received until about midnight of the 17th. The two regimental commanders agreed that this order now was out of date because messages, signed later in the day, had promised resupply by air.

Late in the evening of the 17th General Jones consulted the VIII Corps commander and at 0215 the next morning sent out an order: "Panzer regtl CT on Elmerscheid-Schönberg-St. Vith Rd, head near St. Vith. Our mission is to destroy by fire from dug in positions of Schönberg-St. Vith Rd. Am, food and water will be dropped. When mission accomplished, move to area St. Vith-Wallerode-Weppler. Organize and move to W." This message reached the 423d Infantry, which alone had some sporadic radio link with the division, about 0730; it reached the 422d Infantry about half an hour later. The regimental commanders decided to begin the move to the west at 1000, with their regiments abreast (although the only contact was by patrol) and in column of battalions. As understood, the mission was to advance across the Bleialf-Schönberg road and attack from the south side of the road between Schönberg and St. Vith, that is, bypassing Schönberg.

From the time of this joint decision there was little contact between the regiments. The 423d destroyed its kitchens and excess equipment, left the wounded with medical aid men in the regimental collecting station, and started off on the road through Oberlascheid and Radscheid. About 1130 Puett's 2d Battalion, leading, met the Germans near the Schönberg-Bleialf road. With the aid of its heavy weapons company, whose mortars did yeoman service, the battalion began to push the enemy back toward Bleialf. Meanwhile Colonel Cavender had gone forward to see what the situation was, but en route he received a radio message from General Jones telling him that the relief attack by the American armor would not take place and ordering the two regiments to shift their move to Schönberg. Cavender passed word of this new mission to Colonel Descheneaux and ordered his own 3d Battalion to come up on Puett's right. At noon Puett sent an urgent plea for help, but none arrived at this critical point in the firefight and the attack finally lost momentum. The 3d Battalion had advanced across the Ihren Creek and dug in perhaps 1,000 to 1,500 yards from the edge of Schönberg, but in doing so lost touch with both its own regiment and the 422d Infantry. About dusk the 1st Battalion was put in on the left of the 2d to help clear the German infantry from the woods astride the Bleialf-Schönberg road, but the psychological moment had passed.

The last message from the division (actually dispatched at 1445 the day before) was heard an hour or so before midnight, "It is imperative that Schönberg be taken." Colonel Cavender already had decided to disengage his two left battalions, in light of the next mission, and shift northward to support a dawn attack by the 3d Battalion. By this time the 423d was going it alone, for all attempts to reach the sister regiment had failed. During the night the regiment pulled itself together in some semblance of order along Ridge 536, just southeast of Schönberg. Losses had been high—some 300 casualties (including 16 officers). No more rounds were left for the 81-mm. mortars, most of the machine guns were gone, there was little bazooka ammunition, and rifle clips were low.

The surrounding enemy forces were surprised that the American regiments made no move to counterattack during the night of 18-19 December; one report says:

"In the Kessel absolute quiet reigned." The troops actually ringing the pocket were relatively few: the 293d Infantry Regiment, the 18th Volks Grenadier Division Replacement Battalion (which had come over the Schnee Eifel), and the newly arrived 669th Ost Battalion. Since the roads at the Schönberg bottleneck were jammed, the LXVI Corps commander could bring only one battalion of field guns that far forward; therefore the corps artillery was instructed to concentrate fire on the pocket during the 19th.

The 423d still was attempting to form for the attack, when, an hour or so after dawn on 19 December, German field pieces along the Bleialf-Schönberg road opened fire, sweeping the southeastern slope of Ridge 536. Soon the shelling ceased and the enemy infantry closed in, overrunning the 590th Field Artillery Battalion and other heterogeneous units which had been moving in the rear of the rifle battalions. Despite this blow Lt. Col. Earl F. Klinck's 3d Battalion jumped off in good order at 1000. One company was cut off and captured, but two rifle companies reached the environs of Schönberg, then had to retire in a storm of antiaircraft fire. The 1st Battalion was able to put one company in the advance, but by midafternoon it was eliminated. When brought forward on the right the 2d Battalion became separated and was subjected to fire from the 422d Infantry, then about 400 yards to the north. At last, with tactical control gone, only five to ten rifle rounds per man, no supporting weapons, and an increasing number of wounded untended (despite yeoman effort by the regimental surgeon, Maj. Gaylord D. Fridline, and his staff), the commander of the 423d Infantry surrendered his regiment. The time was about 1630.

The experience of the 422d Infantry was very similar to that of its sister regiment. Largely quiescent during the 17th, the 422d acted as promptly as possible when the division order was received on the following morning. Colonel Descheneaux, acting in concert with the 423d, ordered an advance in column of battalions, the axis to the northwest in the direction of Schönberg. Excess equipment was destroyed, the wounded were left with an aid man, the regimental cannon company fired its last smoke rounds into Auw (as a slight deterrent to enemy observers), then spiked the pieces. In two columns—one made up of foot troops lugging all portable weapons, the other made up of regimental vehicles—the movement encountered nothing but small groups of the enemy. Reconnaissance had been confined to the map, although the I and R Platoon was used as point during the march, and when the two columns reassembled at dusk the 422d was lost. A wood had been selected on the map as a suitable assembly area from which to launch a coordinated attack against Schönberg, this about one and a half miles from the village. In fact, however, the regiment had bivouacked northeast of Oberlascheid in a wood about three miles from its objective—nor apparently was anyone the wiser.

During the early evening the I and R Platoon reported that contact had been made with the neighboring regiment, which intended to attack Schönberg. No further liaison was made. While gunfire sounded off to the west and northwest the rifle battalions marched through the darkness to three smaller woods, preparatory for an attack at daylight on the 19th. The dispositions now taken were farther to the north, facing the Bleialf-Auw road, with the battalions deployed so that the 1st Battalion was farthest north, the 2d Battalion in the center, and the 3d Battalion on the south. At daybreak the three battalions moved out abreast, advancing in approach march formation toward the objective—Schönberg—believed to be little more than a mile distant. The leading troops were just crossing the Bleialf-Auw road when they were hit by machine gun and tank fire coming from the north. At this point the road curved to the east, and the enemy apparently had taken a position in woods north of the bend which allowed him to enfilade the straightway. The 1st Battalion commander ordered his men to turn back from the road and move southward. In the meantime the 2d and 3d Battalions had jumped off, but at the road their lead companies also came under severe frontal and flanking fire.

It will be recalled that the 422d and its sister regiment to the south had no contact. While the right wing battalion of the 423d was attempting to advance northwestward, it was discerned by the left flank troops of the 422d who, mistaking this movement for a German flanking attack, poured bullet fire into the draw where the men of the 423d were moving. In the brief exchange of fire which followed both these inner flank units became considerably disorganized.

But finally it was fire superiority in the hands of the enemy which checked further movement. About 1400, tanks were heard approaching from the north. In a last desperate flare of optimism the Americans thought that these were friendly tanks—but they were not. By a stroke of ill fortune the Fuehrer Begleit Brigade had been ordered forward to support the LXVI Corps attack on St. Vith. En route from Auw to Schönberg, the panzers arrived at the fork where the road split toward Schönberg and Bleialf just in time to give the coup-de-grâce. The tanks rolled through the battalions on the right while the German infantry poured in from the woods. At 1430 the regimental commander decided to surrender that part of his regiment which was disorganized and entrapped. After negotiations to determine that the Germans would feed the Americans and provide care for the wounded, the surrender was completed about 1600.

A group of about 400, however, were reorganized by the 2d Battalion executive officer (Maj. Albert A. Ouellette) in the woods which had been the 2d Battalion assembly area. This group attempted to move southwest the following day, but it too was surrounded. After destroying weapons and equipment Ouellette's people surrendered on the morning of 21 December. Another band, representing most of the vehicular column, had attempted to break out through Bleialf on the late afternoon of 19 December but was halted by a mine field at the edge of the village, surrounded, and forced to capitulate. Not more than 150 men of the 422d Infantry succeeded in escaping to the American lines.

The number of officers and men taken prisoner on the capitulation of the two regiments and their attached troops cannot be accurately ascertained. At least seven thousand were lost here and the figure probably is closer to eight or nine thousand. The amount lost in arms and equipment, of course, was very substantial. The Schnee Eifel battle, therefore, represents the most serious reverse suffered by American arms during the operations of 1944-45 in the European theater. The Americans would regard this defeat as a blow to Allied prestige. The Germans would see in this victory, won without great superiority in numbers, a dramatic reaffirmation of the Schlieffen-Cannae concept.

The fate of the two regiments was not immediately known to the 106th Division and the VIII Corps. The last message radioed out of the pocket had been dispatched at 1535 on 18 December, simply saying that the regiments had started to comply with the orders for an attack to the northwest; it was received at St. Vith on the morning of the 19th. By the night of the 20th the division must have given up hope, what with the German reinforcements from the east congregating in front of St. Vith, but one last attempt to reach the 423d Infantry by radio was made two days later.

The Question of Air Resupply

One question mark still dangles over the fate of the two regiments captured in the Schnee Eifel. Why were they not resupplied by airdrop? General Jones and the two regimental commanders made their wants known as early as the 17th and evidently had some reason to believe that ammunition, medical supplies, and other necessities would be delivered to the encircled regiments before they essayed the final attempt at escape. Although most of the processing involved in handling the 106th Division requests was by telephone and without record, two facts are certain: General Jones did all in his power to secure air resupply; the weather did permit planes to fly on 18 December when resupply was most needed.

At 1051 on 17 December the commander of the 423d Infantry radioed a request for an airdrop. Relayed through the division artillery net, this request was logged in at the 106th Division headquarters at 1500. In the meantime Jones apparently decided to act on his own and asked the VIII Corps air officer to arrange a resupply mission. The time of this conversation cannot be fixed, but by 1345 a message was en route from St. Vith to the 423d Infantry promising a drop in the vicinity of Buchet "tonight." Within a quarter of an hour a second message was on the air for the 422d. The VIII Corps air officer (Lt. Col. Josiah T. Towne) meanwhile had relayed Jones's request through the IX Fighter Command to the IX Tactical Air Command. At this point the chain of events and the chain of responsibility both become unclear.

The IX Tactical Air Command normally would have referred the request to First Army for clearance. The report of the G-4 at the latter headquarters simply says that on the afternoon of 17 December the plight of the two regiments was made known by telephone calls and that preparations for supply by air "were promptly set in motion." Since carrier planes would have to come from the United Kingdom it was necessary at some stage to bring CATOR (Combined Air Transport Operations Room) at SHAEF into the picture. How many telephone calls were made before the First Army request reached CATOR and how many headquarters were involved cannot be determined.

The IX Troop Carrier Command, whose planes would fly the mission, got the word from CATOR sometime during the early morning of the 18th with orders to prepare forty planeloads of ammunition and medical supplies. The 435th Troop Carrier Group, at Welford, drew this assignment and loaded up with parapacks and door bundles. Orders were precise. The group was to fly to the airfield at Florennes, Belgium, and there be briefed on the mission and meet its fighter cover. The Welford base was closing in when—at an unspecified time—the first serial took off. Nonetheless twenty-three C-47's arrived in the air over Florennes. This field, it is reported, was "too busy to take care of the 435th formation," which was ordered to another field near Liège. The commander and his wingman landed at Florennes, however, only to find that there was no information for a briefing, nobody had the map coordinates for the scheduled drop, and no fighter escort had been arranged. During this time the 435th had been diverted again, finally landing at Dreux in France. Here the planes would stay until 23 December, their original mission on-again, off-again daily. Somewhere along the line additional requests from the 106th Division had swelled the mission to 138 planeloads and ultimately it was decided to make this larger drop with planes from the United Kingdom. The entire mission was canceled on 22 December in order to support the 101st Airborne Division at Bastogne.

Two melancholy facts emerge from this story: fixed responsibility and coordination were lacking; supplies prepared for airdropping had to come from the

United Kingdom, despite the fact that Allied ground troops were at the German border. Attempts to prevent a similar fiasco were initiated in a matter of days, but too late to help the dispirited Americans marching into German captivity. On 21 December the 12th Army Group issued an order "confirming" the procedure for airdrops to ground troops. This of course could be only a palliative so long as air and ground coordination remained in abeyance. A day later the commanding officer of the Communications Zone, Lt. Gen. John C. H. Lee, requested SHAEF to set up stocks of ready-packed supplies, capable of air delivery, at airfields strategically located on the Continent. This proposal was accepted.

Perhaps the coordination of separate services and the proper application of new military techniques must always be learned the hard way. If so, the cost is very dear and the prospect in future wars depressing.

Chapter VIII. The Fifth Panzer Army Attacks the 28th Infantry Division

The battle plans and tactics of the Fifth Panzer Army, more than those of any other German army that took part in the Ardennes counteroffensive, bore the very strong personal imprint of its commander, General Manteuffel. As a junior officer in the prewar panzer troops, Manteuffel had made a mark as an armored specialist. His record in North Africa and Russia, where he achieved a reputation for energetic leadership and personal bravery, brought him to Hitler's attention and promotion directly from a division to an army command. Despite the failure of his Fifth Panzer Army in the Lorraine campaign against Patton's Third Army, Manteuffel was listed by Hitler for command in the Ardennes. His staff, carefully selected and personally devoted to the little general, was probably the best German staff on the Western Front.

Manteuffel had found himself in almost complete disagreement with the original operations plan handed down by Jodl in November. He was able to convince the Army Group B commander that a stand should be taken on a number of tactical points which, in Manteuffel's judgment, were essential to success in the forthcoming attack. In the last planning conference held at Hitler's headquarters, Model and Manteuffel combined forces in a forthright appeal that carried the day on a series of tactical decisions although it failed to sway the Fuehrer from his strategic decision for the Big Solution. The Fifth Panzer Army commander was bitterly opposed to that part of the plan which called for a tremendous opening barrage at 0800 and a two-hour artillery preparation before the attack jumped off. He argued that the enemy literally must not be awakened and that the assault forces should move forward the moment the guns sounded. This point was conceded when Hitler ruled that the artillery fires along the entire front would begin at 0530. Manteuffel also held strongly for infiltration tactics by small detachments, such as were conventionally employed by both opponents on the Eastern Front. Hitler himself seems to have favored this concept (it is found in the first Fuehrer operations order), but only in the Fifth Panzer attack would assault detachments be found inside the American positions when the initial barrage opened up.

Manteuffel likewise opposed the concept proposed by Jodl in which the attack would be carried by two panzer corps advancing in column. He wanted an attack on a broad front with both tank corps in the line at the opening gun—this point Hitler conceded. Viewing the ground in front of his right armored corps as especially difficult, Manteuffel would give Generaloberst Walter Krueger's LVIII Panzer Corps a fairly narrow front for the initial assault. Believing that once across the Our River, his left armored attack force, General der Panzertruppen Heinrich Freiherr von Luettwitz's XLVII Panzer Corps, would find the going better than on the right, he assigned Luettwitz a rather wide front. In final form, the LVIII Panzer Corps' mission was to cross the Our River on both sides of Ouren, drive west on the Houffalize axis, and create a bridgehead over the Meuse River in the neighborhood of Namur and Andenne. At the same time the XLVII Panzer Corps would cross the Our in the vicinity of Dasburg and Gemünd, push west via Clerf, seize the vital road center at Bastogne, form in a deep column echeloned to the left and rear, then race for the Meuse River crossings south of Namur. Manteuffel had two armored formations in reserve, the Panzer Lehr Division and the Fuehrer Begleit Brigade. These he intended to throw in behind the armored corps which made the first bridgehead at the Our. Although success or failure would turn on the operations of the two armored corps, the Fifth Panzer Army had been given a small infantry corps of two divisions to flesh out its right shoulder. This was General der Artillerie Walther Lucht's LXVI Corps. In early planning there had been some question as to whether the Americans in the Schnee Eifel should be left to the Fifth or the Sixth. Unhappy about this thorn in his side, Manteuffel won the assignment of the Schnee Eifel heights to his army and personally developed a scheme to mop up resistance in this sector at the earliest possible moment. Despite the general dictum that defended towns would be bypassed, Manteuffel wanted St. Vith as a blocking position and so ordered Lucht to capture it. Once through St. Vith the LXVI would follow Krueger to Andenne, but if things grew rough on the left wing Manteuffel intended to switch Lucht's corps to the south.

The Fifth Panzer commander seems to have been fairly optimistic, although he gave little ear to Hitler's promise of air support. He personally rated four of his armored divisions as good attack formations (the 116th, 2d, Panzer Lehr, and Fuehrer Begleit), and his panzer corps commanders were of his own choosing. Krueger and Luettwitz were old hands at mechanized warfare, had learned their business as commanders of the 1st and 2d Panzer Divisions, respectively, and had fought side by side in Lorraine. Krueger was the elder of the two and lacked something of Luettwitz' dash. The latter was a hard-driving commander, daring and tenacious, and had a reputation of giving help to neighboring formations without debate.

With this team Manteuffel hoped to win a quick penetration and get rolling. His first concern would be to gain the ridge west of the Our and thus cover the armor crossings, for he recognized that it would be a difficult stream to bridge. He expected that the tactics of predawn infiltration would pay off and that his assault detachments would have reached the crest line, Lascheid-Heinerscheid-Roder-Hosingen, before noon on D-day. He hoped that the armored debouchment into the bridgehead would commence during the early afternoon. Manteuffel had no precise schedule for his right wing but after the war was over would say that he had hoped for the seizure of St. Vith on the first day of the attack. One thing clearly worried him: would the Seventh Army keep pace and cover his left flank to Bastogne? His appeal for a mechanized division to be given the neighboring Seventh the Fuehrer personally denied.

The 110th Infantry Sector 16-18 December

On the second day of December, a staff officer from General Luettwitz's XLVII Panzer Corps arrived at the headquarters of the Fifth Panzer Army to receive the highly secret word of a great counteroffensive in the Ardennes sector. At the moment Luettwitz's corps was fighting in the bogs and swamps of southwest Holland, where the 30 British Corps and the U.S. 84th Division had essayed an attack in the sector around Geilenkirchen intended to erase the salient retained by the Germans on the left flank of the US Ninth Army. Earlier the XLVII Panzer Corps headquarters had taken part in the Fifth Panzer Army counterattack against the US Third Army in September, had been given new divisions to spearhead the brief spoiling attack in late October against the British and American advance in southwest Holland, and had returned to the line in this sector in mid-November to bolster the failing German defenses. Luettwitz turned the Geilenkirchen sector over to the XVII SS Corps on 6 December and moved with his staff to Kyllburg, close to the Fifth Panzer Army headquarters, where a few trusted officers set feverishly to work on plans for Christrose, the code name for the coming offensive.

The mission given Luettwitz conformed to his reputation for drive and audacity. The XLVII Panzer Corps, if all went well, would cross the Our and Clerf Rivers, make a dash "over Bastogne" to the Meuse, seize the Meuse River crossings near Namur by surprise, and drive on through Brussels to Antwerp. Two things were necessary to success. First, Luettwitz could not allow any slackening to an infantry pace by frontal attacks against strongly defended American positions. Second, he had to disregard his own flanks, particularly on the south, and resolutely refuse to detach any force for flank protection until the main body was west of the Meuse. The only security for the southern flank would have to come from an advance in echelon and such protection as the less mobile divisions of the Seventh Army could offer on the left.

Intelligence reports indicated that the elements of the US 28th Infantry Division likely to be encountered during the first hours of the attack were battle-weary, small in number, and widely dispersed. The problem then, as seen by Manteuffel and Luettwitz, was not how to achieve the initial breakthrough at the Our and Clerf Rivers, but rather how to employ the armor once these two rivers lay behind. The roads in the corps zone of attack were narrow, twisting, and certain to be muddy; they were particularly bad on the axis assigned to Luettwitz's southern columns. Just east of Bastogne the roads straightened somewhat, but good tank-going could not be expected until the Marche-Rochefort line was reached midway between Bastogne and the Meuse. The road center at Bastogne presented a special problem, a problem recognized in the first German plans. Luettwitz and the army commander ran at least two map exercises to arrive at a solution, but Bastogne lay nineteen air-miles west of the German jump-off positions on the Our River and the final orders to Luettwitz's divisions were couched in very general terms. One thing was agreed upon: Bastogne had to be taken before the bulk of the XLVII Panzer Corps moved beyond it to the west.

The sector at the Our River in which Luettwitz's corps would begin the attack was a little over seven miles wide, the villages of Dahnen on the north and Stolzembourg on the south serving as boundary markers. This initial zone was roughly equivalent to the American defensive position manned west of the Our by the 110th Infantry, the center regiment of the 28th Infantry Division, although the width of the 110th front was about two miles greater than the front assigned the panzer corps. The latter consisted of three divisions. The 26th Volks Grenadier

Division (Generalmajor Heinz Kokott) already was deployed in the Eifel sector of the West Wall adjacent to the Our where it covered not only the XLVII Panzer Corps zone but a wide frontage beyond. An old line division, the 26th had fought on the Eastern Front from July 1941 to the last days of September 1944, winning many decorations but little rest. Finally, after a grueling battle in the Baranôw-Warsaw sector the division was relieved for the first time since the beginning of the Russian campaign and brought back to Poznan, there receiving the title of Volks Grenadier (regarded as somewhat less than an honor by the survivors of the old regular army 26th Infantry Division).

To the surprise of the division staff the task of re-equipping and replenishing the 26th went amazingly fast for the beginning of the sixth year of the war. Replacements, mostly from the Navy, were whipped into shape by the "Old 26th," and first-rate equipment replaced that lost in the east. The division commander, officers, and noncoms were veterans; training throughout the division was reported as adequate. Ration strength was more than 17,000, and forty-two 75-mm. antitank guns supplemented the weapons organic to the conventional Volks Grenadier division. Like all such units, however, the 26th was geared to foot power and horsepower; there were 5,000 horses in the division, including a few of the tough "winterized" Russian breed. The new mission given General Kokott was this: the 26th would force the crossings at the Our and Clerf Rivers on the left of the corps, hold open for the armor, then follow the more mobile panzer units to Bastogne. At that crucial point the infantry had to take Bastogne as quickly as possible, with or without the help of the armored divisions. Once this barrier was passed the 26th would be responsible for covering the left flank of the corps while the armored divisions made the Meuse crossings.

The initial penetration by the corps' right was charged to the armored infantry of the famous 2d Panzer Division (Colonel Meinrad von Lauchert), a unit that had fought the Allies all the way from Normandy back to the German frontier. When the 2d Panzer Division was relieved at the end of September its tanks were gone, but there remained a large cadre of veterans who had escaped to the West Wall on foot. In the weeks that followed, the division rested and re-formed in the Bitburg-Wittlich area, its units moving constantly to escape Allied observation. Replacements, generally better than the average, were brought in from Austria (the home station for the 2d Panzer Division was Vienna), and new-model Panther tanks, equipped for night fighting with the new infrared sighting apparatus, arrived fresh from assembly plants near Breslau. On the eve of commitment the two tank battalions were about full strength, with 27 Mark IV's, 58 Panthers, and 48 armored assault guns in the division tank parks. Sufficient trucks were available to motorize most of the division, but there was a shortage of tracked cross-country vehicles. One battalion of armored infantry was given bicycles, and would move so slowly through the mud and over the hills that its function during the drive to the west was simply that of a replacement battalion, feeding into the more mobile units up ahead.

Once the 2d Panzer Division had thrown a bridge across the Our at Dasburg and the 26th Volks Grenadier Division had put a bridge in at Gemünd, the well-known Panzer Lehr Division would be ready to roll, advancing behind the two forward divisions until the corps had cleared the Clerf River, then pushing ahead of the infantry on the corps left in the race to Bastogne. The Panzer Lehr (Generalleutnant Fritz Bayerlein) was one of the divisions earmarked in November for use in the Ardennes counteroffensive, but the American offensive in Lorraine and Alsace had forced OKW to release the Panzer Lehr from its position in the strategic reserve. Hitler had committed Bayerlein's tanks in an abortive counterattack designed to roll up the exposed flank of the American Third Army on the Saar. This Panzer Lehr thrust failed, and at the beginning of December Bayerlein's command was brought north to the Eifel district for an emergency attempt at refitting. Losses in equipment had been particularly heavy. Tanks, tank destroyers, and guns were rushed up from the depots at Mayen, but on 15 December the two panzer grenadier regiments were still missing 60 percent of their regular rifle strength and the panzer regiment had ready only one of its two battalions (with 27 Mark IV's and 30 Panthers). To compensate for the armored weakness of the battered division, two battalions of armored tank destroyers and an assault gun brigade were given Bayerlein just before the attack to the west began. The best troops and newest equipment were placed in the division reconnaissance battalion, heavily reinforced, which was slated to join the reconnaissance battalion of the 26th Volks Grenadier Division in spearheading the advance once the Clerf River had been crossed.

With three divisions, and added corps troops, the XLVII Panzer Corps possessed a considerable amount of shock and firepower. Manteuffel allotted Luettwitz the 15th Volks Werfer Brigade (108 pieces), the 766th Volks Artillery Corps (76 pieces), the 600th Army Engineer Battalion, and the 182d Flak Regiment, all motorized. Each division was reinforced with additional self-propelled assault guns or tank destroyers and each had a full complement of divisional artillery (four battalions for the infantry division and three motorized battalions in the armored divisions). Finally Luettwitz was promised two 60-ton bridges—capable of carrying his Panthers—and very considerable support from the Luftwaffe. Both Luettwitz and Manteuffel had been "promised" air support on numerous occasions before; so it is questionable whether either of them expected the Luftwaffe to make good. Luettwitz, at least, pinned his faith on bad flying weather, night operations, and the large number of flak guns dispersed through his columns.

The sector designated for the XLVII Panzer Corps breakthrough was held by the 1st and 3d Battalions of the 110th Infantry (28th Infantry Division), commanded by Col. Hurley E. Fuller. This regiment formed the division center, with the 112th Infantry on the north and the 109th Infantry aligned to the south. Battered and fatigued by weary, bloody fighting in the Hürtgen Forest, the 28th Division came into the quiet front on the Our during mid-November. 5 During the division attack of 21 November in the Schmidt-Vossenack sector the 28th had taken 6,184 casualties. The task of rebuilding the rifle companies, repairing battle damage, and training replacements was of necessity a slow one. But by the middle of December the 110th Infantry had almost a full roster—a roster numbering many men and some officers who yet had to see their first action. The 109th and 112th were in like status.

Fuller had only two battalions at his disposal because the 2d Battalion, located at Donnange, constituted the division reserve. Anything even remotely resembling a continuous line across the 9- to 10-mile regimental front was beyond the strength of the 1st and 3d Battalions. As a substitute, a system of village strongpoints—each manned in about rifle company strength—was set up on the ridge line separating the Our and Clerf Rivers, which here is traced by the excellent north-south highway connecting St. Vith and Diekirch. This highway (known to the Americans as the Skyline Drive) and the garrison line paralleled the Our at a distance of one and a half to two and a half miles. Each battalion was responsible for five outposts along the west bank of the Our, but these vantage points were occupied only during daylight hours and then in squad strength. At night the strip between the ridge and the river became a no man's land where German and American patrols stalked one another. Even in daytime it was possible for German patrols to move about on the west bank, using the cover provided by the deep, wooded draws.

The Our, in many places, was no more than forty feet wide and easily fordable, but the roads leading to the river made circuitous and abrupt descent as they neared its banks. In the 110th zone four roads ran from the German border at the Our, up and over the Skyline Drive, and down to the Clerf. The American strongpoints were therefore located with an eye to blocking these entry ways while at the same time defending the lateral ridge road which connected the 110th with its neighboring regiments and provided the main artery sustaining the entire division front. The northernmost of the four roads had a good all-weather surface, was the only main through road running east to west through the area, and gave direct access to Clerf and Bastogne. The Germans planned to connect this route to their own supply lines by bridging the Our at Dasburg. The remaining roads through the 110th sector normally were poor but were made worse by the rains prior to 16 December; the 26th Volks Grenadier Division intended to enter the two southernmost roads by throwing a bridge across at Gemünd.

The Americans had identified the 26th long since as the unit garrisoning the West Wall bunkers on the German bank. The presence of two panzer units on the 110th Infantry front was not suspected. General Cota and the 28th Division Staff were prepared for some kind of German effort west of the Our, but the intelligence coming down from higher headquarters pointed only to the possibility of a limited German attack against the 109th Infantry and the American communications running north from Luxembourg City. There was no hint from any source that the enemy was about to strike squarely into the center of the 8th Division and in overwhelming array.

In the late afternoon of 15 December General Luettwitz gathered his division commanders in the XLVII Panzer Corps forward headquarters at Ringhuscheid for final instructions and introduction to the new commander of the 2d Panzer Division, Colonel von Lauchert, who had been selected at the last moment by the Fifth Panzer Army leader to replace an incumbent who was not an experienced tanker. Lauchert arrived too late to meet all of his regimental commanders, but the 2d Panzer, like the rest of the corps, was already in position to move the moment darkness came. Apprehensive lest the Americans be prematurely warned, Army Group B had forbidden the movement of any troops across the Our in advance of the opening barrage set for 0530 on 16 December. Conforming to these instructions the 2d Panzer Division moved its assault columns to Dasburg during the night of 15-16 December but halted in assembly areas east of the river.

On the corps left, however, General Kokott and the 26th Volks Grenadier Division jumped the gun. Kokott's screening regiment, the 78th, had been in the habit of throwing out an outpost line west of the Our from nightfall till dawn. On the evening of 15 December the outpost troops, considerably reinforced, crossed to the west bank as usual and moved cautiously forward. About 0300 engineers manning pneumatic rubber boats began ferrying the 80-man assault companies and heavy infantry weapons across the river. As each company debarked it marched inland to the line of departure which the outpost force now held close to the American garrison points. The 77th Regiment formed on the right near Hosingen and the 39th, echeloned to the left and rear, assembled in the woods north of Wahlhausen. With surprise almost certainly assured and the knowledge that the Americans had no cohesive line of defense, General Kokott had ordered the 77th Regiment to circle north of Hosingen and head straight for the Clerf bridges at Drauffelt, while the 39th cut cross-country, avoiding the villages on the western side of the ridge line, and seized the road junction and bridges at Wilwerwiltz on the Clerf. The eye of the division commander would be on the assault echelons of his right wing regiment, for they would make the main effort to reach the Clerf. The timetable for the 26th Volks Grenadier Division advance called for both its attacking regiments to reach the Clerf River by nightfall of the first day. Adherence to this schedule meant that the villages garrisoned by the American companies would have to be avoided or captured quickly.

The units of the 110th Infantry were disposed as follows to face three full German divisions. On the left of the regimental zone, the 1st Battalion (Lt. Col. Donald Paul) held the intersection of the Skyline Drive and the Dasburg-Bastogne main highway at Marnach, employing Company B and a platoon from the 630th Tank Destroyer Battalion. To the southwest, Company C and the regimental cannon company were deployed in and around Munshausen, guarding the side road which cut cross-country from Marnach to Drauffelt. Company A, at Heinerscheid, was on the extreme left flank of the 110th and so lay outside the path of the XLVII Panzer Corps attack, as did Company D at Grindhausen. The 3d Battalion (Maj. Harold F. Milton) formed the regimental right, with its companies on both sides of the ridge line. Company K, reinforced by Company B, 103d Engineer Combat Battalion, garrisoned Hosingen, a village on the Skyline Drive overlooking two of the four roads which wound from the Our up over the ridge. To the south Company I held Weiler-les-Putscheid, a hamlet in a knot of trails and byroads on the forward slopes of the ridge line. The 110th Antitank Company was in Hoscheid just to the west. Both of these positions lay adjacent to the prospective boundary between the XLVII and LXXXV Corps. West of the ridge, Company L in Holzthum and the headquarters company and Company M in Consthum barred a direct approach to the Clerf crossing site at Wilwerwiltz. Behind the Clerf River and to the west of the regimental command post in the town of Clerf the 2d Battalion (Lt. Col. Ross C. Henbest) lay in divisional reserve. Separated of necessity by the width of the front and the requirements of some depth in the defenses athwart the east-west roads, the units of the 110th could offer little reciprocal support against an enemy attacking in any force.

Chapter IX. The Attack By The German Left Wing: 16-20 December

The massed guns and Werfers of the XLVII Panzer Corps which roared out at 0530 on 16 December gave the Americans their first warning. But the tactical effect of this artillery preparation was considerably less than the German planners had anticipated. The telephone wires connecting the American-held villages were shot out in the first few minutes and Fuller could not reach any of his battalions; artillery radios, however, continued to function. The German barrage, with a limited number of rounds at the guns, dwindled away after about half an hour to sporadic salvos and stray single shots, leaving the advancing infantry without cover while they were still short of the American positions.

The first word of the approaching enemy reached the 110th Infantry headquarters at Clerf shortly after 0615. Company L, on the western side of the ridge at Holzthum, reported figures in the half-light but, peering through the ground fog, which clung all along the division front, could not be sure whether they were American troops passing through the area or the enemy. In fact, detachments of the 39th Regiment had crossed the Skyline Drive unobserved and were moving in to surprise Holzthum. To some extent, then, Kokott's decision in favor of premature assembly west of the Our had gained ground for the 26th. Fuller, however, was able to get a warning message through to the 28th Division command post about 0900.

As the morning passed the small German detachments west of the ridge increased in strength. Before noon five separate assaults had been made at Consthum, but all were beaten off by small arms, .50-caliber, and artillery fire. Finally the Germans took the village, only to be driven out again. A German attempt to cut the road between Consthum and Holzthum failed when Capt. Norman G. Maurer, of the 3d Battalion, leading a sortie of twenty men, surprised the enemy and drove him back with very heavy casualties. Between Holzthum and Buchholz, Battery C of the 109th Field Artillery was hit hard but held its positions, firing the 105-mm. howitzers with one- and two-second fuzes. The battery commander and fifteen gunners were casualties of the close-range fight before help arrived. This came late in the morning, after the 28th Division commander, General Cota, ordered a tank platoon from the 707th man infantry out of the Battery C area.

The 26th Volks Grenadier Division poured more troops into the 3d Battalion sector, compressing the American companies in the village positions. At the crossroads village of Hosingen atop the Skyline Drive, the leading detachments of the 77th swung to the north, cutting the road but moving on in the direction of the Clerf. The 2d Battalion of the 77th, under the cover provided by German artillery, drove in to the south edge of Hosingen, contrary to orders, and there grappled in house-to-house fighting with Company D and Company B, 103d Engineer Battalion. Meanwhile the 39th Regiment, echeloned to the left of the 77th, ran into a snag. The 1st Platoon of Company I had been deployed along the Wahlhausen road on the forward slope of the ridge, covering an observation post. From this point the American artillery observers could see the enemy assembling in the woods just to the north. Accurately adjusted fire held the enemy battalion at bay and forced it to call on neighboring battalions, attacking Weiler, to help outflank the thin infantry line on the Wahlhausen road.

The defenders at Weiler would not be easily pushed aside. Company I (minus the platoon at Wahlhausen), a section of 81-mm. mortars, and an antitank platoon repelled wave after wave of attacking German infantry. When the mortar crews and antitank platoon had used all their ammunition they joined the infantry in the center of the village and fought as riflemen. Twice during the morning the attackers were allowed to send in aid men and remove their wounded. At 1330 the enemy ceased fire and sent forward a white flag, with an offer for the Americans to surrender. When this was refused the Germans systematically set to work to surround the village; by dark they had ringed Weiler.

In the 1st Battalion zone to the north the advance detachments of the 2d Panzer Division moved straight for Marnach, attempting with one quick blow to clear the Americans obstructing the through road from Dasburg to Clerf. While the German engineers labored at the Dasburg site to bring their heavy tank bridging equipment down to the river, the 28th Panzer Engineer Battalion and the 2d Battalion, 304th Panzer Grenadier Regiment, crossed the Our in rubber boats and moved west through the predawn darkness. The advance was delayed somewhat when the grenadiers marched into an American mine field, but by 0800 the leading Germans had reached Marnach. Company B and a platoon of the 630th Tank Destroyer Battalion were well entrenched there and gave the Germans a warm reception, although themselves under fire from batteries east of the Our. Minus his heavy weapons, the enemy failed to knock the Marnach garrison out of the way, but an hour later Company B radioed that three hundred Germans were northwest and southwest of Marnach. The 1st Battalion commander had already ordered Company A, located three miles farther north on the Skyline Drive at Heinerscheid, to send a patrol south and make contact with Company B. In midmorning Paul ordered Company C to march north from Munshausen, leaving the cannon company there, and counterattack the Germans in the Company B area.

By this time, however, the advance infantry detachments of the 2d Panzer Division were not only involved in a battle to knock out Marnach but were pushing past the village en route to Clerf. The 24-man patrol from Company A ran into the German flank at Fishbach, about 1120, and had to withdraw under intense fire. Two hours later the enemy struck at Company A, apparently an attempt to clear the north-south Skyline Drive, but artillery fire beat him off. In the meantime the Company C advance north toward Marnach also ran into trouble: persistent small arms fire forced the infantry to leave the road and move slowly across country. Tanks, ordered up from the division reserve, had not yet arrived. In Marnach the hard-beset garrison fought on, now under the command of the battalion executive officer, Capt. J. H. Burns, who had taken over when the company commander was wounded.

Back to the west, in the 28th Division command post at Wiltz, General Cota took what steps he could to help the 110th Infantry. The bulk of his very limited reserve consisted of the 2d Battalion, 110th Infantry, and the 707th Tank Battalion. By the middle of the morning it was apparent that the VIII Corps was under attack all along the front and that the 28th Division would have to make out with what it had. Radio communication, which was functioning fairly well, showed that the division center was most endangered. About 1000, therefore, General Cota ordered Companies A and B of the 707th Tank Battalion to reinforce the 110th Infantry, with the intention of clearing up the deepest enemy penetrations and sweeping the ridge road clear. Although Fuller pled for the return of the 2d Battalion to his regiment, Cota refused to release this last division reserve.

Shortly before noon a platoon of Company B's tanks reached the hard-pressed field artillery battery near Buchholz and reported the situation in hand. But the enemy here represented only the probing forefinger of the main attack. Company B moved east to aid the 3d Battalion, and Company A, less a platoon in mobile reserve at Clerf, moved to the northern sector. At nearly every point the American tanks would have to fight their way down the roads to reach the infantry holding the villages. To the east, at Dasburg, the German engineers were straining to finish the tank bridge which would bring the German armor into play. Time was running out for the American companies: ammunition was low and the short winter day was drawing to a close—with the likelihood that the small garrisons would be overwhelmed in the darkness by sheer weight of numbers.

On the Wahlhausen road the 3d Battalion observation post, defended by the Company I platoon, called for ammunition and was told that tanks were being sent with resupply. At Weiler the rest of the company and the antitank platoon, their supply of ammunition dwindling, also awaited the tanks. For some reason the tank platoon sent from the 707th had not reached the Company I area when night fell.

About 1830 troops at the battalion observation post reported that enemy vehicles were attacking with multiple 20-mm. guns and asked for American artillery fire on their own positions. This was the end. Only one man escaped. At Weiler the Americans, with only a few rounds left, were completely surrounded and decided to fight their way out. They divided into two groups and headed west through the enemy lines.

On the west slopes of the ridge a platoon of medium tanks was committed early in the afternoon to drive the Germans off the side road linking Holzthum and Consthum. Co-ordination between small packets of infantry and armor, hard at best, was made most difficult by this kind of piecemeal commitment. The tankers had been told that there were no friendly troops on the road and just Outside Holzthum knocked out an antitank gun placed there by Company I. After some delay, while the tank platoon and the infantry identified themselves, the tanks rolled south to the 3d Battalion headquarters at Consthum. At Hosingen, on the ridge road, Company D and Company B were fighting German infantry hand to hand inside the village. In response to their call for reinforcement and ammunition four tanks fought their way through the German infantry along the Skyline Drive, arriving in Hosingen about 2200 — but with no rifle ammunition.

In the 1st Battalion sector, late in the afternoon, two tank platoons arrived in Munshausen to support Company C, already on its way north to relieve Company B in Marnach. Company C had been driven off the road, and the tanks, missing the infantry entirely, rolled into Marnach. One tank platoon remained there to bolster the defense, while the other turned back to the south, picked up Company C, and, on orders, returned with the infantry to Munshausen. About dusk the Marnach garrison radioed that half-tracks could be heard moving toward the village. This was the last word from Marnach. Late in the afternoon, Colonel Fuller had ordered Company D, a platoon of heavy machine guns, and a provisional rifle company hastily assembled from men on pass in Clerf, to move to Reuler and protect Battery B of the 109th Field Artillery Battalion, then firing in support of the troops in Marnach and very hard pressed by the enemy. These reinforcements arrived at Reuler in time to take a hand against the Germans pouring past Marnach toward Clerf and its bridges. But Battery A of the battalion was swept up by the Germans who had bypassed the left wing anchor of the regiment at Heinerscheid.

During most of this first day of attack the German infantry had fought west of the Our without heavy weapons, although the bulk of two regiments from both the 26th Volks Grenadier Division and the 2d Panzer Division had crossed the river and taken some part in the fight. Shortly before dark the 60-ton bridges were completed at Gemünd and Dasburg (inexperienced engineers and the difficulties attendant on moving the heavy structures down to the river bed had slowed construction markedly), and the German tanks and assault guns moved across to give the coup de grâce to the villages still defended by the 110th Infantry. On the left the 26th Volks Grenadier Division finally achieved contact with the 5th Parachute Division, which had been advancing cautiously along the boundary between the 109th and 110th Infantry and had done nothing to help Kokott's southern regiment, the 39th. With an open left flank and under artillery fire called down by the American observation post on the Wahlhausen road, the 39th swerved from the westward axis of attack and became involved at Weiler, contrary to orders. There the American tank platoon from Company B, 707th Tank Battalion, hit into the German flank while attempting to reach Weiler and, it would appear, caused disorganization and confusion. Kokott's right, the 77th Regiment, pushed elements beyond Hosingen (actually moving between the 1st and 3d Battalions of the 110th Infantry), but these detachments, stopped by the American 105-mm. howitzers and the tank platoon near Buchholz, again had to sidestep in the drive to the Clerf. Back at Hosingen the attempt to break American resistance had won an early lodgment in the south edge of the village, but had achieved no more. The 26th Volks Grenadier Division needed Hosinen badly. Without it the western exit road from the Gemünd bridge was hopelessly blocked; through Hosingen ran the main divisional supply route to the Clerf. Just before dark, therefore, Kokott threw a part of his replacement training battalion into the action; these fresh troops succeeded in forcing their way into the north edge of the village, although with heavy losses.

A whole series of monkey wrenches had been thrown into the well-oiled machinery of the 26th Volks Grenadier Division. The American infantry had made excellent use of the ground and had held their positions, refusing to buckle under the weight of numbers. The 39th Regiment had got involved in local actions and been diverted from the westward axis—sustaining high losses in the bargain. The 77th had been unable to win a quick decision at Hosingen. Now, at the end of the day, the armored reconnaissance battalion of the Panzer Lehr Division found itself crawling rather than racing west from the Gemünd bridge. The road to Hosingen was muddy and winding; but worse, at the western exit of the bridge an American abatis and a series of bomb craters blocked the flow of traffic. A few light tanks and self-propelled guns got forward late in the evening, but the bulk of the Panzer Lehr reconnaissance battalion remained backed up at the bridge. Kokott's infantry would have to carry the battle through the night. The 39th regrouped and turned to assault Holzthum and Consthum in force. The 77th marched toward Drauffelt on the Clerf River, leaving the replacement training battalion to continue the fight at Hosingen. Kokott's reserve regiment, the 78th, crossed the Our at dusk and moved forward between the two assault regiments. On the right its 1st Battalion marched on Hosingen, bringing flame throwers and self-propelled guns to blast the Americans from the village; the 2d Battalion moved straight for the Clerf River, aiming at control of the crossings and road net at Wilwerwiltz. The 26th Volks Grenadier Division was across the Our River in force but had failed to gain its first-day objective, control of the Clerf River crossings. The German infantry would have to fight step by step; the hope of a quick breakthrough had proven illusory.

The story in the 2d Panzer Division zone was the same. There the infantry driving toward the town of Clerf had been stopped short of their objective. Marnach remained in American hands, even after the Dasburg bridge was completed and the leading tanks of the 3d Panzer Regiment entered the fight. The 304th Regiment had suffered severely at American hands: the regimental commander was a casualty and one battalion had been badly scattered during the piecemeal counterattacks by the American tank platoons.

General Luettwitz was none too pleased with the progress made by his two attack divisions on this first day. But the credit side of the ledger showed a few entries. The two heavy tank bridges where the Americans obviously were weakening, and the 2d Panzer Division had been able to move its tanks forward on the relatively good road in the northern part of the corps zone. Luettwitz concluded that the Clerf River now would be crossed not later than the evening of the second day.

Across the lines General Cota had little reason to expect that the 110th Infantry could continue to delay the German attack at the 28th Division center as it had this first day. But at dark he ordered his regimental commanders to hold their positions "at all costs" and began preparations to commit his remaining reserves to restore the situation in the Marnach sector and block the road to Clerf. This seemed to be the most endangered sector of the whole division front, for here the 2d Panzer Division had been identified and here was the main hard-surface road to Bastogne. As yet, however, the Americans had no way of knowing that the bulk of the 2d Panzer Division actually was moving down the road to Clerf or that a counterattack would collide with any such German force.

Meanwhile, General Middleton, the VIII Corps commander, issued a holdfast order to all his troops. All VIII Corps units were to hold their positions until they were "completely untenable," and in no event would they fall back beyond a specified final defense line. In the 110th Infantry sector this line ran through Lieler and Buchholz to Lellingen. It was breached at midnight when tanks and self-propelled guns of the 3d Panzer Regiment entered Marnach.

General Cota still had in hand a reserve on the night of the 16th, but it was the last reserve of the 28th Division. It consisted of the 2d Battalion, 110th Infantry, at Donnange and the light tank company of the 707th Tank Battalion, which was located at Weiswampach behind the division north flank in support of the 112th Infantry. By the late evening the picture as seen at the division command post had cleared to this extent: the two flank regiments, the 109th and 112th, had lost relatively little ground; the 110th was very hard pressed; and German tanks were moving along the main road to Bastogne by way of Marnach. At 2100, therefore, General Cota turned the reserve rifle battalion back to the 110th Infantry, minus Company G which was moved to Wiltz to defend the division command post, and agreed with Colonel Fuller's proposal that the battalion be used in an attack eastward to restore American control at Marnach. At the same time the light tank company in the 112th area was alerted by division headquarters for an attack south along the Skyline Drive, also directed toward Marnach, as soon as daylight came. To complete the concentration against the enemy in or around Marnach, Colonel Fuller ordered the medium tank platoon in Munshausen to attack to the northeast with a rifle platoon from Company C. When Fuller heard of the light tanks, he ordered Colonel Henbest to delay the 2d Battalion attack next morning until the incoming tank detachment was ready to attack on the Skyline Drive.

There was still hope on the morning of 17 December that at least one platoon from Company B was holding on in Marnach. About 0730 the two rifle companies of the 2d Battalion jumped off at the ridge east of Clerf. In a matter of minutes the left company ran into a strong German skirmish line, deployed at the edge of a wood, which was supported by tanks and self-propelled artillery firing from around Marnach. The battalion commander ordered his right company down to block the paved road from Marnach to Clerf, but this road was in the hands of the 2d Panzer Division, whose tanks were rolling toward wing of the 110th, had been overrun or forced to displace. Only one battery of the 109th Field Artillery Battalion was firing during the morning and it ran low on ammunition. This battery was driven from Buchholz with the loss of half its howitzers. By noon the 2d Battalion, helpless against massed tanks and without artillery support, was held in check along the ridge running southwest from Urspelt to the Clerf road, only a thousand yards from its line of departure.

The southern prong of the three-pronged counterattack to shut off the German armored drive moving through Marnach toward Clerf also was outgunned and outnumbered but did reach Marnach, only to report that no friendly infantry could be found. About 1000 the small tank-infantry team was allowed to return to its original position at Munshausen, and Fuller then ordered the tank platoon to fight its way to Clerf and help defend the town. These two attacks from west and south had made no headway but were not too costly.

The attack by the light tank company of the 707th along the Skyline Drive was disastrous. About 0720 the company crossed into the 110th Infantry zone, where the ground rose away from the highway and forced the tanks to advance in column on the road. As the column emerged from the village of Heinerscheid, concealed high-velocity guns opened on the skimpily armored light tanks, picking them off like clay pipes in a shooting gallery. Eight tanks were knocked out by the enemy gunners and in the confusion three more fell prey to bazooka fire. The entire action lasted ten minutes. Two of the American tanks destroyed during the German assault later in the day. The company commander withdrew the remaining five tanks on a side road and reached Urspelt, taking position near the 2d Battalion command post.

The American pincers action had failed to constrict at Marnach. Yet there was still an opportunity to retard the 2d Panzer march along the road to Bastogne. Less than two miles west of Marnach lay the Clerf River and the town of Clerf, the latter the headquarters of the 110th Infantry. The town itself lies in a horseshoe bend of the river. From town and river rise wooded and precipitous slopes, particularly sharp and difficult to the east. Descent to the town and its bridges is made on this side by two winding roads. The main paved road from Marnach approaches Clerf through a shallow draw, passing just to the south of the little village of Reuler, which perches on the high ground overlooking the river bend. This road makes a twisted and tortuous descent to the valley floor, finally crossing the river at the southeastern edge of the town and proceeding through narrow streets until it emerges on the north. A secondary road, on the right of the through highway to Bastogne, approaches Clerf from the hamlet of Urspelt. A sharp hairpin turn breaks the descent; then the road crosses the river into the northern edge of Clerf near the railroad station and enters the main highway. In sum, the way through Clerf would be none too easy for an armored division.

Colonel Fuller's command post was in a hotel only a few yards from the north bridge. Across town the regimental headquarters company was billeted in an ancient château, now partially modernized but retaining the heavy stone walls behind which, since the twelfth century, fighting men had dominated the river bend and controlled the main bridge site. In the late evening of 16 December German artillery began to range into Clerf, apparently covering the advance of patrols from Marnach. About 0345 the German artillery quieted. Small detachments with burp guns now crept down through the dark and engaged the troops in and around the château. At dawn a single tank or self-propelled gun began firing from the curving road to the south; more enemy infantry joined the firefight near the château as the morning advanced.

Then rolling down the Marnach road came the German advance guard, perhaps two platoons of Mark IV tanks and as many as thirty half-tracks filled with armored grenadiers. Colonel Fuller had ordered a platoon of the 2d Battalion to swing south and bar the road, but it was already dominated by the German armor. About 0930 the 2d Platoon of Company A, 707th Tank Battalion, climbed out of Clerf to meet the German Mark IV's. At the top of the ascent the tanks met: four German tanks were knocked out, three American tanks destroyed. The 1st Platoon of Company A, which had returned to Munshausen after the unsuccessful attempt to reach Marnach, moved north meanwhile to help the 2d Platoon. A radio message alerted the commander to the danger of a direct approach; so the platoon and some accompanying infantry entered Clerf by a secondary road along the river. German tanks opened fire on them, but a direct hit stopped the leading Mark IV, for the moment effectively blocking the serpentine approach from Marnach. At the château, however, headquarters company still was hard pressed by riflemen and machine gunners in the houses nearby. And German tanks still fired from the eastern height. Shortly before noon German pressure noticeably relaxed. East of Clerf the left flank of the 2d Battalion started to move forward against an enemy assembly point in a woods northeast of Reuler. This threat north of the Marnach road seems to have caused the German commander some concern. Then too, some welcome tank support had arrived on the scene. On General Middleton's order, CCR, 9th Armored Division, had put a task force backstop position behind the threatened center of the 28th Division. Company B of the 2d Tank Battalion, en route to set up a roadblock northeast of Clerf, was appropriated by General Cota and sent to support the 110th Infantry. It arrived in Clerf with nineteen medium tanks. Colonel Fuller set one platoon to clearing the Germans out of the south end of town, sent one platoon to Reuler to help the 2d Battalion, and, sent one to the 1st Battalion at Heinerscheid where the light tanks of the 707th Tank Battalion had been smashed earlier in the day. The appearance of the Shermans in Clerf cooled the ardor of the German infantry.

The 2d Panzer Division advance guard had taken a bloody nose on the Marnach road, but more tanks and infantry were arriving hourly and maneuver was possible. During the afternoon the Germans pressed the 2d Battalion back through Reuler, the Americans fighting stubbornly with the aid of the dwindling tank force from the 9th Armored Division and the few remaining towed tank destroyers of Company B, 630th Tank Destroyer Battalion. A platoon of self-propelled tank destroyers had arrived early in the afternoon but left precipitately, losing one gun as it careened down the road back through Clerf. Shortly before dusk Companies E and F dug in on a ridge north of Reuler under a rain of German shells. On their left German tanks were wiping out the last posts of the 1st Battalion. At Heinerscheid, Company A had been overrun in midafternoon, leaving open an avenue into the 2d Battalion left flank. Then the enemy grenadiers encircled the American roadblock at Urspelt, whereupon the light tank platoon destroyed its single remaining tank and withdrew on foot to Wiltz—the 2d Battalion flanks were wide open.

Colonel Lauchert was worried about the slow rate of the 2d Panzer advance. He even dispatched a kampfgruppe to seize a bridge considerably south of Clerf apparently intending to swing his attack column to a poorer road in the event that Clerf continued to hold. But now the north road into the town was open. A small tank-infantry team blasted the single 57-mm. antitank gun in the path and crossed the bridge at the railroad station. At the same time a tank platoon, shrouded in darkness and with no American tanks left to contest the passage, wound its way into the south end of Clerf. At 1825 Colonel Fuller phoned the 28th Division chief of staff that his command post was under fire and that enemy tanks occupied the town. Fuller and some of his staff made their escape, hoping to join Company G, which had been released at division headquarters and was supposed to be coming in from the west. Later Colonel Fuller was captured, with a group of stragglers he commanded, while attempting to break through to the west. At 1839 the sergeant at the regimental switchboard called the division to report that he was alone—only the switchboard was left.

This was not quite the end in Clerf. At the château by the south bridge 102 officers and men of the regimental headquarters company still were in action. Around them Clerf was crawling with tanks, for most of the Mark IV Battalion of the 3d Panzer Regiment had assembled in the town during the night. Perhaps the tankers were too busy looting the American freight cars and supply dumps to bother with the little force in the château. Perhaps they did not care to risk bazooka fire in the dark. In any case the defenders made radio contact (their last) with the 28th Division as late as 0528 on the morning of 18 December. The final word on the defense of Clerf would come from the enemy.

At dawn the Panther Battalion of the 3d Panzer Regiment came clanking into Clerf, after a night move from the Our River, and found tanks from the Mark IV Battalion playing cat and mouse with the Americans in the château. Bullet fire from the old stone walls was no menace to armored vehicles, bazooka teams sent down from the château were killed or captured, and the German tank battalions moved on, north and west toward Bastogne. But the German infantry were more vulnerable and their march was delayed for several hours before engineers and self-propelled 88's finally set the riddled château afire and forced the Americans to surrender. It is impossible to assess in hours the violence done the 2d Panzer Division timetable at Clerf, but it is clear that the race by this division to Bastogne was lost as the result of the gallant action by the 110th Infantry in front of and at the Clerf crossings.

On 18 December what was left of the 110th Infantry was wiped out or withdrew to the west. Survivors in the north headed toward Donnange and, with Company G, joined elements of the 9th Armored Division to make a stand. Those in the south fell back toward Wiltz, the division command post. The 2d Battalion, surrounded on the ridge east of Clerf, attempted to filter through the enemy lines in the early morning hours. Seven officers and fifty to sixty men did reach Donnange. Of the 1st Battalion, only a part of Company C retained its organization. It had held on at Munshausen, with the 110th Cannon Company and a section of tank destroyers, all through the 17th. The riflemen and cannoneers made a fight of it, barricading the village streets with overturned trucks, fighting from house to house. After the Germans captured the howitzers, a bazooka team of a company officer and a sergeant held the enemy tanks at bay, destroying two which ventured into the village. Before daybreak on 18 December the survivors, now only a handful, started west.

Remnants of the 3d Battalion had assembled at Consthum, the battalion headquarters. The garrison of a hundred or so was reinforced by Company L, ordered back from Holzthum to avoid entrapment. After dark on 17 December a captain led in about twenty-five men of Company I from Weiler, after a desperate march, narrow escapes, and an ambuscade. Only Company K in Hosingen was yet to be heard from. For two days and nights Company K and Company B of the 103d Engineer Combat Battalion fought off all enemy attempts to eradicate this block on the Skyline Drive. On the morning of the 17th German tanks had set the town ablaze, but the few American Shermans had held them at bay. By that night the defenders were without ammunition, but they continued the battle with hand grenades, withdrawing slowly and stubbornly from house to house. The American artillery by this time had displaced to the west and was out of range. Finally, on the morning of 18 December, the surviving members of the garrison sent out a last radio message; they had no choice but surrender.

After the fall of Hosingen the 3d Battalion elements in Consthum offered the last organized resistance in the 28th Infantry Division center east of the Clerf River. Col.

Daniel Strickler, the regimental executive officer, who now had assumed command at Consthum, organized a perimeter defense of the town, set out mines along the approaches, and disposed his three effective tanks and three armored cars to watch for the enemy armor known to be on the road from Holzthum. Some artillery support was still available from a battery of the 687th Field Artillery Battalion, whose shells swept the open fields between the two villages. A half hour before dawn on 18 December German guns and mortars opened heavy fire. With daylight the fire lifted and the enemy infantry advanced, attacking in one wave after another as the morning progressed but making no headway. About 1300 a thick, soupy December fog rolled in on the village. Under this natural smoke screen German tanks and grenadiers poured into Consthum. While tanks dueled in the street like gunmen of the Old West the 3d Battalion made its orderly way out the west side of the town, reorganized, and as night descended marched to Nocher. There it dug in to defend the battery which had given aid during the battle. The Bofors crews belonging to the 447th Antiaircraft Artillery lingered on near Consthum as a rear guard, discouraging all pursuit with their fast, accurate fire. The next day General Cota ordered the battalion to Wiltz, where it would take part in the defense of the division headquarters.

The 112th Infantry Sector 16 – 20 December

The German attack to penetrate the front lines of the 28th Division succeeded on the first day of the offensive in splitting the 112th Infantry from the rest of the division. For this reason the fight put up by the 112th Infantry on the north flank of the division had little or no effect on the operations of its sister regiment east of Bastogne. Furthermore, lack of communication between the 28th Division and its northern regiment would ultimately force the regimental commander, Col. Gustin M. Nelson, to act on his own. The action of the 112th Infantry in this part of the 28th Division story stands therefore as an episode in itself until, after four days' fighting, the regiment joins the forces arrayed in defense of St. Vith.

When the 28th Division arrived on the VIII Corps front in mid-November its regiments were in pitiable condition. The fight in the Schmidt area had cost the 112th Infantry alone about 2,000 killed, wounded, missing, and nonbattle casualties. In a month's time the flow of replacements had brought the regiment to full strength. The regimental commander believed that morale had been restored to a high degree and that the new officers and men now were fairly well trained.

The sector held by the 112th Infantry was approximately six miles wide. Most of the positions occupied lay on the east or German bank of the Our River. In the north, contact was maintained with the 106th Infantry Division at a point northwest of Lützkampen. The regimental position, really a series of squad and platoon posts, followed a ridge line south through Harspelt and Sevenig, then bent back across the Our and followed the western slopes of the river nearly to Kalborn. Here in the south daylight patrols also operated to maintain control of the eastern bank, although the main positions were around Lieler and Lausdorn.

The 229th Field Artillery Battalion was emplaced behind the north flank near Welchenhausen on the German side of the river. Two rifle battalions manned the main battle positions east of the Our: the 1st facing Lützkampen, the 3d occupying and flanking Sevenig. The 2d Battalion manned observation posts and operated patrols across the river but was deployed in a refused position west of the Our. It was accounted the regimental reserve, having fixed schemes of employment for support of the two battalions in the north by counterattack either northeast or southeast.

Hills intersected by wooded draws marked the terrain in this sector. Extensive pine forests covered much of the area, making observation difficult. In general the ground on the east bank commanded. The road net was adequate, although mired by constant rain, but the two forward battalions had to be supplied at night because of German fire. The 3d Battalion positions on the German bank were built around captured pillboxes, for here earlier American advances had pierced the first line of the German West Wall. Since most of these works were "blind" the final protective line turned on foxholes and extensive patches of barbed wire which the battalion itself had constructed. Because the West Wall angled away to the east near Lützkampen the 1st Battalion was denied pillbox protection but, at the insistence of the regimental commander, had constructed a foxhole line with great care.

Aside from patrol activity (generally small raids against individual pillboxes) the 112th Infantry sector had been quiet. Men in the observation posts watched the enemy move about his daily chores and reported flares and occasional rounds of mortar or artillery fire. Early in the month the Germans had undertaken what appeared to be a routine relief in their forward positions. On the nights of 14 and 15 December, sounds of horse-drawn vehicles and motors moving in slow gear drifted to the American outposts; but since the same commotion had attended an earlier relief in the German lines, it was reported and perfunctorily dismissed.

The stir and movement in the enemy lines during the two nights prior to 16 December was occasioned by troops moving in and troops moving out. The 26th Volks Grenadier Division, which had allowed the 112th to go about its training program with only very minor interruption, marched south to join the XLVII Panzer Corps and take part in the attack for Bastogne. Its pillboxes and supporting positions were occupied in greater strength as the LVIII Panzer Corps (Krueger) moved in. In the first German blueprint for the Ardennes counteroffensive the latter corps had been assigned four divisions and the mission of driving to and across the Meuse River on the right of its old comrade, the XLVII Panzer Corps. The mission remained, but the troops available on 16 December were less than half the number promised: one armored division, the 116th Panzer Division, and two-thirds of an infantry division, the 560th Volks Grenadier Division.

The 116th had fought itself out in almost continuous battles during the withdrawal across France and the defense of the West Wall but had a fine reputation and was fairly well refitted. It had ninety-two Panthers and forty-seven Mark IV tanks; perhaps 40 percent of its organic vehicles were missing. The 560th, activated from inexperienced garrison units in Norway and Denmark, had been tagged for the Russian front. Directed to the west by Hitler's orders, the division would see its first action in the Ardennes. One rifle regiment and part of the division engineers were still in Denmark. The artillery supporting the LVIII Panzer Corps consisted of five battalions plus two Werfer battalions, and a few batteries of heavy guns. It appears that the corps had only moderate support in the way of engineers and bridge trains.

The immediate mission of Krueger's corps, like that of the XLVII Panzer Corps on its left, was to seize crossings at the Our River. The areas selected by the two corps for their main efforts were some six to seven air-line miles apart — an indication of the weight to be thrown against the American 28th Infantry Division. The line of departure for Krueger's corps began across the Our from Kalborn and extended north to a point east of Burg Reuland. The bulk of his two divisions, as a consequence, faced the 112th Infantry, albeit the corps zone overlapped somewhat the sectors of the 106th Infantry Division in the north and the 110th Infantry in the south. Krueger had based his plan of attack on the intelligence reports dealing with the Our bridges. Since the American troops east of the Our were deployed in the Lützkampen-Sevenig area, Krueger determined that his main effort should be made there. Roads and bridges, he reckoned, must be in shape to support the American troops east of the river. These roads and bridges he intended to seize by surprise.

On the corps right, then, the 116th Panzer Division (Generalmajor Siegfried von Waldenburg) had orders to attack north of Lützkampen; at least two or more bridges crossed the Our in this sector. The 560th Volks Grenadier Division (Generalmajor Rudolf Langhaeuser) was assigned two specific bridges as targets, one just north of Ouren, the other a stone arch a little to the south of the village. Because surprise was essential in this stroke for the bridges, artillery fire on the American forward positions in the first moments of the assault was forbidden.

The heavy barrage and the pyrotechnic display which opened elsewhere on the 28th Division front on 16 December was viewed at first with some detachment by the men at the 112th observation posts. They heard, and duly reported, heavy artillery to the south, they saw searchlights and flames lighting up the sky, but again in the south. About 0620, however, the 1st Battalion phoned to say that shells were coming over the battalion command post. The German guns and Werfers had finally opened fire to neutralize or destroy the rearward artillery and reserve positions in the 112th sector. As the enemy gun layers dropped their range back to the river and then to the American positions, the searchlights blinked on, searching out pillboxes and bunkers. When daylight came, the German infantry already were stealing through the draws behind and around the forward platoons, aiming to assemble in the wooded areas to the rear.

The 3d Battalion (Maj. Walden F. Woodward), in the regimental center, was hit by the 1130th Regiment of the 560th Volks Grenadier Division. This German blow fell on either side of Sevenig, held by Company L. The American barbed wire line had not been completed across the draws to the north and south of the village; through these gaps the shock companies advanced. The company leading the left battalion surprised a platoon of Company L at breakfast, overran the company kitchen (which was only 800 to goo yards behind the rifle line) and killed the platoon commander. Leaderless, the platoon broke. A part of the German company, perhaps a platoon in strength, succeeded in reaching the stone bridge over the Our south of Ouren, but was dispersed.

The bulk of the 3d Battalion held their positions despite surprise, defending from pillboxes and foxholes. Later the Americans in this sector reported that the attackers must have been "awfully green"—as indeed they were. The enemy attempt to capture or destroy the American command posts, kitchens, and observation posts was only partially successful, although the grenadier assault parties were well inside the 3d Battalion positions when day broke. Two company kitchens were captured and one or two observation posts cut off, but the artillery observer inside Sevenig was able to direct the 229th Field Artillery howitzers onto the Germans in the draw. Meanwhile the mortar crews took a hand from their foxholes on the hill behind Sevenig, dropping mortar shells into the hollows where the Germans congregated or picking them off with carbines.

Early morning reports of considerable German penetration and the threat to the Our bridges in the 3d Battalion area led the regimental commander to put one of his counterattack plans into operation. At 0930 two companies of the 2d Battalion (Lt. Col. J. L. MacSalka) assembled in a draw between Ouren and Lieler (west of the river), crossed the bridges the German patrol at the stone bridge had evaporated under machine gun fire-and moved toward Sevenig. The Germans in the way quickly withdrew to the east. By nightfall the 3d Battalion line on the Sevenig ridge had been restored while the commander of the 1130th reported that his regiment, despite many attempts, had not been able "to get going."

The main effort launched by the LVIII Panzer Corps on 16 December was assigned the 116th Panzer Division. This attack aimed at the bridges near Burg Reuland (in the 106th Division sector) and Oberhausen, in the rear of the positions manned by the left battalion of the 112th. General Waldenburg committed his infantry here, in the predawn hours, hoping that the 60th Regiment would break through on the right or that the 156th Regiment would reach the river on the left and so secure a bridgehead through which his tank regiment could be passed. The lay of the ground and defenses in the area north of Lützkampen were such that Waldenburg's right regiment had to move northwestward at an oblique to the axis of his left wing advance.

In common with the German assault tactics employed all along the front on 16 December, both regiments led off with a predawn advance by shock companies eighty men strong. The company from the 60th ran into trouble almost immediately when it was immobilized in some woods northwest of Berg by flanking fire from Heckhuscheid, in the 424th Infantry sector. Later reports indicate that this group was almost wiped out. The assault company from the 156th was initially more fortunate in its advance west of Lützkampen. By 0630 the grenadiers were behind the command post of the 1st Battalion (Lt. Col. William H. Allen) in Harspelt; the first sign of their presence was a kitchen truck ambushed while journeying to the rear. The advance party of grenadiers had moved along the wooded draw between the two companies holding the 1st Battalion line.

When day came the Americans caught the troops following the advance party of the assault company out in the open. Interlocking machine gun and rifle fire blocked off the German reinforcements some sixty were captured and the rest dug in where they could. Company D, in its support position on the high ground overlooking Lützkampen, meanwhile commenced mopping up the enemy who had filtered between the companies on the line. By noon Company D had so many prisoners that it "couldn't handle them all!" Nonetheless some part of the assault wave had broken through as far as the battery positions near Welchenhausen, where they were repelled by the .50-caliber quadruple mounts of the antiaircraft artillery.

Shortly before noon the advance guard of the 60th Panzer Regiment, rolling along the Lützkampen-Leidenborn road, appeared on the knoll west of Lützkampen. The seven tanks counted here strangely enough made no effort to attack (perhaps the rough terrain and dragon's teeth along the American bunker line did not appear too promising). After a brief pause they wheeled back into Lützkampen. About dark infantry from Lützkampen attacked in close order formation against Company B. Maps picked up from dead Germans showed that the American machine gun positions had been exactly plotted — but as they had existed up to a change made just before the 16th. The enemy made three attacks in the same close formation over the same ground before they discovered the error of their ways. Company B, however, had been badly shot up during the engagement and probably somewhat shaken by the presence of two or three flame-throwing tanks — a new experience to most American troops on the Western Front. Nevertheless by midnight the 1st Battalion front had quieted down, although there still were small groups of the enemy crawling about in the gap breached that morning Lützkampen would continue as a sally port for sorties against the 1st Battalion and the best efforts by the American field pieces to flatten the village failed to still the men and vehicles moving in its streets.

The German plans had been altered during the day, but of course some time was needed for orders to reach the frontline troops. Bad tank going in the West Wall maze north of Lützkampen and the initial reverse suffered by the assault company of the 60th Regiment led the corps commander to order the 116th Panzer Division to pivot its weight on Lützkampen in a drive southwestward toward Ouren. Leaving only a screening force behind, the 60th Regiment started a march intended to bring it east of Sevenig on the left of the 156th Regiment. Although the left division (the 560th Volks Grenadier Division) had not fared too well in the attack on Sevenig, farther to the south its 1128th Regiment had seized a blasted bridge three kilometers east of Heinerscheid and established a bridgehead over the Our at the boundary between the 112th Infantry and the 110th Infantry. This had been accomplished by noon on the first day—as usual a boundary line had proved a point of little resistance—and the German engineers moved in. The approach road on the east bank was blocked with trees and mines, the bridge debris would have taken much effort to clear, and to Krueger's disappointment there was no assurance that a bridge could be in before the night of 17 December. On the evening of 16 December, therefore, the German commander ordered the corps to continue the attack for the bridges at Ouren. Meanwhile he dispatched the Reconnaissance Battalion of the 116th Panzer Division to cross the XLVII Panzer Corps bridge at Dasburg and commence a sweep along the western bank calculated to take the Ouren crossings from the rear.

At the close of this first day the 112th Infantry remained in its positions east of the Our. The 2d Battalion had not yet been seriously engaged, although one company had been detached to reinforce the 3d. Both flanks of the regiment, however, were in process of being uncovered by enemy thrusts against the neighboring units—although this effect may not have been immediately apparent. A gap remained in the center of the 1st Battalion line and small groups of the enemy were wandering along the Our River.

Considerable damage had been done the German assault forces. Although the 116th Panzer Division losses were moderate, the inexperienced 560th Volks Grenadier Division had suffered an estimated 1,000 casualties—a figure, however, that included the reinforced fusilier company which got lost in the woods southwest of Sevenig and was not seen again for two days. Perhaps the Americans had some reason for elation on the night of 16 December, but all knew that harder blows would be dealt on the morrow. Wrote one in his diary: "Nobody able to sleep and no hot meals today. This place is not healthy anymore."

The presence of enemy tanks in Lützkampen constituted a distinct threat, even to infantry in pillboxes. Colonel Nelson's antitank reserve, Company C, 630th Tank Destroyer Battalion, was deployed on the ridge west of the river, but these were towed guns, dug in and relatively immobile. Even so, the unit accounted for six tanks on the 16th and broke up two panzer assaults of company size. On the afternoon of the 16th the division commander had loaned Neslon the light tank company of the 707th Tank Battalion, but after a sweep through the 1st Battalion area in which not a shot was fired the tanks recrossed the river. Subsequently General Cota ordered them to go to the aid of the hardpressed 110th Infantry. This move was made early in the morning with disastrous results recorded earlier. Some additional help for the 112th did arrive before daybreak on 17 December, four self-propelled tank destroyers out of the 811th Tank Destroyer Battalion borrowed from Combat Command Reserve, 9th Armored Division, at Trois Vierges. Finally, the regimental antitank and cannon companies were disposed around Ouren guarding the bridges, the roads, and the regimental command post.

Through the early hours of 17 December American outposts reported sounds of tank movement in Lützkampen. This was the Mark V Battalion of the 116th Panzer Division assembling to lead the attack toward the Ouren bridges. About an hour before dawn eleven searchlights flicked on, their rays glancing dully from the low clouds back onto the Lützkampen-Sevenig ridge. The German artillery could take a hand this morning, particularly since a number of forward observers had wormed into the American positions. First the Werfers and guns pounded the front line, particularly the 1st Battalion positions. Then as the attack got moving they were raised to lay heavy counterbattery fire on the 229th Field Artillery Battalion (Lt. Col. John C. Fairchild). With the first light some eighteen Mark V tanks started down the ridge spur pointing toward Ouren; at the same time the 1130th Regiment and the 156th Regiment resumed the attack to cut off and destroy the forward American companies. Company A, directly in the way, lost a platoon to tanks rolling and firing methodically along the foxhole line. Through this gap the panzers moved in on the support positions held by Company D.

Earlier a German infantry company in close order had been caught in the glare of its own headlights atop a hill and been massacred by Company D sections lying on the reverse slope, but at 0755 Company D was forced to send out an urgent plea for help "and damn quick." West of Harspelt the self-propelled tank destroyer platoon from the 811th arrived in time to destroy four of the panzers, but at the cost of all but one of its own guns. Colonel Nelson sent back request after request for air support. The first American planes arrived at 0935, immobilizing the German tanks momentarily. Company D positions had been taken by assault only a few minutes earlier. About this time a German tank platoon appeared on the ridge less than a thousand yards from the regimental command post in Ouren. Five hundred yards from the Germans, on the far side of a draw, the cannon company gunners quickly bore-sighted their pieces, loaded reduced charge, and with direct fire knocked out four of the panzers. A scratch platoon of less than fifty men collected from the regimental headquarters and Ouren held the supporting German infantry at bay along the ridge east of the village.

The tank thrust through the 1st Battalion center pushed parts of companies C (a platoon of which had joined the battalion from training), A, and D back through the woods toward Welchenhausen. Here about ten o'clock, Battery C of the 229th came under direct tank fire but stopped the tanks with howitzer fire at close range while Company C of the 447th Antiaircraft Artillery Battalion used its quad mount machine guns to chop down the infantry following behind.

About noon the 2d Battalion counterattacked and German pressure along the 112th front began to wane. The 229th Field Artillery Battalion pounded the German assembly point at Lützkampen as hard as limited stock of shells permitted and fighter-bombers plastered the village: "air tremendously effective" reported the expectant ground observers. But there were too few guns and too few air sorties to keep the enemy immobilized for long. Probably by this time a good share of the 116th tanks had been committed. Certainly the enemy infantry were spreading rapidly through the woods and draws between the American front line and the Our River. By 1315 the howitzers around Welchenhausen again were firing at their minimum range.

Three-quarters of an hour later the regimental commander ordered the artillery to displace behind the river; Colonel Fairchild moved the battalion across the river without losing a piece and immediately resumed firing.

Throughout this entire action the 229th gave the 112th Infantry such support as to elicit from the regimental commander the opinion that "it was the best artillery in the army," an expression which would be used by other infantry commanders about other artillery units during these trying days. In this case, as in many others during the American withdrawal, the full story is that of the cooperation of the combined arms. The field artillery commander in his turn would credit the ably served .50-caliber machine guns and 40-mm. Bofors of the protecting antiaircraft company with saving his howitzers.

News of the battle on the right and left of the 112th Infantry sector had been sparse. During the afternoon General Cota radioed Colonel Nelson to be especially watchful of his northern flank, but added that if his own position became untenable he should withdraw at dark behind the Our. About 1515 Nelson sent his executive officer, Lt. Col. William F. Train, to the 28th Division command post with orders to report personally on the regiment's position. Cota, as it turned out, already had phoned the corps commander and asked permission to bring the 112th back to the high ground west of the river. General Middleton agreed, but with the proviso that the regiment should remain close enough to the river to deny an enemy crossing.

Although this final word seems to have reached Ouren about 1600, Colonel Nelson did not act immediately on the order because he still had hopes that the entrapped 1st Battalion could be reached. The 3d Battalion, fighting mostly against infantry, had held its own through the day, aided greatly by the possession of the pillbox line, far stronger than the defensive positions in the 1st Battalion sector. Then, too, the 2d Battalion had once again used the stone bridge south of Ouren to launch a counterattack across the river and, during the afternoon, materially restored the 3d Battalion positions. But the German tanks were fanning out as the day drew to a close, turning attention to the south as well as the west. Patrols could not reach the 1st Battalion and at dusk the 3d Battalion reported that the panzers finally were in position to rake its ridge defenses with fire from the north—the pillbox line no longer was tenable. Colonel Nelson gave the order to withdraw behind the river under cover of darkness.

The regimental command post staff left Ouren even while the enemy was filtering into the village and moved to Weiswampach. The speed of the German attack caught most of the regimental medical company and troops from the headquarters and cannon companies. The 3d Battalion commenced its withdrawal at 2200 under orders to pull back through Ouren. Fortunately Major Woodward, the battalion commanding officer, was suspicious of this route. His suspicions were confirmed when a patrol sent into the town failed to return. The 3d Battalion then crossed the river farther to the south, circled and finally dug in along the OurenWeiswampach road, where its flank would be covered by the refused line of the 2d Battalion. A patrol which had been sent from the 3d Battalion to carry the withdrawal order to the 1st Battalion command post, still holding on at Harspelt, failed to get through. Fortunately radio contact was re-established from Weiswampach shortly after midnight and the 1st Battalion was given orders to withdraw through the former 3d Battalion positions. Company B, on the extreme north flank, had been forced back into the 424th Infantry area, but about 235 men withdrew cross-country toward Ouren.

Near the village a patrol found that the stone bridge was guarded by only a half squad of Germans. The Americans lined up in German formation and, while an officer shouted commands in German, marched boldly across the bridge. The next morning Colonel Nelson was able to tell General Cota, "Very good news. 1st Battalion has worked [its] way back." The little group from regimental headquarters which had been deployed on the ridge line at Ouren was less successful. Completely surrounded by the enemy, it had hoped to join the withdrawal of the line companies. The group never established contact, however, and most of its members were captured when they attempted to break away the following morning.

Although the enemy had seized all of the ground which the 112th Infantry was occupying east of the Our and finally had secured a bridgehead at Ouren, the cost to him on 17 December had been high. At least fifteen tanks had been disabled or destroyed on the first day and German sources indicate that this figure may have doubled on the 17th. The Americans had taken 186 prisoners and killed or wounded two or three times that number; the losses in the 1130th Regiment were "very high," said the enemy reports. It is impossible to give an accurate count of losses in the 112th Infantry, but they seem to have been moderate. Most members of the 1st Battalion, for example, eventually found their way back to the regiment.

The degree of tactical success achieved by the 112th Infantry and the fact that it was able to hold intact as a regiment may be explained by a number of factors. The ground east of the river was favorable to the defender, who was well entrenched as the result of careful planning and inspection by Nelson and his staff, and whose guns covered the few routes of mechanized advance. The numerous pillboxes provided a substantial amount of cover; the 3d Battalion, for example, was not seriously endangered until the attacking tanks maneuvered close enough for direct fire. The refused positions of the 2d Battalion allowed fairly free use of a regimental reserve during both days and good counterattack plans were ready. Equally important, the green 1130th Regiment (incorporated into the 116th Panzer Division attack on the second day) had failed to follow closely in the path of the tanks and so gave American riflemen and machine gunners time to get set after the tanks rolled past.

Even before the seizure of Ouren the LVIII Panzer Corps had shifted its interest to the south. By the second day it was apparent that the combination of stubborn resistance and poor approach roads would delay the projected crossing at Ouren. The orders given the 116th Panzer Division on the night of 16 December to switch to the left were altered on the 17th to start its infantry regiments marching still farther south to the Dasburg bridgehead held by the neighboring corps. Although delayed by inadequate deliveries of POL and the traffic jam on the damaged Dasburg-Marnach road the entire division, including its tank regiment, assembled on the west bank around Heinerscheid during the night of 17-18 December. The main body of the 560th Volks Grenadier Division also had detoured around the stubborn men and difficult ground in the 112th Infantry area, extending the bridgehead which the 1128th Regiment had seized east of Heinerscheid on 17 December. Only the weakened 1130th Regiment and the division fusilier company, once again in touch with its fellows, were left behind to extend the bridgehead formed at Ouren.

All this gave the 112th Infantry a chance to get its breath on 18 December. A few attacks were started against the new American line, which now covered Beiler, Lieler, and Lausdorn, but none were energetic. Throughout the day the American outposts watched masses of foot troops and vehicles defile westward through Heinerscheid, only some two thousand yards to the south. The regimental cannon company also provided some interested spectators, who trained their howitzers on Heinerscheid with such good effect that enemy records take rueful note of this harassing fire from the north.

Communication between the 112th and division headquarters had been sketchy since 16 December, depending on artillery radio nets and liaison officers. Early in the afternoon of 18 December a radio message finally arrived at the division command post asking that the regiment be given instructions. General Cota had been trying through most of the morning to reach Nelson with an order to hold in essentially the positions which the regiment now occupied. But the situation east of Bastogne was growing more precarious and the division commander decided to bring the 112th back to join in the defense of Bastogne. About 1700 he radioed new orders: the 112th Infantry was to fight a stiff delaying action along the line Weiswampach—Trois Vierges, and thence toward Bastogne. Two hours later the 112th Infantry acknowledged receipt of these instructions.

Colonel Nelson decided to pull back through Huldange since enemy tanks were known to be in Trois Vierges. Early on 19 December the 112th Infantry and 229th Field Artillery Battalion moved under cover of a heavy fog and assembled without hindrance around Huldange, the defensive front now facing south. Here Nelson received a message from the 28th Division which ordered the regiment to hold the line LausdornWeiswampach-Beiler, which the 112th Infantry had just abandoned. Colonel Nelson at this moment had two contradictory orders and would have to risk his regiment if he carried out either.

Through the roundabout artillery channels he asked permission to join the 106th Infantry Division, only a little distance away to the north. Nelson also reported to General Jones at Vielsalm and set the problem before him. Jones attached the 112th Infantry to his own division on the spot, assuring Nelson that he would assume full responsibility. The sequence of events in this story of difficulties in command and communication is none too clear, but the VIII Corps commander approved the attachment. On the morning of the 20th Jones ordered the regiment to sideslip back to the east, reoccupy Beiler, and dig in along the eastwest ridge line, Leithum-Beiler-Malscheid. Thus deployed on the right of the 424th Infantry, the 112th was another piece filling out the fast developing "island defense" of St. Vith.

The Fall of Wiltz

The total impact of the severe German blows dealt the 110th Infantry in the late afternoon and evening of 17 December was not felt at the division and corps headquarters for several hours. Information on the hard-pressed battalions and their companies was sketchy and secondhand. At 2013 General Cota phoned the VIII Corps commander to say that the situation was critical, that routes were open for the German tanks to come through, and that "there is some question in regard to the 110th Infantry CP." He added, however, that he had "three battalions now trying to counterattack from Clerf to Marnach." (By this hour, of course, the story was quite different: the 1st Battalion was cut to pieces, most of the 2d Battalion was surrounded, and the 3d Battalion was holding at Consthum and Hosingen only by the skin of its teeth.)

The corps commander was loath to yield ground to the enemy. Nonetheless he advised Cota to withdraw the 110th back of the Clerf, that "under the circumstances it was necessary." Furthermore, Middleton instructed Cota to use his tanks and tank destroyers to block the roads west of the river.

The 28th Division commander agreed to pull back where he could, but by the morning of the 18th it was apparent that to re-establish any sort of front behind the Clerf was impossible. The bridges at Clerf and Wilwerwiltz were in German hands (no preparations had been made to destroy them); most of the sixty tanks committed in the central sector were destroyed. No help could be expected from either the right or left wing regiments in shoring up the division center. The 109th Infantry was losing ground on its north flank and soon would be forced back fanwise into the 9th Armored Division zone. The 112th Infantry south wing was giving way under heavy attack, and during the day all communications between the regiment and division were lost.

Miscellaneous troops of the 110th Infantry had joined with units of Combat Command R of the 9th Armored Division (briefly under operational control of the 28th Infantry Division) to defend along the main road to Bastogne in the area west of Clerf. The responsibility for command here was assumed directly by the VIII Corps. General Cota, as a result, decided to concentrate what was left to him—headquarters troops, engineers, stragglers, and the handful of organized units moving back from across the Clerf—in defense of Wiltz, the 28th Division command post. This sizable town lay in a bend of the Wiltz River valley, southwest of Clerf and some three miles away from the enemy-held crossings at Wilwerwiltz. Next to the paved through highway via Clerf, the Wiltz valley offered the best avenue westward. The road center at Wiltz and the bridges there were only about twelve miles from Bastogne. It would be natural, therefore, for the Germans debouching from the Wilwerwiltz bridgehead to defile through the Wiltz valley.

About 1000 on 18 December, General Cota received the welcome word that a combat command of the 10th Armored Division was moving forward to his assistance, probably to be in position to give support by the late afternoon. Middleton had ordered the 44th Engineer Combat Battalion (Lt. Col. Clarion J. Kjeldseth) to Wiltz on the previous evening with about six hundred men (it had been operating sawmills and rock crushers, working on roads, and the like). This unit now relieved the provisional battalion, hastily formed from the 28th Division headquarters, by setting up positions north and east of the town. There were also available some tanks and guns to help the engineers, bandsmen, telephone linemen, and paymasters who composed the defense. All that remained of the 707th Tank Battalion—some six crippled tanks and five assault guns—was gathered in Wiltz after a rear guard action in Wilwerwiltz. Six three-inch towed tank destroyers from the 630th Tank Destroyer Battalion, weapons of the 447th Antiaircraft Battalion, and light armored cars of the 28th Reconnaissance Troop reinforced the perimeter. Southeast of the town the undergunned batteries of the 687th Field Artillery Battalion held firing positions along the road, sited to cover the Wiltz perimeter or support the 3d Battalion, 110th Infantry, fighting at Consthum.

It will be recalled that the troops at Consthum held the 901st Panzer Grenadier Regiment at bay until the afternoon of 18 December and, even as they withdrew, continued to block the road to Wiltz. The northern regiment of the Panzer Lehr Division, the 902d, made better progress. The capitulation of the gallant garrison at Hosingen, during the morning, removed this threat to the 902d supply road. The 26th Volks Grenadier Division, having completed its initial mission by seizing an undamaged bridge across the Clerf at Drauffelt during the night, made way for the Panzer Lehr Division to strike for Bastogne. The Panzer Lehr Reconnaissance Battalion, earlier withdrawn from the fight at Holzthum, reverted to its parent command and crossed the river first. The 902d, advancing by way of Munshausen, now cleared of Americans, followed. Despite harassing fire from American guns and mortars the Germans moved swiftly. At the crossroads east of Eschweiler the Reconnaissance Battalion turned to the left and bore down on Wiltz. The 902d, led in person by the division commander, continued toward the west, although briefly delayed in a fight with a few towed antitank guns and armored cars near Eschweiler.

German field guns, by this time west of the Clerf, opened fire on Wiltz at noon. Two hours later tanks and self-propelled guns struck the 44th Engineers, which was outposting the little hamlets northeast of Wiltz. A section of tank destroyers, supporting the forward outpost, was overrun by the more mobile German tanks, but the engineers held their fire for the German infantry on the heels of the panzers and then cut loose, with satisfying results. The American howitzers, south of Wiltz, also took a hand in slowing the German attack. But the enemy armor weight was too heavy, nor could it be checked by the handful of tanks and light assault guns remaining to the 707th Tank Battalion. By dusk the American line had been pushed back nearly to Weidingen when orders came to withdraw behind the Wiltz River and destroy the bridge at Weidingen. For some reason the bridge was not blown. But the pressure on the Wiltz perimeter relaxed briefly as the Panzer Lehr Reconnaissance Battalion turned back toward the north to rejoin its division in the race for Bastogne. Infantry of the 26th Volks Grenadier Division took over the attack on the northeast (probably the 39th Volks Grenadier Regiment).

On German operations maps Wiltz lay athwart the boundary which divided the attack zones of the XLVII Panzer Corps and the LXXXV Corps. On 19 December the right wing division of the latter, the 5th Parachute Division, took over the attack on Wiltz, or perhaps more accurately, drifted into a fight for the town. On the evening of the 18th Col. Ludwig Heilmann, commander of the 5th Parachute Division, knew that the divisions on his right and left were well ahead of his own. In fact the troops of the 26th Volks Grenadier Division sent against Wiltz from the northeast were acting under orders to protect the flank and rear of Panzer Lehr against possible American counterattack from the Wiltz valley. Heilmann, therefore, had decided to bypass Wiltz on 19 December with his entire division but now found that he could not get his regiments back in hand. The 5th Parachute Division commander had already experienced great difficulty in maintaining control of his units in action. His staff and regimental commanders, appointees of Generaloberst Kurt Student, had formed a clique against the previous commander and were hostile to Heilmann. Furthermore, troops and troop leaders were poorly trained, coming as they had only recently from Luftwaffe ground units. Even on the first day of the offensive one of Heilmann's regiments had been lost for several hours. This experience, events would show, had borne little fruit.

On the morning of 19 December the headquarters of the 28th Infantry Division transferred from Wiltz to Sibret, southwest of Bastogne. The provisional battalion which had been recruited from the headquarters staff remained in Wiltz. Meanwhile General Cota had ordered Colonel Strickler to move in the 3d Battalion, 110th Infantry, from Nocher. The battalion, perhaps 200 strong, arrived in Wiltz about noon and Strickler assumed command of the forces in the town. During the morning the 26th Volks Grenadier Division engaged in desultory action, moving troops around to the north. Since the Wiltz bridge had not been destroyed, the American assault gun platoon was ordered back to Erpeldange, covering the northeastern approach to the bridge and the engineer outposts. Four of the 707th tanks that had been crippled the previous day were drawn up on the ridge east of Wiltz to give what help they might as more or less stationary artillery. The Americans were not too worried by the flanking move because tanks of the 10th Armored Division were expected momentarily.

The German infantry on the north side of town aligned for the assault about 1400. A sharp attack drove a provisional platoon, made up from the 28th Division band, off the high ground to the northwest, thus exposing the engineer line. The 44th was hit from the northeast and east by infantry armed with machine pistols charging in alongside single tanks. As American riflemen and machine gunners cut down the German assault teams, they saw their own ranks thinning. In this fight the crossroads near Erpeldange changed hands four times. The assault gun platoon gave good support wherever the line was threatened, but by the end of the afternoon its fuel and ammunition were nearly gone and the gunners, after four days of nearly continuous action, were approaching complete exhaustion. When darkness finally came, the 44th withdrew with the assault guns into Wiltz, having lost four officers and 150 men. This time the bridge was blown. On orders, the three remaining assault guns went back to cover the wrecked structure. Their fate is unknown.

While elements of the 26th Volks Grenadier Division were attacking on the north side of the Wiltz, detachments of the 5th Parachute Division struck the American perimeter on the south and southeast. This timing might seem to indicate a co-ordinated attack. In fact it represented Heilmann's failure to gain control of his division, for the orders were to bypass Wiltz. The division advance guard from the 15th Parachute Regiment (supposedly on its way to capture Sibret) somehow became confused, wandered away northward, and about 1500 struck the 687th Field Artillery Battalion, whose batteries had displaced to a road angling southeast from the town. Battery A met the tanks leading the German column with direct fire, disabled or destroyed them, and briefly slowed the advance toward Wiltz. But menaced as they were, the artillery commander could not risk his howitzers further. Battery B fired its few remaining rounds to cover the other batteries, the battalion assembling during the evening at a crossroad southeast of Harlange.

By nightfall the American perimeter had been pierced at many points and the defenders pushed back into the center of Wiltz. Most of the tanks and assault guns were out of action, there were insufficient machine guns to cover the final protective line, radio communication between the desperate units was practically nonexistent, searchlight rays glancing from the low clouds lighted the path of the attackers, and ammunition was running very low.

Attempts during the evening to send a task force of stragglers and trains forward from the 28th Division headquarters at Sibret were abortive; the roads east to Wiltz now were blocked every few kilometers by enemy infantry and self-propelled guns.

On the ridges which look down over Wiltz more Germans appeared in the early evening, apparently eager to be in at the kill. The 14th Parachute Regiment, which had been moving slowly westward (the 5th Parachute Division commander ascribed its dilatory movement to the habit of attacking small villages in order to have billets for the cold December nights), entered the fight via a climb onto the eastern ridge overlooking the town. At least a third of the 5th Parachute Division was finally engaged at Wiltz contrary to Heilmann's orders.

Colonel Strickler decided to evacuate Wiltz by infiltration and regroup at Sibret, but with the Germans pressing in from all sides and no means of reaching his units except by runner the actual withdrawal would be difficult to control. It was his intention, however, to move the provisional battalion first, leaving the 3d Battalion to keep the escape exits open while the 44th Engineers acted as rear guard. The 687th Field Artillery Battalion pulled out to the southwest and the 3d Battalion also started to move, under the impression that this was the plan. When orders finally arrived to hold in place, the 3d Battalion had reached a trident crossroad southwest of the town. After a long wait the battalion commanding officer, Major Milton, went back into Wiltz to get further orders; when he returned most of his battalion had disappeared. With the few troops remaining, Milton successfully made his way cross-country to the west.

The bulk of the provisional battalion, inside Wiltz, started southwest an hour or so before midnight, some on foot, the rest riding on trucks, half-tracks, and tank destroyers. A few hundred yards had been traversed when, at the first crossroad, the leading half-track ran into a patch of mines laid in front of a German roadblock and exploded. An unidentified crew of a 447th Antiaircraft Artillery half-track drove straight onto the mines, its .50-caliber fire searching out the enemy riflemen. The half-track was demolished, but the field had been exploded and the covering infantry cleared away. As the column turned northwest on the main Bastogne highway enemy fire increased; some in the column turned back from the gantlet in hopes of finding another escape route by retracing their steps through Wiltz. About four and a half miles west of the town, a second block was encountered and a German self-propelled gun lashed out at the lead vehicles while machine gunners blazed away from positions around it. A platoon of Negro troops came to the head of the column and, attacking through the dark with grenades and bayonets, cleared the position.

Only a short distance beyond, at a third block, fire swept into the column from all sides. This was the end: shots, blazing vehicles, and screaming wounded. Those who could left the road, scattering in small parties into the dark. In the darkness and confusion many stragglers made their way into Bastogne and Vaux-lez-Rosières. (Strickler made it to the latter point where General Cota placed him in charge of the defense.) Farther to the south the 687th Field Artillery Battalion was surrounded at a crossroad about seven miles from Wiltz. The gunners and their attached antiaircraft artillery unit made a stand with their carbines, Colts, and a few .50-caliber machine guns. For nearly two hours enemy flares methodically picked out targets for mortar and bullet fire, while the Americans were so closely beset that the Bofors and murderous quad mounts could not retaliate without cutting down their own people. Only three of the howitzers left could be withdrawn and losses among the cannoneers and drivers were high. The 44th Combat Engineers, the rear guard unit at Wiltz, probably suffered most, the enemy accounting for 18 officers and 160 men during the final withdrawal.

The fall of Wiltz ended the 28th Division's delaying action before Bastogne. Other American troops now had to take over the actual defense of that all-important road center, but without the gallant bargain struck by the 110th Infantry and its allied units — men for time — the German plans for a coup-de-main at Bastogne would have turned to accomplished fact. The cost had been high, much higher than American units expected to pay at this stage of the war: the 110th Infantry virtually destroyed, the men and fighting vehicles of five tank companies lost, the equivalent of three combat engineer companies dead or missing, and tank destroyer, artillery, and miscellaneous units engulfed in this battle. In the last analysis the losses inflicted on the enemy may have equaled those sustained by the Americans — certainly the Germans paid dearly for their hurried frontal attacks against stonewalled villages and towns — but the final measure of success and failure would be in terms of hours and minutes won by the Americans and lost to the enemy.

Chapter X. The German Southern Shoulder Is Jammed

In the first week of December the 4th Infantry Division (Maj. Gen. Raymond O. Barton) left the VII Corps after a month of bloody operations in the Hürtgen Forest. Having lost over 5,000 battle casualties and 2,500 nonbattle casualties from trench foot and exposure, the division now had to be rebuilt to something approaching its former combat effectiveness. It moved south to Luxembourg, "the quiet paradise for weary troops," as one report names it, taking over the 83d Infantry Division positions on the right flank of the VIII Corps (and First Army) while the 83d occupied the old 4th Division sector in the north. The 35-mile front assigned to the 4th Division conformed to the west bank of the Sauer and Moselle Rivers. Across these rivers lay a heterogeneous collection of German units whose lack of activity in past weeks promised the rest the 4th Division needed so badly. The division completed its concentration within the Grand Duchy of Luxembourg on the 13th, its three regiments deployed as they would be when the German attack came. The 12th Infantry was on the left (next to the 9th Armored Division) and fronting on the Sauer; the 8th Infantry was in the center, deployed on both the Sauer and Moselle; the 22d Infantry reached to the right along the Moselle until it touched the First and Third Army boundary just beyond the Luxembourg border. Of the three regiments only the 12th Infantry (Col. Robert H. Chance) lay in the path of the projected German counteroffensive.

As soon as it reached the quiet VIII Corps area, the 4th Infantry Division began to send groups of its veterans on leave — to Paris, to Arlon in Belgium, even a fortunate few to the United States. Rotation in the line allowed others a few hours in Luxembourg City, ice cream in several flavors, well-watered beer, and the dubious pleasure of hearing accordionists squeeze out German waltzes and Yankee marching songs of World War I vintage. Replacements, now by order named "reinforcements," joined the division, but by mid-December the regiments still averaged five to six hundred men understrength. Infantry replacements were particularly hard to obtain and many rifle companies remained at no better than half strength. Equipment, which had been in use since the Normandy landings, was in poor condition. A number of the divisional vehicles had broken down en route to Luxembourg; a part of the artillery was in divisional ordnance shops for repair. When the Germans attacked, the 70th Tank Battalion, attached to the 4th Division, had only eleven of its fifty-four medium tanks in running condition.

Neither the 83d Division, which the 4th had relieved, nor any higher headquarters considered the Germans in this sector to be capable of making more than local attacks or raids, and patrols from the 4th Division found nothing to change this estimate. Even so General Barton made careful disposition of his understrength and weary division, even ordering the divisional rest camps, originally back as far as Arlon, to be moved to sites forward of the regimental command posts. Since any static linear defense was out of the question because of the length of the front and the meandering course of the two rivers, Barton instructed his regimental commanders to maintain only small forces at the river outpost line, holding the main strength, generally separate companies, in the villages nearby. Each regiment had one battalion as a mobile reserve, capable of moving on four-hour notice. Each regiment, by standard practice on such a wide front, had one of the division's 105-mm. howitzer battalions in direct support. General support was provided by the division's own 155-mm. howitzer battalion and two additional medium battalions belonging to the 422d Field Artillery Group, but even this added firepower did not permit the 4th Division massed fire at any point on the extended front. Mobile support was provided by those tanks of the 70th Tank Battalion which were operational, the self-propelled tank destroyers of the 803d Tank Destroyer Battalion, and the towed tank destroyers of the 802d. The plans to utilize these positions were briefed by General Barton to his commanders on the 13th. Barton was apprehensive that the enemy would attempt a raid in force to seize Luxembourg City, and in the battle beginning on the 16th he would view Luxembourg City as the main German objective.

Intelligence reports indicated that the 4th Division was confronted by the 212th Volks Grenadier Division and miscellaneous "fortress" units, deployed on a front equal to that held by the 4th. Until the night of 14 December this estimate was correct. As yet no American troops had had opportunity to try the mettle of the 212th (Generalmajor Franz Sensfuss). After three years of campaigning on the Eastern Front the division had been so badly shattered during withdrawals in the Lithuanian sector that it was taken from the line and sent to Poland, in September 1944, for overhauling. The replacements received, mostly from upper Bavaria, were judged better than the average although there were many seventeen-year-olds. Unit commanders and noncommissioned officers were good and experienced; morale was high. Although the 212th was at full strength it shared the endemic weaknesses of the volks grenadier division: insufficient communications and fewer assault guns than provided by regulation (only four were with the division on 16 December).

Brandenberger rated the 212th as his best division. For this reason the 212th was assigned the mission of protecting the flank of the Seventh Army, just as the latter was responsible for guarding the flank of the forces in the main counteroffensive. More specifically, the Seventh Army plans called for the 212th to attack over the Sauer on either side of Echternach, reach and hold the line of the Schlammbach, thus eliminating the American artillery on the plateau in the Alttrier-Herborn-Mompach area, and finally to contain as many additional American troops as possible by a thrust toward Junglinster. Radio Luxembourg, the powerful station used for Allied propaganda broadcasts, was situated near Junglinster. As in the case of the 276th Volks Grenadier Division, there is no indication that the LXXX Corps expected to send the 212th into Luxembourg City, although the Germans knew that the 12th Army Group Headquarters and the advance command post of the Ninth Air Force were located there.

On the night of 13-14 December the 212th commenced to strip its extended front in concentration for its part in the counteroffensive. The 423d Regiment made a forced march from the sector southwest of Trier and by daylight had bivouacked on the right wing of the 212th. The following night all three regiments assembled behind a single battalion which acted as a screen along the Sauer between Bollendorf and Ralingen, the prospective zone of attack. On the final night (15-16 December) the division moved into the position for the jump-off: the 423d on the right, north of Echternach; the 320th on the left, where the Sauer turned east of Echternach; and the 316th in army reserve northeast of the city. The long southern flank of the old 212th Volks Grenadier Division sector had been drastically weakened to permit the concentration at Echternach. Only two Festung battalions were left to cover the twelve miles south to the boundary between the Seventh and First Armies, but in this denuded sector the Sauer and Moselle Rivers afforded a considerable natural defense.

The Germans had excellent intelligence of the 4th Infantry Division strength and positions. The Luxembourg-German border was easily crossed, and despite the best efforts of the American Counter Intelligence Corps and the local police the bars and restaurants in Luxembourg City provided valuable listening posts for German agents. It is likely that the enemy had spotted all the American outpost and artillery positions; it is certain he knew that the 212th Volks Grenadier Division would be opposed only by the 12th Infantry during the first assault phase.

The German Thrust Begins

When the German artillery opened up on the 12th Infantry at H-hour for the counteroffensive, the concentration fired on the company and battalion command posts was accurate and effective. By daybreak all wire communication forward of the battalions was severed. Many radios were in the repair shops, and those at outposts had a very limited range over the abrupt and broken terrain around Echternach and Berdorf, Luxembourg's "Little Switzerland." Throughout this first day the 12th Infantry would fight with very poor communication. The problem of regimental control and coordination was heightened by the wide but necessary dispersion of its units on an extended front and the tactical isolation in an area of wooded heights chopped by gorges and huge crevasses. In accordance with the division orders to hold back maximum reserves, the 12th Infantry had only five companies in the line, located in villages athwart the main and secondary roads leading southwest from the Sauer River crossings to the interior of the Grand Duchy. These villages, at which the crucial engagements would be fought, were Berdorf, Echternach, Lauterborn, Osweiler, and Dickweiler. Actually, only a few men were stationed with the company command post in each village; the rifle platoons and weapon sections were dispersed in outposts overlooking the Sauer, some of them as far as 2,000 yards from their company headquarters.

The leading companies of the two German assault regiments began crossing the Sauer before dawn. Apparently the crews manning the rubber boats had trouble with the swift current, and there were too few craft to accommodate large detachments. The immediate objective of the northern regiment, the 423d, was the plateau on which stood the village of Berdorf; beyond this the regiment had orders to cut the road running west from Lauterborn and Echternach and link forces with the 320th Regiment. The latter crossed east of Echternach, its first objective being the series of hills north of Dickweiler and Osweiler. Once in possession of these hills the 320th was to seize the two villages, then drive on to join the 423d.

General Barton had warned his regiments at 0929 to be on the alert because of activity reported to the north in the 28th Division area, intelligence confirmed by a phone call from General Middleton. But the first word that the Germans were across the river reached the 12th Infantry command post in Junglinster at 1015, with a report from Company F, in Berdorf, that a 15-man patrol had been seen approaching the village a half-hour earlier. At Berdorf most of Company F (1st Lt. John L. Leake) had been on outpost duty at the four observation posts fronting the river. The company radio was back for repair but each of the artillery observers, forward, had a radio. Either these sets failed to function or the outposts were surprised before a message could get out. The 1st Battalion, 423d Regiment, overran three of the outpost positions, captured the company mortars, machine guns, and antitank guns sited in support of the forward detachments, and moved in on Berdorf. Outpost 2 at Birkelt Farm, a mile and a half east of Berdorf, somehow escaped surprise. Here the 2d Platoon (with twenty-one men and two artillery observers) held out in the stone farm buildings for four days and from this position harassed the Germans moving up the ravine road to Berdorf. Direct assault failed to dislodge these Americans, and the attempt was abandoned pending the arrival of heavy weapons from across the river.

At Berdorf itself, Lieutenant Leake gathered about sixty men in the Parc Hotel as the enemy closed in. The Parc was a three-storied reinforced concrete resort hotel (indicated in the guidebooks as having "*confort moderne*") surrounded by open ground. Leake's force had only one .50-caliber machine gun and a BAR to reinforce the rifles in the hands of the defenders, but the Germans were so discouraged by the reception given their initial sorties that their succeeding attempts to take the building were markedly halfhearted.

Meanwhile the 7th Company, 423d Regiment, pushed forward to cut the Echternach-Luxembourg road, the one first-class highway in the 12th Infantry sector. This company struck Lauterborn, on the road a mile and a half southwest of Echternach, and cut off the Company G outposts. By 1130 the remainder of Company G, armed with rifles and one BAR, was surrounded but still fighting at a mill just north of the village, while a platoon of the 2d Battalion weapons company held on in a few buildings at the west edge of Lauterborn. Company E, in Echternach, likewise was surprised but many of the outpost troops worked their way back to a hat factory, on the southwestern edge of the city, which had been organized as a strongpoint. The first German assault here did not strike until about 1100, although Echternach lay on low ground directly at the edge of the river. Attempts by the 320th Infantry to make a predawn crossing at Echternach had been frustrated by the swift current, and finally all the assault companies were put over the Sauer at Edingen, more than three miles downstream.

This delay brought the advance troops of the 320th onto the hills above Osweiler and Dickweiler well after daylight, and almost all of the American outposts were able to fall back on the villages intact. Late in the morning two enemy companies attacked Dickweiler, defended by Company I, but were beaten off by mortar fire, small arms, and a .50-caliber machine gun taken from a half-track. The Germans withdrew to some woods about 800 yards to the north, ending the action; apparently the 320th was more concerned with getting its incoming troops through Echternach. Osweiler, west of Dickweiler, thus far had seen no enemy.

With wire shot out, radios failing, and outposts overrun, only a confused and fragmentary picture of the scope and intent of the attack was available in the 4th Infantry Division headquarters. By noon, however, with Berdorf and Echternach known to be under attack, Dickweiler hit in force, and Lauterborn reported to be surrounded, it was clear that the Germans at the very least were engaged in an extensive "reconnaissance in force," thus far confined to the 12th Infantry sector. Artillery, normally the first supporting weapon to be brought into play by the division, had very limited effect at this stage. The field artillery battalions were widely dispersed behind the various sections of the long 4th Division front; only fifteen pieces from the 42d Field Artillery Battalion and the regimental cannon company were in range to help the 12th Infantry. The one liaison plane flying observation for the gunners (the other was shot up early on 16 December) reported that "the area was as full of targets as a pinball machine," but little could be done about it. Radio communication, poor as it was, had to serve, with the artillery network handling most of the infantry and command messages in addition to its own calls for fire. The gunners nevertheless began to get on the targets, and the German infantry reported very punishing artillery fire during the afternoon.

At noon the picture of battle had sharper definition; so General Barton authorized the 12th Infantry to commit the 1st Battalion (Lt. Col. Oma R. Bates), the regimental reserve. At the same time he gave Colonel Chance eight medium tanks and ten light tanks, leaving the 70th Tank Battalion (Lt. Col. Henry E. Davidson, Jr.) with only three mediums and a platoon of light tanks in running order. Small tank-infantry teams quickly formed and went forward to relieve or reinforce the hard-pressed companies. Unfortunately rain and snow, during the days just past, had turned the countryside to mud, and the tanks were bound to the roads. Later Barton phoned the corps commander to ask for reinforcements. Middleton had nothing to offer but the 159th Engineer (Combat) Battalion, which was working on the roads. He told Barton that if he could find the engineers he could use them.

Company A, mounted on a platoon of light tanks, was ordered to open the main road to Lauterborn and Echternach which supplied the 2d Battalion (Maj. John W. Gorn). This team fought through some scattered opposition southwest of Lauterborn, dropped off a rifle platoon to hold Hill 313 (which commanded the southern approach), and moved through the village to the Company G command post, freeing twenty-five men who had been taken prisoner in the morning. By nightfall the Germans had been driven back some distance from Lauterborn (they showed no wish to close with the tanks), but the decision was made to dig in for the night alongside Company G rather than risk a drive toward Echternach in the dark. Companies A and G together now totaled about a hundred officers and men.

Early in the afternoon Company B mounted five light and five medium tanks and set out to reach Company F. At the southern entrance to Berdorf, which is strung out along the plateau road for three-quarters of a mile, the relief force ran into a part of the 1st Battalion, 423d Regiment, which opened bazooka fire from the houses. When darkness fell the Americans still were held in check, and the infantry drew back, with two tanks in support, and dug in for the night. The rest of the tanks returned to Consdorf for gasoline and ammunition.

The morning situation in the sector held by the 3d Battalion (Maj. Herman R. Rice, Jr.) had not seemed too pressing. The 320th had not reached Osweiler and the first assault at Dickweiler had been repulsed handily. But Colonel Chance sent out all of the usable tanks in Company B, 70th Tank Battalion—a total of three—to pick up a rifle squad at the 3d Battalion command post (located at Herborn) and clear the road to Osweiler. When this little force reached Osweiler, word had just come in that Dickweiler was threatened by another assault. The tanks and riflemen proceeded to run a 2,000-yard gauntlet of bursting shells along the high, exposed road to Dickweiler (probably the enemy guns beyond the Sauer were firing interdiction by the map).

The little column came in on the flank of the 2d Battalion, 320th Regiment, which was in the process of moving two companies forward in attack formation across the open ground northwest of Dickweiler. The tanks opened fire on the German flank and rear, while all the infantry weapons in the village blazed away. Thirty-five of the enemy, including one company commander, surrendered; the commander of the second company was killed, as were at least fifty soldiers. Later the 4th Infantry Division historian was able to write: "This German battalion is clearly traceable through the rest of the operation, a beaten and ineffective unit."

But the 320th Regiment, although badly shaken in its first attempts to take Dickweiler, was rapidly increasing the number of its troops in this area, spreading across the main road and encircling the two villages. About an hour after dark a message from the 3d Battalion reached the 12th Infantry command post: "Situation desperate. L and I completely surrounded." Colonel Chance took Company C, the last troops of the 12th Infantry, and sent them to the 3d Battalion command post for use on the morrow.

The 12th Infantry had rigidly obeyed the division commander's order that there should be "no retrograde movement," despite the fact that nine days earlier it had been rated "a badly decimated and weary regiment" and that on 16 December its rifle companies still were much understrength. The 42d Field Artillery Battalion in direct support of the 12th, though forced to displace several times during the day because of accurate counterbattery fire, had given the German infantry a severe jolting.

In the face of the German build-up opposite the 12th Infantry and the apparent absence of enemy activity elsewhere on the division front, General Barton began the process of regrouping to meet the attack. There was no guarantee, however, that the enemy had committed all his forces; the situation would have to develop further before the 4th Division commander could draw heavily on the two regiments not yet engaged. The 2d Battalion of the 22d Infantry, in regimental reserve, was alerted to move by truck at daylight on 17 December to the 12th Infantry command post at Junglinster, there to be joined by two tank platoons. The 9th Armored Division loaned a medium tank company from the 19th Tank Battalion, also to report to the 12th Infantry on the following morning. Three battalions of 155's and two batteries of 105-mm. howitzers began the shift north to reinforce the fifteen howitzers supporting the 12th Infantry. And the division reserve, the 4th Engineer Combat Battalion and 4th Cavalry Reconnaissance Troop, concentrated behind the 12th Infantry lines. Most important, just before midnight the corps commander telephoned General Barton that a part of the 10th Armored Division would leave Thionville, in the Third Army area, at daybreak on 17 December. The prospect must have brightened considerably at the 4th Division headquarters when the promise of this reinforcement arrived. The 4th Division would not be left to fight it out alone.

On the second day of the battle both sides committed more troops. As yet the 212th had no bridge, for the American artillery had shot out the structure erected on the 16th before it could be used. The 4th Division switched all local reserves to the threatened left flank to block further penetrations and to reinforce and relieve the garrison villages in the north. The 212th Volks Grenadier Division took a shock company from the 316th Regiment, which was still held in reserve under Seventh Army orders, and moved it into the fight. The division fusilier battalion was committed against the 12th Infantry center in an attempt to drive a wedge through at Scheidgen while a part of the 23d Festung Battalion crossed the Sauer near Girst to extend the left flank of the German attack.

During the night of 16 December searchlights had been brought down to the river opposite Echternach to aid the German engineers attempting to lay spans on the six stone piers, sole relic of the ancient bridge from whose exit the people of Echternach moved yearly in the "dancing procession" on the feast of St. Willibrord. American shellfire finally drove the enemy away from the bank, necessitating a new effort in broad daylight farther to the north. The enemy infantry would outnumber the Americans opposing them in the combat area, but on 17 December the Germans in the bridgehead would meet a far greater weight of artillery fire than they could direct against the Americans and would find it difficult to deal with American tanks. The superiority in tanks maintained by the 4th Infantry Division throughout this operation would effectively checkmate the larger numbers of the German infantry.

Fighting on 17 December took place along the axes of three principal German penetrations: on the American left flank at Berdorf, Consdorf, and Müllerthal; in the center along the Echternach-Lauterborn-Scheidgen road; and on the right in the Osweiler-Dickweiler sector.

About three hours before dawn, General Barton, concerned over his left flank, dispatched the 4th Engineer Combat Battalion and 4th Cavalry Reconnaissance Troop to Breitweiler, a small village overlooking the wishbone terminus of the Schwarz Erntz gorge and the ganglia ravine roads which branched thence into the 12th Infantry flank and rear. The Schwarz Erntz gorge lay within the 4th Infantry Division zone but in fact provided a natural cleavage between the 4th Division and the 9th Armored Division. Both units would therefore be involved in guarding the cross-corridors and ravines which stemmed from the gorge itself. The advance of the 423d Regiment across the Berdorf plateau on 16 December had reached the winding defile leading down into the gorge west of Berdorf village, there wiping out a squad of infantry and one 57-mm. antitank gun which had been placed here to block the gorge road. When the 4th Division reserves arrived in Breitweiler on the morning of 17 December the threat of a flanking move through the gorge was very real but the Americans had time to dig in.

At 0936 American observers reported a very large force moving along the bottom of the gorge, and at 1044, "5 companies counted and still coming." What had been seen were troops of the 987th Regiment, the reserve regiment of the 276th Volks Grenadier Division, then attacking in the 9th Armored Division sector. Company C, 70th Tank Battalion, now had eight tanks in running condition and these were hurried to Breitweiler to reinforce the cavalry and engineers. Two platoons from Company A, 19th Tank Battalion, which had just arrived from the 9th Armored, the assault gun and mortar platoons of the 70th Tank Battalion, a battery of 105-mm. howitzers, the reconnaissance company of the 803d Tank Destroyer Battalion, and the 2d Battalion, 8th Infantry, were hastily assembled in Colbet, a mile and a half south of Müllerthal, and organized at 1104 as Task Force Luckett (Col. James S. Luckett) .

An hour earlier the tank destroyer reconnaissance company had begun a long-range firefight but the German advance guard, despite heavy shelling from three field artillery battalions and every self-propelled piece which could be brought to bear, drove straight on to Müllerthal. Consdorf, the command post of the 2d Battalion, 12th Infantry, was left open to an attack from Müllerthal up the Hertgrund ravine. Major Gorn organized a hasty defense with a few cooks, MP's, stragglers, and one tank, but the blow did not fall. The 987th Regiment failed to emerge from the gorge and even may have withdrawn from Müllerthal, after beating off the counterattack launched there in the afternoon by elements of the 9th Armored Division.

The failure on the part of the 987th to push past Müllerthal on 17 December or to overflow from the gorge onto the flanks of the two American units remains a mystery. Possibly this failure is explained by the lack of heavy weapons needed to blast a way up from the gorge bottom. Possibly the American artillery and self-propelled guns had disorganized and disheartened the German infantry; prisoners later reported that shell fragments from the tree bursts in the bottom of the wooded gorge "sounded like falling apples" and caused heavy casualties. Whatever the reason, this enemy penetration went no further than Müllerthal. By early afternoon, however, a new threat was looming in the Consdorf area, this time from an enemy penetration on the right along the Scheidgen section of the main highroad to Echternach. This turned out to be only a patrol action and the enemy was quickly beaten off.

Early in the day Company B and ten tanks from the 70th Tank Battalion renewed the attack at Berdorf in an attempt to break through to Company F, still encircled at the opposite end of the village. This time the tanks deployed on the roads and trails south of Berdorf and moved in with five riflemen on each tank deck. The five medium tanks drove through to the northeastern edge and just before noon began shelling the Parc Hotel in the mistaken belief that it was held by the enemy. One of the Company F men had been rummaging about and had found an American flag. This was unfurled on the shattered roof. Contact thus established, an assault was launched to clear Berdorf. But the Germans defending the houses were heavily armed with bazookas and the tanks made little progress. At dark the Americans drew back to the hotel, while the Germans plastered the area with rockets, artillery, and mortar shells, lobbed in from across the river.

In the central sector Companies A and G, with five light tanks, started from Lauterborn along the road to Echternach. The enemy here was in considerable strength and had established observation posts on the ridges ringing Lauterborn and bordering the road. Heavy and accurate shellfire followed each American move. When the day ended the relief force had accomplished no more than consolidating a defensive position in Lauterborn. In Echternach Company E, 12th Infantry, had occupied a two-block strongpoint from which it harassed the German troops trying to move through the town. No large-scale assault was attempted this day, apparently because the enemy was still waiting for guns to cross the river. Troops from the 320th Regiment and fusilier battalion circled around Echternach and Lauterborn meanwhile in an attempt to cut the main road at Scheidgen. The platoon from Company A, 12th Infantry, which had been posted on Hill 313 the day before, fell back to Scheidgen and there was overwhelmed after a last message pleading for tank destroyers. At the day's end only the regimental antitank company, numbering some sixty men, stood between the enemy and the 2d Battalion command post at Consdorf.

Although the German penetrations on the left and in the center of the 12th Infantry sector deepened during the day, the situation on the right was relatively encouraging. At the break of day on 17 December Company C, the 12th Infantry reserve, moved out of Herborn en route to join the two companies beleaguered in Osweiler. As Company C worked its way through the woods south of Osweiler the left platoon ran head on into the 2d Battalion, 320th Infantry; all the platoon members were killed or captured. By some chance the two platoons on the right missed the German hive. In the meantime the 2d Battalion, 22 Infantry (Lt. Col. Thomas A. Kenan), had arrived in the 12th Infantry zone. Company F was mounted on tanks from the 19th Tank Battalion, which had just come in from the 9th Armored Division and also set out for Osweiler. This force arrived on the scene shortly after the enactment of the German ambush fought a short sharp engagement, rescued some of the prisoners from Company C, and pushed on into Osweiler.

With this reinforcement a new defensive line was organized on the hills just east of the village. The original defenders had taken a large bag of prisoners the previous day; these were sent back to Herborn with a tank platoon. In midafternoon the remaining companies of the 2d Battalion, 22d Infantry, started for Osweiler, advancing in column through the woods which topped a ridge line running southwest of the village. While the American column moved in a northeasterly direction, a German column, probably a battalion in strength suddenly intersected the 2d Battalion line of march. In the fire fight which followed the 2d Battalion companies became separated, but the early winter darkness soon ended the skirmish. The Americans dug in for the night, and the Germans passed on toward Scheidgen.

In Dickweiler the troops of the 3d Battalion, 12th Infantry, had been harassed by small forays from the woods above the village. The three tanks which had come up the evening before, and very effective fire by American batteries, put an end to these German efforts. Thus both Osweiler and Dickweiler remained tight in American hands. Toward the close of day Company C of the 12th Infantry took position on some high ground between and slightly south of the two villages, thus extending the line here on the right.

General Barton's headquarters saw the situation on the evening of 17 December as follows. The 3d Battalion and its reinforcements had "a semblance of a line" to meet further penetration in the vicinity of Osweiler and Dickweiler. On the opposite flank things were temporarily under control, with Task Force Luckett not yet seriously engaged and the enemy advance thus far checked at Müllerthal. However, there was a present danger that the large German force might turn the 4th Division flank by a successful attack through the 9th Armored Division blocking position at Waldbillig. All that could be said of the 12th Infantry center was that the situation was fluid, for here the road junction at Scheidgen was in enemy hands and German detachments were on the loose.

Across the river at the headquarters of the 212th Volks Grenadier Division there was little realization of the extent to which the American center had been dented. General Sensfuss told his superiors that the 212th had made little progress beyond completing the encirclement of Echternach. Despite the complete surprise won by the 212th on 16 December, it had been unable to effect either a really deep penetration or extensive disorganization in the 12th Infantry zone. With the close of the second day it may be said that the German opportunity to exploit the initial surprise and attendant tactical gains commenced to fade.

On the morning of 17 December the 10th Armored Division (General Morris) had moved out of Thionville for Luxembourg, the first step (although at the time not realized) which General Patton's Third Army would make to intervene in the battle of the Ardennes. General Morris drove ahead of his troops and reported to General Middleton at Bastogne. The VIII Corps commander originally had intended to use a part of the 10th Armored in direct support of the 28th Division, but now he instructed Morris to send one combat command to the Bastogne area and to commit the remainder of the 10th Armored with the 4th Infantry Division in a counterattack to drive the Germans back over the Sauer. General Middleton regarded the German advance against the southern shoulder of his corps as potentially dangerous, both to the corps and to the command and communications center at Luxembourg City. There was, of course, no means by which the VIII Corps commander could know that the Seventh Army scheme of maneuver was limited to a swing only as far as Mersch, eight miles north of the city.

General Morris left Bastogne and met the 4th Infantry Division commander in Luxembourg. The two were of one mind on the need for counterattack tactics and arranged that CCA (Brig. Gen. Edwin W. Piburn), the leading combat command, should make an immediate drive to the north between the Schwarz Erntz gorge and the main Echternach-Luxembourg road. CCA made good speed on the 75-mile run from Thionville, but the leading armor did not arrive in the 12th Infantry area until late in the afternoon of 17 December. Apparently some troops went at once into the line, but the actual counterattack was postponed until the next morning. Then, so the plan read, CCA would advance in three task forces: one through the Schwarz Erntz gorge; one on the Consdorf-Berdorf road; and the third through Scheidgen to Echternach. The infantry to the front were alerted for their role in the combined attack and half-tracks with radios were moved close to the line of departure as relay stations in the tank-infantry communications net.

The counterattack moved off on the morning of 18 December in a thick winter fog. On the left, Task Force Chamberlain (Lt. Col. Thomas C. Chamberlain) dispatched a small tank-infantry team from Breitweiler into the gorge. The Schwarz Erntz, taking its name from the rushing stream twisting along its bottom, is a depression lying from three to five hundred feet below the surrounding tableland. At several points canyonlike cliffs rise sheer for a hundred feet. The floor of the gorge is strewn with great boulders; dense patches of woods line the depression and push down to the edge of the stream. In time of peace the gorge of the Schwarz Erntz offered a picturesque "promenade" for holiday visitors in the resort hotels at Berdorf and Beaufort, with "bancs de repos" at convenient intervals. In December 1944, the gorge represented a formidable military obstacle, difficult of traverse for both foot troops and vehicles, capable of defense by only a few.

The entrance to the gorge was so narrow that the tanks had to advance in single file, and only the lead tank could fire. The accompanying infantry were under constant bullet fire; and when the lead tank was immobilized by an antitank projectile some time was required to maneuver the rest of the column around it. With every yard forward, bazooka, bullet, and mortar fire increased, but the enemy remained hidden. Finally, the Americans halted near the "T" in the gorge road just south of Müllerthal.

It was clear that to capture Müllerthal, or even to block the southern exit from the gorge, the surrounding hills and tableland had to be won. The infantry and engineers belonging to Task Force Luckett were given this mission, advancing in the afternoon to bypass Müllerthal on the west and seize the wooded bluff standing above the gorge road north of Müllerthal. Tanks pumped seven hundred rounds into the woods to shake the Germans there, but little time was left in the short winter day and the foot soldiers only got across the Müllerthal-Waldbillig road.

The center task force (Lt. Col. Miles L. Standish), which had been assigned to help the 2d Battalion, 12th Infantry, clear the enemy from Berdorf, had little better success. Elements of Task Force Standish were strafed by a pair of German planes but moved into Berdorf against only desultory opposition and before noon made contact with the two companies and six tanks already in the village. Then the German gunners laid down smoke and a bitter three-hour barrage, disabled some tanks and half-tracks, and drove the Americans to cover. When the fire lifted the attack was resumed, but the enemy fought stubbornly for each house. This house-to-house assault gained only seventy-five yards before darkness intervened. Meanwhile the sixty-some members of Company F remained in the Parc Hotel, whose roof and upper story had been smashed in by German shelling. Pole charges or bazooka rounds had blasted a gaping hole in one side of the hotel, but thus far only one man had been wounded. Morale was good, bolstered superbly by the company cook who did his best to emulate the *"cuisine soignée"* promised in the hotel brochures by preparing hot meals in the basement and serving the men at their firing posts.

While part of Task Force Standish was engaged in Berdorf, another team attacked through heavy underbrush toward Hill 329, east of Berdorf, which overlooked the road to Echternach. Despite the presence of the tanks, which here could maneuver off the road, the infantry were checked halfway to their objective by cross fire from machine guns flanking the slope and artillery fire from beyond the Sauer. About forty men were wounded, creating a problem for evacuation by this small force.

The third task force from CCA, 10th Armored (led by Lt. Col J. R. Riley), made good progress in its attack along the Scheidgen-Lauterborn axis. Scheidgen was retaken early in the afternoon virtually without a fight (the German battalion which had seized the village had already moved on toward the south). Five tanks and two companies of the 159th Engineer Combat Battalion, which Barton had located on the road job as promised by Middleton, then launched a surprise attack against the Germans on Hill 313, overlooking the road to Lauterborn. The tanks rolled down the road from Scheidgen with their motors cut and caught the enemy on the slopes while the engineers moved in with marching fire. But a thick winter fog rolled in before the Americans could occupy the hill. Other elements of Task Force Riley meanwhile had advanced to the mill beyond Lauterborn where the command post of Company G was located. Two tanks and two squads of riflemen continued along the main road to the hat factory at the southwestern edge of Echternach where Company E, 12th Infantry, had established itself. Here the company was found to be in good spirits, supplied with plenty of food and wine, and holding its own to the tune of over a hundred of the enemy killed. The tank commander offered to cover the withdrawal of Company E from the city, but Capt. Paul H. Dupuis, the senior officer in Echternach, refused on the ground that General Barton's "no retrograde movement" order of 16 December was still in effect. As darkness settled in, the small relief force turned back to the mill north of Lauterborn, promising to return on the morrow with more troops.

While CCA, 10th Armored, gave weight to the 4th Division counterattack, General Barton tried to strengthen the 12th Infantry right flank in the Osweiler-Dickweiler sector. The 2d Battalion, 22d Infantry, which had met the German column in the woods west of Osweiler the day before, headed for the village on the morning of 18 December. The last word to reach Osweiler had been that the 2d Battalion was under serious attack in the woods; when the battalion neared the village the American tanks there opened fire, under suspicion that this was a German force. After two hours, and some casualties, a patrol bearing a white flag worked its way in close enough for recognition. Osweiler now had a garrison of one tank company and four understrength rifle companies.

As the American reinforcements stiffened the right flank and the armored task forces grappled to wrest the initiative from the enemy on the left, German troops widened and deepened the dent in the 12th Infantry center, shouldering their way southward between Scheidgen and Osweiler. The burden of this advance was carried by battalions of the 320th Regiment (which explains the relaxing of pressure in the Osweiler-Dickweiler area), and the advance guard of the 316th Regiment which General Sensfuss had pried from the Seventh Army reserve by reporting the arrival of the 10th Armored Division.

The first appearance of any enemy force deep in the center occurred near Maisons Lelligen, a collection of two or three houses on the edge of a large wood northwest of Herborn. The 12th Infantry cannon company was just moving up to a new position when fire opened from the wood. The drivers and gunners dived for cover and returned fire. After a few minutes of this exchange Sgt. J. C. Kolinski got up, ran back to a truck, fixed a round, and fired it from a howitzer still coupled to the truck. This idea caught on and other men started to serve the howitzers, awkward as the technique was, some firing at ranges as short as sixty yards. Ammunition at the pieces ultimately gave out, but a volunteer raced to the rear of the column and drove an ammunition truck, its canvas smoldering from German bullets, up to the gun crews. The action lasted for over three hours At last two howitzers were manhandled into a position from which they could cover the company; guns and vehicles were laboriously turned around in the mud, and the company withdrew.

Farther to the west another part of the German force which had come from Scheidgen surrounded the rear headquarters of the 2d Battalion, 22d Infantry, and a platoon of towed tank destroyers in Geyershof. Tanks en route to Osweiler got word of this situation, picked up twenty-five cannoneers from the 176th Field Artillery Battalion, and intervened in the fight. Covered by this counterattack the battalion headquarters withdrew to Herborn.

The engagements at Geyershof and Maisons Lelligen were comparatively minor affairs, involving only small forces, but German prisoners later reported that their losses had been severe at both these points. This fact, combined with the American pressure on either shoulder of the penetration area, may explain why the enemy failed to continue the push in the center as 18 December ended.

The net day's operations amounted to a standoff. The Americans had strengthened the Osweiler-Dickweiler position, but the Germans had extended their penetration in the 12th Infantry center. Elsewhere neither side clearly held the field. Enemy artillery had interdicted many of the roads in the area and had been very effective at Berdorf. American artillery, now increased in the 12th Infantry zone, gave as good support as communications permitted and succeeded in destroying a pontoon bridge at the Echternach site before it could be put in use. Both sides were forced to rely largely upon radio communication, but it would appear that the Germans had particular difficulty: prisoners reported that "nobody seems to know where anybody else is."

American intelligence officers estimated on 17 December that the enemy had a superiority in numbers of three to one; by the end of 18 December the balance was somewhat restored. Losses and stragglers, however, had reduced the American infantry companies, already understrength at the opening of the battle. The two companies in Berdorf reported a combined strength of seventy-nine men, while the 2d Battalion of the 22d Infantry listed an average of only sixty in each company. The American makeweight would have to be its armor. Lacking tanks and self-propelled artillery, the 212th Volks Grenadier Division had to rely on the infantry. Accordingly, the 316th Infantry began to cross the Sauer, moving up behind the center of the parent division.

During the night of 18-19 December the 9th Armored Division withdrew to a new line of defense on the left of the 4th Infantry Division. Actually the 9th Armored did not abandon the right flank anchor at Waldbillig and so continued direct contact with the friendly forces deployed near the Waldbillig-Müllerthal road. The problem of dealing with the 987th Regiment and clearing the enemy out of the Schwarz Erntz gorge, or containing him there, was left to the 4th Division and CCA, 10th Armored. As a result, these two units faced four German regiments in the 12th Infantry sector.

Of the 4th Division, it must be remembered, four rifle battalions still were retained on guard along the twenty miles of the division front south of the battle area.

When the Americans resumed the counterattack early on 19 December Task Force Luckett made another attempt to bring forward the extreme left flank in the gorge sector. As before, the maneuver was a flanking movement designed to seize the high ground overlooking Müllerthal. Troops of the 2d Battalion, 8th Infantry (Lt. Col. George Mabry), with tanks and armored field artillery firing in support, first attacked east from Waldbillig to take the wooded nose around which looped the Waldbillig-Müllerthal road. This advance was made across open fields and was checked by extremely heavy shellfire. Next Mabry shifted his attack to the right so as to bring the infantry through the draw which circled the nose. Company E, which had about seventy men and was the strongest in the battalion, led off. By now the German artillery was ranged inaccurately. The casualties suffered by Company E cannot be numbered, but have been reported as the most severe sustained by any company of the 4th Division in the battle of the Ardennes. Casualties among the officers left a lieutenant who had just joined the company in command. Despite its losses Company E drove on, clearing the Germans from the lower slopes before the recall order was given.

The division commander now called off the attack and assigned Task Force Luckett the mission of denying the enemy the use of the road net at Müllerthal, a task which could be accomplished in less costly fashion. Colonel Luckett deployed his troops along the ridge southwest of the Müllerthal-Waldbillig road, and a log abatis wired with mines and covered by machine guns was erected to block the valley road south of Müllerthal. Task Force Chamberlain, whose tanks had given fire support to Task Force Luckett, moved during the afternoon to a backstop position near Consdorf.

The tank-infantry counterattack by Task Forces Standish and Riley in the Berdorf and Echternach areas also resumed. The enemy resisted wherever encountered, but spent most of the daylight hours regrouping in wooded draws and hollows and bringing reinforcements across the river, stepping up his artillery fire the while. Intense fog shielded all this activity. Apparently the assembly of the 316th Regiment behind the 212th Volks Grenadier Division center was completed during the day. A few rocket projectors and guns were ferried over at the civilian ferry site above Echternach, and about the middle of the afternoon a bridge was finished at Edingen, where the 320th Regiment had crossed on 16 December. The American counterattack on the 19th, then, first would be opposed by infantry and infantry weapons, but would meet heavier metal and some armor as the day ended.

At Berdorf a team from Task Force Standish and a platoon of armored engineers set to work mopping up the enemy infantry who had holed up in houses on the north side of the village. This proved to be slow work. First a ten-pound pole charge would be exploded against a wall or house; then a tank would clank up to the gap and blast away; finally the infantry would go to work with grenades and their shoulder weapons. At dark the Germans had lost a few houses, but were in the process of being reinforced by Nebelwerfers and armored vehicles.

Other troops of Task Force Standish returned to the attack at Hill 329, on the Berdorf-Echternach road, where they had been checked by flanking fire the previous day. Sharp assaults destroyed the German machine gun positions and the attack reached the ridge leading to Hill 329. Then the advance had to be halted short of the objective in order to free the tanks and half-tracks for use in evacuating the large number of wounded. This ambulance convoy was en route to Consdorf, in the late afternoon, when a radio message reported that the Germans had cut the road north of Consdorf and bazooka'd two tanks on their way back from Berdorf for ammunition. The wounded were left in Berdorf and the task force tanks, hampered by milling civilian refugees, began a night-long firefight with the 2d Battalion, 423d Regiment, which had concentrated to capture Consdorf.

Task Force Riley sent tanks carrying infantry into the edge of Echternach on the morning of 19 December. There they re-established contact with Company E and covered the withdrawal of outlying detachments to the hat factory. The 12th Infantry commander already had given permission for Company E to evacuate Echternach, but communications were poor — indeed word that the tanks had reached Company E did not arrive at the 12th Infantry command post until four hours after the event — and the relief force turned back to Lauterborn alone. The tanks were hardly out of sight before the Germans began an assault on the hat factory with bazookas, demolition charges, and an armored assault gun. Two volunteers were dispatched in a jeep to make a run for Lauterborn, carrying word that enemy tanks were moving into the city and asking for "help and armor." The two, last of the Americans to come out of Echternach, made the run safely despite direct fire aimed by the German assault gun. At Lauterborn, however, they were told that the tanks could not be risked in Echternach after dark. American artillery observers by the failing light saw "troops pouring into Echternach." Orders were radioed to Company E (a fresh battery for its radio had been brought in by the tanks) to fight its way out during the night. It was too late. The defenders had been split up by the German assault and the company commander had to report that he could not organize a withdrawal. Through the night of 19-20 December Riley's tanks waited on the road just north of Lauterborn, under orders from the Commanding General, CCA, not to attempt a return through the dark to Echternach.

Although the fighting on 19 December had been severe on the American left, a general lull prevailed along the rest of the line. The enemy made no move to push deeper in the center. The combat engineers in Scheidgen returned to Hill 313 and occupied it without a fight. A few small affrays occurred in the Osweiler-Dickweiler sector, but that was all. By nightfall the situation seemed much improved — despite the increased pressure on the 4th Division companies closely invested in the north. Both flanks were nailed down, and the German attack seemed to have lost momentum.

Elsewhere on the VIII Corps front the enemy advance was picking up speed and reinforcements were rolling forward to widen the avenues of penetration behind the panzers. Reports that two new German divisions were en route to attack the 109th Infantry and 9th Armored Division had reached General Morris, coming by way of the 12th Army Group intelligence agencies. If this additional weight should be thrown against the thin American line immediately to the north of the 4th Infantry Division, there was every likelihood that the line would break.

It was imperative that the line be held. Troops of the Third Army were already on the move north, there to form the cutting edge of a powerful thrust into the southern flank of the German advance. The 109th Infantry, the 9th Armored Division, the 4th Infantry Division, and CCA, 10th Armored Division, had to win both the time and the space required for the assembly of the American counterattack forces. General Patton, commanding the Third Army, to which the VIII Corps was now assigned, gave General Morris a provisional corps on 19 December, composed of the

10th Armored Division, the 9th Armored, the 109th Infantry, and the 4th Infantry Division. Morris, now charged with unifying defensive measures while the Third Army counterattack forces gathered behind this cover, alerted CCA, 10th Armored Division, early on the morning of 20 December, for employment as a mobile reserve. Morris had already dispatched one of his armored infantry battalions to help the 9th Armored in an attack intended to retake Waldbillig. Task Force Chamberlain had been placed in reserve the previous day, but it was not immediately feasible to withdraw the two task forces that were still engaged alongside the 4th Division, for it would take General Barton's division a few hours to reorganize on a new line and plug the gaps left by the outgoing armored units.

While General Morris made plans to hold the ground needed as a springboard for the projected counterattack, General Beyer, commanding the German LXXX Corps, prepared to meet an American riposte. Higher German headquarters had anticipated the appearance of some American reinforcements opposite the LXXX Corps as early as the third day of the operation. Intervention by elements of the 10th Armored Division on 18 December, as a result, was viewed only as the prelude to a sustained and forceful American attempt to regain the initiative. It cannot now be determined whether the German agents (V—Leute), who undoubtedly were operating behind American lines, had correctly diagnosed the beginning of the Third Army shift toward Luxembourg and Belgium, or, if so, whether they had been able to communicate with the German field headquarters.

In any event the LXXX Corps commander decided on the night of 19 December to place his corps on the defensive, his estimate of the situation being as follows. His two divisions generally had reached the line designated as the LXXX Corps objective. The force available was insufficient to continue the attack. On the north flank there was a dangerous and widening gap between the LXXX Corps and the LXXXV Corps. The supply situation was poor and could become critical, in part because of the Allied air attacks at the Rhine crossings, in part because of the Allied success—even during poor flying weather—in knocking out transportation and forward supply dumps in the Trier-Bitburg area. A large-scale American counterattack against the LXXX Corps could be predicted, but lacking aerial reconnaissance German intelligence could not expect to determine the time or strength of such an attack with any accuracy. General Beyer's orders for 20 December, therefore, called upon the 212th and 276th Volks Grenadier Divisions to crush the small points of resistance where American troops still contended behind the German main forces, continue local attacks and counterattacks in order to secure more favorable ground for future defense, and close up along a coordinated corps front in preparation for the coming American onslaught.

On 20 December there was savage fighting in the 4th Infantry Division zone despite the fact that both of the combatants were in the process of going over to the defensive. The 4th Division and 10th Armored sought to disengage their advance elements and regroup along a stronger main line of resistance, and the enemy fought to dislodge the American foothold in Berdorf and Echternach. At the same time elements of the 276th Volks Grenadier Division struck through Waldbillig, the point of contact between the 4th Division and the 9th Armored, in an attempt to push the right wing of the LXXX Corps forward to a point where the road net leading east to the Sauer might be more easily denied the gathering American forces.

The team from Task Force Standish had made little progress in its house-to-house battle in Berdorf. Company F, 12th Infantry, retained its position in the Parc

Hotel, despite a German demolition charge that exploded early in the morning of the 20th and blew in part of one wall. After a short melee in the darkness American hand grenades discouraged the assault at this breach and the enemy withdrew to a line of foxholes which had been dug during the night close to the hotel. When the fight died down one of the defenders found that the blast had opened a sealed annex in the basement, the hiding place of several score bottles of fine liquor and a full barrel of beer. Lieutenant Leake refused permission to sample this cache, a decision he would regret when, after withdrawal from Berdorf, he and twenty-one of his men were returned to the foxhole line with neither their coats nor blankets.

At daylight on 20 December the 1st Battalion, 423d Regiment, which had been brought in from the Lauterborn area, initiated a counterattack against the team from Task Force Standish at the edge of Berdorf and recovered all the ground lost during the previous two days. The American artillery forward observer's tank was crippled by a bazooka and the radio put out of commission, but eventually word reached the supporting artillery, which quickly drove the enemy to cover. Although the evacuation of Berdorf was part of the 4th Division plan for redressing its line, the actual withdrawal was none too easy. The Germans had cut the road back to Consdorf; so the right team of Task Force Standish was withdrawn from the attack on Hill 329 and spent most of the afternoon clearing an exit for the men and vehicles in Berdorf. Finally, a little after dark, Companies B and F (12th Infantry), ten engineers, and four squads of armored infantry loaded onto eleven tanks and six half-tracks and made their way past burning buildings to the new 4th Division line north and east of Consdorf.

The elements of Task Force Riley, which had waited outside of Lauterborn through the night of 19-20 December in vain expectation that Company E would attempt to break out of Echternach, received a radio message at 0823 that Company E was surrounded by tanks and could not get out. Through the morning rumors and more rumors poured over the American radio nets, but there was no sign of Company E. About noon Colonel Riley agreed to send a few tanks in one final effort to reach the infantry in Echternach, provided that the 12th Infantry would give his tanks some protection. Company G, therefore, was assigned this task. At 1330 a report reached the 12th Infantry that Company E had gotten out. Half an hour later this report was denied; now a message said the company was coming out in small groups. Finally, in the late afternoon, Colonel Chance sent a call over the radio relay system: "Where is Riley?" Thirty minutes later the answer came back from CCA: a section of tanks and some riflemen were fighting at the outskirts of Echternach.

This was the last effort. Night had come, Echternach was swarming with Germans, and the 10th Armored Division headquarters had ordered all its teams to reassemble behind the 4th Division lines preparatory to moving "in any direction." Since most of Task Force Riley by this time had reverted to the reserve, Lauterborn, the base for operations against Echternach, was abandoned. Company G, now some forty men, and the last of Riley's tanks withdrew to the new main line of resistance. It is probable that the Americans in Echternach were forced to surrender late on 20 December. General Sensfuss had determined to erase the stubborn garrison and led the 212th Fusilier Battalion and some assault guns (or tanks) in person to blast the Americans loose. The commander of the 212th Volks Grenadier Division received a slight wound but had the satisfaction of taking the surrender of the troublesome Americans, about 111 officers and men from Company E, plus 21 men belonging to

Company H. On this same day the Company F outpost which had held out at Birkelt Farm since 16 December capitulated.

Finally the enemy had control of most of the northern section of the road net between the Sauer River and Luxembourg—but it was too late. The new American line, running from Dickweiler through Osweiler, Hill 313, Consdorf, to south of Müllerthal, was somewhat weak in the center but solidly anchored at the flanks. The German attack through the 9th Armored sector beyond Waldbillig had been checked. At the opposite end of the line enemy guns and mortars worked feverishly to bring down Dickweiler around the ears of the defenders, but the Americans could not be shelled out. (When one blast threw a commode and sink from a second story down on the rear deck of a tank the crew simply complained that no bathing facilities had been provided.) At Bech, behind the American center, General Barton now had the 3d Battalion, 22d Infantry, in reserve, having further stripped the 4th Division right. And in and around Eisenborn, CCA, 10th Armored Division, was assembling to counter any German attack.

Barton's troops and Morris' tanks had brought the 212th and the 276th Volks Grenadier Division to a halt, had then withdrawn most of their advance detachments successfully, and now held a stronger position on a shortened line. The southern shoulder of the German counteroffensive had jammed.

Southern Flank – A Summing Up

The Seventh Army had thrown three of its four divisions into the surprise attack at the Sauer River on 16 December. The Americans had met this onslaught with two infantry regiments (the 12th and 109th), an armored infantry battalion (the 60th), and an understrength tank battalion (the 70th), these units and others attached making the total approximately division strength. The stubborn and successful defense of towns and villages close to the Sauer had blocked the road net, so essential to movement in this rugged country, and barred a quick sweep into the American rear areas.

In like manner the enemy had failed in the quick accomplishment of one of his major tasks, that is, overrunning the American artillery positions or at the least forcing the guns to withdraw to positions from which they could no longer interdict the German bridge sites. General Barton, it may be added, had refused absolutely to permit the artillery to move rearward. The failure to open the divisional bridges over the Sauer within the first twenty-four hours had forced the German infantry to continue to fight without their accustomed heavy weapons support even while American reinforcements were steadily reducing the numerical edge possessed by the attacker. Further, the German inability to meet the American tanks with tanks or heavy antimechanized means gave the American rifleman an appreciable moral superiority (particularly toward the end of the battle) over his German counterpart.

It should be added that Seventh Army divisions suffered as the stepchild of the Ardennes offensive, not only when bridge trains failed to arrive or proved inadequate but also in the niggardly issue of heavy weapons and artillery ammunition, particularly chemical shells. Perhaps these German divisions faced from the onset the insoluble tactical dilemma, insoluble at least if the outnumbered defenders staunchly held their ground when cut off and surrounded. Strength sufficient to achieve a quick, limited penetration the German divisions possessed, so long as the assault forces did not stop to clean out the village centers of resistance. Strength to exploit these points of penetration failed when the village centers of resistance were bypassed.

Successful the American defense in the Sauer sector had been, but costly too. In six days (through 21 December, after which the Americans would begin their counterattack) the units here on the southern shoulder lost over 2,000 killed, wounded, or missing. German casualties probably ran somewhat higher, but whether substantially so is questionable. In any case, about 800 German prisoners were taken and nonbattle casualties must have been severe, for German commanders later reported that the number of exposure and trench foot cases had been unusually high, the result of the village fighting in which the defender had the greater protection from cold and damp.

Chapter XI. The 1st SS Panzer Division's Dash Westward, and Operation Greif

The bulk of the fourteen divisions under First U.S. Army command on 16 December were deployed north of the Belgian Ardennes. Behind them, roughly in the triangle formed by the cities of Liège, Verviers, and Spa, lay the supply installations built up through the autumn to support the advance toward the Rhine. At Spa, which had served the German Emperor as headquarters in World War I, the First Army had established its command post surrounded on every side by service installations, supply dumps, and depots. Liège, twenty miles northwest of Spa, was one of the greatest American supply centers on the Continent. Verviers, an important and densely stocked railhead lay eleven miles north of Spa.

General Hodges' First Army headquarters, set up in the déclassé resort hotels and casinos of the once fashionable watering place, was remote from sound of battle on the morning of 16 December, but in a matter of hours the slashing thrust of the 1st SS Panzer Division roughly altered its ordered existence. The nature of the ground along which the Americans would attempt to defend the myriad headquarters and service installations, railheads, and depots, must be explained. Southeast of Spa runs the Amblève River, the creation of a series of tributaries flowing south from the springs and swamps of the rugged Hohes Venn. The Amblève, bending westward, is joined by the Salm, a north-flowing tributary, at the town of Trois Ponts, then angles northwest until it meets the Ourthe River and finally the Meuse at Liège. The Amblève and the Salm are narrow and rather minor streams; the valleys through which they course are deep-cut, with long stretches of steep and rocky walls. A line on the map tracing the course of the Amblève River and its initial tributaries will pass from northeast to southwest through three important bridgeheads and road centers, Malmédy, Stavelot, and Trois Ponts. From the first two, roads led north to Spa, Verviers, and Liège. Although both Malmédy and Stavelot were administrative centers of importance (Stavelot contained the First Army map depot with some 2,500,000 maps), the most important item hereabouts was the great store of gasoline, over two million gallons, in dumps just north of the two towns.

The 1st SS Panzer Division (SS Oberfuehrer Wilhelm Mohnke) was the strongest fighting unit in the Sixth Panzer Army. Undiluted by any large influx of untrained Luftwaffe or Navy replacements, possessed of most of its T/O&E equipment, it had an available armored strength on 16 December of about a hundred tanks, equally divided between the Mark IV and the Panther, plus forty-two Tiger tanks belonging to the 501st SS Panzer Detachment. The road net in the Sixth Panzer Army would not permit the commitment of the 1st SS Panzer as a division, even if two of the five roads allocated the army were employed. The division was therefore divided into four columns or march groups: the first, commanded by Colonel Peiper, contained the bulk of the 1st Panzer Regiment and thus represented the armored spearhead of the division; the second was made up from the division's Reconnaissance Battalion; the third and fourth each comprised armored infantry and attached heavy weapons; the heavy Tiger detachment was left to be fed into the advance as occasion warranted.

Kampfgruppe Peiper on the Move

On the morning of 16 December Colonel Peiper journeyed to the advance command post of the 12th Volks Grenadier Division, whose troops were supposed to make the gap in the lines of the American 99th Infantry Division north of the Schnee Eifel through which his armor would be committed. To Peiper's disgust the infantry failed in their assigned task and the day wore on with Peiper's column still waiting on the roads to the rear. The blown bridge northwest of Losheim increased the delay; for some reason the engineers failed to start repair work here until noon or later. This was not the end. In midafternoon the horse-drawn artillery regiment of the 12th Volks Grenadier Division was ordered up to support the infantry, hopelessly clogging the approaches to the bridge. Peiper himself took over the job of trying to straighten out this traffic Jam but more time was lost. It was not until 1930 that the armored advance guard was able to reach Losheim, the village which gave its name to the gap at the northern terminus of the Schnee Eifel. At this time Peiper received a radio message saying that the next railroad overpass was out, that the engineers would not get up in time to make repairs, and that he must turn west to Lanzerath in the 3d Parachute Division sector. This move was completed by midnight, although a number of tanks and other vehicles were lost to mines and antitank fire while making the turnabout at Losheim. At Lanzerath Colonel Peiper discovered that the 3d Parachute also had failed to punch any sizable hole through the American line, although the 1st SS Panzer Division had taken Krewinkel and so helped the 3d Parachute forward. Irritated by the hours frittered away, Peiper took an infantry battalion, put two of his Panther tanks at the point of the column, and at 0400 attacked toward Honsfeld. Opposition had evaporated. Honsfeld was surprised and taken with ease.

The original route assigned Peiper's kampfgruppe ran west to Schoppen. This was a poor road, bogged with mud from the winter rains, and since the 12th SS Panzer Division had not yet come up Peiper pre-empted the latter's paved route through Büllingen. Also he had been told that there were gasoline stores in Büllingen, and a great deal of fuel had been burned during the jockeying around Losheim. Sure enough, the gasoline was found as predicted. Using American prisoners as labor, the Germans refueled their tanks. They scooped up much other booty here and destroyed a number of artillery planes on a nearby field. When American gunners commenced to shell the village the column was already moving on, although it suffered some casualties. By this time Peiper and his staff believed that the breakthrough was complete; no American troops appeared on the sensitive north flank, and only an occasional jeep scuttled away to the west of the column.

It was between noon and one o'clock of 17 December, on the road between Modersheid and Ligneuville, that the German advance guard ran into an American truck convoy moving south from Malmédy. This was ill-fated Battery B of the 285th Field Artillery Observation Battalion. The convoy was shot up and the advance guard rolled on, leaving the troops to the rear to deal with the Americans who had taken to the woods and ditches. About two hours after, or so the dazed survivors later recalled, the Americans who had been rounded up were marched into a field where, at a signal, they were shot down by machine gun and pistol fire. A few escaped by feigning death, but the wounded who moved or screamed were sought out and shot through the head. At least eighty-six Americans were massacred here. This was not the first killing of unarmed prisoners chargeable to Kampfgruppe Peiper on 17 December. Irrefutable evidence shows that nineteen unarmed Americans were shot down at Honsfeld and fifty at Büllingen.

The Malmédy massacre would have repercussions reaching far wider than one might expect of a single battlefield atrocity in a long and bitter war. This "incident" undoubtedly stiffened the will of the American combatants (although a quantitative assessment of this fact is impossible); it would be featured in the war crimes trials as an outstanding example of Nazi contempt for the accepted rules of war; and it would serve a United States Senator as a stepping-stone toward a meteoric career. But the Malmédy massacre and the other murders of 17 December did not complete the list chargeable to Peiper and the troops of the 1st SS Panzer Division. By 20 December Peiper's command had murdered approximately 350 American prisoners of war and at least 100 unarmed Belgian civilians, this total derived from killings at twelve different locations along Peiper's line of march.

So far as can be determined the Peiper killings represent the only organized and directed murder of prisoners of war by either side during the Ardennes battle. The commander of the Sixth SS Panzer Army took oath in the trials of 1946 that, acting on Hitler's orders, he issued a directive stating that the German troops should be preceded "by a wave of terror and fright and that no human inhibitions should be shown." There is conflicting testimony as to whether the orders finally reaching Peiper specifically enjoined the shooting of prisoners. There is no question, however, that some of Peiper's subordinates accepted the killing of prisoners as a command and that on at least one occasion Peiper himself gave such an order. Why Peiper's command gained the bestial distinction of being the only unit to kill prisoners in the course of the Ardennes is a subject of surmise. Peiper had been an adjutant to Heinrich Himmler and as a battalion commander in Russia is alleged to have burned two villages and killed all the inhabitants. The veteran SS troops he led in the Ardennes had long experience on the Eastern Front where brutality toward prisoners of war was a commonplace. On the other hand Peiper's formation was well in the van of the German attack and was thus in position to carry out the orders for the "wave of terror" tactic—which might be excused, or so Peiper claimed, by the rapid movement of his kampfgruppe and its inability to retain prisoners under guard.

The speed with which the news of the Malmédy massacre reached the American frontline troops is amazing but, in the emotional climate of 17 December, quite understandable. The first survivors of the massacre were picked up by a patrol from the 291st Engineer Combat Battalion about 1430 on that date. The inspector general of the First Army learned of the shootings three or four hours later. Yet by the late evening of the 17th the rumor that the enemy was killing prisoners had reached as far as the forward American divisions. There were American commanders who orally expressed the opinion that all SS troops should be killed on sight and there is some indication that in isolated cases express orders for this were given. It is probable that Germans who attempted to surrender in the days immediately after the 17th ran a greater risk than would have been the case during the autumn campaign. There is no evidence, however, that American troops took advantage of orders, implicit or explicit, to kill their SS prisoners.

The point of Peiper's column reached Ligneuville sometime before 1300, in time to eat the lunch which had been prepared for an American detachment stationed in the village. Here the road divided, the north fork going to Malmédy, the western leading on to Stavelot. Although it was agreed that the armored columns should have considerable leeway in choosing the exact routes they would follow, a general boundary line gave the 1st SS Panzer Division the southern part of the zone assigned the I SS Panzer, while the 12th SS Panzer Division advanced in the northern sector. The 12th SS Panzer Division, of course, was still back at the line of scrimmage, nor would it break into the clear for many hours to come, but all this was unknown to Peiper. He did know that the Americans thus far had shown no disposition to throw punches at his north flank. Furthermore, the 3d Parachute Division had a clear field to follow up and protect his line of communications, while the 2d Panzer Division — so Peiper understood — was moving fast in the south and roughly abreast of his own advance.

Peiper had a precisely defined mission: his kampfgruppe was to seize the Meuse River crossings at Huy, making full use of the element of surprise and driving west without regard to any flank protection. The importance of this mission had been underlined during the initial briefing at the command post of the 1st SS Panzer Division on 14 December when Peiper had been assured that his command would play the decisive role in the coming counteroffensive. There seems to have been some hope expressed among the higher German staffs that the advance guard elements of both the 1st SS Panzer Division and the Fifth Panzer Army's 2d Panzer Division would reach the Meuse within twenty-four hours of the time of commitment. The distance by road, on the 1st SS Panzer Division axis, was between 125 and 150 kilometers (about 75 to 95 miles). Peiper himself had made a test run on 11 December to prove that it was possible for single tanks to travel 80 kilometers (50 miles) in one night. Whether an entire tank column could maintain this rate of progress for a day and a night in enemy country and on the sharp turns and grades of the Ardennes road net was a matter of guesswork.

Whatever schedule Peiper was using, if indeed he had any precise timetable in mind, the kampfgruppe of the 1st SS Panzer Division was making good progress and the element of surprise, as shown by the lack of any formal resistance, was working to German advantage. His path lay straight ahead, through Stavelot, Trois Ponts, Werbomont, Ouffet, Seny, Huy — a distance of some 50 miles, from where the head of the 1st SS Panzer Division column stood in Ligneuville, to Huy and the Meuse. Only a few short miles to the north lay Malmédy and the road to Spa and Liège. Malmédy and the Meuse crossing sites in the vicinity of Liège, however, were in the zone assigned the 12th SS Panzer Division. Peiper stuck to his knitting.

About 1400 the column resumed the march, taking some time to negotiate the sharp turns and narrow streets in Ligneuville. At the western exit the point of the column ran onto the trains belonging to CCB, 9th Armored Division, which was preparing to move east in support of the combat command then engaged in the St. Vith sector. A couple of Sherman tanks and a tank destroyer made a fight for it, demolishing the leading Panther and a few other armored vehicles. Peiper's column was delayed for about an hour.

Advancing along the south bank of the Amblève, the advance guard reached Stavelot, the point where the river must be crossed, at dusk. Looking down on the town the Germans saw hundreds of trucks, while on the opposite bank the road from Stavelot to Malmédy was jammed with vehicles. Although the Germans did not know it, many of these trucks were moving to help evacuate the great First Army gasoline dumps north of Stavelot and Malmédy. March serials of the 7th Armored Division also were moving through Stavelot en route to Vielsalm.

The small town of Stavelot (population 5,000) lies in the Amblève River valley surrounded by high, sparsely wooded bluffs. Most of the town is built on the north bank of the river or on the slopes above. There are a few scattered buildings on the south bank. Like most of the water courses in this part of the Ardennes, the Amblève was no particular obstacle to infantry but the deeply incised valley at this point offered hard going to tanks, while the river, by reason of the difficult approaches, was a tougher than average tank barrier. Only one vehicular bridge spanned the river at Stavelot. The sole approach to this bridge was by the main highway; here the ground to the left fell away sharply and to the right a steep bank rose above the road.

Stavelot and its bridge were open for the taking. The only combat troops in the town at this time were a squad from the 291st Engineer Combat Battalion which had been sent from Malmédy to construct a roadblock on the road leading to the bridge. For some reason Peiper's advance guard halted on the south side of the river, one of those quirks in the conduct of military operations which have critical import but which can never be explained. Months after the event Peiper told interrogators that his force had been checked by American antitank weapons covering the narrow approach to the bridge, that Stavelot was "heavily defended." But his detailed description of what happened when the Germans attacked to take town and bridge shows that he was confused in his chronology and was thinking of events which transpired on 18 December. It is true that during the early evening of the 17th three German tanks made a rush for the bridge, but when the leader hit a hasty mine field, laid by American engineers, the others turned back—nor were they seen for the rest of the night.

Perhaps the sight of the numerous American vehicles parked in the streets led Peiper to believe that the town was held in force and that a night attack held the only chance of taking the bridge intact. If so, the single effort made by the German point is out of keeping with Peiper's usual ruthless drive and daring. Perhaps Peiper accepted the word of his leading troops and failed to establish the true situation for himself. Perhaps he was interested at this moment only in closing up his third column, which in march formation extended for fifteen miles. Perhaps, as he says, Peiper was waiting for his infantry. Whatever the reason—and it never will be known—the German kampfgruppe came to a halt on the night of 17-18 December at the Stavelot bridge, forty-two miles from the Meuse.

During the night the First Army fed reinforcements into Malmédy, for it seemed impossible that the Germans could forfeit the opportunity to seize the town. As part of the defense being organized here a company of the 526th Armored Infantry Battalion and a platoon of 3-inch towed tank destroyers were ordered to outpost Stavelot. Maj. Paul J. Solis, commanding this detachment, began moving his troops into position just before daybreak: two platoons on the south bank of the river (with a section of tank destroyers at the old roadblock); one platoon with three 57-mm. antitank guns and the second section of tank destroyers in reserve around the town square north of the river.

Before the riflemen could organize a defense the German infantry attacked, captured the tank destroyers south of the river, and drove the two platoons back across the bridge. Taken by surprise, the Americans failed to destroy the bridge structure, and a Panther made a dash about 0800 which carried it onto the north bank.

More tanks followed. For some while the Germans were held in the houses next to the river; an antiaircraft artillery battery from the 7th Armored Division wandered into the firefight and did considerable damage before it went on its way. A company from the 202d Engineer Combat Battalion entered the town and joined in the fray. By the end of the morning, however, the German firing line had been built up to the point where the Americans could no longer hold inside the village proper, particularly since the hostile tanks were roving at will in the streets.

Solis ordered his detachment to retire to the top of the hill above Stavelot, but in the confusion of disengagement the remaining antitank weapons and all but one of the rifle platoons fell back along the Malmédy road. With German tanks climbing behind the lone platoon and without any means of antitank defense, Solis seized some of the gasoline from the Francorchamps dump, had his men pour it out in a deep road cut, where there was no turnout, and set it ablaze. The result was a perfect antitank barrier. The German tanks turned back to Stavelot—this was the closest that Kampfgruppe Peiper ever came to the great stores of gasoline which might have taken the 1st SS Panzer Division to the Meuse River. Solis had burned 124,000 gallons for his improvised roadblock, but this was the only part of the First Army's POL reserve lost during the entire Ardennes operation.

While the engagement in Stavelot was still in progress, Peiper turned some of his tanks toward Trois Ponts, the important bridgehead at the confluence of the Salm and the Amblève. As Peiper puts it: "We proceeded at top speed towards Trois Ponts in an effort to seize the bridge there.... If we had captured the bridge at Trois Ponts intact and had had enough fuel, it would have been a simple matter to drive through to the Meuse River early that day." One company of Mark IV tanks tried to reach Trois Ponts by following a narrow side road on the near bank of the Amblève. The road was almost impassable, and when the column came under American fire this approach was abandoned. The main part of the kampfgruppe swung through Stavelot and advanced on Trois Ponts by the highway which followed the north bank of the river. Things were looking up and it seemed that the only cause for worry was the lowering level in the panzer fuel tanks. Missing in Peiper's calculations was an American gun, the puny 57-mm. antitank weapon which had proven such an impuissant answer to German tanks.

Trois Ponts gains its name from three highway bridges, two over the Salm and one across the Amblève. The road from Stavelot passes under railroad tracks as it nears Trois Ponts, then veers sharply to the south, crosses the Amblève, continues through the narrow valley for a few hundred yards, and finally turns west at right angles to cross the Salm and enter the main section of the small village. A number of roads find their way through the deep recesses of the Salm and Amblève valleys to reach Trois Ponts, hidden among the cliffs and hills. Most, however, wind for some distance through the gorges and along the tortuous valley floors. One road, a continuation of the paved highway from Stavelot, leads immediately from Trois Ponts and the valley to the west. This road, via Werbomont, was Peiper's objective.

Company C, 51st Engineer Combat Battalion, occupied Trois Ponts, so important in the itinerary of the kampfgruppe. Quite unaware of the importance of its mission, the company had been ordered out of the sawmills it had been operating as part of the First Army's Winterization and Bridge Timber Cutting Program, and dispatched to Trois Ponts where it detrucked about midnight on 17 December. Numbering around 140 men, the company was armed with eight bazookas and ten machine guns. Maj. Robert B. Yates, commanding the force, knew only that the 1111th Engineer

Group was preparing a barrier line along the Salm River from Trois Ponts south to Bovigny and that he was to construct roadblocks at the approaches to Trois Ponts according to the group plans. During the night Yates deployed the company at roadblocks covering the bridge across the Amblève and at the vulnerable highway underpass at the railroad tracks north of the river. On the morning of 18 December a part of the artillery column of the 7th Armored Division passed through Trois Ponts, after a detour to avoid the German armor south of Malmédy; then appeared one 57-mm. antitank gun and crew which had become lost during the move of the 526th Armored Infantry Battalion. Yates commandeered the crew and placed the gun on the Stavelot road to the east of the first underpass where a daisy chain of mines had been laid.

A quarter of an hour before noon the advance guard of Peiper's main column, nineteen or twenty tanks, came rolling along the road. A shot from the lone antitank gun crippled or in somewise stopped the foremost German tank, but after a brief skirmish the enemy knocked out the gun, killed four of the crew, and drove back the engineers. The hit on the lead tank checked the German column just long enough to give warning to the bridge guards, only a few score yards farther on. They blew the Amblève bridge, then the Salm bridge, and fell back to the houses in the main part of town. In the meantime one of the engineer platoons had discouraged the German tank company from further advance along the side road and it had turned back to Stavelot.

Frustrated by a battalion antitank gun and a handful of engineers, Kampfgruppe Peiper now had no quick exit from the valley of the Amblève. With but one avenue remaining the column turned northward toward La Gleize, moving through the canyons of the Amblève on the east side of the river. At La Gleize there was a western exit from the valley, although by a mediocre, twisting road. Nearby, at the hamlet of Cheneux, the Germans found a bridge intact over the Amblève. This stroke of good luck was countered by bad when the weather cleared and American fighter-bombers knocked out two or three tanks and seven half-tracks, blocking the narrow road for a considerable period. When night came the armored point was within some three miles of Werbomont, an important road center on the main highway linking Liège and Bastogne.

Then, as the Germans neared a creek (the Lienne) a squad of Company A, 291st Engineer Combat Battalion, blew up the only bridge. Reconnaissance north and south discovered other bridges, but all were too fragile to support the Tiger tanks which had come forward with the advance guard. During the evening one detachment with half-tracks and assault guns did cross on a bridge to the north and swung southwest toward Werbomont. Near Chevron this force ran into an ambush, set by a battalion of the 30th Division which had been sent to head off Peiper, and was cut to pieces. Few of the Germans escaped. Since there was nothing left but to double back on his tracks, Peiper left a guard on the bridge at Cheneux and moved his advance guard through the dark toward the town of Stoumont, situated on the Amblève River road from which the abortive detour had been made during the afternoon. Scouts brought in word that Stoumont was strongly held and that more American troops were moving in from Spa. There was nothing left but to fight for the town.

All through the afternoon of the 18th, liaison planes from the First Army airstrip at Spa had been skidding under the clouds to take a look at Peiper's tanks and half-tracks. One of these light planes picked up the advance at Cheneux and called the Ninth Air Force in to work over this force. By the evening of 18 December

Peiper's entire column, now spread over many miles of road had been located and the word flashed back to First Army headquarters. The element of surprise, vital to the German plan of a coup de main at the Meuse, was gone. American forces from the 30th Infantry Division were racing in on Peiper from the north, and the 82d Airborne Division was moving with all possible speed to the threatened area.

It is doubtful that Peiper realized how the American net was being spread for a cast from the north, but he had experienced enough reverses on 18 December to feel the stiffening of opposition in his path. Radio contact between Peiper and the higher German headquarters had broken down, the armored sending apparatus failing to carry over the Ardennes terrain, and the Sixth Panzer Army was forced to follow Peiper's progress through intercepted American radio messages. Peiper, on the other hand, had little or no information as to what was happening behind him and where the following kampfgruppen of his own division were located. A Luftwaffe ultrahigh-frequency radio set was rushed to Peiper by liaison officer late this day, but its possession did no alter the relative independence and isolation of Peiper's command.

Sometime during the night of 18-19 December the radio link with the headquarters of the 1st Panzer Division was restored. By this means Peiper may have learned what he already must have suspected, that the 30th Infantry Division was on the move south from the American Ninth Army sector. German reconnaissance and intelligence agencies opposite the US Ninth Army had been alert from the first hours of the counteroffensive for any sign that troops were being stripped from the Roer front for intervention in the south. The first two divisions to leave the Ninth Army area, the 30th Infantry and 7th Armored, actually were in reserve and out of contact, but when the two started moving on 17 December the word was flashed back to OB WEST almost at once. Again American radio security had failed.

Operation Greif

During the last days before the great offensive which would send the German armored spearheads plunging west, Hitler belatedly set about replicating the winning combination of rapid and deep armored penetration, paratroop attacks in the enemy rear, and infiltration by disguised ground troops which had functioned so effectively in the western campaign of 1940 and the Greek campaign of 1941. To flesh out this combination, a special operation named Greif (or Condor) was hurriedly organized as an adjunct to the armored operation assigned the 1st SS Panzer Division.

The plans for the ground phase of Greif consisted of three parts: the seizure intact of at least two bridges across the Meuse by disguised raiding parties, the prompt reinforcement of any such coup de main by an armored commando formation; and an organized attempt to create confusion in the Allied rear areas through sabotage carried out by jeep parties clad in American uniforms. Later it would be rumored that a feature of Operation Greif was the planned assassination of Allied leaders, notably General Eisenhower, but there is no evidence of such plotting in the plan.

The idea for the ground operation was probably Hitler's and the leader, Lt. Col. Otto Skorzeny, was selected personally by Hitler. Skorzeny had achieved a considerable reputation as a daring commando leader, had rescued Mussolini from the Italians, and had seized the Hungarian Regent, Admiral Miklós von Nagybánya Horthy, when the Hungarian regime began to waver in its loyalties. For Operation Greif, Skorzeny formed the special Panzer Brigade 150 (or Brandenburger) numbering about two thousand men, of whom one hundred and fifty could speak English. Captured Allied equipment (particularly tanks and jeeps), uniforms, identification papers, and the like were hastily collected at the front and sent to Skorzeny's headquarters. The disguised jeep parties did go into action with varying degrees of success on 16 December, but the Brandenburger Brigade would be engaged as a unit only in a single and abortive skirmish near Malmédy five days later.

The airborne phase of Operation Greif, whose code name was Hohes Venn, seems to have been completely an afterthought, for the orders setting up the operation were not issued until 8 December. Hitler, like most of the higher German commanders, had lost confidence in airdrop tactics after the many casualties suffered by the German paratroopers in the Crete jump. Then too, in late 1944 the necessarily lengthy training for paratroop units was a luxury denied by the huge drain of battlefield losses. Apparently it was Model who suggested that paratroop tactics be tried once again, but undoubtedly Hitler seized upon the proposal with alacrity although there was no longer a single regular paratroop regiment active in the Wehrmacht. Model wanted the jump to be made in the Krinkelt area, and one may wonder what effect such a vertical attack might have had on the fight put up at the twin villages by the American 2d and 99th Infantry Divisions. Hitler, however, had one of his intuitive strokes and ordered the jump to be made north of Malmédy.

His choice for commander devolved on Col. Friedrich A. Freiherr von der Heydte, a distinguished and experienced paratroop officer then commanding the Fallschirm Armee Waffen school where the nominal parachute regiments were being trained as ground troops. Colonel von der Heydte was ordered to organize a thousand-man parachute formation for immediate use. Four days later von der Heydte received his tactical mission from the Sixth SS Panzer Army commander during an uncomfortable session in which Dietrich was under the influence of alcohol. The paratroopers were to jump at dawn on D-day, first opening the roads in the Hohes Venn leading from the Elsenborn-Malmédy area toward Eupen for the armored spearhead units, then blocking Allied forces if these attempted to intervene. Colonel von der Heydte was told that the German armor would reach him within twenty-four hours.

The preparations for Operation Hohes Venn were rushed to completion. The troops received their equipment and a little jump training (many had never attended jump school); 112 war-weary Junkers troop-carrier planes were gathered with an ill-assorted group of pilots, half of whom had never flown combat missions; 300 dummy figures were loaded for drops north of Camp Elsenborn to confuse the Americans (this turned out to be about the most successful feature of the entire operation); and the pilots and jumP-masters were given instructions—but no joint training. It must be said that these preparations for what would be the first German paratroop assault at night and into woods left much to be desired.

On the evening of 15 December Colonel von der Heydte formed his companies to entruck for the move to Paderborn, where the planes were assembled. The trucks never arrived—they had no fuel. Now the jump was ordered for 0300 on the 17th. This time the jump was made on schedule, although not quite as planned and into very bad crosswinds. One rifle company was dropped behind the German lines fifty kilometers away from the drop zone, most of the signal platoon fell just in front of the German positions south of Monschau, and the bulk of the command and the weapons packages were scattered almost at random. Despite this bad beginning about one hundred paratroopers reached the rendezvous at the fork in the Eupen road north of Mont Rigi. Since this group was obviously too weak for open action, Colonel von der Heydte formed camp in the woods and sent out patrols to pick up information and harass the Americans in the vicinity. These patrols gathered in stragglers until some three hundred paratroopers had assembled, but it was now too late to carry out the planned operation. On the night of the 21st the paratroopers were ordered to find their way back to the German lines believed to be at Monschau. Von der Heydte was taken prisoner two days later. The tactical effect of this hastily conceived and ill-executed operation proved to be almost nil although American commanders did dispatch troops on wildgoose chases which netted little but a few paratroopers, empty parachutes, and dummies.

Chapter XII. The First Attacks at St. Vith

St. Vith lay approximately twelve miles behind the front lines on 16 December. This was an average Belgian town, with a population of a little over 2,000 and sufficient billets to house a division headquarters. It was important, however, as the knot which tied the roads running around the Schnee Eifel barrier to the net which fanned out toward the north, south, and west. Six paved or macadam roads entered St. Vith. None of these were considered by the German planners to be major military trunk lines, although in the late summer of 1944 work had been started to recondition the road running east from St. Vith to Stadtkyll as a branch of the main military system, because normally the Schnee Eifel range served as a breakwater diverting heavy highway traffic so that it passed to the north or south of St. Vith.

In German plans the hub at St. Vith was important, but it was not on the axis of any of the main armored thrusts. The German armored corps advancing through the northeastern Ardennes were slated to swing wide of the Schnee Eifel and St. Vith, the I SS Panzer Corps passing north, the LVIII Panzer Corps passing south. But despite admonitions from the German High Command that the armored spearheads should race forward without regard to their flanks it was obvious that St. Vith had to be threefold: to insure the complete isolation of the troops that might be trapped on the Schnee Eifel, to cover the German supply lines unraveling behind the armored corps to the north and south, and to feed reinforcements laterally into the main thrusts by using the St. Vith road net. The closest of the northern armored routes, as these appeared on the German operations maps, ran through Recht, about five miles northwest of St. Vith. The closest of the primary armored routes in the south ran through Burg Reuland, some five miles south.

St. Vith is built on a low hill surrounded on all sides by slightly higher rises. On the south the Braunlauf Creek swings past St. Vith and from the stream a draw extends to the west edge of the town. About a mile and a half to the east a large wooded hill mass rises as a screen. This is crossed by the road to Schönberg, which then dips into the Our valley and follows the north bank of the river until the Schönberg bridge is reached, approximately six miles from St. Vith.

On the morning of 16 December the messages reporting the initial German attacks in the 106th Division positions were punctuated for the division staff by occasional large-caliber shells falling in St. Vith. This fire was quite ineffectual and there was little comprehension in of the German attack. The attachment of CCB, 9th Armored Division, to the 106th Division late in the morning promised such aid as then seemed necessary, but Hoge's command post was at Monschau and he would not receive his orders from Jones until about 1800. As a result CCB began its move for St. Vith about 2000 on the 16th.

As the size and direction of the first enemy effort began to assume some shadowy form on the situation maps in the corps and division headquarters, General Middleton advised the 106th Division commander that he could use the 168th Engineer Combat Battalion, which was engaged in routine duties around St. Vith and Vielsalm. This battalion (Lt. Col. W. L. Nungesser) was at about half strength—attendance at schools or special assignments accounted for the rest. The men had not been given any recent training in the use of bazookas or machine guns; a large percentage of the machine gunners would therefore be killed in the fight for St. Vith. At 1030 on 17 December, reports of the German penetration from the east led General Jones to send the 168th out the St. Vith-Schönberg road with orders to defend astride the road at the village of Heuem. While en route, the engineers met troopers of the 32d Cavalry who had been involved in a running fight along the road west of Schönberg. Heuem, they reported, was in enemy hands and a German column was heading straight for St. Vith.

On the morning of the 17th Colonel Slayden, VIII Corps' assistant G-2, and Lt. Col. Earle Williams, the 106th Division signal officer, while doing independent scouting east of St. Vith, had seen the enemy and tapped the signal wire to ask for artillery interdiction of the highway. The combat engineer battalion deployed about two miles east of St. Vith along the outer edge of a pine forest fringing the ridge mask over which climbs the road from Schönberg. Here forty men or so of the 81st Engineer Combat Battalion (106th Division) joined the 168th. CCB, 9th Armored Division, had passed St. Vith en route to aid the 424th Infantry, and a platoon of Troop C, 89th Cavalry Squadron, was commandeered to reinforce the watch east of the town. This little force was digging in when, at noon, the first enemy patrols were sighted.

The 7th Armored Division Move to St. Vith

When the counteroffensive began, the 7th Armored Division (Brig. Gen. Robert W. Hasbrouck) was in the XIII Corps reserve, planning for possible commitment in the Ninth Army Operation DAGGER intended to clear the Germans from the west bank of the Roer River once the dams were destroyed.

The division, assembled about fifteen miles north of Aachen, had taken no part as a unit in the November drive toward the Roer, although companies and battalions on occasion had been attached to attacking infantry divisions. The period of rest and refitting, after heavy fighting at Metz and in Holland, had put the 7th Armored in good condition. When General Bradley and the 12th Army Group staff met in the afternoon of the 16th to make a tentative selection of divisions which could be taken from other fronts to reinforce the Ardennes sector, the choice in the north fell on Hasbrouck's command. Actually there were armored divisions in the First Army closer to the scene, but they had been alerted for use in the first phases of the attacks planned to seize the Roer River dams (a design not abandoned until 17 December) and as yet little sense of urgency attached to reinforcements in the VIII Corps area.

General Hasbrouck received a telephone call at 1730 alerting, his division for movement to the south (it took five more hours for the 7th Armored G-2 to learn that "three or four German divisions were attacking"). Two hours later while the division assembled and made ready, an advance party left the division command post at Heerlen, Holland, for Bastogne where it was to receive instructions from the VIII Corps. Vielsalm, fourteen miles west of St. Vith by road, had already been designated as the new assembly area. At Bastogne General Middleton outlined the mission: one combat command would be prepared to assist the 106th Division, a second could be used if needed, but under no circumstances was the third to be committed. The decision was left to General Hasbrouck, who first was to consult with the 106th Division as to how and when his leading combat command would be employed. Even at this hour the scope of the German counteroffensive was but dimly seen and the 7th Armored Division advance party was informed that it would not be necessary to have the artillery accompany the combat command columns—in other words this would not be a tactical march from Heerlen to Vielsalm.

The movement plans prepared by the First Army staff assigned General Hasbrouck two routes of march: an east route, through Aachen, Eupen, Malmédy, and Recht, on which CCR would move; a west route, through Maastricht, Verviers, and Stavelot, which would be used by the main body of the division. The division artillery, which had been firing in support of the XIII Corps, was not to displace until the late morning of 17 December, when it would move on the eastern route. Shortly after midnight the Ninth Army was informed that the two columns would depart at 0330 and 0800; actually the western column moved out at 0430. The estimated time of arrival was 1400, 17 December, and of closure 0200, 18 December. A couple of hours earlier the First Army headquarters had told General Middleton that the west column would arrive at 0700 and close at 1900 on the 17th, and that the combat command on the east road would arrive at 1100 and close at 1700. It was on this estimate that General Middleton and the 106th Division commander based their plans for a counterattack by a combat command of the 7th Armored east of St. Vith early on 17 December.

Although this failure to make an accurate estimate of the time of arrival in the battle area bore on the fate of the two regiments on the Schnee Eifel, it was merely a single event in the sequence leading to the final encirclement and lacked any decisive import. The business of computing the lateral movement of an armored division close to a front through which the enemy was breaking could hardly attain the exactness of a Leavenworth solution complete with march graphs and tables. None of the charts on traffic density commonly used in general staff or armored school training could give a formula for establishing the coefficient of "friction" in war, in this case the mass of jeeps, prime movers, guns, and trucks which jammed the roads along which the 7th Armored columns had to move to St. Vith. Also, the transmittal of the 7th Armored Division's own estimate of its possible progress was subject to "friction." This estimate was received at the headquarters of the VIII Corps at 0500 on 17 December, the first indication, it would appear, that the leading armored elements would arrive at 1400 instead of 0700 as planned. Thus far the Ninth Army had given Hasbrouck no information on the seriousness of the situation on the VIII Corps front.

The advance party sent by General Hasbrouck reached St. Vith about 0800 on 17 December, reporting to General Jones, who expected to find the armored columns right behind. Brig. Gen. Bruce Clarke, in advance of CCB, agreed with Jones's recommendation that his combat command be organized upon arrival into two task forces and committed in an attack to clear the St. Vith-Schönberg road. At Schönberg the 7th Armored task forces would turn south to join CCB of the 9th Armored Division, already engaged along the road to Winterspelt. If successful, the attack by the two combat commands would provide escape corridors for the beleaguered regiments of the 106th.

CCB of the 7th Armored had meanwhile been making good progress and arrived at Vielsalm about 1100, halting just to the east to gas up. Although Vielsalm was only fourteen miles by road from St. Vith, it would be literally a matter of hours before even the lightly armored advance guard could reach St. Vith. The mass of artillery, cavalry, and supply vehicles moving painfully through St. Vith to the west—with and without orders—formed a current almost impossible to breast. Although the mounted military police platoon in St. Vith had orders to sidetrack the withdrawing corps artillery when the armor appeared, the traffic jam had reached the point where the efforts of a few MP's were futile.

General Jones, beset by messages reporting the German advance along the Schönberg road, sent urgent requests for the armor to hurry. At 1300 German vehicles were seen in Setz, four and a half miles from the eastern edge of St. Vith. Half an hour later three enemy tanks and some infantry appeared before the 168th Engineer Battalion position astride the St. Vith road. Carelessly dismounting, one tank crew was riddled by machine gun fire; a second tank received a direct and killing blast from a bazooka; the third tank and the infantry withdrew. Another small German detachment deployed in front of the engineers an hour later was engaged and was finally put to flight by American fighter planes in one of their few appearances over the battlefield on this day.

About the same time the 87th Cavalry Reconnaissance Squadron, temporarily under the command of Maj. Charles A. Cannon, Jr., reported to General Clarke in St. Vith, the first unit of the 7th Armored to reach the 106th Division. Troop B was sent out the east road to reinforce the engineers, but the main body of the reconnaissance battalion deployed to screen the northeastern approaches to the Wallerode area. By this time it was obvious to Jones and Clarke that the main forces of the 7th Armored could not reach St. Vith in time to make a daylight attack. General Hasbrouck reached St. Vith at 1600—it had taken him all of five hours to thread his way through the traffic jam between Vielsalm and St. Vith. He found that General Jones already had turned the defense of St. Vith over to Clarke and the 7th Armored Division. After a hasty conference the counterattack was postponed until the following morning.

It was just turning dark when the assistant G-2 of the 7th Armored led a company of tanks and another of armored infantry into St. Vith. This detachment had literally forced its way, at pistol point and by threatening to run down the vehicles barring the road, from Vielsalm to St. Vith. About this time the Germans made another attempt, covered by artillery fire, to thrust a few tanks along the east road. Three American tank destroyers which had been dug in at a bend in the road were abandoned—their crews shelled out by accurate enemy concentrations but the attack made no further headway and perhaps was intended only as a patrol action. The 106th Division now could report, "We have superior force in front of St. Vith."

Why did the LXVI Corps fail to make a determined push toward St. Vith on 17 December? German assault guns or tanks had been spotted west of Schönberg as early as 0850. By noon German infantry were in Setz, with at least five hours of daylight remaining and less than five miles to go, much of that distance being uncontested. By mid-afternoon the enemy had reached the 168th Engineer positions less than two miles from St. Vith. Yet at no time during the day did the Germans use more than three assault guns and one or two platoons of infantry in the piecemeal attacks west of Schönberg. The successive concentrations laid by the American artillery on Schönberg and both sides of the road west—from 9 o'clock on—must have affected enemy movement considerably. The bombs dropped on Schönberg and its narrow streets late in the day may have delayed the arrival of reinforcements, and air attack certainly helped to scatter the most advanced German troops. The stand made by Troop B, 32d Cavalry Squadron, near Heuem and the later fight by the engineers gave the German point an excuse to report—as it did—the presence of "stubborn resistance" east of St. Vith.

It seems likely, however, that only small German detachments actually reached the Schönberg-St. Vith road during the daylight hours of 17 December. The German corps commander, General Lucht, had ordered the Mobile Battalion of the 18th Volks Grenadier Division up from reserve during the previous night with orders to advance via Andler. (It will be remembered that the 18th Volks Grenadier Division was charged with the encirclement and capture of St. Vith.) The Mobile Battalion (comprising three platoons of assault guns, a company of engineers, and another of fusiliers) did not arrive at Schönberg until after noon. During the morning the division commander had led a battalion of the 294th Regiment to Schönberg, but seems to have halted there (perhaps to secure the Schönberg bridge against recapture), sending only small detachments against Troop B at Heuem. With the arrival of the assault guns some attempt was made to probe the American defenses east of St. Vith. This, however, was not the main mission assigned the advance guard of the 18th Volks Grenadier Division, for the original plan of advance had called on the Mobile Battalion to seize the high ground at Wallerode, northeast of St. Vith, which overlooked the valley road from Schönberg. The bulk of the German advance guard, as a result, toiled through the woods toward Wallerode, arriving there in the early evening.

An opportunity had been missed. Perhaps the German command did not realize the full extent of the gains won in the St. Vith area and was wedded too closely to its prior plans. In any case the German armored reserve was not available. Tanks of the Fuehrer Begleit Brigade, theoretically attached to the LXVI Corps but subject to commitment only on army orders, would not be released for use at St. Vith until too late for a successful coup de main.

On the movement of the main body of the 7th Armored Division on 17 December hung the fate of St. Vith. Behind the reconnaissance and advance elements the bulk of the division moved slowly southward along the east and west lines of march, forty-seven and sixty-seven miles long, respectively. The division staff knew little of the tactical situation and nothing of the extent to which the German armored columns had penetrated westward. It is probable that night-flying German planes spotted the American columns in the early hours of the 17th, but it is doubtful that the tank columns of the Sixth Panzer Army traveling west on roads cutting across the 7th Armored routes were aware of this American movement. Actually CCR of the 7th Armored, on the eastern route, came very close to colliding with the leading tank column of the 1st SS Panzer Division south of Malmédy but cleared the road before the Germans crossed on their way west. The western column made its march without coming in proximity to the west-moving German spearheads, its main problem being to negotiate roads jammed with west-bound traffic.

The division artillery, finally released in the north, took the east route, its three battalions and the 203d Antiaircraft Battalion moving as a single column. Early on the afternoon of the 17th the 440th Armored Field Artillery, leading the column, entered Malmédy, only to be greeted with the sign THIS ROAD UNDER ENEMY FIRE. The town square was a scene of utter confusion. Trucks loaded with soldiers and nurses from a nearby hospital, supply vehicles, and civilians of military age on bicycles eddied around the square in an attempt to get on the road leading out to the west; a battalion from a replacement depot threaded its way on foot between the vehicles, also en route to the west. All that the artillery could learn was that a German tank column was south of Malmédy. This, of course, was the panzer detachment of the 1st SS Panzer Division.

The 440th Armored Field Artillery Battalion, unable to reverse itself, turned west to Stavelot and subsequently joined the western group on its way to Vielsalm. Alerted by radio from the 440th, Maj. W. J. Scott (acting in the absence of the artillery commander who had gone ahead to report at the division headquarters) turned the column around in the square and to avoid the narrow and congested road led it back toward Eupen, cutting in to the western divisional route at Verviers. This roundabout move consumed the daylight hours and through the night the gun carriages streamed along the Verviers-Vielsalm road. The main artillery column again missed the 1st SS Panzer Division by only a hair's breadth. As Battery D, 203d Antiaircraft (AW) Battalion, at the tail of the column, rolled through Stavelot about 0800 on the morning of 18 December, it found itself in the middle of a fire fight between the advance guard of the 1st SS Panzer Division and a small American force of armored infantry, engineers, and tank destroyers. The battery swung its quadruple machine guns around for ground laying and moved into the fight, firing at the enemy assembling along the banks of the Amblève River, which here ran through the south edge of the town. After an hour or so the battery turned once again and, taking no chances, circled wide to the west. It finally arrived in the division assembly area east of Vielsalm late in the afternoon. The bulk of the artillery column closed at Vielsalm during the morning, although the last few miles had to be made against the flow of vehicles surging from the threatened area around St. Vith.

While the 7th Armored Division artillery was working its way onto the west road during the evening of 17 December, most of the division assembled in the St. Vith area along positions roughly indicative of an unconsciously forming perimeter defense. From Recht, five miles northwest of St. Vith, to Beho, seven miles to the southwest of the 106th Division headquarters, the clockwise disposition of the American units was as follows. At Recht were located the command post of CCR and the rear headquarters of CCB, with the 17th Tank Battalion assembled to the southeast. The disorganized 14th Cavalry Group was dispersed through the area between Recht and Poteau. East of Hünningen the 87th Cavalry Reconnaissance Squadron had formed roadblocks to bar the northern and northeastern approaches to St. Vith. To the right of the cavalry the most advanced units of CCB had reinforced the 168th Engineer Combat Battalion on the Schönberg road and pushed out to either side for some distance as flank protection. During the night, CCB, 9th Armored Division, and the 424th Infantry withdrew across the Our River and established a defensive line along the hill chain running from northeast of Steinebrück south to Burg Reuland; these troops eventually made contact with the advance elements of CCB, 7th Armored Division. Some six or seven miles west of Burg Reuland, CCA of the 7th Armored had assembled near Beho.

West of St. Vith, in position to give close support, were located the 275th Armored Field Artillery Battalion (Lt. Col. Roy Udell Clay) and the remainder of CCB. The 275th, reinforced by the 16th Armored Field Artillery Battalion, and three batteries of corps artillery, fired through the night to interdict the eastern approaches to St. Vith; this was all the artillery support remaining to the American troops in this sector. The 112th Infantry, now beginning to fold back to the north as the center of the

28th Division gave way, was no longer in contact with the 424th Infantry, its erstwhile left flank neighbor, but the axis of withdrawal ultimately would bring the 112th Infantry to piece out the southern sector of the defense slowly forming around St. Vith.

While it is true that an outline or trace of the subsequent St. Vith perimeter was unraveling on the night of 17-18 December, this was strictly fortuitous. General Jones and General Hasbrouck still expected that CCB would make its delayed drive east of St. Vith on the morning of the 18th. The strength of the German forces thrusting west was not yet fully appreciated. Information on the location of the enemy or the routes he was using was extremely vague and generally several hours out of date. Communication between the higher American headquarters and their subordinate units was sporadic and, for long periods, nonexistent. Late in the evening of the 17th and during the morning of the 18th, however, the scope and direction of the German drive thrusting past St. Vith in the north became more clearly discernible as the enemy struck in a series of attacks against Recht, Poteau, and Hünningen.

The Enemy Strikes at the St. Vith Perimeter

The 1st SS Panzer Division, forming the left of the I SS Panzer Corps advance in the zone north of St. Vith, had driven forward on two routes. The northern route, through Stavelot and the Amblève River valley, carried the main strength of the division, led by its panzer regiment. It was the first group in this northern column which CCR had unwittingly eluded and from which the tail of the 7th Armored artillery column had glanced at Stavelot. The southern route, through Recht and Vielsalm, was assigned to a kampfgruppe of the 1st SS Panzer Division made up of a reinforced panzer grenadier regiment and a battalion of assault guns. This group had been delayed by poor roads and American mine fields west of Manderfeld, and by the end of 17 December it was some hours behind the north column.

The headquarters of CCR, 7th Armored, opened in Recht in midafternoon of the 17th. At that time the combat command retained only the 17th Tank Battalion (assembled to the southeast) because its armored infantry battalion had been diverted to St. Vith. About 2045 CCR got its first word of the Germans it had so narrowly missed when the driver for the division chief of staff, Col. Church M. Matthews, appeared at the command post with the report that during the afternoon he had run afoul of a large tank column near Pont and that the colonel was missing. These Germans, of course, were part of the northern column. Lt. Col. Fred M. Warren, acting commanding officer, sent the driver on to division headquarters to tell his story, and at the same time he asked for a company of infantry. He then ordered the 17th Tank Battalion (Lt. Col. John P. Wemple) to send a tank company into Recht. Warren and Wemple studied the road net as shown on the map and agreed to try to hold Recht through the night. Stragglers came pouring through Recht in the meantime with rumors and reports of the enemy just behind them. The headquarters and tank company had little time to get set, for about 0200 the advance guard of the southern German column hit the village from the east and northeast. Unwilling to risk his tanks without infantry protection in a night fight through narrow streets, and uncertain of the enemy strength, Warren ordered a withdrawal after a sharp 45-minute engagement. CCR headquarters started down the road southwest toward Vielsalm, and the tanks rejoined Wemple.

Made cautious by the collision at Recht, the German column moved slowly, putting out feelers to the southeast before the main force resumed the march southwest along the Vielsalm road. Wemple and his tankers were able to repel these probing attempts without difficulty. CCR headquarters had meanwhile become ensnarled with the remnants of the 14th Cavalry Group and the residue of the corps artillery columns at the little village of Poteau, where the roads from Recht and St. Vith join en route to Vielsalm. This crossroads hamlet had been the worst bottleneck in the traffic jam on 17 December; indeed the situation seems to have been completely out of hand when the CCR headquarters arrived in the early morning hours and succeeded in restoring some order.

On the afternoon of 17 December the 14th Cavalry Group commander had ordered the remnants of his two squadrons to fall back to Recht. Through some confusion in orders both squadrons got onto the St. Vith-Poteau highway, although three reconnaissance teams did reach Recht and took part in the action there. About midnight orders from the 106th Division arrived at the group headquarters which had been set up in Poteau: the cavalry were to return to Born, which they had just evacuated, and occupy the high ground. By this time most of the 32d Squadron had threaded their way south through Poteau, apparently unaware that the group had established a command post there. Shortly after dark Colonel Devine departed with most of his staff for the 106th Division command post, but this command group was ambushed near Recht (Colonel Devine and two of his officers escaped on foot).

Early on the 18th, Lt. Col. Augustine Duggan, senior of the remaining staff, intercepted elements of the 18th Squadron, part of Troop C, 32d Squadron, and the one remaining platoon of towed 3-inch guns from the 820th Tank Destroyer. These were placed under the command of Maj. J. L. Mayes as a task force to comply with the orders from division. With great difficulty the task force vehicles were sorted out, lined the road, and then turned about and faced toward Recht. Mayes's group moved out from the crossroads at first light on 18 December but had gone only some two hundred yards when flame shot up from the leading light tank and an armored car, the two struck almost simultaneously by German bazooka fire. The glare thrown over the snow silhouetted the figures of enemy infantrymen advancing toward the Poteau crossroads. The task force pulled back into the village and hastily prepared a defense around the dozen or so houses there, while to the north a small cavalry patrol dug in on a hill overlooking the hamlet and made a fight of it. By this time the last of the milling traffic was leaving Poteau; eight 8-inch howitzers of the 740th Field Artillery Battalion were abandoned here as the German fire increased, ostensibly because they could not be hauled out of the mud onto the road.

All through the morning the enemy pressed in on Poteau, moving his machine guns, mortars, and assault guns closer and closer. At noon the situation was critical, the village was raked by fire, and the task force was no longer in communication with any other Americans. Colonel Duggan finally gave the order to retire down the road to Vielsalm. Three armored cars, two jeeps, and one light tank were able to disengage and carried the wounded out; apparently a major part of the force was able to make its way to Vielsalm on foot.

During the early morning Headquarters, CCR, set out from Poteau, heading down the valley road toward Vielsalm. At the small village of Petit Thier it was discovered that a lieutenant from the 23d Armored Infantry Battalion, separated from his column on the march south, had heard the firing at Poteau and had rounded up a collection of stray tanks, infantry, cavalry, and engineers to block the way to Vielsalm. The CCR commander took over this roadblock and, as the force swelled through the day with incoming stragglers and lost detachments, extended the position west of the village. The German column at Poteau, however, made no attempt to drive on to Vielsalm. The main body of the 1st SS Panzer Division needed reinforcements. The panzer grenadier regiment and the assault guns therefore were ordered off their assigned route and turned northeast to follow the column through Stavelot.

The 7th Armored counterattack from St. Vith to relieve the two trapped regiments of the 106th Division had been postponed on the 17th, not canceled. During the early morning hours of 18 December preparation was completed for the attack on Schönberg by the 31st Tank Battalion and the 23d Armored Infantry Battalion, now brigaded under CCB. This was risky business at best. The divisional artillery would not be in position to support the attack. The similar effort by CCB, 9th Armored Division, had been called off and the American forces south of the 422d Infantry and 423d Infantry had withdrawn behind the Our. That the German strength was increasing was made apparent by the events during the night of 17-18 December, but the 7th Armored light observation planes were not available for scouting the enemy dispositions or movements east of St. Vith. General Clarke was well aware of the chancy nature of this enterprise and, at 0645, when reporting to Colonel Ryan, the division chief of staff, pointed out that General Hasbrouck still had the option of canceling the attack.

It would be the enemy, however, and not a command decision that forced the abandonment of the proposed effort. About 0800 the Germans launched a reconnaissance in force northeast of St. Vith, advancing from Wallerode toward Hünningen. Here, only two thousand yards from St. Vith, two troops of the 87th Cavalry Reconnaissance Squadron and a few antiaircraft half-tracks offered the sole barrier to a thrust into the city. Who made up the enemy force and its strength is uncertain—probably this was the Mobile Battalion of the 18th Volks Grenadier Division, making the preliminary move in the scheme to encircle St. Vith. In any event enough pressure was exerted during the morning to drive the small American screening force back toward St. Vith.

As the cavalry commenced its delaying action a hurried call went out to CCB, 9th Armored, for tanks and antitank guns. Moving through St. Vith, two companies from the 14th Tank Battalion (Maj. Leonard E. Engeman) and one from the 811th Tank Destroyer Battalion took over the fight. One company of Shermans circled in the direction of Wallerode, falling on the enemy flank while the tank destroyers contained the head of the German column on the Hünnange road. Both American units were able to drive forward and the Shermans knocked out six light panzers or assault guns. By this time the 7th Armored plans for the Schönberg attack were definitely off and a company from the 31st Tank Battalion joined in the affair. American losses were small, the German foray was checked, and before the day closed the Hünningen position was restored, but it was clear that the enemy now was concentrating to the north as well as to the east of St. Vith.

Like the probing thrust at Hünnange, the German efforts on the road east of St. Vith during 18 December were advance guard actions fought while the main German force assembled. The 18th Volks Grenadier Division, charged with the initial attack against St. Vith, actually was riding two horses at the same time, attempting to close up for a decisive blow at St. Vith while maintaining the northern arc of the circle around the Americans on the Schnee Eifel. This tactical problem was made more difficult for the 18th Volks Grenadier Division and the LXVI Corps by the traffic situation on the roads east and north of Schönberg where columns belonging to the

Sixth SS Panzer Army were swinging out of their proper one. Although the corps commander, General Lucht, personally intervened to "rank" the intruders out of the area he seems to have been only moderately successful. Then, too, the artillery belonging to the division had been turned inward against the Schnee Eifel pocket on 18 December; only one battalion got up to the Schönberg-St. Vith road.

The attacks made east of St. Vith on 18 December were carried by a part of the 294th Infantry, whose patrols had been checked by the 168th Engineers the previous day. Three times the grenadiers tried to rush their way through the foxhole line held by the 38th Armored Infantry Battalion (Lt. Col. William H. G. Fuller) and B Troop of the 87th astride the Schönberg road. The second attempt, just before noon, was made under cover of a creeping barrage laid down by the German artillery battalion near Schönberg and momentarily shook the American firing line. But the armored infantry, rallied by their officers and aided by Nungesser's engineers, drove back the attackers. The last German assault, begun after a two-hour firefight, made a dent in the center of the 38th Armored Infantry line. Again the 168th Engineers gave a hand, the bulk of the 23d Armored Infantry Battalion appeared to reinforce the line east of St. Vith, and by dark all lost ground had been retaken. During this entire action the 275th Armored Field Artillery Battalion, emplaced along the Recht road northwest of St. Vith, fired concentration after concentration against the enemy thrusting against the 38th and the engineers. Observation was poor—the 18th was a day of low-hanging fog—but the nine hundred rounds plunging onto the Schönberg road did much to check the grenadiers.

Although the 18th Volks Grenadier Division was able, on this third day of the counteroffensive, to push some of its troops close in toward St. Vith, the 62d Volks Grenadier Division on the left had moved more slowly. Despite the American withdrawal from the WinterspeltHeckhuscheid area and the promptings of the impatient commander of the LXVI Corps, the 62d only tardily brought itself into conformity with the forward kampfgruppen of the 18th Volks Grenadier Division. The 164th Regiment, reinforced by engineers and assault guns, apparently took some time to re-form after its fight with the 9th Armored Division counterattack force on 17 December. Although German patrols continued up the road to Steinebrück, attempting in vain to seize the bridge during the night, the attack was not pressed until after daylight on the following morning. Two of the three Our bridges chosen for capture in the LXVI Corps' plan now were in German hands, but the bridge at Steinebrück still had to be taken.

The bend in the Our River near Steinebrück necessitated a switch in the new American positions on the far bank; thus while the main frontage held by the 424th and CCB, 9th Armored, faced east, the line at Steinebrück faced south, then swung back until it again faced east. In this sector Troop D, 89th Cavalry Reconnaissance Battalion, plus a light tank platoon and an assault gun platoon, was deployed along the 3,000 yard stretch between Steinebrück and Weppler, its left flank in the air at the latter village, its right more or less secured by a provisional company from the 424th Infantry west of Steinebrück.

On the morning of 18 December General Hoge, CCB commander, was ordered to hurry to the 106th headquarters where he was told of the threat developing north of St. Vith. When he sent back orders for the emergency task force from CCB to hasten north, the cavalry troop was included. Covered by one reconnaissance platoon and the cavalry assault guns, sited near the bridge, the remaining platoons of Troop D had left their positions and started filing toward the Steinebrück-St. Vith road when suddenly the movement order was canceled. The cavalry had been under fire since daybreak, and when the 2d Platoon attempted to return to its position on a commanding hill between Steinebrück and Weppler it was forced to move dismounted in a rain of bullets and shells. At the Steinebrück bridge the enemy increased in number as the morning progressed, slipping into positions on the south bank under cover given by exploding smoke shells. To counter this threat the light tank platoon moved into Steinebrück, leaving the American left uncovered. About the same time the provisional rifle company west of Steinebrück took off and one of the cavalry platoons had to be switched hastily to cover this gap.

Thus far the all-important bridge had been left intact, for there was still some hope that the 423d Infantry, at the least, might free itself from the Schnee Eifel trap. By noon the situation was such that the little group of troopers dared delay no longer. On General Hoge's order a platoon of armored engineers went down and blew the bridge—almost in the teeth of the grenadiers on the opposite bank.

An hour later the platoon west of the village saw an enemy column of horse-drawn artillery driving into position. The American gunners in the groupment west of Lommersweiler immediately answered the cavalry call for aid, apparently with some effect; yet within the hour at least a part of the twenty-two enemy guns counted here were in action, firing in preparation for an assault across the river. It would seem that a German rifle company first crossed into Weppler, now unoccupied, then wheeled and encircled the 2d Platoon on the hill. Only five Americans escaped. Two or more companies crossed near the blasted bridge and by 1530, despite the continual pounding administered by the 16th Armored Field Artillery Battalion and the rapid fire from the cavalry tank, assault, and machine guns, had nearly encircled Troop D. A cavalry request for medium tanks perforce was denied; the tank companies sent north to Hünningen had not yet returned and General Hoge had no reserve. A company of the 27th Armored Infantry Battalion, however, was put in to cover the cavalry left flank. With the enemy infantry inside Steinebrück and excellent direct laying by the German gunners picking off the American vehicles one by one, the cavalry withdrew along the St. Vith road.

The CCB position at the Our (where two companies of armored infantry, a company each of light and medium tanks, plus the reconnaissance company, were deployed on a front over 4,000 yards) was no longer tenable. There had been no contact whatever with the 424th Infantry to the south. General Hoge conferred with General Jones at St. Vith and the two decided that the combat command should withdraw from the river northwest to slightly higher ground. Commencing at dark, the move was made without trouble and CCB settled along an arc whose center was about two and a half miles southeast of St. Vith. In this position the combat command blocked the main Winterspelt-St. Vith highway and the valley of the Braunlauf Creek, a second natural corridor leading to St. Vith. The gap between Hoge's command and CCB, 7th Armored, which at dark had been 3,000 yards across, closed during the night when a light tank company and an anti-aircraft battery came in. Later, liaison was established with the 424th Infantry on the right, which had been out of contact with the enemy during the day and remained in its river line position. Although the 62d Volks Grenadier Division was quick to occupy the ground vacated by CCB, no attempt was made to follow into the new American position.

During the afternoon of 18 December while the combat commands of the 7th and 9th Armored Divisions were fighting holding actions along the eastern front of the St. Vith area, General Hasbrouck engaged in an attempt to restore the northern flank of the 7th Armored in the Poteau sector. The opportunity for a decisive American counterattack toward Schönberg was past, if indeed it had ever existed, and Hasbrouck's immediate concern was to establish his division north flank in a posture of defense in the St. Vith-Vielsalm area. The loss of the vital road junction at Poteau, earlier in the day, made the connection between the forces of the division at St. Vith, around Recht, and in the Vielsalm assembly area, more difficult and tenuous. Then too, it appeared that the enemy was concentrating in Recht and might try an attack through Poteau to Vielsalm. CCA (Col. Dwight A. Rosebaum), watching the southern flank of the 7th Armored around Beho, had not yet met the Germans (who were in fact driving past to the west, but on roads south of Beho). General Hasbrouck decided to leave a small force as observers around Beho and commit CCA to recover Poteau.

At noon the 48th Armored Infantry Battalion and the 40th Tank Battalion, representing the bulk of CCA, rolled through St. Vith and out along the Vielsalm road. As the leading tank platoon hove in sight of Poteau it came immediately under small arms and assault gun fire. The few houses here were separated by an abandoned railroad cut, just south of the crossroads, which ran east and west. Colonel Rosebaum sent the tank platoon and an armored infantry company to clear the houses south of the cut. This action continued through the afternoon, while tanks and assault guns played a dangerous game of hide-and-seek from behind the houses and the American infantry tried to knock out the German machine guns enfilading the railroad cut. Toward dark the Americans crossed the northern embankment and reached the road junction. Rosebaum posted the infantry company—now supported by an entire tank company—to hold the village, cheek by jowl with the Germans in the northernmost houses. Thus far CCA had no contact with CCR headquarters and its scratch force to the west at Petit Thier because the road from Poteau was under fire.

With the Poteau crossroad more or less in the hands of the 7th Armored, with a defensive arc forming north, east, and southeast of St. Vith, and with the Vielsalm-Petit Thier area under control in the west, the next step was to block the possible routes of approach from the south and southwest. Nearly all the American units in the St. Vith area were already committed; all that General Hasbrouck could do was to station a light tank company, a company of armored engineers, the headquarters battery of an antiaircraft battalion, and a reconnaissance troop piecemeal in a series of small villages south and west of Beho. At best these isolated detachments could serve only as pickets for the 7th Armored, but fortunately the German columns continued marching west. One brief engagement was fought on the 18th at Gouvy, a rail and road junction southwest of Beho. The headquarters battery, 440th Antiaircraft (AW) Battalion (Lt. Col. Robert O. Stone), and a light tank platoon had been sent to set up an outpost at the village. As they approached Gouvy station, a railroad stop south of the village, they ran afoul of three German tanks which were just coming in from the south. The Germans started a dash to sweep the column broadside, but the first shot knocked out an air—compressor truck whose unwieldy hulk effectively blocked the road. After firing their last rounds at the town and the column, the German tanks withdrew. When Stone took a look around he found himself in charge of a railhead stock of 80,000 rations—which had been set ablaze by the depot guards—an engineer vehicle park, and 350 Germans in a POW cage. Fortunately the fire could be checked without too much damage. Stone then organized a defense with the engineers, ordnance, and quartermaster people on the spot. Unwittingly, in the process of "freezing" this heterogeneous command, Stone stopped the westward withdrawal of badly needed engineer vehicles (carrying earth augers, air compressors, and similar equipment) which the VIII Corps commander was attempting to gather for work on a barrier line being constructed by the corps engineers farther to the west.

The artillery battalions of the 7th Armored Division were in firing positions north and east of Vielsalm at the close of 18 December. They could not give aid to CCB, east of St. Vith, but there the 75th Armored Field Artillery Battalion was in range and already had given a fine demonstration of effective support. The 7th Armored trains, which had reached Salmchâteau by the western route on the morning of the 18th, were sent twenty-two miles west of La Roche, partly to keep them out of enemy reach but also because of the possibility that the division might soon have to retire behind the Ourthe River. The reserve available to General Hasbrouck was scant for such wide-flung positions: some 90-mm. guns from the 814th Tank Destroyer Battalion and the provisional squadron being formed from the remains of the 14th Cavalry Group.

Late in the day General Jones moved the 106th command post to Vielsalm, setting up near General Hasbrouck's headquarters. The orders given the 7th Armored Division still held—to assist the 106th Division. In fact, however, there was little left of the 106th; so responsibility tended to devolve on the junior commander, Hasbrouck.

The two generals had only a vague idea of what was happening beyond their own sphere. Telephone service to the VIII Corps headquarters at Bastogne ended on 18 December when that headquarters moved to Neufchâteau. But Hasbrouck had no doubt that General Middleton counted on the continued defense of the St. Vith road center—this part of the mission needed no reiteration. Since the VIII Corps itself was in possession of only fragmentary information on the German strength and locations there was little to be passed on to the division commanders.

Liaison and staff officers coming from Bastogne brought word of only meager American reinforcements anywhere in the neighborhood of St. Vith. One regiment of the 30th Infantry Division was in Malmédy, thirteen or fourteen miles to the north, but the intervening countryside was swamped German columns heading west. The 82d Airborne Division, it was estimated, would reach Werbomont (about the same distance northwest of Vielsalm) on the morning of 19 December, but it was apparent that in this area also the enemy barred any solid contact with the St. Vith defenders. At Bastogne the 101st Airborne Division was arriving to take over the fight at that critical road junction, but there were no additional reinforcements which General Middleton could employ in plugging the gap between St. Vith and Bastogne.

The problem of maintaining control over the heterogeneous formations in the St. Vith-Vielsalm area or of giving complete tactical unity to the defense was very difficult. Under sustained German pressure a wholly satisfactory solution never would be achieved. The piecemeal employment of lower units, made unavoidable by the march of events, resulted in most involved methods of communication. A tank company, for example, might have to report by radio through its own battalion headquarters, some distance away, which then relayed the message on other channels until it reached the infantry battalion to which the tank company was attached. The homogeneity of the battalion, in American practice the basic tactical unit, largely ceased to exist, nor did time and the enemy ever permit any substantial regrouping to restore this unity. It is surprising that under the circumstances control and communication functioned as well as they did. But the 7th Armored Division was a veteran organization; the general officers in the area dealt with one another on a very cooperative basis; and within the sub-commands established around the coalescing perimeter, the local commanders acted with considerable freedom and initiative.

Although all intention of attempting to breach the German ring around the two regiments of the 106th Division had been abandoned on 18 December and the mission no longer was counterattack, but rather defense in place, there still was a faint hope that the 422d and 423d somehow might be able to fight their way out through Schönberg as General Jones had ordered. During the early morning hours of 19 December messages from the 423d Infantry (dispatched at noon on the previous day) finally reached Vielsalm. From these Jones learned that both regiments had begun the attack westward, but no word on the progress of the attack followed nor did the American outposts on the Schönberg road catch any sound of firing moving west. Finally, late in the evening, a radio message arrived from the VII Corps: bad weather had intervened; the supplies promised the entrapped troops had not been dropped. By this time the last bit of hope for the lost regiments must have gone.

There was one fortunate but unexpected event on the 19th. The exact location and strength of the 112th Infantry, somewhere south of the 424th, were unknown. That a gap existed on the right of the 424th was known. Early on 19 December word reached General Jones by way of liaison officer that, as of the previous evening, the 112th Infantry was cut off from the 28th Division and had fallen back from the Our to the neighborhood of Weiswampach. A few hours later more information filtered back to Vielsalm: the 112th had withdrawn to Huldange, thus coming closer to the 7th Armored and 106th. Finally, in midafternoon, Colonel Nelson (commanding the 112th) appeared at the 106th Division command post and reported his situation, and the regiment was taken over by General Jones—a solution subsequently approved by General Middleton. Colonel Nelson brought a welcome addition to the St. Vith forces. His regiment had lost most of its vehicles, radios, and crew-served weapons but had suffered relatively light casualties and lost but few stragglers. It was well in the hand of its commander and ready to fight. Jones ordered the 112th Infantry to draw northward on the night of 19-20 December and make a firm connection with the southern flank of the 424th.

Throughout the 19th there were sporadic clashes with the enemy around the perimeter. The threatened sector remained the line from Poteau to St. Vith, and from St. Vith along the eastern front covered by CCB, 7th Armored, and CCB, 9th Armored. At Poteau CCA brought more troops into and around the village, while the enemy fired in from the hill to the north rising alongside the Recht road. The southern column of the 1st SS Panzer Division, which first had captured the town, was long since gone, hurrying west. But the newly committed 9th SS Panzer Division, following in its wake via Recht, threw a large detachment of panzer grenadiers into the woods around Poteau, either to retake the crossroad or to pin the Americans there. The resulting state of affairs was summed up when the executive officer of CCA reported to the division G-3: "The CO of CCA wanted these facts made known. He is extended and cannot protect the right flank of the zone between Recht and Poteau. He cannot protect Poteau. He needed two companies of infantry deployed and one in reserve. He is getting infiltration in his rear from the vicinity of Recht. The woods are so thick that he needs almost an infantry platoon to protect three tanks sitting out there. Dismounted infantry in foxholes control the intersection at Poteau but [it is] covered by enemy fire." Nevertheless the Poteau road junction was denied the enemy, and by the close of day patrols had established contact between CCR, to the west, and CCA.

At St. Vith enemy pressure failed to increase during the 19th, and the American commanders took advantage of the breathing spell to reassess their dispositions for defense. The two CCB commanders, Clarke and Hoge, given a free hand by General

Jones and General Hasbrouck, agreed that in the event of any future withdrawal CCB, 9th Armored Division, might be trapped as it then stood because Hoge's combat command, deployed southeast of St. Vith, had no roads for a direct move westward and would be forced to retire through St. Vith. Clarke would hold as long as possible east of the town, but with both combat commands in its streets St. Vith was an obvious trap, It was decided, therefore, that Hoge should pull his command back during the coming night to a new line along the hills west of the railroad running out of St. Vith, thus conforming on its left with CCB, 7th Armored.

The withdrawal was carried out as planned. A small German attack hit the right flank just as the move was being made but was checked by fire from the American tank guns and mortars. The armored infantry were now disposed in the center with the medium tank companies, which had circled through St. Vith, at either flank. The draw extending from the south to the west edge of town served as a boundary between the two CCB's. Because this piece of the front was regarded by both commanders as potentially dangerous, a tank company and a platoon of tank destroyers were placed to back up the troops at the junction point. As part of the reorganization on the 19th, CCB, 7th Armored, took over the 17th Tank Battalion, which had been holding the road southeast of Recht. This fleshed out a more or less connected but thin line running as a semicircle from south of Recht to a point about a thousand yards east of St. Vith, then curving back to the southwest where the 424th Infantry and CCB, 9th Armored, met near Grufflange.

During the 19th the two CCB's had been operating with very limited artillery support, although the 275th Armored Field Artillery Battalion and the 16th Armored Field Artillery Battalion had done yeoman service for their respective combat commands. The arrival of an additional field artillery battalion belonging to the 7th Armored and two 155-mm. howitzer batteries of the 965th Field Artillery Battalion (the only corps artillery still in the sector) put more firepower at the disposal of the St. Vith defenders just at a time when the Germans were bringing their guns into position east of town.

Supply routes to the 7th Armored Division trains were still open, although menaced by the roving enemy and obstructed by west—moving friendly traffic. Having set up installations west of La Roche, the trains' commander (Col. Andrew J. Adams) used his own people and all the stragglers he could find to man roadblocks around the train area. About 1700 two German tanks and a rifle platoon suddenly struck at one of these positions south of La Roche manned by Company C, 129th Ordnance Maintenance Battalion. The ordnance company beat off the Germans, but the appearance this far west of enemy troops (probably from the 116th Panzer Division) indicated that not only the 7th Armored Division trains but the entire division stood in danger of being cut off from the American force gathering around Bastogne.

At the forward command post of the 7th Armored in Vielsalm, the Division G-4 (Lt. Col. Reginald H. Hodgson) sent a message back to Colonel Adams, depicting the view of the situation taken by the St. Vith commanders and their staffs as the 19th came to a close:

"All division units holding firm. Units to south have apparently been by—passed by some Boche. Army dump at Gouvy was abandoned by Army but D/40th Tank Battalion took the town over.... 82 Parachutists (82d Airborne Division) now coming up so we can probably get some ammo....I have no contact with Corps ... but Corps has ordered us to hold and situation well in hand....Hope to see you soon: have sent you copy of all messages sent you. Hope you don't think I'm crazy. CG was well pleased with everything you have done. Congrats. Don't move til you hear from me."

The defense of the St. Vith-Vielsalm area had taken form by the night of 19 December. The troops within the perimeter occupied an "island" with a German tide rushing past on the north and south and rising against its eastern face. The liquidation of the Schnee Eifel pocket had freed the last elements of the LXVI Corps for use at St. Vith; General Lucht now could concentrate on the reduction of that town.

During the day the commanders of Army Group B and the Fifth Panzer Army joined General Lucht at the command post of the 18th Volks Grenadier Division near Wallerode Mill. The LXVI Corps commander left this conference with orders to encircle St. Vith, putting his main weight in enveloping moves north and south of the town. Bad road conditions, the blown bridge at Steinebrück, and continued attempts by Sixth Panzer Army columns to usurp the corps main supply road at Schönberg combined to delay Lucht's concentration. Lucht ordered a barrier erected at Schönberg to sift out the interlopers (Lucht and his chief of staff personally helped make arrests), but this was of little assistance. Corps and division artillery was brought forward piece by piece whenever a break in a traffic jam occurred, but the appearance of these horsedrawn guns in the motorized columns only succeeded in further disrupting the march order. Like the Americans on 17 December, jammed on the St. Vith-Vielsalm road, the Germans lacked adequate military police to handle the situation.

Even so, by the evening of 19 December the two infantry divisions of the LXVI Corps were in position to launch piecemeal attacks at or around St. Vith. The 18th Volks Grenadier Division, on the right, had fed the foot troops of its 295th Regiment in between the Mobile Battalion, deployed around Wallerode, and the 294th, astride the St. Vith-Schönberg road. The 293d Regiment, having aided in the capture of the Schnee Eifel regiments, filed into Schönberg during the night. The division artillery might be in firing position by the morning of the 20th. The 62d Volks Grenadier Division, to the south, finally brought its inner flank into echelon with the left of the 18th near Setz by pivoting the 190th Regiment west. The division left wing was formed by the 164th Regiment, which had occupied Lommersweiler and Hemmeres following the withdrawal of CCB, 9th Armored. The main body of the 183d remained in reserve at Winterspelt. During the night of 19-20 December the Germans completed a division bridge at Steinebrück near that destroyed by the American armored engineers, and division artillery and heavy vehicles began their move north and west.

The real punch in the forthcoming attack would be delivered by the tanks belonging to the Fuehrer Begleit Brigade. This armored brigade, commanded by Col. Otto Remer, had been hastily thrown together around a cadre composed of Hitler's former headquarters guard. When the Fuehrer's command post on the Eastern Front was closed by Hitler's return to Berlin, in November, Remer was given some additional troops and shipped to the west. The final composition of the brigade was roughly equivalent to a reinforced American combat command: three grenadier battalions, a battalion of Mark IV tanks from the Grossdeutschland Panzer Division (a unit that caused Allied intelligence no end of trouble since Grossdeutschland was known to be on the Eastern Front), a battalion each of assault and field guns, and eight batteries of flak which had formed the antiaircraft guard for Hitler. Despite repeated requests by General Lucht, this brigade was not released to reinforce the LXVI Corps until late afternoon on 18 December. Colonel Remer reached the corps headquarters that same night, but the movement of his complete brigade from Daun via Prüm to St. Vith would take considerable time. The orders he received from General Lucht were these: the Fuehrer Begleit Brigade would take part in the St. Vith attack but would not get too involved in the fight; once the town fell the brigade must drive posthaste for the Meuse River. After a personal reconnaissance east of St. Vith on 19 December Remer concluded that a frontal attack in this sector was out of the question. He decided, therefore, to flank the St. Vith defenses from the north as soon as his brigade, scheduled to arrive on 20 December, was in hand.

Chapter XIII. VIII Corps Attempts To Delay the Enemy

CCR, 9th Armored Division, and the Road to Bastogne

CCR, 9th Armored Division, the armored reserve of the VIII Corps, had been stationed at Trois Vierges on 13 December in position to support the corps left and center. It consisted of the 52d Armored Infantry Battalion, 2d Tank Battalion, 73d Armored Field Artillery Battalion, and the conventional task force attachments. By the afternoon of 17 December German armored gains at the expense of the 28th Division, forming the center of the corps front, caused General Middleton to start gathering what anti-mechanized means he could find for commitment; this included the platoon of self-propelled tank destroyers from CCR which, as described earlier, he dispatched toward Clerf.

When the second day of the battle came to a close, it had become apparent that the German columns advancing in the central sector were aiming at the road system leading to Bastogne. Delayed reports from the 28th Division indicated that an enemy breakthrough was imminent. The 9th Armored Division commander already had sent CCR south to Oberwampach, behind the 28th Division center, when General Middleton ordered the combat command to set up two strong roadblocks on the main paved road to Bastogne "without delay." This order came at 2140, ten minutes after word that the enemy had crossed the Clerf reached the VIII Corps command post.

The two roadblock positions selected by the corps commander lay on Highway N 12, which extended diagonally from St. Vith and the German border southwestward to Bastogne. Both positions were on the line which General Middleton would order held "at all costs." Earlier, Middleton had directed the commander of the 106th Division to watch the northern entrance to this road, but the immediate threat on the night of the 17th was that the mobile spearheads of the German attack would gain access to this road much closer to Bastogne. One of the blocking positions was the intersection near the village of Lullange where the hard-surfaced road from Clerf entered that leading to Bastogne. Clerf and its bridges were only five miles away from this junction and, on the evening of 17 December, already under German fire. The second position, three miles to the southwest on Highway N 12 near the village of Allerborn, backed up the Lullange block. More important, the Allerborn road junction was the point at which a continuation of Highway N 12 turned off to the southeast and down into the Wiltz valley where advance patrols of the main German forces, albeit still on the far bank of the Clerf, had appeared. The Allerborn block was only nine miles from Bastogne.

A little after midnight CCR had manned these two important positions, under orders to report to the VIII Corps command post the moment they were brought under assault. Off to the east, however, the 110th Infantry continued the unequal contest with an enemy whose strength was growing by the hour. The force in the hands of the CCR commander, Col. Joseph H. Gilbreth, was small. Now split into two task forces and the supporting CCR headquarters group, the whole was spread thin indeed. Task Force Rose (Capt. L. K. Rose), at the northern roadblock, consisted of a company of Sherman tanks, one armored infantry company, and a platoon of armored engineers. The southern roadblock was manned by Task Force Harper (Lt. Col. Ralph S. Harper), which consisted of the 2d Tank Battalion and two companies of the 52d Armored Infantry Battalion.

In midmorning the troops peering out from the ridge where the northern roadblock had been set up saw figures in field gray entering a patch of woods to the east on the Clerf road, the first indication that the enemy had broken through the Clerf defenses. These Germans belonged to the Reconnaissance Battalion of Lauchert's 2d Panzer Division, whose infantry elements at the moment were eradicating the last American defenders in Clerf. Lauchert's two tank battalions, unaffected by the small arms fire sweeping the Clerf streets were close behind the armored cars and half-tracks of the advance guard.

Two attempts by the Reconnaissance Battalion to feel out Task Force Rose were beaten back with the help of a battery from the 73d Armored Field Artillery Battalion whose howitzers were close enough to give direct fire at both American roadblocks. About 1100 the first Mark IV's of the 2d Battalion, 3d Panzer Regiment, appeared and under cover of an effective smoke screen advanced to within 800 yards of the Shermans belonging to Company A, 2d Tank Battalion. The Germans dallied, probably waiting for the Panzer Battalion, which finally arrived in the early afternoon, then deployed on the left of the Mark IV's. Taken under direct fire by the enemy tank guns, the American infantry withdrew in the direction of the southern roadblock and Rose's tanks now were surrounded on three sides.

Colonel Gilbreth, whose combat command was directly attached to VIII Corps and who was charged with the defense of the entry to the Bastogne highway, could not commit his tiny reserve without the approval of the corps commander. A telephone message from Gilbreth to the VIII Corps command post, at 1405, shows the dilemma in all tactical decisions made during these hours when a few troops, tanks, and tank destroyers represented the only forces available to back up the splintering American line.

"TF Rose ... is as good as surrounded. ... have counted 16 German tanks there. ... TF is being hit from 3 sides. Recommend that they fight their way out. They could use 2 platoons of A/52d Armd Inf Bn [the last rifle reserve in CCR]—everything else is committed.... Did not commit any of the TDs, will wait until the over-all plan is known. Plan to push TF Rose toward the other roadblock. If the decision is to stay, some units will be sent there to help them out."

The corps commander refused to let Rose move; and even if adequate reinforcement for Task Fore Rose had been at hand the hour was too late. A flanking move had driven back the American howitzers, German assault guns saturated the crest position with white phosphorus, and when the Shermans pulled back to the rear slope the panzers simply ringed Rose's company. CCR headquarters got the word at 1430 that the northern roadblock and its defenders had been overrun, but despite the loss of seven Shermans Company A continued to hold. It had been forced back from the road junction, however, and the bulk of the 3d Panzer Regiment was moving out onto the Bastogne highway. The early winter night gave the Americans a chance. Captain Rose broke out cross-country with five tanks and his assault gun platoon, rolling fast without lights through little villages toward Houffalize, near which the detachment was ambushed. A few vehicles and crews broke free and reached Bastogne.

The southern roadblock came under German fire in the late afternoon, light enemy elements seeping past the beleaguered block at the northern junction. The Mark IV's and Panthers actually did not reach Task Force Harper until after dark. Sweeping the area with machine gun fire to clear out any infantry who might be protecting the American tanks, the panzers overran and destroyed two tank platoons of Company C, 2d Tank Battalion. Perhaps the weight of this night attack had caught the American tankers off guard: the enemy later reported that only three Shermans at the Allerborn block were able to maneuver into a fighting stance. The armored infantry, about 500 yards from the Shermans, had no better fortune. The panzers set the American vehicles afire with tracer bullets, then picked out their targets silhouetted by the flames. During this action Colonel Harper was killed. What was left of Task Force Harper and stragglers from Task Force Rose headed west toward Longvilly, where CCR headquarters had been set up.

Longvilly, five and a half miles from Bastogne, was the scene of considerable confusion. Stragglers were marching and riding through the village, and the location of the enemy was uncertain, although rumor placed him on all sides. About 2000 an officer appeared at Gilbreth's command post and, to the delight of the CCR staff, reported that a task force from the 10th Armored Division (Team Cherry) was down the Bastogne road. The task force commander, Lt. Col. Henry T. Cherry, he then announced, had orders not to advance east of Longvilly. This word abruptly altered the atmosphere in the command post.

Two armored field artillery battalions (the 73d and 58th) still were firing from positions close to Longvilly, pouring shells onto the Allerborn road junction from which Task Force Harper had been driven. A handful of riflemen from the 110th Infantry, including Company G which had been ordered to Clerf and the remnants of the 110th headquarters which had been driven out of Allerborn, were still in action. These troops, together with four tank destroyers from the 630th Tank Destroyer Battalion, had formed a skirmish line to protect the firing batteries of the 58th south of the village.

Late in the evening firing was heard behind the CCR position. This came from Mageret, next on the Bastogne road, where German troops had infiltrated and cut off the fire direction center of the 73d Field Artillery Battalion. The firing batteries nevertheless continued to shell the road east of Longvilly, tying in with the 58th Field Artillery Battalion. Both battalions were firing with shorter and shorter fuzes; by 2315 the gunners were aiming at enemy infantry and vehicles only two hundred yards to the front. Somehow the batteries held on. A little before midnight Colonel Gilbreth ordered what was left of CCR and its attached troops to begin a withdrawal via Mageret. A few vehicles made a run for it but were ambushed by the Germans now in possession of Mageret. When a disorderly vehicle column jammed the exit from Longvilly, Gilbreth saw that some order must be restored and stopped all movement until morning light.

Under orders, the 73d Armored Field Artillery Battalion displaced westward, starting about 0400, one battery covering another until the three were west of

Longvilly firing against enemy seen to the east, north, and south, but giving some cover for the CCR withdrawal. The 58th Field Artillery Battalion and its scratch covering force were hit early in the morning by a mortar barrage, and very shortly two German halftracks appeared through the half-light. These were blasted with shellfire but enemy infantry had wormed close in, under cover of the morning fog, and drove back the thin American line in front of the batteries. About 0800 the fog swirled away, disclosing a pair of enemy tanks almost on the howitzers. In a sudden exchange of fire the tanks were destroyed.

About this time CCR started along the Bastogne road, although a rear guard action continued in Longvilly until noon. The 58th Field Artillery Battalion, with cannoneers and drivers the only rifle protection, joined the move, Battery B forming a rear guard and firing point-blank at pursuing German armor. The head of the main column formed by CCR was close to Mageret when, at a halt caused by a roadblock, hostile fire erupted on the flanks of the column. There was no turning back, nor could the vehicles be extricated from the jam along the road. The melee lasted for several hours. Company C of the 482d Antiaircraft Artillery Battalion (Capt. Denny J. Lovio) used its mobile quadruple machine guns with effect, working "heroically," as CCR later acknowledged, to hold the Germans at bay. The two batteries of the 8th Armored Field Artillery Battalion that had been able to bring off their self-propelled howitzers went into action, but the fog had thickened and observed fire was wellnigh impossible. At long last the dismounted and disorganized column was brought into some order "by several unknown officers who ... brought leadership and confidence to our troops."

In midafternoon CCR headquarters, the remnants of the 58th, and the stragglers who had been accumulated in the Longvilly defense made their way around to the north of Mageret, thence to Foy, and finally to Bastogne, this move being made under cover of fire laid down by paratroopers from the 101st who seemed to materialize out of nowhere. The losses sustained by CCR cannot be accurately determined, for a part of those listed in the final December report were incurred later in the defense of Bastogne. 2 The 58th Armored Field Artillery Battalion had lost eight of its howitzers; the 73d Armored Field Artillery Battalion had lost four. That these battalions were self-propelled accounts for the fact that so many pieces, closely engaged as the batteries had been, were saved to fire another day.

While the battle for the roadblocks and Longvilly was going on, a third task force from CCR (Lt. Col. Robert M. Booth) had been separately engaged. As a guard against tank attack from the north, the CCR commander sent Booth with the headquarters and headquarters company of the 52d Armored Infantry Battalion, plus a platoon from the 811th Tank Destroyer Battalion, and a platoon of light tanks to occupy the high ground north of the Allerborn-Longvilly section of the main highway. During the night of 18-19 December Booth's position received some enemy fire but did not come under direct assault. Communications with CCR had broken down, however, and German tanks had been identified passing to the rear along the Bourcy road.

Booth decided that the best chance of escaping encirclement lay in moving out to the northwest. At daylight on the 19th the column started, picking up stragglers from the original roadblocks as it moved. The light tank platoon dropped off early in the march to fight a rear guard action against the enemy who was closing in on the column and to protect a number of half-tracks which had bogged down. Hard pressed and unable to disengage its vehicles, the rear guard finally escaped on foot.

The main column dodged and detoured in a series of small brushes with the Germans, who by this time seemed to be everywhere, until it reached Hardigny, three miles northwest of the starting point. German tanks and infantry were waiting here, and in the ensuing fight the column was smashed. About 225 officers and men escaped into the nearby woods and after devious wanderings behind the German lines, some for as long as six days, finally reached Bastogne.

The Advance of the XLVII Panzer Corps

Luettwitz' XLVII Panzer Corps was coming within striking distance of Bastogne by the evening of 18 December. The 2d Panzer Division, particularly, had picked up speed on the north wing after the surprising delay at Clerf. Luettwitz' mission remained as originally planned, that is, to cross the Meuse in the Namur sector, and the capture of Bastogne remained incidental—although none the less important—to this goal.

Having erased the two roadblocks defended by CCR, General Lauchert turned his 2d Panzer Division to the northwest so as to swing past the Bastogne road nexus and maintain the momentum of the westward drive. This maneuver was according to plan for there was no intention to use the 2d Panzer Division in a coup de main at Bastogne. Lauchert's column followed the remnants of Task Force Harper from the Allerborn roadblock, then turned off the Bastogne highway near the hamlet of Chifontaine and headed toward Bourcy and Noville. It was the 2d Panzer tanks which Task Force Booth had heard rolling in its rear on the night of 18-19 December and with which its rear guard collided on the 19th. Although Task Force Booth and the Germans at first missed each other, the subsequent American attempt to circle around the northwest and thus attain Bastogne threw Booth's column straight into the German path. Lauchert's advance guard had hit Noville but found it strongly held and was forced to withdraw. As a result a strong detachment moved north to Hardigny, before a flanking attempt against the Noville garrison, and here encountered and cut to pieces Booth's column.

The American troops defending in and around Longvilly were given a period of grace by Lauchert's decision to turn off on the Bourcy road. A second on-the-spot decision by another German commander added a few hours' breathing space. Bayerlein's Panzer Lehr Division was slowly climbing out of the Wiltz valley on the afternoon and evening of 18 December, en route to an assembly point at Niederwampach. The division had met little resistance but the roads were poor (the corps commander had caviled against the zone assigned the Panzer Lehr even during the planning period), and march control was further burdened by the fact that the 26th Volks Grenadier Division was marching two of its rifle regiments toward the same assembly area. Theoretically the mobile columns of Panzer Lehr now should have been ahead of the infantry division. In fact the foot troops of the 26th were making nearly as much speed as the armor. Horse-drawn artillery was mixed up with armored vehicles, the roads had been pounded to sloughs, and the German timetable for advance in this sector had gone out the window.

In the early evening Bayerlein himself led the advance guard of the Panzer Lehr (four companies of the 902d Panzer Grenadier Regiment and some fifteen tanks) into Niederwampach. On the march the advance guard had heard the sounds of battle and seen gunfire flaming to the north, "an impressive sight," Bayerlein later recalled. This was the 2d Panzer Division destroying the Allerborn roadblock defense. Bayerlein had two choices at this point. He could direct his division south to the hardsurfaced road linking Bras, Marvie, and Bastogne, or he could risk an unpaved and muddy side road via Benonchamps which would put the Panzer Lehr onto the main Bastogne highway at Mageret, three miles east of Bastogne. Bayerlein decided on the side road because it was shorter and he believed that it probably was unguarded.

A kampfgruppe (a dozen tanks, a battalion of armored infantry, and one battery) was sent on to seize Mageret and arrived there an hour or so before midnight. The Americans occupied the village, but only with a small detachment of the 158th Engineer Combat Battalion, which had been ordered in to block the road, and a few of the service troops belonging to CCR. Fighting here continued sporadically for an hour or two as Americans and Germans stumbled upon each other in the dark. By 0100 on 19 December the enemy had set up his own roadblock east of the village, for about that time ambulances evacuating wounded from Longvilly were checked by bullet fire. Thus far the Panzer Lehr advance guard had run into no serious trouble, but a friendly civilian reported that American tanks had gone through Mageret earlier, en route to Longvilly. These tanks belonged to Team Cherry from CCB of the 10th Armored Division.

Team Cherry on the Longvilly Road
On the evening of 18 December Team Cherry moved out of Bastogne on the road to Longvilly. Since he had the leading team in the CCB, 10th Armored, column, Cherry had been assigned this mission by Colonel Roberts because of the immediate and obvious enemy threat to the east. Cherry had Company A and two light tank platoons of his own 3d Tank Battalion, Company C of the 20th Armored Infantry Battalion, the 2d Platoon of Company D, 90th Cavalry Reconnaissance, and a few medics and armored engineers. His headquarters and headquarters company was established in Neffe, just east of Bastogne; his trains, fortunately as it turned out, remained in Bastogne. The VIII Corps commander had designated Longvilly as one of the three positions which CCB was to hold at all costs. Cherry knew that CCR, 9th Armored Division, was supposed to be around Longvilly, but beyond that he was totally in the dark. Even the maps at hand were nearly useless. The 1:100,000 sheets were accurate enough for a road march but told little of the terrain where the team would deploy.

About 1900, after an uneventful move, 1st Lt. Edward P. Hyduke, commanding the advance guard, reached the western edge of Longvilly. Seeing that the village was jammed with vehicles, he halted on the road. An hour later Cherry and his S-3 arrived at the headquarters of CCR where they learned that the situation was "vague." CCR had no plans except to carry out the "hold at all costs" order, and at the moment its southern roadblock had not yet been overrun. Cherry went back to Bastogne to tell the CCB commander, 10th Armored Division, how things were going, leaving orders for the advance guard to scout and establish a position just west of Longvilly while the main force (Capt. William F. Ryerson) closed up along the road with its head about a thousand yards west of the town. Hyduke's reconnaissance in the meantime had convinced him that the main gap in the defenses around Longvilly was in the south, and there he stationed the cavalry platoon, four Sherman tanks, and seven light tanks.

Just before midnight Lieutenant Hyduke learned that CCR intended to fall back toward Bastogne (although, in fact, the CCR commander later curtailed this move) and radioed Colonel Cherry to this effect. When Cherry got the message, about two hours later, he also learned that Mageret had been seized by the Germans and that his headquarters at Neffe now was cut off from the team at Longvilly. Team Hyduke was in the process of shifting in the dark to cover Longvilly on the east, north, and south. Ryerson had sent a half-track load of infantry to feel out the situation at Mageret, while independently CCR headquarters (9th Armored Division) had dispatched a self-propelled tank destroyer from its platoon of the 811th Tank Destroyer Battalion on the same mission. After apprehensive and belated recognition the two crews agreed that the road through Mageret could be opened only by force. This word ultimately reached Cherry who sent back orders, received at 0830, that Ryerson should fight his way through Mageret while the erstwhile advance guard conducted a rear guard defense of Longvilly.

During the night small German forces had tried, rather halfheartedly, to get into Longvilly or at least to pick off the weapons and vehicles crowded in the streets by the light of flares and searchlights directed on the town. As yet the German artillery and heavy mortars had not come forward in any number and Longvilly was shelled only in desultory fashion. The two right-wing regiments Of the 26th Volks Grenadier Division were reoriented to the northwest in a move to reach the Noville-Bastogne road and place the division in position for a flanking attack aimed at penetrating the Bastogne perimeter from the north. On the extreme right the 77th Grenadier Regiment had bivouacked near Oberwampach, its orders to advance at daybreak through Longvilly and head for Foy. Its left neighbor, the 78th, was to make the main effort, swinging around to the north of Mageret and attacking to gain the high ground beyond Luzery.

This plan failed to recognize the limitations of physical stamina and supply. With the dawn, the two regimental commanders reported that their troops must be rested and resupplied before the advance could resume. Shortly after 1000 the 77th was ready to start its advance guard through Longvilly, believing that the town was in German hands. In light of the way in which troops of the 26th Volks Grenadier Division, Panzer Lehr, and 2d Panzer Division had poured into the area east of Bastogne during the night, crossing and recrossing boundary lines which now existed mostly on paper, it is not surprising that General Kokott and his commanders were a little vague as to whose troops held Longvilly.

The 77th was close to the town, advancing in route column when patrols suddenly signaled that the Americans were ahead. It was too late to bypass the town; so the German regimental commander hastily organized an attack behind a screen of machine guns which he rushed forward, at the same time borrowing some tanks from the 2d Panzer Division for a turning movement northeast of Longvilly. The division commander, however, ordered the attack held up until it could be organized and supported, made arrangements with the Panzer Lehr Division to join by a thrust from the southwest, and hurried guns and Werfers up to aid the infantry. General Luettwitz, the corps commander, also took a hand in the game, without reference to Kokott, by ordering the 78th Grenadier Regiment to turn back toward the east in support of the 77th. When Kokott heard what had been done with his left regiment the 78th already was on the road, and it took until early afternoon to get the regiment turned around and moving west. An hour or so after noon the reinforced 77th was ready to jump off from the attack positions south, east, and northeast of Longvilly.

By this time the bulk of CCR (9th Armored Division) and the mass of stragglers who had attached themselves to CCR were jammed in an immobile crowd along the road to Mageret, but a few riflemen were still holed up in the houses at Longvilly and the third platoon of Company C, 811th Tank Destroyer Battalion, was manfully working its guns to cover the rear of the CCR column. The main action, however, devolved on the tanks and armored infantry which Hyduke had shifted during the night to form a close perimeter at Longvilly.

The first indication of the nearing assault was a storm of Werfer and artillery shells. Then came the German tanks borrowed from the 2d Panzer Division, ramming forward from the north and east. In the confused action which followed the American tankers conducted themselves so well that Lauchert later reported a "counterattack" from Longvilly against the 2d Panzer flank. But the Shermans and the American light tanks were not only outnumbered but outgunned by the Panthers and the 88's of a flak battalion. The foregone conclusion was reached a little before 1400 when the last of the light tanks, all that remained, were destroyed by their crews who found it impossible to maneuver into the clear. The armored infantry were forced to abandon their half-tracks. The same thing happened to the three tank destroyers. At least eight panzers had been destroyed in the melee, but Longvilly was taken.

Lieutenant Hyduke's team, acting under orders to rejoin Captain Ryerson's main party, threaded a way west on foot and in small groups through the broken and burning column now in the last throes of dissolution, in the woods along the road, under a rain of shells and bullets. Ryerson's team, which Colonel Cherry had instructed early in the morning to withdraw to the west, had been hard put to reverse itself and negotiate the cluttered road leading to Mageret. The leading American tank had reached a road cut some three hundred yards east of Mageret when a hidden tank or antitank gun suddenly opened fire, put a round into the Sherman, and set it aflame. The road into Mageret was closed and all possibility of a dash through the village ended.

Protected somewhat by the banks rising on either side of the road the Americans spent the day trying to inch forward to the north and south of the village. Some of the gunners and infantry from the CCR (9th Armored Division) column attempted to take a hand in the fight and help push forward a bit, but constant and accurate shelling (probably from Panzer Lehr tanks which had been diverted northward from Benonchamps to aid the 26th Volks Grenadier Division) checked every move. At dark a small detachment from Ryerson's team and CCR reached the houses on the edge of Mageret. The village was held in some strength by detachments of the 26th Reconnaissance Battalion and Panzer Lehr. Ryerson had to report: "Having tough time. [The Germans] are shooting flares and knocking out our vehicles with direct fire." But the Americans held onto their little chunk of the village through the night.

While the bulk of Team Cherry was engaged at Longvilly and Mageret, the team commander and his headquarters troops were having a fight of their own at Neffe, a mile and a quarter southwest of Mageret. Here, cut off from his main force, Colonel Cherry had waited through the small hours of 19 December with the comforting assurance that troops of the 101st Airborne Division were moving through Bastogne and would debouch to the east sometime that day. At first light a detachment of tanks and infantry from the Panzer Lehr hit the Reconnaissance Platoon, 3d Tank Battalion, outposting the Neffe crossroads. The platoon stopped one tank with a bazooka round, but then broke under heavy fire and headed down the Bastogne road. One of the two American headquarters tanks in support of the roadblock got away, as did a handful of troopers, and fell back to Cherry's command post, a stone château three hundred yards to the south.

The enemy took his time about following up, but just before noon moved in to clear the château. For four hours the 3d Tank Battalion on command post group held on behind the heavy walls, working the automatic weapons lifted from its vehicles and checking every rush in a blast of bullets. Finally a few hardy Germans made it, close enough at least to pitch incendiary grenades through the Window. Fire, leaping through the rooms, closed this episode. Reinforcements, a platoon of the 501st Parachute Infantry, arrived just in time to take part in the withdrawal. But their appearance and the covering fire of other troops behind them jarred the Germans enough to allow Cherry and his men to break free. Before pulling out for Mont, the next village west, Colonel Cherry radioed the CCB commander this message: "We are pulling out. We're not driven out but burned out."

Through the afternoon and evening of 19 December Captain Ryerson and the little force clutching at the edge of Mageret waited for reinforcements to appear over the ridges to the south, for CCB had radioed that help (from the 101st Airborne Division) was on the way. Finally, after midnight, new word came from CCB. Ryerson was to withdraw northwest to Bizory at dawn and join the 501st Parachute Infantry there. A little after daybreak Team Ryerson took its remaining vehicles, its wounded, and the stragglers who had paused to take part in the fight and pulled away from Mageret. Forty minutes across country and it entered the paratrooper lines. The total cost to Team Cherry of the engagements on 19 December had been 175 officers and men, one-quarter of the command. Matériel losses had included seventeen armored half-tracks and an equal number of tanks. Team Cherry records fifteen German tanks destroyed in this day of catch-as-catch-can fighting, a likely figure since the 2d Panzer Division counted eight of its own tanks knocked out in one spot north of Longvilly.

The story here set down has been one of mischance and confusion. But regard the manner in which CCR, 9th Armored Division, and Team Cherry altered the course of the German drive on Bastogne. Through the night of 18-19 December General Luettwitz hourly expected word that the advance guard of the XLVII Panzer Corps had reached Bastogne and the road there from north to Houffalize. This good news failed to arrive. While it was true that the resistance in the sector held by the American 110th Infantry had finally crumbled, the cost to the Germans had been dear in men, matériel, and tactical disorganization, but most of all in time. Fatigue too was beginning to tell. Yet Luettwitz had some reason to expect, as he did, that the road to the west at last was clear and that the lost momentum would shortly be restored. Instead, as the record shows, the XLVII Panzer Corps continued to encounter irritating delays, delays compounded by American resistance, fatigue among the attacking troops, disintegrating roads, a general loss of control on the part of the German commanders, and, most telling of all, a momentary thickening of the "fog of war." On the right wing of the corps the fight waged at the Lullange road junction by Task Force Rose cheated the 2d Panzer Division of vital daylight hours. More time was lost in reducing the Allerborn roadblock, and Lauchert's advance guard found itself on the Bourcy-Noville road in the middle of the night. It is not surprising that the German advance was cautious and further attack to the northwest delayed. The whole affair added up to several extra hours that allowed the American defenders at the Noville outpost of Bastogne until midmorning on the 19th to get set.

The story of events at Longvilly and on the Longvilly-Mageret road merits particular attention by the student of tactics. Here was a confused and heterogeneous force whose main concern on the night of 18-19 December and the following day was to find a way out of the German trap whose jaws were in plain view. Further resistance by either CCR or Team Cherry was intended strictly as a rear guard action. Yet the mere physical presence of these troops in the Longvilly area caused a confusion in German plans and a diversion of the German main effort on 19 December out of all proportion to the tactical strength or importance of the American units involved. The "discovery," on the morning of 19 December, that American troops were in and around Longvilly cost the 26th Volks Grenadier Division at least four hours of precious daylight, first in setting up an attack for the 77th Grenadier Regiment and then in straightening out the 78th. As a result when night came the right wing of the 26th Volks Grenadier Division was only a little over two miles beyond Longvilly, and the left, which had crossed to the north side of the Bastogne road in the late afternoon, reached Bizory too late for a fullscale daylight assault.

Although the main advance guard of the Panzer Lehr Division continued to the west on 19 December, where it ran afoul of Cherry's headquarters group at Neffe, a considerable part of the Panzer Lehr armored strength was diverted north from Benonchamps to use its tank gun fire against the Americans seen along the road east of Mageret and later to attack that village. Troops of both the 901st and 902d were thrown in to mop up the woods where the CCR column attempted to make a stand and they did not complete this job until midafternoon. So, although the Panzer Lehr elements had helped free the Longvilly-Mageret road for the belated advance by the 26th Volks Grenadier Division to the northwest, the Panzer Lehr advance west of Bastogne was not the full-bodied affair necessary at this critical moment. The sudden blow at Bastogne which the commander of the XLVII Panzer Corps had hoped to deliver failed to come off on 19 December. Some American outposts had been driven in, but with such loss of time and uneconomical use of means that the remaining outposts in front of Bastogne now were manned and ready.

The 101st Airborne Division Moves Into Bastogne

After the long, bitter battle in Holland the 82d and 101st Airborne Divisions lay in camp near Reims, resting, refitting, and preparing for the next airborne operation. General Ridgway's XVIII Airborne Corps, to which these divisions belonged, constituted the strategic reserve for the Allied forces in western Europe. Although the Supreme Allied Commander had in the past attempted to create a SHAEF Reserve of a size commensurate with the expeditionary forces under his command, he had been continually thwarted by the demands of a battle front extending from the North Sea to Switzerland. On 16 December, therefore, the SHAEF Reserve consisted solely of the two airborne divisions in France.

Less than thirty-six hours after the start of the German counteroffensive, General Hodges, seeing the VIII Corps center give way under massive blows and having thrown his own First Army reserves into the fray plus whatever Simpson's Ninth could spare, turned to Bradley with a request for the SHAEF Reserve. Eisenhower listened to Bradley and acceded, albeit reluctantly; the two airborne divisions would be sent immediately to the VIII Corps area. Orders for the move reached the chief of staff of the XVIII Airborne Corps during the early evening of 17 December and the latter promptly relayed the alert to the 82d and 101st. There seems to have been some delay in reaching the corps commander in England, where he was observing the training of a new division (the 17th Airborne), but a couple of hours after midnight he too had his orders and began hurried preparations for the flight to France.

The two divisions had little organic transportation—after all they were equipped to fly or parachute into battle—but in a matter of hours the Oise Section of the Communications Zone gathered enough 10-ton open trucks and trailers plus the work horse 2 ½-tonners to mount all the airborne infantry. Because the 82d had been given a little more rest than the 101st and would take less time to draw its battle gear and get on the road, it was selected to lead the motor march into Belgium. Ridgway would be delayed for some hours; so General Gavin, commanding the 82d, assumed the role of acting corps commander, setting out at once for the First Army headquarters where he arrived in mid-morning on the 18th. Since Maj. Gen. Maxwell D. Taylor was on leave in the United States, Brig. Gen. Anthony C. McAuliffe, artillery commander of the 101st, prepared to lead this division into battle.

To alert and dispatch the two veteran airborne divisions was a methodical business, although both moved to the front minus some equipment and with less than the prescribed load of ammunition. This initial deployment in Belgium presents a less ordered picture, blurred by the fact that headquarters journals fail to square with one another and the memories of the commanders involved are at variance, particularly as regards the critical decision (or decisions) which brought the 101st to Bastogne and its encounter with history.

General Middleton, the VIII Corps commander, had his headquarters in Bastogne when the storm broke in the east. The city quite literally commanded the highway system lacing the southern section of the Belgian Ardennes. Middleton, having done all he could on the 16th and 17th to assemble his meager reserve of tanks and engineers in last-ditch positions on the roads entering Bastogne from the east, read the pattern of the enemy advance in these terms on the 17th. The number of German divisions and the speed at which they were moving would require the acquisition of a much larger road net than the Germans had thus far used. If St. Vith held and the V Corps shoulder did not give way, the enemy would attempt to seize the excellent highway net at Bastogne. Middleton therefore planned to hold the original VIII Corps positions as long as possible (in accordance with orders from General Hodges), and at the same time to build strong defenses in front of St. Vith, Houffalize, Bastogne, and Luxembourg City.

For the second stage of his plan he counted on prompt assistance from the First and Third Armies to create the defenses for St. Vith and Luxembourg, while the two airborne divisions—which Hodges had assured him would be forthcoming—took over Bastogne and Houffalize. Middleton reasoned that a strong American concentration in the Bastogne-Houffalize sector would force the enemy to come to him, and that in any case he would be in strength on the German flank and rear. At midnight on the 17th the VIII Corps commander had a telephone call from Hodges' headquarters and heard the welcome word that he probably would get the 82d and 101st Airborne Divisions "immediately." Middleton's plan, it seemed, could be put in effect by the morning of the 19th.

Eisenhower's order to commit the two airborne divisions did not specify exactly how they would be employed. Bradley and Hodges were agreed that they would be thrown in to block the German spearhead columns, but Lt. Gen. Walter Bedell Smith, the SHAEF chief of staff, seems to have selected Bastogne as the initial rendezvous point in Belgium without any knowledge of the First Army and VIII Corps plans. In any event Smith expected both of the airborne divisions to assemble around Bastogne.

The subsequent order of events is rather uncertain. When Gavin reported at Spa on the morning of the 18th, he found the First Army staff gravely concerned by Peiper's armored thrust toward Werbomont and he was ordered to divert the incoming 82d, then en route to Bastogne, toward Werbomont. Initially both Gavin and McAuliffe were under the impression that the 101st was to go to Werbomont; actually McAuliffe started with his advance party to report to Gavin at that point but detoured with the intention of first getting Middleton's view of the situation. Middleton, on the other hand, expected that the 82d Airborne would be put in at Houffalize to seal the gap opening on the north flank of the VIII Corps. McAuliffe reached Bastogne about 1600.

The VIII Corps roadblocks east of Bastogne had meanwhile begun to give way. Middleton got Bradley's permission to divert the 101st to the defense of Bastogne, whereupon Hodges turned the 101st over to Middleton and ordered him to withdraw his corps headquarters from the threatened city. Middleton, however, remained with a few of his staff to brief Ridgway, who reached Bastogne in the early evening, and to help McAuliffe make his initial dispositions, the latter selecting an assembly area around Mande-St. Etienne, some four miles west of Bastogne. The VIII Corps commander telephoned Bradley that he had ordered the 101st to defend Bastogne, that there was no longer a corps reserve, and that the 101st might be forced to fight it out alone.

Turning the motor columns of the 101st was catch-as-catch-can. At the village of Herbomont two main roads extend southeast to Bastogne and northeast of Houffalize (en route to Werbomont). When the leader of the 101st column, Col. Thomas L. Sherburne, Jr., reached Herbomont about 2000 he found two military police posts some two hundred yards apart, one busily engaged in directing all airborne traffic to the northeast, the other directing it to the southeast. This confusion was soon straightened out; the last trucks of the 82d roared away in the direction of Werbomont and Sherburne turned the head of the 101st column toward Bastogne. The story now becomes that of the 101st Airborne Division and of those units which would join it in the fight to bar the way west through Bastogne.

The 501st Parachute Infantry Regiment (Lt. Col. Julian J. Ewell) headed the 101st Division columns rolling into Belgium, followed by the 506th Parachute Infantry (Col. Robert F. Sink), the 502d Parachute Infantry (Lt. Col. Steve A. Chappuis), and the 327th Glider Infantry Regiment (Col. Joseph H. Harper) to which was attached the 1st Battalion of the 401st Glider Infantry. (The 1st Battalion from the 401st is carried as the "3d Battalion" in the journals of the 327th and this designation will be used throughout the narrative.)

The division was smaller than a conventional infantry division (it numbered 805 officers and 11,035 men), but the organization into four regiments was better adapted to an all-round or four-sided defense than the triangular formation common to the regular division. The 101st had three battalions of light field pieces, the modified pack howitzer with a maximum effective range of about 8,000 yards. In place of the medium artillery battalions normally organic or attached to the infantry division, the airborne carried one battalion of 105-mm. howitzers. Also the airborne division had no armor attached, whereas in practice at least one tank battalion accompanied every regular division. The odd bits and pieces of armored, artillery, and tank destroyer units which were en route to Bastogne or would be absorbed on the ground by the 101st would ultimately coalesce to provide a "balanced" combat force in the defense of Bastogne.

Three of these ancillary units retained their tactical identity throughout the fight at Bastogne. The 705th Tank Destroyer Battalion (Lt. Col. Clifford Templeton) was in Germany with the Ninth Army when it received orders on the evening of the 18th to go south to Bastogne. By the time the column reached the Ourthe River, German tanks were so close at hand that Templeton had to detour to the west. To protect his trains he dropped off two platoons to hold the Ortheuville bridge, one of those accidents of war which have fateful consequences. On the night of the 19th the battalion reached Bastogne. The 705th was equipped with the new self-propelled long-barreled 76-mm. gun which would permit a duel on equal terms with most of the German tank guns.

The 755th Armored Field Artillery Battalion (Lt. Col. William F. Hartman) was sent from Germany on the evening of the 18th with equally vague orders to proceed to Bastogne. The battalion reached its destination the following morning to find Bastogne jammed with vehicles. Middleton ordered Colonel Hartman to keep his bulky prime movers and 155-mm. howitzers out of the city until, in the evening, some traffic order had been restored.

The 969th Field Artillery Battalion (Lt. Col. Hubert D. Barnes), also equipped with medium howitzers, joined the Bastogne defense more or less by chance. Originally assigned to support the 28th Division artillery, the battalion had been ordered to displace west as the enemy broke into the open. Sent hither and yon by liaison officers who apparently knew no more of the situation than did the cannoneers, the battalion was moving out of the Bastogne sector when orders came to emplace and fire by map on German troops along the road entering Noville from the north. Thus the 969th joined the Bastogne battle. Ordered by McAuliffe into the slowly forming perimeter, it took firing positions at Villeroux near the 755th and the 420th Armored Field Artillery Battalions. These three battalions together would form a groupment firing from the west around the entire sweep of the Bastogne perimeter.

The 101st move from Camp Mourmelon to Bastogne was made in rain and snow flurries; for the later serials most of the 107-mile trip was in darkness. All parts of the column were forced to buck the mass of vehicles streaming back to the west. But the move was made in good time, the 501st in the van taking only eight hours before it detrucked at midnight. By 0900 on 19 December McAuliffe had all four regiments in hand

There could be no prolonged pause for an integrated division deployment, for all through the night messages of apprehension, defeat, and disaster—none too precise—came into Bastogne. Middleton counted on CCB of the 10th Armored Division (Col. William Roberts) to heal the breach—for a time at least—opened on the main road east of Bastogne. He expected McAuliffe to support this force, but as yet the enemy dispositions and intentions were too uncertain to permit any wholesale commitment of the 101st.

Chapter XIV. The VIII Corps Barrier Lines

On the morning of 16 December General Middleton's VIII Corps had a formal corps reserve consisting of one armored combat command and four engineer combat battalions. In dire circumstances Middleton might count on three additional engineer combat battalions which, under First Army command, were engaged as the 1128th

Engineer Group in direct support of the normal engineer operations on foot in the VIII Corps area. In exceptionally adverse circumstances, that is under conditions then so remote as to be hardly worth a thought, the VIII Corps would have a last combat residue—poorly armed and ill-trained for combat—made up of rear echelon headquarters, supply, and technical service troops, plus the increment of stragglers who might, in the course of battle, stray back from the front lines. General Middleton would be called upon to use all of these "reserves." Their total effect in the fight to delay the German forces hammering through the VIII Corps center would be extremely important but at the same time generally incalculable, nor would many of these troops enter the pages of history.

A handful of ordnance mechanics manning a Sherman tank fresh from the repair shop are seen at a bridge. By their mere presence they check an enemy column long enough for the bridge to be demolished. The tank and its crew disappear. They have affected the course of the Ardennes battle, even though minutely, but history does not record from whence they came or whither they went. A signal officer checking his wire along a byroad encounters a German column; he wheels his jeep and races back to alert a section of tank destroyers standing at a crossroad. Both he and the gunners are and remain anonymous. Yet the tank destroyers with a few shots rob the enemy of precious minutes, even hours. A platoon of engineers appears in one terse sentence of a German commander's report. They have fought bravely, says the foe, and forced him to waste a couple of hours in deployment and maneuver. In this brief emergence from the fog of war the engineer platoon makes its bid for recognition in history. That is all. A small group of stragglers suddenly become tired of what seems to be eternally retreating. Miles back they ceased to be part of an organized combat formation, and recorded history, at that point, lost them. The sound of firing is heard for fifteen minutes, an hour, coming from a patch of woods, a tiny village, the opposite side of a hill. The enemy has been delayed; the enemy resumes the march westward. Weeks later a graves registration team uncovers mute evidence of a last-ditch stand at woods, village, or hill.

The story of the units that were retained under tactical control and employed directly by General Middleton in the attempt to form some defense in depth in the VIII Corps center has been partially recorded and therefore can be narrated. The effect that these units had in retarding the German advances, a course of action evolving extemporaneously, must be considered along with the role played by the uncoordinated frontline formations in the haphazard sequence of their delaying actions from east to west. For convenience sake the VIII Corps action is recounted here in independent detail.

With the very limited forces at his disposal prior to 16 December the VIII Corps commander found it physically impossible to erect any of the standard defenses taught in the higher army schools or prescribed in the field service regulations. The best he could do to defend the extended front was to deploy his troops as a screen, retaining local reserves for local counterattack at potentially dangerous points. In effect, therefore, the main part of Middleton's reserve consisted of the battalions and companies assembled in or close to the villages which formed the strongpoints of the screen. Under the circumstances there could be no thought of an elastic defense with strong formations echeloned in any depth behind the forward positions. In the event of a general attack in great strength delivered against all parts of the corps front simultaneously, Middleton had little choice but to carry out the general directive to "defend in place." With four engineer battalions and one small armored combat command as the only corps reserve behind an elongated and brittle linear defense Middleton's commitment of this last reserve would turn on the attempt to plug a few of the gaps in the forward line, slow the enemy columns on a few main roads, and strengthen by human means two or three of the natural physical barriers deep in the corps rear area.

Middleton's First Moves

During the daylight hours of 16 December the direction of the German main effort and the weight of the forces involved was only vaguely perceived by the VIII Corps and higher commands. In the front lines the troops actually grappling with the enemy initially reported piecemeal and seemingly localized attacks. As the day progressed and the attackers appeared in greater numbers the changing situation duly was reported through the chain of command. By this time, however, communications had been so disrupted that the time lag as represented on the situation maps in corps and army headquarters was a matter of several hours. As a result CCR, 9th Armored Division, and the four engineer combat battalions received alert orders and carried out assembly, but only the 168th Engineer Combat Battalion was committed and it had a string attached that restricted its free employment by the 106th Infantry Division. Of the three army engineer battalions in the VIII Corps zone under the 1128th Engineer Group, one, the 299th Engineer Combat Battalion, already was in the battle area. During the day its sawmills at Diekirch received a part in a First Army security plan, prepared a fortnight earlier. About one o'clock on the morning of the 16th the 299th was put on alert status with other units in the army rear area to meet expected landings of German paratroops. Through the first day of the counteroffensive, therefore, the 1128th had most of its men reinforcing the guards at rear area headquarters and installations or manning observation points.

During the night of 16 December communications deteriorated still further, particularly from regimental command posts forward. The outline of the German attack began to emerge, and the pattern tentatively pointed to Liège as the enemy objective and made the size of the German effort more or less apparent. But the growing hiatus in time between the initial contact with enemy troops at a given point and the ultimate "fix" in grease pencil on the acetate overlays in the higher American headquarters made any true and timely picture of the extent of the German penetrations impossible. Enough information filtered into the VIII Corps command post at Bastogne, nevertheless, to enable Middleton to formulate his countermoves. The defensive plan he adopted consisted of two phases: first, to defend in place along the corps front as long as possible, thus carrying out the existing First Army directive; second, to deny the enemy full and free use of the Ardennes road net by building the strongest possible defense, with the limited force at hand, in front of the key communications centers, St. Vith, Houffalize, Bastogne, and Luxembourg City. Although General Middleton counted on reinforcements from outside his own command to garrison these four key points, it would fall to the VIII Corps to deny the enemy access thereto during the hours or days which would pass before reinforcements could take over.

St. Vith and Bastogne appeared to be in the greatest immediate danger as cracks commenced in the linear defense on the 17th. Friendly armor was hurrying down from the north to bolster the 106th Division and St. Vith; so, having turned one of his engineer battalions over to General Jones, the corps commander directed his attention to the approaches to Bastogne, a natural thing in view of the dangerous condition of the VIII Corps center. Thus a pattern was forming in which the meager resources at Middleton's disposal would be committed to delaying actions in the southwestern part of the corps area while a vacuum formed south of St. Vith and to the rear of that sector.

By the afternoon German advances at the expense of the 28th Division center forced Middleton to deploy the bulk of his reserve along the road net east of Bastogne. The presence of enemy reconnaissance at the Clerf River indicated that the main crossings would be made near Clerf and Wilwerwiltz. From the Clerf bridgehead a main, hard-surfaced highway led into Bastogne. The Wilwerwiltz bridgehead gave entry to the Wiltz valley and a complex of secondary roads wending toward Bastogne. CCR, 9th Armored (which earlier had sent some tank destroyers to Clerf), drew the assignment of blocking the Clerf-Bastogne highway. One engineer battalion, the 44th, was ordered to reinforce the headquarters force of the 707th Tank Battalion for the defense of Wilwerwiltz, but events were moving too fast and the battalion was diverted to the 28th Division command post at Wiltz. There remained the problem of barring the way to Luxembourg City, east of which the 4th Infantry Division was having a hard time. Already in the area, the 159th Engineer Combat Battalion was attached to Barton's division in the late afternoon and headed for Consdorf.

Of what might be considered the formal reserve of the VIII Corps, General Middleton had left, by 1600 of 17 December, only the 35th Engineer Combat Battalion; he retained in addition a partial voice in the disposition of the 28th Engineer Group. The corps engineer officer, meanwhile, had proposed a plan for defending a line from Foy to Neffe which would screen the eastern entries to Bastogne. To form this screen the 35th and the 158th Engineer Combat Battalion, the latter taken from the 8th Group, assembled their companies, vehicles, and equipment. Both battalions had been dispersed in numerous working parties; their trucks were hauling road-building stores, timber, and the like. Weapons long in disuse had to be collected and checked—land mines and explosives had to be gathered. Furthermore the 35th had the responsibility of guarding the VIII Corps headquarters and could not be released immediately.

At the close of day other engineer units were on the move. Pontoon and light equipment companies pulled onto the roads leading west with orders to take their bridges, air compressors, graders, and other paraphernalia out of enemy reach. Some of these units, like the 626th Engineer Light Equipment Company, would find themselves directly in the path of the German advance. At Diekirch the 299th Engineer Combat Battalion, under orders to rejoin its group in the west, shut down the sawmills and entrucked under artillery fire. As yet no large numbers of foot stragglers had come from the front lines, but the roads to the rear were crowded with supply vehicles, medium and heavy artillery, service and headquarters trucks, jeeps, and command cars. Around the headquarters and installations farther to the west, clerks, mechanics, truck drivers, and the like stripped the canvas from truck-mounted machine guns, filled the ammunition racks on deadlined tanks, listened to hurried explanations of bazooka mechanisms, or passed in inspection before sergeants who for the first time in weeks were seriously concerned with the appearance of each carbine and pistol.

At daylight on 18 December the 158th Engineer Combat Battalion commenced digging on its designated position northeast of Bastogne between Foy and Neffe. In addition barriers manned in platoon strength were set up at Neffe, Mageret, and

Longvilly on the Clerf highway. By dint of borrowing right and left 950 anti-tank mines could be used to strengthen the 158th position. At Bizory, northwest of Mageret, a part of Company C, 9th Armored Engineer Battalion, had been loaned by CCR and during the morning dug in on the high ground facing toward the Bastogne road.

Help was on the way to the VIII Corps, two airborne divisions and one armored. Of these reinforcements the 101st Airborne Division and the 10th Armored Division were expected to assemble in the neighborhood of Bastogne. The problem then, during the 18th, was to extend the slim screen already in position east of Bastogne so as to provide cover north and south of the city against any enemy interruption of the assembly process. On the south side the 1102d Engineer Group gathered ordnance, quartermaster, signal, and engineer units, placing them east of the highway running to Arlon. At the moment, however, this sector gave no cause for immediate concern, for the southern flank of the corps still was holding.

North of Bastogne a German threat was beginning to take shape. During the morning word reached the VIII Corps command post that the 740th Field Artillery Battalion had been overrun by the 1st SS Panzer Division at Poteau, west of St. Vith. Also, the left wing of the 28th Infantry Division had been forced back across the Our River and it appeared that a penetration was in progress south of St. Vith. To head off any roaming German reconnaissance units north of Bastogne, a collection of antiaircraft, tank destroyer, ordnance, and engineer units moved to intersections and bridges along the Bastogne-La Roche road. In the latter bridgehead town the 7th Armored Division trains took over responsibility for blocking the roads which there united to cross the Ourthe River. East of this line lay Houffalize, one of the four key road centers designated by Middleton for defense, but the 82d Airborne Division was en route to the battle and the VIII Corps commander expected that it would be deployed in the Houffalize sector. The Germans were moving too fast. At 1400 on the eighteenth a radio message reached Bastogne that the enemy had overrun the rear command post of an engineer company at Steinbach, just east of Houffalize.

There remained the very real threat of a coup de main against Bastogne from the east. In the afternoon bad news from this sector came thick and fast: at 1405 a telephone call from the commander of CCR, 9th Armored Division, reported that his most advanced roadblock force (Task Force Rose) was "as good as surrounded"; at 1430 the Germans were reported advancing on the second roadblock; at 1525 came confirmation that Task Force Rose had been overrun. On the Clerf highway, then, the enemy was less than nine miles from Bastogne. Troops of the 28th Division continued to hold the town of Wiltz, but they could not bar the valley corridor to the Germans. An officer patrol, in armored cars taken out of ordnance workshops, made an attempt to reconnoiter a proposed barrier line between CCR and Wiltz. Toward evening their report reached Bastogne: the Germans were west of the proposed line. The project was dropped.

As ordered by General Hodges, most of the VIII Corps headquarters moved during the day to Neufchâteau, about eighteen miles southwest of Bastogne, but General Middleton and a small staff remained in the city to brief the incoming airborne and armored commander and to maintain what little control still could be exercised over the course of battle. The 35th Engineer Combat Battalion, headquarters guard, was more urgently needed east of Bastogne; at 1800 Middleton ordered the battalion to move in on the right of the 158th. With two battalions in line there was a screen, albeit very thin, extending from the Houffalize-Bastogne road to the Arlon-

Bastogne road. Then, since the center of gravity for the corps was rapidly shifting to the southwest, Middleton took his last two engineer battalions, the 1278th and 299th, to establish a screen facing generally north between Libramont and Martelange. Behind this screen, southwest of Bastogne, he hoped to assemble the stragglers and broken units of his corps.

The situation as seen by Middleton and his staff on the night of the 18th was this. CCB of the 10th Armored had arrived from the Third Army and taken positions between Bastogne and Wiltz. Some part of CCR, 9th Armored, remained intact at Longvilly astride the Clerf road. The 101st Airborne Division was detrucking in its concentration area west of Bastogne. The Germans had achieved a clear penetration in the corps center and for all practical purposes the American forces in the St. Vith sector were separated from those under Middleton's immediate control. The deep and dangerous penetration made by the armored columns of the 1st SS Panzer Division in the V Corps sector north and west of St. Vith had forced the First Army and 12th Army Group commanders to choose between an attempt to restore the breach between Bastogne and St. Vith and one to stop the 1st SS Panzer Division.

The decision, made during the afternoon, was to assemble the 82d airborne Division at Werbomont, instead of Houffalize as Middleton had intended. Houffalize would have to go and without a fight. Rumors in the early evening already placed it in German hands. Since there was no force at hand to close the Houffalize gap the most that could be done was to vulcanize the edges of the tear by holding on at St. Vith and Bastogne. Perhaps, too, the enemy rushing through the gap might be caused some difficulty and delay by the creation of a barrier line along the Ourthe River and its tributaries. Plans for such a barrier line already were in execution in heterogeneous units hurrying to outpost bridges, villages, and road intersections between La Roche and Bastogne.

The night of 18 December was rife with rumor. By the quarter hour new reports came in from excited truck drivers, jeep patrols, or lonely clerks on unfamiliar outpost duty, placing the Germans in some village or on some road actually well to the west of the real locations of the most advanced enemy spearheads. The rear areas of the corps—if one could continue to speak of any "rear" area—was crawling with vehicles. Supply points, truckheads, and medical installations were moving to the westsome for the third time in as many days. New collecting points for the dead were opening. And closer to the vague and fragmentary front line, roads, trails, and paths carried stragglers singly or in large herds, toiling painfully on foot or clinging tenaciously to some vehicle, back to Bastogne or beyond to the west.

The Gap North of Bastogne

The action east of Bastogne during the night of 18 December, the absorption of the engineer screen into the larger defending forces, and the final fate of CCR, 9th Armored, has already been described. Here the focus is on the attempt to impede the probing advance guards and reconnaissance parties of the Fifth Panzer Army pushing into the gap north of Bastogne.

Construction of a really tough barrier line along the Ourthe River hardly could be expected. The stream itself, even when swollen by the winter snows, was narrow. At some points the approaches to the crossing sites were difficult to negotiate and lent themselves to blocks and barriers, but there were many bridges and numerous fords which an enemy could use to bypass a barred crossing site. At best only a very few companies of engineers could be found for the business of preparing bridge demolition charges, erecting barriers, laying antitank mines, and blasting craters in the roads. Some engineer tools and equipment had been lost to the enemy, but there was probably as much available as the small number of engineers could properly use. It was one thing to strengthen the physical barriers in the path of the oncoming enemy; it was quite another to defend at these barriers with sufficient rifle strength and antitank weapons. The men and weapons required for a continuous defensive line along the Ourthe simply were not available. On the other hand the German columns would not hit the Ourthe line in a coordinated and general attack; furthermore their initial appearance could be predicted along the well-defined and major routes westward.

On the morning of 19 December reconnaissance troops of two German armored divisions, the 2d Panzer Division and the 116th Panzer Division, funneled through a narrow corridor, only two miles in width, between Noville and Houffalize. The southern wall of this corridor was formed by the American troops who had pushed the rapidly forming Bastogne perimeter as far out as Noville. In the north where the town of Houffalize had been abandoned the corridor wall was formed by nature, for Houffalize was a bridgehead on the east-west channel of the Ourthe River. The two corps whose armored divisions were leading the Fifth Panzer Army pack in the race for the Meuse were strung out for miles behind the foremost reconnaissance forces. The main forces of the two armored divisions, although relatively close to the reconnaissance teams, were still a few hours behind.

On the German left the 2d Panzer Division, leading the XLVII Panzer Corps, collided with the Noville defenses early on the 19th. Partly by chance and partly by design, for General Lauchert needed more road room in which to pass his division around Bastogne, the 2d Panzer Division column became involved in a fight which extended from Noville east to Longvilly and lasted all through the day and following night. Caught up in this fight the advance elements of the division did not push beyond the Houffalize-Bastogne road until darkness had fallen. On the German right the reconnaissance battalion of the 116th Panzer Division moved along the south side of the Ourthe swinging wide to avoid Houffalize (this before noon), then turning to the northwest with the intention of crossing the Ourthe and seizing the La Roche bridges from the rear. This advance, though unopposed, was slow. Shortly after noon a few light reconnaissance vehicles reached Bertogne, from which a secondary road led across the Ourthe and on to La Roche.

General Middleton had spotted Bertogne as one of the chief approaches to the Ourthe and La Roche. Having been promised the 705th Tank Destroyer Battalion, en route south from the Ninth Army, he ordered the battalion to erect roadblocks at both Bertogne and La Roche. The 705th, coming by way of Liège, was a few hours distant when the German scouts entered Bertogne. Across the river the commander of the 7th Armored Division trains had taken independent action to protect his trucks and supplies gathered in the neighborhood of La Roche by installing outpost detachments and roadblocks to the south and east. Someone (who is not clear) had blown the Ourthe bridge northwest of Bertogne. To prevent the reconstruction of this bridge Colonel Adams sent Company C, 129th Ordnance Maintenance Battalion, and a couple of antiaircraft half-tracks mounting 37-mm. guns to form a block on the near bank about a half mile from the village of Ortho.

It was midafternoon when the enemy reached the far bank. A self-propelled gun at the head of the small German column got in the first blow, its shells knocking out the half-track crews. Capt. Robert E. Spriggs withdrew his company to a ridge overlooking the river and radioed for reinforcements. The enemy would not risk a daylight crossing, nor could the German engineers repair the damaged span while under direct fire. In the early evening five more half-tracks from the 203d Antiaircraft Battalion and a pair of self-propelled tank destroyers from the 705th Tank Destroyer Battalion came up.

It must have been about this time that the 116th Panzer Division commander received the unwelcome news that he had no bridge on which to cross the western branch of the Ourthe. The forward combat teams of the division were west of the Houffalize-Bastogne road but not yet up to the river. They had defiled with difficulty on the limited road net north of the Bastogne outworks, and a part of the tank regiment had stopped by the way to aid the 2d Panzer Division at Noville. In the twilight reconnaissance troops who had pushed west along the Ourthe after the setback at the Bertogne crossing discovered a Bailey bridge, still standing, at Ortheuville. Whether the bridge could be captured in usable condition was yet to be seen, but as soon as this find was radioed to the 116th Panzer Division commander he directed the advance guard of the division toward Ortheuville.

The Ourthe River resembles a misshapen Y in which the down stroke runs east to west and the open arms extend toward the northwest and southwest. The bifurcation in this Y comes about five miles west of Houffalize. The west branch of the Ourthe, as Belgian hydrographers name it, was the obstacle confronting the German armored spearheads on the night of 19 December. All during that day engineers from the VIII Corps and First Army had toiled to make a barrier line of the two arms west of Houffalize, blowing bridges which were not on the main American supply lines, fixing charges for future destruction of others, planting antitank mines at possible fording sites, erecting and manning roadblocks on roads and in the villages along the main approaches to the river. On the north branch, that is the line Durbuy-Hotton-La Roche, the 51st Engineer Combat Battalion (Lt. Col. Harvey R. Fraser) was hard at work. Only three companies were on hand to prepare this twelve-mile stretch of the river barrier, for Company C had been hurried northeast to Trois Ponts where it would administer a severe setback to Kampfgruppe Peiper of the 1st SS Panzer Division. South of La Roche, whose important bridges were outposted by the 7th Armored trains, the 9th Canadian Forestry Company had left sawmills and logging tracts to prepare demolitions and guard the crossing sites on a tributary of the Ourthe. The steps taken to bar the western branch of the Ourthe northwest of Bertogne and the initial reverse imposed on the enemy reconnaissance there have already been noted. Strung across the land neck between La Roche and the bridgehead at Ortheuville were a few platoons of the 1278th Engineer Combat Battalion.

At Ortheuville one of the main VIII Corps supply roads (Bastogne-Marche-Namur) crossed the western branch of the river by means of a heavy Bailey bridge. Shortly after noon on the 19th a platoon or less of the 299th Engineer Combat Battalion arrived in Ortheuville to prepare this important span for destruction. Although the VIII Corps staff had given priority to defense at this bridge, there was little enough that could be put in the effort. Three companies of the 299th and a small portion of the 1278th Engineer Combat Battalions comprised all the troops available for a barrier line now being constructed from Martelange northwest along Highway N46 to the Ourthe River, thence on both banks of the river to Ortheuville—a distance of about twenty-seven miles.

In the meantime the 158th Engineer Combat Battalion (Lt. Col. Sam Tabets) which, as part of the screen east of Bastogne, had been in a firefight throughout the morning, was relieved by the 501st Parachute Infantry, the battalion leaving the sector about 1430. The companies of the 158th were returning to their separate and original bivouacs when corps orders suddenly arrived dispatching the battalion to the Ourthe line. It would take some while to reassemble the battalion but Company C was reached and diverted to Ortheuville. Here it closed about 1900. To his surprise and relief the engineer company commander found that he would have some antitank support—desultory shellfire already was falling on the village and it was known that German armor was close at hand. The 705th Tank Destroyer Battalion, which Middleton had attached to the 101st Airborne Division, was on the move to Bastogne. Originally ordered to use the road through Bertogne, the battalion had been forced to detour when the battalion commander found the enemy there. The 705th, following the near bank of the Ourthe west to St. Hubert, dropped off eight tank destroyers to bar an enemy crossing while its trains passed through Ortheuville. These guns, as it turned out, would not reach Bastogne for a number of days.

So things stood as the evening advanced: the engineers and tank destroyer crews waiting for some enemy move to take the bridge; the German self-propelled guns and tanks lobbing in a shell now and again to keep the Americans away from the bridge and perhaps with hopes of cutting the wires on the demolition charges. Back to the east the advance guard of the 116th Panzer Division was marching toward Ortheuville.

At this point General Krueger, the LVIII Panzer Corps commander, made his fateful decision. The bridge northwest of Bertogne was gone, the bridge at Ortheuville probably would be blown in any attack, and furthermore it would be difficult to squeeze the entire corps through the small opening between the east-west channel of the Ourthe and Noville. Late in the evening he ordered the 116th Panzer Division advance guard, then at Salle three miles southeast of the Ortheuville bridge, to a halt. Then he sent orders to the division commanders and corps troops which would countermarch the forces west of the Houffalize-Bastogne road and turn the entire LVIII Panzer Corps to the north, through the Houffalize bridgehead, and away from the western branch of the Ourthe.

A flurry of enemy activity a little before midnight on the roads northwest of Bastogne masked the withdrawal of the LVIII Panzer Corps. Armored cars and half-tracks raced up and down the roads shooting up small convoys, sparring with American outposts, and engendering a flock of rumors which placed German spearheads in a half dozen spots beyond the Ourthe. In truth the only serious efforts to cross the west branch in the late evening were those made by roving reconnaissance elements of the 2d Panzer Division, whose main combat strength remained tied down in the fight for Noville. An hour before midnight these scouts did appear in front of a bridge at Sprimont, which crossed a tributary of the Ourthe south of Ortheuville; for their pains the American engineers blew the bridge in their faces.

A few engineers, ordnance troops, and antiaircraft and tank destroyer crews on 19 December had contributed mightily to the German decision which turned an entire armored corps from the road west and plunged it into profitless adventures in a side alley. Of all the disappointments suffered by the Fifth Panzer Army on this day, and there were many, perhaps the greatest stemmed from the reverses suffered in fact at the bridge beyond Bertogne and in anticipation at the Bailey span in Ortheuville.

While Krueger's corps turned in its tracks during the night of 19 December, General Luettwitz issued commands to his XLVII Panzer Corps, whose forward column was bunching up around Bastogne. Reports from the troops pressing onto the city from the north and east led Luettwitz to conclude that hard-hitting tactics in the coming day might break the will of the defenders, loosen their grip on the Bastogne road net, and give the armor of the 2d Panzer Division and Panzer Lehr a clear highway west. Luettwitz put a time limit on the attack prepared for the 20th, instructing his armored divisions to be ready to bypass Bastogne. His reconnaissance pushed around the city, meanwhile, both north and south, and tangled with the defenders of the makeshift, attenuated barrier lines.

At Ortheuville a lull developed shortly after midnight as the light armor screening the 116th Panzer Division finally pulled away. The engineers patrolled across the river along the Bastogne road but found no one except American wounded whose trucks had been shot up by German raiders earlier in the night. Just before dawn, light tanks and armored infantry from the 2d Panzer Division arrived to take their turn at the bridge. After some time spent probing the bridge defenses by fire, the German infantry rushed forward behind a careening scout car. As much to their surprise as to that of the American engineers the bridge remained intact. For some reason, perhaps the enemy shelling a few hours earlier, the demolition charges on the span failed to explode when the plunger went home. At the first shock the defenders had fallen back across the bridge to the houses by the river bank and started firing. They had only a few minutes to wait before a column of German vehicles led by a light tank appeared on the opposite bank. When the leader started across the span, one of the two American tank destroyers which had been run down close to the bridge got a direct hit, thus blocking the span. Peculiarly enough the enemy made no further attempt to win a way across. In the afternoon, when the troops of the 158th and the 9th Canadian Forestry Company undertook a counterattack across the river they found no trace of the enemy. So confused was the location of friend and foe that for a few hours two-way traffic between Marche and Bastogne was resumed.

The capture of Noville during the afternoon freed the 2d Panzer Division to continue the advance toward the Meuse. On the other hand, Luettwitz' corps was having trouble bringing gasoline forward on the crowded, winding supply roads in its sector; furthermore, the 2d Panzer Division would take some time to reassemble for the move on Marche.

It remained for the division reconnaissance battalion, reinforced by artillery and engineers, to make the next foray against the Ortheuville crossing site. The reconnaissance troops got there about 2200. For two hours German howitzers, mortars, and machine guns pummeled the American defenses on the far bank, setting buildings aflame and tying the engineers and tank destroyers to their positions. At midnight the enemy infantry forded the river, attacking from out of the darkness against defenders whose movements were etched by the light of flares and burning houses. While those who had waded the river circled to the engineer flanks, more Germans crossed into the village, this time by way of the bridge. Earlier the Americans had rewired demolition charges and installed the detonator in a foxhole close to the span, but for some reason there again was no explosion.

The bridge defenders were in contact with the 1128th Engineer Group headquarters through the Belgian telephone system (which continued in operation although its wire ran through the German lines). A request for infantry support could not be filled and the commanding officer of the 1128th ordered the defenders to fall back southwest to St. Hubert. Most of the 158th Engineer Combat Battalion reached St. Hubert. As a parting gesture the tank destroyers, which had seen no tank targets, laid indirect fire on the bridge. A muffled explosion led the engineers to report that the span was at least severely damaged.

If so, the German engineers were quick to make repairs, for the advance guard of the 2d Panzer Division began to roll almost immediately on this and other temporary bridges thrown across east of Ortheuville. When daylight came the 2d Panzer Division was bunched up in assembly area with its head across the river near Tenneville and its rear guard, arrayed to meet a counterattack from Bastogne, near Salle. Inexplicably, so far as the American patrols were concerned, the 2d Panzer Division did not bestir itself during the 21st to employ its victory at Ortheuville for a move on Marche, in which the advance regimental combat team of the 84th Infantry Division was assembling. The answer here was logistical, not tactical: Lauchert's armor would have to waste the entire day waiting for gasoline.

Defense Southwest of Bastogne

Throughout the 21st the VIII Corps had worked hard to strengthen the engineer barrier line in front of Neufchâteau and Arlon, centers around which the corps was re-forming, because the presence of German patrols south and southwest of Bastogne gave ample warning of imminent attack. Actually it is incorrect to consider these defenses in the sense of a line. There was no continuous natural barrier on which to build. The defense of this sector, as a result, consisted of erecting obstacles at important road crossings, bridge demolitions, cratering concrete and macadam road surfaces, and mining fords and narrow stretches of roads. The troop detachments to cover these barriers remained small and heterogeneous, their weapons usually no more than carbines, rifles, machine guns, and bazookas. Heavy antitank weapons—a handful of tank destroyers, headquarters tanks, and howitzers—would be found in ones and twos at the most important points. In general these defensive positions were organized with an eye to barring the roads which approached Neufchâteau (the VIII Corps headquarters) and Arlon (the western gateway to Luxembourg City) from the north.

Strongpoints—the term is relative—had been created at St. Hubert, Libramont, Sibret, and Martelange, of which the last two were in the most imminent danger. Sibret, where remnants of the 28th Infantry Division had reorganized as Task Force Caraway, lay only four miles southwest of Bastogne. Martelange, on the highway to Arlon, was thirteen miles due south of Bastogne. Possession of this town was of pressing importance.

General Middleton asked his troops, at 1600, to hold the barrier line in front of Neufchâteau and Arlon for forty hours, or until help could come, and he specifically named Martelange. Here a branch of the Sure River provided a natural hindrance to troops advancing from the north; but here also an enemy penetration would endanger the assembly of reinforcements coming up through Luxembourg and Arlon and would lay bare the right flank of the VIII Corps screen.

At dusk a platoon from Company B, 299th Engineer Combat Battalion, which was holding Martelange, came under attack by tanks and infantry. The platoon blew the two bridges in the center of the town and withdrew. In great confusion the corps hastily gathered more engineers to defend the road to Arlon by a counterattack, but the Germans remained quietly in the town and made no attempt to repair the bridges. An advance in force south on Arlon was no part of the XLVII Panzer Corps plan. The foray at Martelange had been made by column from the assault gun brigade attached to the 5th Parachute Division, the division itself being strung out around Wiltz, which it had taken earlier. Poor communications, by this time as baneful an influence on the operations of the XLVII Panzer Corps as on those of the American VIII Corps, gave the 5th Parachute Division commander an extremely muddled picture of what had happened at Martelange. Heilmann did not know for sure who had the town until the next afternoon and in the interim became gravely worried about his exposed south flank, which at this moment was the left anchor of both the corps and army. In a postwar account Heilmann concluded that in the Martelange action "quite a few things had gone wrong," a conclusion which General Middleton could have shared.

The next engagement in the new VIII Corps sector took place at Sibret. As the enemy closed on Wiltz General Cota had withdrawn the 28th Division command post, setting it up in Sibret on the night of 19 December. A straggler line established around Neufchâteau brought in some troops, and these were placed at roadblocks between Bastogne and Sibret. The 630th Tank Destroyer Battalion, having supported the 28th Infantry Division from 16 December on, took station at a road junction south of Sibret. The battalion, be it said, consisted of parts of Company B and the headquarters — but without their guns. North and west of Sibret a number of artillery outfits belonging to the 333d Field Artillery Group and the 28th Division had gone into firing positions from which to support the 101st Airborne troops around Bastogne. Some were intact, others were no more than headquarters batteries with a few pieces and a collection of cannoneers armed with rifles or carbines. Cavalry, tank, and tank destroyer units which had come back as the 28th Division center withdrew also were present with the artillery, but they too were remnants of battalion and company headquarters with few men and few weapons. In Sibret General Cota had perhaps two hundred men, mostly stragglers and strangers, for his headquarters and service people had been organized as a provisional battalion and thrown in to help hold Wiltz. There were three howitzers near the village, but the main antitank defense consisted of two bazookas which the assistant division commander, Brig. Gen. George A. Davis, ordered held "in reserve." Sibret, then, was a "strongpoint" in the VIII Corps screen but could be so considered only in relation to the surrounding roadblocks manned by squads and sections.

Renewed Drive Around Bastogne

Around the eastern arc of the Bastogne perimeter the events of the 20th had convinced the Fifth Panzer Army that no more time should be wasted here and that the westward momentum of the XLVII Panzer Corps must be revived. The command solution to the Bastogne problem called for the 2d Panzer Division to shake loose and hurry past the city in the north. This move, highlighted by the seizure of the Ortheuville bridge, began late on the 20th. Luettwitz divided the armor of the Panzer Lehr Division, one kampfgruppe to swing south of Bastogne and on to the west, one to stay behind for a few hours and aid the 5th Parachute Division in reducing the city. The latter division would be left the unpleasant and difficult task (as General Kokott, the commander, saw it) of containing the American forces in and around the city while at the same time shifting the axis of attack from the east to the south and west.

On the afternoon of the 20th General Kokott gave orders to set the first phase of this new plan in motion. The 39th Regiment, attacking on the south side of Bastogne, was told to continue across the Bastogne-Martelange highway and capture the high ground in the vicinity of Assenois. The 26th Reconnaissance Battalion would assemble, pass through the rifle regiment at dark, swing around Bastogne, and seize and hold the village of Senonchamps immediately west of Bastogne. From this point the battalion would lead an attack into the city. The 26th's commander had high hopes for this admittedly risky foray. The reconnaissance battalion was in good condition and its commander, Major Kunkel, had a reputation for daring. Kokott expected the battalion to reach Senonchamps during the morning of the 21st.

Through the dark hours General Kokott waited for some word from Kunkel's kampfgruppe. At daybreak the first report arrived: the reconnaissance battalion was in a hard fight at Sibret, two miles south of its objective. Next came an irate message from the corps commander: the 5th Parachute Division had captured Sibret and what was the 26th Reconnaissance Battalion doing hanging around that village? Kokott, his pride hurt, sent the division G-3 jolting uncomfortably on a half-track motorcycle to find out what had gone wrong.

From very sketchy German and American sources the following broad outline of the fight for Sibret emerges. When Kunkel crossed the Bastogne-Neufchâteau road, he came upon a stray rifle company of the 5th Parachute Division which was engaged south of Sibret in a fire fight. About 0300 this German company had reached the road junction at which the remnants of the 630th Tank Destroyer Battalion formed their roadblock. The American gunners, fighting on foot with rifles, apparently delayed the Germans for a couple of hours. Then the rifle company and troopers from Kunkel's command advanced through the dark to the south edge of Sibret, while German mortar fire started falling in the village. The first rush carried a group of the enemy into the solidly built gendarmerie at the southern entrance. Probably it was this initial success which was credited to the 5th Parachute Division.

General Cota went through the streets rounding up all the troops he could find for a counterattack against the gendarmerie, but the building could not be taken by unsupported riflemen. It was well after daybreak now, but very foggy; the armored vehicles of the German battalion were closing on the village and it was necessary to reoccupy the gendarmerie as a barrier. The three howitzers in the village defense had been overrun by tanks, but a battery of the 771st Field Artillery Battalion remained emplaced some two thousand yards northwest of the village. After much maneuvering to attain a firing site where there was no minimum elevation, the battery opened on the Germans barricaded in the gendarmerie. At almost the same time the enemy started a very heavy shelling. It was about 0900 and Kampfgruppe Kunkel was well behind schedule. The garbled radio messages reaching the XLVII Panzer Corps retracted the early report that Sibret had been taken and told of heavy fighting in the "strongly garrisoned" village. But the Germans could not be shelled out of the gendarmerie, tanks moved in on the American battery, and General Cota ordered his small force to retire south to Vaux-lez-Rosières; there he set up his division command post.

Meanwhile the staff of the 771st Field Artillery managed to get two guns into position to meet the enemy advance north of Sibret, but both guns and their tractors were put out of action by direct shelling. Kampfgruppe Kunkel rode roughshod into the artillery assembly areas north and west of Sibret, coming upon guns hooked to their prime movers, motors turning, and all the signs of hurried exodus. Kunkel reported the capture of more than a score of artillery pieces, much ammunition and many prisoners. Quickly the kampfgruppe moved on Senonchamps, leaving only a small force to protect its left flank by a drive toward Chenogne.

The 26th Reconnaissance Battalion was not alone west of Bastogne. During the previous night the reconnaissance battalion of the Panzer Lehr Division had been relieved at Wardin, strengthened by the attachment of the division engineer battalion, and started on a march around the south side of Bastogne as advance guard in the resumption of the Panzer Lehr attack toward the Meuse. This Panzer Lehr task force had orders to scout in the direction of St. Hubert, the key to the road complex west of Bastogne. Following the 26th Reconnaissance Battalion through Sibret, the Panzer Lehr column turned northwest and fanned out on the eastern side of the Ourthe River in the neighborhood of Amberloup and Tillet. There were numerous fords and crossing sites along this stretch of the river, but the enemy was concerned with securing good roads and bridges for the heavy columns following.

The approaches to St. Hubert were defended on the 21st by the 35th Engineer Combat Battalion (Lt. Col. Paul H. Symbol), which had barricaded the northern entrance from Ortheuville and erected a strongpoint (held by Company C) at a crossroad in a loop of the Ourthe north of the village of Moircy. This latter defense barred the most direct line of march between Bastogne and St. Hubert. A company of German infantry and four tanks appeared in front of the Company C abatis and foxholes before 0900, but two of the tanks were rendered hors de combat by a bazooka team and the action turned into a small arms duel. For some reason the attackers were not immediately reinforced, perhaps because there were other and more attractive targets in the vicinity. The 724th Engineer Base Depot Company, earlier manhandling supplies in the depots at St. Hubert, marched in to thicken the American firing line, and by noon the fight had dwindled to an occasional exchange of shots. During the lull of early afternoon the 158th Engineer Combat Battalion and the tank destroyers which had retreated from Ortheuville to St. Hubert were ordered south to take over the defense of Libramont. The 35th was left alone to blockade and delay a possible thrust by the 2d Panzer Division forces now crossing at Ortheuville or the more direct threat from the east.

During the morning roving detachments of the Panzer Lehr task force had enjoyed a field day. For one thing they seized a large truck convoy, perhaps sixty to eighty vehicles, en route to Bastogne. They also surrounded the 58th Armored Field Artillery Battalion near Tillet, although no serious attempt was made to eradicate it. The bulk of the German task force crossed the Ourthe north of the Company C strongpoint but found that the American engineers had done a remarkably thorough job of blocking the roads leading to St. Hubert. Abatis (mined and boobytrapped), blown culverts, stretches corduroyed with felled trees, and extensive minefields prompted reports to the Panzer Lehr Division commander that it would be some time before the eastern and northeastern approaches to St. Hubert could be cleared.

In the late afternoon the Panzer Lehr task force brought artillery into position and started shelling the Company C position. By this time the VIII Corps line no longer ran north and south in front of the German drive but was forming from east to west with the enemy passing across the corps front. A single battalion of engineers and miscellaneous antiaircraft and depot troops could not be expected to hold what remained of the barrier line on the western branch of the Ourthe. Fearful lest the engineers be cut off, VIII Corps headquarters ordered the 35th to hold as long as feasible, then rejoin the VIII Corps in the south. Using several hundred pounds of

TNT which had arrived in the afternoon the engineers prepared demolitions to be blown coincident with the withdrawal through St. Hubert and Libramont. The enemy, hindered by darkness, mines, craters, and abatis, did not interfere with the engineers, and the latter fell back through Libramont, entrucked, and by midnight were in a new assembly area at Bouillon close to the French frontier.

Somewhat earlier a German detachment had seized a bridge over the Ourthe at Moircy, to the south of the Company C strongpoints. This bridge gave access to a back road which entered St. Hubert from the southeast. Despite the fact that this secondary route was relatively free from the craters and obstacles which cluttered the main roads, the Panzer Lehr task force made no move to strike for the town but instead spread out farther north. The 902d Regiment of the division had been relieved near Neffe during the evening of 21 December and been assigned an advance via St. Hubert. The light armor of the task force remained nearly immobile for the next twenty-four hours, and it was left to the main body of the division to utilize the Moircy road.

With the withdrawal of the 35th Engineer Combat Battalion the VIII Corps no longer had elements directly in the path of the main German drive, always excepting, of course, the troops defending Bastogne, which by this time were cut off from the rest of the corps. The outposts of the corps at Recogne (held by the 7th Tank Destroyer Group) and at Vaux-lez-Rosières (defended by a scratch force from the 28th Division, reinforced by the 527th Engineer Light Pontoon Company) thus far had escaped the attention of an enemy moving west, not southwest. General Middleton was concerned about his open left flank and as his engineers came back ordered a barrier line formed along the Semois River. On the VIII Corps right, in the area south of Bastogne, reinforcements from the Third Army were concentrating under the command of the III Corps. The VIII Corps tactical air command post, which had been moved to Florenville on the 21st, continued to receive rumors and half-true reports of German forces turning southwest against its front, but it was fairly clear that the main threat was past.

To meet the German forces scouting and probing along the corps sector General Middleton organized a counter-reconnaissance screen. Behind this were collected stragglers and strays, many of whom had crossed the French border and got as far as Sedan. What was left of the corps artillery, mainly the 402d Field Artillery Group, assembled for tactical control and re-equipment. Other field artillery battalions, as well as tank destroyer battalions, engineer regiments, and the like, were arriving to reinforce the corps and help make good its losses. New infantry formations were on the way to restore the striking power of the corps and the Third Army commander already was planning the employment on the offensive—of a revitalized VIII Corps.

There remained one more battle to be fought by the residue of General Cota's command, gathered around the outpost position at Vaux-lez-Rosières on the Bastogne-Neufchâteau road. During the night of 21 December some two hundred survivors of the 110th Infantry fight at Wiltz reached the 28th Division command post. Those who could be provided with clothes and weapons were put back into the line. Cota had in addition the engineer light pontoon company, retained as riflemen over the protests of the corps engineer, a few howitzers sited as single pieces around the village perimeter, and a platoon of self-propelled 76-mm. tank destroyers from the 602d Tank Destroyer Battalion, which had just come up from the Third Army. While the stragglers were being organized, about 0800 on the 22d, German shells commenced to burst over the perimeter. Enemy riflemen opened fire and an incautious light tank poked its nose into range of an American tank destroyer, which destroyed it. One prisoner was taken before this first flurry ended, a rifleman from the 5th Parachute Division.

The 5th Parachute Division, it will be recalled, had the mission of extending westward the cordon which the Seventh Army was to erect to forestall American counterattack against the south flank of the Fifth Panzer Army. The terminus of this extension was intended as the line Sibret—Vaux-lez-Rosières—Martelange, at which point the 5th Parachute Division would go over to the defense. Colonel Heilmann's troops had taken Martelange, the eastern anchor for this projected line, late on the 21st while small detachments reconnoitered to the west; it was one of these which briefly engaged the 28th Division perimeter at Vaux-lez-Rosières.

When the dispositions of the XLVII Panzer Corps around Bastogne were altered on the 21st, Heilmann expected that his division would be given a more ambitious mission. For this reason he ordered reconnaissance to be pushed south from Martelange and southwest toward Libramont on the 22d. That morning, however, a new corps commander, General der Kavallerie Edwin Graf von Rothkirch, arrived on the scene. He advised Heilmann to be "foresighted," advice which the latter, drawing on his battle experience in Italy, interpreted as a warning to secure the original defensive line in preparation for imminent American counterattack. Sibret and Martelange were held by the 5th Parachute; so Heilmann started his leading regiment, the 14th, for Vaux-lez-Rosières. It was growing dark when the German advance guard appeared northeast of the village.

General Cota had placed his tank destroyers here, anticipating correctly the point of greatest danger, but this precaution was useless. The enemy pushed to the fore a platoon of long-barreled 88-mm. assault guns mounted on an old model Tiger body with exceptionally heavy armor. The armor-piercing shells fired by the American 76-mm. guns had no effect whatever. The 28th Division headquarters flashed a radio warning to the VIII Corps command post, reported that it had five bazookas left, and affirmed that these weapons could stop Tiger tanks, so much had the American infantryman's respect for the bazooka grown in the trying days of the Ardennes. But the troops manning the perimeter were untrained engineers or men exhausted by constant battle and retreat, thrown again into a fight where the odds were with the enemy and organized in pitifully small groups with strange officers and companions. Vaux-lez-Rosières fell to the Germans, and the 28th Division command post moved once more, this time to Neufchâteau.

There is a footnote to the events west of Bastogne on 22 December—the story of the 58th Armored Field Artillery Battalion. This battalion, commanded by Lt. Col. Walter J. Paton, had taken part in the fight at Longvilly and the ensuing withdrawal to Bastogne. With eight guns left the 58th went into position west of the town to fire for the 101st Airborne. On the afternoon of the 21st, with the enemy on the prowl in every direction, the battalion moved close to Tillet. Here it was cut off by enemy reconnaissance units, and Colonel Paton ordered his drivers and gunners to dig a foxhole circle around guns and vehicles. Shortly after midnight a radio message came through: the battalion was to try to reach Bastogne. The column formed but had gone only a little way when the tank at its head was knocked off by an antitank gun; then mortars and machine guns raked the road. Returning to the position which it had just left, the battalion waited for daylight.

In the meantime strong forces of the Panzer Lehr Division were on the move west and troops were detached to wipe out this "strongpoint." For most of the morning the encircled Americans stood to their guns or fought from their foxholes. As one participant in the bitter fight phrased it, "We gave them everything we had and they gave it back just as fast." Only one of the eight self-propelled howitzers was in firing condition when Colonel Paton gave the order to destroy all equipment and make a break for it. Moving in little groups, shielded by trees and falling snow, most of the battalion succeeded in reaching the VIII Corps lines.

There is a German peroration to this action. The commander of the Panzer Lehr Division recalling the route taken by his division as it marched toward St Hubert drafts a detour showing the advance guard swerving close to Tillet to engage an American "armored unit." And late on the night of the 22d a gray-clad staff officer posting the situation map in the operations section of OKW makes a heavy pencil stroke. It is under the name Tillet.

No accurate computation can be made of the hours added to the German march tables by the efforts of the engineers, artillery, and other small detachments who fought to delay the enemy advance through the rear areas of the VIII Corps. But there is no question that the LVIII Panzer Corps was diverted from the main stream of the western advance by these efforts—halving, for many hours, the spearhead strength of the Fifth Panzer Army. Students of the retrograde action fought by the VIII Corps between 16 and 22 December will wish to examine the question as to the most profitable use of engineer troops who formed the backbone of the rear area defense in such circumstances. The "magnificent job" which General Middleton later ascribed to the engineers credits the engineers in their role as infantry. The VIII Corps engineer and the various engineer group commanders at that time and later believed the engineer battalions and companies could have done more to impede the German advance if they had been denied the eastern firing line and employed in a tactically unified second line of defense in the western part of the corps area. For this latter purpose General Middleton would have had some 3,300 engineers in addition to those organic in the divisions. But it is questionable whether the 7th Armored Division would have had time to establish itself at St. Vith, not to speak of the 101st Airborne Division at Bastogne, without the intervention of the engineer battalions. Nonetheless, the story of the Ardennes barrier lines does make clear that the use of engineers in their capacity as trained technicians often paid greater dividends than their use as infantry, and that a squad equipped with sufficient TNT could, in the right spot, do more to slow the enemy advance than a company armed with rifles and machine guns.

Chapter XV. The German Salient Expands to the West

The reaction of rifle companies and battalions to the German surprise attack on the morning of 16 December was an automatic reflex to an immediate threat. The speed of reaction in higher American headquarters was appreciably slower since the size of the enemy threat and its direction could be determined only when the bits and pieces of tactical information, ascending the command ladder echelon by echelon, began to array themselves in a credible manner. The fact that the German High Command had chosen to make the main effort on the north flank contributed to an early misreading of the scope of the attack, for in this sector of the Allied line there were two possible German military objectives which were tactically credible and compatible with the

Allied preconception of a limited objective attack. These were, first, a spoiling operation to neutralize the gains of the 2d and 99th Infantry Divisions in the advance into the West Wall, and, second, a line-straightening operation to reduce the salient held by the 106th Infantry Division within the old West Wall positions. Either or both of these interpretations of the initial German effort could be made and would be made at corps and higher headquarters during the 16th.

The chain reaction during the early hours of the attack followed two paths, one via Gerow's V Corps and the other via Middleton's VIII Corps. The first report of enemy action on the 16th seems to have come to Gerow from the 102d Cavalry Group in the Monschau sector. The second report reaching V Corps was initiated by the 393d Infantry and was circumstantial enough to indicate a German penetration on the front of the 99th Division. By noon Gerow had sufficient information to justify a corps order halting the attack being made by the 2d and 99th. Although the First Army commander subsequently disapproved Gerow's action and ordered a resumption of the advance for 17 December, the American attack in fact was halted, thus permitting a rapid redeployment to meet the German thrust. Gerow's decision seems to have been taken before V Corps had any certain word from the 394th Infantry on the corps right flank. Neither Gerow nor Middleton was given prompt information that contact between the 99th Division and the 14th Cavalry Group had been broken at the V-VIII Corps boundary.

Since Middleton's corps had been hit on a much wider front than in the case of its northern neighbor, a somewhat better initial appreciation of the weight of the attack was possible. Even so, Middleton and his superiors had too little precise information during most of the 16th to assess the German threat properly. Middleton seems to have felt intuitively that his thinly held corps front was being hammered by something more serious than local and limited counterattacks. By 1030 he had convinced General Hodges that CCB, 9th Armored Division, should be taken out of army reserve and turned over to the VIII Corps, for he had no armor in reserve behind the corps left flank. Shortly after noon telephone conversations with his corps liaison officers at the 106th headquarters in St. Vith convinced Middleton that he had to be ready to commit his own available corps reserves, four battalions of combat engineers and CCR, 9th Armored Division. By 1400 the 168th Engineer Combat Battalion was assembling at St. Vith and within the next few hours the remaining engineers and CCR were alerted and assembled, the latter moving up behind the corps center where, Middleton learned at 1415, all regiments of the 28th Division were under attack.

The sequence of events in the hours before midnight on the 16th is difficult to time. Middleton talked with the commander of the 106th Division by telephone and apparently believed that he, Middleton, had sanctioned a withdrawal of Jones's exposed two regiments and that such a withdrawal would be made. Impressed with the growing strength of the German attack, Middleton drafted a "hold at all costs" order which left his command post at 2120 and which set the final defense line generally along the west bank of the Our, Clerf, and Sure Rivers. General Bradley, whose 12th Army Group headquarters in Luxembourg City had a better telephone link to the VIII Corps than had the First Army command post at Spa, talked with Middleton, then telephoned General Patton that the 10th Armored Division would have to come north to help Middleton's corps. At midnight General Hodges ordered the 26th Infantry attached to V Corps and set it marching for Camp Elsenborn. About the same time Hodges alerted part of the 3d Armored.

It is unlikely that the responsible American commanders slept soundly on the night of the 16th, but as yet they had no real appreciation of the magnitude of the enemy attack. The tactics followed by the Germans in the first hours had made it very difficult for even the frontline commanders to gauge the threat. The disruption of the forward communications nets by German shellfire on the morning of the 16th had led to long periods of silence at the most endangered portions of the front and a subsequent overloading, with consequent delays, of those artillery radio networks which continued to function. The initial enemy employment of small assault groups, company-size or less, had led the combat commanders on the line to visualize and report a limited-scale attack. The broken and wooded nature of the terrain in the area under attack had permitted extensive German infiltration without any American observation, which also contributed to an erroneous first estimate of the enemy forces. Finally, the speed with which the American observation or listening posts were overrun and silenced had resulted in large blank spaces on the G-2 maps in the American headquarters.

At the close of this first day of battle, therefore, the only certain view of the enemy was this: German forces were attacking all along the line from Monschau to Echternach; they had succeeded in making some dents in the forward American positions; at a number of points the defenders seemed to need reinforcement; and the amount of German artillery which had been used was suspiciously large for only a limited objective attack. During the night of 16 December the German assault waves overran or destroyed a large number of communications points and much radio or wire equipment in the forward areas, drastically slowing the flow of information to higher American headquarters.

To many American units 17 December opened as just another day. Company B of the 341st Engineer General Service Regiment, for example, went that morning to work on a railroad bridge under construction at Butgenbach. (Before noon the surprised engineers were shelled out.) As the morning progressed, however, the higher American headquarters began to comprehend that the enemy was making a full-scale attack and this with no limited objective in mind. By 0730 the V Corps commander had sufficient information to convince him that the enemy had broken through the lines of the 99th Division. At 0820 the VIII Corps artillery radio reported to Middleton that German troops were approaching St. Vith along the Schönberg] road. Two hours later the American command nets were jammed with Allied air force reports of large enemy vehicular columns moving westward. Even more significant was the fact that the fighter-bomber pilots were having to jettison their bomb loads in order to engage increasingly large flights of German planes.

Two other key pieces helped fill out the puzzle picture of enemy forces and intentions. Prisoners had been taken from a number of units known to belong to the Sixth Panzer Army, a formation long carried in Allied G-2 estimates as the German strategic reserve in the west. Second, some ninety Junker 52's had been counted in the early morning paratroop drop, an indication that the Germans had planned a serious airborne assault. By late morning of the 17th, therefore, it can be said that the American commanders had sufficient information to construct and accept a picture of a major German offensive. It would take another thirty-six hours to produce a really accurate estimate of the number of German divisions massing on the Ardennes front.

The 12th Army Group commander, General Bradley, had gone to Paris to discuss the replacement problem with General Eisenhower, when, on the afternoon of the 16th, a message from his own headquarters in Luxembourg City gave word of the

German attack. Eisenhower suggested that Bradley should move the 7th Armored Division down from the north and bring the 10th Armored Division up from the Third Army. The 12th Army Group had no strategic reserve, but plans already existed to move troops in from Patton's Third Army and Simpson's Ninth in the unlikely event that the undermanned VIII Corps front was threatened. Bradley telephoned Patton and told him to send the 10th Armored Division north to help Middleton. Patton, as Bradley expected, demurred. His own army was readying for a major attack on 19 December, an attack which had been the subject of controversy between Eisenhower and Montgomery and which represented the Third Army's last chance to be the chief ball carrier in the Allied push to cross the Rhine. Bradley, however, was firm and Patton at once gave the order to assemble the 10th Armored.

Bradley's second call went to General Simpson whose grueling attack to close along the Rhine River had come to a halt on 14 December beside the muddy western banks of the Roer. Here the choice fell, as Eisenhower had suggested, on the 7th Armored Division, which was resting and refitting in the rear of the XIII Corps zone. The 7th was turned over to the First Army and now Bradley had a fresh armored division moving in to shore up each of the endangered VIII Corps flanks. More troops, guns, and tanks would be moved out of Simpson's army on 16 and 17 December, but the authorization for these reinforcements is hard to trace. In many cases the transfer of units would be accomplished in simple fashion by telephone calls and simultaneous agreement between the higher commanders concerned. Hodges and Simpson had been comrades in World War I, and when Hodges asked for assistance Simpson acted promptly and generously. On the 16th, for example, Simpson offered the 30th Infantry Division and the 5th Armored on his own initiative.

Prior to the invasion of Normandy there had been a great deal of staff planning for the creation of a SHAEF strategic reserve for use in the first ninety days of the operation in western Europe. The Allied successes during the summer and autumn put these plans in mothballs and the subject was not reopened until early December when Eisenhower ordered that a strategic reserve be assembled and placed under the 12th Army Group, but for employment only at his direction as Supreme Allied Commander. Two days before the Ardennes attack the SHAEF operations section submitted a plan calling for a strategic reserve of at least three divisions. The concept, quite clearly, was to amass a force capable of exploiting a success on any sector of the Allied front without diverting divisions from other parts of the front. Some operations officer, possibly imbued with the Leavenworth doctrine of "Completed Staff Work," inserted the observation that "a strategic reserve could be used to repel a serious breakthrough by German forces," but hastened to add: "In view of current G-2 estimates, it is unlikely that such employment will become necessary."

To understand fully the position in which the Supreme Commander found himself on 16 December, it should be remembered that American troops were in constant movement to Europe and the higher staffs tended to look upon the next few troopships as containing a reserve which could and would be used by the Supreme Commander to influence the direction of the battle. Four U.S. infantry divisions and one armored division were scheduled to arrive on the Continent in December, with an equal number slated for January. Of the December contingent two infantry divisions (the 87th and 104th) were already in the line when the Germans struck. There remained en route the 11th Armored Division and the 66th and 7th Infantry Divisions, the 75th having already crossed the Channel on its way to the front. Two additional US divisions were training in the United Kingdom and waiting for equipment, but neither was expected to cross the Channel during December: the 17th Airborne was scheduled for France in January, and the 8th Armored Division, still missing many of its authorized vehicles, was not as yet on a movements list.

The only combat-wise divisions ready to the hand of the Supreme Commander were the 82d and 101st Airborne Divisions, which had been brought back to France after the long, tough battle in the Netherlands and were not expected to regain full operational status until mid-January. By the 17th, however, it was clear that the First Army had to be heavily reinforced, and promptly. General Eisenhower reluctantly gave the airborne troops to Bradley.

From this point on the immediate reinforcements needed to meet and halt the German counteroffensive would have to come from the armies in the field. (Simpson had already thrown the 30th Infantry into the pot, in addition to the 7th Armored.) Late in the evening of the 17th Bradley telephoned Patton, who was starting to move his troops into assembly areas for the Third Army attack on the Saar, and told the latter that two more divisions might have to go north. By midnight of 17 December approximately 60,000 men and 11,000 vehicles were on the move to reinforce Hodges' First Army. In the following eight days three times this number of men and vehicles would be diverted from other areas to meet the Germans in the Ardennes.

One piece of military thinking dominated in all the higher US military headquarters and is clearly traceable in the initial decisions made by Eisenhower, Bradley, and the army and corps commanders. The Army service schools during the period between the two World Wars had taught as doctrine—a doctrine derived from the great offensives of 1917 and 1918 on the Western Front—that the salient or bulge produced by a large-scale offensive can be contained and finally erased only if the shoulders are firmly held. The initial movements of the American reinforcements were in response to this doctrine.

The 30th Division Meets Peiper

The 30th Division (Maj. Gen. Leland S. Hobbs) was resting in the neighborhood of Aachen, Germany, after hard fighting in the Roer River sector, when a call from the XIX Corps informed its commander of the German attack along the V and VIII Corps boundary. At this time (the evening of 16 December) the situation did not seem too ominous and the division commander merely was told that he should alert his units in the rest area. Shortly before noon of the following day the corps commander, Maj. Gen. Raymond S. McLain, telephoned to say: "I don't know any of the details but you are going south. I think it is only temporary." The 30th Division was to move to an assembly area north of Eupen where the V Corps commander, General Gerow, would issue detailed orders. Gerow's instructions, actually received at noon, directed the 30th Division to relieve the 18th Infantry (1st Division) around Eupen and prepare for a counterattack to the southeast in support of the 2d and 99th Divisions farther south. The rapid advance of Kampfgruppe Peiper, however, would catch the division in midpassage, drastically changing the manner of its ultimate commitment.

At 1630, on 17 December, the division started the forty-mile trip to its new assembly area moving by combat teams prepared to fight. The 30th Reconnaissance Troop, the 119th Infantry, 117th Infantry, and 120th Infantry moved in that order, with tanks and tank destroyers interspersed between the regiments. Despite the presence of a few German aircraft which picked up the column early in the move and hung about dropping flares or making futile strafing passes, the leading regiment closed by midnight. Meanwhile the V Corps commander, apprehensive lest the 1st SS Panzer

Division column thrusting south of Malmédy should destroy the last connection between his own and the VIII Corps, ordered General Hobbs to switch his leading combat team to Malmédy at daylight.

Since the 119th had detrucked and bedded down for the night, the assistant division commander, Brig. Gen. William K. Harrison, Jr., caught the 117th Infantry on the road and directed it toward Malmédy. Its way fitfully lighted by enemy flares, the 117th (Col. Walter M. Johnson) moved cautiously south from Eupen. In early morning the head of the regimental column was bucking the heavy stream of traffic leaving Malmédy when new orders arrived: one battalion was to go to Stavelot, erect a roadblock, and prevent the Germans from advancing north of the Amblève River. Colonel Johnson hurried his 1st Battalion toward Stavelot, deployed the 2d Battalion on the ridge between Stavelot and Malmédy, then organized the defense of Malmédy with the 3d Battalion and the troops already in the town.

At daybreak on 18 December the remainder of the 30th Division was on the road to Malmédy with the 120th Infantry in the lead, under new orders for a division attack to the southeast. The V Corps G-3 had told General Hobbs that he expected this attack to be made not earlier than 19 December. But the German attack on Stavelot during the morning caused consternation in both the corps and army headquarters, from which erupted a stream of orders and demands for greater speed. Harassed by confusing and contradictory directions, Hobbs finally had to ask that he be given orders from but one source. As it was, the 119th Infantry, still in Eupen, was alerted for Stavelot while the 120th Infantry, painfully slipped and slid along the muddy roads to Malmédy. Before trucks could arrive for the 119th Infantry Stavelot had fallen to the enemy. The First Army commander called Hobbs to Spa about noon. Before leaving Eupen, General Hobbs instructed the 119th Infantry (Col. Edward M. Sutherland) to meet him at Theux, five miles north of Spa, at which time he expected to have new orders.

General Hodges had just finished a conference with the acting commander of the XVIII Airborne Corps, Maj. Gen. James M. Gavin, whose two divisions, the 82d and 101st Airborne, had started advance parties from France for the Bastogne area where, according to the initial orders from SHAEF, the divisions were to be employed. The First Army commander, under whose orders the XVIII Airborne Corps now fell, determined to divert the 82d Airborne Division to Werbomont as a backstop in case Kampfgruppe Peiper succeeded in crossing the Amblève and Salm Rivers. The 82d, however, would not be in position before 19 December at the earliest. Meanwhile the 30th Division commander reached the First Army headquarters. In the midst of a discussion of new plans, word came in that the First Army liaison planes scudding under the clouds had seen the German armor moving north from Trois Ponts in the direction of La Gleize and Stoumont. It was apparent that the enemy had two choices: he could continue north along the Amblève valley, thus threatening the rearward installations of the First Army; or he could turn west toward Werbomont and so present a grave menace to the assembly of the 82d. Hobbs, then, met Colonel Sutherland with First Army orders which would split the 119th Infantry, sending one force along the valley of the Amblève, the other to Werbomont and thence to Trois Ponts.

The 119th left General Hobbs and traveled south to Remouchamps. At this point it divided, one detachment made up of the 2d Battalion and the cannon company heading for Werbomont, the second and stronger column winding along the road that descended into the Amblève valley. The 2d Battalion reached Lienne Creek after dark and threw up hasty defenses on the hills about three miles east of Werbomont. The Germans under Peiper had been stopped at the creek earlier, it will be recalled, but the battalion was in time to ambush and destroy the separate scouting force in the late evening. The 3d Battalion, leading the truck column carrying the bulk of the combat team, reached Stoumont after dark and hurried to form a perimeter defense. Patrols pushing out from the village had no difficulty in discovering the enemy, whose pickets were smoking and talking not more than 2,000 yards away. At least forty German tanks were reported in bivouac east of the village. Under cover of darkness the remainder of the American force assembled some three miles northwest of Stoumont, while the 400th Armored Field Artillery Battalion, picked up during the march, moved its batteries forward in the dark. Both Americans and Germans, then, were ready with the coming of day to do battle for Stoumont.

The 117th Infantry, first of the 30th Division regiments to be fed into the line, had been deploying on the morning of 18 December around Malmédy. Its 1st Battalion (Lt. Col. Ernest Frankland), under orders to occupy Stavelot, circled through Francorchamps to approach the town from the north. On the road Colonel Frankland met officers of the 526th Armored Infantry Battalion who told him that the enemy was in Stavelot. About this time word of the German success reached the V Corps headquarters, where it was assumed that the 1st Battalion would perforce abandon its mission. Frankland, on the contrary, kept on going. He made contact about 1300 with a rifle company of the 26th Armored Infantry Battalion remaining near Stavelot, then detrucked his battalion north of the still-flaming gasoline roadblock and started south toward the town.

All this while Peiper believed that the 3d Parachute Division was close behind his column. Expecting it to reach Stavelot by the evening of 18 December, he had left only a small holding force in the town. In fact, the 3d Parachute Division had been held up by a combination of jammed roads and unexpectedly tenacious American resistance. The Sixth Panzer Army therefore did not expect the advance guard of the 3d Parachute Division to arrive in Stavelot before 19 December. At this point the failure of communications between Peiper and rearward German headquarters began to influence the course of operations, to the distinct disadvantage of the Sixth Panzer Army. Although without artillery support, Colonel Frankland launched his attack at Stavelot. On the slope north of the town a platoon of 3-inch towed tank destroyers from the 823d Tank Destroyer Battalion made good use of positions above the Germans to knock out a brace of Mark VI tanks and a few half-tracks. The two leading companies of the 1st Battalion had just reached the houses at the northern edge of the town when ten hostile tanks, returning in haste from Trois Ponts, counterattacked.

It might have gone hard with the American infantry but for the fighter-bombers of the IX Tactical Air Command and XXIX Tactical Air Command which opportunely entered the fray. During the afternoon the American planes had worked east from the La Gleize area, where the little liaison planes had first signaled the presence of German columns, and struck wherever Peiper's tanks and motor vehicles could be found. Perhaps the trail provided by the rearward serials of Kampfgruppe Peiper led the fighter-bombers to Stavelot; perhaps the 106th Tactical Reconnaissance Squadron, which broke through the clouds to make one sweep over the town, tipped off the squadrons working farther west. Before the German tanks could make headway, planes from the 365th Fighter Group, reinforced by the 390th Squadron (366th) and the 506th Squadron (404th), plunged in, crippled a few enemy vehicles, and drove the balance to cover, leaving the infantry and tank destroyers to carry out the cleanup inside Stavelot on more equitable terms. By dark the two American companies held half of the town, had tied in with the 2d Battalion between Stavelot and Malmédy, and were reinforced by a tank platoon from the 743d Tank Battalion. Also the riflemen had the comforting knowledge that they could call for and receive artillery support: the 118th Field Artillery Battalion had moved through bullet fire and set up northeast of the town.

The fight for Stavelot continued all through the night of the 18th with German tanks, now free from the air threat, working through the streets as far as the town square. At daybreak the 1st Battalion and its tanks went to work and by noon had reclaimed all of the town down to the Amblève River. Twice during the afternoon tank-led formations drove toward the town, but both times the American gunners dispersed the field gray infantry and the tanks decided not to chance the assault alone. It is not surprising that the German infantry gave over the field. The 118th cannoneers fired 3,000 shells into the assault waves, working their guns so fast that the tubes had to be cooled with water.

By the night of 19 December the 1st Battalion had a firm grip on Stavelot—but, in the most telling stroke of all, its attached engineers had dynamited the Amblève bridge across which Peiper's force had rolled west on the morning of 18 December. The armored weight of the 1st SS Panzer Division could make itself felt only if it continued punching westward. Without fuel the punch and drive were gone.

Without the Amblève bridge and a free line of communications through Stavelot there was no fuel for Peiper. Without Peiper the freeway to the Meuse which the 1st SS Panzer Division was to open for the following divisions of the Sixth Panzer Army remained nothing more than a cul-de-sac.

Could the 30th Division surround and destroy Kampfgruppe Peiper before German reinforcements from the east reopened the way to their now isolated comrades? Would the 30th Division, its rear and right flank partially uncovered, be left free to deal with Peiper? The latter question was very real, even with the 82d Airborne moving in, for on the morning of 19 December the V Corps commander had warned the 30th Division chief of staff (Col. Richard W. Stephens) that large German forces had slipped by to the south and were moving on Hotton. An additional question plagued the 30th Division: where was the 7th Armored? Patrols sent out toward Recht on the 19th could find no trace of the tankers.

While the 1st Battalion, 117th Infantry, was busily severing the lifeline to Kampfgruppe Peiper on 19 December, Peiper was engaged with the bulk of his troops in an attempt to blast a path through Stoumont, the barrier to the last possible exit west, that is, the valley of the Amblève. Battle long since had been joined at Stoumont when scouts finally reached Peiper with the story of what had happened to his line of communications.

The kampfgruppe, whose major part was now assembled in the vicinity of La Gleize and Stoumont, consisted of a mixed battalion of Mark IV tanks and Panthers from the 1st SS Panzer Regiment, a battalion of armored infantry from the 2d SS Panzer Grenadier Regiment, a flak battalion, a battalion of Tiger tanks (which had joined Peiper at Stavelot), a battery of 105-mm. self-propelled guns, and a company from the 3d Parachute Division which had ridden on the tanks from Honsfeld. The force had suffered some losses in its breakthrough to the west, but these were not severe. By now the critical consideration was gasoline. A few more miles on the road or a few hours of combat maneuvering and Peiper's fuel tanks would be bone dry.

When the 119th Infantry (minus the 2d Battalion) moved into the Stoumont area on the night of 18 December, the rifle companies of the 3d Battalion (Lt. Col. Roy G. Fitzgerald) deployed in a hastily established line north, south, and east of the town. The 3d was backed up by light 3-inch towed tank destroyers belonging to the 823d Tank Destroyer Battalion, two 90-mm. antiaircraft guns detached from the 143d Antiaircraft Battalion, and three battalion 57-mm. antitank guns. The 1st Battalion, it will be remembered, dismounted in an assembly area about three miles northwest of Stoumont, where Colonel Sutherland located the regimental command post. The moment patrols had established the proximity of the large German force Sutherland was alerted, and he promised a tank company as reinforcement first thing in the morning. For the rest of the night the troops around Stoumont dug foxholes, planted mines, and waited uneasily for day to break.

Stoumont and the American lines lay on a bald hill mass rising on the north bank of the Amblève. La Gleize, the enemy assembly area, shared a similar situation on the road east of Stoumont. The road itself, some distance from the river bank, approached Stoumont through patches of trees, which gave way at the eastern edge of the town to a border of level fields. The whole lent itself admirably to the employment of armor.

As the first light came on 19 December Peiper threw his infantry into the attack, supporting this advance from the east with tanks firing as assault guns. The grenadiers and paratroopers were checked by fire from the American lines as they crossed the open fields. But the gunners of the 823d, who could not see fifty yards from the muzzles of their guns and whose frantic calls for flares to be fired over the German tanks went unheeded, could not pick out the enemy armor. The panzers, formed in two columns, moved toward the foxhole line and the American company on the east edge of Stoumont fell back to the houses, uncovering the outnumbered and immobile towed tank destroyers, all eight of which were captured. At this moment the ten tank from the 743d Tank Battalion promised by Sutherland arrived and went into action. The enemy thereupon reverted to tactics successfully employed in reducing village resistance on the march west, sending two or three of the heavy-armored Panthers or Tigers in dashes straight along the road and into the town. At least six German tanks were crippled or destroyed in this phase of the action, two of them by antiaircraft crewmen, Private Seamon and Pvt. Albert A. Darago, who were handling bazookas for the first time and who were awarded the DSC for their bravery. (An infantry officer had showed the antiaircraft crew how to load and fire the bazooka just before the battle began.) One of the two 90-mm. antiaircraft guns also did yeoman service in the unfamiliar ground-laying role and destroyed two tanks from Peiper's heavy Mark VI battalion before the German infantry got in close enough to force its abandonment.

The Germans took some two hours to force their way inside Stoumont, but once the panzers ruled the streets the fight was ended. The rifle company on the south was cut off and the company in the town liquidated. The third company withdrew under a smoke screen laid down by white phosphorus grenades, reaching the reserve position manned by the 1st Battalion about noon. The tanks, commanded by 1st. Lt. Walter D. Macht, withdrew without loss, carrying survivors of the center company on their decks. The 3d Battalion had lost most of its equipment, as well as 267 officers and men.

This engagement had seen the Americans fighting without the artillery support so essential in American tactics. The 197th Field Artillery Battalion, assigned the direct support mission, did not reach firing positions in time to help the 3d Battalion. The

400th Armored Field Artillery Battalion was finally able to place one battery where it could give some help, but by this time the battle had been decided and the cannoneers fired only a few missions.

Word that the fight was going against the troops at Stoumont impelled Colonel Sutherland to alert his reserve battalion. Company C, dispatched as reinforcement, had reached the village of Targnon when it began to pass men of the 3d Battalion moving to the rear. The company dismounted from its trucks and marched as far as the entrance to Stoumont. Failing to find the 3d Battalion commander the riflemen joined the tanks, which by this time had no infantry cover and were running low on ammunition. The newly wedded tank-infantry team yielded ground only in a slow and orderly withdrawal. The impetus of the German advance was considerably reduced when a 90-mm. antiaircraft gun, sited at a bend in the road west of Stoumont, knocked out a couple of German tanks and momentarily blocked the highway.

The situation was precarious—and not only for the force left to Sutherland. The only armor between the 119th Infantry command post and Liège was a detachment of ten Sherman tanks which had been whipped out of the First Army repair shops, manned with ordnance mechanics, and dispatched through Aywaille to block the Amblève River road. In front of the 119th command post the ten tanks of the 743d had but few rounds left in their ammunition racks.

At 1035 the 30th Division commander, who was in Sutherland's command post, called the First Army headquarters to ask for the 740th Tank Battalion. The S-2 of the 119th Infantry had discovered that this outfit, a new arrival on the Continent, was waiting to draw its tanks and other equipment at an ordnance depot near Sprimont, about ten miles north of the 119th command post. The First Army staff agreed to Hobbs's request, but the unit it handed over was far from being ready for combat. The depot had few fully equipped Shermans on hand and the first tank company drew fourteen Shermans fitted with British radios (unfamiliar to the American crews), five duplex drive tanks, and a 90mm. self-propelled gun. While Hobbs was on the phone trying to convince the army staff that he must have the tanks, his chief of staff, Colonel Stephens, was being bombarded by army demands that some part of the 119th should be pulled out and shifted north to cover the road to Spa and First Army headquarters. This was out of the question for the moment, for Sutherland had only a single battalion at his disposal.

All this while the little tank-infantry team held to its slow-paced withdrawal along the river road, lashing back at the Panthers in pursuit. Retreating through Targnon and Stoumont Station the force reached a very narrow curve where the road passed between a steep hill and the river bank. Here Lt. Col. Robert Herlong, who now had all of his 1st Battalion engaged, ordered the tanks and infantry to make their stand. It was about 1240. Fog was beginning to creep over the valley. A forward observer from the 197th Field Artillery Battalion, whose pieces now were in position, saw three German tanks leave Targnon and head down the road. A call sent a salvo crashing down on the western side of the village just as a large tank column started to follow the German point. Followed by more shells these tanks turned hurriedly back into Targnon. One of the point tanks did reach the American position, poked its nose around the bend in the road, got a round of high explosive uncomfortably close, and took off.

It is true that Herlong's tanks and infantry held a naturally formidable roadblock. And the presence of artillery once again showed what it could do to alter the course of battle. But Peiper's object in the advance beyond Stoumont was not to crush his way through the 119th Infantry and move north through the defiles of the Amblève valley. His object, thus far unachieved, was to climb out of the valley confines and resume the westerly advance toward Huy and the Meuse. Peiper had been thwarted at Trois Ponts and at Lienne Creek in turn. The advance through Stoumont offered a last opportunity, for midway between Targnon and Stoumont Station lay an easy approach to the river, a bridge as yet untouched, and a passable road rising from the valley to join the highway leading west through Werbomont, the road from which Peiper's force had been deflected. With this bridge in German hands, Peiper had only to contain the 119th Infantry which had been retiring before his tanks while his main column crossed to the west. But Peiper knew by this time that his supply line had been cut at Stavelot. "We began to realize," he says, "that we had insufficient gasoline to cross the bridge west of Stoumont."

Unaware of the enemy predicament, the 119th Infantry took advantage of the lull which had followed the single German pass at the roadblock position to reorganize the remnants of the 3d Battalion. About 1530 the leading platoon of the conglomerate company taken from the 740th Tank Battalion arrived, but the additional infantry for which Colonel Sutherland had pleaded were not forthcoming. Indeed, his weakened 3d Battalion was already earmarked for use in the event the enemy turned north on the secondary road running from Stoumont directly to Spa and the First Army headquarters. However, Sutherland was told that the 2d Battalion, 119th Infantry, was in process of turning its position east of Werbomont over to the 82d Airborne Division and would be available in a few hours.

Anxious to feel out the enemy and establish a good line of departure for an attack on 20 December, Sutherland ordered the 1st Battalion commander to push out from the roadblock, using Capt. James D. Berry's untried and conglomerate tank company. About 1600 Herlong started east, Company C advancing on both sides of the road and tanks moving in the center. Just west of Stoumont Station three Panthers were sighted and destroyed in quick succession, one by a fluke shot which glanced from the pavement up through the tank flooring. The dead tanks blocked the road; so Herlong sent his infantry on alone and organized a line at the western edge of the station. There was no further contact with the Germans. Peiper, whose mechanized force by this time was nearly immobile, had withdrawn his advanced troops back to Stoumont, about two and a half miles east of the station. As for the road leading from Stoumont to Spa, a matter of grave concern to First Army headquarters on 19 December, Peiper, acutely conscious of his lack of mobility, never gave it a serious thought.

In midafternoon the 119th Infantry and the 740th Tank Battalion (Lt. Col. George K. Rubel) had been detached from the 30th Division and assigned to the operational control of the XVIII Airborne Corps, which at the same time took back its 82d Airborne Division from the V Corps and in addition received the 3d Armored Division. The XVIII Corps commander thus had an entire airborne division, more than half of an armored division, and a reinforced regimental combat team to employ in checking a further westward drive by the Germans assembled in the La Gleize-Werbomont-Stoumont area.

The subsequent operations of the XVIII Airborne Corps would be molded in considerable degree by events prior to its appearance in the battle area. Already set forth have been the engagements in the Stoumont sector with two battalions of the 119th Infantry committed. The 2d Battalion of the 119th Infantry had left the regiment on 18 December with the independent mission of blocking the Germans at Werbomont and Trois Ponts, thus covering the assembly of the 82d Airborne. Late in the afternoon the battalion reached Werbomont, found no sign of the enemy, and detrucked for the march to Trois Ponts. About dusk the column reached the Lienne Creek in the vicinity of Habiemont, a village on a bald summit overlooking the Lienne. Here Maj. Hal D. McCown, the battalion commander, learned that German tanks had been sighted at Chevron, another hamlet a mile or so north on the Lienne. McCown, whose battalion was reinforced by a platoon each of tanks, tank destroyers, and infantry cannon, turned north only to find that the bridge near Chevron had been destroyed by friendly engineers and that no hostile crossing had been made. He moved north again but this time encountered fire from across the creek. Uncertain as to the situation and with darkness upon him, McCown ordered the battalion to deploy on the bare ridge line rising west of the creek.

Some time later the Americans heard tracks clanking along the road between their position and the creek; this was the reconnaissance detachment which Peiper had sent north and which had found a bridge, albeit too weak a structure for the German tanks. A brief fusillade from the ridge and the Germans fled, leaving five battered half-tracks behind. One prisoner from the 2d SS Panzer Grenadier Regiment was taken. His company, he told interrogators, was the advance guard of a four company detachment whose mission was to reconnoiter toward Werbomont and take that town. But no other attempt was made that night to run the 2d Battalion gauntlet. Screened by McCown's force, the 82d Airborne Division was free to detruck and assemble around Werbomont, as the night progressed, according to plan.

Recall that on the morning of 18 December the 82d Airborne Division started for Bastogne but was diverted short of its destination and ordered to Werbomont. General Gavin had gone from the First Army headquarters to Werbomont and made a personal reconnaissance of the ground as far as the Amblève River. This, of course, was on the morning of the 18th so that he saw none of the enemy forces who at that moment were turning in the direction of Werbomont. The advance party of the 82d arrived in the village at dark and opened the division command post. Although there was now serious question whether the convoys of the 82d would reach Werbomont in force before the Germans, the bulk of the division moved without opposition into the area during the night of 18 December. The following morning Maj. Gen. Matthew B. Ridgway, who had resumed command of the airborne corps, opened his corps command post near that of the 82d, once again under Gavin.

Later in the morning at the First Army headquarters (which had moved to Chaudfontaine), General Hodges gave Ridgway the directive which would make the airborne corps operational and flesh it out with troops. The corps' mission was to block further German advance along an irregular line extending from the Amblève through Manhay and Houffalize to La Roche on the Ourthe River, placing the corps' right boundary twenty miles northwest of Bastogne. Three threatened areas were known to be in the newly assigned zone of operations: the Amblève River sector, where the 119th Infantry was deployed; the Salm River sector, especially at Trois Ponts where a lone engineer company still barred the crossings (although this information was unknown to the 82d); and the general area north of the Ourthe River where a vague and ill-defined German movement had been reported. But beyond checking these specific enemy advances the XVIII Airborne Corps had the more difficult task of sealing the gap of nearly twenty miles which had opened between the V and VIII Corps.

During the morning of 19 December the 504th and 505th Parachute Infantry Regiments marched out of the Werbomont assembly area under orders to push to the fore as far as possible, relieve the 2d Battalion, 119th Infantry, and improve the American defense line by adding a bridgehead across the Lienne Creek. There were no Germans here and by noon the initial deployment was close to completion. Meanwhile rumors had reached the First Army command post that the enemy had cut the main north-south highway running between Bastogne and Liège in the neighborhood of Houffalize. More rumors, mostly from truck drivers whose missions on the rear area roads usually gave them first sight of the westernmost German spearheads, put the enemy somewhere near Hotton, ten miles northwest of the XVIII Airborne Corps boundary marker at La Roche. Hastily complying with First Army orders, the 3d Battalion of the 325th Glider Infantry Regiment and a tank destroyer platoon set off southwestward to block the approaches to Hotton. By nightfall the battalion was in place, stuck out alone on the corps' right wing and waiting for troops of the 3d Armored to appear. A couple of hours before midnight a patrol did meet the armored "point" — Maj. Gen. Maurice Rose, the 3d Armored commander, riding in a jeep far in front of his tank columns.

The main body of the 82d Airborne Division began to push toward the east and south in midafternoon. With the 508th Parachute Infantry in support, the 504th and 505th moved along the roads toward La Gleize and Trois Ponts respectively. This proved to be only a route march, for the Germans were nowhere about. By midnight the 505th had a battalion each in the villages of Haute-Bodeux and Basse-Bodeux, effectively backstopping the small American force which still held Trois Ponts. The 504th, which had marched northeast, occupied the village of Rahier with two battalions. The 325th Glider Infantry, minus the battalion sent to Hotton, remained in and around Werbomont as corps and division reserve. One of its companies moved during the evening to the crossroads at Manhay, due south of Werbomont, a crossroads which General Ridgway styled "of vital significance." And a company of the 508th meanwhile established an outpost position on the Manhay-Trois Ponts road at Bras.

By the morning of 20 December, therefore, the 82d Airborne Division had pushed a defensive screen north, east, south, and west of Werbomont. It is true that to the south and west the screen consisted only of motorized patrols and widely separated pickets in small villages, but now there was a good chance that any major enemy thrust could be detected and channelized or retarded. Thus far, however, the XVIII Airborne Corps was making its deployment against an unseen enemy. Indeed, so confused was the situation into which Ridgway had been thrust that at midnight on 19 December he was forced to send an urgent message to Hodges asking for information on any V or VIII Corps units in his zone. But his corps was substantially strengthened by the next morning. CCB of the 3d Armored Division had reached Theux, about ten miles north of Stoumont, and was ready for immediate use. The 3d Armored Division (minus CCA and CCB) had reached the road between Hotton and Manhay on the corps' right wing.

Ridgway had detailed plans for continuing the pressure along the corps front from northeast to southwest. CCB, 3d Armored, was to clear the east and north banks of the Amblève and establish contact with the 117th Infantry, which had its hands full in Stavelot. The reinforced 119th Infantry was to secure the Amblève River line from Stoumont to La Gleize. The 82d Airborne Division was to take over the Salm River bridges at Trois Ponts, drive the enemy from the area between the Amblève and the

Werbomont-Trois Ponts road, and make contact with CCB when the latter reached Stavelot, thus completing the encirclement of such enemy forces as might be left to the north. The 3d Armored Division was to fan out and push reconnaissance as far as the road between Manhay and Houffalize, locating and developing the shadowy German force believed to be bearing down on the sketchy corps right wing somewhere north of Houffalize.

The immediate and proximate threat, on the morning of 20 December, was Peiper's force of the 1st SS Panzer Division, now concentrated with its bulk in the Stoumont-La Gleize area, but with an outpost holding the light bridge over the Amblève at Cheneux and its tail involved in a fight to reopen the rearward line of communications through Stavelot. Kampfgruppe Peiper, it should be noticed, was considerably weakened by this piecemeal deployment; furthermore, it lacked the gasoline to undertake much maneuver even in this constricted area.

CCB (Brig. Gen. Truman E. Boudinot) moved south past Spa on the morning of the 20th in three task forces, using three roads leading to the Stoumont-La Gleize-Trois Ponts triangle. The largest of these detachments, Task Force Lovelady (Lt. Col. William B. Lovelady), had been given a complete tank battalion, reinforced by a company of armored infantry, and the important job of cutting the Stavelot-Stoumont road. Colonel Lovelady, then, led the force which formed the left jaw of the vise forming to clamp down on Kampfgruppe Peiper. His task force, proceeding on the easternmost of the three routes, reached the junction of the Trois Ponts-Stoumont roads without sign of the enemy. Just as the column was making the turn south toward Trois Ponts, a small enemy column of artillery, infantry, and supply trucks appeared, apparently on its way to reinforce Peiper's main body.

Since Trois Ponts and Stavelot were both in American hands, the appearance of this train was surprising. What had happened was this: German engineers had reinforced a small footbridge east of Trois Ponts, at least to the point that it would sustain a self-propelled gun carriage, and since the night of 18 December supply trucks and reinforcements had used the bridge to slip between the two American-held towns. German records indicate that some much-needed gasoline reached Peiper through this hole in the American net, but the amount was insufficient to set the kampfgruppe rolling again even if the road west had been free. As to this particular German column, the Americans disposed of it in short order. Task Force Lovelady continued on its mission and established three roadblocks along the main road between Trois Ponts and La Gleize. The Germans in the Stoumont sector were definitely sealed in, albeit still active, for four Shermans were destroyed by hidden antitank guns.

The two remaining task forces of CCB and companion units from the 30th Division were less successful. Task Force McGeorge (Maj. K. T. McGeorge), the center column, made its advance along a road built on the side of a ridge which ran obliquely from the northeast toward La Gleize. Most of the ridge road was traversed with no sight of the Germans. At Cour, about two miles from La Gleize, Task Force McGeorge picked up Company K of the 117th Infantry and moved on to assault the latter town. Midway the Americans encountered a roadblock held by a tank and a couple of assault guns. Because the pitch of the ridge slope precluded any tank maneuver, the rifle company circled the German outpost and advanced as far as the outskirts of La Gleize. A sharp counterattack drove the infantry back into the tanks, still road-bound, and when the tanks themselves were threatened by close-in work McGeorge withdrew the task force for the night to the hamlet of Borgoumont perched above La Gleize. It was apparent that the Germans intended to hold on to La Gleize, although in fact the greater part of Peiper's command by this time was congregated to the west on the higher ground around Stoumont.

The attack on Stoumont on the 20th was a continuation of that begun late on the previous afternoon by the 1st Battalion of the 119th Infantry. The maneuver now, however, was concentric. The 1st Battalion and its accompanying tank company from the 740th Tank Battalion pushed along the road from the west while Task Force Jordan (Capt. John W. Jordan), the last and smallest of the three CCB detachments, attempted a thrust from the north via the Spa road, which had given the First Army headquarters so much concern. Task Force Jordan was within sight of Stoumont when the tanks forming the point were suddenly brought under flanking fire by German tanks that had been dug in to give hull defilade. The two American lead tanks were knocked out immediately. The rest of the column, fixed to the roadway by the forest and abrupt ground, could not deploy. Search for some other means of approach was futile, and the task force halted for the night on the road.

The 1st Battalion, 119th Infantry, and the company of medium tanks from the 740th Tank Battalion found slow but steady going in the first hours of the attack along the western road. With Company B and the tanks leading and with artillery and mortars firing rapidly in support, the battalion moved through Targnon. The Germans had constructed a series of mine fields to bar the winding road which climbed up the Stoumont hill and had left rear guard infantry on the slopes north of the road to cover these barriers by fire. At the close of day the attacking column had traversed some 3,000 yards and passed five mine fields (with only two tanks lost), the infantry advance guard climbing the wooded hillside to flank and denude each barrier.

Now within 800 yards of the western edge of Stoumont and with darkness and a heavy fog settling over the town, Colonel Herlong gave orders for the column to close up for the night. One of the disabled tanks was turned sidewise to block the narrow road, while Companies B and C moved up the hill north of this improvised barrier to seize a sanatorium which overlooked the road and the town. The main sanatorium building stood on an earthen platform filled in as a projection from the hillside rising north of the road. Its inmates, some two hundred sick children and old people, had taken to the basement. After a brief shelling the American infantry climbed over the fill and, shrouded in the fog, assaulted the building. The German infantry were driven out and four 20-mm. guns taken. Companies B and C dug in to form a line on the hillside in and around the sanatorium, and Company A disposed itself to cover the valley road. Four tanks were brought up the slope just below the fill and in this forward position were refueled by armored utility cars. The enemy foxhole line lay only some three hundred yards east of the companies on the hill.

An hour before midnight the Germans suddenly descended on the sanatorium, shouting "Heil Hitler" and firing wildly. On the slope above the building German tanks had inched forward to positions from which they could fire directly into the sanatorium. American tanks were brought up but could not negotiate the steep banks at the fill. One was set afire by a bazooka; two more were knocked out by German tanks which had crept down the main road. The flaming tanks and some outbuildings which had been set afire near the sanatorium so lighted the approach to the building that further American tank maneuver on the slope was impossible. By this time German tanks had run in close enough to fire through the windows of the sanatorium. The frenzied fight inside and around the building went on for a half hour or so, a duel with grenades and bullet fire at close quarters. About thirty men from

Company B were captured as the battle eddied through rooms and hallways, and the attackers finally gained possession of the main building. However, Sgt. William J. Widener with a group of eleven men held on in a small annex, the sergeant shouting out sensings—while American shells fell—to an artillery observer in a foxhole some fifty yards away. (Widener and Pfc. John Leinen, who braved enemy fire to keep the defenders of the annex supplied with ammunition, later received the DSC.)

Although the German assault had won possession of the sanatorium and had pushed back the American line on the slope to the north, accurate and incessant shellfire checked the attackers short of a breakthrough. About 0530 the enemy tried it again in a sortie from the town headed for the main road. But tank reinforcements had arrived for the 1st Battalion and their fire, thickening that of the artillery, broke the attack before it could make appreciable headway. When day broke, the Americans still held the roadblock position but the enemy had the sanatorium. In the night of wild fighting half the complement of Companies B and C had been lost, including five platoon leaders.

Despite the setbacks suffered during the American advance of 20 December on the Stoumont-La Gleize area, the net had been drawn appreciably tighter around Peiper. The German line of supply—or retreat—was cut by Task Force Lovelady and the Americans in Stavelot. The roads from Stoumont and La Gleize north to Spa were blocked by tank-infantry teams which had pushed very close to the former two towns. The 1st Battalion of the 119th Infantry had been checked at the sanatorium but nonetheless was at the very entrance to Stoumont and had the 2d Battalion behind it in regimental reserve.

Also, during the 20th, the 82d Airborne Division moved to close the circle around Peiper by operations aimed at erasing the small German bridgehead at Cheneux on the Amblève southeast of Stoumont. The 82d had planned an advance that morning to drive the enemy from the area bounded on the north by the Amblève River and by the Trois Ponts-Werbomont road on the south. The two regiments involved (the 504th Parachute Infantry on the left and the 505th on the right) marched to their attack positions east of Werbomont with virtually no information except that they were to block the enemy, wherever he might be found, in conjunction with friendly forces operating somewhere off to the north and south. The first task, obviously, was to reconnoiter for either enemy or friendly forces in the area.

Patrols sent out at daybreak were gone for hours, but about noon, as bits of information began to arrive at General Gavin's headquarters, the picture took some shape. Patrols working due north reached the 119th Infantry on the road west of Stoumont and reported that the countryside was free of the enemy. Civilians questioned by patrols on the Werbomont-Stoumont road told the Americans that there was a concentration of tanks and other vehicles around Cheneux. Working eastward, other patrols found that Trois Ponts was occupied by Company C, 51st Engineers, and that the important bridges there had all been damaged or destroyed. This word from Trois Ponts came as a surprise back at General Gavin's headquarters where the presence of this single engineer company at the critical Trois Ponts crossing site was quite unknown.

The most important discovery made by the airborne infantry patrols was the location of the 7th Armored Division troops in the gap between the XVIII Airborne Corps and Bastogne. The whereabouts of the westernmost 7th Armored Division positions had been a question of grave import in the higher American headquarters for the past two days. Now a patrol from the 505th Parachute Infantry came in with information that they had reached a reconnaissance party of the 7th Armored in the village of Fosse, a little over two miles southwest of Trois Ponts, and that troops of that division were forming an outpost line just to the south of the 505th positions.

Once General Gavin had a moderately clear picture of the situation confronting his division he ordered the two leading regiments forward: the 504th to Cheneux, where the enemy had been reported, and the 505th to Trois Ponts. The 505th commander, Col. William E. Ekman, already had dispatched bazooka teams to reinforce the engineer company at the latter point and by late afternoon had his 2d Battalion in Trois Ponts, with one company holding a bridgehead across the Salm.

Acting under orders to reach Cheneux as quickly as possible and seize the Amblève bridge, the 504th commander, Col. Reuben H. Tucker, 3d, sent Companies B and C of his 1st Battalion hurrying toward the village. The leading company was nearing the outskirts of Cheneux in midafternoon when it came into a hail of machine gun and flak fire. Both companies deployed and took up the fire fight but quickly found that the village was strongly defended. Ground haze was heavy and friendly artillery could not be adjusted to give a helping hand. Dark was coming on and the companies withdrew to a wood west of Cheneux to await further orders.

The 1st Battalion had not long to wait. New plans which would greatly extend the 82d Airborne Division front were already in execution and it was imperative that the German bridgehead on the north flank of the division be erased promptly. Colonel Tucker ordered the 1st Battalion commander (Lt. Col. Willard E. Harrison) to take the two companies and try a night attack. At 1930 they moved out astride the road west of Cheneux, two tank destroyers their only heavy support. The approach to the village brought the paratroopers across a knob completely barren of cover, sloping gradually up to the German positions and crisscrossed with barbed wire. The hostile garrison, from the 2d SS Panzer Grenadier Regiment, was heavily reinforced by mobile flak pieces, mortars, machine guns, and assault artillery.

To breast this heavy fire and rush the four hundred yards of open terrain, the two companies attacked in four waves at intervals of about fifty yards. The moment the leading American assault waves could be discerned through the darkness the enemy opened an intense, accurate fire. Twice the attackers were driven back, both times with gaping ranks. The first two waves were almost completely shot down. Company C ran into the wire and, having no wire cutters available, was stalled momentarily. Finally the two tank destroyers worked their way to the front and began to shell the German guns. With their support a third assault was thrown at the village. This time a few men lived to reach the outlying houses. In a brief engagement at close quarters the Americans silenced some of the flak and machine guns, then set up a defense to guard this slight toehold until reinforcements could arrive.

The West Flank of the XVIII Airborne Corps, 20 December
The general advance of the XVIII Airborne Corps on 20 December included the mission assigned to the 3d Armored Division of securing the Bastogne-Liège highway between Manhay and Houffalize, thus screening the right or western flank of the corps. The bulk of the 3d Armored was engaged elsewhere: CCA deployed as a defense for the Eupen area, CCB driving with troops of the 30th Infantry Division against Kampfgruppe Peiper. When General Rose moved his forward command post to Hotton on 20 December, the residue of the 3d Armored was assembling between Hotton and Soy, a force numbering only the small reserve combat command and the 83d Reconnaissance Battalion. Nothing was known of any friendly troops to the front,

nor did information on the location and strength of the enemy have more than the validity of rumor. Since it was necessary to reconnoiter and clear the area west of the important section of the north-south highway, now his objective, General Rose decided to divide his limited strength into three columns, two attacking via generally north-south routes and then swinging eastward; the third, on the extreme left, driving east to the Manhay crossroads and then turning south on the main highway.

This was a risky decision, as the 3d Armored commander well knew, for the zone of attack was very broad and if one of the small columns ran into a superior enemy force the best it could do would be to fight a delaying action on its own. Terrain and weather, however, would aid the reconnaissance somewhat, for although the area was laced by back roads and trails German maneuver would be drastically curtailed and a German advance limited to the few open and passable roads. General Rose tried to retain as much flexibility as he could, in view of the vague status of the enemy and the width of the front to be covered. The three task forces, or more properly reconnaissance teams, assigned to Lt. Col. Prentice E. Yeomans each had a reconnaissance troop, a medium tank company, a battery of armored field artillery, and a platoon of light tanks. The reserve, commanded by Col. Robert L. Howze, Jr., was made up of an armored infantry battalion, two companies of light tanks and one of mediums, plus a company of engineers. This reserve would follow the middle task force.

The attack or reconnaissance, time would tell which, began in early afternoon. On the right Task Force Hogan (Lt. Col. Samuel M. Hogan) set out along a secondary road surmounting the ridge which rose on the east bank of the Ourthe River and extended south to La Roche, the boundary for the XVIII Airborne Corps right wing. The Ourthe River, then, would form a natural screen on this flank. Hogan's column met no opposition en route to La Roche and upon arrival there found that the town was defended by roadblocks that had been thrown up by the 7th Armored Division trains. At this point the route dropped into the river valley, following the twists and turns of the Ourthe toward the southeast. Hogan sent on a small scouting force which covered some three miles before it was confronted by a German roadblock. There was no way around, daylight was running out, and the force halted.

The road assigned Task Force Tucker (Maj. John Tucker), the center column, followed the Aisne River valley southward. At the village of Dochamps this route began an ascent from the valley onto the ridge or tableland where lay the town of Samrée. At Samrée Task Force Tucker was to make a left wheel onto the La Roche-Salmchâteau road (N28), which followed a high, narrow ridge line to the east, there crossing the main Liège-Bastogne highway. This intersection, the Baraque de Fraiture, would have a special importance in later fighting.

Tucker's column moved unopposed through the Aisne valley but at Dochamps, where began the ascent to the Samrée highland, it was engaged by a German force of unknown strength. In an attempt to continue the reconnaissance Major Tucker split his command in three. One force circled west and south to Samrée where, it had only now been learned, a part of the 7th Armored Division trains was fighting to hold the town. The second group turned east and finally made contact with Task Force Kane. Tucker's third group moved back north to Amonines.

Late in the afternoon General Rose learned that the 3d Armored tanks sent to Samrée had been knocked out and the town itself lost to the enemy. The elevation on which Samrée stood and its importance as a barrier on the highway from La Roche to the division objective made recapture of the town almost mandatory. Rose ordered

Colonel Yeomans to regain Samrée and hold it; for this mission two companies of armored infantry from the reserve combat command were detailed to Lt. Col. William R. Orr. Colonel Orr picked up the remaining elements of Task Force Tucker and arrived outside of Dochamps a little before midnight, setting up a roadblock for the remainder of the night.

Task Force Kane (Lt. Col. Matthew W. Kane), on the left in the three column advance, found easy going on 20 December. Acting as the pivot for the swing south and east, Kane's column was charged with the occupation of Malempré, about 3,000 yards southeast of the vital Manhay crossroads. This latter junction on the Liège-Bastogne highway represented a position tactically untenable. Hills away to the east and west dominated the village, and to the southeast an extensive woods promised cover from which the enemy could bring fire on the crossroads. By reason of the ground, therefore, Malempré, on a hill beyond the woods, was the chosen objective. Kane's task force reached Manhay and pushed advance elements as far as Malempré without meeting the enemy.

The three reconnaissance forces of the 3d Armored Division by the close of 20 December had accomplished a part of their mission by discovering the general direction of the German advance northwest of Houffalize and, on two of the three roads, had made contact with the enemy. It remained to establish the enemy's strength and his immediate intentions. As yet no prisoners had been taken nor precise identifications secured, but the G-2 of the 3d Armored Division (Lt. Col. Andrew Barr) made a guess, based on earlier reports, that the three task forces had met the 116th Panzer Division and that the 560th Volks Grenadier Division was following the former as support.

Action in Front of the XVIII Airborne Corps Right Wing on 20 December

As the 3d Armored Division assembled for advance on the morning of 20 December, and indeed for most of the day, it was unaware that little groups of Americans continued to hold roadblocks and delay the enemy in the area lying to the front of the XVIII Airborne Corps right wing. These miniature delaying positions had been formed on 18 and 19 December by men belonging to the 7th Armored Division trains, commanded by Colonel Adams, and by two combat engineer battalions, the 51st and 158th. As the 7th Armored advanced into combat around St. Vith on 18 December and it became apparent that German thrusts were piercing deep on both flanks of this position, Adams received orders to move the division trains into the area around La Roche and prepare a defense for that town and the Ourthe bridges. Most of the vehicles under Adams' command were concentrated west of La Roche by 20 December, but large stores of ammunition, rations, and gasoline had just been moved to dumps at Samrée.

The 51st Engineer Combat Battalion (Lt. Col. Harvey R. Fraser) had arrived at Hotton on 19 December with orders to construct a barrier line farther south which would utilize the Ourthe River as a natural obstacle. The battalion was minus Company C, which, at Trois Ponts, did much to slow the pace of Kampfgruppe Peiper's westward march. It did have the services of the 9th Canadian Forestry Company, which took on the task of preparing the Ourthe crossings south of La Roche for demolition. From La Roche north to Hotton and for several kilometers beyond, the remaining two companies worked at mining passable fording sites, fixing explosives on bridges, and erecting roadblocks; but the extensive project was far from complete on 20 December. The sketchy barrier line on the Ourthe was extended toward Bastogne by the 158th Engineer Combat Battalion. To the 7th Armored trains and the engineers were added little groups of heterogeneous composition and improvised armament, picked up by the nearest headquarters and hurried to the Ourthe River line in answer to rumors of the German advance over Houffalize. It is hardly surprising, then, that the 3d Armored Division began its advance unaware of efforts already afoot to delay the enemy.

While little American detachments worked feverishly to prepare some kind of barrier line on the Ourthe River and around La Roche and Samrée, the north wing of the Fifth Panzer Army was coming closer and closer. Krueger's LVIII Panzer Corps pushed its advance guard through the Houffalize area on 19 December, while the rear guard mopped up American stragglers and isolated detachments on the west bank of the Our River. Krueger's orders were to push as far west as possible on the axis Houffalize-La Roche while his neighbor on the left, the XXXVII Panzer Corps, cut its way through Bastogne or circled past the road complex centered there.

The Reconnaissance Battalion of the 116th Panzer Division, several hours ahead of the main body of Krueger's corps, had reached Houffalize on the morning of 19 December, but because Krueger expected the town to be strongly defended and had ordered his reconnaissance to avoid a fight there the battalion veered to the south, then west toward La Roche. This brief enemy apparition and sudden disappearance near Houffalize probably account for the conflicting and confusing rumors as to the location of the Germans in this sector which were current in American headquarters on 19 December. Between Bertogne and La Roche the Reconnaissance Battalion discovered that the bridge over the west branch of the Ourthe had been destroyed. At this point the Germans had a brush with one of the roadblocks put out by the 7th Armored troops in La Roche and thus alerted Colonel Adams. Adams had no other information of the enemy.

It seemed to Adams, as a result of the skirmish, that the German advance toward La Roche was being made on the northwest bank of the main branch of the Ourthe River and that the final attack would come from the west rather than the east. He therefore moved the 7th Armored dumps from locations west of La Roche to Samrée, from which point he hoped to maintain contact with and continue supplies to the main body of the division at St. Vith. By early morning of 20 December the transfer had been completed. Adams now was confronted with the necessity of pushing his defenses farther east to protect the new supply point. He dispatched part of a battery of the 203d Antiaircraft Artillery Battalion to the Baraque de Fraiture crossroads formed by the intersection of the Samrée-Salmchâteau road and the main Liège-Bastogne highway, the same junction which had seemed so important to the XVIII Airborne Corps commander in his map reconnaissance of this area. Upon arrival there the newcomers found that some gunners from the 106th Infantry Division, commanded by Maj. Arthur C. Parker, already had dug in to defend the vital crossroads.

The German appearance at the broken bridge which altered Colonel Adams' plans had even greater effect in General Krueger's headquarters. Krueger had no bridging available in the corps trains when the word reached him on the night of the 19th. The fact that he had to rely on the limited capacity of the 116th Panzer Division engineers meant that the western branch of the Ourthe could not be spanned before the evening of 20 December. Such a delay was out of the question. To sidestep to the south would bang the corps against very strong resistance forming around Bastogne and would scramble the vehicular columns of Krueger's armor with the 2d Panzer

Division. By this time the 116th Panzer Division rear guard had occupied Houffalize without a fight. The main body of the division, having marched unopposed nearly to the road which runs from Bastogne northwest to Marche, was preparing to seize a second bridge over the west branch of the Ourthe at Ortheuville. Krueger had no faith that any stroke of fortune would deliver the Ourtheuville bridge untouched. This was the end of the fourth day of the German advance and the Americans, he reasoned, were long since on guard against a coup de main there.

Weighing the apparent American strength in the Bastogne sector against the total absence of resistance at Houffalize the LVIII Panzer Corps commander decided, late in the evening of the 19th, to shift his advance to the north bank of the Ourthe River and reroute the 116th Panzer Division toward Samrée by way of Houffalize. The order to halt his division and countermarch to Houffalize was a distinctly unpleasant experience for General von Waldenburg. (He would later say that his decision was "fatal to the division.") The business of reversing a mechanized division in full swing under conditions of total darkness is ticklish at best; when it is conducted by tired officers and men unfamiliar with the road net and is hampered by supply and artillery trains backing up behind the turning columns it is a serious test for any unit. Nevertheless the 116th sorted itself out, issued supplies, refueled its vehicles, and by early morning was en route to Houffalize. Meanwhile the 1128th Regiment, leading the 560th Volks Grenadier Division, had been closing up fast on the 116th Panzer Division in a series of forced marches (that later won for the 560th a commendation for its "excellent march performance"). By noon of 20 December the bulk of the 116th Panzer Division followed by a large portion of the 560th Volks Grenadier Division had defiled through Houffalize and was on the north bank of the Ourthe River.

The maneuver now to be executed was a left wheel into attack against Samrée and La Roche, with the main effort, carried by the tank regiment of the 116th Panzer Division, made at Samrée. The right flank of the attack would be covered by the 560th Volks Grenadier Division As the morning drew along the Americans had made their presence felt by increasingly effective artillery fire from the north. German scouts reported that there were tanks to be seen near Samrée (actually the American garrison there had only one) but that the ground would sustain a German tank attack The 60th Panzer Grenadier Regiment assembled under cover of the woods south of the town, and the tanks (from the 16th Panzer Regiment) moved out onto the Samrée road. Advance patrols, which had started a firefight in the late morning, were able to occupy a few houses when a fog settled in shortly after noon.

All this time the 7th Armored Division quartermaster, Lt. Col. A. A. Miller, had been issuing rations, ammunition, and gasoline as fast as trucks could load. The force he had inside Samrée was small: half of the 3967th Quartermaster Truck Company, the quartermaster section of the division headquarters, part of the 440th Armored Field Artillery Battalion's Service Battery, two sections of D Battery, 203d Antiaircraft Artillery Battalion, armed with quadruple-mount machine guns, plus a light tank and a half-track from the 87th Cavalry Reconnaissance Squadron. About noon word reached Samrée that the 3d Armored Division was sending a task force to the town. The German patrols had not yet entered the town; so, heartened by the approach of the friendly armor, Miller gave orders that no supplies were to be destroyed. About 1430 the firefight quickened. Hearing that the 3d Armored tanks had reached Dochamps, Miller drove to find the task force and insure that he would get immediate aid. Not more than a half hour later the Germans swarmed in under a sharp barrage of rocket fire. By this time the one tank was out of ammunition, the machine gunners manning the .50-caliber weapons on the quartermaster trucks were also running low, the antiaircraft outfit had lost three of its weapons and fired its last round, and the division Class III officer had ordered the units to evacuate. A majority of the troops got out with most of their trucks and the remaining artillery ammunition, but 15,000 rations and 25,000 gallons of gasoline were left behind.

Shortly after, the detachment sent from Task Force Tucker appeared. Two armored cars, at the point, entered the north edge of the town, but the six medium tanks following were quickly destroyed by German armor coming in from the east. During the shooting the armored cars were able to pick up the surviving tankers and escape to La Roche. The 7th Armored Division headquarters received word of the fight, and from La Roche the commander of the Trains Headquarters Company, 1st. Lt. Denniston Averill, hurried to Samrée with two medium tanks and a self-propelled tank destroyer. Averill's little party attempted to enter Samrée, but was not heard from again.

Off to the east, at Salmchâteau, Troop D of the 87th Cavalry Reconnaissance Squadron also got orders sending it to Samrée. Passing the friendly outpost at the Baraque de Fraiture the troop came within two and a half miles of Samrée when it encountered a German roadblock, not well defended. Smashing it, the troop moved on. Shortly it struck a second block formed by abandoned American trucks and defended by a large force of German infantry (two companies of the 560th Volks Grenadier Division). Having felt out the enemy and with night drawing on, the cavalry commander pulled his troop back a little to the east to await the morning. Later in the evening radio orders came from the 7th Armored Division headquarters telling him to arrange a co-ordinated attack with the 3d Armored Division task force north of Dochamps.

The action at Samrée had delayed Krueger's corps considerably. But the gasoline stores captured there had refueled all the vehicles of the 116th Panzer Division; despite assurances by American prisoners that sugar had been mixed with the gasoline the enemy drivers reported that it suited the German motors very well.

The Net Closes on Peiper

General Hobbs's division and CCB, 3d Armored Division, had a job to do before the XVIII Airborne Corps could be free to direct all its strength into a drive to re-establish contact with the VIII Corps and close the gap between Houffalize and Bastogne. Kampfgruppe Peiper, estimated as comprising at least half of the 1st SS Panzer Division, had to be eradicated north of the Amblève River. This force, whose rapid drive to the west had caused such alarm only a few hours before, appeared to be pocketed in the Stoumont-La Gleize sector. Effectively blocked off on the west the trapped Germans would probably try to cut their way to the rear via Stavelot or at least establish a bridgehead there as a potential escape hatch. Probably, too, the troops in the pocket would receive some aid from new German units moving along the north flank of the St Vith salient through the gap between Malmédy and Recht.

The operations designed for 21 December left the 30th Division and its reinforcing armor to finish off Peiper by tightening the net spread the day before. Thereafter the 30th had orders to link up with the 82d Airborne at Trois Ponts and prepare to join in the XVIII Airborne Corps advance by pushing south. The varied indications that the Germans were moving in some force toward Malmédy, the pivot point for both the corps and division left wing, seemed to be no reason for reverting strictly to the defensive. Malmédy had been prepared for defense since the scare of 17 December, the reports of enemy forces thereabouts were rather vague, and six American artillery battalions were in position to give support where needed. In detail, then, the plans prepared by Hobbs and his staff were formulated against the Germans in the pocket.

On the morning of 21 December the American forces in and around Malmédy were substantial: the 120th Infantry (minus a battalion in division reserve); the "Norwegians," that is, the 99th Infantry Battalion; the 526th Armored Infantry Battalion; a company from the 291st Engineer Battalion; a tank company from the 740th; and two platoons from the 823d Tank Destroyer Battalion. The American infantry line formed an arc south of the town, swinging to east and west. On the left this line touched the 1st Infantry Division outposts near Waimes; on the right it had a tenuous connection with the 117th Infantry at the junction of the road from Stavelot and the road running north to Francorchamps. In passing it must be said that the responsibilities of the two sister regiments at the vaguely defined interregimental boundary were none too explicit. All roads leading to Malmédy had been blocked by mines and barricades or were barred by outpost detachments.

The first action of 21 December, as it turned out, was neither against Peiper nor at the pocket, but an engagement at Malmédy with new German troops thus far unidentified as a regular tactical unit. The night before, an enemy force had assembled in Ligneuville, five miles south of Malmédy. This was the notorious 150th Panzer Brigade which, under the command of the equally notorious Colonel Skorzeny, had been especially trained to seize the Meuse bridges as a part of Operation Greif. When the German plans to reach the Hohes Venn on the second day of the counteroffensive miscarried and the regular German formations were checked so far from the Meuse as to make a dash by this special task force out of the question, Colonel Skorzeny sought for some other road to fame and glory. His recommendation, made to the Sixth Panzer Army commander, that the group be reassembled and committed as an ordinary combat unit was accepted, and the capture of Malmédy was assigned as its first mission.

The troops that gathered in Ligneuville must have made a motley crew. Some were completely equipped with American uniforms and dogtags; others had olive drab trousers and American combat boots surmounted by field gray tunics; still others wore the German field uniform. Their vehicles were an assortment of German makes; captured American armored cars, tanks, and jeeps; and German models which had been given a facelifting job by the addition of dummy turrets, decks, and fronts to simulate an American equivalent. Despite this ragtag appearance Skorzeny's command was composed of tough, picked men, abundantly armed with automatic and heavy weapons.

Skorzeny divided his brigade into three groups, two for the assault and one in reserve. About two hours before dawn the right group struck straight north along the Ligneuville road in an effort to seize the bridge south of Malmédy. The assault force was engaged by the 1st Battalion of the 120th Infantry and the 3d Battalion joined the fire fight as well; but it was left to the artillery to "plaster" the Germans, as the infantry were quick to acknowledge. Two hours later the attackers had disappeared. The morning came with a dense fog floating out from the Amblève River. Attacking under this cover the left German assault group, two rifle companies, and a tank company rolled in column along a secondary road which would bring it west of Malmédy against the 3d Battalion of the 120th. One detachment turned toward the town but came to a sudden halt when the lead vehicles hit a minefield in front of B

Company, 99th Infantry Battalion. It took only minutes for mortars, machine guns, and artillery to dispel this assault.

Here, on the first day of use of the new POZIT fuze, the Germans were roughly dealt with. Nearly a hundred were killed by the shellbursts and for a moment panic spread among them, some running forward into the fire shouting "Kamerad." But Skorzeny's troops were tough and tried repeatedly to break Lt. Col. Harold D. Hansen's "Norwegians," an outfit characterized in the German intelligence reports as "old men." German machine gun crews tried to set up their pieces right in front of the railroad embankment where B Company lay but were shot down or blasted by hand grenades. Several times the enemy infantry reached the foot of the embankment, but could go no farther. Finally the assault died down.

The main enemy detachment headed for the Malmédy-Stavelot road, pushing its infantry to the fore. In the fog it encountered K Company of the 120th Infantry, knocked out a platoon deployed at a roadblock, and, using its tanks, drove the remaining American infantry back some distance to the north. Four 3-inch towed tank destroyers covering the road were abandoned after their crews removed the firing pins.

Not all the Americans fell back, however. One who stayed was 1st Lt. Kenneth R. Nelson, who decided to hold on with a few men left in his section and did so, savagely beating back the attackers. Nelson led the fight until he died of the wounds he had suffered. He received the DSC posthumously. T/Sgt. John Van Der Kamp then took command, although wounded, and held the position until ordered to withdraw. He was awarded the DSC. Part of K Company withdrew to a nearby factory, where Pfc. Francis Currey essayed a series of gallant deeds for which he later received the Medal of Honor. He knocked out a tank with bazooka fire, drove the German crews out of three tanks with antitank grenades, with a bazooka blew in the front of the house where the enemy tankers had taken refuge, and turned a half-track machine gun on the house with such effect as to silence the German fire and permit the escape of five Americans who had been cornered by the enemy.

This confused fight in the fog, taking place as it did on the boundary between the 120th and the 117th, had repercussions out of all relation to the event. By noon garbled reports and rumors placed German tanks (erroneously as it proved) in villages northwest of Malmédy; the 117th Infantry was worried that the Germans were left free to strike their left flank at Stavelot; the staff of the 120th Infantry was trying desperately to find out exactly what had happened; two battalions of antiaircraft artillery with 90-mm. guns were hurriedly taking positions to build a defense in depth as far back as the division command post; the 120th Infantry reserve was rushed west to Burnenville—but found no Germans. The much-touted German penetration finally boiled down to one tank and a half-track which had driven up and down the road in the fog with an English-speaking soldier shouting out lurid promises of warm female companionship for the Americans if they only would surrender.

The German thrust along the boundary between the two American regiments, as the event showed, had become jammed in the narrow corridor and most of its armor destroyed by cross fire coming in from the flanks. Deprived of tank support and followed unrelentingly by the new variety of shellbursts, the enemy infantry had withdrawn. Skorzeny, by this time fully aware of the defending strength at Malmédy, ordered his brigade to pull back to the south Thus ended the first and the last attack on Malmédy. The lines of the 3d Battalion were restored and two of the abandoned tank destroyer guns recovered and placed in action. Nonetheless, the unexpected strength of the German attack on Malmédy had impacts all up and down the American chain of command. At Hodges' First Army headquarters there had been a continuing question as to whether the enemy would try to shake loose in the north and drive for Liège. Momentarily it looked as if this indeed was the German intention.

To the west at Stavelot, a detachment from the rearward march echelons of the 1st SS Panzer Division made an abortive attempt to cross to the north bank of the Amblève preparatory to reopening the route leading to Kampfgruppe Peiper. The Americans holding the major section of the town had blown the last bridge, and the panzer grenadiers were forced to take to the icy stream. This crossing brought a hundred or so of the assault force in front of B Company, 117th Infantry, whose riflemen picked off most of the attackers while they still were in the stream. Beyond this one alarm the day passed quietly at Stavelot—although one major disaster occurred when a section of the 743d Tank Battalion fired high explosive into a building and set it afire, only to learn that it was filled with champagne and cognac.

The march echelons of the 1st SS Panzer Division en route to relieve Peiper were slow in assembling and their concentration area, southeast of Stavelot, was under constant interdiction by artillery fire. The 1st SS Panzer troops trapped to the west were closely engaged, and as yet Peiper had no orders which would permit a retrograde movement. On the American side the skirmish at Stavelot, coupled with German counterattacks in the La Gleize-Stoumont sector, made for bewilderment. General Hobbs dryly stated the prevailing opinion on the intentions of the trapped enemy, "They are trying to get out forward or backward or something."

The main task for the 30th Division and its reinforcing armored task forces remained that of eradicating all German troops north of the Amblève. The general plan was a continuation of the one set in operation the day before: the 119th Infantry (reinforced), now organized under the assistant division commander, General Harrison, as Task Force Harrison, to capture Stoumont and continue its eastward drive as far as La Gleize; the 3d Battalion of the 117th Infantry (reinforced) and the two 3d Armored task forces to carry through the concentric attack to seize La Gleize.

The latter maneuver got under way on 21 December. Task Force Lovelady, which had cut south between Stavelot and La Gleize on the previous day, reversed its course and moved north from the Trois Ponts area with the intention of securing the ridge which overlooked La Gleize from the southeast. Task Force McGeorge, stopped cold the evening before on the narrow ridge road which angled to La Gleize from the north, resumed the attack with K Company, 117th Infantry, trying to pry out the German block to the front. South of the Amblève, Task Force Lovelady was screened by the low-hanging fog from the strong enemy patrols working through the area; on the north bank, however, it ran into trouble while advancing on the sunken La Gleize road. Two leading tanks were crippled when they hit a patch of mines. Then German tanks or antitank guns knocked out the last two tanks in the column. At this point, therefore, the road was effectively blocked against further American or future German counterattacks. The infantry with Lovelady and a tank company spent the remainder of the day mopping up in the small villages along the river bank, finding evidences of revolting atrocities earlier perpetrated on the defenseless Belgians by Peiper's troops. Attempts to mount the ridge were checked by machine gun fire, and it became evident that the enemy had a strong force concentrated in this sector.

Task Force McGeorge and riflemen of the 117th Infantry likewise were unable to make much headway in extending the northern arm of the planned envelopment. The

German barrier interposed by dug-in tanks and assault guns at a little stream about a thousand yards north of La Gleize could not be taken by maneuver, for McGeorge's tanks were unable to get off the road, or by single-handed infantry assault. The American column then drew back along the valley road. About a mile east of La Gleize the task force turned west to cross the valley and approach the town but was halted at a curve in the road by fire from dug-in tanks and antitank guns. The riflemen formed a line of skirmishers in front of the German block and the task force halted for the night.

The drive to pinch out the western contents of the Peiper pocket at Stoumont got off to a late start on the 21st. General Harrison's original plan called for a coordinated attack in the early morning. The 1st Battalion, 119th Infantry, was to continue the drive to enter the town from the west (after recapturing the sanatorium and the high ground flanking the entrance). The 2d Battalion would swing wide through the woods north of the town, block the escape route to La Gleize, and then attack from the east. Task Force Jordan and the reorganized 3d Battalion (which earlier had been thrown out of Stoumont) would attack from the north as soon as the sanatorium, which overlooked the northern entrance to the town as well as the western, was wrested from enemy hands. The sanatorium, then, and the rise on which it stood held the final control of Stoumont.

Peiper did not wait for the counterattack which might lose him the sanatorium. Sometime before 0500 the lull which had succeeded the night of fierce fighting was broken by a German assault against the 1st Battalion positions on the roadway west of the town. The road itself was blocked by a tank platoon from the 740th Tank Battalion, the infantry dug in behind. The first tank facing the enemy fell to an antitank gun; in the darkness three more were set aflame by Panzerfausts in the hands of the infiltrating enemy infantry. The Germans were finally thrown back but they had succeeded in disorganizing the 1st Battalion to the point where General Harrison felt that his own attack would have to be postponed. The division commander agreed to Harrison's proposal that the attack be launched at 1245 instead of 0730 as planned. In the meantime the regimental cannon company and the 197th Field Artillery Battalion set to work softening up the Germans.

At the new hour the 1st and 2d Battalions jumped off. The 1st Battalion assault drove the enemy infantry out of some of the sanatorium rooms, but when a heavy German tank moved in on the north side (where it was screened from the Americans) and started blasting through the windows the Americans withdrew under smoke cover laid down by friendly mortars. Although the 2d Battalion made some progress in its advance through the woods the battalion commander, Major McCown, was captured while making a personal reconnaissance, and his troops fell back to their original position. The American tanks, unable to advance along the narrow sunken road under the guns of the Panthers and Tigers, remained north of the town.

A call from the division commander in late afternoon for "the real picture down there" elicited a frankly pessimistic answer from General Harrison. Two battalions, the 1st and 3d, had been cut down and demoralized by earlier enemy counterattacks; they were "in pretty bad shape." As to the armored detachment: "The trouble is the only places where tanks of any kind can operate are on two sunken roads. The Germans have big tanks, so tanks have been of no help to us." Further, Harrison told Hobbs, he would advise against continuing the attack on the morrow: "That place [Stoumont] is very strong. I don't think those troops we have now, without some improvement, can take the thing. That is my honest opinion. They are way down in strength. The trouble is that we can only get light artillery fire on the town, and the Germans can shoot at us with tank guns and we can't get tanks to shoot back unless they come out and get hit." To this forthright opinion there was little to add. General Hobbs cautioned Harrison to be on the lookout for a German attempt to break out during the night and head west, and told him that an attempt would be made to work out a scheme with General Ridgway for an attack by the 82d Airborne Division against the southern side of the Stoumont-La Gleize pocket.

Earlier in the day Hobbs had assured the corps commander that if the 82d Airborne cleared out the south bank of the Amblève no further help would be needed. His request that evening for an attack by the 82d from the Trois Ponts sector came at a time when the situation along the entire corps front had drastically altered and in part deteriorated. To the south the XVIII Airborne Corps was heavily engaged, the 7th Armored Division was being pushed out of the St. Vith salient, and even in the Trois Ponts area there had been a sudden enemy resurgence. Furthermore a frontal attack from the south would be almost suicidal so long as the Germans held the higher ground on the north bank of the Amblève.

Hobbs's diagnosis of the problem as "the physical proposition of human beings" may have been a truism but it was sound. On the one side a tough force of cornered Germans weighted the scales, fighting in desperate fashion and given physical and moral backing by heavily armored tanks mounting a superior gun and able to employ hull defilade, blocking a few well-defined and straightened avenues of approach. On the other side the counterweight consisted of a relatively few tanks whose crews knew that their tanks were not heavy enough for a headlong attack and their guns could not match the German tank guns in long-range dueling, and who were working with infantry whose strength was no longer sufficient to pry the Panthers and Tigers out of their lairs. Nonetheless the "human being" could not be exactly equated at a discount rate against machines. Pfc. Jack Gebert demonstrated the point when he advanced through machine gun fire, destroyed a German tank with a bazooka round, climbed onto a US tank, and directed its fire until shot down. He was awarded the DSC posthumously.

The answer seemed to be air attack. The missions set up to aid the 30th Division had been canceled on the morning of 20 December because of bad weather. The First Army air officers, however, had told Ridgway and Hobbs that there was a fair chance of flying weather on the morning of the 22d. Hobbs assured the corps commander that he "could use up to sixteen groups in one day," that his own air support officer would have the targets ready. Here the matter rested in the lap of the weather gods.

Although there was little direct help that the 82d Airborne Division could give the 30th Division while the Germans still held Stoumont, it had aided the attack north of the Amblève on December by soldering the southern link in the bank around Kampfgruppe Peiper and by beating off the relief detachments of the 1st SS Panzer Division who were trying to lever an opening in this ring. The two companies of the 1st Battalion, 504th Parachute Infantry, that fought their way into Cheneux on the 20th, had endangered Peiper's only remaining foothold on the south bank of the Amblève. Since the companies B and C, had suffered very severe losses from the waist-high fire of the German .20-mm. self-propelled flak pieces while making the assault across the open ground around the village, Colonel Tucker ordered in G Company and in the hours after midnight effected some reorganization. Fighting continued inside the village all through the night, for the most part a hunt with knife and grenade to destroy the crews of the antiaircraft half-tracks (the flak wagons) which had punished the paratroopers so badly. During the battle Pfc. Daniel Del Grippo, who had been painfully wounded, attacked and killed the crew of a self-propelled gun. S/Sgt. William Walsh, leading a platoon which became pinned down by flanking fire from a flak wagon, rushed the Germans and destroyed them with a grenade, although he was so badly wounded that a comrade had to arm the grenade. Both of these soldiers received the DSC.

When morning dawned General Gavin turned the entire regiment over to Tucker with orders to "wipe out" the Germans at Cheneux. The 3d Battalion (Lt. Col. Julian A. Cook) made a wide flanking movement in a six-hour march over rough ground and entered the village from the north side; by late afternoon the fight was ended. The Americans had lost 225 dead and wounded, mostly from the two assault companies. Company B had 18 men left and no officers; C Company had 38 men and 3 officers. Few Germans were captured. The rear guard fought to the end, but most of the garrison still living had withdrawn during the night leaving scores of dead behind. Booty taken here included fourteen flak wagons and a battery of 105-mm. howitzers, as well as many vehicles. Only one German tank was taken a clue to the ability of the few survivors from the initial assault to hang on in the village till help arrived.

Peiper's bridgehead was gone. Lacking the gasoline to make an advance out of it on 19 December, and hoping that some resupply would be forthcoming, he had ordered it held as a possible future sally port, from which to resume the westward drive. But even as the bridgehead was torn from the hands of his kampfgruppe, so the German relief forces were stopped before they could reopen the line of communications behind Peiper. In this feat also the 82d Airborne had a share on 21 December by defending the Salm River line.

Chapter XVI. One Threat Subsides; Another Emerges

The Attempt To Relieve Peiper's Kampfgruppe

The quick and cheaply won victories which had taken Peiper's armored kampfgruppe so close to the Meuse bridges in so short a time may have blinded the higher German staffs for a while to the fact that Peiper was in danger. By the 21st, however, the most strenuous efforts were being made to save the ground he had won north of the Amblève and to rescue the men and matériel in his command. What happened to leave the kampfgruppe stranded and alone?

The 1st SS Panzer Division had begun its drive west in four march groups moving independently. The bulk of the 1st Panzer Regiment, a motorized battalion of armored infantry, a mobile company of engineers, and a battery of self-propelled artillery (as well as most of the gasoline available) had gone to Peiper with the expectation that the armored weight and the mobile character of this spearhead detachment would permit a quick breakthrough and exploitation even to the Meuse River. The balance of the division was to follow hard on Peiper's heels, provide reinforcement as required, and keep the line of communications open until such time as following divisions could take over and be prepared to re-form as a unit at the Meuse. By noon of 17 December Peiper's kampfgruppe was out of touch with the second and third march columns of the division and was racing alone toward the west. The strongest of the rearward columns, the fourth, which amounted to a reinforced armored infantry regiment, had been held up by mines at the entrance to its designated route' and in fact never made a start until 18 December. The student of first causes may wish to speculate on the fateful role of the unknown cavalry, engineers, and foot soldiers who laid the mines between Lanzerath and Manderfeld, thus delaying most of the 1st SS Panzer Division armored infantry for a critical twenty-four hours.

By 19 December, it will be recalled, Peiper was over the Hohes Venn highlands, had crossed to the north bank of the Amblève River, and had secured the Stoumont-La Gleize area. At the same time he had almost completely drained his fuel tanks. On that same day radio communication of a sort had been re-established between Peiper and the 1st SS Panzer Division headquarters, so that his plight was known. The second march group, the mobile Reconnaissance Battalion, had come up and engaged the Americans at Stavelot, getting through some reinforcement to Peiper but failing in the larger task of keeping the door open behind Peiper. Meanwhile the third march group was moving slowly toward Stavelot while the fourth, following the southern route through Recht, had become involved at roadblocks on the north flank of the 7th Armored Division salient.

The hardening American resistance ahead of Peiper and on his exposed north flank, plus reports that his fuel supply was low, prompted the Sixth Panzer Army commander and staff to undertake new plans and orders calculated to get the kampfgruppe rolling once again. The army chief of staff was particularly concerned lest Peiper be forced to face north so as to protect his endangered flank and line of communications—as in fact happened. The nearest intact formation was the 3d Parachute Division. But if this division were taken out of its blocking position south of Waimes the road would be open for American reinforcements from the north to reach St. Vith. The 12th SS Panzer Division, originally scheduled to be the 1st SS Panzer Division's running mate on the north, had been taken out of the fight at Krinkelt-Rocherath but was engaged in refitting and a very roundabout move to get back onto the road west. There was no chance now that the 12th SS could reach the Malmédy sector as planned and so cover Peiper's flank. Peculiarly enough (and a commentary on the state of communications), both Peiper and the commander of the 3d Parachute Division thought that the 12th SS Panzer Division actually was in the vicinity of Malmédy, there covering the north flank. The II SS Panzer Corps, whose two armored divisions were supposed to form a second wave behind the I SS Panzer Corps, was still in the army rear and could not reach the Stoumont-La Gleize sector for three or four days, even if committed at once.

The glaring fact was that the Sixth Panzer Army had failed to crack a gap in the American front wide enough for the passage west of the two armored divisions supposedly leading the I SS Panzer Corps or for the quick forward movement of the infantry divisions that were earmarked for the northern block protecting the line of communications to the west. The best the Sixth Panzer Army could do on the 19th and 20th was to order supply troops and a small reconnaissance detachment of the 12th SS Panzer Division to guard the north flank between the 3d Parachute Division positions and Peiper, tell General Priess (the I SS Panzer Corps commander) to collect the 1st SS Panzer Division for an attack to relieve Peiper, and urgently request the Luftwaffe to drop gasoline and ammunition for the isolated kampfgruppe. (One air resupply mission was flown on the night of 21 December. But it was difficult to hit the constricted zone in darkness, and the kampfgruppe got only enough gasoline to keep its radios going and to move a few of its tanks to more favorable firing positions. Thereafter the Luftwaffe refused all Sixth Army requests for such missions.)

On the morning of 21 December SS-Oberfuehrer Mohnke, the 1st SS Panzer Division commander, had collected most of his third and fourth march groups in the area south of Stavelot and east of Trois Ponts. To reach Peiper it would be necessary to get onto the north bank of the Amblève and strike northwest or to cross the Salm and then turn north. What Mohnke's intentions actually were is hard to tell. Apparently he sent part of his infantry to ford the Amblève between Trois Ponts and Stavelot about the same time that Task Force Lovelady crossed to the north bank. The two forces probably missed each other in the morning fog, but it seems certain that the sizable German detachment encountered by Colonel Lovelady when he attempted to push away from the north bank and up the ridge was that sent by Mohnke. Meanwhile, when the Germans tried to cross heavy assault guns on the temporary bridge above Trois Ponts the frail structure collapsed out of hand. Attempts to put in bridges at other points were all frustrated by artillery fire.

Mohnke made his main effort with a westward thrust at the Salm River line, first in the direction of Trois Ponts, then as a groping attempt to find some weak spot farther south. His force would collide with the 505th Parachute Infantry, now spread along an 8,000-yard front reaching from Trois Ponts south to Grand Halleux. The initial German attack was thrown against E Company of the 505th Parachute Infantry, which had organized a small bridgehead on the cliff across the river east of Trois Ponts the day before. Fleeing civilians halted by patrols on the morning of the 21st bore word of German tanks and infantry assembling in Wanne. Shortly before noon a company led by self-propelled guns appeared through the fog along a road running past the rise held by the paratroopers. An 8-man bazooka section knocked out the assault guns, but its members were captured or killed. The howitzers of the 456th Parachute Field Artillery Battalion west of the river went to work and for a time disorganized the enemy. Tanks were seen moving about and more German infantry were heard gathering in the woods and draws.

The commander of the 2d Battalion, 505th Parachute Infantry (Lt. Col. Benjamin H. Vandervoort) tried unsuccessfully to reach his regimental commander by radio. In the absence of specific instructions as to the bridgehead, he then dispatched Company F to climb the cliff across the river. Company F moved into the woods on the right of Company E, while a jeep towed a single 57-mm. antitank gun across stringers laid atop the broken bridge structure. This gun, manned by Lt. Jake Wurtich, fought an unequal duel with the panzers—its shells bouncing off the German armor—until it was knocked out and Wurtich killed. The tanks, however, could not maneuver on the soggy, snow-covered ground and the fight broke into a series of hand-to-hand engagements swirling around little knots of infantrymen.

The American rifle line was steadily decreasing in strength, denuded by casualties and carrying parties laboriously moving the wounded down and ammunition up the cliff. Vandervoort put one more platoon across the river. By this time the assistant division commander and the regimental commander both had reached Trois Ponts and it was agreed that Ekman could withdraw his troops from the minuscule bridgehead. Having a third of his regiment committed at this single point on his extended and exposed front, Colonel Ekman decided to chance a daylight withdrawal. Some troops came back over the bridge but many, hard pressed, leaped off the cliff into the river. A number of the enemy, in close pursuit, crossed behind the Americans by fording or swinging along the broken bridges.

Before the 2d Battalion could reorganize on the west bank, at least two German platoons had crossed the river. They were immediately knocked back, however.

To the south of Trois Ponts the 3d Battalion of the 505th had been deployed on a wide front which was extended still more as its neighboring battalion concentrated at Trois Ponts. Near the three or four houses of the hamlet of La Neuville a bridge still spanned the Salm, covered by a platoon roadblock on the east bank. At dark a German column of tanks (or assault guns) and infantry approached the bridge. The platoon called for artillery, engaged in a short exchange of fire, withdrew, and blew the bridge. Four large enemy fighting vehicles remained at the bridge site when the rest of the thwarted column turned away. They were too close for shellfire; so a four-man patrol armed with Gammon grenades crossed in the dark to deal with them, but as the patrol reached the east bank the tanks turned and lumbered off. During the evening enemy foot soldiers also tried to sneak across the wreckage of the railroad bridge south of Trois Ponts, an attack quickly ended when shellfire caught them right at the river.

Although most of the night of 21 December passed quietly it was a time of strain because the 505th line at Trois Ponts was thin, the enemy was known to be strong, and the river was fordable. The 82d Airborne Division as a whole was too widely dispersed to permit immediate and large-scale help in the Trois Ponts sector. General Gavin, who had been in and out of the regimental command post all day long, could give Colonel Ekman only one rifle company and a battery of groundmount .50 caliber machine guns for help on the morrow.

When 22 December dawned the XVIII Airborne Corps still was engaged in maneuvering to create a solid barrier along its 45-mile front against the Germans heading for the Meuse. Things were not going too well. The St. Vith salient had been dealt heavy blows and the lines there were crumbling. The enemy had pushed as far along the Ourthe River valley as Hotton and was gathering to the west of that river. General Hobbs, whose 30th Division was holding the corps north flank, felt that his sector now was secure although he knew that enemy reinforcements had crossed the Amblève. But he was concerned lest the Germans bring off a successful eccentric attack north of Trois Ponts which would separate the 30th Division from the 82d Airborne. This he told General Ridgway in a telephone conversation on the morning of the 22d, but Ridgway gave him Gavin's assurance that the paratroopers would hold, that nothing would get through to the west. To the corps commander the priority project in this sector remained that of eliminating the La Gleize-Stoumont pocket as rapidly and as thoroughly as possible, freeing the 30th Division and its attached armor for urgent work elsewhere.

After a quiet night in most of the 30th Division lines the day came with intense cold, falling snow, and heavy overcast. Veteran troops by this time had learned that beautifully clear weather at the foxhole line often meant bad flying weather back at the air bases; but they knew too that close tactical support necessitated a decent modicum of clear weather. At 0806 the 30th Division air officer learned that his targets had been approved and that a fighter-bomber group would be on hand "weather permitting." At almost the same moment General Hobbs got the word that he could expect no help from the air. The resumption of the attack to deflate the pocket would depend on ground troops and guns, most of all guns. The artillery, however, was finding it difficult to get into good firing positions, and the American troops were so near the target towns as to require the nicest type of precision ranging. Prospects for the attackers seemed as discouraging as the weather.

The plan of 22 December included the continuation of the drive to take La Gleize and Stoumont plus an attack to mop up the 1st SS Panzer Division relief detachment which had dug in north of the Amblève between Stavelot and Ster. This latter group was established on the nose of a ridge, from which its fire swept north, west, and south, and in surrounding woods. Two rifle companies of the 3d Battalion, 117th Infantry, working from the north, and the rifle company of the 120th Infantry attached to Task Force Lovelady, attacking from the west, found every move checked by mortars, Werfers, and bullet fire. Finally a rifle company was sent from Stavelot to hit the Germans in the rear. Thereafter the Americans were able to converge on the ridge, but as day ended pockets of the enemy still remained in the woods. During the day other enemy troops had crossed the Amblève and for a time isolated one of Lovelady's roadblocks north of Trois Ponts. But at no time on the 22d did organized units of the relieving force of the 1st SS Panzer Division succeed in breaking through to Peiper in La Gleize.

At the west end of the Peiper pocket the night of 21 December had witnessed the final reduction of the sanatorium, opening the way for a direct attack on Stoumont by Task Force Harrison. Early that evening an officer of the 740th Tank Battalion had crawled into the enemy lines, scouting for a way to bring tanks around to the northwest of the building. Returning to his own lines he called for volunteers to build a ramp over the fill, or embankment, which had barred direct assault earlier in the fight. The ramp, constructed from shell castings, worked, and by midnight four Shermans were firing into the sanatorium. Shortly thereafter the Germans left the place. When the Americans entered the basement, they found that none of the civilian inhabitants had been killed or injured.

General Harrison felt that it would be possible to bring in his attached armor and the 3d Battalion, 119th Infantry, from the north, now that the enemy flanking position on the high ground was gone. He set up this attack to precede the final assault from the west. Patrols, groping their way through the morning snowstorm, found Stoumont strangely quiet, but Harrison was well aware that the 119th had been seriously weakened and went ahead with plans for pounding the town with artillery preparatory to the all-out infantry-armor push he had ordered for 1300. At noon the storm was beginning to break and visibility promised to improve, a necessity if the artillery was to give support by fire so close to the American lines. At 1320 the guns opened the fifteen-minute drum fire intended to pave the way for the northern assault. Almost at once shells began to explode in the American assembly areas, and there was nothing to do but call off the barrage. The 3d Battalion and the tanks nevertheless started forward. By 1410 they were at the edge of Stoumont, and the 1st Battalion had started in from the west.

No German fire was received—the occupants of Stoumont were wounded Germans and Americans left in the houses. Peiper had withdrawn his last forces in Stoumont during the night and early morning with the intention of fighting a last-ditch action at La Gleize where the ground permitted an easier all-round defense. La Gleize, be it added, lay closer to the area where the remainder of the 1st SS Panzer Division had assembled. But it seems likely, as Peiper himself later said, that Peiper's decision to abandon the western town had been prompted to great degree by the threat, posed by the 2d Battalion, 119th Infantry, on 21 December, to the line of communications linking Stoumont and La Gleize. Despite General Hobbs's insistence that Task Force Harrison push on promptly to La Gleize the advance was halted just east of the recaptured town. It was now late in the day, and patrols had discovered German tanks operating as rear guard on the road to La Gleize.

Elsewhere on the northern edge of the Peiper pocket the status quo had obtained through most of the day. A little after noon Task Force McGeorge, blocked on the valley road east of La Gleize, saw a column of German tanks and infantry move out to the north along the ridge road on the opposite side of the valley, the same route McGeorge's column had been forced to abandon the day before. This reconnaissance, for it seems to have been no more, was driven off by a few artillery concentrations. Later in the day Task Force McGeorge made a pass at the block barring the river road in the bend but lost its two lead tanks. Colonel Johnson of the 117th Infantry, commanding in this sector, advised General Hobbs that tanks could not get past the bend and into La Gleize, that foot soldiers would have to do the job.

To the south along the Salm River line the 1st SS Panzer Division made a number of attempts on 22 December to seize a bridge, build a bridge, or in some manner gain a crossing. The 505th Parachute Infantry had little trouble in wiping out the few small detachments that actually made it across, but with so much enemy activity apparent on the east bank the 505th anticipated momentarily the launching of a full-scale assault. Mohnke, it appears, was trying to do too much with too little and so dissipated his limited strength that a forthright blow was not struck at any one point during the 22d. The strongest effort came late in the evening when two of his companies tried to seize the bridge at Grand Halleux; this bridge was blown when the leading Germans actually were on the span. On the whole the day had gone as badly for the 1st SS Panzer Division as for Peiper. It is true that few of the American riflemen had had German infantry in their sights, but the artillery supporting the 30th Division and 505th by interdiction fire had taken heavy toll in the enemy assembly areas and on the roads, as later attested by the Germans themselves.

Priess, the I SS Panzer Corps commander, had reasoned with the Sixth Panzer Army staff that Peiper should be given a chance to break out to the east while his force still was reasonably intact. The higher German commands, all the way up to OKW, remained convinced on 22 December that despite the growing strength of the Americans on the north flank the build-up there would not reach dangerous proportions before their own armored columns had reached and crossed the Meuse. Peiper, therefore, had to hold until such time as reinforcement and resupply could once again set his kampfgruppe on the way west.

During the night of 22 December twenty Luftwaffe planes carrying gasoline and ammunition flew to the trapped force. Probably the pilots had been briefed on the assumption that Peiper still held Stoumont, for many of the gasoline containers parachuted into American hands there. Peiper certainly was helped little by this minor and mistaken effort. On this occasion, as it turned out, the American air-warning net worked a bit too well. Both the 30th Division and the 82d Airborne were placed on alert against an airborne attack (although General Hobbs avowed that such an attack made little sense in this heavily forested and broken country). The numerous antiaircraft artillery batteries backing up the divisions stood to their guns all night long, and the infantry were given little sleep as rumors ran wild of parachutists sighted hither and yon.

Interrogation of prisoners and artillery observer reports had indicated that the Germans were moving troops into the sector south of Malmédy reviving the earlier American concern that a hard blow might be dealt there at the 30th Division. As a result General Hobbs was able to hold onto all the reinforcements which had accumulated to the 30th, as well as CCB, 3d Armored Division. The Malmédy threat seems to have been raised by a few troops of the 3d Parachute Division, who had moved west of Waimes, and by rumors rife in the German camp that the 12th SS Panzer Division (held up by the Sixth Army attempt to seize the Elsenborn ridge) was moving in to support the 1st SS Panzer Division. Actually the 23d passed quietly in the Malmédy-Stavelot sector. Opposite the 505th Parachute Infantry the enemy contented himself with sporadic firing across the river. Mohnke, it would appear, lacked the strength needed for resumption of the attack to free Peiper. At least his corps commander, Priess, asked the II SS Panzer Corps to deflect the 9th SS Panzer Division, coming forward on the left, and throw it in at Stavelot. This request was denied.

Major action on 23 December did flare up at La Gleize and along the north bank of the Amblève, where a part of the 1st SS Panzer Division relief force still maintained a foothold. In the latter sector six American rifle companies were assembled to clear out the woods and restore the cut made by the enemy on the road between Trois Ponts and Stavelot. Regrouping in the heavy woods took nearly all day and was marked by some sharp clashes. At Petit Coo, close by Stavelot, S/Sgt. Paul Bolden and T/Sgt. Russell N. Snoad decided to attack a house from which the Germans were firing. While his companion fired to cover him, Bolden rushed the door, tossed in a pair of hand grenades, then went in firing his Tommy gun. Bolden killed twenty of the enemy, then withdrew. A blast of fire killed Bolden's comrade and wounded the sergeant, but he dashed back into the house, killing fifteen more of the enemy. (Bolden later received the Medal of Honor and Snoad was awarded the DSC posthumously.)

As for La Gleize the story once again was one of frustration and failure. Most of Peiper's troops were driven to the cellars of the town by the incessant shellfire, increasing in the afternoon as the American attack brought forward observers closer to the target, and made even more effective by the new POZIT fuze which the 113th Field Artillery was using. But wherever and whenever the attacking tanks and infantry tried to move along the roads and trails winding up the ridge nose to La Gleize, they encountered mine plots swept by direct fire from deeply dug in tanks and antitank guns. Progress then was slow; the leading American tank would be knocked out or burned by a direct hit with armor-piercing ammunition, eventually the infantry would work around and destroy or neutralize the German weapon, the engineers would remove the mine field, and the advance would continue.

Harrison decided that a flanking move through the woods to the north might work and in the afternoon elements of the American rifle companies reached the edge of La Gleize, only to come under machine gun and 20-mm. fire from streets and houses. General Harrison's main worry was the heavy German tanks gathered in the center of the town. Would they break out in a desperate counterattack against the lighter and more vulnerable Shermans? Would they slip through the net and bludgeon their way to the Amblève? To deal with the tanks, Allied planes were promised for a strike at the town square. They came as promised but hit Malmédy instead of La Gleize, their bombs burying a number of civilians in one of the hotel buildings before the strike could be called off.

Peiper had yet to be driven out of La Gleize; the 1st SS Panzer Division bridgehead force north of the Amblève (which had cut off a part of Task Force Lovelady) still had to be liquidated. But this fight in the bend of the Amblève had become anticlimactic, dwarfed by far more important operations elsewhere on the northern shoulder of the Ardennes salient. Through the early evening of the 23d the telephone wires connecting the headquarters of the First Army, the XVIII Airborne Corps, and the 30th Division were busy: the First Army insisting that Hobbs must release CCB, 3d Armored, for immediate return to its hard-pressed division; the 30th Division commander protesting that the loss of the combat command would leave La Gleize open on two sides and make it impossible to mop up the bridgehead force; General Ridgway for his part essaying on the scene the role of the honest broker. The final decision was favorable to Hobbs: General Boudinot, the CCB commander, would start his trains moving but at least two-thirds of the command would be left for the final tough fight envisaged for the coming morning.

The net had been drawn tight around Peiper, as tight as it could be drawn in this complex of woods and hills. But on the morning of the 24th most of the quarry had flown. Late the previous afternoon Mohnke had radioed Peiper permission to break out. Peiper knew that he could not take his vehicles or his wounded, that the escape would have to be made at night and on foot. Leaving a rear guard to demolish the tanks, trucks, and guns, Peiper and some eight hundred of his command started at 0100 in single file through the woods fringing La Gleize on the south, crossed the river, and as day broke took cover among the densely wooded hills north of Trois Ponts. On the night of the 24th Peiper's force crossed the Salm, briefly engaging troops of the 82d Airborne Division in a brisk exchange of fire, and on Christmas morning rejoined the 1st SS Panzer Division south of Stavelot.

The 30th Division commander, under pressure from corps and army to finish the job at La Gleize and release Boudinot's armor, had made no promises that La Gleize would fall on the 24th but had urged his unit commanders to get the attack rolling early and finish off the defenders. To tired troops who had expected a desperate last stand it must have been gratifying to find the town open for the taking. They liberated about 170 Americans, most of whom had been captured at Stoumont on 19 December. The prisoners they took, nearly all wounded, numbered 300. Twenty-eight tanks, 70 half-tracks, and 25 artillery pieces were found in the town. This booty, plus the German tanks and guns destroyed earlier in the operation, accounted for nearly the entire heavy equipment of the 1st SS Panzer Regiment. Although those of Peiper's troops who had escaped were back in the line with the reconstituted 1st SS Panzer Division, that elite unit could no longer be considered an armored division.

In an epilogue to the taking of La Gleize, foot troops of the 117th and 120th Infantry Regiments began the slow work of beating the woods in the triangle formed by the Salm and the Amblève where a part of the 1st SS Panzer Division relief force continued to hold out. In the woods north of La Gleize some fifty Germans who apparently had not received the orders to withdraw tried to fight it out. All were killed. What German strength had seeped into this appendix at the rivers no one knew. Rumors of twenty-five enemy tanks hiding in the road cuts north of Trois Ponts had the result of delaying the relief of CCB of the 3d Armored Division. That some armored vehicles had crossed to the north bank of the Amblève by improvised bridging seems certain, but most succeeded in escaping to the south. By the 26th the last Germans had been captured, killed, or driven off from the north bank of the Amblève. The satisfaction which the 30th Division could take in giving the quietus to Kampfgruppe Peiper was alloyed by untoward events at Malmédy on the 24th and 25th. On these days American planes bombed the 120th Infantry (at least thirty-seven Americans lost their lives on the first day), killed a considerable number of civilians, and set the town afire. A mass flight started by the population was halted only with great difficulty.

The 3d Armored Division Is Checked, 21-23 December

Still minus two of its combat commands the 3d Armored Division was prepared, on the morning of 21 December, to retake Samrée, the communications and supply center on the middle route of the 3d Armored advance which had been seized by the enemy the previous afternoon. With this intent General Rose sent a part of his very small reserve to reinforce the center task force (now Task Force Orr) north of the village of Dochamps. During the previous night Rose had asked General Ridgway for respite from his main mission, that is, the advance to the Liège-Bastogne highway and an attempt to re-establish contact with the VIII Corps, until the situation at Samrée could be cleared up. At 0815, however, Rose assured Ridgway that the 3d Armored was moving once again to accomplish its major mission. Less than a half-hour later German tanks were discovered moving toward Hotton, where the rear command post and installations of the 3d Armored Division were located. The immediate result of this threat was to nullify the reinforcement readied for dispatch from Soy, where the combat reserve held by Colonel Howie was located, to the Samrée sector.

General Krueger, the LVIII Panzer Corps commander, had reason to congratulate himself at the close of the 20th for the decision to back away from the Ourthe River line northwest of Bastogne. In turning north his corps had crossed the east-west segment of that river without trouble, had discovered large stocks of gasoline at Samrée, and had met so little opposition as to indicate a general retrograde move on the part of the Americans. Krueger determined to strike while the iron was hot, drive northwest at top speed to the bridgehead town of Hotton, recross the Ourthe River at that point, and concentrate his corps on the far bank before the Americans could establish a blocking line. Thus far Krueger's advance guard had fought only outpost or patrol actions with the 3d Armored Division and there was little reason, as Krueger saw it, to anticipate much resistance during the next twenty-four hours. He did know, from radio messages intercepted by OB WEST, that one combat command of the 3d Armored Division had moved into the Werbomont area on 19 December.

After the seizure of Samrée, Krueger dispatched an armored task force (Kampfgruppe Bayer) from the 116th Panzer Division to gain control of the road between Soy and Hotton preliminary to seizure of the latter bridgehead town. During the night of 20 December this task force marched northwest along a secondary route parallel to and between the roads on which Task Force Hogan and Task Force Orr had made their advance during the day. Just at daybreak members of an American patrol operating out of the Combat Command Reserve headquarters at Soy were fired upon. They reported that they "thought" they had heard German voices. This was the first evidence that the enemy had penetrated to the 3d Armored rear. The next message from Soy to reach the division command post at Erezée came at 0850: "many enemy tanks" had debouched astride the Soy-Hotton road and were heading west toward Hotton. Actually the attack at Hotton had already begun.

The town of Hotton (about ten miles northwest of La Roche) is built astride the main channel of the Ourthe at a point where the valley widens. Here a series of roads converge to cross the river and proceed on the west bank to the more important junction center at Marche from which roads radiate in all directions. In the center of Hotton the river was spanned at this time by a class 70 two-way wooden bridge. In the buildings east of the river were installed about two hundred men from the service detachments of the division and CCR headquarters. There were, in addition, one light and one medium tank. On the west bank at the bridge exit a platoon of the 51st Engineer Battalion (Capt. Preston C. Hodges) was deployed, reinforced by two 40-mm. antitank guns, a 37-mm. antitank gun, and a Sherman tank. A squad of engineers guarded a footbridge at Hampteau, two thousand yards south of the town.

At dawn mortar and small arms fire suddenly gave notice of the enemy. Despite casualties and confusion a defense was hastily set up by the executive officer of the 23d Armored Engineer Battalion (Maj. Jack W. Fickessen), engineer trucks were driven out to block the roads, and bazookas and machine guns were distributed for a close-in defense of the town. Taking advantage of the woods that came right up to the eastern edge of Hotton, four or five enemy tanks rumbled forward to lead the assault. The two American tanks east of the river were knocked out at once; but on the opposite bank a 90-mm. tank destroyer "appeared from nowhere," got a direct hit on a Panther and perhaps a second German as well. The enemy infantry were able to take about half the buildings on the near bank but were checked short of the bridge by the rifles, bazookas, and machine guns in the hands of men on both banks of the river. (A "hailstorm of fire," say the Germans.) The engineer squad guarding the footbridge south of Hotton was overrun, apparently by Germans wearing American uniforms, but fortunately this bridge could bear no vehicles.

By the middle of the morning the defenders, now recovered from their initial surprise, were holding their own and the vehicles in the town were evacuated to the north along with most of the medical personnel and ambulances. Two or three more German tanks were destroyed by bazookas (one was even chalked up to the account of the 37-mm. antitank gun). For some reason the enemy had not thrown all of his tanks into the battle at once, a fortunate circumstance. By 1400 the tanks still in town joined those on the hill east of Hotton against the counterattack which Colonel Howze had launched along the Soy road. About this time Howze was able to get a small group of tanks and infantry around to the north of the attackers and into Hotton, redressing the balance somewhat. As yet it was impossible to bring any friendly artillery to bear, and the foot troops continued to rely largely on their own weapons for the rest of the day.

General Rose, as already indicated, had at his immediate disposal a very limited reserve. Although he had ordered Howze to counterattack with the entire force of the Combat Command Reserve it became apparent as day wore on that this would be insufficient. The ground over which the counterattack from Soy had to move gave every advantage to the Germans. Maneuver was restricted by the cuts through which ran the Hotton road, by a stream bordering the road on the south, and by the German position atop the nose of the hill between the two towns which gave observation and fire over the barren ground to the north. Since General Rose had been promised the use of a battalion from the 517th Parachute Infantry, he decided to hold up the drive from Soy until it arrived. Also it appeared that the defenders of Hotton would shortly be reinforced by part of the leading RCT of the 84th Infantry Division, moving via Marche under orders from Ridgway to secure the Ourthe River line south of Hotton.

This help was slow in coming. As early as 0900 the 51st Engineer Battalion commander had asked the 84th to send aid to Hotton but the staff of the latter seem to have taken rather skeptically reports of the enemy strength involved. Two platoons finally arrived in Hotton late in the afternoon but by this time the German infantry were leaving the town and loading into their half-tracks as if the fight were over.

Through the night American mortars in Hotton laid down a defensive barrage of illuminating shell and high explosives, but the enemy made no move to return to the assault.

The commander of the 116th Panzer Division, as well as General Manteuffel, would later pay tribute to "the bravery of the American engineers" at Hotton. They had reason for this acknowledgment (in which they could have included signal and service troops, unknown gun and tank crews) because the failure to secure the Hotton bridge was decisive in the future history of the LVIII Panzer Corps. Credit must also go to the Combat Command Reserve at Soy whose fire, as the enemy acknowledged, caught Kampfgruppe Bayer in the flank and checkmated its single-minded employment against Hotton. Finally, a share in the successful defense of the Hotton bridge should be assigned those elements of the three 3d Armored task forces which, on the 21st, had engaged the bulk of the 116th Panzer Division and 560th Volks Grenadier Division and prevented a wholesale advance into the Hotton sector.

Krueger's original intention had been to risk a thrust for the Hotton bridge without regard to flank security. The armored task force moving on Hotton accordingly contained most of the forward combat elements of the 116th Panzer Regiment and 60th Panzer Grenadier Regiment. But the presence of American armor and infantry in the a between Soy and Dochamps, as this became apparent during the morning of 21 December, forced Krueger to face much of the strength of the two regiments to the east and northeast so as to form a protected corridor for the drive into Hotton.

Through this corridor the 156th Panzer Grenadier Regiment, which had been in reserve south of Samrée, moved late in the afternoon to an assembly area around Beffe. At the base of the corridor, that is, around Dochamps, the 1128th Regiment of the 560th Volks Grenadier Division made an attack to widen the path northwest to the Ourthe crossing. Early in the day the grenadiers collided with Task Force Orr while the latter was trying to eradicate the roadblock which barred the road up to Dochamps and Samrée. In a sharp action at a hairpin turn in the road at the base of the Dochamps hill the German infantry infiltrated close enough to bazooka three tanks but themselves took a beating from the American artillery. Twice during the day Orr had to order a withdrawal, the last bringing the task force to Amonines, three miles southeast of Soy. Here on a slight rise overlooking the Aisne valley road Orr's column formed a perimeter defense for the night.

Task Force Hogan, checked the previous day in the winding Ourthe valley southeast of La Roche, came under attack early on the 21st by small enemy groups striking out from the roadblock. The LVIII Panzer Corps commander had no intention of taking La Roche unless it could be occupied without a fight and had committed only a fraction of the 60th Panzer Grenadier Regiment to throw out a screen here. Later in the day part of the Reconnaissance Battalion, 116th Panzer Division, arrived from Houffalize and started running combat patrols through the woods in front of La Roche. Hogan, under orders to hold up his own advance until Orr could take Samrée, finally received a change in orders about 1300 which directed his task force to fall back on Amonines. It was crystal clear by this hour that there could be no advance to Samrée. Hogan's column moved north, skirmishing with small German forces along the way, but at twilight ran into machine gun fire and lost its lead tank to a German bazooka just at the edge of the hamlet of Beffe. Without realizing the fact, the Americans had hit the assembly area of the 156th Panzer Grenadier Regiment. There was nothing for it at this time of day but to pull away.

Task Force Hogan retired to the south and bivouacked on a hill near Marcouray. Although their plight was not immediately apparent, Hogan and his 400 men had been cut off from the rest of the 3d Armored Division.

The eastern column, Task Force Kane, alone of the 3d Armored forces passed the morning of the 21st without enemy contact. As planned, Kane sent a detachment south to the important crossroads at Baraque de Fraiture, on the Vielsalm-Samrée route, to reinforce the mixed group of Americans already there and to take part in the final attack on Samrée. This detachment reached the crossroads in the middle of the afternoon and there met the 7th Armored Division cavalry which had come in from Vielsalm the previous evening. Caught up in the fight already started at the crossroads, the tanks and armored cars were unable to proceed to Samrée. The remaining troops of Task Force Kane received orders during the afternoon to move on Dochamps as part of a projected concentric maneuver to retake Samrée and did advance about a mile south of Grandménil before darkness closed in.

The 3d Armored Division had met a superior force on the 21st, had failed to retake Samrée, had been forced to use its reserves in a fight to reopen the road to Hotton, and had seen its western and center task forces pushed back. But there were some reasons to expect an improvement in what had been a deteriorating situation. The Hotton bridge had been held and there was word that the 84th Infantry Division would lend a hand. The 3d Armored Division was going to get back its own CCA, although under a corps prohibition against using it save in dire circumstances, and during the night of 21 December CCA did close north of Manhay. At least a battalion of the 517th Parachute Infantry was on its way to reinforce the Combat Command Reserve at Soy. The eastern flank had been more or less secured by contact made between Task Force Kane and the 82d Airborne Division during the day. All this was heartening, but there remained the worry as to what the full enemy strength and intentions might be.

Operations maps posted on the night of the 21st in the bunkers housing the Wehrmachtfuehrungsstab showed the LVIII Panzer Corps as the most advanced unit of all the German forces driving west, with its 116th Panzer Division at Hotton, only twenty air-line miles from the Meuse River. But the fight at Hotton, despite what the operations map might show, had convinced the LVIII Panzer Corps commander that, instead of finding a quick and easy way to cross the Ourthe by his shift to the northwest, he stood an excellent chance of running his corps into a cul-de-sac. Unwilling to continue down what might turn into a blind alley, if the Americans continued to defend Hotton as staunchly as they had during the day, General Krueger revised his plans. His southern neighbor, Lauchert's 2d Panzer Division, was reported to have seized a bridge across the western arm of the Ourthe and might be expected to move so rapidly into the Marche sector, on the west side of the main channel, that the American barrier line which Krueger had feared at the Ourthe could not be placed in operation. Krueger, therefore, ordered the 116th Panzer Division to disengage on the Soy-Hotton road, pull back as rapidly as possible to the south, and cross the Ourthe at La Roche. This town had been abandoned by the Americans during the afternoon when the 7th Armored Division trains, threatened with encirclement, crossed the river and moved to Marche, leaving only some pickets to guard the roadblocks at the various bridges.

Krueger intended to use the 560th Volks Grenadier Division to continue the attack northwest, aiming for the Ourthe crossings at Han north of Hotton. At twilight the leading elements of the 2d SS Panzer Division were in position on the right flank of the 560th. This fresh division, when assembled, was to pass to the LVIII Panzer Corps and could be used to cover the exposed eastern flank—a source of continuous concern to the corps commander. General Krueger, an experienced and intelligent officer, may not have been as hopeful of success as his plans for 22 December would indicate. He records that his command had suffered very heavy casualties during the fighting of the 21st, that troop morale was flagging, that fatigue was beginning to tell, and that, for the first time, the advance had begun to decelerate.

While Krueger laid plans for shifting the LVIII Panzer Corps armor to the west bank of the Ourthe, his opponent, General Ridgway, was issuing orders designed to strengthen and extend the XVIII Airborne Corps right wing west of the Ourthe. At dawn of the 22d, CCA of the 3d Armored Division had just completed its move to rejoin General Rose when the corps commander ordered Rose to throw out a screen on the west bank between La Roche and St. Hubert as cover for the American concentration in process around Marche. By noon a task force from CCA was en route to carry out this mission. Of the reinforcement that General Rose had counted on only one tank battalion and one company of armored infantry were left. The 3d Armored Division would have to continue the battle to establish a holding position with forces hardly stronger than those which had been driven back on the 21st. The final orders for the day were "counterattack": first, to drive the enemy out of the Soy-Hotton sector, second, to retake the hill mass at Dochamps-Samrée in the center of the division zone. The job of dealing with German penetration between the Ourthe and the Aisne Rivers fell to CCR (and Task Force Hogan). For this Colonel Howze would get the battalion from the 517th Parachute Infantry as soon as it arrived. Those troops of CCA still in the division commander's hand (Task Force Richardson) would serve as backstop behind the two remaining task forces, Orr and Kane, which were charged with the capture of Dochamps.

Task Force Orr was at the vortex of the action on the 22d, standing as it did in the path of the main movement by the 560th Volks Grenadier Division. The 116th Panzer Division, on the German left, would have to disengage its forward units during the coming night, and in order to effect the relief the 560th had to be brought forward. This German advance, begun by two regiments abreast, started at daylight, its object the command of the Erezée-Soy-Hotton road. Meanwhile Colonel Orr led his counterattack force out of Amonines, heading down the Aisne valley road for Dochamps. One company of armored infantry had been left to defend the base at Amonines. The detachment with Orr consisted of a company of armored infantry plus three medium and three light tanks.

About 0900 the small American column saw an enemy column coming up the road from Dochamps, and each halted to size up the other. Task Force Orr's opponent was the 1128th Regiment which, though reduced to a combat strength of seven hundred, was the strongest unit in the 560th Volks Grenadier Division. As it happened a part of the German force had been pinned down by an attack against flank and rear thrown in by Task Force Kane, but this intelligence was unknown to Orr. The German commander disengaged from Kane, put in his engineer battalion to hold Dochamps, then moved to the ridge east of the valley road and began the firefight. Shortly after noon Orr's scouts on the ridge west of the valley reported more German troops moving northwest. This looked like a trap of some sort and Orr withdrew his column to the starting point on the crest at Amonines, where he was reinforced by infantry and tank destroyers. The 1128th did not follow in force (Task Force Kane still threatened from the east) but was content to fire smoke shells onto the American position and probe with patrols. The troops in field gray seen moving west of the valley were the 1129th Regiment en route to Beffe to relieve the 116th Panzer Division. They paid no attention to Task Force Orr.

Task Force Kane, easternmost of the 3d Armored detachments, obviously was playing an important part in delaying the German advance toward Amonines. The attack toward Dochamps, started the previous afternoon and resumed on the 22d, was hampered by the necessity of keeping a blocking force at the Manhay junction and reinforcing the scratch defense farther south at the Baraque de Fraiture crossroads. Despite the fact that Task Force Kane was fighting with its left arm tied down, by noon the drive toward Dochamps reached the village of Lamorménil. During these morning hours the American tanks proved too much for the German infantry; it is probable that an entire battalion of the 1128th was engaged and siphoned away from the attack against Orr.

The terrain beyond Lamorménil, however, was distinctly adverse to armored tactics. A single road wound southward through a narrow semiwooded valley until, about eight hundred yards east of Dochamps, it climbed abruptly up the east face of a bare hill to reach the village. As soon as Kane's tanks reached the foot of the hill German antitank guns started to work. Maneuver on the soft earth flanking the road promised that the tanks would bog down; attack straight along the road was suicidal. After futile attempts at counterbattery against the enemy gunners the tanks withdrew to the north. Kane's column had been short of infantry, and Dochamps presented a problem to which the answer was infantry.

Just after dark there appeared in the American bivouac six trucks carrying two officers and eighty men belonging to the 1st Battalion, 517th Parachute Infantry. Lost from its convoy the detachment had been passed around from headquarters to headquarters, finally ending up with Kane. The paratroopers were handed the job of taking Dochamps, this time by an attack from the north guiding on a narrow-gauge railway which approached the village. Twice the detachment moved forward, only to meet machine gun fire from front and flank. The second try ended when the Germans counterattacked from a hill northwest of the village. More than a handful of infantry would be required if the 3d Armored Division was to regain control of the Dochamps-Samrée heights.

The story of Task Force Hogan on the 22d is quickly told. Cut off at Marcouray, Hogan received radio orders to try once more to break out northeast through Beffe. Little aid could be spared by the Americans in the north, but a small task force from CCA was organized to drive toward Hogan. There proved to be simply too many Germans between Beffe and the Soy-Hotton road. In any case, Hogan, who had been rushed into action with his tanks half full, was running out of gasoline. In early afternoon his column retired to Marcouray and sent out requests for fuel, surgical supplies, and reinforcements. All this while the enemy knew Hogan's exact whereabouts but paid him scant attention. When the 116th Panzer Division moved out on the night of 22 December, the commander of the 560th detailed some of his engineers to watch Hogan's laager.

The armored German kampfgruppe astride the road between Soy and Hotton was content to remain on the defensive pending its withdrawal southward, but the German tanks and antitank guns ruled as "King of the Rock" on the crest overwatching the road. Grooved by the road, the first American attack from Soy toward Hotton slammed straight into direct fire and lost six medium and two light tanks. Cross-country maneuver by infantry was indicated. Long awaited, the 1st

Battalion of the 517th Parachute Infantry and a company from the 643d Tank Destroyer Battalion arrived in Soy at twilight. Howze had expected to use the paratroopers in a daylight attack to reopen the Hotton road, but the division commander demanded an immediate commitment. Thrown into assault over strange ground, only half an hour after crawling out of their trucks, the paratroopers made little headway against six German self-propelled guns and clusters of machine gun nests. By 2000 the attack west from Soy was stopped dead still.

An alarm from Hotton, suddenly assailed after a day of quiet, forced a second try. This time Howze ordered two of the paratroop platoons, tank supported, to circle around and into Hotton from the north, intending a squeeze play by attack in the dark from both Soy and Hotton. But neither claw was able to grip the enemy holding the core high ground. So the night ended. During its course the 560th Volks Grenadier Division had made a smooth and unperceived relief of the 116th Panzer Division. At dawn the grenadiers held an irregular front reaching from the Ourthe River east to the Baraque de Fraiture crossroads athwart the Liège-Bastogne highway. This sector from river to highway now formed the center of the LVIII Panzer Corps with the 2d SS Panzer Division moving in on the east and the 116th Panzer Division circling to form the western wing beyond the Ourthe.

Events of the 22d had shown a movement of large German forces to the west, consequent to the fall of St. Vith, and brought the threat—epitomized by the appearance of the 2d SS Panzer Division—of a large-scale buildup for an attack to push through the XVIII Airborne Corps in a climactic, dramatic bid for Spa and Liège. The orders issued by General Ridgway on the night of 22 December, it will be remembered, were a detailed expression of the larger Allied plan to halt and then amputate the German forces swelling the western end of the salient, orders to hold the line or win more favorable positions while the VII Corps assembled on the right flank and a counterattack to regain St. Vith formed on the left.

Between the Ourthe River and the Liège-Bastogne road the single combat command of the 3d Armored Division, now reinforced, had the mission on the 23d of building a forward line along the Salmchâteau-La Roche road as a breakwater against the anticipated German surge to the north. From the head of the enemy salient, between Soy and Hotton, to the Salmchâteau-La Roche road was a distance of eleven miles. Attempts to get this counterattack moving in the night battles near Hotton and Dochamps had failed. Strength to do the job had increased somewhat but far from enough to guarantee success. With the main force of CCA west of the Ourthe and CCB still mopping up in Kampfgruppe Peiper's stronghold, General Rose had available three tank battalions and four armored infantry companies of his own division. Newly arrived reinforcements had swelled the rifle contingent by two battalions, the 1st Battalion of the 517th Parachute Infantry and the 509th Parachute Infantry Battalion. Total artillery support consisted of the 105-mm. self-propelled howitzers belonging to the 54th and 83d Armored Field Artillery Battalions, plus three self-propelled 155-mm. guns from the 991st Field Artillery Battalion—any unbalance of force favorable to the Germans hardly would be redressed by the weight of American gun metal. In conference on the morning of the 23d the commanders of the XVIII Airborne and VII Corps agreed that Rose needed more troops. But the one battalion of the 75th Infantry Division assigned could not reach the scene for some hours.

The story of the 23d is one of local counterattacks to hold or restore existing positions against an enemy who retained the initiative and maintained the momentum of the attack rolling northward. The critical point would be the Baraque de Fraiture crossroads at the boundary between the 3d Armored Division and the 82d Airborne Division, a point marking the thrust line along which the 2d SS Panzer Division intended to proceed north. The action at this road junction, "Parker's Crossroads," requires independent treatment. It has bearing at this point because the small combat reserve available to the 3d Armored Division would be drained away here and because American operations set in train to east and west would be conditioned by the shaky character of the 3d Armored left flank.

In front of Dochamps Task Force Kane resumed the attack broken off in the early morning. German mortars lobbing down 81-mm. and 120-mm. shells stopped the infantry on the slopes, and direct fire knocked out an entire platoon of Sherman tanks when they tried to ascend the hill road. The plain fact was that Kane lacked the men, tanks, and guns to take Dochamps. But this was not all. During the day a part of the task force had to be diverted to man roadblocks along the valley north to Grandménil which was both Kane's flank and line of communications. In the afternoon the 1130th Regiment (possibly reduced to battalion strength) and an assault gun platoon moved in from the west to cut the Dochamps-Grandménil road. Fighting at Freyneux and Lamorménil was touch and go, but the enemy suffered badly and failed to gain the road. This maneuver from the west had been given top priority by the 560th Volks Grenadier Division whose command was as anxious to erase the Dochamps salient as General Rose was to pinch out the Hotton bulge.

Sometime after dark the Germans hit the valley route again, but this time farther north and from the opposite side. Five light tanks and a squad of riflemen posted at Odeigne were set upon by enemy infantry who lighted their targets by flares and moved in with self-propelled 40-mm. guns to make the kill. The Americans held their ground until nearly surrounded, then—when so ordered—withdrew. This foray came from the Baraque de Fraiture crossroads sector, where the 2d SS Panzer Division finally had broken through, and was made by elements of the 3d Panzer Grenadier Regiment moving with much difficulty along the narrow forest trails south of Odeigne. Now Task Force Kane would have to battle to hold its narrow corridor against an enemy closing in from both flanks and circling to the rear.

In the center sector, at Amonines, Task Force Orr waited for CCR to wipe out the enemy between Soy and Hotton, then turn south in an attack with the two forces abreast. With the exception of the maneuver to clear the Americans out of the territory north of Dochamps described earlier, the 560th Volks Grenadier Division was in no hurry to attack those American positions where the defenders seemed willing and able to put up a stiff fight. After all, the German corps commander had promised the support of fresh assault troops. Therefore, although the Germans pressed in around Amonines they made no move to tackle Task Force Orr.

The vise created the night before to close on the German hill positions astride the Soy-Hotton road compressed very slowly on the 23d, nor did the jaws meet. Radio communication between the two American assault forces failed to function in the morning, the Hotton group was forced to spend much of the day mopping up the enemy who had seeped into the village during the night battle, and both the eastern and western groups—when the attack finally started moving—were too weak to make headway against German tanks and antitank guns firing from hull defilade on the high ground. Four tanks from the Soy force were knocked out in five minutes; there was little point in courting such losses and in any case there was only a single tank still operating so the battle was left to the infantry.

Lacking the numbers needed to envelope the German position, the infantry turned to a firefight that lasted well into the night. Pfc. Melvin Biddle, a paratrooper, tried to carry the fight to the enemy by advancing in front of his own troops to throw grenades and pick off the enemy infantry with his rifle. (Later he was awarded the Medal of Honor.) But there was no apparent diminution in the enemy firepower and toward dawn the fight dwindled away. The rifle battalion promised from the 75th Infantry Division had not arrived.

Task Force Hogan, out of gasoline and immobile in its ridge road laager at Marcouray, was not hard pressed by the encircling German pickets. Enemy parlementaires appeared during the afternoon with a demand for immediate surrender but were politely told that if they wanted Marcouray they could come and take it. To underline the isolation of the American force, a detachment of enemy infantry started an assault; this promptly was blasted by slugs pouring from the multiple .50-caliber machine guns carried by a half-track section of the 486th Antiaircraft Artillery Battalion.

Hogan had accompanied his radio report of the German surrender demand with a request for "maximum support." CCR was having its hands more than full in its own backyard on the 23d, and the Germans obviously could not be left to one side while a relief party went to aid Hogan. The immediate question then was how to supply the task force and keep it in being until the tactical situation improved. The 54th Armored Field Artillery Battalion was near enough to Marcouray for an attempt to shoot medical supplies into Hogan's lines. The gunners loaded howitzer shells with medical packets, using the same technique as with propaganda leaflets, but the supplies were so damaged on impact as to be worthless. Resupply by airdrop went awry.

The position of the 3d Armored Division was measurably more difficult by the end of the 23d. As in the days just past General Rose had the promise of some addition to his command, but thus far piecemeal reinforcement had failed to keep pace with growing enemy strength, much less create a balance. Late in the afternoon the 3d Armored Division was assigned to the VII Corps, which had assumed the conduct of operations west of the Ourthe. Tactically the transfer made no marked change. Rose's command east of the Ourthe remained tied to the 82d Airborne Division and the XVIII Airborne Corps, sharing the same terrain compartment and facing the same major enemy maneuver. General Collins, the VII Corps commander, managed to provide some assistance to the 3d Armored, during the night attaching the 290th Infantry of the 75th Division and the 188th Field Artillery Battalion, whose 155-mm. howitzers would provide a weight and range sadly deficient in the artillery supporting Rose.

Even so, the coming day promised to be grim. All plans for counterattack to regain the La Roche-Salmchâteau line were dismissed. The critical hour was at hand. General Rose told the CCR commander, "Impress on every individual that we must stay right here or there will be a war to be fought all over again, and we won't be here to fight it." The 560th Volks Grenadier Division could be held, had been held. Could the 3d Armored Division and the troops forming the western wing of the 82d Airborne Division throw back the fresh 2d SS Panzer Division, which had already punched a deep hole at the interdivision boundary, and hold other German forces believed to be moving into the battle zone?

The Fight at the Baraque de Fraiture Crossroads, 23 December

Baraque de Fraiture is a handful of buildings at a crossroads south of the Belgian hamlet of Fraiture. There are many such crossroads in the Belgian Ardennes, but this crossing of ways stands on one of the highest summits of the Ardennes, a small shelf or tableland at an elevation of 652 meters (2,139 feet). The roads which here intersect are important: N15, the north-south road, is the through paved highway linking Liège and Bastogne; N28, the east-west road, is classed as secondary but is the most direct route for movement along the northern side of the Ourthe River, connecting, for example, St. Vith with La Roche. The crossroads and the few buildings are on cleared ground, but heavy woods form a crescent to the north and west, and a fringe of timber points at the junction from the southeast. In the main the area to south and east is completely barren. Here the ground descends, forming a glacis for the firing parapet around the crossroads.

The tactical stature of the Baraque de Fraiture intersection was only partially derived from the configuration of roads and terrain. The manner in which the XVIII Airborne Corps had deployed its units in the initial attempt to draw a cordon along the northwest flank of the German advance was equally important. The mission assigned the three reconnaissance forces of the 3d Armored Division had been to close up to the Liège-Bastogne highway (with the crossroads as an objective), but it had not been carried out. East of the same highway the 82d Airborne had deployed, but with its weight and axis of advance away from the crossroads. Circumstance, notably the direction of the German attacks from 20 December onward, left the Baraque de Fraiture crossroads, and with it the inner flanks of the two divisions, to be defended on a strictly catch-as-catch-can basis.

On the afternoon of 19 December Maj. Arthur C. Parker III, led three 105-mm. howitzers of the ill-starred 589th Field Artillery Battalion on the crossroads. The rest of the battalion had been cut off on the Schnee Eifel or ambushed during the withdrawal to St. Vith. Parker's mission was to establish one of the roadblocks that the 106th Division was preparing behind St. Vith. The next day, four half-tracks mounting multiple .50-caliber machine guns arrived from the 203d Antiaircraft Artillery Battalion, now moving in with the 7th Armored Division to establish the defensive lines around St. Vith. That night, for the first time, vehicles were heard moving about to the south along the road to Houffalize. (They probably belonged to the 560th Volks Grenadier Division, which that afternoon had taken part in the capture of Samrée.) Before dawn an 80-man enemy patrol came up the road from Houffalize, stumbled onto the American half-tracks, and was cut to pieces by streams of bullet fire. The dead and prisoners were grenadiers from the 560th, but among them was an officer from the 2d SS Panzer Division, scouting out the route of advance for his incoming division. In the afternoon D Troop of the 87th Cavalry Squadron, earlier dispatched by the 7th Armored to aid Task Force Orr in the projected counterattack at Samrée, came in to join the crossroads garrison. The troop leader had gone to Dochamps to meet Orr but, finding Germans in the town, disposed his men and vehicles under orders from General Hasbrouck that the crossroads must be held.

Fog settling over the tableland in late afternoon gave the enemy a chance to probe the defense erected at the crossroads, but these jabs were no more than a warning of things to come. Meanwhile eleven tanks and a reconnaissance platoon arrived from Task Force Kane. The Americans spent the night of 21 December ringed around the crossroads, tanks alternating with armored cars in a stockade beyond which lay the rifle line. There was no sign of the enemy despite reports from all sorts of sources that German armor was gathering at Houffalize. Messengers coming in from the headquarters of the 3d Armored and 82d Airborne Divisions brought the same message, "Hold as long as you can."

General Gavin was especially concerned by the threat to the 82d flank developing at the crossroads and went to talk the matter over with Rose at his command post in Manhay. The 3d Armored commander assured Gavin that his troops would continue to cover the western wing of the 82d Airborne. Gavin nevertheless acted at once to send the 2d Battalion, 325th Glider Infantry, from his division reserve to defend Fraiture, the latter on a ridge three-quarters of a mile northeast of Parker's crossroads position. In addition, having made a personal reconnaissance of the area, Gavin told Col. Charles E. Billingslea, the regimental commander, to dispatch a company of the glider infantry to reinforce the crossroads defenders. The 2d Battalion reached Fraiture before dawn on the 22d, and Capt. Junior R. Woodruff led F Company into the circle around the crossroads just before noon. This slight reinforcement was negated when Kane took away his tanks to stiffen the attack going on in front of Dochamps.

The day of 22 December was spent in waiting. The 2d SS Panzer Division was having fuel troubles and moving in fits and starts. Mortar fire, laid on by the German reconnaissance screen left in this area as the 560th Volks Grenadier Division advanced northwest, from time to time interrupted movement in and out of the crossroads position. That was all. During the day the 3d Armored had received some reinforcements; these were parceled out across the front with a platoon from the 643d Tank Destroyer Battalion going to the crossroads. En route south from Manhay on the night of the 22d the tank destroyer detachment lost its way and halted some distance north of the crossroads. German infantry surprised and captured the platoon in the early morning. Already the 2d SS Panzer Division was moving to cut off and erase the crossroads garrison. Attack was near at hand, a fact made clear when an officer patrol from the 2d SS was captured at dawn in the woods near the American foxholes.

At daylight, shelling increased at the crossroads as German mortar and gun crews went into position; yet the long awaited assault hung fire. The reason was lack of fuel. The 2d SS Panzer Division had only enough gasoline to move its Reconnaissance Battalion on the 21st and this had been committed near Vielsalm. All through the 22d the division waited in its final assembly areas. Toward evening enough fuel arrived to set the 4th Panzer Grenadier Regiment, some tanks, and an artillery battalion to moving. In the course of the night the grenadiers relieved the small reconnaissance detachments of the 560th, which had been watching the crossroads, and filed through the woods to set up a cordon west and north of Baraque de Fraiture. The commander of the 4th Panzer Grenadier had placed his 2d Battalion on the right of the main north-south highway, while his 3d Battalion deployed around and to the rear of the crossroads. In the dark hours before dawn of the 23d the first move came, as the 2d Battalion made a surprise attack on Fraiture and was driven back after a bitter fight with the paratroopers.

The surprise attack at Fraiture having aborted, the Germans settled down to hem in and soften up the crossroads defense. Radios that had been taken from captured American vehicles were used to jam the wave band on which the American forward observers were calling for fire. Whenever word flashed over the air that shells were on their way, enemy mortar crews dumped shells on American observation posts—easily discernible in the limited perimeter—making sensing virtually impossible. Late in the morning Lt. Col. Walter B. Richardson, who had a small force backing up Kane and Orr, sent more infantry and a platoon of tanks toward the crossroads. By this time the German grenadiers occupied the woods to the north in sufficient strength to halt the foot soldiers. The American tanks, impervious to small arms fire, reached the perimeter at about 1300, whereupon the rifle line pushed out to east and south to give the tankers a chance to maneuver.

But at the crossroads time was running out. Shortly after 1600 the German artillery really got to work, for twenty minutes pummeling the area around the crossroads. Then, preceded by two panzer companies (perhaps the final assault had waited upon their appearance), the entire rifle strength of the 4th Panzer Grenadier Regiment closed upon the Americans. Outlined against new-fallen snow the line of defense was clearly visible to the panzers, and the Shermans had no maneuver room in which to back up the line. The fight was brief, moving to a foregone conclusion. At 1700 the commander of F Company asked Billingslea for permission to withdraw; but Gavin's order still was "hold at all costs." Within the next hour the Germans completed the reduction of the crossroads defense, sweeping up prisoners, armored cars, half-tracks, and the three howitzers. Three American tanks managed to escape under the veil of half-light. Earlier they had succeeded in spotting some panzers, who were firing flares, and knocked them out. A number of men escaped north through the woods; some got a break when a herd of cattle stampeded near the crossroads, providing a momentary screen. Company F of the 325th Glider Infantry suffered the most but stood its ground until Billingslea gave permission to come out. Ultimately forty-four of the original one hundred sixteen who had gone to the crossroads returned to their own lines. Drastically outnumbered and unable to compensate for weakness by maneuver, the defenders of the Baraque de Fraiture crossroads had succumbed, like so many small forces at other crossroads in the Ardennes.

The dent made here at the boundary between the 3d Armored and the 82d Airborne Divisions could all too quickly develop into a ragged tear, parting the two and unraveling their inner flanks. The next intersection on the Liège road, at Manhay, was only four miles to the north. From Manhay the lateral road between Trois Ponts and Hotton would place the Germans on the deep flank and rear of both divisions. Generals Rose and Gavin reacted to this threat at once; so did General Ridgway. Order followed order, but there remained a paucity of means to implement the orders. The deficit in reserves was somewhat remedied by the troops of the 106th Division and the 7th Armored who, all day long, had been pouring through the lines of the 82d Airborne after the hard-fought battle of St. Vith. General Hoge, CCB, 9th Armored commander, had been told at noon to send his 14th Tank Battalion to bolster the right flank of the 82d. One tank company went to the Manhay crossroads; the rest moved into Malempré, two miles to the southeast and off the Liège highway. Coincident with the German attack at Baraque de Fraiture General Hoge received a torrent of reports and orders. By this time Hoge was not sure as to either his attachment or mission. He finally gathered that the Baraque de Fraiture crossroads had been lost and CCB was to join the defense already forming on the road to Manhay.

As darkness settled and the enemy reformed to continue the attack beyond the crossroads, Maj. Olin F. Brewster formed a strongpoint at the north edge of a fringe of woods about 3,000 yards north of Baraque de Fraiture. There he placed Company C of the 509th Parachute Infantry Battalion, which earlier had failed to break through from the north with Richardson's tanks, a platoon of armored infantry, and a tank platoon. With straggling tanks and infantry drifting in from the south and a platoon of tank destroyers sent in by General Hoge, Brewster's force grew. All through the night German infantry tried to filter past and on toward Manhay, but when morning came Brewster's command still stood between the 2d SS Panzer Division and Manhay. A new and critical phase of operations was about to open — the battle for the Manhay crossroads.

Chapter XVII. St. Vith Is Lost

The Defenders of St. Vith Pass to the XVIII Airborne Corps

On the morning of 20 December the Americans defending St. Vith held the easternmost position of any organized nature in the center sector of the Ardennes battleground. The most advanced elements of the German drive by this time were twenty-five airline miles to the southwest of St. Vith. The St. Vith perimeter, now of substantial size, continued to act as a breakwater holding the LXVI Corps in check while other German units forged westward past its northern and southern extensions. As yet the enemy forces passing to the north and south had failed to coalesce to the west of the St. Vith perimeter. The northern penetration, represented at its tip by the 1st SS Panzer Division, remained narrow and road-bound. Well to the rear of the 1st SS the 9th SS Panzer Division, reinforced by the 519th Heavy Antitank Battalion, was toiling slowly westward on the single, free main road which served as the main supply route for two armored 4 and two infantry divisions. The advance guard had arrived near Recht the previous evening. The southern advance, which had carried a mass of German armor and infantry from the XLVII and LVIII Panzer Corps toward Bastogne and Houffalize, had the troops and the maneuver room to constitute a real threat to the southern and western sections of the St. Vith perimeter. The German successes in this area had already isolated the St. Vith forces from the remainder of the VIII Corps, although a slim connection remained between the 7th Armored Division rear installations at La Roche and the VIII Corps headquarters at Bastogne. Communication between the 7th Armored rear headquarters and the St. Vith command post (thirty-five miles by road) was extremely difficult. Communication between the VIII Corps headquarters and the St. Vith command post was almost nonexistent, even by radio.

The road to Spa and the First Army headquarters, albeit roundabout and hazardous, remained open on the morning of the 20th. Thither the 7th Armored Division commander sent a liaison officer (Lt. Col. Frederic Schroeder) with a letter to the First Army chief of staff, Maj. Gen. William B. Kean, and orders to explain that St. Vith was out of touch with the VIII Corps. The letter, safely delivered, gave the First Army its first definite picture of events in the far-removed St. Vith sector:

"Dear Bill:

"I am out of touch with VIII Corps and understand XVIII Airborne Corps is coming in.

"My division is defending the line St. Vith-Poteau both inclusive. CCB, 9th AD, the 424th Inf Regt of the 106th Div and the 112th Inf Regt of the 28th Div are on my right and hold from St. Vith to Holdingen. Both infantry regiments are in bad shape. My right flank is wide open except for some reconnaissance elements, TDs and stragglers we have collected and organized into defense teams at road centers back as far as Cheram [Chérain] inclusive. Two German Divisions, 116 Pz and 560 VG, are just starting to attack NW with their right on Gouvy. I can delay them the rest of today maybe but will be cut off by tomorrow.

"VIII Corps has ordered me to hold and I will do so but need help. An attack from Bastogne to the NE will relieve the situation and in turn cut the bastards off in rear. I also need plenty of air support. Am out of contact with VIII Corps so am sending this to you. Understand 82AB is coming up on my north and the north flank is not critical.

"BOB HASBROUCK"

The First Army headquarters was in process of drafting plans for uniting the XVIII Airborne Corps and the St. Vith force when General Hasbrouck's letter arrived. General Hodges' answer, dispatched at 1230, stated:

"Ridgway with armor and infantry is moving from west to gain contact with you. When communication is established you come under command of Ridgway. You retain under your command following units: 106th Inf Div, RCT 112, and CCB 9th Armed Div.... [Ridgway] holds Malmédy, Stavelot and Trois Ponts...."

For the first time since forming the St. Vith perimeter the force there knew what measures were under way for its reinforcement or relief as well as the precise status of command within the force. Thus far General Hasbrouck and General Jones, the two division commanders, had directed the units in the perimeter on a basis of mutual agreement, although Hasbrouck, with the largest force in his own command, made most of the decisions. As the 7th Armored commander phrased it: "I never knew who was in my command. I just did everything I thought necessary. The command status was more or less of an assumption." Actually the perimeter held from St. Vith westward was so large and the defending units so thoroughly mixed that command functioned on an area basis, even after the receipt of the First Army order, with the 106th Division headquarters continuing to direct the defense south and southwest of St. Vith.

To the surprise of the St. Vith forces this day (the 20th) passed rather quietly. Only a few feeble German jabs were directed against the American line, which on its eastern face had been strengthened by a series of withdrawals to more favorable ground during the previous night. The American positions were much better integrated than on previous days: the 7th Armored Division artillery and attached battalions—of particular importance the one medium tank battalion—were tied in closely with the troops they supported. Finally, the enemy was under compulsion to reconnoiter anew the outlines of the American eastern front which had been redrawn during the night of 19 December. German reports covering activity on the 20th assume the defense of the St. Vith area as much stronger than it was in fact. The enemy was much impressed by the collection of American armor confronting him—"tanks were everywhere," said the 18th Volks Grenadier Division—and by the amount of artillery fire his every movement attracted.

It must be added, however, that Lucht's LXVI Corps was not in position to bring off the smashing attack against St. Vith which had been set tentatively for the 20th. The Fuehrer Begleit Brigade, whose tanks were supposed to add new punch to operations of the infantry corps, was still strung out along the jammed and miry roads east of St. Vith. Its commander, Colonel Remer, impatient with delay, had ordered an assault west of Wallerode at midnight on the 19th, but the small detachment of armored infantry and assault guns at hand came under shellfire each time it formed for attack and Remer finally gave over the whole idea. Before daylight some of his tanks arrived in the woods west of Born. Having convinced the corps commander that direct attack on St. Vith from the east was no longer feasible, Remer tried to make good on his own favored plan for an armored flanking attack in the north even at the risk of a piecemeal effort.

Taking advantage of a heavy fog which rose in midafternoon, Remer sent a tank company through Ober-Emmels and up the slope west of Hünningen. American 90-mm. tank destroyers from the 814th Tank Destroyer Battalion, waiting on the reverse slope, caught the first wave of four Panthers in their sights, fired seven rounds, and knocked out all four. Remer's battalion of armored infantry and two assault gun batteries, waiting in reserve in the valley below, never were committed. This then was the extent of the Fuehrer Begleit effort on the 20th; Remer decided to await the arrival of the full brigade.

East of St. Vith the 18th Volks Grenadier Division was regrouping as it waited for its artillery and trains, involved in the traffic jam caused by the Fuehrer Begleit columns. As usual, attempts to bring up the horse-drawn caissons past the armor only resulted in more delay and confusion. The division commander, General Hoffmann-Schönborn, did try a piecemeal attack on the high ground north of the Schönberg road with the intent to seize the St. Vith railroad station. He personally accompanied the 295th Regiment in the assault. The attacking troop assembled in Wallerode toward midmorning where they offered wonderful targets for the artillery supporting CCB, 7th Armored. The gunners, as infantry observers reported, "threw everything at Wallerode but the shoes on their feet." Within half an hour the German regimental commander was hors de combat and the attack dissipated.

South of St. Vith, where CCB, 9th Armored, had redressed its lines during the previous night consonant with the 7th Armored position on the left and taken over a five-mile front, the enemy made some attempt to press westward. The 62d Volks Grenadier Division had been given the mission of cutting the possible escape routes southwest of St. Vith by an advance through Grufflange and Maldingen. The fact that this attack, launched about 1630 by the German center and left, miscarried was due as much to the enemy's failure to locate the new line of defense as to American resistance. The 190th Regiment advanced in close formation toward the 27th Armored Infantry Battalion, almost as if in route march, and took a terrible beating from artillery, mortars, tank destroyers, antitank guns on ground mounts, and machine guns. The 164th Regiment, advancing opposite the southern flank of CCB, reported success while moving unopposed through Maspelt and across ground which had been abandoned the previous night, but at a crossroads in the Grufflange woods American shells suddenly poured in and the advance came to a dead stop. Prisoners subsequently told of very severe losses here in the forest.

Although action had flared up on 20 December along the eastern face of the St. Vith perimeter, the feature of this day was the series of rearrangements to tighten the perimeter on the north and south. Hasbrouck earlier had been "suspicious" of what was happening in the northern sector around Recht and Poteau, but he was no longer too apprehensive after the successive march groups of the 1st SS Panzer Division had bounced off the 7th Armored Division roadblocks. The gap between the western anchor of the north flank at Vielsalm and the eastern outposts of the 82d Airborne Division was closed toward the end of the day when patrols from the 505th Parachute Infantry met a reconnaissance party from the 7th Armored south of Trois Ponts. In addition light tanks belonging to the 87th Cavalry Reconnaissance Squadron had established radio contact with the 3d Armored task force north of Samrée. On the whole it appeared that the north flank of the St. Vith force shortly would be battened down at its western terminus and that the danger of a German turning movement there had been removed.

The main danger, apparent since 19 December, was the open south flank of the St. Vith defense hanging on the air at Holdingen. It was known that a German move northwest toward this open flank was in process—indeed the 116th Panzer Division and the 560th Volks Grenadier Division had been identified. Furthermore the 7th Armored trains had reported signs of an enemy force far to the west of the 7th Armored outpost positions. Acutely aware of the threat now forming, General Hasbrouck stripped such elements as he dared from his north flank, added the remnants of the 14th Cavalry Group, and created Task Force Jones (Lt. Col. Robert B. Jones, Commanding Officer, 814th Tank Destroyer Battalion) to guard the south and southwestern flank. Admittedly this scratch force was too weak to make a serious defense in the endangered sector, but it could be expected to block the key road junctions and sound a warning should the enemy attempt any flanking movement.

Colonel Jones organized three small detachments to occupy Deifeld, Gouvy, and Chérain, a screening position a little over six miles from east to west. Deifeld was occupied without trouble. The high ground commanding Chérain, seven miles northeast of Houffalize at the junction of the roads from Vielsalm and St. Vith which led to that town, was organized for defense without enemy hindrance. By chance the Chérain detachment received reinforcement late in the afternoon when a company of the 112th Infantry appeared. At an earlier and more optimistic hour this company had been dispatched to Houffalize with orders to make a counterattack southward to relieve the pressure on Bastogne. The company commander was persuaded that the situation had changed somewhat and that he should wait at Chérain for further orders. A little later a company of German infantry was detected marching north along the valley toward Chérain. During the night a few of the enemy entered the village but quickly were driven out. General Hasbrouck decided to wait further developments before committing any of his meager reserves at Chérain.

The detachment which Jones had sent to Gouvy, midway between Deifeld and Chérain, was surprised to find the village occupied by German infantry. On 18 December the 7th Armored had learned in a roundabout way that a "Lieutenant Colonel named Stone" had collected a few troops and was holding Gouvy. Subsequently Hasbrouck sent a platoon of light tanks to help out and an injunction that it was "imperative" that the village be held. All through the day and night of 19 December German vehicles (units of the 116th Panzer Division and the advance guard of the 560th Volks Grenadier Division) had rolled past Gouvy to the south and west, but no attempt had been made to repeat the attack of the previous day. Stone sent out one of his staff to try to line up some help; this officer discovered the command post of the 965th Field Artillery Battalion, near the town of Beho, and put forth the case of the Gouvy defenders "who were attempting to hold the line despite their not being trained infantrymen." Battery C had been assigned to support the 112th Infantry and with the consent of the latter shifted its 155-mm. howitzers to give Stone's men a hand.

Actually the pick-up force of quartermaster troops, light tanks, and stragglers under Stone's command was deployed so as to defend the railhead stocks at Gouvy Station east of the village proper, but this fact was unknown to the 7th Armored Division headquarters. During the night of 19 December the bulk of the 1130th Regiment, 560th Volks Grenadier Division, bivouacked in and west of the village of Gouvy. This regiment, which had sent combat patrols against Stone's force on the

18th, was at the tail end of the LVIII Panzer Corps columns pushing past Houffalize. It had become embroiled with the 112th Infantry at Sevenig, had suffered intensely (the fighting strength of the regiment now was between five and six hundred), and had been unable to disengage in the Our River sector as quickly as the rest of the division. The LVIII Panzer Corps commander was anxious to get the 1130th up to cover his right rear and had ordered the regiment to seize and block the St. Vith-Houffalize road in the neighborhood of Gouvy and Chérain.

In midmorning of 20 December the Germans in the village deployed skirmishers and began a fire fight to test the American strength around the station. After three hours of this the Americans observed the enemy going into attack formation in an open field next to the village church. Using the church spire as a reference point the cannoneers of Battery C opened fire, their 155-mm. howitzers scattering the German formation in every direction. When the 7th Armored detachment arrived to set up the Gouvy roadblock, it found the Germans inside the village. The detachment drove them out in a sharp fight but at nightfall withdrew to a road junction a mile and a half to the west, here blocking any further German move toward the north. Stone's group was incorporated in Task Force Jones. The next day it was able, with some pride, to turn over to the 7th Armored Division the 350 German prisoners it had guarded since 18 December and the stores at the railhead.

Possession of the First Army ration dumps at Gouvy Station was a boon to the units in the St. Vith-Vielsalm defense, for by 20 December the 7th Armored Division trains for all practical purposes were cut off from the forward combat elements. On this day it was necessary to instruct all unit commanders that the rations, water, and gasoline on hand must be made to last for three days. The eight battalions of field artillery taking part in the defense were put on a strict ration, seven rounds for each 105-mm. howitzer, to fire only on the most urgent and well-defined targets. Harassing and interdiction fire, therefore, was turned over to the mortar crews, who mixed high explosives and white phosphorous shells to make the supply last. Fortunately the stock of artillery shells was replenished (for the first time in three days) from the Samrée dump before it was overrun by the enemy. An attempt to give greater weight to the artillery in the St. Vith-Vielsalm area failed when the 4.5-inch guns of the 770th Field Artillery Battalion were cut off at Samrée en route from La Roche.

Even when separated from the 7th Armored trains the St. Vith front was considerably stronger and better organized than it had been. Incidentally, the quick and forceful reaction to all German probing during the day and the fact that Hasbrouck had kept only a very small reserve out of the line had created an impression of American strength in the enemy headquarters well beyond the fact. The front held by the 7th Armored Division, CCB of the 9th Armored, and attached units by this time had expanded to about thirty-two miles. Traced on the map the line assumed the form of a horseshoe, the bend at St. Vith, the open prongs facing west. This opening had been partially covered by the advance southeastward of the 82d Airborne Division, but a gap of some five miles still existed north of the Chérain outpost set up by Task Force Jones.

The VIII Corps passed to General Patton's Third Army during the 20th. Word of this, handed down by Colonel Ryan who had been at the VIII Corps headquarters in Neufchâteau and had worked his way back to the division trains, caused a little confusion as to the exact status of the units attached to the 7th Armored Division. In the early evening CCB, 9th Armored Division, received orders to revert to the VIII

Corps and move that same night to St. Hubert, seventeen miles west of Bastogne. The loss of this combat command would create a wide breach in front of the enemy congregating south of St. Vith, a breach which hardly could be filled by the last reserves at Hasbrouck's disposal. The 7th Armored commander, at Hoge's request, got Middleton to cancel the order, and CCB, 9th Armored, subsequently was taken under the First Army command. The attachment already existing was thus legalized. What Hasbrouck needed now he tersely relayed in a message through the 7th Armored trains to the XVIII Airborne Corps: "We can hold if no troops are taken away from us and our right rear is given protection."

The addition of the 7th Armored Division to the XVIII Airborne Corps had contributed greatly to the phenomenal expansion of a corps front which measured only some twenty-five miles on 19 December but which represented a sector of approximately eighty-five miles on the evening of 20 December. On the 19th most of Ridgway's troops had engaged in patrolling with no enemy contact; on the 20th the XVIII Airborne Corps faced the westernmost elements of the I SS Panzer Corps, the entire LXVI Corps, and the LVIII Panzer Corps. Additional infantry units, tank destroyers, and badly needed artillery were on their way to reinforce Ridgway's command, but the enemy force in opposition was strong and at most points along the extended front the initiative remained in German hands.

Whether the XVIII Airborne Corps could maintain the freshly added burden imposed by the 7th Armored Division salient remained to be seen. But that the XVIII Airborne Corps lacked the strength to close the gap of thirteen road miles between the VIII Corps and itself (that is, the gap between the 7th Armored Division detachment at Chérain and the elements of the 101st Airborne at Foy) was rapidly becoming apparent to all. The corps' mission, as it had devolved by the end of the day, would be this: pivoting on Malmédy, to continue the advance to the southeast and east with "utmost vigor," driving back the German forces found west of the line Malmédy—Pont-Vielsalm—Hebronval—Houffalize.

That the enemy was prepared to contest this move all intelligence reports affirmed. True, Kampfgruppe Peiper had been pretty well bottled up on the corps left wing; but this effort had been made by thinning the line between Malmédy and Trois Ponts. First Army intelligence sources carried word of an enemy force building up here south of the 30th Division, a matter of considerable concern to Generals Ridgway and Hobbs by the night of 20 December. Furthermore, it was recognized that Peiper might try to break out through Stavelot. German documents, taken in the fight at Gouvy, showed clearly the intention of the LVIII Panzer Corps to drive on Hotton, at the moment the location of the 3d Armored Division command post. Already the advance guard of this force had pushed beyond Samrée. The St. Vith salient, where the 7th Armored Division was to remain on the defensive during the XVIII Airborne advance, was confronted with growing German forces on three sides. Prisoners had reported that the Grossdeutschland Panzer Division, previously identified on the Eastern Front, had joined the LXVI Corps before St. Vith. Even though the new armored outfit did not prove to be the famous division but Remer's much weaker panzer brigade, the report was of particular concern.

The Enemy Closes on the St. Vith Salient

The St. Vith salient looked like this by the morning of the 21st: on the north and east the line was as well organized as the forces available would permit; the southern flank had been somewhat reinforced and prolonged by a covering screen extending westward; the 82d Airborne Division was in position to give some support in the northwestern segment of the gap to the rear of the 7th Armored and 106th Infantry Division; and there was a fair number of light batteries supporting the front and flanks of the salient. Although rationing had begun, there was no immediate threat that food, gasoline, or ammunition would fail. The piecemeal German attacks on the 20th had been turned back with little loss or difficulty. Command relations under the XVIII Airborne Corps had been clarified (the 106th was no longer attached to the 7th Armored) and communications established. For the first time the two divisions holding the salient had some clear picture of the dispositions and plans of neighboring friendly units. No one could say with certainty, of course, what strength the enemy was preparing for the final assault to gain St. Vith.

The Fifth Panzer Army, constantly prodded by the higher staffs and acutely aware that the St. Vith road net must be opened to allow forward movement of the reinforcements needed to maintain the momentum of the advance toward the Meuse, was in no mood for further delay. General Manteuffel was anxious to free the LXVI Corps and hurry it forward to the Salm River sector as right wing cover for the two panzer corps. General Model hoped to shake the corps free and use Remer's armor to help the Sixth Panzer Army get moving in the north. Lucht, therefore, was ordered to make an all-out attack and take St. Vith itself on 21 December, whether or not the Fuehrer Begleit Brigade was ready. This, one of his division commanders opined, was easier said than done.

The course of battle on 21 December initially affirmed the pessimistic view with which most of German unit commanders seem to have started the attack. Remer, still missing most of his tanks, had been instructed to drive from Nieder-Emmels straight south into St. Vith. South of Nieder-Emmels the St. Vith road crossed the ridge where, the day before, the American tank destroyers had broken the back of the German attack before it could get rolling. The Fuehrer Begleit commander, with the independence that characterized the actions of a man who stood ace-high with Hitler, decided to shift the attack and take Rodt (Sart-lez-St. Vith), about two and a half miles west of his assigned objective. The rifle battalion assigned to carry out this mission happened to come under American artillery fire while assembling west of Nieder-Emmels before dawn, or thus Remer explains the failure to strike Rodt. So he compromised by sending a large combat patrol into the woods west of that village with orders to find a covered route along which the tanks might advance on Vielsalm once they arrived.

The section of the main St. Vith-Vielsalm supply road west of Rodt was guarded by two American medium tank companies spread over a distance of three miles. It was easy for the German infantry to move unnoticed through the heavy timber. They even succeeded in ambushing enough vehicles, passing back and forth along the road, to promise motorization of the brigade's bicycle battalion. The American tankers caught on to what had happened when messengers and liaison officers failed to arrive at their destinations, but by this time the Germans had journeyed on to the southwest. Near Hinderhausen they attempted to surprise the 275th Armored Field Artillery Battalion, an outfit that had been exposed to close-quarter fighting before. With the help of two tanks and an antiaircraft artillery half-track mounting the dreaded .50-caliber quad, the artillerymen beat off the attack. When the raiders turned back to rejoin Remer they found the American tankers waiting; however, evasion in the woods was easy, although at this point the prized vehicles were abandoned and most of the captured Americans escaped. Meanwhile Remer's armored group had arrived north of St. Vith and the brigade was ready for attack as soon as darkness came.

On most of the front held by the 7th Armored and the troops of the 9th Armored and 106th the morning passed in ominous quiet. Patrols working in front of the American lines came back with reports of enemy activity and movement; some kind of an attack was in the offing but it seemed slow in coming. Apparently the German corps command had some difficulty in organizing a co-ordinated and well-timed advance over the broken and wooded ground around St. Vith. In fact, he had not reached the commanders of his two infantry divisions with orders until daylight. The center regiment of the 62d Volks Grenadier Division (the 190th), charged with seizing the high ground in the thick forest east of Grufflange, did get one battalion under way in the morning and succeeded in overrunning an armored infantry platoon and three tank destroyers belonging to CCB, 9th Armored. Once the element of surprise was lost the Germans made no further headway in the forest; artillery and bullet fire held them until a platoon of American tanks arrived, whereupon they withdrew.

The American defense of St. Vith itself was based on the possession of ridge lines and hills masking the town to the northeast, east, and southeast. Two draws cut through this shield of high ground, one on the north represented by the highway running from Büllingen into St. Vith, the other angling from the southeast and traversed by the road and railroad line from Prüm. Directly east of St. Vith ran the Schönberg highway, which had been the avenue of the very first German attacks, but this road ran over a ridge just outside St. Vith where the Americans had stood successfully to meet all previous enemy thrusts. Much of the area here described was covered with dense stands of timber spaced irregularly with clearings between. Connecting the Büllingen and Schönberg approaches a spider web of secondary roads and trails ran back and forth, centering at the hamlet of Wallerode (two miles northeast of St. Vith) behind which lay a large forest. It was here that the unsuccessful attacks launched earlier by the 18th Volks Grenadier Division and the Fuehrer Begleit Brigade had formed.

Faced with the problem of organizing and integrating a defensive line which had come into being piecemeal and with little regard to the integrity of the tactical units involved, the Americans divided command responsibility along easily discerned map features. Thus the draws coming in from the southeast marked the boundary between CCB of the 9th Armored and CCB, 7th Armored, while the northern defile and the Büllingen road designated the boundary between two sector commands within CCB, 7th Armored. The easternmost defenses, as a result, were in the sector bounded by the Prüm road on the right and the Büllingen road on the left, susceptible to penetration at either flank or both. This sector was under Lt. Col. William H. G. Fuller (commanding officer of the 38th Armored Infantry Battalion), whose command consisted of four companies of armored infantry, Troop B of the 87th Reconnaissance Squadron, and some four hundred men remaining from the 81st and 168th Engineer Combat Battalions (the men who had taken the first enemy blows at St. Vith), backed up by a tank company and a platoon of self-propelled 90-mm. tank destroyers.

The frontal attack planned by the LXVI Corps commander, under pressure for a quick victory, would be mounted by the 18th Volks Grenadier Division and the 62d Volks Grenadier Division, whose highly successful envelopment tactics east of St. Vith had bagged prisoners finally counted on this day as approaching eight thousand. The main effort would be made by the 18th in the north and the 183d Regiment from the right wing of the 62d, this force attacking in the sector outlined by the two draws where Colonel Fuller's command was deployed. To the right of the main effort Remer's brigade was under orders to enter St. Vith by direct assault from the northwest via the Hünningen road, orders which he subsequently disobeyed. To the left the two remaining regiments of the 62d were to attack due west with the object of reaching the road between St. Vith and Maldingen; they would take no part, however, in the assault on St. Vith.

By prodigious effort the LXVI Corps artillery finally had been wormed through the traffic jam east of St. Vith, and towed and manhandled into position. Around 1400 the German guns and Werfers opened up against Fuller's positions in front of the town. West of Wallerode the 295th Regiment started into the assault, possibly only as a feint, but withdrew as the guns supporting CCB, 7th Armored, went into action. This gambit was succeeded by a fifteen-minute artillery concentration; as it raised westward the main German attack moved forward. It was now about 1600 hours.

One of the heaviest and longest-sustained barrages the veteran American combat command had ever encountered tied the troops of CCB to their foxholes, and even there tree bursts claimed many a victim. On both sides of the main Schönberg road the 294th Regiment moved groups of forty to fifty men forward in bounds through the woods. A platoon of Sherman tanks stationed just north of the road was caught in the thickest of the German concentrations. Three lost their commanders and the platoon withdrew. The first German waves then hit between Company A of the 38th Armored Infantry Battalion and Company A of the 23d Armored Infantry Battalion. Meanwhile the 293d Regiment had pushed south of the Schönberg highway toward Company B of the 38th Armored Infantry Battalion, Troop B, 87th Reconnaissance Squadron, and Company A, 81st Combat Engineers, left to right. Only two medium tanks were barring the road. For some reason this attack never fully developed—later German reports indicated that the assault waves lost their direction while moving through the thick woods. Suddenly, about 1700, the German pressure along the Schönberg road eased. The enemy had found a soft spot and was regrouping while his tanks and assault guns moved forward. General Lucht ordered the commander of the 18th Volks Grenadier Division to throw everything he had behind the 294th and continue the attack.

North of the threatened area the 295th Regiment had come out of the woods behind Wallerode and started an advance southwest, covered by assault gun or tank fire from the ridge west of the town. This move brought the grenadiers across open ground and under flanking fire from American tanks located by the railroad underpass just north of St. Vith. At the same time Company A of the 38th Armored Infantry Battalion fired into their ranks from the front. American artillery joined in, the attack broke, and the 295th streamed back from whence it had come.

At 2000 the battle along the Schönberg road flared up again. This was the end. Most of the American troops were killed or captured, so that only a conditional reconstruction of the German breakthrough east of St. Vith can ever be made. The American units flanking the road had been badly understrength before the 21st, but the lengthy and destructive barrage laid down by the enemy had caused very severe casualties and shaken the defenders. Sustained shelling had also destroyed all means of communication, except by runner, and left the little groups isolated and unable to support one another. Troop B of the 87th Reconnaissance Squadron and Company A of the 81st Engineer Combat Battalion, both directly in the German path, probably numbered less than forty men apiece when the final blow fell. It appears that if there were any mines left on the Schönberg road they had been lifted in preparation for a promised counterattack by American tanks.

Actually there were only three Shermans on the main road, remnant of a reserve platoon which had been commandeered when the initial tank support had decamped. During the earlier lull the enemy infantry worked through the thick woods, penetrating the thin and disordered American line at a number of points. The final assault, made by the 294th and one or two platoons of Tigers, simply peeled the Americans back on both sides of the road. The three Shermans had aimed their guns to blast the first tanks as they came over the ridge where the American foxhole line had been drawn. In the darkness, and with radios and wire no longer functioning, the first sign of the enemy armor was a volley of flares fired in flat trajectory from the Panthers. Silhouetted in light and with blinded crews the Shermans were disposed of in one, two, three order. In a matter of minutes German infantry and tanks were to the rear of the foxhole line. Lt. Col. Thomas J. Riggs, Jr., commander of the 81st Engineer Combat Battalion, who had tried to organize a counterattack to wipe out the earlier penetrations was lost trying to organize a last-ditch defense in the hamlet of Prümerberg on the main road. No withdrawal orders reached the troops now behind the enemy. Some held where they were; some stampeded blindly through the woods in search of an exit to the west.

A double column of enemy troops and vehicles marched along the road into St. Vith. On the right of Colonel Fuller's sector Company B of the 23d Armored Infantry Battalion and a platoon of the 814th Tank Destroyer Battalion, after having withstood almost continuous assault for four hours, succumbed about the same time to the 183d Regiment, which attacked along the draw from the southeast between CCB, 7th Armored, and CCB, 9th Armored. The 183d Regiment now poured through the draw into St. Vith. Two of the American tank destroyers reached St. Vith and here blocked the main street until nearly midnight, when one was destroyed by a bazooka round. Of the force originally commanded by Colonel Fuller in the eastern sector only some two hundred escaped, and half of these had to be evacuated for wounds or exhaustion. The loss here of the four armored infantry companies would be keenly felt by CCB, 7th Armored Division.

General Clarke, the CCB, 7th Armored Division, commander, could do little to influence the course of the battle. Communications were gone and he had no reserves. About 2130 he ordered what was left of his command to fall back to the high ground west of the city, planning to anchor the new line on those of his troops who were still intact in the Nieder-Emmels sector, northwest of St. Vith. The troops east of St. Vith simply had to be written off (at least 600 officers and men) although some later would be able to work their way back through the German lines.

The new defense ordered by Clarke began to form shortly before midnight. It was a ragged, piecemeal affair about two miles long, running south from Hünningen along the chain of hills a thousand yards west of St. Vith. Lt. Col. Robert C. Erlenbusch (Commanding Officer, 31st Tank Battalion) was charged with the organization of this new position. He and Lt. Col. Robert L. Rhea (Commanding Officer, 23d Armored Infantry Battalion), who had taken over from Colonel Fuller when the latter was evacuated because of exhaustion, were able to restore some measure of confidence and order. CCB, 7th Armored Division, be it remembered, was a battle-tested outfit of superior morale—as was the entire division—so credit also must go to the unnamed officers, noncoms, and men who withdrew in good order to the new line. Fortunately, the enemy, too, had to regroup before he resumed the battle.

CCB, 9th Armored, also made readjustments to meet the new situation. General Clarke had informed General Hoge, whose command post was close at hand, that his command was moving back to re-form west of St. Vith. Since the shift would leave Hoge's northern flank open, it was agreed that contact between the two combat commands would be re-established at Bauvenn, necessitating that Hoge's left be pulled back some two thousand yards. This was accomplished. The remainder of CCB, 9th Armored Division, remained in the positions on the ridge line west of the Braunlauf Creek and draw.

About 2200 General Clark reached General Hasbrouck with word of what had happened at St. Vith and the latter immediately informed the XVIII Airborne Corps. But this was not all that the 7th Armored Division commander had to report. Earlier, Task Force Jones (deployed on the southern flank of the salient) had captured a German engineer officer who, under questioning, said that his division, the 2d SS Panzer Division, was moving toward Gouvy. Thus far the 2d SS Panzer Division had not been located. Its presence on the weak southern flank (in case the captured officer was not a "plant") was disturbing. Apparently General Hasbrouck accepted the veracity of the report (he could hardly risk the chance that it was not true) and so recommended that General Ridgway send the 3d Armored Division east and south to meet this new enemy. Already Hasbrouck had ordered Task Force Jones to shorten its line because the last reserve available behind the southern wing (the 17th Tank Battalion) was en route to reinforce CCB. Without Wemple's tanks, or with them, Task Force Jones was no match for any large detachment of the 2d SS Panzer Division.

The First Army commander still expected, on the night of the 21st, that Ridgway's corps would shortly gain contact with the 7th Armored—but the situation was deteriorating at a fast clip. After a hasty meeting of his corps staff the XVIII Airborne commander sent new orders to Hasbrouck (it was now about 0200 on the 22d). The 424th and 112th Infantry Regiments were to withdraw from their positions. The entire force under Generals Hasbrouck and Jones was to form a defensive ring west of St. Vith and east of the Salm River. By early morning of the 22d the withdrawal of the southernmost units was under way and the circle was beginning to form. The command situation finally was "regularized" when Ridgway gave Maj. Gen. Alan W. Jones the command of the 7th Armored Division (he ranked Brig. Gen. Robert W. Hasbrouck) in addition to his own division and its attachments. Actually this change had no effect on the conduct of subsequent operations and was effective for only a few hours.

A perimeter defense by units cut off from the rest of the XVIII Airborne Corps was a very temporary expedient; the ground now occupied, in the opinion of the local commanders, could not be held for long. General Clark later phrased the problem thus:

"In studying the map of the area it will be noted that the troops were to be disposed surrounding a forest through which there was a paucity of roads. There was practically no possibility of being able to shift forces to meet a threat at any point How units were to be supplied in such a situation is not understood. Air supply of such a large and scattered force would have been most difficult. Without supply the force would have been through in two or three days."

Fortunately for the forces in the salient the withdrawal to the "goose egg" defense, a move made with extreme difficulty on muddy and congested roads and trails, was unhampered in its first phases by any German reaction. The occupation of St. Vith had considerably disorganized the attacking division, whose regiments jammed into the town from east, north, and south. Orders given the 18th Volks Grenadier Division early on the 22d to continue the attack along the main road through Rodt and Poteau toward the Salm River could not be carried out for some hours. On the left the bulk of the 62d Volks Grenadier Division was still confronted with an unbroken defense. The only force in position for an immediate exploitation was Remer's Fuehrer Begleit Brigade, whose tanks finally had arrived on the evening of 21 December.

The Final Withdrawal from the St. Vith Sector

The raid made by Remer's infantry past Rodt now paid dividends. Having found a negotiable route for his heavy vehicles, Remer prepared to capture Rodt, cut the main road between that village and Vielsalm, and overrun such of the American batteries as remained in the way. In the midst of a snowstorm, sometime around midnight of the 21st, Remer's tank group and his armored infantry started along the narrow trails winding through the thick woods north of the Rodt-Vielsalm road. By daybreak the Fuehrer Begleit advance guard had arrived at the edge of the forest north of Rodt. This small village, 4,000 yards west of St. Vith, lay on the reverse slope of a ridge line along which extended the north flank of the 7th Armored Division. Here a number of secondary roads entered the St. Vith-Vielsalm highway, one from Recht in the north, others from Hinderhausen and Crombach in the south. As a result of the regrouping under way in the 7th Armored zone, Rodt was the junction point between CCA, still holding the division north flank, and CCB, raising a new line along the low hill chain that extended south of the village. The ground at Rodt, then, overlooked the flank and rear of CCB.

The village itself was garrisoned by the service company of the 48th Armored Infantry Battalion and some drivers belonging to the battalion whose vehicles were parked there. Astride the woods road running north to Recht were small blocking detachments of tanks, engineers, and antitank guns. Between Rodt and the next village to the west, Poteau, two companies of medium tanks patrolled the main road and watched the trails running in from the north. To the northeast the troop from CCB which originally had held the left wing of the St. Vith sector around Hünningen was still in position; as yet it had not sustained any heavy blows.

As light broke, the right battalion of Remer's brigade attacked to cut the main western road close to Poteau. The German assault here was beaten off by the drivers in a vehicle park who used the .50-caliber machine guns on their two-score half-tracks in a withering fusillade. In the east, at Rodt, Remer's left battalion tried to rush the village from the woods but ran straight into artillery fire. Some of the Germans made it to the houses and defended themselves in the cellars, but most of the battalion finally had to pull back. A number of prisoners were later rounded up by the Americans on the Recht road. The second German assault was made in a more methodical manner. First, mortars went to work against houses and foxholes. Then the German tank group, which had been delayed by a mine field, and an infantry company or two swung to the west and rolled down the main road into the village. The Sherman tanks on the Recht road were caught in masked positions from which they could not return the panzer fire coming in from higher ground, and the troops in

Rodt could not stand alone against the Panthers. The enemy took the village quickly, and with it many of the half-tracks belonging to the 48th Armored Infantry Battalion.

Word that the St. Vith-Vielsalm road had been cut at Rodt reached Lt. Col. Vincent L. Boylan, Commanding Officer, 87th Cavalry Reconnaissance Squadron, who took charge of the few troops of CCB remaining north of St. Vith on the wide open flank. Boylan got orders from Clarke to withdraw south at once. Despite a brush with Remer's group and the loss of several tanks in the swampy ground south of Rodt the command reached Crombach and Hinderhausen, where General Clarke was building a second line of defense. This line was now gravely endangered on its open north flank by the German position astride the ridge at Rodt.

In the meantime, Colonel Rosebaum, the CCA commander, sent two of his tank companies east of Poteau to engage Remer's tanks. In a long distance duel along the ridge the Shermans were out-ranged. Rosebaum asked for some tank destroyers, hoping to stop the Panthers if they should turn west from Rodt. Remer's objective, however, was not in that direction.

All during the morning of 22 December American observers had watched enemy troops and vehicles milling around Recht, just to the north of Poteau. Here the first identification was made of the 9th SS Panzer Division. This fresh armored division was in fact moving its main strength west from Recht toward the Salm River and collision with the 82d Airborne Division, but a kampfgruppe had been dropped off to cover the south flank of the division by attacking in the direction of Vielsalm. With the discovery of this new enemy force in the north and the knowledge that the only route of withdrawal remaining to CCA was along the road from Poteau to Vielsalm, Colonel Rosebaum gave over the effort against the Fuehrer Begleit armor and gathered the major part of his command in a circular defense around the Poteau crossroads. As yet he had only vague information of the serious situation confronting the American troops in the south and southeast.

The capture of Rodt left General Clarke no alternative but further withdrawal. In the early afternoon the sketchy line just west of St. Vith was abandoned and CCB fell back to the secondary position which had been under preparation since the early morning hours. The villages of Hinderhausen and Crombach, on which this position was based, both offered emergency exits to the west along dirt roads and trails. The three task forces organized along the new line nominally represented a total of five medium tank companies, a light tank company, three platoons of 90-mm. tank destroyers, two troops of cavalry, and the equivalent of four or five rifle companies. But unit integrity had been lost, the armored components were far below strength, and many of the armored infantry were weary, ill-equipped stragglers who had been put back in the line after their escape from St. Vith. General Clarke's plea for reinforcements brought in a rifle company, a company of tank destroyers, and a few light armored vehicles. That was all. Supplies were running short and the ground now occupied was not well adapted to defense. Still worse, CCB had no friendly contact on the north, and a patrol sent to establish connection with CCB, 9th Armored, on the south had disappeared. The fact was that the 62d Volks Grenadier Division had thrust a force through the woods and along Braunlauf Creek into the gap between the two combat commands.

It will be recalled that on the night of 21 December General Hoge had set in motion a withdrawal of the northern flank of CCB, 9th Armored, to conform with Clarke's first defensive position just west of St. Vith. In blinding snow, on slippery roads, 9th Armored tanks and infantry headed for Bauvenn, designated as the linkage point for the two combat commands. Confusion, darkness, and mud slowed the move, but by morning a medium tank company and a platoon of riflemen had reached the village.

Bauvenn, no more than a jog in the road, lay three-quarters of a mile north of the natural corridor through which flowed the Braunlauf Creek, the corridor at whose eastern entrance the enemy had attacked the night before in severing the connective tissue between the 7th and 9th Armored combat commands. The course of the valley westward proffered a natural line of advance, and through it, in the early hours of the 22d, pushed small detachments of the 62d Volks Grenadier Division. Undetected, a German rifle company reached Neubrueck, in the valley southwest of Bauvenn, where the command post of the 27th Armored Infantry Battalion was located. About 1000 the enemy rushed the village and killed or captured the entire battalion staff. A counterattack thrown in by a scratch force of infantry and tanks from Bauvenn drove the Germans out and freed those Americans still alive. In a subsequent readjustment of the CCB line to round out the goose egg, Hoge's tanks and infantry were arrayed from Neubrueck south and west through Grufflange and Maldingen. Late in the afternoon a battalion of the 424th Infantry was added to the line, but as yet the enemy made no appearance in force in this sector.

The LXVI Corps was in no position to capitalize with speed and immediate effect on its capture of St. Vith. As the intermingling of roadways at St. Vith had made it possible for the defenders to bar the way west, so now this knot in the Belgian-German road prevented a quick transfer of men and guns in pursuit. Of the LXVI Corps only those units which had swung wide of the city during the attack were able to maintain pressure on the Americans: the Fuehrer Begleit Brigade, executing its semi-independent turning movement, and the advance guard of the 190th Grenadier Regiment, inserting a company or so between the two CCB's. In the course of the night battle at St. Vith the German assault units had become badly scrambled. The problem involved in extricating and reforming these units was enhanced by the natural desire of the German soldiers to make the most of this opportunity to sleep for a little while in warm billets. Service and army troops, with and without orders, jammed into the city in a kind of scavenger hunt for anything usable that the Americans had left behind.

The Sixth Panzer Army, thus far unable to win enough roads for a mass movement to the west, turned its reserve formations into the roads threading into the city. The traffic jam thus created was made worse by the horde of officers and men driving American vehicles captured in the Schnee Eifel who were grimly determined to hang onto their loot. By midmorning of 22 December the flood of vehicles streaming into St. Vith was out of control. For some hours the columns could move neither forward nor back, and when Field Marshal Model arrived on the scene he was forced to dismount and make his way into the city on foot. Corps and division military police, too few in number for a traffic problem of this magnitude, were brushed aside. The volks grenadier officers who tried to restore some semblance of order found the SS officers of the army units truculent and unyielding. Divisional and corps artillery; emplaced with great effort in the woods east of the city, now had to be snaked out along the narrow, muddy, woods trails and wedged piece by piece onto the overburdened roads entering St. Vith, Even the batteries supporting the 62d Volks Grenadier Division on the south flank were brought to a standstill in the mire on the bypass through Galhausen.

To the commander of the 18th Volks Grenadier Division, whose men had taken St. Vith, the events of 22 December spelled catastrophe; to the Americans falling back from the city they were a godsend. Given this breathing spell, the Allies now faced the question of whether the tired, depleted, and divided forces trying to form a new perimeter should make a lone and desperate stand or fall back to join the XVIII Airborne Corps. This decision rested with Field Marshal Montgomery, the newly assigned commander of all Allied forces north of the German salient, who had been authorized by the Supreme Commander to give up such ground as was necessary in order to assemble sufficient strength for a decisive counterattack. During the morning of the 22d a red-tabbed British captain arrived at General Hasbrouck's headquarters, introducing himself as one of the field marshal's liaison officers. Politely he asked Hasbrouck what he thought should be done with the 7th Armored. The general answered that the division naturally would continue to defend if its present position was considered to be vital but that he personally favored withdrawal.

Hasbrouck's answer and a report on the existing state of the American forces were taken to Montgomery. Meanwhile Hasbrouck dispatched a memorandum to the XVIII Airborne Corps commander setting forth the hard facts of the case already put to the British captain.

". . . Unless assistance is promptly forthcoming I believe our present position may become serious for several reasons, namely: a. Our supplies must come in through a bottleneck over a bridge near Vielsalm. b. We may become subjected to enemy artillery fire from practically any direction. c. The road net within our position is totally inadequate to the troops and vehicles concentrated therein. The map shows many roads, but on the ground, the majority of these are mere tracks on which even a jeep bogs down if more than two or three travel on it. d. If the 2d SS Panzer Division attack should succeed in driving back the two RCTs of the 82d Airborne Division now between Salmchâteau and Hebronval even as little as 3000 yards we will be completely severed from any source of supplies.

"Since the chances of assistance in the immediate future do not seem bright, I would like to suggest that consideration be given to withdrawal of the 7th Armored and 106th Divisions to a position to the right (west) of the 82d Airborne Division where they may be of assistance in halting a possible advance north by the 2d SS Panzer.

"The withdrawal of CCB, 7th Armored Division, last night from St. Vith was expensive. So far we are missing at least one half of Clarke's force. Of course many of them will show up, but they will be minus weapons, ammunition, blankets and rations as well as at a low physical level. *I don't think we can prevent a complete breakthrough if another all-out attack comes against CCB tonight* [italics supplied] due largely to the fact that our original three infantry battalions have at present melted to the equivalent of only two very tired battalions."

It was about an hour before noon. Hasbrouck had not yet sent his message to Ridgway when word came of the German advance against the north flank of CCB, 7th Armored, in the Rodt sector. General Hasbrouck now had a postscript to add, one bringing tenseness and urgency to the precise military form and phraseology of the main text.

"P.S. A strong attack has just developed against Clarke again. He is being outflanked and is retiring west another 2,000 yards refusing both flanks. I am throwing in my last chips to halt him. Hoge has just reported an attack. In my opinion if we don't get out of here and up north of the 82d before night, we will not have a 7th Armored Division left. RWH."

This message reached Ridgway's headquarters ten minutes before noon.

Hasbrouck was not alone in this apprehensive view of things to come. Over the field telephone General Jones concurred in the opinion furnished Montgomery and Ridgway, but at 1250 Jones dispatched a memo to Ridgway saying, "My intentions are to retain the ground now defended." Without further orders the two commanders, their staffs, and subordinates set to work on plans for demolitions and a rear guard stand to keep the escape routes to the Salm open. During the afternoon the 7th Armored Division trains, whose officers and men had done a remarkable job in supporting the troops in the salient, got through one last supply column of ninety vehicles to Salmchâteau. The arrival of gasoline, rations, ammunition, and the presence of a few replacement vehicles in the division park would make the last-ditch stand or withdrawal, whichever it might be, a little easier.

In the middle of the afternoon the order came — withdraw. Montgomery had consulted with General Hodges, the First Army commander, and here showed the ability to honor the fighting man which had endeared him to the hearts of the Desert Rats in North Africa: "They can come back with all honor. They come back to the more secure positions. They put up a wonderful show." The First Army commander, tired and worried from the strain under which he had lived since 16 December, agreed to the withdrawal.

In the chain of command only General Ridgway demurred. He still hoped to counterattack and restore the line Malmédy-St. Vith. As an airborne commander thoroughly indoctrinated in the concept of isolated action by units cut off from friendly ground contact and supply he took a sanguine view of the ability of the goose-egg defenders to hold until the projected corps counterattack relieved them. This optimism, as the record shows, was not shared by the commanders in the ring itself. At 1500 a radio message from the XVIII Airborne Corps headquarters informed Hasbrouck that the "request of CG, 7 AD" for withdrawal had been approved.

With this concrete mission assigned, planning began for the extremely difficult job of disengaging from an enemy who might continue the attack at any moment. Even as a logistical exercise withdrawal presented a tricky staff problem. The roads to be used were few and in poor state, the troops and vehicles to be moved were so numerous that a thirty minute gap in a column on any one of the roads would be serious. The 7th Armored Division, CCB of the 9th Armored, the remnants of the 106th Division, and the sizable attached units all would have to make their westward exit through a 3,000-yard-wide bottleneck with only two bridges, those spanning the Salm River at Vielsalm and Salmchâteau. To achieve the tight control needed in this type of operation General Ridgway ordered General Hasbrouck to take charge of all the troops in the ring, General Jones becoming assistant to the corps commander and General Hoge being named deputy commander of the 7th Armored.

The plan for withdrawal, slowly and carefully worked out by Hasbrouck and Colonel Ryan on the evening of the 22d, envisaged a progressive siphoning from the units farthest to the east in which these troops passed gradually into the main routes leading to the bridges while rear guard forces staged holding actions in echelon along the roads and trails. Originally three routes were chosen: a northern route along the Poteau-Vielsalm road; a center route from Commanster to the Vielsalm bridge (nothing more than a poor woods road); and a southern route via Maldingen, Beho, and Bovigny, thence north along the Salm valley road to the Salmchâteau bridge and east along the Salmchâteau-La Roche road by way of the Baraque de Fraiture crossroads, which at this time was still in American hands.

General Ridgway estimated that Hasbrouck's troops would have fourteen hours of darkness in which to make their getaway. But at least four hours were consumed in drafting the plan and dispatching liaison officers, who had to memorize the general plan and the specific instructions for the unit to which they were sent. At 0030 on the 23d General Hasbrouck informed General Hoge that his combat command, which was to initiate the move west, would begin withdrawal at 0200. By this time both Hoge's and Clarke's combat commands were under attack. The two commanders consulted, agreed that Hoge could not break loose and thus expose Clarke to encirclement from the rear, and telephoned Hasbrouck at his command post in Vielsalm that the withdrawal must be delayed. Meanwhile the hours of darkness were slipping away.

The bulk of the LXVI Corps remained wedged in the streets of St. Vith or backed up along the roads funneling in from the east. But the combat echelons of the two regiments of the 62d Volks Grenadier Division which had bypassed the city on the south were in position by the night of the 22d to renew the attack. A few tanks, light armed reconnaissance troops, most of the division engineers, and considerable rifle strength struck through the dark against the eastern arc of the loosely organized American ring. At first there was no artillery forward to give weight to the assault, but densely wooded approaches and darkness gave the advantage to the attackers.

At Crombach, in the sector held by CCB, 7th Armored, the attack came in along the railroad, and the American tanks again were blinded by high velocity flares which gave the first clear shot to the enemy armor. East of the village American infantry and engineers were aided by friendly gunners, for the 434th Armored Field Artillery Battalion had received some ammunition when the trains came in and its forward observers were well posted. A protective barrage dropped in a half moon, sometimes no more than three hundred yards in front of the American foxholes, checked part of the 190th Grenadier Regiment east of Crombach. But some Germans filtered into town from the north and started hunting down the American tanks and assault guns. With little protection against the German bazooka teams a number of the fighting vehicles pulled out of danger. Colonel Wemple and other officers restored a line, but when daylight came it was hard to tell whether friend or foe really held Crombach.

The left battalion of the 190th made use of the predawn hours on the 23d to renew the push along Braunlauf Creek (on the north flank of Hoge's combat command), which had been beaten back by the American tankers early in the day. This time the enemy gained Neubrueck and held it, feeding in more troops hourly from the assembly area of Galhausen. Horse-drawn artillery succeeded in getting into position nearby and had a share in the action. The left flank of CCB, 7th Armored, folded back to the southwest. Then Hoge's center was hit, at this point by the 164th Grenadier Regiment whose troops got into Grufflange in the darkness and overran a medium tank platoon. The situation at Grufflange was so confused that neither Americans nor Germans reacted to the fight there, either to seal off the sector or to continue the penetration. Meanwhile, as dawn drew near, the left wing of the 164th moved against Thommen, where a cavalry platoon held an outpost to the south of the main CCB, 9th Armored, lines. A heavy barrage (the 62d Volks Grenadier Division by this time had a number of pieces in firing position) and a massed infantry assault drove the troopers out. When ordered back into the village the cavalrymen found it jammed with German infantry.

By daylight small hostile groups had pushed far to the west in the sectors of the two armored combat commands. Some had even climbed out of the Braunlauf valley and engaged in scattering fire against the battalion of the 424th Infantry in the reserve position at Maldingen. In general, however, the battle was waning all along the eastern arc, bringing a brief respite to the men in the foxholes, now subjected to a freezing, blasting wind after hours of fighting in snow and slush. Although no major disruption had occurred in the ring defense, the night attacks had developed cracks in the line at Crombach and in the valley of the Braunlauf which would widen under a little more pressure. Most important, the 62d Volks Grenadier Division had robbed the Americans of their chance for a night withdrawal.

At Vielsalm General Hasbrouck waited impatiently for word that the two harassed combat commands were ready to disengage. He was acutely conscious of the narrow margin of protection afforded by the 82d Airborne Division and worried lest a northward attack by the incoming 2d SS Panzer Division beat back the west flank of the 82d and close off the Salm River exits once and for all. Finally, at 0500, this message went out from the command post of the 7th Armored Division:

"The situation is such on the west of the river south of [the] 82d that if we don't join them soon the opportunity will be over. It will be necessary to disengage whether circumstances are favorable or not if we are [to] carry out any kind of withdrawal with equipment. Inform me of your situation at once particularly with regard to possibility of disengagement and execution of withdrawal."

General Hoge, whose combat command was first in the march table, was able to give a favorable answer, but all this last-minute improvisation took time. As a result, orders charging CCB, 9th Armored, to pull out at 0600 were received in Hoge's command post at 0605. About ten minutes later the withdrawal commenced, running smoothly to conclusion. One tank company was left as rear guard north of Maldingen, there blocking the approach from the German concentration area at Galhausen, but the enemy reacted slowly and the rear guard got away with the loss of only two tanks. A small cavalry detachment, Task Force Lindsey (Capt. Franklin P. Lindsey, Jr.), remained through the morning, screening the exit route at its Maldingen entrance. The first phase of the withdrawal had been auspicious. Be it noted, however, that the southern route (via Beho, Salmchâteau, and through the 82d Airborne lines at Lierneux) followed a hard-surfaced motor road, that as yet there was little traffic congestion, and that the enemy efforts prior to the withdrawal had not disorganized the command but had simply forced its left flank closer to the avenue of escape.

The southern force of CCB, 7th Armored, under Colonel Wemple, was next to go, the plan calling for a move south through Braunlauf and onto the route traveled by Hoge's columns. Wemple's task had been complicated by the events of the night, since the Germans had won partial control of Crombach and were sitting across the road in the rear of the American tanks and riflemen to the east of the village. But the assault guns which had pulled out of Crombach and gone south during the night battle now came handily into play. At 0718 Wemple sent the guns blazing into the western side of the village in an attempt by smoke and shell to drive the Germans off the streets.

The enemy grenadiers and gunners refused to stay put. When the American tanks rolled in from the east, two of the leaders were hit by antitank fire and left helplessly blocking the road. Fate took a hand to save the rest of the column. During the night a quick freeze had hardened the ground just enough to allow the tanks and half-tracks from the east, covered with clinging foot troops, to swing cross-country and south to the Braunlauf road. Even so, a number of vehicles mired and had to be abandoned at the soft banks of a small stream. At Braunlauf the column found a company of the 424th Infantry in a firefight with German infantry who had sneaked in during the night. The tankers, mindful of their passengers, could not use the tank cannon; so the column rolled through the streets with the infantry riders firing wildly in every direction. The Germans were somewhat disconcerted, but snipers accounted for two American officers. The rest of the journey behind Hoge's columns into the 82d Airborne lines was without incident. By noon most of the 424th Infantry and Wemple's force were across the Salm. Of the southern half of the original ring there remained only the rear guard and covering forces strung along the roads east of Salmchâteau.

The bulk of CCB, 7th Armored Division, represented by Task Force Lohse (formerly Erlenbusch), commanded by Maj. Leslie A. Lohse, and Task Force Boylan, started to withdraw shortly after daybreak, Boylan's command acting as the division rear guard. Maneuver by these elements of CCB was rigidly constricted by the presence of the Fuehrer Begleit armor in the north around Rodt and by the German hold on Crombach. Access to the Poteau-Vielsalm route in the north or the Beho-Salmchâteau route in the south was no longer possible. There remained a narrow, rutted trail running from Hinderhausen (around which Task Force Boylan was deployed) west through the woods to the crossroads at Commanster, from which a secondary road ran to the bridge at Vielsalm. This jeep trail—it was no more—had been reconnoitered by General Clarke on the 22d and designated (with much misgiving) as an emergency exit. The emergency had arrived, fortunately along with the sudden freeze that gave a surface hard enough to bear the weight of armored vehicles. Even so the one-way trail was a poor and precarious road to safety; a sudden thaw or one tank askew could trap both Lohse and Boylan.

While Boylan's men took positions to defend Hinderhausen against attack from Rodt, Lohse's heavy column formed to enter the trail at Hinderhausen. It consisted of four tank companies, two cavalry reconnaissance troops, a company of tank destroyers, and many foot soldiers hitchhiking on the vehicles. The move had no more than started when the Fuehrer Begleit Brigade descended on Hinderhausen. While Boylan took on the Germans, Lohse's column circled the village, then funneled slowly into the woods. One tank threw its track on the one-way stretch but obligingly coasted off the trail and into the trees. At Commanster a traffic jam started. Most of the nine field artillery battalions in the ring had been grouped in this area and their displacement—while some batteries remained to keep up fire—was a slow, painful process. General Clarke took a hand here as a kind of super traffic cop until the jam cleared. By noon Task Force Lohse and most of the artillery had crossed the river at Vielsalm.

Having cut the St. Vith-Vielsalm road by capturing Rodt in the late morning of the 22d, Remer's Fuehrer Begleit Brigade made no serious attempt to push beyond Rodt, either against CCA, 7th Armored Division, to the west or CCB to the south. Remer's heavy Panthers had made bad going of the muddy roads north of Rodt. Only a few arrived in time to take part in the battle there; for the rest of the day and far into the night the Panthers crawled into the Rodt assembly area. The Fuehrer Begleit trains could not negotiate the churned and mired trails at all. They would have to be threaded through the St. Vith bottleneck.

In the early morning of 23 December Remer gathered a truck-mounted battalion of armored infantry, put some tanks at their head, and started them for Hinderhausen, with the intention of cutting south across the rear of the Americans. About 0800 the Panthers engaged the small covering force at Hinderhausen. A brace of 90-mm. tank destroyers knocked out two of the lead tanks, temporarily halting the attack and giving Lohse's column time to reach Commanster. When the Germans finally maneuvered into position to renew the attack, the Americans broke free and fell back toward Commanster. German infantry and a few tanks pursued but were held off until the last of the CCB column had been pushed through the village and was on its way northwest to the Vielsalm bridge.

Colonel Boylan led the rear guard back toward the bridge but then was ordered, because of a traffic jam at the bridge, to hold on the east bank until the 7th Armored Division headquarters could cross. This covering force consisted of a few light tanks, a couple of tank destroyers and a few rifle squads from the 112th Infantry. The Fuehrer Begleit Brigade did not follow CCB. Remer's orders were to join the LVIII Panzer Corps west of the Salm, and his immediate design was to reach the paved road leading to Salmchâteau. The motorized rifle battalion, now led by an assault gun company, headed south toward the road center at Beho, found it free of American troops, and there joined a part of the 62d Volks Grenadier Division. The time now was midafternoon.

Task Force Lindsey, whose cavalry and infantry had screened the main withdrawal of the southern segment of the ring, had come under damaging shellfire as the 62d Volks Grenadier Division artillery got into position. About 1315 the task force fell back through Beho and proceeded west to Salmchâteau, picking up other small blocking groups as it went. Thus far events in the southern sector had gone well for the Americans. There remained the task of evacuating the blocking force which for so long had held the southernmost outposts of the St. Vith salient. This was Task Force Jones, assembling in the middle of the afternoon at Bovigny some three and a half miles south of Salmchâteau on the west side of the Salm River. To protect the valley corridor through which Task Force Jones would have to move some companies of the 112th Infantry were still left east of the river in the villages of Rogery and Cierreux.

When CCB of the 9th Armored, the 424th Infantry, and the larger part of CCB, 7th Armored, had peeled away in layers from the ring, the last two combat commands of the 7th Armored defending the Poteau-Vielsalm highway had to be drawn off. At Poteau, five miles from the river, CCA stood facing the enemy to north, east, and south. CCR maintained its cordon along the valley road. The Americans did not know that the troops of the 9th SS Panzer Division, who in past days had made raids from Recht southwest toward Poteau, were few in number and that only the day before the main body of the 9th SS Panzer Division had started on a forced march to the northwest in an attempt to break through to Kampfgruppe Peiper, now nearing the end of its tether. The German force left at Recht was no more than a screen, although under orders to maintain pressure on Poteau.

To the east of CCA, 7th Armored Division, however, some part of the 293d Regiment of the 18th Volks Grenadier Division finally had worked its way through St. Vith, arriving during the night of 22 December at Rodt. After some confusion in getting through the Fuehrer Begleit Brigade around Rodt on the morning of 23

December, the 293d continued along the road to Poteau. Again a confused command situation took its price. The infantry and assault guns in the 9th SS Panzer Division screen mistook the newcomers for a withdrawing American column and poured in heavy flanking fire. It was some hours later—and the Americans had decamped—when the 293d finally entered Poteau.

Poteau lends itself well to defensive action. It stands at the entrance to the valley road which leads to Vielsalm, and mechanized attack from either Recht or Rodt had to funnel through the narrow neck at this crossroads, vehicle maneuver off either of the two approaches being almost impossible. Away from the crossroads the ground rises sharply and is cluttered with thick stands of timber. The formation adopted by CCA was based on a semicircle of ten medium tanks fronting from northwest to east, backed by tank destroyers and with riflemen in a foxhole line well to the front. About 1035 the blocking troops left by the 9th SS Panzer Division made an attack. Tank and artillery fire stopped the Germans just as it had on previous days. Perhaps the enemy would have returned to the fray and made the final withdrawal hazardous, but shortly after noon some P-38's of the 370th Fighter Group, unable to make contact with the 82d Airborne Division control to which they were assigned, went to work for the 7th Armored Division, bombing and strafing along the road to Recht. The enemy recovery was slow.

At 1345 Hasbrouck sent the signal for CCA to pull out. In an hour the armored infantry were out of their holes and their half-tracks were clanking down the road to Vielsalm. Forty minutes later the tanks left Poteau, moving fast and exchanging shots with German tanks, while the 275th Armored Field Artillery fired a few final salvos to discourage pursuit. When the last vehicle of CCA roared over the Vielsalm bridge (at 1620) the remaining artillery followed; then came the little force from CCR which had held the road open while CCA made its withdrawal. Darkness descended over the Salm valley as CCR sped across the Vielsalm bridge.

The vacuum which had existed for some hours in the northern reaches of the one-time ring had filled rapidly in the late afternoon as the 18th Volks Grenadier Division brought its infantry out of St. Vith. Through most of the confusion and immobility characterized the St. Vith bottleneck. But the process of disentangling this mass of men and vehicles was speeded up considerably during the afternoon when the 402d and 485th Squadrons (370th Fighter Group) winged their bombs onto the city and its approaches. By dark the 293d Regiment was marching through Poteau and the rest of the infantry formations of the division were jumbled along a five-mile front on the east side of the Salm. Control, as the 18th's commander later reported, was almost nonexistent. As a result the small body of riflemen from the 112th Infantry and Boylan's tiny armored rear guard were able to see the headquarters of the 7th Armored safely across the Vielsalm bridge and to withdraw themselves through that city without much interference from the enemy closing along the river. This was sometime after 1900.

Although troops of the 18th Volks Grenadier Division or the 9th SS Panzer Division fired on Boylan as his detachment reached the river, they made no attempt to rush the bridge—a fortunate circumstance, as it turned out, for when the 82d Airborne engineers tried to blow the bridge the charge failed to explode. It was after midnight when the engineers finally reported that the charge had been replaced and successfully detonated. Even then the span was only partially wrecked and was still capable of bearing foot troops; but the German tanks milling about the burning buildings east of the river would have to find other means of crossing the Salm.

As for the last American troops extricated from the ring, Task Force Jones, it will be recalled, had assembled at Bovigny, south of Salmchâteau and on the west bank of the river, while elements of the 112th Infantry waited east of the river at Rogery and Cierreux for the withdrawal order from General Hasbrouck. The Germans driving on Salmchâteau were held in tighter control than those advancing toward Vielsalm and moved with greater speed and coordination. Around 1500 the mobile column of the Fuehrer Begleit Brigade appeared in front of Rogery. There two companies of the 1st Battalion, 112th Infantry, were deployed, guarding a draw and secondary road which provided quick access to the Salm valley at a point midway between Jones's assembly area at Bovigny and Salmchâteau. Lacking armored or other antitank means, the American infantry fell back in some confusion through the draw to Cierreux, less than a half-mile east of the river. General Hasbrouck was apprised of this new enemy threat; by what he later remembered as "one of the funniest orders I ever issued," the 7th Armored commander sent his "division reserve" — two tank destroyers — hurrying south from Vielsalm. One of the tank destroyers arrived just as a German tank platoon hove into sight at Cierreux, hit the two leaders, and drove off the five remaining tanks. During the lull that followed, a platoon of light cavalry tanks and a section of towed tank destroyers came east from the river road to give a hand.

Colonel Nelson, commanding the 112th Infantry, had sent a radio message some time around 1300 telling Hasbrouck that the withdrawal east of the river had been completed, that only the 112th covering force remained. Nelson waited for three hours for the division order to withdraw (a liaison officer with such an order had left Hasbrouck's command post at 1345). Then, with German tanks only two hundred yards from the regimental command post, lacking any communication with the 7th Armored headquarters, and out of touch with what was happening elsewhere, he gave the word to pull out of Salmchâteau. By this time Task Force Jones was moving along the Bovigny-Salmchâteau road which traversed the narrow defile cut by the Salm River. The infantry, considerably disorganized, had just crossed the river west of Cierreux and started feeding into the 2,500-yard-long column on the valley road when word passed down the line that the light tanks in the van had been hit by enemy fire as they entered Salmchâteau. Here was the column, straitjacketed on the valley floor by high ridges to either side, unable to move forward or back, and with the enemy apparently closing in from every side. But Colonel Nelson his executive officer, Col. William F. Train, and a few other officers set to work to organize a breakout.

Actually the column was blocked at Salmchâteau before the pursuing troops of the Fuehrer Begleit Brigade caught up with the tail. This bridgehead village lay in the outpost line of the 508th Parachute Infantry. Just north, the wing of the 82d Airborne defense running west to the Baraque de Fraiture crossroads (and junction with the 3d Armored Division) rested on the Salm River. In the late afternoon of the 23d the single company of the 112th Infantry at the eastern end of the Salm River bridge had been attacked by a larger force from the 62d Volks Grenadier Division. The Americans had blown the bridge and fallen back through Salmchâteau to the lines of the 82d, whereupon a few of the Germans crossed the river and entered the village. The stopper was more firmly seated in the bottleneck just at dark with the arrival of a detachment from the 2d SS Panzer Division coming in from the southwest.

While the 2d SS Panzer Division was awaiting the gasoline needed for its projected attack north along the seam between the 82d Airborne Division and the 3d Armored in the Baraque de Fraiture sector, the reinforced Reconnaissance Battalion

(Maj. Ernst Krag) had been dispatched on the 22d to cut the main road between Salmchâteau and the Baraque de Fraiture crossroads. Krag's detachment attacked straight north, driving in the American outposts in villages south of the road and dropping off small parties en route to form blocking positions covering the eastern flank of the division advance. An attack to seize the village of Joubiéval, on the main road, was launched late in the day but was repulsed by the American artillery. Krag decided to shift his advance toward Salmchâteau and there possibly link up with friendly forces he knew to be coming from St. Vith. He had available nearly three reconnaissance troops and an assault gun battalion. His accompanying battalion of self-propelled artillery was within range of Salmchâteau. A sharp attack in the late afternoon brought Krag's detachment through the American outposts in the hamlets west of Salmchâteau and by nightfall he had a troop in the south section of the town, its task made easier by the preliminary shelling laid in by the battalion of field guns. From this point on Kampfgruppe Krag fought two battles, one to mop up the town, the other to capture American vehicles trying to break out of the valley road in the south.

As the evening wore on, the leading Americans bottled up in the defile hastily organized an attack to open the exit through Salmchâteau, but there was little room to deploy, and this attempt failed. At the tail of the column disaster, in the form of the Fuehrer Begleit advance guard, suddenly struck. The light tanks and tank destroyers, earlier disposed at Cierreux, and now brought back to form the column rear guard, were spotted by German scouts and set upon in the dark by assault guns that lighted their targets with high velocity flares. Several of the American fighting vehicles were destroyed before they could return fire. To make matters worse some engineers blew a culvert, trapping the tail of the column. In sharp fighting most of the mechanized force at the tail was destroyed.

This was not to be the end. A trail had been discovered leading west out of the valley, and most of the middle of the column, led by a light tank company, escaped over it. Fortunately bright moonlight allowed some maneuver. Striking northwest and fighting off the small blocking forces left behind by Kampfgruppe Krag, the bulk of this part of the column succeeded in reaching the 82d Airborne. By midnight on the 23d over two hundred men from the column had reached the 508th Parachute Infantry and many others straggled in before daylight. How many vehicles and men were captured by the enemy is impossible to say.

There is a postscript to this story. During Task Force Jones's disengagement the 440th Armored Field Artillery had emplaced to give covering fire and protect the flank of the task force. When the 440th commenced its withdrawal word came in that the Germans had blocked the designated crossing site at Salmchâteau. Thereupon the 440th formed in column, cut loose with every available machine gun, knifed through the startled enemy, and roared over the bridge at Vielsalm.

The troops under General Hasbrouck's command who came back across the Salm River were greeted by a warm letter of commendation from the Supreme Commander and orders to return at once to the fight. It is difficult to determine with surety how much of the 7th Armored Division, CCB, 9th Armored, 424th Infantry, 112th Infantry, and the numerous attached units had been lost during the fight for St. Vith and in the subsequent withdrawal. Many records were destroyed during the final retreat, units were put back in the line on the 23d with no accounting of their existing strength, and the formations of the 106th Division and 14th Cavalry Group had taken very severe losses before the defense of St. Vith began. Casualty figures subsequently compiled for the 7th Armored Division, and the 14th Cavalry Group list 3,397 officers and men either killed, wounded, or missing, Statistics on losses suffered by the various artillery, engineer, and tank destroyer units have never been compiled. The 7th Armored Division (by fairly accurate reckoning) had lost 59 medium tanks, 29 light tanks, and 25 armored cars.

The losses sustained by the defenders of St. Vith must be measured against their accomplishments. They had met an entire German corps flushed with easy victory and halted it in its tracks. They had firmly choked one of the main enemy lines of communication and forced days of delay on the westward movement of troops, guns, tanks, and supplies belonging to two German armies. They had given the XVIII Airborne Corps badly needed time to gather for a coordinated and effective defense. Finally, these units had carried out a successful withdrawal under the most difficult conditions and would return again to the battle.

Chapter XVIII. The VII Corps Moves To Blunt the Salient

Thus far the story of the German counteroffensive has been developed on a geographical pattern generally from east to west with particular attention given the initial battles fought by the American forces attempting to hold the shoulders of the salient, the defense of St. Vith, the VIII Corps' attempt to form a barrier line across the area of penetration, and the First Army's efforts to extend the north flank alongside the expanding bulge. While these bitter defensive battles were being waged, American forces were already moving to go over to the offensive in the south for as early as 19 December General Eisenhower and his field commanders had laid plans for a major counterattack. But before this counterattack, by the Third Army, takes stage center, three important developments are unfolding: the division of the Ardennes battlefield between Field Marshal Montgomery and General Bradley, the assembly and intervention of the VII Corps in an extension of the American north shoulder, and the initial defense of the Bastogne sector.

Division of the Battlefield

Late on Tuesday evening, 19 December, Maj. Gen. Kenneth W. D. Strong, the SHAEF chief of intelligence, went to Maj. Gen. J. F. M. Whiteley, deputy chief of staff for operations at SHAEF, with a proposal which would have very audible repercussion. The German drive, said Strong, showed no sign of turning northwest toward Liège but seemed to be developing on a thrust line directly to the west. This meant, in his opinion, that the American forces north and south of the growing salient would be split by its further expansion toward the Meuse. It was his idea, therefore, that two commands should be created to replace General Bradley's 12th Army Group control of the divisive battle front, General Bradley to retain command of the troops on the southern shoulder of the salient, Field Marshal Montgomery to take those in the north under the wing of the British 21 Army Group. Strong's proposal seemed sound to Whiteley. Although both officers were British neither had broached this idea to the field marshal.

Whiteley immediately took his colleague in to see the SHAEF chief of staff, Lt. Gen. Walter Bedell Smith. General Smith, famous in the headquarters for his hair-trigger temper, first reacted negatively and with considerable heat, then cooled off and admitted the logic of the proposal. Sometime that same evening Smith telephoned Bradley. Bradley was none too sympathetic toward the idea but did concede that Montgomery would be more apt to throw British reserves into the battle under such a command arrangement. The next morning Smith brought up the matter in the Supreme Commander's usual meeting with his staff. Eisenhower in his turn telephoned Bradley, who agreed to the division of command.

The new Army Group Boundary line, now ordered by Eisenhower, would extend from Givet, on the Meuse, to St. Vith. (That both these locations would be Montgomery's responsibility was not clarified until nearly twenty-four hours later.) The reorganization placed the U.S. First and Ninth Armies under Montgomery's 21 Army Group. Bradley would command all forces to the south of the salient—which in effect meant Patton's Third Army—and eventually he might add Devers' 6th Army Group. The reorganization required a like shift in the Allied air forces, meaning that the US IX and XXIX Tactical Air Commands (Maj. Gen. Elwood R. Quesada and Maj. Gen. Richard E. Nugent) were put under the operational control of the British Second Tactical Air Force commanded by Air Chief Marshal Sir Arthur Coningham. Because the British had very strong forces of fighter-bombers, enough of these planes were taken from IX Tactical Air Command to give Brig. Gen. Otto P. Weyland's XIX Tactical Air Command, slated to support Patton's counterattack into the German bulge, ten fighter-bomber groups.

The decision to pass the US First and Ninth Armies to British command must have been hard to make, since both Eisenhower and Smith were acutely conscious of the smoldering animosity toward the British in general and Montgomery in particular which existed in the headquarters of the 12th Army Group and Third Army, not to mention the chronic anti-British sentiment which might be anticipated from some circles in Washington. This decision involved no question of Bradley's ability as a commander—that had been abundantly proven—but rather was a recognition of the communications problem presented by the German thrust between Bradley's headquarters in Luxembourg City and Hodges' headquarters, which had been moved on the 19th from Spa to Chaudfontaine.

Face-to-face discussion between Bradley and Hodges—let alone Simpson—so needful if the army group commander was to give the continuous encouragement and counsel demanded in these trying days, was already difficult. If German raiders crossed the Meuse, it might become impossible. Bradley had last visited Hodges in the early evening of the 17th by motoring directly from Paris. Further visits would involve traversing three sides of a square: west from Luxembourg across the Meuse (and perhaps as far west as Reims), north into Belgium, then east again behind the none too certain American front. Telephone and radio contact still existed; indeed, Bradley talked half a dozen times on the 18th with Hodges and General Kean, the First Army chief of staff, and at least twice on the 20th. But this was hardly a satisfactory substitute for personal presence.

The 12th Army Group had approximately fifty important wire circuits on 16 December between Luxembourg and First and Ninth Armies, these extending laterally to link the three headquarters in sequence. The mainstay and trunk line of this system was a combination open-wire and buried cable line from Aubange, near Luxembourg, via Jemelle to Namur and Liège. Jemelle was a repeater station (near Marche) and the key to the whole northern network. As it turned out the Germans subsequently cut both the wire line and cable; the signal operators, as well as a rifle platoon and a few light tanks on guard duty at Jemelle, were ordered out when the enemy was in sight of the station. Very high frequency radio stations seem to have been available throughout the battle but transmission did not carry very far and had to be relayed. These stations twice had to be moved farther west to avoid capture. Nonetheless the Signal Corps would succeed in maintaining a minimum service, except for short interruptions, by stringing wire back into France and through the various army rear areas. Whether this would have sufficed for the 12th Army Group to exercise administrative as well as tactical control of the First and Ninth Armies from Luxembourg is problematical.

A British major presented himself at the First Army headquarters about two-thirty on the morning of the 20th. Ushered up to Hodges' bedroom he told the general and Kean that Montgomery was moving 30 British Corps (Lt. Gen. B. G. Horrocks) south into the Hasselt-Louvain-St. Trond area to back up the Meuse line if needed, that four divisions were on the way and a Fifth would follow. Further, he said, the British were taking over the responsibility for the Meuse bridges at Namur, Liège, Huy, and Givet. One of Hodges' main worries could now be shouldered by somebody else. Whether there would be a sufficient force available to halt the German drive if it reached the Meuse River south of Givet was still open to question.

News of the decision to split the American forces battling in the Bulge came to the First Army later in the morning when Bradley telephoned this word. Montgomery himself arrived at Hodges' command post an hour or so after noon, commencing a series of daily visits. He promptly agreed with Hodges that the V Corps' position jamming the German northern shoulder would have to be held at any cost and concurred in the handling of the XVIII Airborne Corps as it had been deployed in the past thirty-six hours. Eisenhower's formal order placing the First and Ninth Armies under Montgomery's command stressed that the flanks of the penetration must be held but added that all available reserves should be gathered to start counterattacks in force. Montgomery's problem, then, was to cover the west flank of the First Army between the XVIII Airborne Corps and the Meuse while reforming his new command for the counterattack mission. It would appear that at this juncture the field marshal was thinking in terms of a counterattack against the western tip of the salient, for he told Hodges that he wanted the most aggressive American corps commander who could be found and sufficient troops to launch an attack from the area southwest of the XVIII Airborne.

As to the first item, the marshal made his wishes very clear: he wanted Maj. Gen. J. Lawton Collins ("Lightning Joe"), whose VII Corps had been carrying the left wing of the December Roer River offensive; nor would he listen to any other names. Where to find the divisions needed was more difficult. But Bradley already had ordered the 84th Infantry Division to leave the Ninth Army and come in on Ridgway's flank, the 75th Infantry Division had just arrived from the United States and would reach the battle zone in a few days, the 3d Armored Division might be available in the proximate future. This, then, was the line-up for the new VII Corps when Collins reported to Hodges in the early morning of the 21st. Collins got the promise of an addition to his putative force when Brig. David Belchem, 21 Army Group chief of operations, who was visiting headquarters, suggested that the 2d Armored Division be taken from the Ninth Army reserve. Collins, who considered the veteran 2d and 3d the best armored divisions in the US Army, accepted with enthusiasm. Later in the day Montgomery met with Hodges and Simpson, confirming the proposed transfer of the 2d Armored from Simpson's command.

The VII Corps Assembles

Along the Roer River front the Ninth Army was being stripped progressively of its reserves as the German threat in the south increased. After the 7th Armored and 30th Infantry Divisions had been rushed to the First Army on 17 December, the next to go would be the 84th Infantry Division (Brig. Gen. Alexander R. Bolling), taken out of the Geilenkirchen sector. Bolling received orders on the night of the 19th to make ready for relief by the 102d Infantry Division, and at noon the next day his leading regimental combat team, the 334th, was on the road to Belgium. At Chaudfontaine the First Army G-3 told Bolling to assemble the 84th in the Marche sector, but the First Army staff could furnish little accurate information as to the location of friendly or enemy troops in that area. Temporarily attached to the XVIII Airborne Corps, Bolling had no knowledge of the embryo attack plan for the VII Corps. He was alerted, however, to be ready to attack northeast or east on order.

Two hours before midnight on 20 December the leading troops of the 84th entered Marche. The remainder of the division was coming out of the line about the same time, ready to begin the seventy-five-mile move from Germany to Belgium. As it stood it would be some twenty-four hours before Bolling could be sure of having the entire division in hand. The 84th had been blooded on the West Wall fortifications in the Geilenkirchen sector and had spent a month in combat before the move south. Battalions had been rotated in the front lines and were less battle-weary than many of the troops thrown into the Ardennes, but losses had been heavy and the division was short 1,278 men.

The area in which the 84th Division (and the VII Corps) would assemble was high and rolling. There was no well-defined system of ridges but instead a series of broad plateaus separated by deep-cut valleys. Although some sections were heavily forested, in general the countryside was given over to farm and pasture land dotted with small wood lots. Concealment was possible in the narrow stream valley and the larger forests. The sector in question was bounded on the east by the Ourthe River, a natural barrier of considerable significance. At a right angle to the Ourthe another and less difficult river line composed of the Lesse and its tributary, L'Homme, ran south of Marche, through Rochefort, and into the Meuse near Dinant. Beyond Marche a plateau suffused with the upland marshes and bogs so common to the Ardennes extended as far south as St. Hubert. Marche was the central and controlling road junction for the entire area between the middle Ourthe and the Meuse. Here crossed two extremely important paved highways; that running south from Liège to Sedan; and N4, the Luxembourg City-Namur road which ran diagonally from Bastogne northwest to Namur and the Meuse with an offshoot to Dinant. Eight miles south and west of Marche the Liège-Sedan highway passed through the town of Rochefort, at which point secondary but hard-surfaced roads broke away to the west, north, and southwest. Rochefort, by road, was approximately twenty miles from Dinant and the Meuse. Marche was some twenty-eight miles from Bastogne and about the same distance from the confluence of the Sambre and Meuse at Namur. The entire area was rich in all-weather primary and secondary roads.

In the small, dark hours of 21 December while the leading regimental team of the 84th Infantry Division was outposting Marche and bedding down in the town, the advance guard of the crack 2d Panzer Division bivouacked on the west bank of the Ourthe only fifteen miles away. Neither of these future antagonists had knowledge of the other. At this point in the battle, the Fifth Panzer Army had taken the lead from the Sixth, whose hell-for-leather Peiper had run his tanks into a net on the north flank. Two armored divisions from the Fifth were driving for the gap which German reconnaissance had found open between the XVIII Airborne Corps and the VIII Corps. In the north the 116th Panzer Division had righted itself, after the countermarch ordered on the night of 19 December, and had pushed the attack over Samrée on the 20th. The order for the following day was to cross the Ourthe in the neighborhood of Hotton, just northeast of Marche, before the Americans could bring troops into the area, and thus open the road straight to the Meuse. The 116th Panzer had lost at least twenty-four hours by the counter-march on the 19th, for on that night its armored cars had been as far west as the Bastogne-Marche road. In the neighboring corps to the south, the 2d Panzer Division finally had taken Noville on the 20th and been ordered to head for Namur, disregarding the fight which had flared up from Bastogne. When its reconnaissance battalion seized the Ourthe bridge at Ortheuville, shortly after midnight, the road to Marche and Namur opened invitingly. Luettwitz, the XLVII Panzer Corps commander, ordered Lauchert to disengage the 2d Panzer Division north of Bastogne and speed for the Meuse.

Here, then, were two armored divisions from two different corps striking out for the Meuse, one in the possession of a crossing on the Ourthe, one expecting to seize a crossing in only a few hours, but both divisions with their flanks uncovered and both uncomfortably aware of the fact. Nonetheless the two corps commanders expected to thicken their armored thrusts within twenty-four hours: Luettwitz was trying to shake the Panzer Lehr loose south of Bastogne; Krueger had been promised that the 2d SS Panzer Division was on its way to the LVIII Panzer Corps. During the 21st, however, the Fifth Panzer Army's advance would be carried only by forward patrols of the 2d Panzer Division and the 116th, the two spearhead formations separated by the Ourthe River and, in ensuing days, fighting distinctly separate battles.

The commander of the 84th Infantry Division set up his command post in Marche on the late afternoon of 21 December under order to assemble his division in this area. The enemy, so far as he knew, was some miles away. The only friendly troops he found in the neighborhood were those of the 51st Engineer Combat Battalion, whose command post was located in Marche. This battalion was part of the small engineer force which the VIII Corps had gathered to construct the barrier line along the Ourthe River. The engineer commander, Colonel Fraser, spread out his two companies at roadblocks and demolition sites all the way from Hotton, on the river, to a point just south of the Champlon crossroads on the Bastogne-Marche highway. This latter roadblock was only three miles north of the Ortheuville bridge, which the 2d Panzer advance guard wrested from the detachment of the 158th Engineer Combat Battalion during the night of 20 December.

A few German patrols probed at the roadblock before dawn but no attempt was made to break through. The German reconnaissance troops bedded down in Tenneville, and batteries of the division flak rolled into position to guard the new bridgehead. For some hours this was all. Lauchert's tanks were waiting for gasoline and literally could not move. Although the 2d Panzer had captured enough American trucks, jeeps, and half-tracks to motorize both of its bicycle battalions, the grenadiers would have to start the march west on foot for the same reason. Furthermore, fatigue had begun to tell; the 2d Panzer troops had been marching and fighting almost without respite since 16 December. Some of the human grit was beginning to slow the wheels of the military machine. But why Lauchert, a ruthless and driving commander, did not prod his reconnaissance and flak forward on the morning of the 21st can only be surmised.

The first word of an attacking enemy reached the 84th Division command post in Marche at 0900, but the attack was being made at Hotton, to the northeast, where the 116th Panzer Division had thrown in an assault detachment to seize the Ourthe Bridge. General Bolling ordered his single RCT, the 334th under Lt. Col. Charles E. Hoy, to establish a perimeter defense around Marche. Meanwhile the 51st Engineer Combat Battalion asked for help in the Hotton fight. But when troops of the 334th reached the scene in midafternoon, the embattled engineers, aided by a few men from the 3d Armored Division, had halted the enemy and saved the bridge—a feat of arms subsequently acknowledged by the German corps and army commanders.

About noon Bolling received word from the XVIII Airborne Corps that the 334th was to hold the enemy south of the Hotton-Marche line, both these villages to be the responsibility of his division. A few minutes later a corps message arrived saying that fifteen German tanks and an infantry company had been reported five miles southeast of Marche in the hamlet of Bande and that they were heading west. By this time General Bolling had a more precise statement of his mission, for he had telephoned army headquarters about eleven o'clock to report the enemy blow at Hotton and to ask whether his single RCT should be committed to battle on the Marche-Hotton line. The answer was "Yes, hold." The question posed by the commander of the 84th had been much in the minds of Hodges and Collins that morning. With the German armored spearheads breaking out toward the west, the risk entailed in assembling the VII Corps piecemeal as far forward as Marche was very real, and the American commanders considered that perhaps the corps concentration should be made farther back to the north. But with the order given Bolling the die was cast.

There remained the question of how best to bring in the rest of the 84th and the bulk of the corps. Collins asked for CCR of the 5th Armored Division, which was at Rötgen under V Corps, to be detailed to help the 3d Armored hold N4, the road from Namur. V Corps, however, still was hard beset and Hodges would not at this moment cut into its reserve. The commander of the 84th, who did not know that a 3d Armored picket still held Hotton, ordered the rest of his division to come in on a road farther to the west. By midnight of the 21st he had his entire division and the attached 771st Tank Battalion assembled and in process of deploying on a line of defense. About dark, as the second RCT detrucked, Bolling relieved the 334th of its close-in defense of Marche and moved the 2d and 3d Battalions out to form the left flank of the division, this anchored at Hotton where troops of the 3d Armored finally had been met. The 335th (Col. Hugh C. Parker) deployed to the right of the 334th with its right flank on N4 and its line circling south and east through Jamodenne and Waha. The 333d (Col. Timothy A. Pedley, Jr.), last to arrive, assembled north of Marche in the villages of Baillonville and Moressée ready to act as cover for the open right flank of the division and army—or as the division reserve.

During the night the regiments pushed out a combat outpost line, digging in on the frozen ground some thousand yards forward of the main position, which extended from Hogne on Highway N4 through Marloie and along the pine-crested ridges southwest of Hampteau. The division now was in position forward of the Hotton-Marche road and that vital link appeared secure. Earlier in the day the 51st Engineer roadblocks on the Marche-Bastogne highway had held long enough to allow the 7th Armored trains to escape from La Roche and reach Marche, but at 1930 the tiny engineer detachments were given orders to blow their demolition charges and fall back to Marche, leaving the road to Bastogne in German hands.

The main task confronting the 84th Division as day dawned on the 22d was to determine the location of the enemy. All through the day armored cars, light tanks, and infantry in jeeps and trucks probed cautiously along highways and byways east, south, and west. Some of these vehicles were shot up and the men came back on foot; others engaged in brief duels with unseen foes hidden in villages and wood lots. No German prisoners were taken, but it was clear that the enemy also was feeling his way. At noon an order from the XVIII Airborne Corps instructed Bolling to block all roads east, southeast, and south of Rochefort (seven and one-half miles from Marche) until the 3d Armored could extend its flank to this area. A rifle company was loaded into trucks and reached Rochefort in the late afternoon without trouble.

Shortly after issuing this order Ridgway extended the mission of the 84th. Earlier General Collins had visited the First Army to express his concern that the enemy might crowd in south and west of Marche, thus interdicting the planned VII Corps concentration. Ridgway's order therefore called for the 84th to extend a counter-reconnaissance screen along the line Harsin-Grupont-Wellin, some ten miles south of Marche, at the same time sending security forces southwest to hold the vital crossroad villages at Rochefort, Wanlin, and Beauraing, the latter nearly twenty miles from the division command post at Marche. It will be recalled, as well, that Ridgway had ordered the newly arrived CCA of the 3d Armored Division to throw out a screen on the west bank of the Ourthe between La Roche and St. Hubert as further protection for the VII Corps assembly. At noon a task force from CCA was on its way but by dark had progressed only a short distance south of Marche. There it halted on word that the 335th Infantry might need help against tanks seen moving north toward Marche. Part of the task force became involved with enemy armored vehicles near Hargimont and in a short, sharp fight accounted for five of them.

Bolling could free two rifle battalions and the necessary motors for what he regarded as the first-priority tasks. Early in the evening the two battalion task forces, augmented with tanks and tank destroyers, started out. The 1st Battalion of the 333d (Lt. Col. Norman D. Carnes) had orders to secure Wanlin and bar the Neufchâteau road to Dinant on the Meuse; the 3d Battalion of the 335th (Maj. Gordon A. Bahe) was to hold Rochefort and cover the road thence to Marche with detachments at Harsin, Hargimont, and Jemelle, the important repeater station. The task force from the 333d tried the Rochefort road to Wanlin but ran into the enemy near Marloie and had to detour back through Marche and roundabout through Haversin, reaching Wanlin at daybreak. The battalion of the 335th bumped into Germans at the same spot, left an infantry company to engage the enemy, then swung back through Marche and Humain, arriving at Rochefort in the early morning to find its own I Company in the town and no sign of the Germans.

Although the enemy obviously was in front of the 84th Infantry Division in some strength and had shown signs of increasing his forces during the 22d, the assembly of the VII Corps was moving rapidly. Having turned over his old sector at Düren and its divisions to the XIX Corps, General Collins and some of the corps troops moved during the day into the new VII Corps area southwest of Liège. Of the divisions promised Collins the 84th was in the line, the "Hell on Wheels" 2d Armored Division closed to the rear in the area before midnight, as did the new 75th Infantry Division. The 3d Armored, of course, was still bitterly engaged as the right wing of the neighboring XVIII Airborne Corps. General Collins and his staff could feel at home in this new sector, for the VII Corps had driven the German forces out of the area during the first two weeks of September. Furthermore Collins had visited Bolling's command post and was convinced that the 84th had matters well in hand.

The First Army commander's deep concern for his open western flank—a concern shared by Collins—was very considerably relieved on the 22d when Field Marshal Montgomery arrived at his headquarters with the welcome news that the British 29th Armored Brigade, equipped with fifty tanks, had taken over the defense of the Namur, Dinant, and Givet bridges, and would move on the morrow to reconnoiter the west flank of the VII Corps assembly area. Because another twenty-four hours would be needed to deploy Collins' divisions and get the corps artillery into position, Montgomery and Hodges agreed that the VII Corps counterattack on which so much depended would commence on Sunday, the 24th. The new corps front (officially assumed by the VII Corps at 1630 on 23 December) would reach from the Ourthe River on the left to the junction of the Lesse and Meuse on the right, approximately fifty miles. The 2d Armored Division (Maj. Gen. Ernest N. Harmon) was intended to flesh out the right wing of the corps when the attack began, the 84th already held the center, and the 3d Armored Division was expected to fight its way farther south and become the left wing. Since the 75th Infantry Division was as yet untried, it was to be kept in reserve.

The 2d Armored Division had small patrols scouting to the west of Marche on the 23d, but the bulk of the division assembled in three combat commands well to the north of Marche astride the main road to Huy. Its 70-mile road march (some units moved nearly a hundred miles) had been completed in twenty-two hours despite a cold rain, hazardous roads, and the delay normal to armored movement in column at night. All told the division had suffered some thirty damaged vehicles in traffic mishaps, including eight tanks. (Later one officer wryly remarked, "We lost more vehicles on the march down here than in the subsequent fighting.")

The 2d Armored assembly had been handled with all possible secrecy and the entire division was under radio blackout, for Collins counted heavily on the combination of surprise and shock in the forthcoming counterattack. Events, however, were racing on to shatter the hope that the VII Corps would be allowed to mount a planned and co-ordinated assault. Harmon was conferring with his commanders an hour or so before noon on the 23d, when a message arrived that one of the armored cars out on patrol had been shot up at a little hamlet near Ciney, which was a critical road center northwest of Marche from which main highways debouched for Dinant and Namur. Without waiting for orders, Harmon dispatched CCA (Brig. Gen. John Collier) to rush full speed for Ciney and cut off any German tanks found there. This proved to be a false alarm; British armored patrols were in the town and there was no sign of the enemy.

By now, however, reports of large enemy forces moving toward Ciney were pouring into the corps and division command posts. There was no longer any point in trying to hide the identity of the 2d Armored and it appeared certain that battle would have to be given without regard to the planned corps counterattack. Harmon started his whole division moving into line west of the 84th, displaced the 14th and 92d Field Artillery Battalions to support CCA, and ordered Collier to continue south on the Ciney-Rochefort road to seize Buissonville, where twenty heavy German tanks had been reported. CCA clanked through the darkness, led by a task force composed of the 2d Battalion, 66th Armored Regiment, and the 2d Battalion, 41st Armored Infantry Regiment. About 2100 the combat command became involved in a scrambling skirmish with some Germans who had dismounted from half-tracks in the village of Leignon, wheeled a few small guns into position covering the road, and were now able to halt the Americans for some little time. By midnight Collier's advance guard of armored infantry was again on the move but this time with a more ambitious mission. The sortie toward Ciney had become a full-scale attack to aid the hard-pressed 84th Infantry Division and relieve those of its units cut off in Buissonville and Rochefort.

German Armor Advances on the VII Corps

When the advance guards of the 2d Panzer Division seized the bridge over the southern arm of the Ourthe at Ortheuville on the 21st, they stood only sixteen miles by road from Marche and less than forty from Dinant and the Meuse. It is difficult to determine whether the 2d Panzer Division and Manteuffel's Fifth Panzer Army were abreast of the German attack schedule or behind it. Certainly Manteuffel was two or three days behind the optimistic predictions generated in Hitler's headquarters, but on the other hand few of the lower field commands had committed themselves to any fixed march calendar. As of the 21st there is no evidence in the German accounts of any pressing concern about the rate at which the Fifth Panzer Army attack was proceeding. After all, Sepp Dietrich's much-touted Sixth Panzer Army had bogged down, the Fifth was well out in front, and German intelligence saw no viable American forces barring the door to the Meuse that had opened between Bastogne and the main valley of the Ourthe.

Manteuffel still had a few problems to solve before he could make the final sprint for the Meuse River in force. Fuel deliveries for his tanks were flagging, his divisions had been fighting day and night since 16 December, a part of his left armored corps was hung up at Bastogne, and his armored corps on the right had been forced to retrace its steps with some appreciable loss in time. Manteuffel's first order, sent to the commander of the XLVII Panzer Corps, was to get the Panzer Lehr out of the Bastogne battle. With the 2d Panzer Division, now free of involvement in the army center, and with the Panzer Lehr and the 116th Panzer Divisions coming up on the left and right, respectively, Manteuffel would have the armor needed for a full-blooded blow northwest to the Meuse, and Dinant. The day of the 22d passed, however, with little activity on the part of the 2d Panzer and with little more than regrouping by Panzer Lehr, which finally had to start the march with part of the division still engaged in the fight for Bastogne.

By the morning of the 23d these two divisions were on the move, but their component parts were widely spaced and strung out over long miles of road. The German troops who hit the 84th Division outposts and patrols during the daylight hours and whose appearance west of Marche brought the 2d Armored Division precipitately into action constituted little more than a screen for the main body of the XLVII Panzer Corps. By the late afternoon, however, the advance guards of the 2d Panzer and Panzer Lehr had come up to the forward screen and were ready for attack. So far only the 84th Division had been identified as being in the way. The 2d Panzer Division, its first objective Marche, had the shortest road to follow but was delayed for several hours by the demolitions at the crossroads west of Champlon touched off by the detachment of the 51st Engineers. Not until early afternoon did the leading battalion of the 304th Panzer Grenadier Regiment overrun the 4th Cavalry Group outpost at Harsin, and it was dark when this battalion fought its way into Hargimont, there severing the road from Marche to Rochefort.

Inexplicably the forward momentum of the 2d Panzer main column ceased early in the evening. When Luettwitz, the corps commander, hurried into Hargimont, he found that the attack had been halted for the night because American tanks were reported north of the village. Stopping briefly to tongue-lash and relieve the colonel in command, Luettwitz put in a fresh assault detachment which pushed west as far as Buissonville and there bivouacked. The appearance of this force was responsible for the reports reaching American headquarters shortly before midnight that Company E of the 333d had been trapped in Buissonville.

Chief protagonist of the advance on the VII Corps thus far chronicled has been the main column of the 2d Panzer Division, which on the night of 23 December had its head at Buissonville and its body snarled in a long traffic jam on the single road through Hargimont, Harsin, and Bande. But German armored cars, tanks, and motorized infantry detachments had been encountered west and southwest of Marche all during the day. These troops belonged to the 2d Panzer reconnaissance battalion that during the night was attempting to reassemble as a homogeneous striking force west of Buissonville astride the road to Dinant. It was the point of this battalion which Collier's armored infantry encountered at Leignon.

Under the new orders to attack toward Rochefort, CCA had driven a few miles south of Leignon when Capt. George E. Bonney, riding at the head of the column in a jeep, heard the sound of motors on the road ahead. Bonney whirled his jeep and rode back along the column of American halftracks, passing the word to pull off the road and let the approaching vehicles through. When the small German column was securely impounded, the Americans cut loose with the .30-caliber machine guns on the halftracks, killing thirty of the enemy and capturing a like number. Bonney had his leg almost cut off by slugs from one of his own tanks farther back in the column. Since the night was far spent, the enemy strength and location were uncertain, and his command had few if any detailed maps, Collier ordered the CCA task forces to reorganize and to laager until dawn. The leading task force by this time was near the village of Haid, eight miles from Rochefort.

On the day before (23 December), the Panzer Lehr had been brought forward on the left wing of the 2d Panzer Division, General Manteuffel himself leading the march from St. Hubert. The immediate objective was the road center at Rochefort, for this town, like Marche, had to be secure in German hands if a major assault with all its impedimenta was to be launched on the roads leading to Dinant. German gunners had shelled the town in the late afternoon without any return fire, and just at dark, scouts came back from Rochefort to report that the town was empty. Apparently the scouts had not entered Rochefort. If they had, they would have learned that the 84th Division had built up a garrison there during the past twenty-four hours. In fact the Rochefort defense under Major Bahe consisted of the 3d Battalion (minus Company L) of the 335th; a platoon each from the 638th Tank Destroyer Battalion, 309th Engineer Combat Battalion, and 29th Infantry; plus two platoons of the regimental antitank company.

The approach to Rochefort by the St. Hubert road lay along a narrow defile between two hills. Perhaps General Bayerlein's military intuition told him that the town was defended and that the ground and the darkness presented some hazard, for he gave the order, "*Also los, Augen zu, und hinein!*" ("OK, let's go! Shut your eyes and go in!") The leading battalion of the 902d rushed forward, only to be hit by cross fire from the hills and stopped cold by a formidable barricade on the road. The Germans took heavy casualties. Bayerlein then set to work in systematic fashion to take

Rochefort. He brought forward his guns to pound the hills and the town, and edged his troops in close as the night lengthened. He did not forget his main task, however, and sent a part of the 902d around Rochefort to find a way across L'Homme River, which looped the town on the north. These troops found one bridge intact, giving the Panzer Lehr access to the Dinant road.

During the night Manteuffel and Luettwitz discussed the plan to seize Dinant. They altered the axis of the 2d Panzer attack to conform with the actual tactical situation, struck Marche from the operations map as an immediate goal, and instructed Lauchert's armor to bypass it on the southwest. Rochefort, it appeared, would have to be taken, but it was intended that the Panzer Lehr would reinforce its bridgehead force promptly and get the attack rolling toward Dinant while battering down the Rochefort defense. Luettwitz, a bold and experienced corps commander, was anxious to push on for the Meuse but worried about his flanks. Marche was an obvious sally port through which the Americans could pour onto the exposed flank of the 2d Panzer Division unless something was done to cut the road north of the town and thus interdict reinforcement. This task had been assigned the 116th Panzer Division, whose main strength was still separated from Luettwitz' divisions by the Ourthe River. Promising that the 116th would come forward to cover the 2d Panzer flank, Manteuffel set out by automobile to give the 116th a little ginger.

The army group commander, Model, had said that the 9th Panzer Division would support the 2d Panzer on 24 December, but neither Manteuffel nor Luettwitz seems to have counted on its appearance. While commanding the 2d Panzer Division in Normandy Luettwitz had learned the hard way about the reliability of flank protection promised by others. He had already begun to strip troops from both of his forward divisions for deployment on the shoulders of the thrust being readied for Dinant. The Panzer Lehr had most of one regiment (the 903d), as well as its antiaircraft and engineer battalions, strung all the way from Moircy (west of Bastogne) to the area southwest of Rochefort as cover on the left for the division attack corridor. Bayerlein had been forced to leave one regiment in the Bastogne battle; so his effective assault force on the 24th consisted of the division reconnaissance battalion, some corps and division artillery, and one reinforced regiment. All of the 2d Panzer Division was available to Lauchert, but the kampfgruppen of the division were widely separated and for every mile forward troops would have to be dropped off to cover the division north flank.

When daylight came on the 24th, the head of the leading kampfgruppe had advanced well to the northwest of the Marche-Rochefort road in considerable strength. In this kampfgruppe were the reconnaissance battalion, one battalion of Panthers from the 3d Panzer Regiment, the 304th Panzer Grenadier Regiment, two artillery regiments, a battalion of heavy guns, and two-thirds of the division flak, the whole extending for miles. The remainder of the 2d Panzer remained on the Harsin road southeast of Marche under orders from Luettwitz to protect the corps right shoulder.

The Main Battle Is Joined 24 and 25 December
Pitched battles and fumbling skirmishes flared up all along the VII Corps front on 24 December. But the VII Corps front was not a homogeneous line, and the German drive was not conducted by division columns whose units were contiguous to each other and flanked by overwatching screening forces on parallel roads. The opposing commanders by this time did have a fairly accurate idea of what formations

were on "the enemy side of the hill," but neither Americans nor Germans were too certain as to where these formations would be encountered. The hottest points of combat on the 24th were Rochefort, Buissonville, and the Bourdon sector east of the Hotton-Marche road.

At Rochefort the Panzer Lehr commander began his main attack a couple of hours after midnight, but the defenders held and made a battle of it in houses and behind garden walls. Companies I and K of the 333d concentrated in and around a large hotel, dug in a brace of 57-mm. antitank guns and a section of heavy machine guns in front of the hotel, and so interdicted the town square. About 0900 on the 24th the 3d Battalion lost radio contact with the division, but four hours later one message did reach Marche: an order from General Bolling to withdraw. By this time a tree burst from a German 88 had put the antitank guns out of action. To disengage from this house-to-house combat would not be easy. Fortunately the attackers had their eyes fixed on the market place in the center of the town, apparently with the object of seizing the crossways there so that armored vehicles could move through from one edge of the town to the other. So preoccupied, they neglected to bar all the exits from Rochefort. Driven back into a small area around the battalion command post where bullet and mortar fire made the streets "a living inferno," the surrounded garrison made ready for a break. Enough vehicles had escaped damage to mount the battalion headquarters and Company M. The rest of the force formed for march on foot.

At 1800 the two groups made a concerted dash from the town, firing wildly as they went and hurling smoke grenades, which masked them, momentarily, from a German tank lurking nearby. Sgt. J. W. Waldron manned a machine gun as a line rear guard, was wounded, but rejoined his company. (He received the DSC.) The vehicular column headed west for Givet, and it is indicative of the widely dispersed and fragmented nature of the German forces on this day that the American column reached the Meuse without being ambushed. The foot column, led by Lt. Leonard R. Carpenter, started north with the idea of reaching the outposts of the 3d Armored task force known to be thereabouts, but here the spoor of the enemy was very strong and movement was slow. During the night some trucks were sent east from Givet and found parts of Companies I and K; two officers and thirty-three men belonging to Company I were picked up in an exhausted state by 2d Armored patrols and brought back to the American lines.

The defense of Rochefort had not been too costly: fifteen wounded men, under the care of a volunteer medic, were left in the town and another twenty-five had been killed or captured. But the Panzer Lehr commander, who had fought in both engagements, would later rate the American defense in Rochefort as comparable in courage and in significance to that at Bastogne. Significantly, the Panzer Lehr Reconnaissance Battalion carried the attack for the Meuse without any help from the rest of the division until after midnight, when the 902d finally reached the Buissonville area.

Buissonville had been the primary objective of the 2d Armored Division when Harmon first propelled his CCA into action. True, Rochefort was the goal when CCA resumed its march on the morning of the 24th, but Buissonville first had to be brought under American control. A glance at the map will show the reason why.

The village lay in a valley where the Dinant-Rochefort highway dipped down, but in addition it controlled the entry to that highway of a secondary road net running west from the Marche-Rochefort road. The hamlet of Humain, four miles to the east, was the nodal point of this secondary system.

During the night the Humain-Buissonville road had been jammed with German columns from the 2d Panzer reconnaissance battalion and advance guard. But now the wealth of good, hard-surfaced roads which characterize this part of Belgium came into play. Entering the main highway at Buissonville, the German units had gone north for about a mile, then made a V-turn back onto a secondary road running straight west to Conjoux, a village four miles south of Ciney. The Belgian telephone operator at Conjoux attempted to get word of this movement to the Americans, but the message had to pass surreptitiously through a number of hands and did not reach the 2d Armored command post until the afternoon of the 24th. The CCA sortie from Ciney, as a result, was being made obliquely to the German axis of advance and would intersect the enemy line of march at Buissonville only after the leading kampfgruppe of the 2d Panzer had passed on to the west.

This is not to say that Collier's task forces encountered no opposition when CCA resumed the attack on the morning of the 24th. Flank guard and blocking detachments backed by tanks had been left to screen the 2d Panzer line of communications on the north and these had to be disposed of. Furthermore, CCA had to proceed with some caution, feeling out to the flanks as it went; indeed General Harmon added a reconnaissance company to Collier's command because "the situation is changing all the time." The leading American task force reached Buissonville in early afternoon and formed for an assault to encircle the village from the north. By chance the second task force, advancing in echelon on the right flank, had run into antitank fire and, in process of maneuvering onto a ridge overlooking the German guns, saw its sister detachment moving into the attack. An enemy column, coming in from Havrenne, appeared about the same time on the opposite side of the village.

While the American attack swept through and round Buissonville, the tank and tank destroyer crews on the ridge opened fire, laying their guns at four thousand yards, and directing the salvos crashing in from the field batteries supporting CCA. The final tally was 38 wheeled vehicles, 4 antitank guns, 6 pieces of medium artillery, 108 prisoners, and a large but uncounted number of German dead. After this action a squadron of P-38's strafed the village, probably on a mission which had been called for before the assault, killing one American officer and wounding another before the airplanes could be diverted.

With Buissonville in hand, Harmon ordered Col. John MacDonald, whose 4th Cavalry Group had just been attached to the 2d Armored, to take Humain and thus put a stopper in the narrow channel between his division and the 84th which led to the west and the rear of the Marche position. MacDonald had only the 24th Squadron—his 4th Squadron was deploying in the west as a screen between CCA and CCB—and in the early evening he sent Troop A into Humain. The troopers experienced little opposition. Mines and booby traps were their greatest hazard, and by midnight they had full control of the village.

All through the day messages had come into the 2d Armored Division headquarters telling of German tanks in increasing numbers in and around Celles, a main crossroads village southwest of Ciney and only four miles from the Meuse River. During the morning the British light armored cavalry patrolling this area had been forced back toward Dinant. At midday two P-51's flew over to take a look at Celles but got an exceedingly warm reception from flak batteries there and were driven off. Further evidence of a large German concentration came in the afternoon when the Belgian report of enemy columns in Conjoux finally reached the Americans.

Harmon had not waited for confirmation of the early British reports, the right and rear of CCA being too exposed for that. At 1045 he ordered CCB (Brig. Gen. Isaac D. White) to secure Ciney — at the moment occupied by some of Collier's troops — "as a base for future operations." At the same time the division artillery commander, Colonel Hutton, sent two battalions of armored artillery into firing positions north of Ciney. (Throughout the day artillery support for both the 2d Armored and the 84th had been rendered under difficult circumstances. The location of friendly units was none too certain and a number of the advanced outpost positions along the VII Corps front were beyond the range of their own guns.)

The eastern flank of the VII Corps was the third area of hot combat on the 24th. On the previous night the 116th Panzer Division finally had begun to build up a bridgehead on the west bank of the Ourthe. Perhaps Manteuffel's visit had had some effect, or, more likely, the 116th had more troops for the attack now that reinforcements were arriving to take on the Americans in the Soy-Hotton sector. The mission set for General Waldenburg's division was of critical importance to the Fifth Panzer Army attack. First, the 116th Panzer was to break through the American position forward of the Hotton-Marche road. Then, having cleaned out Marche in the process, the division was to swing north onto the Baillonville road, which offered good tank going, drive west through Pessoux, and make contact with the 2d Panzer Division in the neighborhood of Ciney. At that point the two divisions would provide reciprocal protection for their inner flanks. Waldenburg was low on fuel for his tanks but attempted to set the ball rolling by sending two rifle companies through the dark to infiltrate the American lines at the junction point of the 334th and 335th Regiments. The tactic — penetration along boundary lines — was a German favorite, attended by success in the initial days of the offensive. The two companies (dismounted troops of the division reconnaissance battalion) stealthily worked their way forward and at dawn were to the rear of the 334th. There they sought cover on a wooded ridge north of Verdenne. This village, outposted by the Americans, was the immediate goal of the attack planned for the 24th. Commanding the Marche-Hampteau road — roughly the line held by the left wing of the 84th Division — it afforded immediate access via a good secondary route to Bourdon on the main Hotton-Marche highway, and its possession would offer a springboard for the German armored thrust.

The 116th Panzer Division did not attack with daylight, for its fuel trucks had not yet appeared. Instead Waldenburg sent detachments of the 60th Regiment into the Bois de Chardonne, the western extrusion of a large wood lot partially held by the Germans southwest of Verdenne. Unusual movement in the Bois was noticed by the Americans during the morning, but this came into really serious light about noon when a prisoner revealed the presence of the two companies behind the 334th. General Bolling gathered the 1st Battalion, 334th, and three tank platoons of the 771st Tank Battalion to trap the infiltrators. It appears that his opponent, General Waldenburg, had postponed the German attack for an hour or so but that this order did not reach the two forward companies. When the American tanks suddenly appeared on the wooded ridge north of Verdenne, they ran head on into the enemy just assembling at the wood's edge in assault formation. The Germans broke and fled, some fifty were captured, and the woods were cleared.

But this was only the first act. An hour later five enemy tanks and two half-tracks carrying or covering a hundred or so grenadiers struck Verdenne from the south, engaged the second platoon of Company I in what Waldenburg later called "a bitter house-to-house battle," finally overwhelmed the Americans, and pushed on to a château a stone's throw north of the village. In a last assault at eventide the attackers drove this wedge deeper. Companies I and K of the 334th fell back to a new line barely in front of the crucial Marche-Hotton road, and German light artillery moved up to bring the road under fire.

Christmas Eve in the far western sector of the Ardennes Bulge found various shadings of uneasiness in the American headquarters and a pall of foreboding, silver-lined by the proximity of the Meuse, in the German. The attack planned for the VII Corps had turned into a defensive battle. On the east wing the 3d Armored (CCB) was hard pressed and some of its troops were surrounded—indeed two regiments of the 75th Infantry Division were en route to help General Rose. The 84th Division, so far as then was known, had lost a battalion in Rochefort, might be driven out of Marche, and stood exposed to an armored exploitation of the penetration made at Verdenne. The 2d Armored Division had had a good day but was not yet securely linked to the 84th on the left and could only surmise what tank strength the Germans had accumulated opposite CCB on the right.

Field Marshal Montgomery, chipper as always but cautious, had taken steps during the day to bring the 1st Division (British) across the Meuse and into backstop position behind the First Army in the sector southeast of Liège. Other British troops were on the move to assist the 29th Armoured Brigade (British) if the enemy should hit the bridges at Givet or Namur. This was good news to the First Army commander and his staff, not to mention that some elation was abroad as the result of Allied air force activity on this clear day and the reports of prisoners and booty taken from the 1st SS Panzer Division at La Gleize.

The gloomy side of the picture was all too readily apparent. The fall of St. Vith had opened the way for fresh forces and new pressure against the army center and right. The 82d Airborne Division was exposed to entrapment in the Manhay sector and in the course of the evening Hodges would order a withdrawal. The situation as it appeared in the VII Corps on the army right wing was, as just described, somewhat of a cliffhanger. On the left wing, in the V Corps sector, the enemy appeared ready to resume strong offensive operations, and after their Christmas Eve supper Hodges and Huebner sat down to plan the evacuation of the corps' heavy equipment in order to leave the roads free in the event that withdrawal to the north became mandatory.

In the higher echelons of German command the attitude on Der Heilige Abend became more somber as the distance between the particular headquarters and the 2d Panzer position at the tip of the Bulge diminished. Rundstedt seems to have become reconciled, with the fatalism and aloofness of the aged and veteran soldier, to whatever the fortunes of war now might bring. Model, the commander of Army Group B, was outwardly optimistic; his order for Christmas Day called for the passage of the Meuse and the capture of Bastogne. This official mien of optimism contrasts sharply with the attitude his personal staff had noted on 18 December when, it since has been reported, he phoned Rundstedt and Jodl to say that the offensive had failed. Perhaps he saw in the events of 24 December the possibility that the Meuse at least might be reached and some degree of tactical success east of the river be attained, thus confirming his earlier opposition to the Big Solution dictated by Hitler and Jodl. Manteuffel, as Fifth Panzer Army commander, was the man in the middle. He was well aware of the exposed and precarious position of the 2d Panzer Division. He had traveled the forward roads at the tip of the salient, and his practiced eye recognized that the narrow corridor to the Meuse must be widened if the last stage of the drive to the river was to be logistically supported. Doubtless he recognized the tactical merit of Luettwitz' suggestion, probably made late in the afternoon of the 24th, that the forward columns of the XLVII Panzer Corps should be withdrawn from their position of dangerous isolation until such time as reinforcements arrived. On the other hand Manteuffel was well aware of the Fuehrer's attitude toward surrendering ground and could not possibly acquiesce in Luettwitz' proposal. During the evening Manteuffel telephoned Jodl with a personal and desperate plea for assistance: he argued that his army, not the Sixth, was carrying the main effort of the offensive and that the divisions in the OKW reserve earmarked for Sepp Dietrich should be released at once to reinforce the attack to the Meuse. It would appear that Jodl spoke reassuringly of divisions en route to the Fifth Panzer Army, but this must have brought very cold comfort to Manteuffel.

Chapter XIX. The Battle of Bastogne

The Initial Deployment East of Bastogne

The one standing order that General Middleton gave General McAuliffe before leaving Bastogne on the morning of 19 December was: "Hold Bastogne." Both generals felt that the enemy needed Bastogne and the entrance it afforded to a wider complex of roads leading west. During the night of the 18th the two commanders met in the VIII Corps command post to confer on the uncertain tactical situation and to give Colonel Ewell, whose regiment would first be committed, his instructions. The map spread out before Ewell showed a few blue-penciled marks east of Bastogne where the American armored groups were believed to be fighting at their original roadblock positions. General Middleton told Ewell that his job would be to make contact with these endangered forward posts. Ewell, however, was interested in the red-penciled lines and circles which showed the enemy between Bastogne and the armored roadblocks. In view of the uncertain situation, he suggested that he be given "mission-type orders" which would permit his 501st Parachute Infantry some flexibility of action. McAuliffe agreed, as did Middleton, but the latter still hoped that the roadblock defenders at Allerborn, eight miles to the east on the Bastogne road, would somehow survive until the 501st reached them. McAuliffe's order, then, was for Ewell to move out at 0600, attack eastward, and develop the situation.

At the appointed hour on 19 December Ewell's 501st Parachute Infantry marched out of the assembly area in column of battalions. Ewell knew that this was no time to engage in the all-out, full-bodied assault tactics to which the paratroopers were accustomed. He told his officers to "take it easy," avoid commitment to an action which would involve their whole force, and deploy to right and left as soon as they hit resistance so that they would not be easily cut off and surrounded.

Hindsight, of course, bestows a view of the American and German dispositions at 0600, when the 101st advance guard marched out, which was denied Ewell and the corps and division staffs in Bastogne. The battles already described were now coming to a close on the roads, in the villages, and through the woods east of the town as the 101st was taking its stance. During the night of 18 December the three small task forces of CCR, 9th Armored Division, which Middleton had ordered Colonel Gilbreth to position on and overwatching the Allerborn-Bastogne road (N 12), were cut to pieces. Some men and vehicles would escape to take a part in the fight for Bastogne, although some of Colonel Booth's command took six days of dodging the enemy before they reached the American lines. At Longvilly, next, and to the west, on the Bastogne road, Gilbreth had gathered what was left of CCR and its attached troops to fight a rear guard action until the 19th dawned and an orderly withdrawal might be effected.

Gilbreth started his guns displacing to the rear some time before daybreak, but the main force commenced to defile through the western exit from Longvilly about 0800, only to be ambushed and thrown into disorder when approaching Mageret, midway between Longvilly and Bastogne. Team Cherry (Lt. Col. Henry T. Cherry) of CCB, 10th Armored Division, which had been sent along the road toward Longvilly the previous evening, found itself involved in a series of disjointed actions as enemy troops cut the highway. Team Hyduke (1st Lt. Edward P. Hyduke) was caught up in the fight east of Mageret, subsequently losing all its vehicles in a sharp and aggressive armored action which the 2d Panzer commander dignified as an American "counterattack." (Late on the afternoon of the 19th Lieutenant Hyduke led his men on foot out of the melee under orders to rejoin CCB. He was afterward killed at Bastogne.)

Team Ryerson (Capt. William F. Ryerson), the main force belonging to Cherry, had laagered during the night between Mageret and Longvilly—and thus would fight an action almost independently of the Longvilly column—but before daybreak Ryerson knew that the enemy was in Mageret and that he would have to punch his way back to the west. Cherry sent orders confirming this withdrawal about 0830. Ryerson found his team outnumbered and outgunned by the Germans holding Mageret, but on the night of the 19th four squads of his armored infantry held a narrow foothold in a few houses on the eastern edge of the village, waiting there for help promised from the west. Colonel Cherry had gone back to Bastogne to see the CCB commander late on the 18th, returning thereafter to his own headquarters outside Neffe (a mile and a quarter southwest of Mageret) with word that the 101st would reinforce his command the next day. On the road back, however, he learned that the Germans were in Mageret and his troops were cut off. About the time Ewell's paratroopers debouched on the Bastogne road, Neffe was hit by tanks and infantry from Panzer Lehr; some hours later Cherry's detachment would pull back to Mont.

On the morning of 19 December, therefore, the job confronting the 501st was that of developing, fixing, and fighting the German detachments, now in strength, which stood to the rear of the erstwhile American blocking positions and presaged the coming main effort to crash the panzer columns through or around Bastogne.

The German High Command was aware that the two American airborne divisions had orders to enter the battle; in the late afternoon of 18 December intercepted radio messages to this effect reached OB WEST. German intelligence knew that the Americans were moving by truck and so estimated that none of these new troops would appear in the line before noon on the 19th. The German staffs believed that the two divisions would be deployed along a front extending from Bastogne to the northeast. In any case the German attack plan was unfolding about as scheduled and three German divisions were bearing down on Bastogne. The 2d Panzer Division's successes during the night of 18 December against the outpost positions east of Longvilly had netted forty American tanks, and the apparent crumbling of the last defenses east of Bastogne promised quick entry to that city on the 9th.

Actually the three German divisions moving toward Bastogne were not all maneuvering to attack the city. Lauchert's 2d Panzer Division had other fish to fry— its objective was the Meuse bridges—and when daylight came on the 19th the division advance guard was working its way to bypass Bastogne in the north. The 2d Panzer's end run, across country and on miserable third-class roads, collided with Maj. William R. Desobry's task force from CCB at Noville (four miles north of Bastogne), then blundered into a series of sharp actions reaching back to Longvilly.

On the left the Panzer Lehr, having seized Mageret during the night, began an attack about 0500 on the 19th designed to take Bastogne; it was a part of this forward detachment of Panzer Lehr which hit Cherry's headquarters at Neffe. Close on the heels of Panzer Lehr, two regiments of the 26th Volks Grenadier Division had made a right wheel with the intention of circling through Longvilly and Luzery so as to enter Bastogne from the north via the Noville road. Kokott's grenadiers, who had accomplished a truly remarkable feat in keeping pace with the mechanized columns of the Panzer Lehr, by now were spent. The regimental trains were far to the rear and resupply had to be made. Furthermore the boundaries and attack plans for the three divisions converging on Bastogne were so confused that it would take some time for the 26th Volks Grenadier Division to orient and coordinate its attack. On the morning of the 19th Kokott's two regiments lay quiescent and exhausted in the scattered woods southeast of Longvilly. Only the advance guard of the Panzer Lehr, therefore, was attacking directly toward Bastogne when the paratroopers of the 501st marched on to the Bastogne-Longvilly road.

Ewell had his 1st Battalion (Maj. Raymond V. Bottomly, Jr.) out as advance guard. The road was curtained at intervals by swirling fog and from time to time rain squalls swept in. Some 2,000 yards out of the city (it now was about 0820) the battalion ran onto a few howitzers from the 9th Armored whose crews were "ready, willing and able," as the journals report it, to support the 501st. Less than a thousand yards beyond, the advance guard encountered the enemy near the railroad station at the edge of Neffe; here was the roadblock which the Panzer Lehr had wrested from Cherry's headquarters detachment.

On the previous evening the VIII Corps commander had sent the 158th Engineer Combat Battalion (Lt. Col. Sam Tabets) to establish a line east of Bastogne between Foy and the Neffe road. Nearly a thousand antitank mines had been scraped together from other corps engineers to aid the 158th, and at least part of these were laid in front of the engineer foxholes during the night. When the 158th reported about 0200 that its outpost at Mageret had been overrun, Middleton sent what help he could—five light tanks taken from ordnance repair shops. At daybreak two enemy rifle companies, led by a few tanks, hit Company B, whose right flank touched the Bastogne highway near Neffe. The engineers succeeded in halting the advance along the road, although at a cost of some thirty casualties. Pvt. Bernard Michin seems to have blocked the panzers when he put a bazooka round into the leader at ten yards' range. Meanwhile Team Cherry had lost its roadblock at the Neffe station but momentarily had stopped the Germans at Neffe village. Enemy pressure then eased somewhat; perhaps the German infantry were waiting for their tanks to break through at Mageret. The fight had slackened to a small arms duel when Ewell's paratroopers came on the scene. Feeling carefully to the north and south of the highway, the 1st Battalion found that the Germans were deployed in some force and that this was no occasion for a quick knockout blow to handle a single roadblock. About 0900 Ewell turned the 2d Battalion (Maj. Sammie N. Homan) off the road in a maneuver on the left of the vanguard intended to seize the higher ground near the village of Bizory and Hill 510, a fairly substantial rise to the east which overlooked both Neffe and Bizory. When the 3d Battalion (Lt. Col. George M. Griswold) came up, Ewell sent it to the right with orders to take Mont and the ridge south of Neffe. By noon the regimental attack had attained most of its objectives. (Bizory already was outposted by troops of the 158th Engineer Combat Battalion.) Hill 510, however, was no easy nut to crack. The enemy held the position with automatic weapons sweeping the bare glacis to west and south—here the paratroopers made no progress. On the right one of Griswold's platoons arrived in time to give Colonel Cherry a hand in the fight at the Neffe château command post and, when the Americans were burned out, the subsequent withdrawal to Mont. The 3d Battalion had not been able to get around Neffe, but Company I did go as far as Wardin, southeast of Neffe, where it ambushed a 25-man patrol.

The appearance of the Americans in this area, little more than a mile south of Mageret, was interpreted immediately as a flanking threat to the two grenadier regiments of the Panzer Lehr which had wheeled to the right and away from Bastogne to engage the American columns transfixed on the Mageret-Longvilly road. Bayerlein detached a part of his reconnaissance battalion to meet this threat. The Americans made a fight of it inside Wardin, retreating from house to house as the long-barreled self-propelled guns blasted in the walls. One paratrooper walked into the street to confront one of the guns with a bazooka; he got the gun, then was cut down. Finally the guns jolted the paratroopers out of Wardin; they had inflicted thirty-nine casualties on Company I, all of whose officers were hit, and killed Capt. Claude D. Wallace, Jr., the company commander.

To the west, near the hamlet of Marvie, lay the tanks and armored infantry of Team O'Hara (Lt. Col. James O'Hara) holding the right of the three blocking positions set up by CCB, 10th Armored, the day before. O'Hara thus far had seen no Germans. His first warning that the fight was expanding in his direction was the "stragglers of airborne around us" and high velocity shellfire directed at his left tank platoon. For some reason the enemy failed to close with O'Hara, perhaps because of the low, clinging fog which had reduced visibility to about seventy-five feet. Ordered to do so by Colonel Roberts, the CCB commander, O'Hara sent tanks back into Wardin, but the village was empty. The tanks retired to the Marvie position as dark came on, and late in the evening Panzer Lehr occupied Wardin.

A message from McAuliffe ended this initial day of battle for the 501st and the regiment dug in where it stood. Ewell now had a fair picture of the enemy to his front but no clear idea of the fate or location of Team Cherry's main force, not to mention the CCR roadblock detachments.

Although the 501st had deployed successfully astride the main road east of Bastogne and had developed a sketchy outline of the most advanced German positions, it had not at any time confronted the main German forces. These, the bulk of Panzer Lehr and the two forward regiments of the 26th Volks Grenadier Division, spent most of the day chopping down the American column trapped between Mageret and Longvilly. Kokott apparently had expected to push his two grenadier regiments unopposed through Longvilly, as soon as they were rested, in a circling march to enter Bastogne from the north, but the German corps commander, General Luettwitz, himself took these regiments out of Kokott's hand and thrust them into the battle with the American rear guard at Longvilly—which held there longer than expected—and against the retreating column en route to Mageret. Suffice it to say that the 501st had been effectively debarred from the Longvilly arena by the Panzer Lehr troops holding Neffe, Hill 510, and the stopper position at Mageret. By the evening of the 19th the American troops east of Mageret were in varying stages of tactical dissolution—all but Team Ryerson, still clutching its piece of Mageret village.

Luettwitz was elated by this victory over the American armor (which as an old tanker he attributed in large part to the superiority of the Panther tank gun), but he realized that a precious day had been lost and with it the chance of an armored coup de main at Bastogne.

At Noville, the left of the three blocking positions, Middleton had assigned Colonel Roberts and CCB. Here Team Desobry, organized around fifteen medium tanks, stood athwart the main paved highway running north from Bastogne to Houffalize. This force had been in position about five hours, reporting all quiet, when at 020 on the 19th German half-tracks hit the American roadblocks. Americans and Germans pitched grenades at each other in the fog and one or two panzers reached the village itself. The enemy—probably a patrol feeling a way in front of Lauchert's 2d Panzer—soon pulled out, and the noise of battle died away.

The VIII Corps commander, much concerned by the gap which he knew existed between his southern troops and those of his corps somewhere to the north, ordered Desobry to investigate the town of Houffalize. (During the night, a patrol Desobry had sent in that direction reported the road open.) Before anything could be done about the Houffalize mission, the Germans unleashed their artillery against Noville. Lauchert, intent on regaining the momentum which the 2d Panzer had lost in the night fighting around Allerborn and Longvilly, and determined to get off the miserable side roads which he had chosen as a quick way around Bastogne, put all the guns that had kept pace with the forward elements into a shoot to blast a way through to the west. At 1000 the fog curtain suddenly parted revealing a landscape dotted with German tanks—at least thirty of them. Fourteen tanks from the 3d Panzer Regiment made a try for Noville, coming in from the north. Several bogged down in a vain attempt to maneuver off the road; others were slopped by Desobry's company of Sherman tanks and by tank destroyer fire. On the east the enemy had started an infantry assault, but the fog lifted before the first waves reached the village and, suddenly divested of cover, most of the attackers turned and ran.

Desobry could not know that Noville was the focus of the entire 2d Panzer maneuver, but he did ask for permission to withdraw. Roberts replied that Desobry should use his own judgment, then added that more tank destroyers were on the way from Bastogne (Desobry had only a platoon from the 609th) and that the 101st was sending a rifle battalion within the half hour. Coincident with Roberts' message the last of the German assault force pulled back. Lauchert had decided that the ground was too poor for tank maneuver, that reinforcements must be brought up for a headlong plunge. Meanwhile the German cannoneers continued to pummel Noville. Desobry had many casualties, but several ambulances had been wrecked by shellfire and it was difficult to get the wounded out.

The reinforcements reaching Desobry consisted of a platoon from the 705th Tank Destroyer Battalion (three companies of which constituted the only corps reserve Middleton had to give the 101st Airborne) and the 1st Battalion (Lt. Col. James L. LaPrade) of the 506th Parachute Infantry. Although McAuliffe assigned the 506th the mission of covering the northern approaches to Bastogne, the remaining two battalions had a string attached as the division reserve, and the regimental commander, Colonel Sink, was under strict orders not to move them from their positions just north of Bastogne. As the paratroopers approached Noville, they came under heavy, well-aimed artillery fire, twenty to thirty rounds exploding on the village every ten minutes. Vehicles and buildings were aflame—this was indeed a hot corner, the village itself practically bare of life. Desobry's detachment was deployed south and west of the village; the Germans were firing from the north and east, a more comfortable position since the higher ground encircling Noville tilted up on the enemy side of the dish.

By 1430 the 1st Battalion was ready to begin the assault against the enemy-held high ground. The center company walked almost immediately into a rain of barrage fire and was stopped with heavy losses. The two remaining companies were met with intense small arms fire but in fifteen minutes worked their way forward in short spurts to a point where one last dash would put them on the crest. As the paratroopers lay here, a mass of green-clad figures suddenly erupted over the hill. Later the 1st Battalion estimated this attack was carried by a rifle battalion backed by sixteen tanks. The American assault had smacked headlong into the attack the 2d Panzer had been readying since mid-morning. As the fight spread, nearly thirty-two panzers were counted on the field. The two antagonists each reported subsequently that "the enemy counterattack halted." Both probably were correct—although both continued to suffer heavy casualties. The German tanks might have decided the issue, but for over half an hour they stayed well back of the rifle line, perhaps fearful lest bazooka teams would reach them in the smoke and fog billowing up the hill, perhaps fearful of the bite in the few Shermans left. When a few of the enemy tanks finally ventured to approach, the American tank destroyers south of the village got on the flank of the panzers and put away five of them at 1,500-yards range.

Now as the smoke and fog increased, only small eddies broke the pall to give a few minutes of aimed fire. Two of the airborne companies fell back to the outskirts of Noville while the third, on the hill to the east, waited for darkness to cover its withdrawal. At one juncture the 1st Battalion was under orders to leave Noville, but Brig. Gen. Gerald J. Higgins, the assistant division commander who was acting alter ego for McAuliffe, told the paratroopers to stay put and promised assault gun and tank destroyer support for the morrow.

To the Noville garrison the dark hours were a nightmare. Every half hour a gust of enemy artillery fire shook the town; one shell crashed near the American command post, killing LaPrade and wounding Desobry. Maj. Robert F. Harwick, a paratrooper, assumed overall command, while Maj. Charles L. Hustead replaced Desobry as the armored team commander. (Desobry, with an agonizing head wound, was placed in an ambulance headed for Bastogne, but the ambulance was captured en route.) Through the night the panzers prowled on the edge of the village and the German grenadiers came out of their foxholes in abortive forays to reach the streets. But the paratroopers held the enemy at arm's length and the enemy tankers showed little inclination to engage Hustead's remaining eight Shermans, which had been brought into the village, in a blindfold duel.

Earlier in the day the 101st commander had planned to establish a defensive line running northwest to southeast in front of Bastogne from which the 501st, tied in with Desobry and Cherry as flank guards, would launch a counterattack. The events of the 19th, as it turned out, showed how little room for maneuver was left the Americans. Colonel Roberts, assessing the reports from CCB in the early evening, advised McAuliffe that "right now the whole front is flat against this town [Bastogne]." Roberts was right; nonetheless there remained two indentations in the fast-forming German line: the thumb sticking out at Noville and Team Ryerson's little enclave on the east edge of Mageret. The latter, however, disappeared during the night hours, for Ryerson, on orders, circled the enemy troops in Mageret and brought his depleted command into the lines of the 501st at Bizory. (Ryerson later was killed at Bastogne.)

General Luettwitz lacked the full German corps he craved to throw against Bastogne on the 20th. The 26th Volks Grenadier Division could count on only two of its regiments. Panzer Lehr had a substantial part of the division immediately east of Bastogne, but at least one infantry regiment, much of its artillery, and the bulk of the division trains were still toiling along the gummy little roads—hardly more than trails—climbing west out of the Wiltz valley. Furthermore, Luettwitz had ordered Bayerlein to hold out a reserve for a dash toward Sibret. The neighboring corps might lend Luettwitz a hand in the north—after all its 2d Panzer either had to break through at Noville or had to retrace its steps—but the Fifth Panzer Army commander had reiterated in no uncertain manner that Lauchert's goal was the Meuse, not Bastogne.

The entire artillery complement of the 2d Panzer was in place to support the attack at Noville when the 20th dawned. Lauchert's armor was in poor repair after the long and rough march A goodly number of tanks had been shot up in the first day's action at Noville, and the combination of muddy terrain and American antitank fire boded no good for a headlong armored assault. Lauchert therefore told his panzer grenadiers to carry the battle in company with small tank packets.

While the German guns plastered the village the grenadiers moved in about 0530 on three sides. Smoke and swirling fog veiled the attackers but the 420th Armored Field Artillery Battalion, firing from northwest of Bastogne, laid down a protective curtain which held the enemy at bay for over an hour. The eight Shermans by this time had run out of armor-piercing ammunition and half a dozen panzers tried to close in. A fresh platoon of tank destroyers from the 705th Tank Destroyer Battalion, sent up by Higgins, took a hand and broke up this sortie. In midmorning, when a promised platoon of quad mount antiaircraft failed to appear, Harwick and Hustead learned that the enemy had cut the road to the rear. The two aid stations could handle no more wounded—most of the medics and aid men were casualties—and the enemy grip obviously was tightening. The word relayed through the artillery net back to Bastogne told the story: "All reserves committed. Situation critical."

McAuliffe and Roberts consulted, agreed that the Noville force should withdraw. To free the troops in Noville would take some doing. General Higgins, in charge of the northern sector, already had acted to meet this crisis by sending the 3d Battalion of the 502d Parachute Infantry (assembled near Longchamps) into an attack northeast against the Germans who had descended on the road linking Noville and Foy. The latter village, 2,500 yards south of Noville on the Bastogne road, had been occupied by the 3d Battalion of the 506th, which had its own fight going. Foy lies at the bottom of a pocket and during the night elements of the 304th Panzer Grenadier Regiment had wormed their way onto the hills overlooking the village from north, west, and east. With this vantage the Germans brought their direct fire weapons to bear and forced the 3d Battalion back onto the high ground south of the hamlet.

But by noon the 101st had a solid base for a counterattack. The 2d Battalion of the 506th covered the right flank of the 3d and was in contact with the 501st on the east. The battalion sent from the 502d was in position west of Foy. Beginning the counterattack at 1400, paratroopers pushed back through Foy and dug in some 200 yards to the north where late in the afternoon they met the column fighting its way back from Noville.

The smoke and fog that run through all reports of the Noville fight did good service as cover when the Americans formed for the march out. The main German barrier force had arrayed itself just north of Foy, complete with armor and self-propelled guns. Four Shermans, in the van with a few half-tracks, were put out of action before they could return fire. While one paratroop company attacked to open the road, Major Harwick sent for two tank destroyers from the rear of the column. Shells were bursting among the troops crouched by the roadside, and the clank of tank tracks could be heard approaching from Noville. But the tank destroyers and their armor-piercing shell did the trick—and an assist must be credited also to the Americans in Foy who were now on the enemy's rear. By 1700 the column was back inside the American lines. The fight at Noville cost the 1st Battalion of the 506th a total of 13 officers and 199 men killed, wounded, and missing. Team Desobry has no record of its casualties but they must have been very heavy, both in men and vehicles. The 506th estimates that the 2d Panzer lost thirty-one vehicles in the Noville fight and perhaps half a regiment of foot. At least the first part of this estimate may be close to the fact, for it is known that one battalion of the 3d Panzer Regiment was badly crippled at Noville.

There is an epilogue. In late afternoon, as his soldiers poked about the ruins of Noville, Lauchert radioed the LVIII Panzer Corps commander for permission to wheel the 2d Panzer into Bastogne. Krueger's answer was prompt and astringent: "Forget Bastogne and head for the Meuse!"

The attack planned for the 19th east of Bastogne and carried out by the Panzer Lehr and 26th Volks Grenadier Divisions had signally failed of success. The soft ground had made it impossible for the German tanks to maneuver easily off the roads—a factor of great worth to the defenders. The Americans had at least five artillery battalions on call in this sector, whereas neither of the two enemy divisions had been able to get any substantial number of guns and howitzers forward. Also, the pellmell, piecemeal deployment east of Bastogne by the advance guard formations was beginning to reap a harvest of delay and tactical confusion. There was some savage fighting here during the day, but uncoordinated—on the part of the enemy—and never pressed in force to a definite conclusion.

On the 20th Luettwitz turned the 78th Volks Grenadier Regiment over to the Panzer Lehr commander for the close-in northern hook at Bastogne planned for execution the previous day. The immediate goal was Luzery, a suburb of Bastogne on the Houffalize highway. The 78th circled north to pass the village of Bizory, the left wing pin for the 501st, but fire from Company F caught the Germans in the flank. This halted the move and forced the 78th to swing wide into the cover given by the woods north of the village. Masked by the woods the enemy proceeded west as far as the Bourcy-Bastogne rail line, then unaccountably stopped. When the 2d Battalion of the 506th came up on the left of the 501st, its disposition was such that it faced this German force, plus its sister regiment the 77th, at the point where the Foy-Bizory road crossed the railroad.

Through most of the daylight hours on the 20th the enemy seemed content to probe the main line occupied by the 501st. During the evening Bayerlein sent his own 902d Panzer Grenadier Regiment against Neffe, but a roving patrol from Team O'Hara happened to spot the tank detachment of the regiment as it filed along the Neffe-Wardin road and brought friendly artillery into play. Between the American gunners and paratroopers the 902d took a formidable beating—very severe casualties were reported by the enemy division commander. A tank destroyer platoon from the 705th used ground flares to sight and destroy three of the panzers reinforcing the infantry assault waves.

When the 501st went into position on the 19th, its southern flank had been none too solidly anchored by the thin counter-reconnaissance screen operated by Task

Force O'Hara and the tired, understrength 35th Engineer Combat Battalion (Lt. Col. Paul H. Symbol). Enemy pressure around Wardin, although subsequently relaxed, indicated that here was a gap which had better be sealed. On the morning of the 20th McAuliffe sent the 2d Battalion of the 327th Glider Infantry from the division assembly area through Bastogne to relieve Company A of the engineers.

The engineers had just climbed out of their foxhole line west of Marvie and turned the position over to the 2d Battalion when one of O'Hara's outposts saw a German column streaming into Marvie. This was the advance guard of the 901st Regiment which had finally extricated itself from the Wiltz valley. With only a single rifle company and four tanks, the Germans never had a chance. In an hour's time O'Hara's mediums had accounted for the panzers and the 2d Battalion had beaten the attackers back in disorder and occupied Marvie. The paratroopers waited through the day for the main attack to come, but the only evidences of the enemy were a smoke screen drifting in from the east and occasional tanks in the distance. Unknown to the Americans a shift in the Panzer Lehr's stance before Bastogne was taking place.

The inchoate American defense forming at Bastogne was conditioned by a set of optimistic premises. The first of these was the promised arrival of the 4th Armored Division from Patton's Third Army in the south. During the night of December the VIII Corps commander, acting on word from Patton, told McAuliffe that one combat command from the 4th Armored was on its way to Bastogne and would be attached to the 101st. At noon McAuliffe and Roberts (who had been promised this initial 4th Armored force) learned that the entire division was to be added to the Bastogne defense. The certainty of the 4th Armored's appearance explains in part the routine and rather cavalier treatment accorded Capt. Bert Ezell and his little team from CCB, 4th Armored, when it arrived in Bastogne shortly after noon. Quite obviously McAuliffe and Middleton anticipated the early appearance of the entire armored division.

A second premise—accepted in most of the 101st planning efforts on 20 December—was that the VIII Corps still had viable forces in and around Bastogne which could be employed in common with the airborne divisions. This idea, of course, went hand in hand with the very real ignorance of enemy forces and locations which obtained both in Bastogne and at Middleton's new headquarters in Neufchâteau. Earlier McAuliffe and his staff had counted on Roberts' 10th Armored combat command to reinforce a counterattack east by the 101st—a vain expectation, as it turned out. There remained the 28th Infantry Division—or at least some part thereof. In midafternoon McAuliffe sent a liaison officer to General Cota, whose headquarters was now at Sibret southwest of Bastogne, with instructions to find out the German dispositions and to ask the question: "Could the 28th attack towards Wiltz in conjunction with the 101st Airborne tomorrow?"

Cota's reply is not even recorded in the 101st Airborne log. After all he could give only one answer: the 28th Infantry Division no longer existed as a division (although two of its regiments would continue in stubborn battle under other commands). The fall of Wiltz on the night of 19 December had written finis to the story of the 110th Infantry, Cota's single remaining regiment. On the morning of the 20th Cota had gone into Bastogne, finding its streets jammed with vehicles, corps artillery trying to bull a way through, and a host of stragglers, including many of the survivors of the 110th Infantry. General Middleton gave Cota permission to get his people out of Bastogne and the latter ordered them out on foot, abandoning to the traffic jam those vehicles still in their possession. (So impressed was General Cota by the traffic choking the streets and alleys of Bastogne, that he advised the VIII Corps commander to keep all contingents of the 4th Armored Division out of the town.)

Despite McAuliffe's failure to secure the immediate assistance which would make a full-bodied counterattack feasible, it seemed that the tactical problem facing the 101st on the evening of 20 December remained linear, that is, the creation of a homogeneous and defensible line barring entrance to Bastogne from the north and east. The corps letter of instructions reaching McAuliffe at noon on the 20th was rather more sweeping in its definition of mission. "There will be no withdrawal"this was clear enough to all concerned. "The [101st Airborne] Division will stabilize their front lines on the front P798945 [that is, Recht] to St. Vith, south along a general line east of [Highway] N15 . . . to connect with the 4th Infantry Division at Breitweiler." It may be assumed that neither Middleton nor McAuliffe took this part of the order either literally or seriously. There had been a few indications, and rumors, of enemy activity west of Bastogne—indeed the 101st had lost some of its trains in the division assembly area during the previous night—but thus far all this could be charged to raiding parties roaming on the loose under cover of night in a fluid and changing battle. In early evening a report reached Bastogne that the road northwest to La Roche and Ortheuville (where two platoons of the 705th Tank Destroyer Battalion now attached to the 101st were operating) was free of the enemy. The roads south to Neufchâteau and Arlon were still open—and waiting for traverse by the 4th Armored. So the situation looked in McAuliffe's Bastogne headquarters at 1900 on 20 December.

Across the lines the German commander, Luettwitz, was none too pleased by the rather dilatory operations of his corps. He knew by this time that the American front east of Bastogne had stiffened and that his troops had been able to find no holes. On the other hand the strength of his corps was increasing by the hour as the two divisions hauled their tails up on the muddy roads—it looked as though he had the forces needed for maneuver. As a last flick of the hand Luettwitz ordered Bayerlein to throw the 902d into the night attack against Neffe. This was at most a diversion, for Luettwitz had decided to envelope Bastogne from the south and west. He intended to use the bulk of the Panzer Lehr, leaving only one of its grenadier regiments to flesh out the eastern front with the foot elements of Kokott's 26th Volks Grenadier Division, but in addition he had in hand the 39th Volks Grenadier Regiment of the 26th which had just come up behind the corps' south flank. All told there was a sizable motorized force for this venture: the reinforced reconnaissance battalion, the engineer battalion, and the 902d (as soon as it could be disengaged) from the Panzer Lehr; plus the reconnaissance battalion and 39th from the 26th Volks Grenadier Division.

The immediate objectives seem to have been clearly stated. The Panzer Lehr spearheads were to advance via Hompré and Sibret to St. Hubert, while the units of the 26th would start the attack from an assembly point at Remonfosse on the Bastogne-Arlon road with the intention of stabbing into Bastogne from the southwest. In fact this night operation developed into a mad scramble in which the troops from the two divisions jockeyed for the lead as if they were in a flat race for high stakes.

Truly the stakes were high. Throughout this maneuver Luettwitz and his superior, General Manteuffel, had an eye single to shaking the armored columns of the XLVII Panzer Corps free for the dash to the Meuse bridges. Bastogne, sitting in the center of the web of hard-surfaced roads, was important—but only as a means to a geographically distant end. Bastogne had failed to fall like an overripe plum when the bough was shaken, but it could be clipped off the branch—or so the German High Command still reasoned—and without using Bayerlein's armor.

The enemy drive across the south face of Bastogne and on to the west during the night of 20 December did not immediately jolt McAuliffe's command; it was rather a disparate series of clashes with scattered and unsuspecting units of the VIII Corps. Central to the story at this point is the fact that by daylight on the 21st the German infantry following the armored troops were ensconced on both the main roads running from Bastogne south, while light forces were running up and down the western reaches of the Bastogne-St. Hubert highway. In the north the circle had been clamped shut during the night when the 2d Panzer seized Ortheuville on the Marche road.

Bastogne Is Encircled

Some of the Bastogne defenders recall in the saga of the 101st Airborne Division that their lone fight began on 20 December. "It was on this day, 20 December," reads the war diary of the 327th Glider Infantry, "that all roads were cut by the enemy . . . and we were completely surrounded." This is only hindsight. The picture of complete encirclement was built up in McAuliffe's headquarters only slowly on the 21st, nor did the ring at first seem to be hermetic and contracting. Doubtless the word passed among the regiments very rapidly—the 501st journal notes at 1030 that the last road is cut—but it was late afternoon before an armored patrol sent out by CCB affirmed that the way south certainly was closed.

What were the means available for defense of the Bastogne perimeter? The 101st Airborne was an elite, veteran outfit at nearly full strength, and well acquainted with isolation as a combat formation. Only five battalions from McAuliffe's four regiments had been seriously engaged in the fight thus far. Its four artillery battalions were reinforced by the 969th and 755th Field Artillery Battalions, armed with 155-mm. howitzers whose range was nearly three times that of the airborne artillery, a very important make-weight for the 101st. In addition the 10th Armored Troops were supported by the 420th Armored Field Artillery Battalion, whose mobility and tactics made it especially useful in a perimeter situation. Also available were stray gun sections and pieces from artillery units which had been decimated during the VIII Corps' withdrawal.

Probably CCB, 10th Armored, and CCR, 9th Armored, had between them some forty operable medium tanks by the 21st. To this number of fighting vehicles should be added the light tanks, cavalry assault guns, and antiaircraft artillery automatic weapons carriers—probably no more than two platoons in each category. A very heartening addition to the Bastogne force, of course, was provided by the 705th Tank Destroyer Battalion.

The highway nodal position which made Bastogne so necessary to the Germans also set up a magnetic field for the heterogeneous stragglers, broken infantry, and dismounted tankers heading west. Realizing this fact, Colonel Robert's got permission to gather all stragglers into his command. Roberts' force came to be known as Team SNAFU 9 and served mainly as a reservoir from which regular units drew replacements or from which commanders organized task forces for special assignments.

It is impossible to reckon accurately the number and the fighting worth of those stragglers who reached Bastogne and stayed there. CCR contributed about two hundred riflemen; CCB may have had an equal number; General Cota culled two or three hundred men from Team SNAFU to return to his 28th Division; and one may guess there were another two or three hundred stragglers whose identity has been lost. Many of these men, given a hot meal and forty-eight hours' rest, could be used and were used, but they appear as anonymous figures in the combat record (thus: "100 infantry left for Team Browne").

McAuliffe now had the advantage of a clearly defined command structure. Before the 20th he and Colonel Roberts had commanded independently, but on that date Middleton gave McAuliffe the "say" (as General Cota had advised after his visit) over all the troops in the Bastogne sector. The presence of Roberts would prove particularly valuable. Early in the war he had been the armored instructor at the Army Command and General Staff School, where his humorously illustrated "Do's" and "Don'ts" of tank warfare showed a keen appreciation of the problems posed by armor and infantry cooperation. The paratroopers were in particular need of this advice for they seldom worked with armor, knew little of its capability, and even less of its limitations, and—as befitted troops who jumped into thin air—were a little contemptuous of men who fought behind plate steel. (During the Bastogne battle Roberts developed a formal memorandum on the proper employment of armor, but this was not distributed to the 101st until 28 December.) On the other hand the tankers had much to learn from commanders and troops who were used to fighting "surrounded."

McAuliffe's logistic means were less substantial than the tactical. The airborne division normally carried less supply than conventional divisions and the 101st had been hurried into Belgium with ammunition and grenade pouches not quite full, much individual equipment missing (overshoes, helmets, sleeping bags, and the like), and only a few truckloads of 105-mm. howitzer shells. In fact some of the first paratroopers into line had to be supplied with ammunition from the CCB trains. Fortunately Roberts' trains were full, and in some major supply items even had overages, when they arrived at Bastogne.

The ability of the 101st to sustain itself had been severely diminished on the night of 19 December when German raiding parties (some reported in civilian garb) surprised and overran the division service area around Mande-St. Etienne. Most of the quartermaster and ordnance troops made their way to the VIII Corps, but the raiders captured or killed most of the division medical company. Only eight officers and forty-four men escaped. This loss of doctors, aid men, and medical supplies was one of the most severe blows dealt the 101st. A number of transport vehicles also were lost in this affray, but about a hundred trucks had been sent to the rear for resupply and so escaped. Very few of these got back to the 101st before the ring closed.

In addition, Roberts had sent the CCB trucks back for resupply just before the roads were closed. There was, of course, a considerable quantity of ammunition, food, and other supplies inside Bastogne which the VIII Corps had been unable to evacuate. (Officers of Middleton's staff bitterly regretted the loss of the wine and liquors which had been carefully husbanded for consumption at Christmas and New Year). Bastogne was sizable enough to have some reserve civilian stocks, and the melange of armor, engineers, and artillery units around the city had supplies and ammunition in their own vehicles. (Pancakes would appear regularly in the rations served during the siege, these concocted from the doughnut flour left in a huge American Red Cross dump.)

Through assiduous scrounging, requisitioning, and an enforced pooling of unit resources, the G-4 of the 101st would be able to work minor logistic miracles—but these alone would not have insured the survival of the Bastogne garrison. The airborne division had been supplied by air during the Holland operation, and when, on the 21st, McAuliffe knew that his command was isolated he asked for aerial resupply. Unfortunately no plans had been worked out in advance for airlift support and the supply records of the Holland campaign—which would have made logistic calculation and procedure easier—were back in France. In the first instance, therefore, the troops in Bastogne would have to take what they got whenever they could get it.

Communications would present no major problem. A corps radio-link vehicle arrived in Bastogne just before the road to Neufchâteau was severed; so Middleton and McAuliffe had two-way phone and teletype at their disposal throughout the siege. Inside Bastogne there were enough armored and artillery units—comparatively rich in signal equipment—to flesh out a speedy and fairly reliable command and artillery net. Tactical communication beyond the Bastogne perimeter, however, as for example with the 4th Armored, had to be couched in ambiguous—sometimes quite meaningless—terms.

Mobile forces racing cross-country, shooting up isolated posts and convoys, do not necessarily make a battle. The German dash around Bastogne was preeminently designed to encircle, not constrict. The German commanders, well aware of the fragmentization of their enveloping forces, did not consider that Bastogne had been surrounded until the evening of the 21st. The major enemy impact on this date, therefore, came as in previous days against the east face of Bastogne. The American perimeter, then taking form, represents basically a reaction to the original German intentions with only slight concessions to the appearance of the enemy in the south and west. The 502d held the northern sector of the American line in the Longchamps and Sonne-Fontaine area. Northeast of Bastogne the 506th was deployed with one foot in Foy and the other next to the Bourcy-Bastogne rail line. To the right of this regiment the 501st faced east—one flank at the rail line and the other south of Neffe. The 2d Battalion, 327th, held the Marvie position with an open flank abutting on the Bastogne-Arlon highway.

The American deployment on through the south and west quadrants could not yet be called a line. In the early afternoon McAuliffe took the 1st Battalion of the 327th (then attached to the 501st) and sent it due south of Bastogne; here tenuous contact was established with the division engineer battalion—the 326th—strung thinly across the Neufchâteau road and on to the west. (The airborne engineers were not well equipped with demolition matériel and this road had to be blocked; McAuliffe phoned the VIII Corps for assistance and in the early dark a detachment from the 35th Engineer Combat Battalion came north and did the job.)

Directly west of Bastogne lay the remnants of the division trains and service companies. Defense here would devolve initially on the 420th Armored Field Artillery Battalion (Lt. Col. Barry D. Browne), which was gathering infantry and tank destroyers and finally would be known as Task Force Browne. The last link in the perimeter was the 3d Battalion of the 327th, holding on a front northwest of Bastogne which extended from the Marche-Bastogne highway to Champs.

The dispositions just described represent the more or less static formations in the Bastogne force, the beef for sustained holding operations. Equally important were the mobile, counter-punching elements provided by the armor, assault guns, and tank destroyers. These units, with constantly changing task force names and composition, would have a ubiquitous, fluid, and highly important role in maintaining the Bastogne perimeter against the German concentric attack. Their tactical agility on the interior line would be greatly enhanced by the big freeze which set in on the 21st.

All through the night of 20 December the troops of the 506th in Foy had been buffeted by German artillery. At dawn the enemy advanced on the village, and the Americans, as they had done earlier, retired to the better ground south of Foy and Recogne. This early effort was not followed up because the 2d Panzer was on its way west and had no further concern in this sector save to neutralize a possible American foray against its rear.

The primary attack of the day came along the Bourcy-Bastogne rail line, right at the seam between the 506th and 501st. During the previous night Kokott had built up the concentration of his 26th Volks Grenadier Division in the woods east of the railroad to include much of the rifle strength of the 77th and 78th Regiments. The two American regiments had failed to make a firm commitment as to tactical responsibility and, indeed, the left flank of the 501st was nearly a thousand yards to the rear of the 506th. At 0830 a 506th patrol chanced upon some Germans in the woods behind the regiment's right flank. Companies D and F attacked promptly to seal the gap at the rail line while the 501st turned its weapons to deny any movement on its side.

Enough of the enemy had infiltrated for McAuliffe to ask Colonel Sink to send in his 1st Battalion, which had been badly hurt at Noville, as a cauterizing force. It took three hours of musketry and, at several points, bayonet work to liquidate the Germans in the pocket; the battalion killed about so, took prisoner 85, and drove a large number into the hands of the 501st. This hot sector of the front cooled off during the afternoon. The 26th Volks Grenadier Division was realigning and extending to take over the ground vacated by Panzer Lehr, and Kokott could not afford two regiments in attack at the rail line.

Through most of 21 December the Germans lashed out at the 501st with artillery and sporadic infantry assaults. On the American left flank Kokott's 77th carried the ball but the main effort was made by the 902d, attacking from an assembly area at Neffe against the 3d Battalion. The records of this battalion were lost in later fighting, but participants in the action speak of a "determined" attack by two German rifle battalions and "vicious close-in fighting." Although Colonel Ewell expected a second all-out assault when daylight ended, this never came. The 902d had its orders to catch up with the Panzer Lehr van in the west and during the night assembled for the march to rejoin General Bayerlein.

South of the 501st positions the enemy seemed content to sit back and shell the headquarters of the 2d Battalion, 327th, at Marvie. The 2d Battalion records no other action than the appearance of some tanks and infantry along the Arlon road forcing a flank extension across the road. German evidence, however, speaks of attacks by the 901st in this sector which "miscarried." If discretion in this particular instance proved the better part of valor, it probably was induced by the CCB tanks which had taken position on the Arlon road.

Farther west the enemy was more aggressive. Having played havoc with the VIII Corps' artillery and trains assembled outside Sibret, Kampfgruppe Kunkel turned north in the late morning toward Senonchamps, a village of some importance since it controlled the secondary road leading onto the Marche-Bastogne highway. The immediate prize before Kunkel, but probably unknown to him, was the American artillery groupment consisting of the 755th and 969th Field Artillery Battalions, emplaced with their 155-mm. howitzers near Villeroux, a crossroads some 2,500 yards south of Senonchamps.

At Senonchamps the 420th Armored Field Artillery Battalion under Colonel Browne was busily engaged in firing against the enemy east and north of Bastogne, but Browne had been able to take some steps to secure his gun positions with a scratch force of infantry and light tanks raised by CCB. Around Villeroux, however, all was confusion and no single officer seemed to be responsible for defense of this sector. As Kunkel sped north from Sibret toward Villeroux he met the 771st Field Artillery Battalion, which abandoned its guns and fled. About this time Team Pyle (a detachment formed from the remnants of CCR and numbering fourteen tanks and a couple of hundred stray riflemen) came south on the Neufchâteau road. Kunkel hit the point of this force east of Villeroux and drove the Americans back in the direction of Senonchamps.

The brief respite given the Villeroux defenders by this encounter enabled the two medium howitzer battalions to "march order" their batteries and head for Senonchamps. German infantry in half-tracks closed on Villeroux before the last howitzers could displace, but visibility by this time had dwindled to a couple of hundred yards and Battery A of the 755th alongside the headquarters battery of the 969th laid down a hail of machine gun fire which momentarily halted the enemy. This small rear guard force itself was saved by the appearance of two American tanks that casually wandered into the fight and out again. Only one howitzer was lost during the displacement to Senonchamps, and it was disabled by a mortar shell.

At the edge of Senonchamps Team Pyle made a stand, for the German drive threatened to strike the 420th Armored Field Artillery Battalion (Team Browne) and the two battalions of 155'S from the rear. When the enemy infantry formed to join their tanks in an assault on the village they came directly under the eyes of Battery B of the 796th Antiaircraft Artillery Battalion, whose .50-caliber "meat choppers" quickly ended this threat. Kunkel decided to delay an attempt for conclusion until the morrow.

North and northwest of Bastogne the day passed quietly, although small German detachments did make a few sorties on the Marche road. The company of the 3d Battalion, 327th, which had been sent on a lone mission to aid the survivors of the division medical company, was attacked and momentarily cut off but succeeded in rejoining the battalion.

The Enemy Begins a Concentric Attack

The evening situation report that reached OB WEST on the 21st made good reading. Rundstedt was convinced that the time was ripe for a concentric attack to crush Bastogne and make this road center available for the build-up required to support the Fifth Panzer Army at or over the Meuse. His order to Manteuffel made the seizure of Bastogne a must, but at the same time stressed the paramount necessity of retaining momentum in the drive west. Manteuffel had anticipated the OB WEST command and during the evening visited the XLVII Panzer Corps' command post to make certain that Luettwitz would start the squeeze on Bastogne the next day—but without involving the mobile armored columns of the Panzer Lehr.

Manteuffel, Luettwitz, and Kokott, who was now made directly responsible for the conduct of the Bastogne operation, were optimistic. For one thing the fight could be made without looking over the shoulder toward the south (where the Luftwaffe had reported heavy American traffic moving from Metz through Luxembourg City), because the right wing of the Seventh Army finally had shouldered its way west and seemed ready to take over the prearranged blocking line facing Neufchâteau, Arlon, and the American reinforcements predicted from Patton's Third Army. The advance guard of the 5th Parachute Division already had crossed the Arlon road north of Martelange. General Brandenberger, the Seventh Army commander, himself came to Luettwitz' command post during the evening to promise that all three regiments of the division would take their allotted positions.

Kokott apparently was promised reinforcement for the attack à outrance on Bastogne but he had to begin the battle with those troops on the spot: his own 26th Volks Grenadier Division, the 901st Kampfgruppe (which had been detached from Panzer Lehr), an extra fifteen Panther tanks, and some artillery battalions. What the 5th Parachute Division could put into the pot depended, of course, on the Americans to the south.

It would take some time to relieve those troops pulling out and redress the alignment of the 26th Volks Grenadier Division's battalions. There was little point to attacking the 101st Airborne in the eastern sector where its strength had been demonstrated, but west of Bastogne the Panzer Lehr and Kokott's own reconnaissance troops had encountered only weak and disorganized opposition. The first blow of the new series designed to bore into Bastogne would be delivered here in the western sector, accompanied by systematic shelling to bring that town down around the defender's ears.

The battle on the 22d, therefore, largely centered along an arc rather roughly delimited by Villeroux and the Neufchâteau highway at one end and Mande—St. Etienne, just north of the Marche highway, at the other. One cannot speak of battle lines in this sector: the two antagonists were mixed higgledy—piggledy and for much of the time with no certain knowledge of who was in what village or at what crossroads. It is indicative of the confusion prevailing that the 501st tried to evacuate its regimental baggage train—which had suffered from enemy shelling—through Sibret after Kampfgruppe Kunkel had cut the road north of the town by the dash into Villeroux. (The 501st lost fifteen trucks and nearly all its bed rolls.)

The arena in question earlier had been the 101st service area and contained in addition a good deal of the VIII Corps' artillery and trains. Much of the fighting on the 22d revolved around two battalions of armored field artillery: Colonel Paton's 58th Armored Field Artillery Battalion, which had emplaced near Tillet—after the Longvilly battle—to support the 101st Airborne; and Browne's 420th, now operating as a combined arms team on a 4,000-yard perimeter in the neighborhood of Senonchamps. Tillet lay about six miles west of Senonchamps. Much of the intervening countryside was in the hands of roving patrols from Panzer Lehr, one of which had erected a strong roadblock midway between the two villages.

On the night of the 21st the Germans encircled Tillet, where Paton, hard pressed, radioed the VIII Corps for help. Middleton relayed this SOS to Bastogne but Browne, himself under attack by Kunkel's 26th Volks Grenadier Division reconnaissance battalion, was forced to say that the 58th would have to get back to Senonchamps under its own power. Nevertheless, Team Yantis (one medium tank, two light tanks, and a couple of rifle squads) moved forward to the German roadblock, expecting to give the 58th a hand when day broke.

Paton and his gunners never reached Team Browne, which had had its hands full. Browne's force not only had to defend a section of the Bastogne perimeter and bar the Senonchamps entry, but also had to serve the eighteen 105-mm howitzers which, from battery positions east and south of Senonchamps, provided round—the—clock fire support for friendly infantry five to eight miles distant. Close-in defense was provided by a platoon of thirty stragglers who had been rounded up by an airborne officer and deployed three hundred yards south of the gun positions. (This platoon held for two days until all were killed or captured.) Browne's main weapon against the German tanks and self-propelled guns was not his howitzers but the seventeen Sherman tanks brought up by Team Pyle and Team Van Kleef the day before. These were disposed with nine tanks facing a series of wood lots west of the battery positions, four firing south, and the remaining four placed on the road to Villeroux.

At daybreak the first task was to clear the enemy from the woods which lay uncomfortably near the firing batteries. Pyle's scratch force of riflemen entered the woods but found only a few Germans. Off to the northwest came the sound of firing from the area known to be occupied by a battalion of the 327th Glider Infantry; so Browne reported to Colonel Roberts that his team would join this fight as soon as the woods were clear. Before the sortie could be organized, a detachment from Kampfgruppe Kunkel struck out from Villeroux against the American flank. Direct tank fire chased the enemy away, but this was only the opener. During the afternoon the enemy made three separate assaults from the woods that earlier had been reported cleared, and again the tanks made short work of the Germans (Van Kleef reported eighteen enemy tanks destroyed during the day).

As the afternoon wore on fog and snow clouded the scene and the tank gunners began to lose their targets. The American howitzer batteries, however, provided a static and by this time a well-defined target for enemy counterbattery fire. At twilight Colonel Browne radioed CCB that his heterogeneous team was taking "terrible casualties." Earlier he had asked for more troops, and McAuliffe had sent Company C of the 327th and Team Watts (about a hundred men, under Maj. Eugene A. Watts) from Team SNAFU. At dark the howitzer positions had a fairly substantial screen of infantry around them, although the enemy guns continued to pound away through the night.

The airdrop laid on for the 22d never reached Bastogne—bad flying weather continued as in the days past. All that the Third Army air liaison staff could do was to send a message that "the 101st Airborne situation is known and appreciated." Artillery ammunition was running very low. The large number of wounded congregated inside Bastogne presented a special problem: there were too few medics, not enough surgical equipment, and blankets had to be gathered up from frontline troops to wrap the men suffering from wounds and shock. Nonetheless, morale was high. Late in the afternoon word was circulated to all the regiments that the 4th Armored and the 7th Armored (so vague was information inside the perimeter) were on their way to Bastogne; to the men in the line this was heartening news.

What may have been the biggest morale booster came with a reverse twist—the enemy "ultimatum." About noon four Germans under a white flag entered the lines of the 2d Battalion, 327th. The terms of the announcement they carried were simple: "the honorable surrender of the encircled town," this to be accomplished in two hours on threat of "annihilation" by the massed fires of the German artillery. The rest of the story has become legend: how General McAuliffe disdainfully answered "Nuts!"; and how Colonel Harper, commander of the 327th, hard pressed to translate the idiom, compromised on "Go to Hell!" The ultimatum had been signed rather ambiguously by "The German Commander," and none of the German generals then in the Bastogne sector seem to have been anxious to claim authorship. Lt. Col. Paul A Danahy, G-2 of the 101st, saw to it that the story was circulated—and appropriately embellished — in the daily periodic report: "The Commanding General's answer was, with a sarcastic air of humorous tolerance, emphatically negative." Nonetheless the 101st expected that the coming day — the 23d — would be rough.

The morning of 23 December broke clear and cold. "Visibility unlimited," the air-control posts happily reported all the way from the United Kingdom to the foxholes on the Ardennes front. To most of the American soldiery this would be a redletter day — long remembered — because of the bombers and fighter-bombers once more streaming overhead like shoals of silver minnows in the bright winter sun, their sharply etched contrails making a wake behind them in the cold air.

In Bastogne, however, all eyes looked for the squat planes of the Troop Carrier Command. About 0900 a Pathfinder team dropped inside the perimeter and set up the apparatus to guide the C-47's over a drop zone between Senonchamps and Bastogne. The first of the carriers dropped its six parapacks at 1150, and in little more than four hours 241 planes had been vectored to Bastogne. Each plane carried some twelve hundred pounds, but not all reached the drop zone nor did all the parapacks fall where the Americans could recover them. Nevertheless this day's drop lessened the pinch — as the records of the 101st gratefully acknowledge. On 24 December a total of 160 planes would take part in the drop; poor flying weather on Christmas Day virtually scrubbed all cargo missions — although eleven gliders did bring in a team of four surgeons and some POL badly needed by Roberts' tanks. The biggest airlift day of the siege would come on the 26th with 289 planes flying the Bastogne run.

The bulk of the air cargo brought to Bastogne during the siege was artillery ammunition. By the 24th the airborne batteries were down to ten rounds per tube and the work horse 420th Armored Field Artillery was expending no more than five rounds per mission, even on very lucrative targets. This battalion, covering a 360-degree front, would in fact be forced to make its original 1,400 rounds last for five days. The two 155-mm. howitzer battalions were really pawing at the bottom of the barrel. The 969th fired thirty-nine rounds on 24 December and two days later could allow its gunners only twenty-seven rounds, one-sixth the number of rounds expended per day when the battle began.

The airdrop on the 23d brought a dividend for the troops defending Bastogne. The cargo planes were all overwatched by fighters who, their protective mission accomplished, turned to hammer the Germans in the Bastogne ring. During the day eighty-two P-47's lashed out at this enemy with general-purpose and fragmentation bombs, napalm, and machine gun fire. The 101st reported to Middleton, whose staff was handling these air strikes for the division, that "air and artillery is having a field day around Bastogne."

The German attack on the 23d was mounted by the 26th Volks Grenadier Division and the attached regiment left behind by Panzer Lehr. Lacking the men and tanks for an assault around the entire perimeter, General Kokott elected to continue the fight at Senonchamps while attacking in two sectors diametrically opposite each other, the Marvie area in the southeast and the Flamierge area in the northwest. By the happenstance of its late and piecemeal deployment the 327th Glider Infantry stood in front of the enemy at both these critical points.

The 5th Parachute Division, now badly fought out and with gaping ranks, could be of little help at Bastogne. Actually this division was scattered on a front of eighteen miles, reaching from Neufchâteau clear back to the Sauer crossings. Indeed, during the day the 26th Volks Grenadier Division had to take over the portion of the 5th Parachute line between Clochimont and Hompré because the American forces from the south threatened to pierce this very thinly occupied segment of the blocking line. Kokott, then, could employ only two regiments and his reconnaissance battalion in the assault, while maintaining what pressure the remaining two regiments might have along the balance of the American perimeter.

The enemy tactics on this and the following days reflect the manner in which Kokott had to husband his resources. Extensive preparatory fires by artillery and Werfers opened the show while the infantry wormed in as close to the American foxhole line as possible. By this time the newfallen snow had put every dark object in full relief; the grenadiers now donned white snow capes and the panzers were painted white. (The Americans replied in kind with wholesale raids on Belgian bed linen and with whitewash for their armored vehicles.) The assault would be led by a tank platoon—normally four or five panzers—followed by fifty to a hundred infantry. If this first wave failed, a second or third—seldom larger than the initial wave—would be thrown in. It is clear, however, that the German commander and his troops were chary of massed tactics at this stage of the game.

The 39th Volks Grenadier Regiment, freshest in Kokott's division, was assembled to the west and northwest opposite Team Browne and the 3d Battalion of the 327th. The latter had maintained an observation post at Flamierge and a string of roadblocks along the Flamierge road well in front of the battalion position. Here the enemy dealt the first blow of the day and got into Flamierge, only to be chased out by a counterattack. Next, the enemy gathered south of Company C—positioned astride the Marche highway—and tried to shoot the Americans out with tank fire. In early evening the Germans moved in for the assault and at one point it was reported that Company C had been lost. This was far from fact for the American artillery beat off the attackers; the 3d Battalion, however, pulled back closer to Bastogne. This enemy effort also extended to embrace Team Browne. More infantry were hurried to Senonchamps on light tanks, and at 1830 McAuliffe sent one half of his mobile reserve (Team Cherry) to give a hand against the German tanks. But the American tanks, tank destroyers, and artillery already on the scene were able to handle the panzers without additional help—and even while this fight was on the cannoneers around Senonchamps turned their pieces to lob shells across the perimeter in support of the hard-driven paratroopers and tankers at Marvie.

During the hours of light the 901st made no move to carry out its scheduled attack between Marvie and the Arlon road. Quite possibly the activity of the American fighter-bombers, once more in the skies, made it necessary to wait for nightfall. Through the afternoon the enemy shelled the 2d Battalion, 327th, and its command post in Marvie. As night came on the barrage increased in intensity, sweeping along the battalion front and onto its northern flank—beyond Marvie—where Team O'Hara stood with its tanks.

At 1845 the 901st (with at least two tank companies in support) commenced a co-ordinated attack delivered by platoons and companies against the front manned by the 2d Battalion and Team O'Hara. One quick rush put an enemy detachment on a hill south of Marvie which overlooked this village. The platoon of paratroopers on the hill was surrounded and destroyed, but when a half-track and a brace of tanks tried to move down the hill into Marvie a lucky shot or a mine disabled the half-track, leaving no way past for the tanks. On the Bastogne-Arlon road a group of tanks (twelve were counted) started north toward the right flank of the 2d Battalion. Here Company F later reported that the tanks "made repeated attempts to overrun our positions but were halted." It is probable that the three medium tanks from Team

O'Hara and the three tank destroyers from the 609th Tank Destroyer Battalion which stood astride the road (not to mention the darkness and artillery fire) had a more chastening effect on the panzers than the small arms fire of the paratroopers.

The Germans seem to have had the village of Marvie as their main objective for by midnight the fight had died down all along the line except at Marvie, where it burst out with fresh virulence. It is estimated that at least one rifle battalion and some fifteen tanks were thrown against Company E (now reinforced by an understrength company of airborne engineers) and Team O'Hara.

Using the hill which earlier had been wrested from Company G as a mounting block, three German tanks made their way into the south edge of Marvie, but O'Hara's tanks and assault guns stopped a major penetration from the east by gunning down the panzers silhouetted in the glare of burning buildings, thus enabling the Americans to hold on in the north half of the village. The threat of a breach here impelled McAuliffe to send the remaining half of Team Cherry to Marvie. Because this switch stripped Bastogne of its last counterattack force, Cherry's detachment, which had gone west to assist Team Browne, was recalled to Bastogne. An hour before dawn on the 24th the battle ended and quiet came to Marvie. O'Hara's troops had accounted for eight panzers in this fight, but the village was still clutched by both antagonists.

The battle on the 23d had been viewed in a somewhat somber light inside Bastogne. That evening, only a few minutes after the German attack began in the Marvie sector, Lt. Col. Harry W. O. Kinnard (the 101st Airborne Division G-3) telephoned his opposite number at the VIII Corps command post. The gist of his report, as recorded in the corps G-3 journal, was this: "In regard to our situation it is getting pretty sticky around here. They [the 4th Armored Division] must keep coming. The enemy has attacked all along the south and some tanks are through and running around in our area. Request you inform 4th Armored Division of our situation and ask them to put on all possible pressure."

The events of the past hours had shown that the force under McAuliffe's command was overextended at a number of points. The artillery groupment west of Bastogne was particularly exposed, and the 327th Glider Infantry had already been forced to shorten its lines. Then too the segments of the perimeter defense were not as well coordinated as they might be. The tankers of CCB complained that they had no idea of the airborne positions, and quite probably the regiments of the 101st were hazy as to the location of the small tank and tank destroyer detachments on their flanks.

Colonel Kinnard, whose sharp tactical sense was rated highly by all the commanders who worked with him during the siege, drew up on 24 December a plan to regroup the Bastogne forces. The plan was put into operation that same evening. Kinnard's scheme placed all four regiments of the 101st Airborne on the line as combined arms teams. Team O'Hara and a platoon of the 705th Tank Destroyer Battalion were attached to the 501st. The 506th, whose sector had been quiet, got two platoons of the 705th but no tanks. The 502d was given two platoons from the 705th and Team Anderson (it is symptomatic of the shoestring defense which perforce had evolved at the perimeter that Captain Anderson's "team" consisted of two cavalry assault guns, one tank destroyer, and two jeeps). The 327th took over the 326th Airborne Engineer Battalion, two platoons of the 9th Armored Engineer Battalion (which had won distinction in the Noville fight), and four platoons of the 705th. Also attached to the 327th was the amalgam of infantry, tank destroyers, and tanks which had grown up around Browne's 420th Armored Field Artillery Battalion and which, on the 23d, had been reorganized as Team Roberts. (Colonel Browne was wounded by a shell fragment on the 24th and died the next day.)

This readjustment of the 101st positions resulted in a taut and tenuous line approximately sixteen miles. (Map 4) That it could not be defended in equal strength at all points was not only a military aphorism but a simple fact dictated by the troops available and the accidents of the ground. Creation of a tactical reserve was therefore mandatory, albeit difficult of accomplishment with the limited mechanized force at McAuliffe's disposal. The 101st reserve, as now organized, consisted of Roberts' CCB; that is Teams Cherry and Arnsdorf (with perhaps nine medium and five light tanks operational at any given time) plus a part of the original Team SNAFU, put together by Colonel Roberts from the remnants of CCR, 9th Armored, and various waifs and strays. (Colonel Gilbreth, the commander of SNAFU, was wounded on the 22d and then hospitalized.)

This reshuffle stripped CCB of its own reserve; so Roberts organized a new formation (Team Palmaccio, commanded by 1st Lt. Charles P. Palmaccio) equipped with four antiaircraft half-tracks, one tank destroyer, and two light tanks. Roadblocks at the entrances to Bastogne were established, each manned by two guns from Company C, 609th Tank Destroyer Battalion. Inside Bastogne itself, McAuliffe had a part of Team SNAFU as a kind of "interior guard," backed up by four self-propelled tank destroyers and forty men from the 705th. All this regrouping tightened and strengthened the rifle line surrounding Bastogne, but the resources at hand for fire fighting enemy armored incursions or for quick, local counterattacks were woefully limited—as shown by the commitment of Team Cherry on opposite sides of the perimeter during 23-24 December.

General Luettwitz, with only a reinforced division to use against Bastogne, was worse off than McAuliffe. He had been given rather vague promises of reinforcement, but no decision was rendered by the High Command until the 23d when Hitler agreed to release two fresh divisions (the 9th Panzer and 15th Panzer Grenadier) from the OKW reserve. Once these troops were handed over to Army Group B, Field Marshal Model decided that they were more sorely needed to shore up the left flank of the Fifth Panzer and Seventh Armies than at Bastogne. One regimental combat team from the 15th Panzer Grenadier Division was all he would give Luettwitz for the Bastogne operation.

On both sides of the line, then, the daylight hours of the 24th were spent in regrouping, this punctuated with heavy gusts of artillery and mortar fire whenever the opponent showed signs of movement. Once again, however, a beautiful flying day gave the Americans an edge. P-47's belonging to the 512th, 513th, and 514th Squadrons of the XIX Tactical Air Command worked around the Bastogne perimeter, at one point, in the Noville sector, bombing so close to the airborne lines that the 101st sent frantic word to the VIII Corps asking that the flight leader be told to call off the mission. The 115th Kampfgruppe from the 15th Panzer Grenadier Division duly arrived for attachment to Kokott's division and took over a sector in the northwest between Flamierge and Givry. The 420th Armored Field Artillery Battalion and the medium howitzer battalions displaced to new firing positions just north of the Marche road and not more than a mile and a half from Bastogne. The Americans abandoned their last roadblock at Mande-St. Etienne—now it was too far out—and drew in the western line held by Team Roberts and the 3d Battalion of the 327th.

Germans and Americans both claimed Marvie, a circumstance which may have accounted for an American air strike on Marvie by P-47's during the afternoon.

In the headquarters at Bastogne McAuliffe's staff had been kept pretty well abreast of the enemy movements indicative of incoming reinforcement. Team Anderson, scouting around Champs, reported armor and tracked vehicles moving into Givry (this was the new 115th Kampfgruppe); other reports noted the movement of German traffic coming from the northeast and moving southward across the American front. All this must have been a headache for the 101st G-2, but aside from shortening the lines and tightening up tactical control there was little the Americans could do but wait for the blow to fall.

Early in the afternoon the VIII Corps relayed a message from General Patton and the Third Army: "Xmas Eve present coming up. Hold on." But there were more tangible items to lessen the nostalgia and depression of the surrounded garrison on Christmas Eve. The second day of air resupply had been "a tremendous morale booster"—so reported CCB and most of the regiments. Allied air activity on the 24th had heartened the men on the ground. When night fell they could see the fires left as aftermath of the fighter-bomber strikes blazing all the way round the perimeter. (Twice during the night of 24 December, however, the Luftwaffe retaliated with very damaging and lethal bombing sorties on Bastogne and the surrounding area.) Less obtrusive but of considerable impact was the confidence that the commanders and the troops had in each other; a lesson for future commanders may be read in the considerable effort put forth by McAuliffe, Roberts, and the regimental commanders to apprise all the troops of the "situation."

Christmas Eve in the German headquarters brought forth some cognac and a few "Prosits" but in the main was devoted to preparations for a major attack on Christmas Day. As late as the evening of the 24th Luettwitz hoped to obtain more troops from the 15th Panzer Grenadier Division, but the Fuehrer had other ideas. Earlier in the day the Fifth Panzer Army commander posed a question which finally reached Jodl and Hitler: should he turn to finish off Bastogne or continue, with the bulk of his divisions, toward the Meuse and seize the Marche plateau in an attempt to widen the German thrust? Hitler's answer, finally relayed by Model, was that the attack to seize the Marche plateau should be continued with all available forces. This answer did nothing to relieve Manteuffel's worries about his thin and endangered southern flank. To leave Bastogne as a sally port onto his left rear made no military sense to this experienced soldier—so Manteuffel ordered that Bastogne be taken on 25 December.

(The attack order read: "Displacement [in this context a kind of euphemism for "destruction"] of the enemy at Bastogne.")

The German order of battle on Christmas Eve was this (read from the north clockwise). The 26th Volks Grenadier engineer battalion and a few antitank guns maintained a security screen in the Foy-Recogne sector. The 78th Fuesiliers, brought back to strength by a large draft of replacements, held on a front extending from Foy to Neffe. The 901st, its ranks much depleted by the fighting just ended, continued the circle past Marvie and to a point west of the Arlon road. The 39th was deployed on both sides of the Neufchâteau road. What earlier had been the "western front"—that is, from Senonchamps north to the Marche road was occupied by the reconnaissance battalion of the 26th Volks Grenadier Division, which had moved onto the ground left free by the American withdrawal on the 24th. The regiment from the incoming 5th Panzer Grenadier Division (Colonel Deckert) was bivouacked west of Flamizoulle.

The 77th Fuesilier Regiment completed the circle, the bulk of its troops concentrated west of Champs. Uneasy about the ability of the 5th Parachute Division to cover his back, Kokott was forced to strip a few companies from his own division and the 901st to form a subsidiary front facing south.

The attack plan for the 25th turned on the fresh strength provided by the 15th Panzer Grenadier. The main effort would be made in the northwest between the Marche road and Champs, the latter point included as an initial objective. It was known that the American hold in this sector was weak, the frozen ground gave good tank going and observation for the artillery, and there were no large villages or woods to hold up the assault. To open a way for the main effort Kokott quietly assembled the major part of his division artillery around Flamierge and Givry. The plan included a heavy blow by the Luftwaffe against Bastogne itself (this eventuated in the two bombing attacks during the night of 24 December which killed a Belgian nurse and a score of wounded paratroopers).

The original time schedule was exceedingly optimistic: to put in the infantry assault at 0400; to break through the American rifle line by 0600, at which time the artillery could see to fire on targets of opportunity and the tanks would be able to move with speed; and to rush an armored group from the 15th Panzer Grenadier into Bastogne between 0800 and 0900 hours before the American fighter-bombers took to the air.

The optimism breathed by this schedule must have expired shortly after it was put on paper although the plan remained. Kokott has recorded his shock and surprise at the weak state of the reinforcements brought in by Deckert: the 115th Regiment (three battalions of fusiliers), the reconnaissance battalion and two armored field artillery battalions of the 15th Panzer Grenadier Division, a company of tank destroyers, and seventeen tanks belonging to the 115th Panzer Battalion. Hitler's failure to name Bastogne as the primary objective had been reflected in the dilatory and contradictory orders issued by the higher commanders for the employment of Deckert's division. True, the second of Deckert's regiments (the 104th) finally had been given to the XLVII Panzer Corps, but on Christmas Eve it was toiling slowly toward the east side of Bastogne and would not arrive in time to join the battle. Col. Wolfgang Maucke, commander of the 115th, objected—as strongly as a colonel would dare—when he received his orders toward dusk on the 24th. He had been given no time for reconnaissance; no coordination had been arranged with the tanks supposed to support the 115th. Maucke's superiors simply pointed out the tremendous advantage that would accrue to a surprise attack on Christmas Day—he had his orders.

The main assault, handed the elements of the 15th Panzer Grenadier, was to be a straight thrust over Flamizoulle into Bastogne with the right wing guiding on the Marche highway, a distance of about four miles. For this Maucke put two battalions in line and one in reserve. The 1st Battalion, with tanks carrying some of the infantry, was to pass through Flamizoulle; the 2d Battalion, supported by the tank destroyer company, would circle Flamizoulle to the north and strike for the northern edge of Bastogne. To the left of Maucke's kampfgruppe the 77th Grenadier Regiment was ordered to attack along the secondary road running through Champs and Hemroulle into Bastogne. Here the 1st Battalion had the job of seizing Champs and opening the way while the 2d Battalion, following to the left and rear, would be prepared to leapfrog forward as Champs fell, the two making the final push into Bastogne abreast. The reconnaissance battalion of the 26th Volks Grenadier Division, south of

Maucke's force, had a special mission: to attack from Senonchamps and pierce the new American position by seizing Isle-la-Hesse, a hamlet standing where the Senonchamps road fed into the Marche highway. Although nearly all the German units surrounding Bastogne had some diversionary mission during the Christmas Day assault, only the 39th Grenadier Regiment had a major attack assigned in support of the effort in the northwest, this to be an advance astride the Neufchâteau-Bastogne highway (which was never carried out).

The Battle on Christmas Day

About 0300 a few German planes droned over the 502d lines and dropped bombs indiscriminately around Rolle, the regimental command post. This seems to have been the Luftwaffe support promised Kokott. A few minutes later the German gunners and mortar crews started to work, their target the American positions at Champs. Here Company A of the 502d was deployed on the northwest edge of the village, its right flank joining the 2d Battalion in a large wood lot midway between Champs and Longchamps. Clad in white snow suits the first German assault party, some fifty grenadiers from the 77th, crept forward under the waning moon toward Champs. At 0400 this group dashed into the village and the German attack began. More of the enemy moved through the woods against the left flank of the 2d Battalion, and within the hour a full German battalion had joined the fight. Company B moved up as a backstop if its sister company should be engulfed or pushed aside, but the confused melee around Champs in the predawn darkness pinned the Germans down.

Meanwhile the two assault battalions of the 15th Panzer Grenadier Division were moving against the 3d Battalion of the 327th. The tank group on the right of the German line drew ahead of its marching partner and an hour and a quarter after the advance began reported to Kokott that the only evidence of American reaction was some tank or tank destroyer fire coming in from the south. Thirty minutes later a brief and optimistic radio message flashed to the rear: the tanks and the infantry battalion festooned thereon had reached the western edge of Bastogne. But elation at the German command post was short lived; word that the German tanks were in the streets of Bastogne never came. The commander of the 115th sent a liaison officer forward to find the battalion or its tanks, but without success. German forward observers were alerted to listen for the sound of German tank fire—but all they could hear was the crash of artillery fire and the crump of exploding mortar shells.

The story of the lost tank group is soon told. The eighteen Mark IV's and the riding grenadiers had broken through the positions held by Companies A and B of the 327th Glider Infantry before dawn and got as far as the battalion command post. Several of the enemy tanks passed straight through battery positions of the 755th Field Artillery Battalion, whose gunners opened up with machine guns as soon as they discerned the distinctive German muzzle-brakes. But the 155-mm. howitzers could not be brought to bear at such close range and the Germans rolled on unscathed. Just west of Hemroulle about half the German tanks wheeled left, defiling along a cart path which led to the road between Champs and Bastogne. As they approached the road the panzers formed in line abreast, now bearing straight toward Companies B and C of the 502d, which were on the march to help the paratroopers in Champs.

Colonel Chappuis had a few minutes to face his companies toward the oncoming tanks, but the initial shock was absorbed by two tank destroyers from Company B of the 705th Tank Destroyer Battalion which were knocked out as they fell back toward the Champs road. As the panzers rolled forward, Company C made an orderly withdrawal to the edge of a large wood lot midway between Champs and Hemroulle. Now it was the paratroopers' turn. They showered the tanks with lead, and the German infantry clinging to the decks and sides fell to the snow. The tank detachment again wheeled into column, this time turning toward Champs. Two of the 705th tank destroyers, which were backing up Company C, caught the column in process of turning and put away three of the panzers; the paratroopers' bazookas accounted for two more.

The half of the enemy tank-infantry formation which had kept on toward Hemroulle after knifing through the 327th foxhole line received its coup de grâce in a fury of cross fire laid down by four of the 705th tank destroyers, tanks from Team Roberts, the 463d Parachute Field Artillery Battalion, and bazookas handled by the glider infantry. As recounted by Col. S. L. A. Marshall after the battle: "The German tanks were fired at from so many directions and with such a mixture of fire that it was not possible to see or say how each tank met its doom." The survivors of those panzer grenadiers of the 1st Battalion who had ridden into battle on the tanks found themselves surrounded and alone, for the American rifle line had sealed itself after the initial armored punctures. About fifty German riflemen who had hidden in a stream bed were captured by cannoneers from the 755th. At noon General Kokott wrote the tanks and the accompanying infantry from the 1st Battalion of the 115th off as lost—why and where remained a mystery to the German headquarters.

The 2d Battalion of the 115th seems to have made good use of the rupture created in the 327th positions west of Hemroulle, advancing almost unperceived and unopposed until daybreak when it was brought under fire by Company C, the 3d Battalion reserve. At first light the American artillery and mortars took on the German infantry starkly outlined against the snow-covered slopes west of Hemroulle. The panzer grenadiers tried digging in but the ground was too hard frozen; so they lay in the snow and took their losses. The regimental commander, Colonel Maucke, began in midmorning to re-form his remaining troops, pulling what was left of the 1st Battalion back to a hill southeast of Flamizoulle (where it took a merciless pounding from Allied fighter-bombers) and sending his reserve battalion into the woods north of the 1st to cover its flank. When night fell Maucke ordered the remnants of the 1st Battalion to sideslip south across the gap left by the disappearance of the tank group. Of the battalion staff all were dead or wounded and the battalion commander was a young lieutenant from one of the rifle companies. Maucke himself went forward to find his lost tanks but was stopped by machine gun fire.

At Champs, where the battle had begun, most of the Germans left the village in the middle of the morning to let their gunners blast the paratroopers out of the houses and surrounding woods. The commander of the 77th, apprehensive of a continued house-to-house battle, asked for and received permission to circle around the village, but the new attack up the slopes toward Hemroulle was shot to pieces. In the early afternoon General Kokott called the German attack to a halt, planning to resume the battle under cover of the night.

This last "desperate effort," as Kokott himself termed it, took long to organize and did not get under way until the morning hours of the 26th. Using the German salient at the Isle-la-Hesse road fork as his base, Kokott sent a small assault group from his own division and ten mobile tank destroyers northeast in the direction of Hemroulle with the intention of circling through Savy into Bastogne. This force wedged its way between the two right flank companies of the 327th but was caught in the open by the howitzers massed west of Bastogne which literally blew the infantry assault apart. Four armored tank destroyers continued toward Hemroulle but were finally brought to a halt by a large ditch. Here, while maneuvering, all were put out of action by artillery and tank destroyer fire at close range.

In midafternoon more bad news reached Kokott's command post. He had counted on the 5th Parachute Division to keep Patton's armor at bay in the south, and to make doubly certain had faced parts of the 901st and 39th away from Bastogne in support of the paratroopers. Now word came that the 5th Parachute Division had broken and that the 39th Regiment was under attack. Kokott had little to give the 39th, only five or six tanks which had just been repaired, and he did not dare put these on the road until darkness sent the American fighter-bombers home. Both Kokott and the corps commander, Luettwitz, still expected the main battle to be fought on the Arlon or Neufchâteau road, but in the late afternoon the commander of the 39th radioed that American tanks had broken through farther to the west at Assenois. Kokott asked Luettwitz for help, but the latter had empty hands. Late that night new orders came from Field Marshall Model: the 26th Volks Grenadier Division would hold the defenders inside the Bastogne perimeter until the tanks of the Fuehrer Begleit Brigade could arrive to sever the narrow corridor opened to the defenders that afternoon by the American armor.

The siege of Bastogne, for purposes of historic record, may be considered ended at 1645 on 26 December when the 326th Airborne engineers reported contact with "three light tanks believed friendly." True, the breach in the German-held ring opened by the 4th Armored Division was narrow and precarious, but it would not be closed despite the most strenuous enemy efforts in coming days. The staunch defense of Bastogne had impeded the Fifth Panzer Army drive to the west, just as the desperate rear guard battle by the 7th Armored at St. Vith had slowed the advance of the Sixth, demonstrating the axiom of World War I that no salient thrust into the defender's position can be expanded rapidly and successfully if the shoulders of the salient are firmly held by the defender. The human cost of the Bastogne battle, therefore, probably was not out of proportion to the military gains achieved. The 101st Airborne Division suffered battle casualties numbering 105 officers and 1,536 men. CCB of the 10th Armored Division had approximately 25 officers and 478 men as battle casualties. There is no means of numbering the killed, wounded, and missing in the miscellany of unrecorded tankers, gunners, infantry, and others who shared in the defense of Bastogne. Nor can any casualty roster now be compiled of those units which fought east of Bastogne prior to 19 December and gave the 101st Airborne Division the time and the tactical opportunity to array itself in the defense of that town.

Chapter XX. The XII Corps Attacks the Southern Shoulder

The End of the Defensive Battle 22 December

Intercepted radio messages, a most fruitful source for German intelligence, had clearly indicated by 9 December that the Americans were moving reinforcements in large numbers toward the Bulge. The OB WEST staff reasoned that the bulk of these new divisions would be committed in the west in defense of the Meuse River or along the north side of the salient. Thus far there was no cause to be concerned about the southern flank. The weak Seventh Army had made progress, although not so much as Hitler wished, and there were no signs of change in the defensive attitude shown by the Americans in this sector. Late in the evening of the 19th, Army Group G reported that the U.S. Third Army was giving ground on the Saar front, but the American move was interpreted as a readjustment which could not bring Third Army reinforcements to the Ardennes before 22 December. The German intelligence staffs again agreed that there was no immediate threat to the Seventh Army, and that the westward advance by the Fifth Panzer Army would necessarily force the Americans to strengthen the battle line there and prohibit any thrust into the deep southern flank.

Although the Seventh Army was in the process of going over to the defensive, it had pushed its right wing forward, according to plan, and on 20 December re-established contact with its northern neighbor, the Fifth Panzer Army. In effect the right wing of the Seventh Army had wheeled to face south, while at the same time elongating the shoulder of the Fifth. This extension had widened the gap between the LXXXV Corps, in the Ettelbruck sector, and the LXXX Corps, west of Echternach, but as yet the higher German headquarters were unconcerned about the thinning line.

The division and corps commanders of the Seventh Army were less sanguine. By intuition, or through the natural apprehension induced by heavy losses, they already flinched mentally from the retaliatory blow. Concerned with their own weakness, rather than the strength and successes of the panzer armies, it seemed logical to them that the Americans would seek to exploit such weakness. Across the lines, as it happened, plans were in process for a counterattack against the German southern flank, but General Patton, charged with this operation, would not have his troops in readiness before 22 December and feared that in the interim the enemy would launch a spoiling attack from the Echternach area.

With the main weight of the Seventh Army echeloned forward on its right (western) wing, pressure to regain contact and to grapple with the 109th Infantry was stepped up during the night of 20 December. The 352d Volks Grenadier Division pushed through Ettelbruck and probed cautiously in the dark, searching to the west and south for the outlines of the 109th's new position. This advance onto the ridge rising in the triangle formed by the Wark Creek and Alzette River had a limited object. Luxembourg, an appetizing target, lay only fifteen miles south of Ettelbruck and on a good road, but the orders received by the 352d aimed solely at the quick acquisition of a good blocking position against any American riposte from the south. The objective of the 352d, therefore, was a line based on the villages of Bettborn and Bissen that would cut the main roads running north and northeast from Luxembourg and Arlon, respectively. Parts of two regiments, the 914th and 916th, went up against the outpost positions of the 106th Infantry on 21 December, gaining ground on both of the open flanks. For the Americans the fight was one to gain time (they permitted no serious penetration of the ridge position overlooking the Wark valley) until, on the morning of 22 December, troops of the incoming 80th Infantry Division headed north through their positions.

To the south and east the 276th Volks Grenadier Division, now some distance from the 352d, re-formed its two leading regiments on a common front and worked feverishly to bring artillery ammunition and supplies forward from bridges which at long last were in operation. It appears that the new division commander of the 276th had ordered a limited attack for 21 December, intended to carry from Waldbillig to Christnach and the more readily defended creek line there. Late on the previous day a few assault guns, probably no more than five or six, had arrived west of the river. These weapons, it was hoped, would lend the tired German infantry the necessary punch.

In the 9th Armored Division sector plans were under way to retake Waldbillig, using Task Force Chamberlain of the 10th Armored Division, which had been reorganized with a strength of thirteen medium tanks and two much understrength armored infantry companies (total: 130 men). Before the German attack got under way on 21 December Task Force Chamberlain attacked toward Waldbillig. The Shermans, protected by tank destroyers overwatching on the flanks, negotiated the dangerous skyline crossing on the ridge between Christnach and Waldbillig and by noon were in Waldbillig.

Reports that the enemy had withdrawn proved erroneous the moment that the supporting infantry started to move up with the tanks. Mortar and rifle fire burst from the village, while Werfers in the neighboring woods joined in. Although the infantry support had a bad time, the tanks were little concerned by this enemy action. Their presence inside the village had some effect: a hundred prisoners were taken from the 988th. About midnight the American artillery laid on a brief, sharp concentration and the few tanks still in Waldbillig made a rapid withdrawal. Then Americans and Germans both shelled the village, by now a kind of no man's land.

To the east, opposite the weakest portion of the 4th Infantry Division line, the 212th Volks Grenadier Division made still another effort to reach its original objective—the good defensive terrain and blocking position in the Consdorf-Scheidgen-Michelshof area. In the afternoon of 21 December the 212th Fuesilier Battalion moved along the main Echternach-Luxembourg road through Lauterborn, which the Americans earlier had abandoned. Just ahead lay Hill 313, overlooking the road south. Here a part of Company C, 159th Engineer Combat Battalion, was stationed, with Company B occupying a smaller hill just to the west. There was no protection for the engineer flanks. About 1300 the Germans started a 30-minute shelling, covering their advance through the draws fringing the American-held heights.

Company B caught the full force of the first assault, the grenadiers erupting from the draws, firing their burp guns, and shouting in broken English, "Kill the sons of bitches." Two platoons fell back from Company B onto Company C, which in turn came under attack by Germans who had worked around Hill 313 and threatened to cut the road back to Scheidgen. The engineers had no working radios and did not know that reinforcements in the shape of a hundred or 50 men from the division headquarters company were on the way. Actually this relief party had to fight its way forward as the engineers struggled to clear a path back, and darkness was coming when the two bodies made contact. Almost out of ammunition, the engineers fell back to Scheidgen, but the Germans made no move to follow.

While the fusilier battalion was gaining ground in its drive toward Scheidgen, other troops of the 212th Volks Grenadier Division were trying, albeit with less success, to make headway to the east and west. Assembling in the woods near Rodenhof, the 320th Grenadier Regiment launched an attack to take Osweiler, but ran into two companies of the 2d Battalion, 22d Infantry, en route to clean out the woods. Neither side was able to advance and the Americans dug in for the night a few hundred yards south of Rodenhof. On the left flank of the 12th Infantry sector a sharp fight flared up in midafternoon when two companies of the 423d Grenadier Regiment tried to take Consdorf. The American tanks and infantry held their fire until the enemy assault formation had cleared its assembly area in the woods and was fully deployed on the bare slope before the town. Then they cut loose. Some sixty Germans were killed and the rest withdrew.

The 212th Volks Grenadier Division made a last attempt to expand the gains achieved in the Scheidgen sector on 22 December, the date on which the American counterattack finally began. A stealthy advance through the draws between the Americans occupying the villages of Scheidgen and Michelshof during the early afternoon was perceived and handily checked by shellfire. At dusk the Germans tried again, debouching from the central ravine in a wedge formation. This effort was suicidal. Tanks, tank destroyers, artillery, engineers, and infantry were all in position and watching the draw like hungry cats in front of a mouse hole. The German point was only a hundred yards from the American foxholes when the first American fired. When the fusillade ended, 142 dead and dying Germans were left on the snow, still in their wedge formation. One lone grenadier, with five bullet holes in him, came forward with his hands held shakily over his head.

This bootless enemy effort on 22 December was no more than a counterattack to cover a general withdrawal which the 212th had begun the night before on corps orders. The defensive period for Americans in the Sauer sector in fact had closed with darkness on 21 December. This six-day battle had given adequate proof of General Barton's dictum, "The best way to handle these Heinies is to fight 'em." It was a battle fought off the cuff in a situation which mimeographed periodic reports would call "fluid" but which, for the most, could better be described as "obscure" seen from either side of the hill.

The XII Corps Moves to Luxembourg

Three days before the beginning of the German thrust into the Ardennes, General Patton and Maj. Gen. Hoyt S. Vandenberg met to discuss plans for a combined air and ground attack to smash through the German West Walltarget date, 19 December. After three or four days of intense bombing by the Ninth Air Force and the Royal Air Force, Maj. Gen. Manton S. Eddy's XII Corps would attack from the Saar River to penetrate the West Wall and start the Third Army, stymied by mud, reinforced concrete, and the wasting effect of the past battles of attrition, once again on the way to the Rhine. Patton was jubilant at the prospect of the biggest blitz (so he fondly referred to the planned air assault) in the Third Army's history. General Eisenhower, however, did not conceive of the attack in the Saar sector as the major Allied effort and had decided "regardless of [the] results," to transfer divisions from this sector, once the attack had been made, to the north for the major assault against the Rhine and Germany itself.

Meanwhile the XII Corps had the task of cleaning out the German positions in the small forests and wood lots between the Saar and the West Wall so that no entanglement in these outworks would dull the full shock of the hard blow which was being readied. For this mission General Eddy employed two infantry divisions, the new 87th and the veteran 35th, their attack to begin on 16 December.

The fighting was extremely bitter, and the enemy made the Americans pay dearly for each yard gained toward the West Wall. The superiority of the attacker in men and matériel, however, as usual was clearing the field, a fact of battlefield life that was all too evident to the German defenders. On the night of 16 December the commander of the XC Corps, facing Eddy's divisions, warned his superiors that the German line was so thin and ragged that if the Americans decided on an all-out attack neither the existing battle line nor the West Wall could be held. But in this instance the calculated risk assumed by Hitler in stripping the Army Group G sector to feed troops and weapons into Army Group B paid off. It turned out that the battered and weakened German divisions in front of the XII Corps had done their job, had held long enough.

To take the pressure off the XII Corps infantry Patton was preparing to bolster the attack with the 6th Armored Division when General Bradley informed the Third Army commander of the day's happenings on the VIII Corps front. The army group commander ordered that the 10th Armored be dispatched to Middleton forthwith. this move from the Third Army to begin on the 17th. General Morris started his division north, and Patton canceled the 6th Armored attack which had been poised in front of Forbach—one of the few occasions on which the Third Army commander called off an attack that he personally had ordered. So far as the Third Army staff knew at this stage, however, the German blow in the Ardennes presented no dire threat and the attack on the 19th would go as scheduled.

But on 18 December Bradley called Patton to his Luxembourg headquarters, and there Patton learned for the first time of the grave situation faced by the First Army. When asked what help he could give, the Third Army commander replied that he could intervene in the battle with three divisions "very shortly." He telephoned the Third Army chief of staff to stop the XII Corps attack forming for the following day and to prepare the 4th Armored and 80th Infantry Divisions for immediate transfer to Luxembourg. The 87th Division halted its slow advance, as did the 35th. On the move out of rest area for assembly in preparation for the XII Corps' attack, the 4th Armored and 80th likewise stopped.

When it became apparent by nightfall of the 18th that the situation on the First Army front had deteriorated beyond expectation, General Bradley decided upon immediate use of the Third Army's resources. Patton had returned to his command post at Nancy when, a couple of hours before midnight, Bradley called with word that conditions on the VIII Corps front were much worse, that the troops promised by the Third Army had to move at once, and that Patton was to attend a meeting with the Supreme Commander the following morning at Verdun.

By midnight one combat command of the 4th Armored Division was on its way north to Longwy; at dawn on the 19th the 80th Infantry Division had started for Luxembourg City. And through the night before the Verdun meeting the Third Army staff worked feverishly to draft plans for the intervention of all or any part of Patton's forces in the battle raging in the north, for Bradley had intimated that Patton was to take command of the VIII Corps and other forces moving to its assistance. Bradley already had directed that the III Corps headquarters would be moved from Metz to take command of an attack to be mounted somewhere north of Luxembourg City. Patton's general staff, therefore, prepared three plans for a counterattack: on the axes Neufchâteau-St. Hubert; Arlon-Bastogne; and Luxembourg-Diekirch-St. Vith. The final attack selected would, as Patton then saw it, be delivered by the VIII and III Corps. When Patton arrived at Verdun on the morning of the 19th, Eisenhower asked how soon the III Corps could launch its counterattack. Patton replied that he could start a piecemeal attack in three days, a co-ordinated attack in six. The Supreme Commander, who seems to have felt that Patton was a bit too confident, subsequently informed Field Marshal Montgomery that the counter-attack from the south would be made on the 23d or 24th.

The master plan outlined by Eisenhower in the Verdun meeting of the 19th turned on a major effort to plug the holes developing in the north and the launching of a co-ordinated attack from the south. To free the force needed for this initial counterattack, Eisenhower ordered all offensive operations south of the Moselle to be halted forthwith and turned over the entire Third Army sector (except for that occupied by Maj. Gen. Walton H. Walker's XX Corps on the border of the Saar) to General Devers' 6th Army Group. This northward extension of Devers' command would spread the American forces in Alsace and Lorraine rather thin, but Devers (who was present at the Verdun meeting on the 19th) was promised some of the Third Army divisions and artillery.

It was now clear that Patton would be responsible for a major effort to knife into the German southern flank, that he would have at least two of the three Third Army corps, six of its divisions, and the bulk of the army troops for the task. (On 20 December, however, after a visit to Middleton's command post, Patton found that the VIII Corps was in such shape that it could not be used offensively and that the two Third Army corps would have to carry the ball.) A telephone call from Verdun, using a simple code which had been arranged before Patton left Nancy, informed the Third Army chief of staff (Brig. Gen. Hobart R. Gay) that the XII Corps was to disengage at once, that the command post of Eddy's corps and an advance command post for the Third Army were to transfer to Luxembourg City, that the 26th Infantry Division was to start north on the following morning, and that the 35th Infantry Division—which had been in the line for 160 consecutive days—was to be relieved as quickly as possible and be sent to Metz for much needed rehabilitation en route to the Ardennes battle. At midnight of the 20th, the XII Corps front was taken over by its southern neighbor, Maj. Gen. Wade H. Haislip's XV Corps. The 4th Armored and 80th Infantry Divisions had that day passed to the command of the III Corps in the Arlon sector south of Bastogne.

The next morning General Eddy and his immediate staff departed for Luxembourg with a new mission: to assume command of the American troops north and east of Luxembourg City who had held so tenaciously along the southern shoulder of the original German penetration. General Eddy's new command, aside from corps troops, consisted of those units already in the area and the 5th Infantry Division, which had been added to the roster of Third Army formations rolling northward. It moved in piecemeal as it was relieved from the XX Corps' bridgehead at Saarlautern. The troops in the line when Eddy took over were the 4th Infantry Division, the 10th Armored Division (less CCB), CCA of the 9th Armored Division, the 109th Infantry, and other smaller units of the 28th Infantry Division.

When the XII Corps took control of its new zone on the 21st, the German thrust into eastern Luxembourg had been pretty well checked. The three German divisions which the Seventh Army had thrown into the initial attack were drastically depleted by then and apprehensive that the Americans might undertake a counterattack in such force as to penetrate this part of the Seventh Army's blocking position on the southern flank of the German salient. The Americans likewise were concerned lest the enemy make a last major try for a breakthrough before the promised reinforcement arrived from the Third Army.

There was, however, a fairly continuous—although jagged—line of defense confronting the enemy. The new corps' front, facing east and north, reached from Dickweiler, near the west bank of the Sauer River, to Schieren, on the Alzette River, due north of Luxembourg City. The eastern wing was defended by the 4th Infantry

Division and task forces from the 10th Armored Division. The northern wing was held by the 109th Infantry and CCA, 9th Armored Division, backed by detachments from the 10th Armored. This wing, at its western tip, had been wide open. But the 80th Infantry Division of the III Corps was moving in to establish an extension of the American line beyond the Alzette and on the 22d deployed to envelop the enemy bridgehead west of Ettelbruck.

General Patton intended to give General Eddy two infantry divisions from the old Third Army front, the 5th and 35th. The latter had seen very rough fighting; it would need some refitting and for this reason had been ordered to Metz to reorganize before rejoining the XII Corps. Maj. Gen. S. LeRoy Irwin's 5th Infantry Division was in good condition. Introduced into Walker's XX Corps bridgehead at Saarlautern to relieve the 95th Division, two of Irwin's regiments had attacked on 18 and 19 December to widen the breach made earlier in the main bunker lines of the forward West Wall position. General Irwin, however, had some inkling that his division might soon leave the bridgehead for on the night of the 19th the corps commander warned that the attack was to be held up, that the situation in the north was very much confused and that the 5th Division might be moved in that direction. The 10th Infantry division reserve was put on one-hour alert to move "in any direction."

General Walker arrived at Irwin's command post toward noon of the following day. He told Irwin that one regiment of the 95 would relieve the 5th Division in the bridgehead and that the XX Corps was pulling back across the Saar except in one small bridgehead. As to the future employment of the 5th Division he had no word. More precise directions shortly came from the corps headquarters, moving the 10th Infantry, the 818th Tank Destroyer Battalion, and the 735th Tank Battalion toward Thionville on the Luxembourg road. The next order bade Irwin bring his 11th Infantry out of the bridgehead during the night.

The withdrawal of the tank and tank destroyer battalions, each of which had two companies west of the river, went forward by ferry in full daylight; by 1700 these battalions were on the road to Luxembourg. The relief of the 11th Infantry, by an extension of the 2d Infantry sector, began as soon as darkness settled. It went well also, only two casualties being incurred. By 1000 the next morning the entire regiment was in trucks en route to Thionville. The enemy was neither in strength nor in frame of mind able to interfere with the American withdrawal, although the 2d Infantry attempt to hide the reduction of the line by increased fire fooled the Germans not one whit. Relieved on the night of 21 December by troops of the 95th Division, the 2d Infantry was already rolling to join its sister regiments when the morning fog blew away.

The XII Corps' Counterattack

That same morning the 10th Infantry initiated the 5th Division fight on a new battleground. Despite confusion, fragmentary orders, and a general sense that the leading columns of the division were moving toward an unknown destination and enemy, the 10th Infantry (Col. Robert P. Bell) transfer to Luxembourg had been accomplished in good time. Two officers of Irwin's staff reached the Third Army headquarters in Luxembourg at 1730 on 20 December and there received an assembly area for the regiment and some maps. Hurrying back down the Thionville road the staff officers met the column, blacked out but moving at a good clip. In the early evening the column rolled through the streets of Luxembourg City, and an hour or so after midnight the first trucks drove into the assembly area near Rammeldange. Then the column closed, the infantry shivering out the rest of the night in the trucks.

The mission of the 5th Infantry Division had not yet been defined, but it was clear that it had moved from one battle to another. A series of meetings in Luxembourg during the morning of the 21st resulted in the decision to place the 5th Division north of the city in the sector briefly occupied by the 80th Division. Further, the XII Corps commander told General Irwin to be prepared to attack north or northeast, or to counterattack in the southeast. Later General Eddy warned that the 10th Infantry might have to go into the line that very afternoon to help the 12th Infantry restore the American positions south of Echternach. The 10th did move forward to Ernzen, but no counterattack order was forthcoming.

In the meantime the 11th Infantry arrived in Luxembourg City, its mission to take over the 80th Division position north of the city between Ernzen and Reuland and cover the deployment of the XII Corps—a rather large order for a regimental combat team. However the regimental commander, Col. Paul J. Black, was forced to halt his column when the 80th Division commander gave him a direct order to keep off the road net then being used by the 80th for a shift west into the III Corps' sector. The regimental S-3 later reported that the 80th Division had used the roads only intermittently during the afternoon and that the 11th Infantry could have moved north without difficulty. But on the other hand Maj. Gen. Horace L. McBride had orders to attack the next morning, and the Third Army commander, as he very well knew, would brook no delay. In any case the halt of the 11th Infantry on the north edge of the city did create a mammoth road jam.

During the evening General Eddy met his commanders at the 4th Division command post. Reports coming in from the 12th Infantry, holding the weakest section of the 4th Division front, were discouraging, for that afternoon the 212th Volks Grenadier Division had made substantial progress in an attack along the main road leading from Echternach toward Luxembourg City. Although the 12th Infantry line had hardened and now held near Scheidgen, General Barton expected that the enemy would try another punch down the road. But, even while the American commanders were meeting, the German LXXX Corps staff was drafting orders for a piecemeal withdrawal by the 212th Volks Grenadier Division to begin that very night.

The enemy gains on 21 December marked the high tide of the advance over the Sauer begun six days before, a fact that could not yet be appreciated by the little group of commanders gathered in the 4th Division command post. General Irwin probably summed up what all were thinking: "Situation on whole front from east of us to north varies from fluid to no front at all. Information is very scanty and the situation changes hourly." Under these circumstances General Eddy decided that the 10th Infantry should be placed under tactical control of the 4th Division and attack around noon the following day to restore the situation on the 12th Infantry front.

Admittedly this was the kind of partial solution frowned upon by the field service regulations. General Irwin noted, "I anticipate too much piecemeal action for a while to get any tangible results." But the 4th Division had undergone six days of heavy fighting, its last reserves had been used up, and the events of the day just ended seemed to presage a hardening of the enemy's resolve.

The critical section of the main line of resistance was that marked by the villages of Scheidgen, Michelshof, and Osweiler. Here the line was defended by elements of the 1st and 3d Battalions, 12th Infantry, the regimental antitank company, and part of the 159th Engineer Battalion. During the afternoon of the 21st the 212th Volks

Grenadier Division had used one rifle regiment and the divisional fusilier battalion (both at low strength) in the attempt to take the three villages and the commanding ground on which they stood, ground that represented the final objective of the 212th. General Barton, therefore, planned to meet the German threat by sending the 10th Infantry into attack astride the road from Michelshof to Echternach, the two attack battalions jumping off at noon from the crossroad Scheidgen-Michelshof. This line of departure was occupied by two rifle companies, four tanks, and five platoons of engineers.

Through the morning of the 22d enemy batteries busily shelled the area just behind the American positions. The attack by the 1st and 2d Battalions of the 10th Infantry never really got going. The 2d Battalion on the left of the road deployed some three hundred yards behind the assigned line of departure and started forward just as the Germans began an assault against the small force dug in on the line. German guns supporting the grenadiers made any movement in formation impossible. As it was, the bulk of the two fresh companies reached the line about the same time that the German assault waves struck. The troops on the line were able to beat the enemy back, but not before the 2d Battalion troops had been deflected to the right and left by the enemy onrush. Considerably disorganized, the two companies hurriedly dug in just to the south of the original American covering force.

On the right of the road the 1st Battalion was faced with thick woods and very rough ground. During the morning reconnaissance parties had come forward to look over the route of advance but had been foiled by a thick ground fog and alert enemy gunners. When the battalion deployed for the advance to the line of departure it ran into trouble, for the company next to the road came under the artillery concentration laid down in support of the German assault just described and suffered a number of casualties. Control in woods and ravines was difficult and the company drifted across the road behind the 2d Battalion. It was growing dark when the 1st Battalion finally reorganized and dug in, still short of the line of departure. The intense artillery and Werfer fire by enemy gunners throughout the day, together with the infantry assault of the afternoon, had been designed to cover the 212th Volks Grenadier Division while it withdrew from the exposed position in the Scheidgen salient. Fresh American reinforcements had been held in check; the German withdrawal had been successful.

General Eddy telephoned General Irwin during the evening to say that he planned to use the 5th Division as part of a corps attack to drive the Germans back over the Sauer in the angle formed by the Sauer and Moselle Rivers. Irwin's whole division was in Luxembourg but somewhat dispersed. The 11th Infantry had taken over the reserve battle positions north of Luxembourg City formerly occupied by the 80th Division. The 2d Infantry, having left the XX Corps' bridgehead with only minor incident, was assembled around Junglinster, ready with trucks and attached tank destroyers for use as the corps' mobile reserve. Given time to assemble, the fresh 5th Division could take over from Barton's battle-weary 4th. That night Irwin and his staff pored over maps and march orders for the attack to clear the enemy from the near side of the Sauer, an attack scheduled for the morning of 24 December.

In the interim the two battalions of the 10th Infantry began their second day of action, a clear day but bitter cold with snow underfoot. On the right the 1st Battalion made some progress, but one company lost its way in the heavy woods and a gap opened between the battalions. The main difficulty encountered by both battalions was that of negotiating the heavy belt of timber which lay to the front and in which a relatively small number of the enemy could put up a fight out of all relation to their actual strength. Further, the American advance followed a series of parallel ridge lines; screened by the woods the Germans could and did filter along the draws separating the American companies and take them on individually.

The 2d Battalion had a particularly rough time. Company F, which entered the forest northeast of Michelshof, at first killed or captured a number of Germans in snow-covered foxholes just inside the woods. Then the German shells began to burst through the trees. The company broke into little groups, turning this way and that to avoid the fire-many were scooped up by Germans who had been waiting in their foxholes. When the company withdrew it numbered forty-six men, but later a large number of stragglers appeared at Michelshof. On the left Company E advanced until it came under fire from a cross-grained ridge just ahead. As the company deployed for the assault a large force of German infantry erupted from the draw on its flank, preceded, as it moved, by a curtain of bursting shells. There was plenty of American artillery on call for such an emergency — six battalions were supporting the 10th Infantry attack — and the Germans were dispersed. A few tough enemy riflemen dug in as best they could on the frozen ground and held their place, forcing Company E to "infiltrate" back to its take-off position. This day, then, had been only moderately successful for the 10th Infantry, in part because it was working without the support of its own 5th Division artillery, but the reserve battalion had not been committed and the division stood waiting to expand to attack.

The final field order issued by the XII Corps called for an attack at 1100 hours on the 24th to seize and hold the line of the Sauer and Moselle Rivers with such enemy crossings as might remain intact. The main effort was delegated to the 5th Infantry Division and the 10th Armored Division, the latter having extracted much of its strength from the line on the left of the 4th Division to form a counterattack reserve. The 4th Infantry Division was to hold in place as the 5th passed through, supporting the 5th's attack by fire wherever possible. Finally, the 2d Cavalry Group (reinforced), which was just moving into the new XII Corps area from the old, would take over the extended Moselle flank on the right of the corps. This had been a constant concern to General Barton during the 4th Division battles and had absorbed battalions of the 22d Infantry badly needed on the fighting line. The artillery support planned for the attack included fifteen battalions of corps artillery plus the organic battalions in the divisions. The mechanized units available represented considerable strength: two combat commands of the 10th Armored Division with CCA of the 9th Armored Division attached; two separate tank battalions; five tank destroyer battalions, of which three were self-propelled; and two cavalry squadrons.

The German LXXX Corps faced the XII Corps with two divisions in the line anchored on the Sauer and no corps reserve. The deep valley of the Schwarz Erntz remained the boundary between these divisions, constituting as it had in earlier fighting an ever present physical obstacle to a homogeneous corps front and coordinated maneuver. On the right the 276th Volks Grenadier Division was engaged in small-scale attacks near Savelborn and Christnach. The extreme left or eastern wing of this division was not solidly anchored, and all attempts to break out of the Schwarz Erntz gorge and bring the left forward in conformity with the advance of the neighboring division had been thwarted. The result was that the 212th Volks Grenadier Division, on the right, occupied a south-facing line stepped forward of the 276th and precariously open at its western end. To cover this gap the 423d Regiment had spread thin, so thin that its main line of resistance was little more than a series of smallish strongpoints. As a result the LXXX Corps' order shortening the 212th line by withdrawal on the night of 21 December was issued with the intention of contracting the 423d to give more body to absorb the American punches when they came.

The Echternach bridgehead, expanded toward Michelshof, was defended by the 320th Infantry and the division fusilier battalion. The far left wing of the division and corps was tied to the Sauer by the 999th Penal Battalion. On paper, General Sensfuss' 212th Volks Grenadier Division had a third regiment, the 316th, but although this unit had helped establish the bridgehead it was the Seventh Army reserve and not even the corps commander could use it freely. The field replacement battalions belonging to the LXXX Corps were almost completely drained by the heavy losses incurred in the infantry regiments. The rifle companies of the two line divisions numbered about forty men apiece. Each division had only one light and one medium field artillery battalion in direct support; the corps had perhaps five battalions, plus one Werfer brigade. Probably the bulk of this firepower had displaced across the river to positions directly behind the divisions. The infantry companies had fought during the first days without the aid of assault guns, but a few of these and two companies of antitank guns reached the LXXX Corps just before the American attack on the 24th.

The Seventh Army, and more particularly Beyer's corps, began the Ardennes battle as the kitchen maid in the scullery and would end it in the same status. Replacements, artillery, armor, and supplies by this stage of the German counteroffensive went first to the two panzer armies. Since there was inadequate transport for resupply in the main battle area, Brandenberger could hardly expect that additional trucks and critical items would reach the tactical backwater where his army was stranded. The German commanders on the Sauer front had recognized as early as the 21st and 22d that the bolt had been shot; they and their weary troops knew that the coming battle already was lost. The ground to be held, however, generally favored the defense, just as it had favored the Americans in the first phase.

There was one notable exception—the natural corridor of the Schwarz Erntz. This corridor could be used to split the two German divisions. Moreover, it led directly to the main corps' bridge at Bollendorf and this bridge, if lost, would leave the bulk of the 276th Volks Grenadier Division stranded on the west bank of the Sauer. So seriously was this threat regarded that on 22 December the Seventh Army started work on a heavy bridge at Dillingen to the rear of the 276th.

The morning of the 24th broke clear and cold, bringing a mixed blessing. The thermometer stood below 20 degrees F, and the American foot sloggers would suffer (trench foot was commencing to appear), but the gunners and fighter-bomber pilots could rejoice. With two fire direction centers handling the corps artillery and with perfect visibility at the observation posts, the battalions fired salvo after salvo for interdiction and destruction. A few woods and villages got special treatment—TOT's with white phosphorus, a killing device for which General Patton had built up some attachment among troops of the Third Army. It seemed to the Americans that the good shooting by enemy gunners in the forty-eight hours past required an answer; so counterbattery work began the moment the infantry jumped off in the attack. During the day and night the XII Corps artillery would fire 21,173 shells to support the attack on a ten-mile front. The 5th Division artillery fired 5,813 rounds, exceeding the daily expenditure during the bitter September battle in the Arnaville bridgehead. General Weyland's XIX Tactical Air Command, old friend of the 5th Division, made good use of beautiful flying weather, but there were many targets to divert the fighter-bombers beyond the XII Corps zone. The 405th Fighter Group flew eight missions during the day, dropping fragmentation and napalm bombs at points along the Sauer, then strafing and bombing the roads east of the river.

At 1100 the ground attack commenced. There must have been an uneasy feeling that the enemy had plenty of fight left because the corps commander told Irwin that should he feel the attack was proving too costly it would be called off. Caution, it may be said, had become less opprobrious in the Third Army since 16 December. The XII Corps G-2, who like many other intelligence officers had miscalculated the German ability to resist during the optimistic days of early September, now estimated that the enemy reserves in front of the corps equaled one infantry and one armored division. At the same time the American staffs had an uncertain feeling that the extremely tenuous connection between the XII and XX Corps along the Moselle would attract German attention.

The 5th Division began the attack with three regiments in line on an 8-mile front reaching from Savelborn on the west to Osweiler on the east. From the line of departure, generally in the rear of the main line of resistance, Irwin would feed his battalions into the 10th Armored line on the left and the 4th Division line on the right, eventually relieving the latter by extending the 5th Division wing, lengthened by the 2d Cavalry Group, to the Sauer. Task forces of the 10th Armored Division were to attack on a northern thrust line, clearing the villages on the south banks of the Sauer as they went. The main effort by the 5th Division, also looking north, aimed in its early stages at high ground overlooking the Echternach bridgehead: Hill 313 southwest of Lauterborn, the scene of much bitter fighting when first the Germans pushed down the road from Echternach; the ridge south of Berdorf commanding the Schwarz Erntz gorge; and, in the old 9th Armored sector north of the gorge, the plateau and village of Haller.

On the right of the division the two battalions of the 10th Infantry continued their attack north of Michelshof. Along the thickly wooded ridges to their front the 320th Infantry, supported by most of the 212th Volks Grenadier Division artillery, was concentrated to block the way to Echternach. The 1st Battalion, advancing to the right of the Michelshof-Echternach highway, once again found the combination of heavy woods, Germans in well-disguised foxholes, and accurate shellfire too much. Two hours after the attack began the enemy retaliated with a counterattack, assault guns paving a way for the infantry. The American gunners quickly disposed of this. The 2d Battalion, to the west, had eight medium tanks belonging to the 737th Tank Battalion and less difficult ground. Four tanks and two platoons of Company G started along the main road, covered by other troops advancing on the ridges to either side of the draw. Shell bursts on the road and bullet fire soon drove the troops to the cover of the trees lining the draw, where others of the battalion were ferreting German riflemen out of camouflaged foxholes. Smoke fired to cover the attack gave added momentum; then the tanks destroyed a pair of machine gun nests on Hill 313. Momentarily, however, the attack wavered when a part of Company G turned west toward a hill mass it mistook for its objective. Brought back, the infantry followed the tanks to the proper objective. The Germans there decided not to engage the Shermans, and by dark the battalion had Hill 313.

The 2d Infantry sector, in the division center, extended from the Scheidgen draw west to the Müllerthal (Schwarz Erntz). Immediately to the north lay the thick forest and rugged ground of the Kalkesbach, an unsavory obstacle. Col. A. Worrell Roffe, the 2d Infantry commander, decided to risk a flanking thrust along the Müllerthal with his 2d Battalion and to use his 3d Battalion in a frontal attack against the

Kalkesbach. For the final punch a tank company and the 1st Battalion lay waiting in Colbet. If all went well the regiment would swing onto the Berdorf plateau and face eastward above the Sauer River.

To gain entrance to the Müllerthal was no simple task. It required an attack due west down into the draw, where artillery could be of no help. Companies F and G undertook the task, and the fight became a manhunt, rifleman against rifleman, stalking one another in crevices, on cliffs, from tree to tree. The quarry, skillfully hidden, had the best of it. Company F ran against a strongpoint on a cliff and was the loser in a firefight. Company G lost direction several times in the maze of cross corridors, but at every point drew sharp fire. At dark the two companies dug in against bullets seemingly whistling in from every direction. It was evident that the tree-covered and rocky floor of the gorge was no place for further attack, and Colonel Roffe ordered the two companies to fight their way out of the gorge at daybreak. The battalion was then to gather in an attack on Doster Farm, which overlooked the road to Berdorf.

The 3d Battalion, north of Scheidgen, also had hard fighting and a slow advance. The terrain over which the attack was made consisted of alternating draws and ridges, cleared ground and timber. Advance by ridge line or draw terminated in cross corridors, natural glacis for the enemy riflemen firing down the slope. At one point Company L suddenly was swept by rifle and machine gun fire, suffered thirty casualties, lost two company commanders in the space of minutes, and became disorganized and unable to move. Lt. Col. Robert E. Connor, the battalion commander, got the division artillery to work on the ridge line confronting the company, sent his S-3, Capt. Frederic C. Thompson, up to sort out the demoralized soldiers and replace the platoon and squad leaders who were hors de combat, then put his reserve, Company K, in to flank the German position. The reserve company made its way to the head of a draw from which the enemy could be taken in enfilade. While this flanking fire swept the German line, Company L (reorganized in two platoons of twenty-five men each) attacked with marching fire. The ridge was gained and most of the defenders killed, but this time the attackers lost only three men. Company I, advancing along a draw on which Werfers were directed, took many losses during the day. All told the 2d Infantry had made only a few hundred yards gain by the close of 24 December.

The 3d Battalion commander reported that the action had been like trying to catch a rat in a maze. The Germans, familiar with the ground, had run back and forth through the draws, popping up in new and unexpected positions. The Americans had lost direction and found maneuver difficult in the dense woods and jagged terrain, while their advance along the more direct paths offered by the draws had given the German batteries easy targets. After the untoward events of this first day the regimental commander instructed his battalions to avoid the draws as much as possible and work along the higher ground by short flanking attacks in which control could be retained.

The 11th Infantry took its attack positions during the night of the 23d in the rear of the 10th Armored screen, the 3d Battalion on the left at Larochette (Fels) and the 1st Battalion southeast of Christnach. Colonel Black had been ordered to put his main effort on the right in an attack up the draws in support of the 2d but decided to throw his weight on the left. The left battalion, draped in white sheets and supported by tanks, made its advance in column of companies on a narrow thrust line bearing north in the direction of Haller and hit squarely between the battalions of the 988th

Regiment. Whenever the enemy stood his ground, artillery and tank fire was brought to bear, quickly followed by infantry assault paced with machine gun fire. Following a level ridge line the 3d Battalion made good time. By midafternoon it held its objective, a wooded rise less than a thousand yards southwest of Haller.

The 1st Battalion had as its objective the wooded table which arose above the Schwarz Erntz northeast of Christnach — the scene of bitter fighting and bloody losses for the Americans when the enemy had held the initiative. Company A, sent down into the Müllerthal gorge while the remainder of the battalion threw in a holding attack on the left, moved slowly but steadily, until after some three hours it was opposite the village of Müllerthal. Here the Germans had dug in, checking the advance with machine gun and mortar fire into the gorge from Waldbillig. Company B came in to help against Waldbillig, moving northwest through one of the cross corridors. As soon as the troops left the cover of the draw they encountered direct fire, and it looked as though the 1st Battalion would find it tough to continue a frontal attack.

The rapid advance by the 3d Battalion on the left appeared a solution to this tactical problem. Colonel Black prepared to alter the 11th Infantry scheme of maneuver on the 25th. The 3d Battalion was to be relieved by the regimental reserve, then wheel to the right, bypass south of Haller, and seize the two hill objectives, the Hardthof and Hohwald, in front of the 1st Battalion. During the night 1st Battalion patrols worked to the edge of Waldbillig, found little indication of enemy strength and by daylight the battalion had a company in the village.

This first day of the 5th Division attack had netted rather limited gains except on the extreme left flank and in the 10th Infantry sector at Hill 313. The six American battalions engaged had lost about two hundred dead and wounded. The enemy generally had held the attackers at arm's length (only nineteen prisoners went through the 5th Division cage) and probably had fewer casualties. The German artillery had been very active and effective, despite heavy counterbattery fire, while the tortuous nature of the ground had robbed the gunners supporting the 5th Division of much good shooting. But something had been accomplished. The 4th Infantry Division at last had been relieved (although it proved difficult to find and make physical contact with some isolated outposts of the 4th Division line), and Col. Charles H. Reed's 2d Cavalry Group took over the quiet portion of the line on the right of the 5th Division.

At the close of day, there were indications at several points that the enemy was pulling away. A German withdrawal actually did take place during the night. The 2d Infantry battle along the floor and sides of the Schwarz Erntz, viewed so pessimistically by those engaged, had convinced General Sensfuss, the 212th Volks Grenadier Division commander, that his extended right flank soon would be pierced or turned.

To form a shorter and thicker line, Sensfuss drew in both flanks and gave up ground at his center, creating a new position which reached from Berdorf across the hills flanking the entrance to Echternach (only 2,500 yards from the center of that town) and west to the Sauer. Meanwhile the miscellaneous troops covering the flank of the 212th west of the river withdrew behind the Sauer, leaving only small outposts behind.

The 10th Armored Division, to which were attached the 106th Infantry and CCA, 9th Armored, put two task forces into the attack on 24 December, their mission to clear the enemy from the Ermsdorf-Gilsdorf road. In keeping with the 5th Division attack on the right, the axis of advance generally ran northeast. Task Force Standish, on the right, was weighted with tanks and armored infantry backed by two armored field artillery battalions. One of its two teams advanced with little opposition, ending the day just northwest of Eppeldorf. The second team came under the German guns while moving across open ground west of Eppeldorf; the first reports said half the team was lost to shellfire and rockets. Driven back to the cover of a wood lot the team reorganized, took on reinforcements, and returned to the attack, this time swinging wide of the town to join the companion team. Later a task force from CCX (as CCA, 9th Armored Division, now was named) seized the high ground west of Eppeldorf.

Task Force Rudder, composed of two battalions (less than half strength) of the 109th Infantry, most of the 90th Cavalry Reconnaissance Squadron, and a company of tank destroyers, found the Germans decamping from the narrow strip they had held south of the Sure River. Most of the fighting involved enemy on the north bank from Ettelbruck to the east. The tank destroyers claimed to have caught and destroyed numerous vehicles and one horse-drawn battery. In Gilsdorf the German rear guard succeeded in gaining a little time, but the attack continued eastward until nightfall, when Rudder's troops paused on the hill west of Moestroff.

While this advance was sweeping the near bank of the Sure the enemy destroyed his foot and pontoon bridges. The 10th Armored attack and the deep thrust achieved by the left wing of the 5th Division in the Haller sector was rapidly crowding the 276th Volks Grenadier Division back on Wallendorf and Dillingen, the crossings over which the division had come on 16 December. On Christmas Eve Colonel Dempwolff moved the command posts of his division and regiments closer to the river—a sign of things to come. By this time there was no real tactical connection between the 276th and the 212th Volks Grenadier Divisions; each had been compressed into the area of its original bridgehead.

Since the river line in the 10th Armored Division zone had been reached on the first day of the XII Corps' attack, Christmas passed quietly on the Ettelbruck-Moestroff-Eppeldorf line except for sounds of the tank destroyers sporadically blasting at German traffic across the Sure on the Diekirch-Bettendorf road. But for the 5th Infantry Division Christmas was no day of celebration. At 0730 the infantry crawled out of their frozen foxholes and moved into the attack. During the first hours they encountered few of the enemy, for the 212th had given up considerable ground during the night withdrawal, but the German assault guns and artillery quickly made their presence known. Although the 10th Infantry right slammed against the new enemy line in the Hardt woods before the day was through, it succeeded in lining up with the 22d Infantry to the east.

The 3d Battalion, which had taken over Hill 313 during the night, found that the Germans had fallen back a few hundred yards to the far side of a fine natural barrier, the Leimerdelt draw. This ravine was some two hundred feet deep and five hundred yards across; its sides were virtually cliffs. Attempts to work around the draw by way of tributary cross corridors failed because the enemy had blocked these routes with machine guns. Lt. Col. Alden Shipley, the battalion commander, asked permission to sideslip westward and flank the draw from higher ground, but the 2d Infantry was engaged in the area Shipley needed for this maneuver and the request had to be denied.

North of Scheidgen, on the 3d Battalion, 2d Infantry, front, American artillery had pounded the enemy all through the night in preparation for the attack, some batteries using the new POZIT fuze. Soon after the infantry started forward, reports came back that much damage had been done the enemy, that his line was softening. By afternoon the battalion had advanced well into the Friemholz woods, but not until the tankers had shelled the enemy out of a foxhole line at the timber's edge. The 2d Battalion, after a rugged night for its main force in the Müllerthal gorge, set about extricating the two companies there in preparation for the attack against Doster Farm. This was no easy task. Rather than work its way the length of one of the exit draws in which Company G had settled during the night, this company attacked up and over the bank, firing and taking its losses. Company F had a hard time disengaging, but got out along the path taken by Company G.

The battalion finally re-formed on Company E, and the three serviceable tanks left in the attached platoon then prepared to attack Doster Farm, a small collection of stone buildings on an open rise. The German infantry had entrenched here, while in the woods to the north a section of antitank guns covered the clearing. One of the enemy guns knocked out a tank but in so doing enabled American observers to direct accurate fire on the gun positions. Once the guns were stilled the tanks and infantry took the farm by assault, then pushed to within a thousand yards of Berdorf.

West of the Müllerthal the 11th Infantry set out on the wheeling movement planned the night before to reduce the stubborn resistance in front of its right flank. Company A of the 91st Chemical Battalion smoked Haller while the 3d Battalion, reinforced by ten Jumbo tanks from the 737th Tank Battalion, crossed the southern face of the village and attacked toward the Hardthof rise. After this rapid and successful advance, the tanks withdrew to help the 1st Battalion drive the enemy off the Hohwald northeast of Waldbillig. Haller itself fell to the reserve battalion, which at twilight sent a rifle company and tank platoon against the village. Nearly two hundred prisoners were rounded up from the 988th, the center regiment of the 276th Volks Grenadier Division.

The 5th Division rate of advance had accelerated appreciably during the second day of action, particularly at those points where tanks were brought into action. Difficult terrain, however, denied rapid exploitation and a clear breakthrough to the Sauer. Then, too, trench foot showed an alarming incidence among the attacking infantry, who found it impossible to keep their feet dry in this attack across the snow-fed streams in the bottom of the draws. The 5th Division, like other veteran divisions, was filled with troops who had returned to duty after evacuation for wounds for sickness, and these "RTD's" were much more susceptible to trench foot than other troops. Still, it was obvious that the enemy was in bad shape and lacked the rifle strength or the heavy weapons to stand for long against tank-infantry assault. General Eddy and General Irwin agreed that the attack was profitable and should continue, although both were anxious to get their troops under cover.

The LXXX Corps could hardly be said to have a line of defense in either of its division bridgeheads on the 26th. Rather there remained an unevenly linked chain of small troop concentrations defending wood lots, hills, or villages — in effect a series of bridgeheads within the two main bridgehead areas. The 212th Volks Grenadier Division was in a particularly hazardous position, for the attack by the 3d Battalion in the 2d Infantry sector had carried to within sight of the Sauer, thus separating the German centers of defense at Berdorf and Echternach. In fact the enemy infantry to the front of the 3d Battalion had been forced to swim the chilly river on the night of the 25th.

The 1st Battalion, 10th Infantry, emerged from the Hardt woods and advanced astride the ridge lines leading north to Echternach. German Teller mines linked with trip wires dotted the trails and the ridge crests, slowing the advance, but by dark the battalion was only a half-mile from the town. The 3d Battalion, stopped the previous day at the Leimerdelt draw, renewed its advance about 0300 with a stealthy descent into the draw, Company L moving on the right to the bend where the draw turned north toward Echternach. Company I, on the left, attacked at daybreak through two tributary draws leading out to the north, each rifleman weighed down with three bandoleers of ammunition. Attacking boldly, firing at every possible enemy hiding place, and never halting for cover, the company killed the Germans in their foxholes or drove them back in flight toward the river. A small detachments of the enemy made a brief stand at Melick Farm, then gave way to artillery shelling and assault by Company L. Company I drove on to the ridge overlooking Echternach and the Sauer, while tanks shelled the woods and draw on the flank.

From this vantage point the artillery observer accompanying the riflemen could see little groups of the enemy paddling across the river in rubber boats. A few were swimming, others were running across a small wooden bridge. Time after time the forward artillery observer called for battalion concentrations, watching the bursts with the POZIT fuze thirty feet over the heads of the fleeing Germans and the murderous effects therefrom. For a while the enemy persisted in using the crossing site, then broke, fleeing into Echternach or along the road to Berdorf. That night patrols entered Echternach but could find no signs of the enemy or of Company E, 12th Infantry, which, it was hoped, still would be holed up somewhere in the town.

In the 5th Division center the 2d Infantry struck at Berdorf and the hill mass next to the Sauer, two companies of the 2d Battalion closing on Berdorf at dawn. There in the half-light Company G, marching on the left, saw troops standing in formation along the main village street while an officer pointed to various houses, apparently disposing his men. The American commander thought that Company E might have come in from the right, but when he called out, "Is that Easy Company?" a gruff voice answered "Yah, das ist Easy Company." The surprised Americans recovered in time to shoot down or capture a number of the enemy, but enough reached the houses to organize a stubborn defense. Nevertheless by dark the 2d Battalion had captured half the town, a few prisoners, a number of decorated Christmas trees, and the cold leftovers of Christmas dinner.

Early in the fight Colonel Roffe decided to employ his reserve, the 1st Battalion, in a drive for the final regimental objective, the woods near Hamm Farm on the ridge north of Berdorf. The reserve battalion marched in column toward Berdorf, expecting to pass through the 2d Battalion, but found a bitter fight in progress and the surrounding area plastered with shellfire. When the 1st Battalion tried to sideslip to the west it ran into a group of Germans in the draw on its left flank and very heavy artillery fire. Company C alone lost thirty-two men while deploying to attack. Not until the morning of 27 December did the final collapse of the Berdorf defense enable the 1st Battalion to reach the woods at Hamm Farm. The 3d Battalion had meanwhile come forward to the east of Berdorf and reached Birkelt Farm, overlooking the river. All that remained were small rear guard detachments, but these put up a real fight in the woods and stone farmhouses. That night many Germans withdrew and swam the river to reach the West Wall lines.

The operations of the 11th Infantry on Christmas Day had forced considerable retraction in the southern flank of the 276th Volks Grenadier Division. Colonel Black ordered the attack continued on the 26th, sending two battalions against what was left o the 987th and 988th Regiments. Before daybreak the 2d Battalion wheeled right and began an attack along the road running from Haller to Beaufort. The leading company encountered the first of the enemy in the wooded ravine of the Hallerbach, well camouflaged in unorthodox positions facing both sides of the ravine so that the attackers found themselves receiving mortar, Werfer, and bullet fire from front and rear.

About 1000 Maj. John N. Acuff, the battalion commander, withdrew his infantry a short distance to see what a mortar barrage could do. The woods were thick, visibility was poor, and mortar fire proved not very effective. When the Americans resumed the assault they in turn were hit by a counterattack. It was dusk when the enemy finally gave way and the 2d Battalion reached the woods north of the ravine. Ordered by Colonel Black to continue the attack through the night, the battalion converged shortly after midnight in a pincers move on the town of Beaufort, located on commanding ground and controlling one of the main exit roads leading to the Dillingen bridge. The enemy held for awhile in the north edge of Beaufort but by daybreak had abandoned the town to the 2d Battalion.

During the morning of 26 December the 3d Battalion had attacked almost without opposition, crossing the Hallerbach ravine and gaining the high ground to the east of Beaufort and overlooking the road to Dillingen. But when the first appetizing target appeared, a column of a hundred or more vehicles heading for the Dillingen bridge, the artillery radios failed to function and a hasty barrage laid on the road by mortars and machine guns caught only the tail of the column. By noon patrols were in position on the river bank to observe the Dillingen bridge site. Calls for artillery fire this time got through to the batteries, but the gunners had difficulty in directing fire into the deep river valley. The division air support party vectored a flight of P-47's over the bridge, but three separate passes failed to gain a hit. Later in the day the artillery observers succeeded in getting high-angle fire on the bridge; one hit registered while the span was crowded with men and vehicles, but the bridge continued in use.

At the end of this third day of the 5th Division attack General Eddy and General Irwin agreed that the mission assigned was as good as accomplished. The west bank of the Sauer had been gained at several points, and the enemy was hastening to recross the river and gain the protection of the West Wall. The Americans had taken over five hundred prisoners in the period of 24-26 December and had recovered much American matériel, lost in the first days of the German advance. There still remained some necessary mopping up in those pockets where the German rear guard held on to cover the withdrawal of the last units of the LXXX Corps as these made their way to safety.

Although the 212th completed its withdrawal over the Bollendorf bridge during the night of 26 December, roving patrols continued to operate on the American side of the river well into January. The 276th Volks Grenadier Division held in some force for another twenty-four hours under specific Seventh Army orders to do so in keeping with the larger army mission of containment. For the 11th Infantry, therefore, there was one last round of fighting, fighting which cost the 1st Battalion dear in attacks against Bigelbach on the 27th. German artillery and Werfers, emplaced on the east bank of the river, made good practice, while the worn grenadiers fought stubbornly wherever they were assailed.

There was one exit through which the German rear guard could hope to escape with minimum loss of men and equipment once its delaying stint was completed — the Dillingen bridge, built by the Seventh Army engineers for just this purpose.

American fighter-bombers made a second effort against the span on 27 December, but reported near misses. Colonel Dempwolff has said that he was much worried about the bridge during the daylight hours of the 27th. Dramatically, the real danger to the division came after dark just as the final withdrawal commenced. Perhaps the law of averages was working, or it may be that an American gunner put some particularly potent spell on this one shell; in any case, a direct hit blasted a gap of about fifteen yards in the bridge structure. When the German engineers hastened to repair the span, they came under small arms fire from American patrols working down toward the river. Then, about 0200, shellfire suddenly increased to feverish intensity and the engineers were driven off the bridge. This shelling finally slackened, the span was repaired, the assault guns, flak, and vehicles filed across, and just after daybreak the Germans blew the bridge.

From 22 December, when the 10th Infantry launched the 5th Division attack toward the Sauer, until 28 December, when the last formal resistance ended, the division took over 800 prisoners. Estimates by burial parties set the number of Germans killed at about the same figure. Losses in the 5th Division totaled 46 officers and 899 men as battle casualties; 22 officers and 598 men were nonbattle casualties — a high ratio but understandable in terms of the continued 20 degree cold and the footslogging advance through countless icy streams. The 276th Volks Grenadier Division lost about 2,000 officers and men between 20 and 28 December, from all causes, and the original division commander had been killed in the action. Many of its companies were reduced to ten-man strength. The average strength of the rifle companies in the 212th Volks Grenadier Division, when they returned to the West Wall, was 25-30 men, but the figure is derived from losses suffered since 16 December. Although this division was better trained than the 276th, it generally had engaged in harder fighting. Its total losses, as estimated by the division commander, were about 4,000 officers and men. The only exact casualty report extant is that of the 988th Regiment, which on 15 December had been at its full strength of 1,868 officers and men. By 28 December the regiment had suffered losses as follows: 190 known killed, 561 missing in action, 411 hospitalized as sick or wounded.

The terrain on which the 4th Infantry Division had defended and over which the 5th Infantry Division had attacked proved to be as difficult as any on which military operations were conducted in the course of the Ardennes campaign. For this reason the battle at the south shoulder of the Bulge merits perusal by the student of tactics. American superiority in heavy supporting weapons, tanks, and tank destroyers never had the full tactical effectiveness on this broken ground which normally would be the case. The military student, however, will have noticed that the psychological effect of American tanks and tank destroyers on an enemy who had no tanks and very few antitank guns was considerable. For this battle German commanders all make much of those periods during the initial American defense and the ultimate counterattack when tanks, even in platoon strength, were employed against them. The relative immobility of the two German divisions, whose flexibility in attack and defense depended almost entirely on the leg power of tired infantry, gave both General Barton and General Irwin a considerable advantage in timing, whether it was in moving troops to counter a thrust or in exploiting weaknesses in the enemy line.

The use of artillery on both sides of the line is one of the features of the XII Corps operations at the Sauer, and in numerous actions German use of the rocket launcher proved particularly disquieting to the Americans. This weapon, whose total weight was only some 1,200 pounds, but which could discharge 450 pounds of high explosive in ten seconds, more than made up for the limited number of conventional artillery tubes that the LXXX Corps had in the bridgehead, and its ease of movement and small silhouette were admirably suited to the broken ground west of the Sauer. The rate and weight of rocket projector fire, plus the fact that the limited German artillery could concentrate to cover well-defined and delimited paths of advance, led the veteran 5th Division to claim that it had been more heavily shelled during these days than in any battle it had sustained. The artillery support furnished the 5th Division, however, had been very effective; German records note it with considerable distaste. As might be expected of this pockmarked and tortuous ground, both sides speak with respect of the enemy's mortars.

By 26 December, the last day of full-fledged attack by the XII Corps against the Sauer salient, the Third Army was fully oriented on its new axis. With the 6th Armored Division en route from the south to join the XII Corps, it was possible to relieve the armor already in the zone and effect a general regrouping calculated to restore some organizational unity. CCA, 9th Armored, therefore, was ordered to Arlon and III Corps control; the 106th Infantry was restored to the 28th Infantry Division, still with the VIII Corps; the 10th Armored Division was directed to hand over its sector to the 6th Armored Division on 27 December and rejoin the XX Corps at Metz. General Patton, wishing to integrate his northern front a little better, redrafted the boundary between the III and XII Corps so that the 80th Infantry Division passed in place to the latter. This new intercorps boundary would originate in the north near Wiltz, run south toward Heiderscheid, and continue to a point below Merzig.

Neither Patton nor Eddy had a definite plan for the employment of the XII Corps once its immediate mission was accomplished and the anchor position of the Third Army opposite the German shoulder was secured. When it became apparent that the fight on the near bank of the Sauer was nearly finished, the corps commander made a tentative plan—probably at Patton's instigation—for an attack north over the Sure River and on toward Bitburg using his new armored division and the 10th Infantry. In addition Eddy asked Irwin's opinion on a river crossing by the 5th Infantry Division. General Irwin agreed that such a follow-up was "worth a thought," reasoning that "the West Wall line in front is weak and we have destroyed much of the garrison."

The Third Army commander finally decided that the 5th and 80th Infantry Divisions would hold the existing line while the 6th Armored moved west to the Bastogne sector and there attacked northward on the left of the 4th Armored Division. The corps front was duly re-formed, the 5th Division edging to the left to join the 80th and the 4th Infantry Division (now commanded by Brig. Gen. Harold W. Blakeley because General Barton had been evacuated by reason of illness) taking over a wider sector on the right. The corps commander did not immediately dismiss the idea of an attack east across the Sauer River and through the West Wall. This project was on-again-off-again until, on 2 January, Patton ordered that plans be made for a corps attack northward. The XII Corps front, however, would remain quiet until 18 January.

Chapter XXI. The III Corps' Counterattack Toward Bastogne

The Verdun meeting on 19 December set in chain the first of a series of actions which the Allies would take to wrest the initiative from the enemy. Nonetheless a few momentous, nerve-shaking days had to elapse before the first gun of the counterattack could be fired. To gain time and save troops the Supreme Commander was willing to let the Allied forces fall back as far as necessary — although it was tacitly understood that the Meuse River must be the limit for any withdrawal. On the 20th General Strong, the SHAEF chief of intelligence, advised General Eisenhower that it looked as if the German command had committed everything it had to the offensive. Flying weather was poor and there was a chance that the Allies now could regroup for a concerted counterattack both north and south without these troop movements being discovered from the air. On this date, therefore, Eisenhower gave Bradley and Montgomery their orders for a counteroffensive against the German salient, to be undertaken as soon as possible.

Air Chief Marshal Tedder, the Deputy Supreme Allied Commander, and a number of others on the SHAEF staff feared that the impetuous Patton would persuade Bradley to let him start the counterattack from the south with only a couple of divisions and that it then would develop piecemeal, as had the German counterattack in Normandy, without a solid tactical base or concrete result. The Supreme Commander himself was well aware of the Third Army commander's penchant for cut and thrust tactics and probably needed little urging to take some action calculated to hold Patton within the constraints of "the big picture." On the other hand Eisenhower recognized that the continued occupation of Bastogne, the key to the entire road net on the south side of the German Bulge, was essential to future offensive operations. Patton, as the SHAEF staff saw it, would make the narrow thrust on the Arlon-Bastogne axis, but any more ambitious plans would have to be subordinated to the larger strategy. Eisenhower, therefore, told Bradley that the American counterattack via Bastogne should be held in check and not allowed to spread, that it was, after all, only a steppingstone for the "main counteroffensive."

Preparations for the Attack

Possibly the "lucky" commander needed some curb on his inherent optimism, but regardless of any pose which Patton may have assumed in the war council at Verdun he and his staff went about the business of mounting this first counterattack coolly and methodically. The direction of attack already had been set by General Eisenhower, that is, north from an assembly area around Arlon. The immediate mission, assigned by the higher command after the Verdun meeting, was the "relief" of Bastogne and the use of its road net as a sally port for a drive by the Third Army to St. Vith in the larger Allied offensive. D-day for the counterattack was 22 December. It must be added that the Third Army order issued the day before the attack was rather ambitious, containing a typical Patton flourish in the prescription of an eventual wheel to the northeast and seizure of the Rhine crossings "in zone." The forces to be employed had been earmarked as early as the night of 18 December when Bradley and Patton agreed to move the new III Corps headquarters (as yet inexperienced and untried) from Metz to Arlon. The divisions given Maj. Gen. John Millikin (the 26th Infantry Division, 80th Infantry Division, and 4th Armored Division) all had been out of the line or in a quiet sector when the Third Army was ordered north, and thus were selected almost automatically.

The area chosen for the III Corps counterattack extended from the Alzette River on the east to Neufchâteau in the west, a front of some thirty miles. Actually these points were not on formal boundaries but rather represent the limits within which the III Corps operation finally developed. This zone, the eastern part lying in Luxembourg, the western in Belgium, contains some of the most rugged ground in the Ardennes. East of the Arlon-Bastogne axis two deeply eroded corridors, cut by the Sure and Wiltz Rivers, form effective barriers to mechanized or motorized advance from the south. The entire area is crisscrossed with rivers and streams, but those of the tableland west of Bastogne lack the gorge-like beds found to the east. Here, as in other parts of the Ardennes, dense woods alternate with rolling fields and clearings. The land is veined with roads, but of varying quality; at their interlacings are found the single farmhouse or the village of a half-dozen dwellings, all promising the phenomenon common to military operations in the Ardennes—the fight for the crossroad. Bastogne, with seven entrant roads, naturally dominates the road complex in this area whether movement be from east to west, as attempted by the XLVII Panzer Corps, or from south to north, as planned for the American III Corps. But in addition to the south-to-north highway from Arlon to Bastogne, there are main roads branching from Arlon to the northeast and northwest, thus offering some flexibility of maneuver. Only one main road south of Bastogne runs east and west, that from Luxembourg City through Arlon to Neufchâteau. This road would form the base of operations for the III Corps.

The enemy situation on the new III Corps front was obscure. The Bastogne garrison knew little of the German deployment beyond the encircling units in direct contact, while the VIII Corps' screen, behind which the III Corps was forming, had been too weak to fight for information. The situation along most of the tenuous and sketchy VIII Corps line was indeed so confused that the location of friendly roadblocks or outposts could hardly be plotted. On the day before the counterattack it was known that the German columns had carried to and beyond Bastogne. It was presumed that the Arlon-Bastogne road had been cut, but this was not certain. Elements of four German divisions were supposed to be in the line opposite the III Corps: the 5th Parachute and the 212th, 276th, and 352d Volks Grenadier Divisions. All but the 5th Parachute had been identified days earlier as belonging to the Seventh Army. What these enemy divisions could do and what they intended to do quite literally was any man's guess. The III Corps attack would have to push off through a fragmentary screen of friendly troops whose positions were uncertain, against an enemy whose exact location was unknown, over terrain which had not been scouted by the Third Army.

The enemy was equally in the dark as to the III Corps capabilities and intentions. The 26th Infantry Division could not be located by German intelligence after it left Metz and would not be identified as present in its new sector until two days after the American drive commenced. The enemy traced the 80th into Luxembourg, but on 22 December believed it was reinforcing "remnants" of the 4th Infantry Division in a purely defensive role.

When General Millikin and his staff settled into the Arlon headquarters on 20 December, with only two days to go before the counterattack target date, the divisions that made up the attack force were either still on the move or were barely completing their shift. The 26th Infantry Division was en route from Metz to Arlon; the 80th Division had just closed into an assembly area near Luxembourg City after a march of 150 miles; the 4th Armored Division had reached Arlon and was trying to find its assembly area on the Arlon-Neufchâteau road. Nor were the three divisions equally ready for return to the fray.

The 26th Division (Maj. Gen. Willard S. Paul) was full of rifle replacements, mostly inexperienced and lacking recent infantry training. This division had seen its first combat in October and had lost almost 3,000 men during bitter fighting in

Lorraine. Withdrawn in early December to take over the Third Army "reinforcement" training program at Metz, the 26th Division had just received 2,585 men as replacements and, on 18 December, was beginning its program (scheduled for thirty days) when the German counteroffensive canceled its role as a training division. The "trainees," men taken from headquarters, antitank sections, and the like, at once were preempted to fill the ranks left gaping by the Lorraine battles. Knowing only that an undefined combat mission lay ahead, the division rolled north to Arlon, completing its move shortly before midnight of the 20th. Not until the next day did General Paul learn that his division was to attack on the early morning of the 22d.

The 80th Division (General McBride) was in good condition. As one of the units being primed by the Third Army for the forthcoming attack against the West Wall, the 80th had been granted priority on replacements, had been rested at St. Avold, and on 18 December was on its way into the line near Zweibrücken when General Patton ordered the move to Luxembourg. There the 80th found itself under the control of the III Corps, its only orders to take up a reserve battle position in the 4th Infantry Division zone. On 21 December McBride first learned that his division would attack the following morning.

The 4th Armored Division (Maj. Gen. Hugh J. Gaffey) had come north under hurried and contradictory orders, the result of the usual time lag between a command decision reached in personal conferences by the top commanders and the receipt of this decision in the lower tactical units. CCB, for example, operated for two days under VIII Corps while the rest of the division was en route to III Corps—a fact that has bearing on the subsequent story of Bastogne. On the night of 18 December General Bradley had told Patton, "I understand from General Ike you are to take over the VIII Corps." That same night CCB, 4th Armored, started for Longwy and the road to Luxembourg. The next day the rest of the division followed, under verbal orders from Patton attaching the 4th Armored Division to the III Corps. These orders were countermanded, then reaffirmed by the 12th Army Group in the course of the 19th.

The advance party of CCB arrived meanwhile at Arlon, and found that the VIII Corps was the only corps operating in the area, the III Corps headquarters not yet having appeared on the scene. Brig. Gen. Holmes E. Dager reported to the commander of the VIII Corps, which was officially under the First Army and would be until noon on 20 December, although all concerned knew that it was to pass to the Third Army. General Middleton perforce had command of this Third Army unit before the anticipated change, whereas Third Army records continued to show the entire 4th Armored Division as assigned to the III Corps. At Dager's request the corps commander agreed to keep CCB together as a tactical unit instead of parceling it out along the front.

The 4th Armored Division had won a brilliant reputation during the autumn battles in Lorraine. It was a favorite of the Third Army commander; so, when its leader, Maj. Gen. John S. Wood, was returned to the United States for rest and recuperation, General Patton named his own chief of staff as Wood's successor. On 10 December the 4th Armored Division came out of the line after five months of incessant fighting. The last phase of combat, the attack in the Saar mud, had been particularly trying and costly. Replacements, both men and matériel, were not to be had; trained tank crews could not be found in the conventional replacement centers—in fact these specialists no longer were trained in any number in the United States. When the division started for Luxembourg it was short 713 men and 19 officers in the tank and infantry battalions and the cavalry squadron.

The state of matériel was much poorer, for there was a shortage of medium tanks throughout the European theater. The division could replace only a few of its actual losses and was short twenty-one Shermans when ordered north; worse, ordnance could not exchange worn and battle-damaged tanks for new. Tanks issued in the United Kingdom in the spring of 1944 were still operating, many of them after several major repair jobs, and all with mileage records beyond named life expectancy. Some could be run only at medium speed. Others had turrets whose electrical traverse no longer functioned and had to be cranked around by hand. Tracks and motors were worn badly: the 8th Tank Battalion alone had thirty-three tanks drop out because of mechanical failure in the 160-mile rush to the Ardennes. But even with battle-weary tanks and a large admixture of green tankers and armored infantry the 4th Armored Division, on its record, could be counted an asset in any operation requiring initiative and battle know-how.

The Ezell Task Force

It is obvious that the Third Army could never have put troops into the Luxembourg area as quickly as it did without a wholesale scuttling of "paper work" and "channels"; that improvisation and reliance on the field telephone as a medium for attaining clear understanding have inherent dangers is equally clear. A bizarre adventure that befell CCB of the 4th Armored in its peregrinations typifies the period of "piecemeal reaction," as some of the participants style it, when Middleton's VIII Corps was trying to plug the yawning gaps in its front with rifle platoons of engineers and mechanics, and before an American riposte could be made in force.

Bradley had told the VIII Corps commander on the night of 18 December that reinforcements were coming up from the Third Army. Sometime later Middleton learned that the 4th Armored Division was heading northward, led by CCB and apparently under attachment to his dwindling command. Another tank command from the Third Army (CCB, 10th Armored Division) had just arrived on the scene, but this Middleton had committed at once to shore up the crumbling defenses between Bastogne and Wiltz. At noon on the 19th (before the VIII Corps had passed to the Third Army) General Middleton telephoned the First Army commander and asked if he might use CCB of the 4th Armored on its arrival. Uncertain of the command situation Hodges referred the request to Bradley, who told the VIII Corps commander that he could employ CCB but only if necessary to hold his position.

By midnight CCB had ended its 150 mile ride and closed in villages on the east side of Vaux-lez-Rosières; all the journal sergeant could enter at this hour was "mission unknown." But by the morning of the 20th the status and duties of Dager's command were really confused, for the III Corps had opened its command post at Arlon and proceeded to give orders on the assumption that the 4th Armored Division in its entirety was reporting to General Millikin. The VIII Corps had ordered Dager to send an officer to Bastogne at daylight on the 20th to determine the exact situation there, but about 0500 that morning someone on the VIII Corps G-3 staff—who it was cannot be determined—ordered Dager to send a tank company, an armored infantry company, and a battery of self-propelled artillery into Bastogne.

Although Dager argued against this fragmentization of his force, at 1030 the small team was on its way, led by Capt. Bert Ezell, executive officer of the 8th Tank Battalion, who earlier had been named the liaison officer to the 101st Airborne. The only mission specified was "to aid CCB of the 10th Armored Division." Since CCB had bivouacked close to the Neufchâteau-Bastogne road this route was used. There had been rumors that the Germans had cut the road, but nobody seemed to know for certain and American reconnaissance was woefully lacking in this sector. En route the team received—or heard—a little small arms fire. In Bastogne Ezell reported to the 101st chief of staff, who turned him over to the division G-3, who passed him on to General McAuliffe, who assigned him to Colonel Roberts, commanding CCB of the 10th Armored. Roberts ordered Ezell to assemble his task force at Villeroux two and a half miles southwest of Bastogne and gave him a number of missions.

About 1400 a radio message from CCB rescinded Ezell's original orders and told him to return to Nives, the 8th Tank Battalion bivouack. This is what had happened. Telephone connection between CCB and General Gaffey's 4th Armored command post had opened, giving Dager an opportunity to express his concern over the way in which his command was being whittled away piecemeal. Gaffey immediately ordered Dager to recall the task force at Bastogne and to move CCB into assembly with the rest of the division northwest of Arlon.

Figuring that someone higher in authority would inform Roberts or McAuliffe, Ezell and his team started for home. On the way into Bastogne the task force had noticed two battalions of field artillery beside the road, the pieces and prime movers jammed together, equipment scattered, and most of the gunners fleeing along the road to the south. This time the task force stopped, found one dead man lying by his prime mover, shot in the head, and an artillery captain single-handedly trying to hitch up the guns and move them to the road. Lieutenant Kiley, who commanded the tank company, hitched three of the pieces to his tanks and left a few of his men to help the anonymous captain. Seven hours after the team set out it was back with CCB. Ezell had counted only three artillery rounds during the trip and had seen signal men calmly laying wire along the highway. At dusk on the 20th, then, the Neufchâteau-Bastogne road still was in friendly hands. Why was CCB as a unit not put in to hold this corridor open? There is no certain answer. The episode of Ezell's task force can be read only through the fog of war as this is generated by the failure of communications, the complexity and unwieldiness of field command, and the natural, human proclivity for overrating (or underrating) the accomplishments of the enemy.

"Drive Like Hell"

General Patton inspected the III Corps dispositions and divisions on 20 December, concluded that the corps concentration was proceeding satisfactorily, and the following day gave the order for attack at 0600 on the 22d. The corps scheme of maneuver, issued to the divisions in the early afternoon, was simple. The III Corps would advance north in the direction of St. Vith. The 80th Infantry Division, on the right, would maintain contact during its advance with the left wing of the XII Corps. The 26th Division would form the center. The 4th Armored Division would advance on the left—Bastogne lay in its zone.

The last of the eleven field artillery battalions which had been taken from active engagement on the old Third Army front to form the corps artillery arrived during the day. They had wheeled north at an average twenty-mile-per-hour clip. In addition the infantry divisions each had a tank battalion and a self-propelled tank destroyer battalion attached. To eke out some cover on the open west flank, Task Force Lyon, consisting of the 178th Engineer Combat Battalion with reinforcements, was assigned the task of erecting roadblocks and preparing bridges for demolition.

The Third Army commander's last instruction to his commanders reflected the admonition against a dribbling attack given by General Eisenhower: he (General Patton) favored an attack in column of regiments, "or in any case lots of depth." As usual Patton was optimistic. He felt certain that the enemy was unaware of the storm about to break, that German intelligence had not spotted the appearance of the 26th Division in the area, and that it did not know the exact location of the other two divisions. "Drive like hell," said Patton.

The 80th Division Advance

Despite hurried preparations the III Corps attack got off at the appointed hour on the 22d. The 80th Division, whose regiments earlier had assembled north of Luxembourg for the defense of that city, had as line of departure the Mersch-Arlon road on a front of five and a half miles. During the night it was learned that the 109th Infantry of the dispersed 28th Division still was facing the enemy near Vichten, five miles to the north. This would give some cover for the development of the 80th Division attack; so McBride ordered his left wing regiment to pass through the 109th Infantry, relieving it in place. There was no artillery preparation (nor were there any certain targets) for the surprise attack.

The two assault regiments, the 319th Infantry on the left and the 318th Infantry on the right, went forward fast on this cold cloudy morning, tramping over a light blanket of snow which had fallen during the night. In two hours the 319th Infantry (Col. William N. Taylor) reached Vichten and relieved the 109th; as the regiment moved on toward Merzig the first few rounds of small arms fire came in. The 318th Infantry (Col. Lansing McVickar) headed for Ettelbruck, constricted to column formation by the Alzette River on the east and a high ridge on the west. South of the bridgehead town enemy shellfire briefly stopped the advance until the German guns were quieted by counter-battery from the 314th Field Artillery Battalion.

The cannonading was brought on by a peculiar circumstance. The 352d Volks Grenadier Division (General Schmidt) on this morning was advancing along the Diekirch-Ettelbruck-Merzig highway in front of but at a right angle to the American advance from the south. Schmidt was under the impression that his division had broken through the American line and was now marching through undefended, unoccupied country. The 914th Regiment had just entered Ettelbruck when the 318th Infantry appeared. It was the artillery regiment of the 352d, bringing up the tail of the division east of the town which ran afoul of the Americans. Quite obviously the Germans did not expect an attack from this direction. The 914th faced left and deployed hurriedly, using the town as a base, but in the process lost its heavy metal, for the German batteries were in no position to engage in an artillery duel, and fell back to Diekirch.

Farther west the rear of the 915th Regiment column was moving directly across the 319th Infantry line of march. To their amazement, troops of the 3d Battalion suddenly saw the Germans filing past, only a few hundred yards away and oblivious of any danger. Tanks, tank destroyers, and the 57-mm. antitank guns of the 1st Battalion ended this serene promenade. Many Germans were killed, a gun battery was blown to pieces, and numerous trucks and horse-drawn weapons were destroyed. The 319th Infantry had knifed between head and tail of the 352d. It now swung right onto the Ettelbruck road and that afternoon reached the villages of Oberfeulen and Niederfeulen. Merzig, however, remained in German hands.

At sundown the 80th Division could look back on a highly successful day. Extensive gains had been the story along the entire III Corps front and Patton was very much pleased. This was, he told General Millikin, a chance to win the war; the attack must be kept rolling through the night. The 319th Infantry put its 2d Battalion, the reserve, into trucks as far as Oberfeulen. There the battalion dismounted about midnight and under a full moon began an advance to take Heiderscheid. The 318th Infantry, which had found it difficult to maneuver on the constricted southern approach to Ettelbruck or to bring its tanks and tank destroyers to bear against the town, at nightfall began a series of successful assaults to gain the hills which looked down upon Ettelbruck from the west. Company B moved with such speed that it reached the houses at the western edge of the town. Although its commander was wounded during the assault his company held on alone. The 80th Division would have to do some bitter fighting before this bridgehead over the Sure and Alzette was cleared of the enemy, but the division had cut one of the main supply routes of the German Seventh Army.

One lone rifle company holding a few houses hardly made for a handhold on Ettelbruck. In and around the town the enemy had a grenadier regiment and many direct-fire heavy weapons. Because the bluffs surrounding the town precluded much maneuver in attack, assault on the west, or American, bank of the Alzette had to be made frontally. Lt. Col. A. S. Tosi had brought the two other rifle companies of his 1st Battalion close to the edge of the town when daylight came on the 24th (B Company still held inside), but three separate attempts to reach the town failed, and with severe casualties. In the afternoon a few tanks were maneuvered into the van, and with their help the 1st Battalion reached the houses and took fifty or sixty prisoners. By this time the battalion had lost the equivalent of a full company, Colonel Tosi had been seriously wounded, and all company leaders had been killed or wounded. One tank reached the streets but found them cluttered with debris and impassable. The division commander decided to call off the attack; at dusk all of the companies withdrew while artillery plastered Ettelbruck. This second day had voided the bright promises of the first, for the 80th Division finally was in contact with the main German forces, well entrenched in towns and villages which could be attacked only over broken and difficult terrain.

In the course of the afternoon General McBride decided to keep the attack rolling by introducing his reserve regiment, the 317th, between the two attacking regiments. The 317th Infantry (Lt. Col. Henry G. Fisher), which had been following the 318th Infantry, was given the mission of clearing the ridge which ran north to Welscheid. Once beyond this town Fisher's troops were to turn east toward the Sure River, thus cutting to the rear of Ettelbruck. When night fell the regiment was on its way, the 2d Battalion in the lead and the 1st Battalion a thousand yards to its rear. Nearing Welscheid sometime after midnight, the forward battalion started into the assault over a series of rough slopes where each man was outlined by the bright moonlight reflecting from the glazed field of snow. The enemy, waiting with machine guns on the reverse slopes, had all the best of it. The American tanks tried but could not maneuver over the broken ground. The battalion commander therefore sent two of his companies to make a wide detour through a deep gorge, their place in the line being taken by the 1t Battalion. But too much time was consumed by this movement, and day broke on the 24th with the two battalions out in the open and dangerously exposed to German fire. The attack had to be abandoned; new plans were made for bypassing the town and striking directly at Bourscheid and the Sure River.

The 319h Infantry had continued its battle by sending the 2d Battalion against Heiderscheid, which lay on the Ettelbruck-Bastogne route and from which a secondary road ran laterally west to Martelange across the 26th Division zone of advance. Just north of Heiderscheid were several crossing points on the Sure River, the chief natural obstacle to be surmounted by the 80th Division in its march northward. The 2d Battalion (Lt. Col. Paul Bandy) reached Heiderscheid about 0230 on the morning of the 23d, but when two rifle companies neared the edge of the village they were stopped by assault gun fire and machine guns firing tracers to point the targets for the gun crews. Infantrymen with submachine guns worked close enough to fire bursts into the positions from which the orange line of the tracers came but could not deal with the German assault guns. Two American tanks belonging to the 702d Tank Battalion came forward only to be checked by a minefield at a crossroad. A German gun took a shot at the tanks but in so doing gave away its own location, and a quick return shot set the assault gun afire. Guided by the light from the blazing gun carriage the American riflemen rushed the gendarmerie, took it, and there barricaded themselves. About this time the explosion of a German shell detonated the minefield, and the tanks ground forward to the village. An hour or so before noon the last of the stubborn defenders had been routed out and the 2d Battalion was north of the village.

The fight was not finished, for at noon two enemy companies converged in a yelling assault on Heiderscheid. Some of the 2d Battalion broke but the rest stood firm, killed the German infantry commander, and wrote quietus to this threat. Then affairs took a more serious turn as eleven enemy tanks hove in sight, decks and cupolas packed with snow for camouflage. While a hurried call was dispatched for armored aid, bazooka teams crawled forward to try their luck. Two of the enemy tanks fell prey to the bazooka teams, led by 2d Lt. Michael Hritsik, 7 whereupon the others showed themselves loath to close in. Friendly tank destroyers appeared in time to account for four more German tanks, and an American tank knocked out a fifth.

By the time the 3d Battalion (Lt. Col. Elliott B. Cheston) came hurrying up the battle was ended. Cheston's battalion, having spent most of the morning rounding up a large enemy detachment in Merzig, now turned northeast from Heiderscheid and marched through a deep defile to reach and take the hamlet of Tadler on the Sure. The Germans blew the nearby bridge, then sat back on the far bank to pound the battalion with rocket salvos. About dark the regimental commander ordered a company to move west along the river and outpost Heiderscheidergrund; admittedly this was poaching in the zone of the 26th Division, but the bridge there was needed. The company found the bridge intact and a stream of German vehicles running back and forth. Organizing an ambush, the company spent the night picking off unwary travelers.

On the eastern flank the 1st Battalion and its tank support spent most of the 23d negotiating the rough ground, dense woods, and deep snow in an advance from Feulen toward Kehmen. From a hill south of Kehmen the advance guard counted twenty-four tanks rolling toward the village from the east, apparently on their way to retake Heiderscheid. Word already had gone back for more tanks, but those with infantry, plus a few tank destroyers, got in the first fire, immobilized two of the leaders, and so surprised the rest that they turned tail and hurried back to Bourscheid—which the 905th Field Artillery Battalion promptly took under fire. Discerning at least a tank platoon backing the grenadiers inside Kehmen, the 1st Battalion waited until after dark for reinforcements—ten tanks formerly attached to the 28th Infantry Division. With their help, the battalion delivered a sharp assault, destroying three German tanks and freeing the village.

The night battles had shown clearly that the 80th Infantry Division faced hard going as the 24th dawned. The advance had carried north to a point where it impinged on the Seventh Army communications leading to the Bastogne battleground. The main fight for the III Corps was that flaring farther west. Henceforth McBride's operation would be subsidiary to the attack by the corps' left and center, an operation designed to interdict the movement of reinforcements heading for Bastogne and to contain the enemy in the Ettelbruck and Bourscheid sectors. Orders from General Millikin, received at the 80th Division command post early on the 24th, underlined the shift of gravity westward: McBride was to send two battalions of the 318th Infantry from Ettelbruck to assist the 4th Armored Division, and at once.

The 26th Infantry Division Attack

The 26th Division advance in the center of the III Corps zone began under circumstances similar to those in the sector of the 80th Division. Before dawn on 22 December the 104th Infantry and the 328th Infantry moved from their assembly areas east of Arlon to the line of departure at the Attert River. A very large number of men in the rifle companies had yet to see their first German, many of them were replacements whose only recent experience with a rifle consisted of a day or two at the Metz training ground. All had heard the current rumors of atrocities perpetrated by the German SS troops and paratroopers; all were steeled, according to the capacity of the individual, to meet a ruthless enemy.

The general axis of advance was Arlon-Wiltz; but there was no main road from the Attert north to Wiltz—indeed the advance would have to reach Eschdorf, seven air miles away, before it could follow a main thoroughfare. There were numerous secondary roads and trails going north, and, the attack would fan out over these. But this network became increasingly difficult to traverse as it descended into the ravines and through the forests leading to the gorges of the Sure River. The ground between the Sure trench and the valley of the Wiltz was equally rugged. Since little was known of the enemy, the division plan simply called for the troops to expand over roads and trails, eliminating German resistance wherever found.

While the 26th Reconnaissance Troop rolled out as a screen several thousand yards to the fore, the 104th Infantry (Lt. Col. Ralph A. Palladino) on the right and the 328th Infantry (Col. Ben R. Jacobs) on the left marched through dense woods and over slushy, muddy trails, finally coming out onto open, rolling fields near the village of Pratz, about three miles by road from the Attert. Unaware of the fact, the Americans were nearing the advance guard of the 915th Regiment, marching out from Ettelbruck. (It was this column of the 352d Volks Grenadier Division whose tail the 80th Division pinched near Merzig.)

The 104th Infantry continued north, assailed only by scattered small arms fire and machine gun bursts fired at long range. A mile farther on a small detachment of enemy tanks and infantry essayed an attack but were repelled by mortar fire.

The first real test of strength came when the leading company was a couple of miles southeast of Grosbous, from which town a road led north to Eschdorf. Here the advance battalion of the 915th Regiment struck so suddenly and with such force that the lead company fell back for at least half a mile. The guns supporting the 104th Infantry were in position, however, and finally bent back the counterattack. In the meantime a handful of riflemen from the 109th Infantry, 28th Division, who had been waging a long battle in Grosbous until driven out by four German tanks, made their way back to the 104th. As it turned out the body of the 352d Volks Grenadier Division was not present here but was in the 80th Division zone. The 915th Regiment consisting of troops now split off from their trains, artillery, and the bulk of the division by the wedge which the 80th had thrust forward west of Ettelbruck, withdrew to make a stand in the neighborhood of Grosbous. Colonel Palladino left Company E to hold in check some Germans who had taken to the nearby woods, while the rest of the 104th Infantry continued tramping north along the road to Grosbous. The village itself was taken a couple of hours after midnight in a surprise attack by a combat patrol from Company G.

The series of blocks thrown against the 352d Volks Grenadier Division by the 80th Division and the 104th Infantry gave the western wing of the 26th Division a clear field. By the middle of the afternoon the 328th had covered nearly six miles without firing or receiving a shot. The advance guard was nearing the village of Arsdorf, from which a series of small roads and trails radiated through ravines and along ridges to the Sure, when a few rounds came in from self-propelled guns firing from a hill to the north. Concurrently reports arrived from the 26th Reconnaissance Troop that there was a strong German force in Rambrouch on the left flank. Night was near and the true strength of the enemy unknown; so the regiment halted while scouts worked their way to the front and flanks.

Who were these German troops? Since it was known that the 352d Volks Grenadier Division could not have reached this point the first guess was that the 5th Parachute Division, believed to be farther north, had pushed down into the area. Actually the 328th Infantry had run into the Fuehrer Grenadier Brigade, which the Seventh Army had borrowed from the OKW reserve, rushing it across the front to bolster this south flank. At first the brigade had been sent in to hold the Sure River line, but the Seventh Army then decided to expand its blocking position well to the south of the river, and so turned the brigade through Bourscheid and Eschdorf to the neighborhood of Arsdorf. This unit contained a battalion of forty Mark IV and Panther tanks, one battalion of mobile infantry, and one of foot, but thus far only a few tanks and the rifle battalion in personnel carriers were on the scene.

The new turn of events caused General Paul some concern about his left flank. The 4th Armored attack had carried abreast of the line held by the 328th Infantry but there remained a gap of three miles, densely wooded, between the two. As a temporary expedient a small task force, organized around Company K, 101st Infantry, and Company A, 735th Tank Battalion, deployed to screen the open left flank of the 26th Division.

Meanwhile Paul's two regiments prepared to continue the attack through the night as the army and corps commanders had ordered. The objective was Wiltz, once the command post of the American 28th Infantry Division, and now the headquarters of the German Seventh Army and the concentration point for enemy troops feeding in from the northeast.

While the 104th moved forward to hit the enemy congregated at Grosbous, the 328th Infantry reorganized to keep the drive going, under somewhat optimistic orders to seize crossings on the Wiltz River. At midnight the 1st and 3d Battalions jumped off to take Grevils-Brésil, from which a fairly good ridge road ran north to Eschdorf. The village was garrisoned by two companies of the Fuehrer Grenadier Brigade, reinforced by several Panthers from the Seventh Army reserve. Unshaken by a half-hour shelling, the Germans held tenaciously to the village all night long.

When daylight came on 23 December the 26th Division had little to show for its night attack. The 104th Infantry held Grosbous, but the 328th was checked at Grevils-Brésil by a company of stubborn German infantry backed up with a few tanks. In the woods south of Grosbous the men of Company E, 104th Infantry, had taken on more than they had bargained for: a couple of hundred riflemen from the 915th Regiment led in person by the regimental commander. (The American regimental commander had to throw in Company I, but even so this pocket was not wiped out until Christmas Eve.)

Although the right wing of the 26th Division was driving along the boundary between the isolated forward regiment of the 352d Volks Grenadier Division and the incoming Fuehrer Grenadier Brigade, only a small part of the new brigade was in contact with the forward American battalions early on the 23d. The German brigade commander had been seriously wounded by a shell fragment while reconnoitering on the previous evening, the hurried march to action had prevented unified commitment, and the heavy woods south of the Sure made control very difficult. Also there were troubles with fuel.

The LXXXV Corps hoped to repel the American attack by means of a coordinated counterattack south of the Sure which would develop as a pincers movement, grappling the American troops who had penetrated into the dense forest north of the Ettelbruck-Grosbous road. For this maneuver, set to open on the 23d, the new 79th Volks Grenadier Division was to attack toward Niederfeulen, secure the Wark River, and hook to the northwest. On its right the Fuehrer Grenadier Brigade would attack in a southeastern direction from Heiderscheid and Eschdorf with Grosbous and union with the 915th Regiment as the immediate objective. This German scheme was slow to come into operation and only a part of the Fuehrer Grenadier Brigade was brought against the 26th Division during the 23d, and then mostly in small packets of infantry supported by a platoon or less of tanks.

The two attacking regiments of the 26th Division continued to fan out over secondary roads and trails, moving very cautiously for fear of ambush as the woods thickened and pressed closer to the roadways. Here the supporting weapons came into play. Detachments of the 390th Antiaircraft Artillery Automatic Weapons Battalion, moving close behind the infantry point, blasted at wood lines, hedges, haystacks, and farm buildings. Their .50-caliber machine guns and the 37-mm. cannon mounted on half-tracks pinned the German infantry down until supporting artillery could be brought to bear, then shifted to a new position before the German gunners could get on target.

The American cannoneers wheeled their pieces from position to position so as to give the closest support possible. At one point the commanding officer of the 102d Field Artillery Battalion, Lt. Col. R. W. Kinney, went forward alone under direct enemy fire to pick out the targets for his guns. (Kinney was awarded the DSC.) When an enemy pocket was discovered in some corner of the woods the self-propelled tank destroyers went into action, spraying the enemy with high explosive. Thus a platoon of the 818th Tank Destroyer Battalion ultimately blasted the lost battalion of the 915th Regiment out of the woods near Grosbous.

It was no more than natural that the 26th Division, full of green troops, wanted the comforting presence of friendly tanks or guns. The 735th Tank Battalion after action report says that the 104th Infantry would not enter Dellen ahead of the tanks.

The 328th Infantry also was slow in moving without tanks ahead. Since through all this day the Americans had little or no idea of the enemy strength that lay ahead or perhaps lurked on the flanks, the lack of swashbuckling haste was not abnormal.

The corps commander shared the feeling that caution was due. At dark he ordered General Paul to keep pushing with small patrols but enjoined him to keep the mass of the two regiments (the third was corps reserve) from getting too far forward. Patrols, Millikin advised, should try to get to the Sure River bridges before daylight of the 24th. As things now stood, the 80th Division had pushed a salient ahead on the right of the 26th Division in the Kehmen sector and was waiting for the center division to come abreast. On the left there remained a fair-sized gap between the 4th Armored Division and the 26th, only partially screened by very small detachments at roadblock positions. Thus far the enemy had failed to recognize or exploit this gap.

The 4th Armored Division Attack

On 21 December the 4th Armored Division, then assembled in the Léglise-Arlon area, learned what its mission would be when the III Corps attacked on the 22d: advance north and relieve Bastogne. Martelange, an outpost of the VIII Corps engineer barrier line on the Sure River, was twelve miles on a hard-surfaced highway from the center of Bastogne. A Sherman tank could make it from Martelange to Bastogne in a half hour—if the road was passable and if the enemy confined his opposition to loosing rifle and machine gun bursts. The task at hand, however, was to "destroy the enemy in zone" and cover the open west flank of the corps.

Of the three divisions aligned to jump off in the III Corps counterattack, the 4th Armored would come under the closest scrutiny by the Third Army commander. Its mission was dramatic. It was also definite, geographically speaking, and so lent itself the more readily to assessment on the map in terms of success or failure. Furthermore, the reputation of the 4th Armored as a slashing, wheeling outfit would naturally attract attention, even though its matériel was not up to par, either in amount or mechanical fitness, and many green troops were riding in its tanks and infantry half-tracks. To all this must be added a less tangible item in evaluating readiness for battle. General Gaffey, the division commander, was a relative newcomer to this veteran and closely knit fighting team; he had as yet to lead the entire division in combat. CCA likewise had a commander who was a stranger to the division, Brig. Gen. Herbert L. Earnest. It might be expected, therefore, that the 4th Armored would take some little time in growing accustomed to the new leaders and their ways of conducting battle.

Theoretically the VIII Corps covered the western flank of the III Corps, but on 22 December the situation in Middleton's area was so fluid and his forces were so weak that no definite boundary or contact existed between the VIII and III Corps. The actual zone of operations for the 4th Armored Division, therefore, proved to be an area delimited by Bigonville on the east and Neufchâteau on the east and Neufchâteau on the west, a front of over fifteen miles. The mission assigned the 4th Armored, rather than zones and boundaries, determined the commitment of the division and the routes it would employ.

Bastogne could be reached from the south by two main approaches, on the right the Arlon-Bastogne road, on the left the Neufchâteau-Bastogne road. General Millikin and the III Corps staff preferred the Arlon route, at whose entrance the 4th Armored already was poised. General Middleton, whose VIII Corps nominally controlled the troops in Bastogne, favored a broad thrust to employ both routes but with the weight placed on the Neufchâteau road. The Arlon-Bastogne road was the shortest by a few miles and on the most direct line from the III Corps assembly area. To control the Arlon approach would block the reinforcement of the enemy troops already south of Bastogne. Attack on this axis also would allow the left and center divisions of the III Corps to maintain a somewhat closer contact with each other. The Neufchâteau-Bastogne route, on the other hand, was less tightly controlled by the enemy, although there was some evidence that German strength was building up in that direction.

The problem facing the III Corps was not the simple one of gaining access to Bastogne or of restoring physical contact with the forces therein, contact which had existed as late as 20 December. The problem was: (a) to restore and maintain a permanent corridor into the city; and (b) to jar the surrounding enemy loose so that Bastogne and its road net could be used by the Third Army as a base for further operations to the north and northeast. The problem was well understood by the 4th Armored Division. General Gaffey's letter of instructions to General Dager, commanding CCB, said, " . . . you will drive in, relieve the force, and *proceed* [italics supplied] from Bastogne to the NE...." The impression held by 4th Armored commanders and staff was that an independent tank column could cut its way through to the city ("at any time," said Dager), but that the opening of a corridor equivalent to the width of the road bed would be self-sealing once the thin-skinned or light armored columns started north to resupply and reinforce the heavy armor which reached Bastogne. The mission set the 4th Armored would require the co-ordinated efforts of the entire division, nor could it be fulfilled by a dramatic ride to the rescue of the Bastogne garrison, although this may have been what General Patton had in mind.

The Third Army commander, veteran tanker, himself prescribed the tactics to be used by Gaffey and the 4th Armored. The attack should lead off with the tanks, artillery, tank destroyers, and armored engineers in the van. The main body of armored infantry should be kept back. When stiff resistance was encountered, envelopment tactics should be used: no close-in envelopment should be attempted; all envelopments should be started a mile or a mile and a half mile back and be made at right angles. Patton, whose experience against the Panther tank during the Lorraine campaign had made him keenly aware of its superiority over the American Sherman in gun and armor, ordered that the new, modified Sherman with heavier armor (the so-called Jumbo) should be put in the lead when available. But there were very few of the Jumbos in the Third Army.

At 0600 on 22 December (H-hour for the III Corps counterattack) two combat commands stood ready behind a line of departure which stretched from Habay-la-Neuve east to Niedercolpach. General Gaffey planned to send CCA and CCB into the attack abreast, CCA working along the main Arlon-Bastogne road while CCB advanced on secondary roads to the west. In effect the two commands would be traversing parallel ridge lines. Although the full extent of damage done the roads and bridges during the VIII Corps withdrawal was not yet clear, it was known that the Sure bridges at Martelange had been blown. In the event that CCA was delayed unduly at the Sure crossing CCB might be switched east and take the lead on the main road. In any case CCB was scheduled to lead the 4th Armored Division into Bastogne.

On the right CCA (General Earnest) moved out behind A Troop of the 25th Cavalry Squadron in two task forces of battalion size. Visibility was poor, the ground was snow-covered, but the tracked vehicles were able to move without difficulty over the frozen terrain—without difficulty, that is, until the eastern task force commenced to encounter demolitions executed earlier by the VIII Corps engineers. The upshot was that both task forces converged on the main Arlon road and proceeded as a single column. Near Martelange a large crater delayed the column for some time. Shortly after noon it was bridged and the advance guard became embroiled in a fire fight with a rifle company of the 15th Regiment (5th Parachute Division) guarding the bridges, now demolished, at Martelange. The town, sprawling on a series of terraces rising from the river, was too large for effective artillery fire and the enemy riflemen held on until about 0300 the next morning when, unaccountably, they allowed a company of armored infantry to cross on one of the broken spans. Most of the 23d was spent in bridging the Sure. The width and depth of the cut through which the stream flowed forbade the use of either pontoon or treadway. Corps engineers came up to fabricate a 90-foot Bailey bridge, but it was afternoon before the tanks could start moving. Delays, however, had not dimmed the general impression that CCA could cut its way through to Bastogne in short order, and at 1500 the III Corps sent word to Middleton that contact with the 101st was expected "by tonight."

On the lesser roads to the west, General Dager's CCB, which had started out at 0430, also was delayed by demolitions. Nonetheless at noon of the 22d the 8th Tank Battalion was in sight of Burnon, only seven miles from Bastogne, nor was there evidence that the enemy could make a stand. Here orders came from General Patton: the advance was to be continued through the night "to relieve Bastogne." Then ensued the usual delay: still another bridge destroyed during the withdrawal had to be replaced, and it was past midnight when light tanks and infantry cleared a small German rear guard from Burnon itself.

Wary of German bazookas in this wooded country, tanks and cavalry jeeps moved cautiously over the frozen ground toward Chaumont, the next sizable village. Thus far the column had been subject only to small arms fire, although a couple of jeeps had been lost to German bazookas. But when the cavalry and light tanks neared Chaumont antitank guns knocked out one of the tanks and the advance guard withdrew to the main body, deployed on a ridge south of the village. Daylight was near. CCB had covered only about a quarter of a mile during the night, but because Chaumont appeared to be guarded by German guns on the flanking hills a formal, time-consuming, coordinated attack seemed necessary.

During the morning the 10th Armored Infantry Battalion and the twenty-two Shermans of the 8th Tank Battalion that were in fighting condition organized for a sweep around Chaumont to west and north, coupled with a direct punch to drive the enemy out of the village. To keep the enemy occupied, an armored field artillery battalion shelled the houses. Then, as the morning fog cleared away, fighter-bombers from the XIX Tactical Air Command (a trusted friend of the 4th Armored Division) detoured from their main mission of covering the cargo planes flying supplies to Bastogne and hammered Chaumont, pausing briefly for a dogfight with Luftwaffe intruders as tankers and infantry below formed a spellbound audience.

While CCB paused south of Chaumont and CCA waited for the Martelange bridge to be finished, the Third Army commander fretted at the delay. He telephoned the III Corps headquarters: "There is too much piddling around. Bypass these towns and clear them up later. Tanks can operate on this ground now." It was clear to all that General Patton's eye was on the 4th Armored Division and his erstwhile chief of staff, General Gaffey, and that he counted on the 4th Armored to cut its way into Bastogne.

At Chaumont the ground assault came about 1330 on the heels of a particularly telling strike by friendly fighter-bombers. German artillery had begun to come alive an hour or so earlier, but with the Jabos in the sky the enemy gunners were quiet. Two rifle platoons mounted on tanks made a dash into the village, where more of the armored infantry soon arrived on foot. Even so, the lunge to envelop Chaumont on the west failed of its intent for the fields were thawing in the afternoon sun and the Shermans were left churning in the mud. A company of the 14th Regiment, 5th Parachute Division, tried to fight it out in the houses, but after a couple of hours nearly all the enemy had been rounded up. Then the scene changed with some abruptness.

During the night a liaison officer carrying the CCB attack orders had taken the wrong turning and driven into the German lines. Perhaps the enemy had seized the orders before they could be destroyed. Perhaps the cavalry foray in the early morning had given advance warning. In any case General Kokott, commanding the 26th Volks Grenadier Division responsible for the Chaumont-Martelange sector, had taken steps to reply to the attack on Chaumont. This village lies at the bottom of a bowl whose sides are formed by hills and connecting ridges. The rim to the northeast is densely wooded but is tapped by a trail leading on to the north. Along this trail, screened by the woods, the Germans brought up the 11th Assault Gun Brigade, numbering ten to fifteen remodeled Mark III carriages bearing 75-mm. guns and with riflemen clinging to their decks and sides. Rolling down the slope behind an artillery smoke screen, the German assault guns knocked out those American tanks they could sight and discharged their gray-clad passengers into the village.

The American riflemen (Lt. Col. Harold Cohen's 10th Armored Infantry Battalion) battled beside the crippled and mired tanks in what Maj. Albin Irzyk, the veteran commander of the 9th Tank Battalion, called the bitterest fighting his battalion ever had encountered. The forward artillery observer was dead and there was no quick means of bringing fire on the enemy assault guns, which simply stood off and blasted a road for the German infantry. Company A, 10th Armored Infantry Battalion, which had led the original assault against Chaumont, lost some sixty-five men. The battle soon ended. In small groups the Americans fell back through the dusk to their original positions, leaving eleven Shermans as victims of the assault guns and the mud. The only officer of Company A left alive, 1st Lt. Charles R. Gniot, stayed behind to cover the withdrawal until he too was killed. Gniot was awarded the DSC, posthumously.

At the hour when the CCB assault first reached Chaumont, the eastern combat command had started moving across the Martelange bridge. Since it would take a long while for the whole column to close up and cross, General Earnest ordered Lt. Col. Delk Oden, commander of the 35th Tank Battalion, to forge ahead with his task force in a bid to reach Bastogne. The road ahead climbed out of the valley and onto a chain of ridges, these ridges closely flanked by higher ground so that the pavement ran through a series of cuts that limited maneuver off the road. The cavalry point had just gained the ridge line when, at a sharp bend, the Germans opened fire. Fortunately the tank company following was able to leave the highway and find cover behind the rise to the west of the pavement. For half an hour artillery worked over the enemy location, and then the artillery observer with the tanks "walked" the fire along the successive ridges while the tanks moved north in defilade. At the same time the half-tracks of Company G, 51st Armored Infantry Battalion, clanked forward along the pavement.

It was growing dark. Oden brought his light tank company and assault guns (used throughout the Bastogne relief as medium tanks) abreast of the medium tank company with orders to continue the advance through the night. The head of the task force now was close to the village of Warnach, which lay to the east of the main road. The light tanks had just come in sight of the village when the company of armored infantry appeared around a bend in the main road. The Germans in Warnach, apparently waiting for such a thin-skinned target, knocked out the first two half-tracks. To bypass the village at night was out of the question. While the assault guns shelled the houses a light tank platoon and a rifle platoon went in. Only one of the tanks got out, although most of the foot troops finally straggled back. Shortly after midnight a company of Shermans tried to get into Warnach but were stopped by antitank fire. Meanwhile tanks and infantry of the task force pushed on to the north, clearing the woods on either side of the main highway (the leading tank company ended up in a marsh).

It was daylight when tanks and infantry resumed the assault at Warnach, driving in from three sides with the riflemen clinging to the tanks. The battle which ensued was the most bitter fought by CCA during the whole Bastogne operation. Heilmann, commanding the 5th Parachute Division, had reasoned that the sector he held south of Bastogne was far too wide for a connected linear defense, and so had concentrated the 15th Parachute Regiment along the Martelange-Bastogne road. Warnach was the regimental command post and there was at least one rifle battalion in the village, reinforced by a battery of self-propelled tank destroyers. Two American artillery battalions kept this enemy force down, firing with speed and accuracy as the Shermans swept in, but once the artillery lifted, a house-to-house battle royal commenced in earnest. Four Shermans were destroyed by tank destroyer fire at close range. The enemy infantry fought desperately, filtering back into houses which had been cleared, organizing short, savage rushes to retake lost buildings, and showing little taste for surrender. But try as they might the German paratroopers could not get past the American armored infantry and at the tanks—only one was knocked out by German bazooka fire. The result was slow to be seen but none the less certain. At noon, when the battle ended, the Americans had killed one hundred and thirty-five Germans and taken an equal number of prisoners. The little village cost them sixty-eight officers and men, dead and wounded.

Chaumont, on the 23d, and Warnach, on the 24th, are tabbed in the journals of the 4th Armored as "hot spots" on the march to Bastogne. Quite unexpectedly, however, a third developed at Bigonville, a village some two and a half miles east of the Bastogne highway close to the boundary between the 4th Armored and the 26th Infantry Division. The gap between these divisions, only partially screened by light forces, suddenly became a matter of more than normal concern on the night of 22 December with reports that a large body of German armor was moving in (actually the advance guard of the Fuehrer Grenadier Brigade which had appeared in front of the left wing of the 26th Division). To protect CCA's open right flank, Gaffey ordered Col. Wendell Blanchard to form the Reserve Combat Command as a balanced task force (using the 53d Armored Infantry Battalion and 37th Tank Battalion) and advance toward Bigonville. Early on 23 December CCR left Quatre-Vents, followed the main road nearly to Martelange, then turned right onto a secondary road which angled northeast. This road was "sheer ice" and much time was consumed moving the column forward.

About noon the advance guard came under fire from a small plot of woods near a crossroads at which point CCR would have to turn due north. The accompanying artillery battalion went into action, pouring high explosive into the woods for nearly an hour. One rifle company then dismounted and went in to clean out the survivors. The company found no serious resistance, returned to the road, and was just mounting its half-tracks when a fusillade of bullets burst from the little wood. Apparently the enemy had withdrawn during the shelling, only to return at the heels of the departing Americans. Tanks were now sent toward the crossroad but were stopped by mines. All this had been time-consuming. Bigonville was still a mile away, and Blanchard ordered a halt. The enemy in the woods continued to inflict casualties on the troops halted beside the road. Even the tankers were not immune — nearly all of the tank commanders of one company were picked off by rifle fire.

In the course of the night the Germans left the wood and fell back to the shelter of the stone houses in Bigonville. The assault on the morning of the 24th followed what had become standard tactics with the 4th Armored. First came a short concentration fired by the artillery. There followed an advance into the village by two teams, each composed of one tank and one infantry company working closely together. As at Chaumont and Warnach there was little trouble from the enemy artillery, for by this time the 5th Parachute Division was rationed to only seven rounds per howitzer a day. Mostly the German infantry held their fire until the Americans were in the streets, then cut loose with their bazookas, light mortars, and small arms. While the two assault companies of the 53d advanced from house to house the tanks of the 37th blasted the buildings ahead, machine-gunned the Germans when they broke into the open, and set barns and out-buildings afire with tracer bullets. One team burst through to the northern exit road and the garrison was trapped. By 1100 the village was clear. Most of the 328 prisoners taken here were from the 13th Parachute Regiment, which had just been released from its flank guard positions farther to the east on Heilmann's insistence that the 5th Parachute Division could not possibly block the American drive north with only two of its regiments in hand.

The pitched battles at Bigonville and Warnach on 24 December made a considerable dent in the front line fighting strength of the 5th Parachute Division but failed to bring CCR and CCA appreciably closer to Bastogne. CCB, the most advanced of the combat commands, had only two platoons of medium tanks left after the affair at Chaumont and had spent the day quietly waiting for replacement tanks from the repair echelons and for the rest of the division to draw abreast. Meanwhile the American paratroopers and their heterogeneous comrades inside the Bastogne perimeter fought and waited, confining their radio messages to oblique hints that the 4th Armored should get a move on. Thus, at the close of the 23d McAuliffe sent the message: "Sorry I did not get to shake hands today. I was disappointed." A less formal exhortation from one of his staff reached the 4th Armored command post at midnight: "There is only one more shopping day before Christmas! "

Perhaps a few of the armored officers still believed that a hell-for-leather tank attack could cleave a way to Bastogne. But by the evening of 24 December it seemed to both Gaffey and Millikin that tanks were bound to meet tough going in frontal attack on the hard-surfaced roads to which they were confined and that the operation would demand more use of the foot-slogger, particularly since the German infantry showed a marked proclivity for stealing back into the villages nominally "taken" by the tankers. Attack around the clock, enjoined by General Patton, had not been notably successful so far as the tank arm was concerned. From commander down, the 4th Armored was opposed to further use of the weakened tank battalions in hours of darkness. Further, night attacks by the two infantry divisions had failed to achieve any unusual gains and the troops were tiring.

The corps commander therefore ordered that his divisions hold during the night of the 24th in preparation for attack early on Christmas day. Two battalions of the 318th Infantry were joining the 4th Armored to give the needed infantry strength in the corps' main effort. Reinforcement by the fighter-bombers had been requested (Gaffey asked the corps for high-priority flights over the 4th Armored as a Christmas present), and good flying weather seemed likely. On the debit side there were indications that reinforcements were arriving to bolster the German line facing the III Corps.

Thus far the Third Army counterattack had tended to be a slugging match with frontal assault and little maneuver. General Patton's insistence on bypassing centers of resistance had been negated by the terrain, the weather, and the wide-reaching impact of the earlier VIII Corps demolitions scheme. Perhaps the pace could be speeded up by maneuver, now that the enemy had been drawn into the defense of the Arlon-Bastogne approach. At Gaffey's request the III Corps commander shifted the boundary between the 4th Armored and the 26th Division, making the infantry division responsible for the Bigonville sector and releasing CCR, on the night of the 24th, for employment on the open west flank of the corps with entry into Bastogne as its primary mission.

The 80th Division Battle in the Woods, 24-26 December

On the morning of 24 December the 80th Division lost the two battalions pre-empted by the corps commander as infantry reinforcement for the 4th Armored Division. This diminution in its rifle strength and successive collisions with German units crossing the front en route to the Bastogne sector in the west constituted the closest link the 80th Division would have with the dramatic effort being made to reach the encircled 101st Airborne. From this time forward the 80th Division attack would be related to the fighting farther west only in that it was blocking the efforts of the Seventh Army to move its reserves into the Bastogne area.

For the next three days the division would wage a lone battle to reach and cross the Sure River, the scene of action being limited to the wedge formed on the north by the Sure and on the east by the Sauer River with a base represented by the Ettelbruck-Heiderscheidergrund road. This area the 80th came to know as the Bourscheid triangle. Within this frame lay thick forests, deep ravines, and masked ridges, the whole a checkerboard of little terrain compartments. Control of a force larger than the battalion would be most difficult, artillery support—except at clearings and villages—would be ineffective, and the maintenance of an interlocking, impervious front nigh impossible. Once a battalion cleared a compartment and advanced to the next the enemy could be counted on to seep back to his original position. Unobserved fire and loss of direction in the deep woods, down the blind draws, and along the twisting ridges made each American unit a potential threat to its neighbors, often forcing the use of a single battalion at a time. The infantryman would be duly thankful when tanks, tank destroyers, or artillery could give a hand or at least encourage by their presence, but the battle in woods and ravines was his own.

On the 23d the enemy forces facing the 80th Division were so weak and so disorganized that the Seventh Army commander, Brandenberger, had feared that the

80th Division would drive across the Sure during the course of the night and sever the main line of communications leading to the west. By the morning of the 24th, however, reinforcements had arrived and the threat of a clean, quick American penetration was on the wane. The LXXXV Corps (Kniess) thus far had faced the American III Corps with only two divisions, the 5th Parachute and the 352d. Despite the Seventh Army apprehension that two divisions would not possibly hold the long blocking line from Ettelbruck to Vaux-lez-Rosières and despite daily requests that OKW release additional divisions to the army to strengthen this line, the German High Command was slow to dip into its strategic reserve.

The two larger units earmarked for employment by the Seventh Army were the Fuehrer Grenadier Brigade and the 79th Volks Grenadier Division. Both were a considerable distance to the rear and both were equipped with the conglomeration of makeshift, battle-weary vehicles that was the lot of those divisions not scheduled to join in the original breakthrough and penetration. Even when they were released from the OKW Reserve, it would be a matter of days — not hours — before the mass of either unit could be placed in the front lines. When OKW finally responded to the pleas of the Seventh Army, the most optimistic estimates placed the Fuehrer Grenadier Brigade and the 79th Volks Grenadier Division in the LXXXV Corps area on the morning of 23 December.

Neither of these two formations was rated as having a high combat value. Theoretically the Fuehrer Grenadier Brigade, a younger brother of the elite Grossdeutschland Panzer Division and like it charged with guarding Hitler's headquarters (albeit as the outer guard), should have been one of the first of the Wehrmacht formations. In fact this brigade was of very recent vintage, had suffered intense losses in East Prussia during its single commitment as a unit, and was not fully refitted when finally sent marching to the west. Replacements, drawn from the same pool as those for the Grossdeutschland and the Fuehrer Begleit Brigade, were hand-picked from the younger classes but had little training. The Fuehrer Grenadier Brigade numbered some six thousand men, had a rifle regiment mounted on armored half-tracks and 1 ½-ton trucks, a reconnaissance battalion, an assault gun battalion, and a mixed tank battalion made up of Mark IV's and Panthers. The 79th Volks Grenadier Division possessed an old Wehrmacht number but, as it stood at the time of its commitment in the Ardennes, was a green division the bulk of whose riflemen had been combed out of headquarters troops in early December. Woefully understrength in both transportation and supporting weapons, it had neither a flak battalion nor an assault gun battalion and would be forced to lean heavily on its artillery regiment.

The Fuehrer Grenadier Brigade, the first to start for the battle front, was ordered to take the road from Ettelbruck to Martelange and there deploy in support of the 5th Parachute Division. Its mission, assigned before the Third Army began its counterattack, was changed on the evening of 21 December, and so was its route, now menaced by the 80th Division advance on Ettelbruck. Trying to cross the Our River at the Roth bridges, the brigade ran into trouble. The bridges had been damaged by attack from the air, and traffic was backed up for miles on both sides of the river. Untrained drivers and mechanical failures further delayed the brigade as its columns entered the icy, narrow, twisting roads of the Ardennes, but by 23 December the reconnaissance battalion, a rifle battalion in armored carriers, and two tank companies had reached Eschdorf and Heiderscheid. Gravely concerned by the rate of the American advance, the Seventh Army commander sidetracked these troops short of the Bastogne sector to restore the gap which was opening between the 5th Parachute Division and the 352d Volks Grenadier Division, and, as already noted, the main body went in on on the 23d to stop the 80th Division at Heiderscheid. A part of the battalion of armored infantry marched south from Eschdorf and succeeded in getting cut off by the 26th Division night attack at Grevels-Brésil.

The heavy losses suffered by the green brigade in its first hours of battle had a marked adverse impact on the morale of the entire command. Many times, in subsequent days of battle, higher commanders would comment on the damage done the brigade by piecemeal commitment and defeat in its baptism of fire. The loss of the brigade commander, Col. Hans-Joachim Kahler, further demoralized the Fuehrer Grenadier. For successive days the command changed hands as new elements of the brigade arrived under more senior officers; this lack of leadership hardly was calculated to restore the shaken confidence of young, inexperienced troops. Yet despite these early reverses in the counterattack role the young soldiers of the brigade would prove tough and tenacious on the defensive.

On the morning of the 24th the Fuehrer Grenadier Brigade, still without artillery and with half of its tanks and infantry still east of the Our River, stood opposite the inner wings of the American 26th and 80th Divisions. The force of perhaps two rifle companies which had been cut off by the 26th Division south of Eschdorf was known to be fighting its way out to the east. The LXXXV Corps commander therefore decided to use his incoming reinforcements—infantry of the 79th Volks Grenadier Division—in a counterattack to regain contact with the lost companies somewhere around Eschdorf. This would be followed by a pivot to the east, intended to strike the Americans in the flank at Heiderscheid. For this maneuver Col. Alois Weber, commanding the 79th, had available one regiment, the 208th, and a single battalion of the 212th. His division, like the Fuehrer Grenadier Brigade, had encountered the traffic jam at the Our River and while crossing on the Gentingen bridge had been further delayed by American fighter-bombers. The assault gun battalion and tanks from the Fuehrer Grenadier were at Weber's disposal, but his artillery regiment was missing, entangled someplace on the road east of the Our. By chance the 79th found an artillery battalion, belonging to the 5th Parachute Division, which had been left behind when its prime movers broke down, and these guns were impressed to support the counterattack toward Heiderscheid.

There remained to the LXXXV Corps the 352d Volks Grenadier Division, by this time reduced to two battered regiments huddled north and east of Ettelbruck. These regiments were needed where they stood for not only did they guard the Ettelbruck bridgehead, covering the flank of the Sauer crossings in the LXXXV Corps sector, but they also represented the only cohesive defense on the north bank of the river in the event that the American XII Corps decided to turn in that direction. The bulk of the 915th Regiment of the 352d, cut off by the American advance on 23 December, could no longer be reckoned with. (The major portion of these troops finally escaped through the thick woods, but would not reach the lines of the 352d until 2 December and then minus most of their equipment.) The fight to bring the American 80th Division to a halt south of the Sure, or at the river itself, would have to be waged by the half-strength 79th Volks Grenadier Division. The battleground, be it said, favored the defender so long as he retained sufficient strength to seal off all penetrations. Whether he could do so remained to be seen.

General McBride continued the attack on 24 December with the 317th and 319th, whose forward battalions had been engaged with the enemy all through the previous night. After the loss of the two battalions from the 318th to the 4th Armored Division, the 317th had simply bypassed Ettelbruck, and the 3d Battalion of the 318th was left to harass the enemy therein with artillery and mortar fire. The immediate division mission remained the same: to root out the enemy south of the Sure River and close in the north along the Sauer.

The 319th, on the left, was in possession of the road net at Heiderscheid and had only a mile to cover before the regiment was on the Sure. Indeed, two companies had spent the night within sight of the river at Heiderscheid although this was in the zone of the 26th Division. The 317th had farther to go because the Sure looped away to the north in its sector. Furthermore the regiment was advancing with its right flank exposed to any riposte coming from east of the Sauer River. Advance northward would have to be made under the eyes of German observers atop two dominating hill masses, one close to the Sure at Ringel, the other rising on the west bank of the Sauer near the bridgehead village of Bourscheid, the initial assembly area of the 79th Volks Grenadier Division. Fortunately for the Americans the 79th lacked the artillery to make full use of such commanding ground, but the German gunners proved to be very accurate.

For the past twenty-four hours the 317th Infantry had been attacking to reach Bourscheid and the high ground there. Although the 2d Battalion lunged ahead as far as Welscheid during the night, it failed to take the village and spent all the daylight hours of the 24th waiting for two companies to extricate themselves from the ridge on whose slope they lay pinned by German fire. (The regimental commander would later remark on the excellent musketry training and first-rate small arms practice of this German unit.)

The 1st Battalion, meanwhile, tried to hook around to the northeast and gain entrance to Bourscheid along the main road. This advance brought the battalion onto open ground where the enemy assault guns spotted farther north could get to work. Then the battalion came under flanking fire from the Germans around Kehmen, in the zone of the neighboring regiment. Mercilessly pounded from front and flank the battalion fell back for half a mile; its casualties numbered 197, mostly wounded. At this point each of the three battalions had taken a crack at punching a way through to Bourscheid. At the close of the 24th the 317th Infantry could report severe losses but no progress and the German tanks and assault guns were raking the Americans wherever they concentrated, even laying with accuracy on the battalion command posts.

While the 317th was being held in check by well-directed gunfire, the 319th attack collided with the enemy counterattack aimed at Eschdorf and Heiderscheid. For this the 79th seems to have assembled at least two battalions of infantry, as well as tanks, assault guns, and armored cars from the Fuehrer Grenadier Brigade. The 319th occupied a triangular position: at the apex the 3d Battalion held Tadler, overlooking the Sure, to the right and rear the 1st Battalion had bivouacked in Kehmen on the Bourscheid road; the 2d Battalion (less its two companies near the Heiderscheidergrund crossing) was stationed as the left wing anchor at Heiderscheid. Colonel Taylor, the regimental commander, wished to bring his right forward to the river. In the dark, on the morning of the 24th, the 1st Battalion (Lt. Col. Hiram D. Ives) marched west out of Kehmen intending to turn north at the next crossroad, two miles away, and push for Ringel on the river.

Daylight was breaking when the head of the column came in sight of the crossroad. About that time two things happened. A German detachment rushed into

Kehmen, which the 1st Battalion had just left, while a German tank suddenly opened fire from a masked position near the crossroad and knocked out two Sherman tanks with the advance guard. The remaining American tanks hastily reversed to the cover of a nearby draw and the infantry deployed along the road. About 0930 one of the attached self-propelled tank destroyers sneaked forward and gave the coup de grâce to the German tank. New orders, however, left the battalion standing at the crossroad, for the 2d Battalion at Heiderscheid was hard hit by the main force of the German counterattack and needed protection on the east. Ultimately fire from the 1st Battalion did contribute to halting an enemy attempt at encircling Heiderscheid.

Colonel Bandy had held his 2d Battalion in Heiderscheid during the night of 23 December while awaiting the return of the two companies that had been sent down to the river. An hour or so before daylight the first German shells came in. After ten minutes of this preparation the enemy, on trucks, armored half-trucks, and armored cars, suddenly appeared at the southwest corner of the village. This was the main counterattack of the day for the 79th Volks Grenadier Division, launched as planned, from Eschdorf. The single American tank in the way was surprised and put out of action, but strangely enough the German armored vehicles, mostly light flak tanks with 20-mm. guns, did not risk a precipitate dash into the village, contenting themselves with racing up and down the road which passed on the south, firing madly at the houses. The Americans, for their part, clustered at the windows and returned the fire with every weapon they could lay hand on.

One tank destroyer was in position to enfilade the road but by a curious chance it had been in the path of a bomb dropped by a stray German plane during the night and the firing mechanism was damaged. The tank destroyer commander tracked his gun on the passing targets, jumped up and down on the firing treadle, swore volubly, and banged the firing mechanism with a hammer but to no avail. Twice the German grenadiers got close enough to pitch grenades through windows. Finally one American tank worked its way around to get clear aim and did destroy four of the enemy armored vehicles. Eventually the enemy foot troops made their way into the streets. With this the forward observer for the 315th Field Artillery Battalion took over, calling for his 155-mm. howitzers to shell the village. For half an hour shells exploded, killing and lacerating the unprotected enemy. When the Germans retired they left 76 dead and 26 badly wounded; their Red Cross had removed many more during the fight.

By midafternoon firing died down all along the 319th front. The hastily organized 79th Volks Grenadier Division counterattack had failed in its larger purpose although it had led Colonel Taylor to recall his advance battalion from its position of vantage close to the Sure. On the whole the 80th Division had been through a hard day's fight, and McBride was more than willing to accept the corps commander's orders to hold up the attack until the following morning.

Across the lines the Seventh Army was bringing in a new, provisional headquarters to assume direction of the battle around Bastogne. The boundary, to be effective on Christmas Day, ran between Eschdorf and Heiderscheid, approximating that between the American 26th and 80th Infantry Divisions. The Fuehrer Grenadier Brigade now passed to the new Corps Rothkirch but would continue to oppose the 26th Division just as the major part of its strength had done on 24 December. The LXXXV Corps was left with the 79th and 352d. On Christmas Eve the last troops of the 352d left Ettelbruck, shelled out by high explosive and white phosphorus. The

German line north and east of the city hereafter would rest on the far bank of the Sauer.

Kniess was not yet ready to withdraw his right wing to the protection of the river barrier, nor would the Seventh Army commander permit it, for the high ground in the Bourscheid bridgehead could still be used to observe and interdict any crossing of the Sauer farther south and at the same time act as an anchor at the eastern end of the Sure. Because the 79th Volks Grenadier Division still lacked much of its infantry and nearly all of its heavy weapons, the corps commander ordered Colonel Weber to defend the bridgehead by concentrating in the heavy woods around Kehmen and Welscheid. With the limited rifle strength at his disposal, Weber was able to man the Burden ridge, his left flank thus adhering to the Sauer, but in the north the right flank of the 79th consisted only of a thin outpost line extending to Ringel Hill and the Sure.

Early on Christmas morning in the bitter cold the 80th Division returned to the attack, its main thrust aimed at Bourscheid. Colonel Fisher sent the 1st and 3d Battalions of the 317th Infantry toward Kehmen and Scheidel, hoping to open the road east into Bourscheid. At Scheidel the attack surprised the enemy infantry; one platoon captured the hamlet and a large number of prisoners. But when the two battalions turned north toward Kehmen the enemy (a battalion of the 266th Regiment) was ready and waiting. Each assault, made across open ground, was repelled by deadly fire from the village and the woods to the north. When General McBride finally intervened to end the attack the assault battalions had lost nearly two hundred officers and men. Kehmen once again had proved a hard nut to crack.

While the 317th Infantry hit head on against the main position held by the 79th Volks Grenadier Division, the 319th Infantry moved north into the gap on the German right flank. The 3d Battalion, which had withdrawn from its location close to the Sure in order to back up the other battalions in the fighting around Heiderscheid on the previous day, simply marched back into Tadler. Since General McBride had ordered the regiment to close up to the Sure but eschew any crossing attempt, the battalion was content to outpost along the river. From Tadler small groups of the enemy could be seen moving about on Ringel Hill, farther to the east. The 90th Field Artillery Battalion dropped a few shells into the village atop the hill; then the 2d Battalion occupied the area with little trouble. The hill position seriously endangered the German bridgehead, but the 79th was too far understrength to mount any sizable counterattack on this flank.

During the afternoon an American outpost saw a small German detachment marching in column of twos up a draw east of Ringel. The men at the outpost could not believe their eyes; they could only conclude that the approaching Germans were coming to surrender. When challenged the little column kept on coming, until a light machine gun put an end to this "counterattack." An hour before midnight more figures were seen approaching from the same direction. What had happened was that the Seventh Army commander had intervened personally to order that Ringel Hill be retaken. Not only was its possession necessary to the defense of the 79th Volks Grenadier Division bridgehead but Brandenberger needed the services of an army engineer brigade that had been committed as infantry on the north bank of the Sure, in the sector overlooked by the hill. If this high ground could be retaken and some command of this stretch of the Sure retained, the engineers could be employed elsewhere.

Since the fight with the 317th Infantry had died down some hours earlier, Colonel Weber was able to gather a substantial force for the counterattack, but there was little ammunition for the few guns supporting the 79th. The Americans, on the other hand, were wired in to their division artillery and by now had a prearranged pattern of fire: four battalions answered the 2d Battalion call for help. A few of the attackers got close to Ringel, only to meet the whistling ricochet of armor-piercing shells fired by a single tank destroyer that rushed around the village like a man stamping out a lawn fire.

Christmas Day witnessed the most artillery activity of the entire division advance; the guns were well forward, the infantry held good ground for observation, and the fighting now surged at many points out of the woods and into the open. 15 The total number of rounds fired by the 80th Division artillery was large when assessed against the terrain: 3,878 rounds and 142 missions. The 80th Division advance ended the day after Christmas, with the 319th Infantry chasing the enemy out of the woods on the near bank of the Sure, the 317th digging in opposite the Bourscheid bridgehead, and the lone battalion of the 318th exchanging fire with the Germans across the Sauer, in the course of which the commander of the 352d was severely wounded.

General Patton was in the process of strengthening the Third Army attack with more divisions. One of these, the 35th Division, was assembling in the rear before joining the III Corps. General McBride's division, as a result, transferred to the XII Corps on 26 December without a change of ground. In the days that followed battalions rotated between the deep snow of the outpost lines and the relative warmth of shell-torn villages, waiting while General Patton debated giving the XII Corps the go sign for an attack across the chill, swollen courses of the Sure and the Sauer.

In the corresponding German headquarters other plans were under consideration, plans to use the Bourscheid bridgehead as a springboard from which to throw a spoiling attack against the flank of the American forces congregated around Bastogne. But neither Brandenberger nor Kniess could scrape up the men, guns, and shells for such an ambitious adventure. The 79th Volks Grenadier Division did what it could with what it had in almost daily counterattacks of small compass, only to be beaten off each time by the American howitzers. Ringel Hill continued as the chief objective in these fruitless and costly attempts, and here the 79th made its last full-blown effort in a predawn attack on 30 December. The previous evening Company E, 319th Infantry, at that time forming the Ringel garrison, learned from prisoners taken on patrol that the attack would be made. The American division arranged for nine battalions of field artillery to give protective fire and the men in the garrison strengthened their outposts. The enemy made the assault, as promised, but with such speed and skill as to enter the village before a single salvo could be fired. One group of Germans penetrated as far as the battalion command post, but Pfc. W. J. McKenzie drove them off, killing the leaders, then taking sixteen prisoners. (McKenzie was awarded the DSC.) Their surprise tactics failed to save the attackers.

Concentration after concentration poured in on the buildings that sheltered the garrison troops, killing, maiming, and demoralizing the grenadiers. Those of the enemy who could not escape surrendered in groups to the first Americans they could find.

When the 80th Division got its orders on 5 January to resume the attack, it could look back on a record of important accomplishment. It had contained and badly mauled two German divisions, had helped delay and cripple the Fuehrer Grenadier Brigade, on its way to enter the Bastogne battle, and had advanced sixteen miles and erased the Ettelbruck bridgehead, so important in the communications system of the Seventh Army.

The 26th Division Fight for a Bridgehead on the Sure, 24-27 December

The 26th Division had not yet been able to push patrols through the woods to the Sure River when morning dawned on 24 December. Two companies of the 80th Division had crossed into the division zone and were waiting on the river near Heiderscheidergrund, but the foremost troops of the 26th Division were at Dellen, three and a half miles away, while the main force still was around Grosbous. Although small pockets of German riflemen fought stubbornly in the woods there seemed to be no cohesive, planned resistance by the enemy. To get the attack rolling and out of the woods, however, the Americans had to open the main road to the Sure. And to open the road they had to capture the town of Eschdorf.

There are many trails and byroads leading to the Sure but they become lost in deep, twisting ravines or run blindly through dense timber. All at this time were clogged by snow and ice. The road to Eschdorf follows a well-defined ridge and for much of its length gives a clear field of vision on both sides. Eschdorf, a town with perhaps two thousand people, is built on three hills which rise well above the surrounding countryside and give excellent observation over open ground for a half-mile to a mile in every direction. The ascent to the town is made across ridge folds. The main road coming in from the south turns away east to Heiderscheid and the Sauer crossing at Bourscheid, but other roads, three in all, continue north to the Sure River, one leading to the bridge at Heiderscheidergrund.

The road net centering at Eschdorf was very important in the German plans to hold the Seventh Army blocking position south of the Sure. Originally Brandenberger hoped to use the town as a concentration point for a counterattack by the Fuehrer Grenadier Brigade along the road to Martelange. The brigade, as recounted earlier, had started this move by piecemeal commitment while the main body still was on the march to the front, but when the 26th Division banged into the Fuehrer Grenadier advance guard southwest of Eschdorf a part of the leading battalion was cut off and the way to Martelange effectively barred. The staff of the LXXXV Corps therefore drew new plans on the night of the 23d to conform with Brandenberger's order that the American attack must be checked south of the Sure. The idea was that the Fuehrer Grenadier Brigade, on the west, and the 79th Volks Grenadier Division, from the east, should launch a concentric drive, pinching off the most forward units in the American advance. Although much of the heavy weapon strength of the brigade was loaned to the 79th, the brigade itself was expected to hold back the Americans south of Eschdorf, at the same time striking in strength east from that town to retake Heiderscheid. But whether the operation ordered for 24 December fared well or ill, the Seventh Army commander was adamant on one point: Eschdorf was to be held.

General Paul was equally convinced of the importance attaching to the command of Eschdorf and its radial roads. As early as the night of the 22d, when the III Corps optimistically prescribed the capture of Wiltz as the next step to be taken by the 26th Division, Paul ordered that a task force be created to leapfrog ahead of the 104th Infantry, capture Eschdorf, and chisel a groove to the Sure. Unwilling to expend his division reserve, Paul took the 2d Battalion, 328th Infantry, as the task force nucleus and turned it over to an officer with the division staff, Lt. Col. Paul Hamilton. A few tanks and tank destroyers were added, but through confusion in orders the engineer company supposed to be attached never joined the task force.

In the first hour of the 23d, Task Force Hamilton left Hostert in trucks. As the column turned north it found the 104th Infantry busy along the roadside with small groups of German infantry who were holding out in the woods. North of Grosbous two German tanks lay in wait just off the road, but were dispatched summarily by an assault gun. The column dismounted about a mile and a half south of Eschdorf, sent back the trucks, and put out pickets for the night. By this time Germans had appeared in some numbers east and west of the task force and their tanks had opened fire, but the 104th was coming up and by agreement was to cover Hamilton's flanks.

At daylight on the 24th scouts on the hills to the front reported much activity around Eschdorf, with vehicles dashing in and out of the town. The Fuehrer Grenadier attack against the 80th Division garrison in Heiderscheid was in full swing, although hardly developing according to plan. The road to Eschdorf, now ahead of Task Force Hamilton, rose and dipped to conform with the ridge folds reaching back to the hills on either side. The leading company had just climbed to the crest of one of these wooded folds when a storm of bullet and tank fire raked into its flank, coming down the length of the main ridge. The second company attempted to swing wide and to the van; it too found the ridge a bullet conductor. About this time the rear of the column came under direct and rapid shellfire from a hill on the right. Boxed in on front and rear, Task Force Hamilton spent most of the day trying to maneuver off the road and across the wooded nose ahead. The 81-mm. mortars got a real workout, churning the woods until they had fired four times their normal load of shells.

Toward sundown help came in the air. P-47's of the 379th Squadron (362d Fighter Group), out on their last mission of the day, swept low over the pine stands on the ridge, dropping fragmentation bombs and strafing. For some fifty Germans, well and wounded, this was the finishing touch; they came straggling out of the woods, hands high. Now that bullet fire no longer shaved the ridge like a razor Task Force Hamilton could move. It took the hamlet of Hierheck, where the woods gave way to the open ground leading up to Eschdorf, and then Hamilton gave orders to dig in for the night—orders which were countermanded almost at once by the division commander, who wanted Eschdorf that night.

While Task Force Hamilton was pinned down, General Paul had notified the III Corps that the 104th Infantry was taking over the task force. In early evening the 104th Infantry received orders for the 1st Battalion (Maj. Leon D. Gladding) to take Eschdorf, while Hamilton went on to secure the Sure crossing. Later the division ordered the 1st Battalion, 104th Infantry, to make the Sure crossing and Hamilton to take Eschdorf. Taking Eschdorf would not be an easy job. When a small group of Hamilton's men started forward to set up an observation post, they encountered enemy fire before they had moved twenty-five yards from their foxholes. The Germans in Eschdorf were alert and waiting.

Colonel Hamilton and Maj. Albert Friedman, the 2d Battalion commander worked as rapidly as they could to devise a plan of attack and bring the task force into assault position, but it was midnight before all was ready. Two companies, E and F, were to lead the attack, moving on either side of Eschdorf with their inner flanks touching, but they were not to enter the village. Company G, with tank support, would follow the assault companies and clear the village. This plan had been adopted in deference to the ground, since Eschdorf rose well above the undulating ridges and there was no higher ground to lend itself to a wider flanking movement.

Forty-five minutes after midnight the two rifle companies started to climb the highest of the three hills on which the town stands, this being the south side. The night was cold and clear, and a full moon was out. As the attackers tramped forward, long, grotesque black shadows followed on the glittering snow. For the first few minutes all was quiet, ominously lovely and peaceful; then, as the first line reached the crest, all hell broke loose. The German rifle line lay along the reverse slope, the grenadiers in white capes and sheets blending unobtrusively with the panorama of snow. Burp guns and rifles cut loose at the splendid targets the Americans provided. In face of such a fusillade the attack wavered, then fell back. Three tanks, all that Hamilton had, churned to the fore through the snow but were checked by a little creek, extended by an antitank ditch, about 300 yards from the nearest building.

A hurried call by Hamilton, who wanted reinforcements to cover his flanks, brought no reply from the division headquarters except "Take Eschdorf." There was little choice but to continue with frontal tactics. At 0400 a second assault started, this time with the tanks and Company G forming the center under orders to drive straight into Eschdorf without pause. Company G got only as far as the crest; the tanks went as far as before, and no farther. But the Germans facing the center were kept occupied long enough to start the wing companies moving. Firing as they went the two companies reached the village. Instead of marching past and around, the men closest to the buildings drifted inward, seeking the shadows and some kind of cover, dragging the two companies in with them.

What then happened cannot be recorded with any certainty. The story of Christmas Day inside Eschdorf was one of confusion at the time and recrimination later. Members of the 104th Infantry subsequently claimed to have captured Eschdorf and believed that no part of Task Force Hamilton held on in the town. Officers and men of the task force, somewhat closer to the scene, have a different story. 16 The men of the two companies that had reached Eschdorf on Christmas Eve were stranded there in the houses while German armored vehicles jockeyed about, firing at doors and windows. In the meantime the bulk of the enemy infantry gathered in the southeastern corner to meet any attempt to reinforce the attackers. When day came the commander of Company E, Capt. Vaughn Swift, took his chances in the gauntlet of bullets and ran out to the American tanks. By some miracle he reached the Shermans alive and led them into Eschdorf. Two were knocked out there, but not before they had quieted the enemy armored vehicles. (Captain Swift was given the DSC.)

As the day went on the two company commanders tried to sort out their men and resume the drive to cut through to the roads entering Eschdorf from the north. Whether this was accomplished remains a matter of debate. Finally, in the late afternoon, the division headquarters responded to Hamilton's urging and instructed the 104th Infantry to send its 1st Battalion and envelop Eschdorf. The instructions were followed. Company C entered the village an hour or so after daylight on 26 December and by 0800 reported Eschdorf clear of the enemy.

Throughout Christmas Day corps and division artillery beat the northern approaches to Eschdorf, hoping to isolate the uncertain dogfight within the town. As it turned out, the Fuehrer Grenadier Brigade had no intention of intervening there but was slipping north through the woods and ravines, while a few rear guard detachments fought on to form a new bulwark to defend the Sure River line. As early as the afternoon of 24 December the 3d Battalion, 104th Infantry (Lt. Col. Howard C. Dellert), had reached Heiderscheid, there secured guides from the 319th, and had gone on to relieve the two companies of the 319th on the river at Heiderscheidergrund.

While the 104th put troops along the river, its sister regiment made a march of three and a half miles over rough country but against little opposition and by nightfall of the 24th was near the bridge site at Bonnal. On the extreme left flank at Bilsdorf, Company C of the 249th Engineer Combat Battalion was on reconnaissance when it was struck by a much larger enemy force deployed in the village. The company commander, Capt. A. J. Cissna, elected to stay behind and cover his men as they withdrew from Bilsdorf; he fought alone until he was killed. Cissna was awarded the DSC posthumously. The 1st Battalion of the 328th (Lt. Col. W. A. Callanan), aided by the 2d Battalion, 101st Infantry, found a rear guard group of the Fuehrer Grenadier Brigade holed up in Arsdorf, near the division west boundary, and spent the night of the 24th digging the grenadiers out of attics and cellars. By midmorning Arsdorf was in hand and the left flank of the 26th Division was fairly secure except for Bigonville, three miles northwest, which now passed into the division zone as CCR, 4th Armored Division, left that village to play a new role on the western flank of the corps.

But the main mission of the 26th Division, to make a crossing at the Sure River, had yet to be accomplished when Task Force Hamilton started the fight at Eschdorf on the night of 24 December. General Paul, beset by incessant urging from the III Corps commander, passed the word to his two forward regiments that the attack must get into high gear, then sent a message to General Millikin that he hoped to seize the Sure crossing before daylight on Christmas Day. Pitched battles at Eschdorf and Arsdorf so entangled the division that the idea of a general movement forward had to be abandoned, particularly when on Christmas Day an additional battalion had to be committed at both of these towns. Although troops of the two attacking regiments were within sight of the river on Christmas Eve they found that there would be no surprise crossing. In the zone of the 104th Infantry the enemy, alerted by the presence of the two companies of the 319th, had strengthened his position at the opposite end of the Heiderscheidergrund bridge and it was apparent that a crossing site would have to be sought elsewhere. On the left the 3d Battalion of the 328th Infantry (Lt. Col. Arthur C. Tillison) reached the bare hill above Bonnal on Christmas morning, just in time to see the last German half-track cross the bridge before it was blown.

The corps commander now released the 101st Infantry from reserve and ordered General Paul to "keep going" and get to Wiltz, four miles the other side of the Sure. Paul planned to relieve the 328th with his reserve regiment, but while arrangements were being made, on the night of the 25th, word flashed back that a bridge had been captured and that the 3d Battalion was crossing. This episode of the Bonnal bridge is an apt—and instructive—example of the "fog of war." The bridge actually had been destroyed eight to ten hours earlier, but it was nearly midnight before the 328th Infantry was able to ascertain that none of its troops had got across the river. Bad news never comes singly. The 104th Infantry had to report that the Germans had blown up one span of the bridge at Heiderscheidergrund.

The Sure River is in itself not too difficult an obstacle, at its widest point no more than twenty-five yards across. The current is not swift, and there are many places where it is possible to wade across. (Plans actually were made for sending an assault party through the bitter cold stream, then wrapping the troops in blankets and thawing them out on the far bank.) The problem is to get down to the river and to get up the steep cliffs to the north bank. So twisting and tortuous is the river course and so blind are its bends that great care must be exercised in choosing a crossing point lest one have to cross the river twice. The approaches to the river, the meanderings of the river bed, and the exits on the north bank combined therefore to dictate where the 26th Division might cross.

Whether the enemy was strong enough to dictate how the division had to cross remained to be seen. The lay of the ground gave three potential crossing sites in the 26th Division zone: from east to west, Heiderscheidergrund, Esch-sur-Sure, and Bonnal. All had stone arch bridges of solid construction—or did prior to 25 December 1944. Heiderscheidergrund normally would present the most attractive of the three crossings because it gave entrance to the main Wiltz road. But the fight for Eschdorf had slowed down the 104th Infantry and prevented a thoroughgoing exploitation of the 319th toehold at Heiderscheidergrund. Furthermore the enemy had first concentrated to defend this, the most obvious of the three crossings. What he was set to do to defend Esch-sur-Sure and Bonnal remained to be tested.

The fragmented commitment of the Fuehrer Grenadier Brigade had resulted in heavy losses and blunted the fighting edge of this "elite" unit. By the very nature of its dispersed and staggered commitment the brigade had succeeded in creating a picture of strength quite out of keeping with reality. The 1st Battalion of the brigade, for example, had first appeared in front of the west wing of the 26th Division headed southwest, then had been turned around, had bumped back across the front of the 328th—fighting here and there in the woods as it went—and then had taken a hand against the 104th. Furthermore the Fuehrer Grenadier Brigade was an amorphous organization which accorded with none of the tables carried in the American handbook on German order of battle. Since its numbering and unit names fitted much of the description of the elder formation, the Grossdeutschland Panzer Division, the brigade had been first identified as the division. It would take much time and numerous prisoners before the 26th Division order of battle team could complete the true picture of the brigade.

When the Seventh Army commander ordered the Fuehrer Grenadier Brigade to withdraw to the Sure on 25 December, he intended the defense to continue on the south bank of the river. But the brigade's rifle regiment, much understrength as the consequence of the rough handling received at Arsdorf, Eschdorf, and in the counterattack at Heiderscheid, could no longer provide the necessary infantry. The bulk of the brigade had apparently crossed to the north side of the river by the morning of 26 December, forming a line—or what passed for a line—east and west of Esch-sur-Sure. The only German reserve in this sector was the army engineer brigade at Nothum, a 2 ½-mile march north of the Bonnal crossing. But General Brandenberger was loath to employ any of his small engineer complement in the firing line except under the direst of circumstances.

There was little artillery to defend the line of the Sure; most of the guns and Werfers which had good prime movers and could be hauled along the crowded roads west of the Our were at work around Bastogne or firing in defense of the Bourscheid bridgehead. One advantage the defenders did have: good observation from the heights overlooking the separate crossing sites.

The morning of 26 December dawned bright and clear with the promise of air support for the 26th Division at the river. On the left the 101st Infantry had relieved the 328th and stood ready to attempt the crossing. The 101st was fresh and its ranks were full. After its first effort to reach the piers of the stone bridge at Bonnal was met by rifle fire, a patrol discovered a good site farther to the west where a river loop curled to the American side. Engineer assault craft reached the 3d Battalion (Lt. Col. James

N. Peale) shortly before noon, but a rumor had circulated that the enemy was lying in wait on the opposite bank and the troops showed some reluctance to move. Col. Walter T. Scott, the regimental commander, took a single bodyguard and crossed the river in a rubber boat, returning without mishap. The battalion then crossed, the silence broken only by the sound of the paddles, an occasional hoarse-voiced command, and a few rifle shots. The 1st Battalion (Maj. Albert L. Gramm), closer to Bonnal, likewise made an uneventful crossing. The enemy, no more than a few stray pickets, did not loiter. Engineers started a Bailey bridge, using the supports of the stone bridge at Bonnal, while the two battalions, tired by their scramble up the steep banks, dug in along the edge of the bluffs. The few enemy planes that tried to strafe along the river were destroyed or driven off by alert fighter-bombers and the 390th Antiaircraft Automatic Weapons Battalion. Nor did a small German counterattack during the evening have any effect.

The eyes of the Fuehrer Grenadier Brigade were fixed on Heiderscheidergrund where the German fighting vehicles and riflemen waited for the main American effort. Although one span of the stone bridge had been blown as a precautionary measure, the enemy threw a trestle over the gap, preserving the bridge as a sally port to the south bank. Twice German tanks and assault guns made a bid to recross and counterattack the 104th Infantry. The first attempt was stopped short of the bridge by rapid shellfire. The second was more successful: four tanks and an assault gun rammed across the bridge but were abandoned by their crews when American guns and howitzers brought salvo after salvo of white phosphorus to sear the near bank. During the 26th, patrols operating in the 104th Infantry sector put their glasses on Esch-sur-Sure. They reported that there was no sign of the enemy in the village, but Colonel Palladino could not risk an immediate crossing on his left while the Germans opposite his right held a bridge and still seemed willing to carry the fight back to the American side of the river.

The troops in the attenuated 101st bridgehead easily repulsed a minor counterattack on the morning of 27 December. As yet there was nothing to indicate an enemy shift to meet this threat to the Sure River position. By midmorning the Bailey bridge was open and tanks and tank destroyers crossed to support the 3d Battalion as it climbed on up the bluffs to Liefrange. Since the two bridges at Esch-sur-Sure had been demolished, the commander of the 104th Infantry arranged for his left battalion to borrow the Bonnal Bailey. As the right battalion put on a demonstration with much firing at Heiderscheidergrund, the left crossed, then swung back toward Kaundorf as if to command the road climbing from Esch-sur-Sure. While this maneuver was in process the engineers constructed a treadway bridge at Esch and tank destroyers were put across to reinforce Palladino's battalion on the far bank. By the close of the day it could be said that the Sure bridgehead was firm and the way open to recapture Wiltz.

The 4th Armored Division Reaches Bastogne

Christmas Day came and went leaving the 4th Armored Division toiling slowly toward Bastogne. The left wing of the III Corps now conformed to the slow, foot-slogging pace of the divisions on the right and in the center. Both CCA and CCB had an additional rifle battalion when the attack resumed on the 25th, for the 1st and 2d Battalions of the 318th Infantry had reported to General Gaffey late on Christmas Eve after a cold, miserable, six-hour truck ride from the 80th Division sector. Both battalions, the 1st attached to CCA and the 2d to CCB, were considerably understrength after the bloody engagements at Ettelbruck. The 1st Battalion, whose officer losses had been very high, had a new commander and so did all of its companies.

During the fight at Warnach a few tanks from CCA had tried to drive on to Tintange but had bogged down. General Gaffey therefore decided to employ a part of his infantry reinforcement with the general mission of attacking to reach Bastogne, and the more immediate job of taking Tintange. After a freezing night bivouacked in the snow, Maj. George W. Connaughton's 1st Battalion, 318th, set off for a line of departure south of the village that was shown on the map as a small creek.

Gaffey had said that the battalion would have to fight for its line of departure. He was right. The two assault companies reached the creek only to discover that they faced a deep gorge, with Germans arrayed to defend it. Somehow the infantry scrambled down and up again while their opponents pitched in hand grenades. Emerging south of the village the attackers came under continuous rifle fire, but what stopped them cold was a single large-caliber assault gun whose shells burst wherever the Americans turned. The support, Company B (Capt. Reid McAllister), was given very special attention by the German gunners. Tired of taking losses where it lay, the company asked permission to take the burden of the assault on its own shoulders. Two platoons advanced through the forward companies and the enemy infantry inside the village immediately opened fire. In so doing the Germans gave away their locations to the third platoon, which had circled in from the east. Return fire coming in from the east momentarily silenced the garrison; galled by its losses Company B rushed the village, captured the maddening assault gun as its crew sought to escape, and took 161 prisoners. This action must be credited to the infantry, but it should be added that eight fighter-bombers from the 377th Squadron had hit Tintange on call, blasting with bombs and rockets just before the riflemen moved in. During the day the 51st Armored Infantry Battalion carried the advance on the west side of the Arlon-Bastogne highway as far as Hollange, pausing here with night coming on and the enemy showing his first intention of making a stand. CCA now had cleared another stretch of woods and villages flanking the Bastogne highway — but the streets of Bastogne still were seven miles away.

The 2d Battalion, 318th Infantry (Lt. Col. Glenn H. Gardner), did its chore of woods clearing and village fighting on Christmas Day alongside the armored infantry and tanks of CCB. Chaumont, scene of the bitter action two days earlier, remained the immediate objective. This time the enemy was deeply dug in, all through the woods south of the village. While tanks from the 8th Tank Battalion edged around the woods firing indiscriminately into the pines, the foot troops routed out the German infantry from holes and log-covered trenches where they sought shelter from the tankers' shells. This was a slow, precarious business. Some of the enemy paratroopers could be persuaded that surrender was the better part of valor, but many had to be finished off with grenades and even bayonets. In this manner the 2d Battalion worked through three successive wood lots, meeting strong rifle and automatic weapons fire in each. Here Sgt. Paul J. Wiedorfer made a lone charge against two German machine guns. He killed the crew serving the first weapon and forced the crew of the second to surrender. (He was awarded the Medal of Honor.)

Chaumont village was less of a problem. Prisoners had reported that a large number of panzers had come in during the night, but in fact there were no tanks, except the derelict Shermans left on the 23d. The American light tanks moved in with the infantry and by dark the village was in American hands — most of the enemy had withdrawn farther north after the struggle in the woods. The 2d Battalion saw nearly a hundred of its men evacuated for bullet wounds, mostly suffered inside the woods. Both here and at Tintange the 5th Parachute troopers had been forced to rely on their small arms; the 318th as a result sustained more casualties from bullet fire than at any time since its frontal attack at the Moselle River in early September.

Artillery and large numbers of fighter-bombers belabored the 5th Parachute Division on 26 December. The advancing Americans of the two combat commands and the attached infantry found that more and more of the enemy were willing to lay down their arms after honor had been satisfied by token resistance, but for each point where the combination of American fighter-bombers, artillery, tanks, and infantry won quick surrender there was a crossroad, a patch of woods, or a tiny collection of houses to which a tough young officer and a few men clung fiercely. Bravery was matched with bravery. Pfc. O. M. Laughlin of the 318th broke up one German position with grenades after he had been hit in the shoulder and could not use his rifle. (He received the DSC.)

Spread across a wide front, CCA and CCB could maintain little contact; nor could the rifle battalions and tank-infantry teams. Much of the American combat strength had to be diverted to screen the flanks of the individual detachments or to circle back to stamp out resistance flaring up unexpectedly in areas supposed to be free of the enemy. (CCA, for example, captured a battalion headquarters and a large number of prisoners in a fight at Hollange, south of Chaumont, which had been taken by CCB the day before.) Mines also made for delay. There were more in the path of the advance than ever before, but they had been laid hastily, were not well concealed, and often lacked fuzes. Again the most lethal and in numerous cases the sole German weapons were the rifle, machine gun, or machine pistol. These served the enemy well, and gaps in the ranks of the attackers widened even as the prisoner bag swelled. Captured paratroopers complained that they no longer had artillery support, that morale was cracking when friendly guns could not be seen or heard; nonetheless the dwindling strength of the 318th and the armored infantry battalions bore witness that the enemy still was in a fighting mood.

Despite all this the lines of the 101st Airborne Division were appreciably closer. By dark the 2d Battalion, 318th Infantry, after bitter battle and very heavy casualties, had reached the woods near Hompré, some 4,000 yards from the Bastogne perimeter. Using green and red light signals, learned from prisoners in the past two days, 1st Lt. Walter P. Carr and a four-man patrol stole through the German lines, reaching the Bastogne outposts at 0430. The return trip, with a situation map marked by the 101st Airborne G-3, wrote finis to a daring and successful mission. But other Americans had beaten Carr to Bastogne.

On Christmas Eve, when it was apparent that no quick breakthrough could be expected on the Arlon-Bastogne highway, the 4th Armored Division commander could look to two possible means of levering the slowing attack into high gear. The two battalions of the 318th were ready to add more riflemen to what had become a slow-paced infantry battle; perhaps this extra weight would tell and punch a hole through which the tanks of CCA and CCB could start rolling again. But General Gaffey was a veteran and convinced armored officer, serving a commander whose name was everywhere attached to feats of speed and daring in mechanized warfare and whose doctrine was simple: if the ground and the enemy combined to thwart the tanks in the area originally selected for attack, then find some other spot where the enemy might be less well situated to face a mechanized thrust.

The command had caught a catnap by 1100, fuel tanks were filled, commanders were briefed, an artillery plane had oriented the gunners—and the drive began. The light tanks and a platoon of tank destroyers from the 704th Tank Destroyer Battalion led off, followed by paired teams of tank and armored infantry companies. The scattered German outposts, members of a replacement engineer battalion, dived for cover as the tanks raced along the road, then hastily surrendered to the infantry following. Beyond Vaux-lez-Rosières the column left the pavement and headed northeast on a secondary road, hoping to find it ill-defended Thus far the teams had leapfrogged, taking turns in dealing with the little villages away from the main route. About 1400 the advance guard was checked at a small creek near Cobreville where the only bridge had just been blown. Abrams called for the battalion bulldozer, always kept close to the headquarters tank in the column. It took an hour for the bulldozer to demolish a stone wall and push the debris into the creek—then on went the column.

CCR of the 4th Armored Division had just taken Bigonville on the division east flank, and was counting its prisoners, waiting for orders, and making plans for feeding its troops a big Christmas dinner when Colonel Blanchard heard from the division commander. The order given was brief: move to Neufchâteau at once. Starting an hour after midnight, the combat command was near Neufchâteau when it received other and more detailed orders—attack toward Bastogne to assist the advance of CCB (then south of Chaumont) and to protect the left flank of the division and corps.

For this task CCR had the 37th Tank Battalion (Lt. Col. Creighton W. Abrams), the 53d Armored Infantry Battalion (Lt. Col. George Jaques), the self-propelled 94th Armored Field Artillery Battalion, and a battery of 155-mm. howitzers from the 177th Field Artillery Battalion. Although CCR normally was not employed as an integral tactical unit in 4th Armored practice, the tank and rifle companies of the two battalions had teamed together in many a fight.

Colonel Blanchard had selected his own route (to avoid blown bridges) and an assembly area southwest of Bercheux village on the Neufchâteau-Bastogne road. Here the column closed shortly before dawn on Christmas Day. Almost nothing was known about the German strength or dispositions along the twelve-mile stretch of road that lay ahead. Inside of Bercheux was a company of First Army engineers, which, as part of the VIII Corps barrier line, was preparing to make a stand. Thus far, however, the Germans had shown little disposition to push much beyond Vaux-lez-Rosières, a mile and a half farther up the road, from which the 28th Division headquarters had been driven on the night of the 22d.

Remonville was next. Perhaps some sixth sense warned that it was full of Germans; maybe a spotter plane had seen movement there or a frightened prisoner had talked. Whatever the reason, Remonville got the treatment. A company of Shermans lined up on the high ground outside the village with their guns trained on the houses. Four battalions of artillery, emplaced close enough to reach the target, opened rapid fire with high explosive and the tanks joined in. For five to ten minutes, long enough for the A Team to race to the village, shells rained down. In the streets the tank crews worked their machine guns until they were hot, while the infantry leaped from their half-tracks and sprinted from building to building. The German garrison, the 3d Battalion, 14th Parachute Regiment, had remained hidden up to this point. Some now emerged—but it was too late. Tank gunners and riflemen cut them down from every side. Hand grenades tossed through cellar windows and down cellar stairs quickly brought the recalcitrant—and living—to the surface. By dusk the job was finished. CCR had taken 327 prisoners.

The light tanks in the advance guard moved on, but only for a few hundred yards. A large crater pitting the road where a small creek made a detour impossible brought the column to a halt as the day ended. CCR had come abreast of CCB, in fact was fearful of using its artillery against any targets to the east. Gaffey still expected CCB to make the breakthrough now that its west flank was protected. To this end General Taylor, impatient to reach his division in Bastogne, had joined General Dager's command post, bringing the first word Dager had that CCR had come up on his left. Even so the general mission for all of the 4th Armored Division remained the relief of the 101st Airborne.

On Christmas night Colonel Blanchard and his officers huddled over a map which had just arrived by liaison plane. This map showed the American disposition in the Bastogne perimeter, only six miles away, and a somewhat hypothetical scheme of the German order of battle as it faced in toward Bastogne and out toward the 4th Armored. The red-penciled symbols representing the enemy were most numerous and precise where they faced north; by now the 101st had had ample opportunity to gauge the German strength and dispositions hemming it in. The red figures farther south were few and accompanied by question marks.

Basing it on this rather sketchy information, Blanchard gave his plan for attack on 26 December. This called for an advance through Remichampagne, a mile and a half away, and Clochimont. Then the combat command would turn northwest to Sibret, thus returning to the Neufchâteau-Bastogne road. At Sibret, which air reconnaissance had reported to be full of troops, the main fight would apparently be made. Fighter-bomber support had been promised for the morning of the 26th, and CCR had seen the sky full of American planes over Bastogne. The four firing batteries with CCR would displace from Juseret to new positions south of Cobreville, but because the exact location of CCB was unknown the howitzers would not be laid on Remichampagne. Immediate targets would be two: a large block of woods west of Remichampagne, for which CCR could spare none of its limited armored infantry; and the road from Morhet, leading east of the Neufchâteau-Bastogne highway, on which spotter planes had observed German tanks.

When CCR started for Remichampagne on the morning of 26 December, the ground was frozen, and tank going was even better than it had been during the summer pursuit across France. The column had just gotten under way when suddenly a number of P-47's appeared. Although the 362d Fighter Group was slated to give CCR a hand, these particular planes, probably from the 362d, had not been called for. Bombing only a few hundred yards in front of the leading tanks, the P-47's shook all ideas of resistance out of the few Germans left in the village or the woods.

Next was Clochimont. CCR was reaching the point where a collision with the enemy main line of resistance could be expected or a strong counterattack be suffered. Carefully then, CCR deployed near Clochimont, moving its teams out to cover the flanks. Colonel Abrams dispatched one tank company northward hoping to uncover the next enemy position or draw fire from Assenois, straight to the fore, or Sibret, the objective on the Bastogne highway. It was about 1500 when these dispositions were completed. Orders called for the attack to be continued toward Sibret, over to the northwest, but this town was probably well defended and German tanks, more likely than not, would be found guarding the main road. The 37th Tank Battalion had lost tanks here and there along the way and had no more than twenty

Shermans in operation. The 53d Armored Infantry Battalion, weak to begin with, now was short 230 men. The two battalion commanders, Abrams and Jaques, stood by the road discussing the next move and watching what looked like hundreds of cargo planes flying overhead en route to drop supplies to the 101st when Abrams suggested that they try a dash through Assenois straight into Bastogne. It was true that Sibret was next on the CCR itinerary, but it was known to be strongly held and Bastogne was the 4th Armored Division objective. Jaques agreed.

Abrams radioed Capt. William Dwight, the battalion S-3, to bring the C Team forward. It was now about 1520. Another message, this time through the artillery liaison officer, gave the plan to the 94th Armored Field Artillery Battalion and asked that the 101st Airborne be told that the armor was coming in. The 94th already was registered to fire on Assenois, but there was little time in which to transmit data to the division artillery or arrange a fire plan. CCR alone among the combat commands had no telephone wire in. Continuous wave radio could not be counted on. Frequency modulation was working fairly well, but all messages would have to be relayed. Despite these handicaps, in fifteen minutes three artillery battalions borrowed from CCB (the 22d, 253d, and 776th) were tied in to make the shoot at Assenois when the call came.

Colonel Abrams had entrusted Captain Dwight with the shock troops (Company C of the 37th Tank Battalion and Company C of the 53d Armored Infantry Battalion), telling him: "It's the push!" By 1620 all was ready and the team moved out, Shermans leading and half-tracks behind. Abrams stayed glued to his radio. At 1634 he checked with the 94th Field Artillery Battalion and asked if he could get the concentration on Assenois at a minute's notice. Exactly one minute later the tank company commander, 1st Lt. Charles Boggess, called from the lead tank. Colonel Abrams passed the word to the artillery, "Concentration Number Nine, play it soft and sweet." A TOT could hardly be expected with existing communications, but the thirteen batteries (an unlucky number for the enemy) sent ten volleys crashing onto Assenois.

Eight antitank guns were sited around the village; here and there a gun crew fired a wild shot before a shell blasted the piece or the furious fire of the Sherman machine guns drove the cannoneers to their holes. At the dip in the road on the village edge Lieutenant Boggess called for the artillery to lift, then plunged ahead without waiting to see whether the 94th had his message. So close did the attack follow the artillery that not a hostile shot was fired as the tanks raced into the streets. The center of the village was almost as dark as night, the sun shut out by smoke and dust. Two tanks made a wrong turn. One infantry half-track got into the tank column; another was knocked out when an American shell exploded nearby. The initial fire plan had called for the battery of 155's to plaster the center of the town, and these shells still were coming in when the infantry half-tracks entered the streets. Far more vulnerable to the rain of shell fragments than the tankers, the armored infantrymen leaped from their vehicles for the nearest doorway or wall. In the smoke and confusion the German garrison, a mixed group from the 5th Parachute and 26th Volks Grenadier Divisions, poured out of the cellars. The ensuing shooting, clubbing, stabbing melee was all that the armored infantry could handle and the C Team tanks rolled on to glory alone.

The "relief column" heading out of Assenois for the Bastogne perimeter now consisted of the three Sherman tanks commanded by Lieutenant Boggess, the one half-track which had blundered into the tank column, and two more Shermans bringing up the rear. Boggess moved fast, liberally spraying the tree line beside the highway with machine gun fire. But a 300-yard gap developed between the first three vehicles and the last three, giving the enemy just time to throw a few Teller mines out on the road before the half-track appeared. The half-track rolled over the first mine and exploded. Captain Dwight then ran his tow tanks onto the shoulder, the crews removed the mines, and the tanks rushed on to catch up with Boggess. At 1650 (the time is indelibly recorded in the 4th Armored Division record) Boggess saw some engineers in friendly uniform preparing to assault a pillbox near the highway. These were men from the 326th Airborne Engineer Battalion—contact with the Bastogne garrison had been made. Twenty minutes later Colonel Abrams (subsequently awarded the DSC for the action at Assenois) shook hands with General McAuliffe, who had come to the outpost line to welcome the relieving force.

Colonel Jaques and the 53d Armored Infantry Battalion missed this dramatic moment; they were involved in a scrambling fight for possession of Assenois— strictly an infantry battle now that the artillery no longer could intervene. This battle continued into the night, the 53d capturing some five hundred prisoners in and around the town. One American, S./Sgt. James R. Hendrix, took on the crews of the two 88-mm. guns with only his rifle, adding crews and guns to the bag in Assenois. (Hendrix was awarded the Medal of Honor). More Germans filtered in along the dense woods which lined the east side of the Bastogne road north of Assenois. Here Company A of the 53d was put in to dig the Germans out, the company commander, Capt. Frank Kutak, directing the fight from his jeep for he had been wounded in both legs. (For bravery here and in other actions Kutak was awarded the DSC.)

An hour or so after midnight enough of the enemy had been killed or captured to give relatively safe passage along the Bastogne road. Over 200 vehicles had been gathered at Rossignol waiting for the road to open, and during the night the light tank company of the 37th Tank Battalion escorted forty trucks and seventy ambulances into Bastogne.

Chapter XXII. The Battle Before the Meuse

The Meuse River Line

Across the western edge of the Ardennes massif runs the Meuse River. This river, throughout history, has been the natural line of resistance against an enemy advancing from east to west over the Belgian highlands. Actually, of course, the river channel changes direction as it passes through Belgium, running south to north between Maastricht and Liège, generally following an east-west line between Liège and Namur, and bending sharply at Namur to assume a south to north orientation. Although rather shallow, the Meuse averages a width of 120 yards in its main course and is fed by so many streams that its current is unusually rapid, particularly in the winter season. There are some fairly level approaches to the Meuse crossing sites; there also are long stretches of steep banks bordering the channel, some of them are cliffs nearly three hundred feet high. As a complement to the natural strength of this barrier the Belgian Government, before World War II, had limited the number of bridges spanning the Meuse. The events of 1940, however, demonstrated that modern armies could cross the Meuse speedily, either by surprise or by an overwhelming concentration of force.

Within forty-eight hours of the launching of the 1944 attack the Allied high command diagnosed the enemy intent as that of driving to the Meuse in the vicinity of Liège. But there could be no certainty in the early phases of the German counteroffensive that such a diagnosis was correct. It was quite possible that the enemy might swerve south at the Meuse, following the historical invasion route past Sedan and on to Paris instead of turning north toward Liège and Antwerp. General Middleton and the VIII Corps staff were concerned particularly with the possibility that the enemy plan might unfold into a thrust southward through the Meuse valley.

Busy with plans and troop movements designed to bolster the threatened sector of the First Army front and harden the shoulders of the corridor through which the German divisions were crowding, SHAEF took its first steps to defend the line of the Meuse (with anything more than local security measures) on 18 December. Late that day General Eisenhower ordered the 17th Airborne and 11th Armored Divisions, both training in the United Kingdom, to move to the Continent without delay. These two divisions were intended for use north and west of the Meuse, but they could not be expected for some days. From Reims, which was designated as concentration area for the airborne division, the airborne could be moved to the west bank; the armored division was slated for use on the north bank. On the 20th, however, the 11th Armored Division was ordered to assemble north of Reims. At the same time SHAEF instructed the 6th Airborne Division (British) to move at once by sea to the 21 Army Group area as a preliminary to strengthening the defense on the north bank of the Meuse.

In the meantime the 1st SS Panzer Division was drawing uncomfortably close to the Huy-Dinant sector of the Meuse and the Fifth Panzer Army had ruptured the VIII Corps center. If the German forces continued to hold their pace westward the reinforcements from the United Kingdom would arrive at the Meuse too late. On 19 December, therefore, Field Marshal Montgomery on his own initiative started troops moving south from the 21 Army Group. The British commander had been in process of shifting the weight of his forces to the north in preparation for an offensive in the Rhineland when the Germans unleashed the attack in the Ardennes; indeed Montgomery's southernmost command, the 30 Corps, already had started its advance parties moving north to the Canadian front. But at 1730 on 19 December the 21 Army Group commander ordered General Horrocks to move his 30 Corps from Boxtel, Holland, into the area between Liège and Brussels and gave him the Guards Armoured Division and the 43d, 51st, and 53d Infantry Divisions, as well as three armored brigades.

Because the situation late on the 19th "remained unpleasantly vague," to use Montgomery's own phrase, the British commander undertook emergency measures to bar the Meuse crossings between Liège and Givet while the 30 Corps made its move. Reconnaissance attachments hastily organized from Special Air Services (British) and tank replacement center troops joined the American Communications Zone personnel to set up cover parties at the bridges between Liège and Givet. British armored cars patrolled the north bank of the river between Liège and Namur. The 29th Armoured Brigade, then refitting with new tanks in western Belgium, was ordered to pick up its old tanks and hurry to defend the Namur-Dinant sector. Reports from the First Army at the close of the 19th led Montgomery to believe that there was "little to prevent German armoured cars and reconnaissance elements [from] bounding the Meuse and advancing on Brussels." That night British troops erected barriers and deployed roadblock detachments to protect the capital city, which had been liberated by the Guards Armoured Division on 3 September.

The rapid deployment of the British screen between Liège and Givet decreased considerably the chance of a surprise crossing on this stretch of the Meuse, and the concentration of the 30 Corps would be accomplished in time to provide a strong counterattack force in the event that the enemy did win a bridgehead. The 120-mile stretch of river from Givet (terminal point of the British line) to Verdun was far less strongly defended than that in the north. It would take approximately a week to bring the 17th Airborne and 11th Armored Divisions from the United Kingdom into the line. Reinforcements moving from the Third and Ninth Armies were already tagged for stiffening the First Army line of battle in the Ardennes. In these first critical days, then, the southern line of the Meuse would have to be guarded on a catch-as-catch-can basis by troops brought up from the depots, supply dumps, administrative installations, and headquarters in France and western Belgium. As late as the 22d there were bridges with no organized defense whatever.

The initial danger, or so it seemed, was posed by saboteurs, parachutists, or small motorized detachments masquerading as Americans or Belgian civilians. The bits of tactical intelligence accumulating as prisoners and documents came into the forward headquarters indicated clearly enough that the enemy had trained and committed special forces to seize the Meuse crossings. Parachutists captured behind the forward lines in the first hours of the battle told lurid tales of the plans to capture General Eisenhower, blow up ammunition dumps, and destroy radio and telephone installations and POL pipelines. When a few bona fide Germans were captured complete with American uniforms, dog tags, and jeeps, the word spread through the battle area and raced from mouth to mouth back into France.

Rumors, grossly elaborated from the few bits of fact, quickly jammed the roads to Paris and Liège with hundreds of jeeps carrying enemy saboteurs or raiding parties in American uniform. Belgian or French café keepers who for weeks had been selling vin ordinaire, watered cognac, and sour champagne to the GI's suddenly were elevated by rumor, suspicion, and hysteria to captaincies in the Waffen-SS. Ladies of no certain virtue who so far forgot themselves as to use some Teutonic phrase picked up from their clients during the years of German occupation found themselves explaining this linguistic lapse to the military police or Counterintelligence Corps agents with far more earnestness than they had ever shown in justifying a moral lapse to agent or flic. The American officer who had the misfortune to appear on the heels of the most recent rumor in some headquarters where he was unknown stood a good chance of being welcomed with a cocked pistol leveled at his belt buckle. Jeep drivers who had forgotten their grade school geography quickly brushed up on the list of the forty-eight state capitals after having been stopped six or seven times by guards who thrust the muzzle of an M1 into the driver's seat with a gruff demand for a quick identification of the capital of Alabama or Oregon. Field grade officers tried once to "rank" their way past a barricade, then resigned themselves to singing the first bars of "Mairzy Doats" for the edification of an adamant young private. And the heavily wrapped, pregnant farm wife who wished to cross any bridge found her delicate condition a cause of considerable embarrassment both to herself and the suspicious bridge guards.

In the first days of the German advance, security measures along the Meuse had been handled by the commanders of installations in the army rear areas. By the 20th this responsibility, particularly along the Meuse south of Givet, had been largely handed over to the Communications Zone and its commander, Lt. Gen. John C. H. Lee. General Lee's responsibility of course reached far west of the Meuse. Guards had to be provided for the great supply dumps and headquarters cities, so also for rail lines, pipelines, supply roads, and the French telephone and telegraph system. Far to the west in Normandy supply troops went on the alert against a possible raid by the German garrisons of the Channel Islands. In Paris, the GI's Mecca, soldiers on leave were rounded up and started back to their units; those who remained in the City of Light found night life drastically curtailed by a rigidly enforced curfew.

Four engineer general service regiments could be assembled for the Meuse line but would require some time to make the move. The commander of the Oise Intermediate Section of the Communications Zone, Brig. Gen. Charles O. Thrasher, had two locally available engineer units, the 354th and 1313th Engineer General Service Regiments, and these were organized as Task Force Thrasher on 20 December, beginning at once the work of preparing the Meuse rail and road bridges for demolition. Shortly afterward General Thrasher was authorized to blow these bridges if their capture appeared imminent. Earlier this decision had rested with the tactical commands. One can only speculate as to what would have happened if a German armored column had kept to schedule and reached one of the important bridges before the bridge guards received authority to destroy the span.

On 22 and 23 December, the 342d, 392d, 366th, and 1308th Engineer Regiments took up positions along the Meuse, reinforced by a field artillery battalion, a regimental antitank company, and six French light infantry battalions provided by the military governor of Metz. These recently organized French troops were poorly equipped with a motley collection of small arms and a few trucks but they proved very useful in screening the military and civilian traffic along the roads leading to the Meuse, both east and west of the river. All of these troops and the responsibility for the sector Givet to Verdun were handed over to the VIII Corps on the 23d by orders of the Third Army commander, who by now had command on the south side of the Bulge.

Even at this late date Middleton and Patton had some apprehension that the enemy columns might make a left wheel on the east or west bank of the Meuse and drive for Sedan. There was no definition of the VIII Corps rear boundary; as the corps commander saw his responsibility, "a vast area was involved." Not only were the corps west flank and rear open to a German turning movement but the main corps supply line, over which Middleton's troops were being re-equipped, could be cut by raids directed against the Semois and Chiers Rivers, eastern tributaries of the Meuse. Corps engineers were stationed at crossings as far west as Bouillon, and the Semois bridges west of Bouillon that had not been destroyed by the Germans during the September retreat were blown.

The enemy did not turn against the VIII Corps east-west line, and the added burden of defending the Meuse between Givet and Semois, accorded Middleton on the 23d, rested more lightly when a part of the 11th Armored Division reached the west bank on the following day. This division, moving by forced marches from Normandy, closed on the 25th; its commander, Brig. Gen. Charles S. Kilburn, took charge of all troops in the sector. The 17th Airborne Division, ordered from the United Kingdom at the same time as the 11th Armored, was delayed by bad weather which grounded its carrier planes. It finally closed at Charleville on 27 December, by which date the threat south of Givet had faded.

The German panzer forces, had actually aimed at crossing the Meuse between Givet and Liège. Montgomery had reacted promptly to the danger posed by the onrushing 1st SS Panzer Division, but with his 21 Army Group caught off balance in the middle of its shift from south to north the plans and orders of the 19th could be implemented but slowly and in sketchy form. The American Communications Zone personnel and the few British troops who took over the bridges were hardly enough to prepare demolitions, screen the traffic passing back and forth over the river in the large bridgehead cities, and maintain patrols, much less make an adequate defense against any crossing attempt in force.

As of noon, 21 December, Brig. Gen. Ewart C. Plank reported that the vital crossings at Liège, Huy, Namur, and Givet were guarded only by the 29th Infantry (a separate regiment assigned to line of communications duty), two antiaircraft gun battalions, two antitank guns, four British scout cars, and a British reconnaissance force of 300 men. The great bridgehead city of Liège had as crossing guards only two rifle companies and two cannon company platoons. The bridges at Liège and other nearby points presented a special problem. The V-bomb barrage directed into the area and German bombing planes made any installation of demolition charges on the bridge structures a hazardous business. Fearful that these important spans would be prematurely destroyed by sympathetic explosion, the engineers could do no more than collect explosives and detonating devices in the vicinity of, but not on, the bridges in question.

Although the crossings north of the bend in the Meuse still were weakly held on the 21st, the danger of a successful enemy penetration beyond the river had lessened. The movement of the 30 Corps, begun late on the 19th, was not designed to erect a linear defense for every yard of the Meuse line but instead was the first phase of Field Marshal Montgomery's plan to create a counterattack force capable of dealing with any German columns which might reach and cross the river. By the afternoon of the 20th the British 43d Division and an attached tank brigade were west of Maastricht, poised to roll up the flank of any penetration across the Meuse.

Next day the new disposition of the 30 Corps was completed. The 29th Armoured Brigade had returned to its battle-worn tanks and armored cars and was established along the river between Namur and Givet. The 2d Household Cavalry Regiment, already on the river line for the past twenty-four hours, crossed the Meuse and pushed reconnaissance as far as Marche and Rochefort, meeting American patrols but no enemy. By the close of the day, General Horrocks could decide and did that now it was possible to hold the enemy at the Meuse line. The British responsibility, be it remembered, extended only as far south as Givet and did not include the actual defense of the bridges at Liège.

On the night of 23 December a jeep load of Germans dressed as Americans appeared at Dinant, one of the few actual materializations of the oft-rumored saboteur parties. The jeep and its crew were captured by a British post. It was a little late for such tactics. By this time each of the main crossings—Givet, Dinant, and Namur—was guarded by an armored regiment and a rifle company, and it is a fair assumption that the opportunity for a German coup de main in the British-held sector was gone by the 23d. In the VIII Corps sector south of Givet the possibility of a surprise stroke still existed on this date, for there remained a number of weak links in the Meuse chain, but the odds were increasing that the defender could at least enforce delay at the Meuse. There remained, of course, the possibility that German armor might reach the Meuse somewhere along its length in sufficient strength to gain by force what no longer could be won easily by stealth or surprise.

The Meuse Seems Within Reach

By Christmas Eve the German counteroffensive showed signs of losing cohesion. The outlines of the overall strategic plan still were discernible, but the higher field commands had begun to extemporize: in a word the German armies had commenced to "react" to the moves made by the enemy or in supposition of what those moves might be. True, some German troops were very close to the Meuse and the advance to the west still had considerable momentum, but the initiative was gradually slipping from German fingers and could not be regained unless the German armies held the Marche plateau as a wider base for the final drive to and over the Meuse.

A résumé of decisions made in the higher German headquarters between 22 December and the night of the 24th will show what was happening. On the 22d OB WEST prepared for Jodl an intelligence appreciation which said that a major Allied counterattack from the north and south by reserves from the U.S. Third and Seventh Armies was unlikely before 1 January, and that a "limited" intervention against the flanks of the Bulge probably could not be attempted before 28 December. OB WEST did recognize that the Allies might assemble a strong force northwest of the Meuse and assumed that they would be able to defend the Meuse in considerable force by 30 December. It appeared from this analysis that time still was on the side of the German armies, time to interject armor from the Sixth Panzer Army into the columns driving for the Meuse and to give the depth to the forces in the van which Rundstedt now regarded as absolutely essential. On the 23d a report that the advance guard of the 2d Panzer Division was only nine kilometers from the Meuse flashed to Model, Rundstedt—and Hitler. The Fuehrer replied with congratulations and, more to the point, released the 9th Panzer and 15th Panzer Grenadier Divisions for free use by OB WEST. That same evening Model phoned Rundstedt to tell of a strong American counterattack forming to relieve Bastogne which must be expected to strike on 24 December; he, Model, would have to retain a kampfgruppe of the 15th Panzer Grenadier for the expanding battle at Bastogne, but the remainder of this division and the new 9th Panzer would be rushed westward to assist the 2d Panzer.

On the morning of the 24th a note of urgency appeared in the orders coming out of Model's command post: the Fifth Panzer Army must take Bastogne at once and "lance this boil" in the southern flank. For this purpose Manteuffel would retain a kampfgruppe of the 9th Panzer southeast of Bastogne as a link with the Seventh Army, now hard pressed by the American counterattack from the south. The sense of urgency heightened as the day wore on—it can almost be plotted like a fever chart in the exchanges between Rundstedt and Model: Rundstedt demanding that the Sixth Panzer Army get its armored divisions forward and alongside Manteuffel's spearhead before the Allies can counterattack from both south and north; Rundstedt ordering that the Allied forces be destroyed east of the Meuse before they can organize a major counter-effort; Model telling Rundstedt that the 2d Panzer has run short of motor fuel and that he has ordered the advance guard to march for the Meuse on foot. (One has the impression—it can never be verified—that as tension mounted Model commenced to turn to the older and more experienced field marshal for moral support.)

General Manteuffel faced a military and political dilemma as day drew to a close on 24 December. Janus-like, his Fifth Panzer Army faced toward the Marche plateau and the road to Dinant and toward Bastogne. Manteuffel later would say that he saw no opportunity for a successful battle west of the Meuse (although he still hoped for military success east of the river), but the decision as to which direction the Fifth Panzer would throw its weight obviously had to be made by Hitler himself. This appeal to the highest German authority was made through various channels by Manteuffel and his chief of staff, Wagener, on the 24th and 25th. Hitler's order, as relayed to the Fifth Panzer headquarters by Jodl early on the 25th, told Manteuffel to put all available forces into the battle for control of the Marche plateau. Manteuffel could hardly disengage from Bastogne and turn the fight over to the Seventh Army (indeed, this was not the Fuehrer's intention), but it was crystal clear that the 2d Panzer Division advance guard had to be reinforced and the narrow wedge it had driven toward the Meuse had to be expanded into a pile driver blow to cross that river.

Manteuffel's immediate tactical problem had four parts: the road to the isolated 2d Panzer advance guard must be reopened, 6 both for tank fuel and reinforcements; the northern flank of the salient reaching toward Dinant would have to be covered at once and in considerable strength; in the southwest where signs of an American concentration were appearing the southern side of the corridor toward the Meuse must be barricaded, perhaps as far back as Bastogne; finally, the assault front in the center required greater width and depth on the Marche plateau. The solution of this problem demanded more strength than the Fifth Panzer Army, with its tail caught in the crack at Bastogne, could amass.

Manteuffel had been promised at least three more divisions, Jodl had assured him that the II SS Panzer Corps was being rushed forward by the Sixth Panzer Army to take over the fight on his right wing east of the Ourthe River, and he had reason to expect that the 9th Panzer Division would arrive in time to take part in the attack planned for Christmas Day. For this attack, primarily designed to reach the "extended index finger" (as one German report calls it) formed by the advance detachment of the 2d Panzer in the woods around Foy-Notre Dame, Manteuffel counted on a drive by the bulk of the 2d Panzer to reach its cut-off troops while the Panzer Lehr attacked Humain and Buissonville to reopen the line of communication.

In addition the Fifth Panzer Army commander had plans to employ the divisions already in this northwestern sector as the vertebrae on which a full-bodied and integrated salient could be developed reaching to and overlapping the Meuse. The right shoulder of the expanding salient would, in Manteuffel's plan, be formed by the 116th Panzer Division. This unit was now in full force on the west bank of the Ourthe, had penetrated the American line at Verdenne, and was in position to bring artillery fire on the Hotton-Marche road. The objective given the 116th Panzer, therefore, was the town of Baillonville (north of Marche), from where it could block an Allied attack southward along the highway from Liège to Marche. The 9th Panzer Division, upon arrival, was ticketed to take position on the right of the Panzer Lehr, thus beefing up the 2d Panzer attack in the center. This was the German plan for 25 December.

The Celles Pocket

Although the VII Corps had become involved in a defensive battle, General Collins still expected to launch the corps counterattack which would signal the beginning of aggressive operations against the north flank of the Bulge. In midafternoon on 24 December General Harmon telephoned the VII Corps command post and asked permission to throw another combat command of his 2d Armored

Division against elements of the 2d Panzer which had been identified in the neighborhood of Ciney and Celles. The corps commander was away from the command post visiting his divisions; so the call was taken by the corps artillery commander, Brig. Gen. Williston B. Palmer. Palmer knew that the First Army had attached strings to any wholesale commitment of Harmon's division and that Hodges' consent and probably Montgomery's would be needed before more of the 2d Armored was unleashed. He therefore told Harmon to wait—it was too late in the day to launch an attack in any case—until the corps commander reached the 2d Armored command post. Harmon was persistent and called again asking for "immediate authority." Palmer, sorely tempted to give Harmon the permission he needed, reluctantly steeled himself and told Harmon to await Collins' appearance at the 2d Armored command post.

A few minutes later Palmer had a call from the First Army chief of staff, General Kean, who said that Collins was authorized to use all his corps and could change his defensive line. In guarded words Kean asked Palmer if he saw "a town A and a town H" on the map and then mentioned a "pivoting move." Palmer, imbued with Collins' attack philosophy and eager to give the green light to the 2d Armored, looked hastily at the map spread before him, picked out two villages southwest of Ciney and forward of the 2d Armored positions: Achêne and (Le) Houisse. This looked like the go signal for the VII Corps and an attack to advance its western wing. Because the wire line to the 2d Armored command post had gone out, Palmer sent his aide with a message for Collins giving his own optimistic interpretation of the conversation with Kean.

The aide had just departed when Kean called again. On further reflection, he said (perhaps Kean had caught a tone of exultation in Palmer's voice), he doubted whether Palmer had understood him correctly. Then came the cold water douche: "Now get this. I'm only going to say it once. Roll with the punch." Palmer's glance flicked over the map, this time to the north; there, thirty miles to the rear of the villages he had selected earlier were the towns of Andenne and Huy. Palmer remembers that this was the only moment in the war when he was "ill with disapproval."

Out went a second messenger with an explanation of Palmer's mistake and an urgent request for Collins to come home. Collins, who had received the first message at Harmon's command post, was just giving the finishing touches to an attack plan for the entire 2d Armored when the second messenger appeared. Telling Harmon to "hold everything" but making clear that the 2d Armored was to go ahead with plans for the attack on Christmas morning, Collins hurried back to his own headquarters. He arrived there about 1830 but nothing more could be done until a liaison officer, promised by Kean, came in from the First Army.

Two hours later the First Army staff officer (Col. R. F. Akers) appeared and confirmed the bad news. Montgomery and Hodges had agreed to shorten the First Army line in order to halt the German advance. The VII corps, therefore, was to go on the defensive and its commander was "authorized" on his own judgment to drop back to the line Andenne-Hotton-Manhay. In any case the VII Corps was to retain a firm contact with the XVIII Airborne Corps, which that evening was withdrawing to the Manhay position.

Although General Collins courteously asked the senior members of his corps staff to give their opinions on the action now to be taken by the corps, neither he nor any of his officers considered giving over the attack planned for the 2d Armored.

During the day Harmon's tanks had inflicted very severe damage on the German columns; the 84th Division had experienced some reverses but seemed to be holding its own. On balance the picture as seen from the VII Corps' point of view was far less gloomy than that apparently prevailing in higher headquarters. Collins recognized that a retrograde move would strengthen the defenses of Huy and Liège. He also knew that such a move would expose Namur and the major Meuse crossings south of that city, for example, those at Dinant. The final decision, made by the corps commander himself, probably could have been predicted: on 25 December the 2d Armored Division would advance as planned; the corps then would continue with limited objective attacks to break up any dangerous concentration of enemy forces on its front.

The boundary between the VII Corps and the XVIII Airborne Corps lay generally along the direct road from Bastogne to Liège, but this was essentially an artificial division and coincided neither with the compartmentalization of the terrain, naturally divided as it was by the Ourthe River, nor with the manner in which the German attack was developing. The ebb and flow of the battle on Christmas Day may best be understood by tracing the movements of three German divisions: the 2d Panzer, the Panzer Lehr, and the 116th Panzer. Perhaps it would be more accurate to say the attempted movements, for the day came bright and clear, bringing the American and British air forces into the skies over the Bulge in one of the greatest demonstrations of tactical ground support ever witnessed by American troops.

By the morning of the 25th the advance kampfgruppe of the 2d Panzer had been split in two, in part by a loss of direction during the night march toward Dinant, in part by the activity of American tank patrols operating out of Ciney, where CCB of the 2d Armored had established its base for future operations. The 2d Panzer reconnaissance battalion and a part of the German artillery column had bivouacked near Foy-Notre Dame, only four or five miles from the bridges at Dinant. Major Cochenhausen, who commanded the main column, including a tank battalion and a regiment of panzer grenadiers, halted at daylight in the woods southwest of Conneaux—perhaps 5,000 meters behind the detachment in Foy-Notre Dame.

Lauchert, the division commander, was acutely aware of the perilous situation confronting his forward troops and knew they had to be reinforced and resupplied at once. His orders, however, were to use the rest of his division to protect the right flank of Luettwitz' XLVII Panzer Corps in the Marche sector until the incoming 9th Panzer Division could take over the task. Since the Americans in and around Marche seemed quiet, Lauchert proposed to Luettwitz that he be relieved of this security mission. While Panzer Lehr attacked west of Marche to reopen the road, Lauchert wanted to switch the main body of his division back through Rochefort, then push northwest to the troops in what German reports already were calling the Conneaux Pocket. At first Luettwitz would not listen to the importunate Lauchert. Probably the refusal made no difference. As Lauchert himself admits, the air was so thick with Allied Jabos that his tactical units could not move during the daylight hours, nor was there a German interceptor plane to be seen this far to the west.

In the early afternoon Manteuffel and his chief of staff visited General Luettwitz. The latter once more proposed that the forward echelons of the 2d Panzer be withdrawn—although he was well aware that such a decision was beyond the power of the Fifth Army commander—and once again was refused. Something might be done, however. Since a kampfgruppe of the 9th Panzer was finally at hand and could be used to relieve Lauchert in the Hargimont sector facing Marche, the 2d Panzer commander received permission to carry out his relief operation. All day long radio reports from Cochenhausen had told of bitter fighting, heavy losses at the hands of Allied planes and tanks, dwindling ammunition, and no fuel. Now, just as Lauchert had his orders in hand, he heard that radio contact with the force cut off at Foy-Notre Dame had ceased.

The attack mapped out by Collins and Harmon late the previous afternoon was launched by CCB at 0800 on Christmas Day, the idea a double-pronged sweep to capture Celles and annihilate the German armor believed to be thereabouts. For this maneuver General White divided his command into two task forces. Task Force A (Lt. Col. Harry Hillyard) had its line of departure on the Achêne road and orders to take the Bois de Geauvelant, a large wood some thousand meters across, which lay midway between Achêne and Celles. It was to assemble for the final assault on high ground northwest of Celles. Task Force B (Maj. Clifton B. Batchelder), starting its move near Leignon, was to make the main envelopment and cut off Celles on the southeast. The 82d Armored Reconnaissance Battalion went in on the open right flank of the attack to screen toward the west and as far forward as the Lesse River, south of Celles. CCB would be supported by artillery emplaced west of Ciney and by both American and British fighter-bombers.

Task Force A, medium tanks to the front, went through the Bois de Geauvelant with almost no opposition. As it debouched it came under fire from a little farm near Foy-Notre Dame and lost three half-tracks. The 370th Fighter Group of the IX Tactical Air Command, flying in support of CCB, then flushed out four Panther tanks and put them out of action, at least temporarily. The column again drew fire near Boisselles, but two platoons of the 67th Armored Regiment moved in and destroyed three Panthers doing the shooting. By the middle of the afternoon Task Force A reached the high ground overlooking Celles, blocking the roads to the west and southwest. Task Force B had a brief battle at Conjoux, then rushed on—knocking out isolated tanks and guns— until it arrived on the ridge 1,300 yards southeast of Celles.

The British 29th Armoured Brigade was conducting its own private battle west of Foy-Notre Dame while pushing reconnaissance toward the Lesse River. The British knocked out three Panthers and some infantry near Sorinne, then shot up more German vehicles and took prisoners around Foy-Notre Dame. In the skirmish near Boisselles a few tanks of the British 3d Royal Tank Regiment and some British gunners gave a hand to Task Force A.

Meanwhile the 82d Reconnaissance Battalion had run into the remnants of the 2d Panzer reconnaissance battalion at Foy-Notre Dame (part of this group had escaped eastward to rejoin the main force huddled in the woods northeast of Celles). These Germans intended to make a fight of it, though at first sight Foy-Notre Dame seemed a peaceful farming village—nothing more. When a platoon from the 82d moved in, the enemy began a fusillade of antitank and machine gun fire from hidden positions. Worse, four Panthers on high ground just south of the village took a hand. The American cavalry suffered some casualties, but Sergeant Rogers used his assault gun to charge a German antitank gun in the middle of the village and the mop-up began. The four Panthers were brought under fire by British gunners, then finally destroyed by air attack. (Probably these were the tanks which had struck Task Force A near the Bois de Geauvelant.) This skirmish marked the end of the German reconnaissance battalion: the commander and 147 others were captured, and much of its remaining equipment was taken.

When General White's two task forces finally sent tanks into Celles they met little resistance. At first it seemed empty except for the townspeople who had gathered in the church; later some 200 dispirited prisoners were rounded up in and near the town. With the capture of Celles the string was drawn on the bag in the forest between that town and Conjoux. Harmon ordered CCB to turn back the next morning and give the coup de grâce to the trapped enemy.

Although Christmas Day had brought much sporadic action and occasional flare-ups like the fight at Foy-Notre Dame the main German pocket simply had been bypassed. It is known that Cochenhausen's tanks had very little gasoline, probably not enough to permit any appreciable skirmishing or tactical movement, but the German sluggishness in the pocket may be credited to the gunners supporting CCB, the army pilots in their flying OP's, and the close coordination between the artillery and the fighter-bombers of the 370th Fighter Group and Royal Air Force 83 Group. At noon, for example, a spotter plane picked up a column of seven enemy tanks north of Celles—all were destroyed by artillery fire. Twelve P38's and an unknown number of British Typhoons, taking time out only to replenish fuel tanks and ammunition racks, worked over the woods where lay Cochenhausen's command and strafed roads and trails whenever vehicles showed signs of making a break for it.

What of the German efforts to reach Cochenhausen's force? Two small forays were attempted during the day by the Panzer Lehr, whose commander had dispatched tanks along the Custinne road toward Celles, but these efforts were foiled by the ubiquitous Allied planes. That night the kampfgruppe with which the 2d Panzer had been blocking in the Hargimont sector was relieved by the 9th Panzer, and Lauchert finally was free to attempt Cochenhausen's relief. The force which he led from the Rochefort road through the Bois de Famenne and Ciergnon was not likely to give much confidence of success: a company or two of tanks, a battalion of armored infantry, a light artillery battalion, two companies of engineers, and part of a flak battalion.

The Germans had neared the twin villages of Petite and Grande Trisogne, little more than a mile from Celles, when they saw the ridge ahead "crawling with tanks." (These may have been British tanks because the 29th Armoured Brigade was blocking behind the CCB lines.) The 2d Panzer never got to launch an attack, for the American guns opened "a hellish fire" (their targets spotted—as Lauchert later recalled—by five artillery planes). Then to top this came the P-38's and Typhoons. On nearby roads more Allied tanks hove in sight but made no concerted attack. Lauchert's group was saved by an order radioed from the XLVII Panzer Corps: he was to return to Rochefort at once; the troops in the pocket would have to destroy their vehicles, leave their wounded, and get out on foot. A Panzer Lehr attempt to reach the pocket via Custinne on 26 December was equally futile, and for the same reasons. Bayerlein's kampfgruppe—at no time in the battles on the Marche front did the Panzer Lehr commander have his entire division in hand—also was ordered back to Rochefort during the night of 26 December.

The story of the 2d Panzer pocket is quickly told. CCB spent two days clearing the thick woods and dense underbrush between Celles and Conjoux. The procedure was simple and effective: first, heavy shelling on a given area, then a slow, methodical advance by the infantry line backed with the tanks. In an extension of the Bois de Geauvelant, where tanks could operate with some freedom, an armored sweep was made which killed about 150 of the enemy. In the main forest near Celles a final squeeze produced 200 prisoners, 12 guns, and 80 vehicles of various types to add to the larger bag. Nonetheless many of the German troops did succeed in escaping on foot. Major von Cochenhausen and nearly 600 of his men ultimately reached Rochefort, but all the equipment of the reconnaissance battalion, the 304th Panzer Grenadier Regiment, the 2d Battalion of the 3d Panzer Regiment, three artillery battalions, and two-thirds of the division flak battalion had to be left behind.

The Fight at Humain

The 2d Armored Division's "limited objective" attack, so carefully planned for Christmas Day, included a drive by CCA straight south from Buissonville on the paved highway to Rochefort, there to relieve the battalion of the 84th Division. This move never was carried through, although Harmon did not learn that the Rochefort troops had escaped until early afternoon. Instead CCA and the 4th Cavalry Group were caught up in a quite unexpected battle whose focal point was Humain, east of Buissonville. During the night of 24 December Troop A of the 24th Cavalry Squadron occupied Humain as an outpost for the CCA assembly area at Buissonville. But the troopers had short tenure in Humain, for across the lines the Panzer Lehr was gathering its few tanks to break the American stranglehold on the throat of the 2d Panzer spearhead. Bayerlein divided his Panthers into two assault groups: a platoon, supported by a rifle company, to seize Humain; a company, reinforced by an understrength rifle battalion, to drive on the left for Havrenne, then Buissonville.

The German blow struck Humain at first light, driving the cavalry out of town. The attack to the west rolled past the burned-out relics of the American successes of the day before-2d Panzer trucks, many armored cars, halftracks, and, near Havrenne, the guns of an entire artillery battalion. Havrenne being empty, the German column moved on toward Buissonville, Here a ruse was tried and worked. A German officer in American uniform went forward to the two Sherman tanks guarding the bridge over which the Havrenne road entered Buissonville; so effective an actor was he that the tank crews obeyed without question his order that they return to their bivouac. Four of the German tanks actually crossed the bridge at daylight, but were driven out by fire from the CCA tanks' guns. On the heels of this skirmish, the leading CCA task force started down the road for Rochefort. Near Havrenne the Panther company attempted to make a stand but was outgunned and lost five tanks. Havrenne fell to the Americans, but CCA discontinued the advance toward Rochefort for by this time it was known that the friendly infantry there had escaped. Meanwhile a considerable threat was looming on the exposed flank at Humain.

Col. John C. MacDonald's 4th Cavalry Group had set about retaking Humain, but his light tanks and tank destroyers were no match for the heavier German Panthers; nor could the American assault guns get a direct shot at them, shielded as they were behind the stone walls of the village. MacDonald tried a dismounted assault, but this failed. Artillery was unable to dislodge the enemy. Late in the afternoon Harmon sent a company of medium tanks to assist the 24h Cavalry Squadron. One last attack was made in the waning daylight—this, too, made no headway. At midnight General Collier, on his own cognizance, ordered the American cavalry to withdraw, blocking the roads to the north and east lest the enemy erupt toward Marche.

When the 26th dawned the defenders had a fresh force in the town. Panzer Lehr, it will be remembered, had been relieved during the night by the 9th Panzer to engage in the sortie toward Celles. The 9th Panzer Division (Brig. Gen. Elverfeldt) had been brought from Holland on 22 December. In view of its exposure to air attack and delays while it waited along the road for tank fuel the division had made very good time, albeit arriving in the battle line a day behind schedule. A veteran of the Arnhem and Aachen battles (it had opposed the 84th Infantry Division at Geronsweiler in the north), the 9th Panzer may have had as many as 90 tanks and 35 self-propelled assault guns or tank destroyers. Apparently the division artillery regiment did not arrive until three or four days later. When the first march column reached the line on the afternoon of the 25th it deployed south of Marche, there taking over the Marloie-Hedree blocking position held by the 2d Panzer.

As more troops arrived the 9th Panzer extended westward, thus including Humain in its bailiwick, but Elverfeldt's fresh division had more than a defensive mission. Although Luettwitz intended to employ this new armor to nourish the drive westward, it is questionable whether the XLVII Panzer Corps commander had anything more in mind than the defeat of the American armor east of the Meuse when he gave the 9th Panzer its orders on the night of 25 December: attack from the Humain sector and take Buissonville.

About 0700 the cavalry observation posts north of Humain saw tanks defiling from the town onto the Havrenne-Buissonville road. This word was flashed to the 2d Armored command post where Harmon ordered Col. Carl Hutton, the division artillery commander, to fire a "serenade" (a TOT) on Humain with all the 155-mm. and 8-inch battalions in range "right away." The avalanche of heavy shells falling in Humain did not disrupt the German attack formation en route to Havrenne but may have prevented its prompt reinforcement. The engagement at Havrenne began within a half-hour, carried by fifteen Panther tanks and a battalion of grenadiers from the 10th Panzer Grenadier riding in armored half-tracks. At the edge of the village the German infantry took over the initial assault, only to be beaten off by tank guns, tank destroyers, and artillery. Company I of the 66th Armored Regiment, with its attached platoons of infantry and tank destroyers, met and threw back three separate attacks during the day. The job was made easier by the capture of the German attack plan and the warm attention paid Humain—the German sally port—by Hutton's artillery and MacDonald's light armor, the latter engaged in shooting up the thin-skinned half-tracks bringing reinforcements into Humain.

It may seem strange that the 9th Panzer, with fresh troops and close to its full tank complement, did not press the attack against CCA. But the 9th, like the 2d Panzer and Panzer Lehr before it, was fighting with one arm behind its back. Luettwitz, gravely concerned that the Americans might break through west of Bastogne and surge north to cut off the divisions in the salient beyond Rochefort, turned the blocking position at Rochefort over to the 9th Panzer, leaving that division with its line bent at a right angle.

All through the night of 26 December the medium and heavy calibers of the 2d Armored Division artillery blasted away at the Germans in Humain. The town had to be retaken, for it presented a continuing point of entry into the left flank of the 2d Armored. But as part of the larger VII Corps' scheme, Harmon had the task of carrying forward the American front to the east-west line of the L'Homme and Lesse Rivers. For this general advance Harmon brought up CCR (Col. Sidney R. Hinds), which had been waiting at Hogne since Christmas Day, and attached it to Collier's CCA. Collier ordered CCR to take on the Panthers in Humain and sent CCA to clear the large forested area and the roads running south to Rochefort and L'Homme. CCB was thus left in the west to eradicate the last remnants of the Celles pocket while extending patrols, in cooperation with the British 29th Armoured Brigade—all of its troops now east of the Meuse—to the line of the Lesse River.

To trap the Humain garrison, Colonel Hinds made his attack on the morning of the 7th with tanks circling south, east, and west of the town, and the armored infantry moving in from the north. The 2d Battalion (Lt. Col. Lemuel E. Pope) of the 67th Armored Regiment had isolated Humain by 1015 but found the Panthers missing, driven out during the night by the artillery bombardment. There remained considerable bite in the Humain defenders and they momentarily halted the American tank column led by Pope. Pope went to the head of the column, reorganized the formation under intense fire, and started the attack moving again. (Colonel Pope was awarded the DSC.) By noon CCR was in Humain, where it took another ten hours to clear the houses of the 150 grenadiers who had been left behind. Even while this fight was in progress Harmon telephoned Collier to "go to the river with abandon."

This was not quite the end of the three-day battle. An artillery spotter plane flying over Hargimont in the early afternoon saw a column of German vehicles gathering for a march down the Humain road. It seems rather appropriate that this last effort against the 2d Armored should have been dealt with by the fighter-bombers whose cooperation had contributed in striking measure to the 2d Armored successes before the Meuse. Fourteen P-38's from the 370th Fighter Group struck Hargimont and, as a cavalry outpost happily reported, "gave them everything they had." Two more flights were vectored in: "much flame and smoke observed." As a final and fitting gesture of Allied cooperation it may be noted that CCR, faced with a stubborn holdout detachment in a large chateau east of Humain, called on the flame-throwing Crocodile tanks of the Scottish Fife and Forfar Yeomanry to apply the finishing touch to the fight for Humain.

The ill-fated battle of the XLVII Panzer Corps in front of Dinant was ended. Luettwitz had new orders: his corps must make one final, all-out effort to take Bastogne, leaving a minimum force in the Rochefort area to guard its back. Across the lines, on 28 December, the 83d Infantry Division and the British 53d Division began to replace the 2d Armored Division combat commands. By 31 December the 2d Armored was in billets, belatedly eating its Christmas dinner. During the brief operation east of the Meuse the 2d Armored Division had racked up a considerable tally: 1,213 prisoners taken, 82 tanks, 83 guns, and 441 vehicles captured or destroyed. The American losses in armor were light: 5 light tanks and 22 mediums. The fight had cost the 2d Armored Division and its attached units 17 killed, 26 missing, and 201 wounded—an illuminating commentary on the use by a veteran formation of the combined arms, the impossibility of striking power inherent in the piecemeal tactics employed by the enemy, the lack of a strong German artillery to counter the weight of metal always available to the Americans, and the complete absence of German attack planes in skies ruled by the American and British fighter-bombers.

The Fight at Verdenne

On the night of 4 December the 84th Infantry Division was deployed along an arc of some twelve miles reaching from Hogne, northwest of Marche, through Waha, south of Marche, thence bowing back to the northeast in front of the Marche-Hotton road. On the right, the 4th Cavalry Group formed a screen masking the infantry line. The center at the moment was quiet, but on the left the 116th Panzer Division had broken through the outpost line and despite the successful American counterattack made late in the afternoon still held an entrant position at Verdenne.

The 116th Panzer faced a lone battle as it prepared to carry out the Fifth Panzer Army orders for attack westward. Thus far the fighting on its right in the sector east of the Ourthe River had not gone too well; neither the 2d SS Panzer nor the 560th Volks Grenadier Division managing to gain ground on the 24th. To the left the attention of the 2d Panzer was centered on Foy-Notre Dame and Celles far to the west. Nonetheless so long as Luettwitz' armor had any chance of breaking through to the Meuse the 116th had to continue its attack to breach the American defenses north of Marche and press forward as a covering shell for the drive to Dinant.

General Bolling knew that some Germans still were around Verdenne on the night of 24 December, but the 84th Division was unaware that the enemy had slipped on into the woods between Verdenne and Bourdon until a lucky fluke revealed the new threat. About midnight Companies A and K of the 334th Infantry and Company L, 333d Infantry, started along the woods trails and byroads to converge in a night assault against Verdenne. Moving in from the west, Company K took a wrong turn and suddenly bumped into a column of six or eight tanks. Sgt. Donald Phelps, marching at the point, went forward to check the lead tank. Suddenly a figure leaning out of the tank shouted, "Halt!" Phelps, recognizing the German accent, took a snap shot at the figure who screamed as the bullet struck. The German tanks opened fire with not only their machine guns but their main armament, and the American infantry file hit the dirt. Severely lacerated before it could break away, the remaining forty men of Company K joined the main assault against Verdenne an hour later.

The Germans inside Verdenne had been softened by an intense preparatory shelling and the American infantry succeeded in getting clear through the village—although fighting resumed in daylight with the dangerous task of house clearing. One enemy tank showed up during the night, but Sgt. E. T. Reineke killed the tank commander with a rifle ball, then tossed a grenade into the open turret. More American infantry arrived in the morning, and by the end of Christmas Day 289 Germans had surrendered.

The seizure of Verdenne cast a loop around the German tanks and infantry in the woods north of the village. At noon on Christmas Day a tank company from the 16th Panzer Regiment tried an assault in staggered formation against Verdenne but found Company B of the 771st Tank Battalion waiting and lost nine tanks—its entire complement. Waldenburg still had hopes that the detachment in the woods could be saved, for during the day the Fuehrer Begleit Brigade came in on his right, freeing the troops he had deployed to watch Hampteau and the Hotton approaches. More than this, Waldenburg apparently expected to use the wedge which would be created in reaching the pocket as a means of splitting the Marche-Hotton line and starting the major advance westward.

The area in which the Germans were hemmed posed a very neat problem in minor tactics. It was about 800 yards by 300, densely wooded, and shaped with an inner declivity somewhat like a serving platter. Guns beyond the rim could not bring direct fire on the targets inside, and tanks rolling down into the pocket would be exposed before they could train their weapons. Tanks inside the pocket would be in the same position if they moved up and over the edge. Assault by infantry could be met with tank fire whether the assault went into or came out of the pocket.

Just such an assault was the first tried by the 333d Infantry, which put Companies A and B into a predawn attack on 26 December. The American skirmish line, its movements given away by the snow crackling under foot, took a number of casualties and was beaten back, but it gave some test of the enemy strength, now estimated to be two rifle companies and five tanks. Actually most of the Germans in the 1st Battalion, 60th Panzer Grenadier Regiment, took part in the fighting at the pocket or in attempted infiltration through the woods to join their comrades there. One such relief party, led by a tank platoon, did cut its way in on the morning of the 26th. Now that the enemy had been reinforced the 333d Infantry decided to try the artillery, although not before Colonel Pedley had been given brass-bound assurance that the gunners would lay their pieces with such minute precision as to miss the friendly infantry edging the pocket. Through the rest of the day an 8-inch howitzer battalion and a battalion of 155's hammered the target area, intent on jarring the panzers loose, while a chemical mortar company tried to burn them out.

On 27 December patrols edged their way into the pocket, to find nothing but abandoned tanks. The previous evening General Waldenburg heard that the Fuehrer Begleit Brigade was being taken away from his right flank and that he must go over to the defensive at once. Still in radio contact with the pocket, Waldenburg ordered the troops there to come out, synchronizing their move with an attack at dusk which would be made toward Ménil, northeast of Verdenne. Perhaps the feint at Ménil served its purpose — in any event most of the grenadiers made their escape, riding out on the tanks still capable of movement.

Although this last sortie against Ménil was only a ruse, Ménil and the surrounding area had been the scene of bitter fighting and stubborn German attacks on 26 December. Krueger, the LVIII Panzer Corps commander, saw in the newly arrived Fuehrer Begleit an opportunity to carve the Hotton garrison, which had been so effectively barring his advance over the Ourthe, down to size. The villages of Hotton, Hampteau, and Ménil form a triangle, Hampteau being the apex of the triangle, if this is pictured as projecting toward the German lines. Krueger's plan was to smash through Hampteau, grab the ridge running back to the west where it overlooked Hotton and Ménil, and take Hotton by attack from the rear, that is, the west bank of the river. Success at Hotton would permit the 116th Panzer to peel the American flank back from the Marche road.

The first contingent from the Fuehrer Begleit came into the line opposite Hampteau at noon, deployed, and at 1400 hit Company G of the 334th Infantry, which was guarding the Hampteau bridge site. This attack seems to have been poorly organized (prisoners said that the attack formation had been wrecked in the assembly area by artillery fire). In any event it crumbled under the shells of tank destroyers and the 84th Division artillery. This proved to be the single pinch-hit performance of the Fuehrer Begleit, for later in the afternoon it was ordered out of the line and sent marching for Bastogne.

At 1830 the German attack shifted toward Ménil, conducted as an envelopment on the east and west by infantry and tanks of the 116th Panzer. The western blade of the scissors ran into trouble when the tanks leading the attacking column were forced off the road by a daisychain of antitank mines. While attempting to re-form, the tanks were suddenly assailed by salvo fire from three field artillery battalions. Six tanks fell prey to the American cannoneers and the attack collapsed. Later the enemy made a demonstration here as part of Waldenburg's feint. On the east side of the town the assault had to be made across 500 yards of bare ground. The enemy fusiliers bravely attempted the passage, attempted it several times during the course of two hours, but unprotected flesh and blood were no match for the 2,000 rounds of high explosive which the 326th Field Artillery Battalion poured down on this killing ground.

By the morning of 27 December the whole Marche-Hotton front had quieted. In the enemy lines the crippled and demoralized 116th Panzer licked its wounds and dug defensive works while its neighbor on the left, the XLVII Panzer Corps, retired to a shortened position in order to free men and tanks for the new fight brewing at Bastogne. The 84th Infantry Division sent out patrols and counted its prisoners—592 for the Verdenne engagement. The entire operation as part of the VII Corps cost the 84th Division 112 killed, 122 missing, and 348 wounded. On New Year's Day the 84th was relieved by the British 53d Division and moved north, prepared to team once again with the 2d Armored Division—but this time for the offensive.

Chapter XXIII. The Battle Between the Salm and the Ourthe, 24 December-2 January

The Sixth Panzer Army had begun the Ardennes counteroffensive with two distinct missions in hand: the first, to cross the Meuse River between Liège and Huy as a prelude to the seizure of Antwerp; the second, to wheel a cordon of divisions onto a blocking line extending due east of Liège to cover the depth of the advancing army and to deny incoming Allied reinforcements the use of the highway complex southeast of Liège. Constricted by the American grip on the Elsenborn Ridge "door post" (as the German High Command called this position), the Sixth Panzer Army had bumped and jostled some of its divisions past Elsenborn and on toward the west, but had failed to achieve the momentum and maneuver room requisite to the assigned missions. The armored gallop for the Meuse had foundered on the north bank of the Amblève River when Peiper's mobile task force from the 1st SS Panzer Division had run squarely against the 30th Infantry Division. The 12th SS Panzer Division, supposed originally to be running mate with the 1st SS Panzer, had become involved in a costly and time-consuming fight to budge the American "door post," failing thereby to keep its place in the German scheme of maneuver. Therefore, the task—and glory—of leading the drive across the Meuse had passed to the Fifth Panzer Army.

But General Sepp Dietrich's SS formations had failed quite as signally to achieve the second mission—to create the blocking line east of Liège. Left free to deploy along the proliferating highway system southeast of Liège, the Americans had been able to throw two fresh corps into defensive array along the Salm, the Ourthe, the Lesse, and L'Homme Rivers, thus still further obstructing the advance of the Sixth Panzer and, more important, endangering the exposed right flank of the Fifth Panzer as it maneuvered before the Meuse.

By 24 December the westernmost armored columns of the Fifth Panzer Army had been slowed to a walk quite literally, for the OB WEST orders on that date called for the advance toward the Meuse "to proceed on foot." In part the loss of momentum arose from supply failure, but basically the slowing process stemmed from the failure of the Sixth Panzer Army to form a protected corridor for its neighbor to the south and so to cover the flank, the rear, and the line of communications for Manteuffel's salient.

It was apparent by the 24th to all of the higher German commanders that the advance must be strengthened in depth and—if possible—enlarged by pushing out the northern flank on the Marche plateau. German intelligence sources now estimated that the Allies were in the process of bringing a total of four armored and seven infantry divisions against the northern flank between the Salm and Meuse Rivers. The Sixth Panzer Army had to transfer its weight to the west. Hitler, who had been adamant that Sepp Dietrich should drive the Americans back from the Elsenborn position, finally granted permission on 24 December to give over the battle there and move in second-line divisions capable only of defensive action. Rundstedt already had gone on record that it was "useless" to keep five divisions in the Elsenborn sector. Neither Rundstedt nor Model had completely given up hope that the point of the Sixth Panzer Army might shake free and start moving again, for the German successes in the Vielsalm area at the expense of the American XVIII Airborne Corps promised much if Dietrich could reinforce his troops on this western flank. Nonetheless, the main play still would be given the Fifth Panzer Army.

The orders passed to Dietrich for 24 December were that his attack forces in the Salm River sector should push hard toward the northwest to seize the high ground extending from the swampy plateau of the Hohes Venn southwest across the Ourthe River. In the opinion of Rundstedt's staff the Fifth Panzer Army was at tactical disadvantage because its westernmost divisions, which had followed the level path of the Famenne Depression at Marche and Rochefort, were under attack from American forces holding command of the high ground on the Marche plateau to the north. It therefore seemed essential for the Sixth Panzer to establish itself on the same high ground if it was to relieve the pressure on Manteuffel's open and endangered north flank. In theory the strategic objectives of the Sixth Panzer were Liège and Eupen, but the German war diaries show clearly that Rundstedt (and probably Model) hoped only that Dietrich could wheel his forward divisions into a good position on defensible ground from which the Fifth Panzer Army could be covered and supported.

On the morning of 24 December the Sixth Panzer Army was deployed in an uneven stairstep line descending southwest from the boundary with the Fifteenth Army (near Monschau) to the Ourthe River, newly designated as the dividing line between the Fifth and Sixth. In the Monschau-Höfen sector the LXVII Corps held a north-south line, the corps' front then bending at a right angle past the Elsenborn ridge line. This corps front coincided almost exactly with that of the American V Corps. The I SS Panzer Corps continued the German line west along the Amblève River where it faced the reinforced 30th Infantry Division, but at the juncture of the Amblève and the Salm the line bent south at a sharp angle, following the east bank of the latter river as far as Vielsalm. This section of the German line opposite the 82d Airborne Division was poorly manned. The 1st SS Panzer Division (the only division available to the corps) had put troops across both the Amblève and Salm, but by the 24th the 1st SS, already badly beaten, was able to do little more than patrol its corner position.

The fall of St. Vith had opened the way for the westernmost corps of the Sixth Panzer Army to form a base of attack running generally west from Vielsalm and the Salm River to the crossroads at Baraque de Fraiture (Parker's Crossroads). This corps, the II SS Panzer, had relieved the 560th Volks Grenadier Division of its attack against the south front of the 82d Airborne and 3d Armored Divisions, the 560th sideslipping further west to take over the front, facing elements of the 3d Armored Division between the Aisne and Ourthe Rivers. The diagonal course of the Ourthe valley and the broken nature of the ground lying east of it posed an organization and command problem for both Germans and Americans. Those elements of the 3d Armored east of the Ourthe, though belonging to Collins' VII Corps, were actors in the story of the XVIII Airborne Corps. The same lack of neat accord between battle roles and order of battle listings was reflected on the German side of the line. There the LVIII Panzer Corps, forming the right wing tip of the Fifth Panzer Army, lay astride the Ourthe with its armor (the 116th Panzer) on the west bank and the bulk of its infantry (the 560th Volks Grenadier Division) on the east bank, echeloned in front of the incoming II SS Panzer Corps.

When, on the night of 22 December, the advance guard of Bittrich's II SS Panzer Corps first descended on the American-held crossroads at Baraque de Fraiture, General Bittrich had only one regiment of the 2d SS Panzer Division available for mounting this new Sixth Panzer Army attack. On 23 December, when the Americans at the crossroads finally succumbed to superior numbers, Bittrich had nearly all of the 2d SS at his disposal and the advance guard of his 9th SS Panzer Division was nearing the east bank of the Salm. Field Marshal Model had just wheeled the two infantry divisions of the LXVI Corps northward with orders to attack astride the Salm valley, thus bolstering Bittrich's right flank, now insecurely held by the decimated 1st SS Panzer Division.

General Bittrich had been promised still more forces for his attack to the northwest. The Fuehrer Begleit Brigade, re-forming after its battles in the St. Vith sector, was en route to join the 2d SS Panzer at the Baraque de Fraiture crossroads. The 12th SS Panzer Division, so Bittrich was told, would be relieved in the Elsenborn sector and hurried to the new Sixth Panzer front. Finally, Hitler himself would order the 3d Panzer Grenadier Division moved from the Elsenborn battle to the fight looming between the Salm and the Ourthe. Bittrich has not recorded any gloomy suspicion of this potential plethora of riches, but as a veteran commander he no doubt recognized the many slips possible between cup and lip: the increasing poverty of POL, Allied air strikes against any and all moving columns, the poor state of the few roads leading back through the narrow Sixth Panzer zone of communications, and, finally, the pressing and probably overriding demands of the Fifth Panzer Army with one foot entangled at Bastogne and the other poised only a few miles from the Meuse.

The German attack plans, formulated during the night of 3 December as the 2d SS Panzer mopped up the last of the defenders around the Baraque de Fraiture crossroads, called for a continuation of the 2d SS Panzer attack northwest, astride the Liège highway on the 24th. The immediate objective was the Manhay crossroads five miles away. Once at Manhay the attack could either peel off along the road west to Hotton, there freeing the Fifth Panzer Army formations hung up at the Hotton-Marche road, or swing northwest to gain the main Ourthe bridge site at Durbuy. The II SS Panzer Corps attack base on the Salmchâteau-La Roche road seemed secure enough. On the left the 560th had driven a salient clear to Soy, a distance of eleven miles. On the right American stragglers from St. Vith were fighting to escape northward through or around Salmchâteau. The 82d Airborne Division still had an outpost line covering much of the road west of Salmchâteau, but the Fuehrer Begleit Brigade was in position to roll back the Americans in this sector. In any case the 9th SS Panzer Division would, in a matter of hours, cross the Salm River in the Vielsalm-Salmchâteau area and swing northwest to march forward at the right shoulder of the 2d SS Panzer. This was the outline plan for 24 December.

On the morning of 24 December the American troops between the Salm and Ourthe Rivers were deployed on a front, if so it can be called, of over thirty miles.

This, of course, was no flankless and integrated position. On the west wing in particular the American line consisted of small task forces from the 3d Armored, each defending or attacking a hill or hamlet in what were almost independent operations. In the Salm sector the 82d Airborne Division faced north, east, and south, this disposition reflecting the topsy-turvy condition encountered when the division first came in to cover the deployment of the XVIII Airborne Corps. The 504th Parachute Infantry (Col. Reuben H. Tucker), on the division north flank, was bent at an angle reaching west and south from the confluence of the Amblève and Salm Rivers, a position assumed while Kampfgruppe Peiper was on the rampage west of Stavelot. The 505th Parachute Infantry (Col. William E. Ekman) overwatched the Salm from positions on the west bank extending from Trois Ponts south past Grand Halleux. The 508th Parachute Infantry (Col. Roy E. Lindquist) held a series of bluffs and ridges which faced the bridge sites at Vielsalm and Salmchâteau, then extended westward overlooking the La Roche highway. The 325th Glider Infantry (Col. Charles Billingslea) held the division right flank and continued the westward line along the ridges looking down on the La Roche road; its wing was affixed to the village of Fraiture just northeast of the crossroads where the 2d SS Panzer had begun its penetration.

From Fraiture west to the Ourthe the American "line" was difficult to trace. Here elements of the 3d Armored Division and two parachute infantry battalions were attempting to hold an extension of the American line west of Baraque de Fraiture, none too solidly anchored at Lamorménil and Freyneux. At the same time the Americans' exposed right wing was counterattacking to erase the German penetration which had driven as far north as the Soy-Hotton road and threatened to engulf Task Force Orr, standing alone and vulnerable at Amonines on the west bank of the Aisne River. Two regimental combat teams from the as yet untried 75th Infantry Division were en route to help shore up the ragged 3d Armored front but probably would not reach General Rose until the evening of the 24th.

There were some additional troops immediately at hand to throw in against the II SS Panzer Corps. All through the afternoon and evening of the 23d the St. Vith defenders poured through the American lines. When the last column, led by Colonel Nelson of the 112th Infantry, reached the paratroopers, some 15,000 men and about a hundred usable tanks had been added to Ridgway's force west of the Salm. Aware of the increasing enemy strength south of Manhay, General Ridgway sent troops of the 7th Armored and the remnants of the 106th Division to extend and reinforce the right flank of the 82d Airborne. At the same time, he ordered CCB, 9th Armored, to assemble as a mobile reserve around Malempré, east of the Manhay road, and to back up the American blocking position just north of the Baraque de Fraiture. Ridgway, however, recognized that the 7th Armored was much below strength and that the rugged, forested terrain on his front was poor for armor; so, on 24 December, he asked Hodges to give him an infantry division.

The Battle at the Manhay Crossroads

By dawn on 24 December Generalleutnant Heinz Lammerding, commander of the 2d SS Panzer, had brought his two armored infantry regiments into line north of the Baraque de Fraiture crossroads. The zone on the west side of the road to Manhay was given over to the 3d Panzer Grenadier, that east of the road to the 4th Panzer Grenadier. Both groups possessed small panzer detachments, but the bulk of Lammerding's tanks were left bivouacked in wood lots to the rear. The terrain ahead was tactically negotiable only by small packets of armor, and in the past twenty-four hours the amount of POL reaching the westernmost German columns had been gravely reduced. Lammerding had to husband his fuel for a short, direct thrust.

The assault, however, was initiated by the right wing of the 560th Volks Grenadier Division, which had provided the cover for the 2d SS Panzer assembly. During the previous night the 1130th Regiment, now reduced to fewer than 500 men, had slipped between the 3d Armored outposts manned by Task Force Kane at Odeigne and Freyneux. The American outpost in Odeigne having been withdrawn, a German assault gun platoon supported by a company or two of grenadiers moved into the open to attack Freyneux. About a dozen American tanks, half of them light, remained quiet in their camouflaged positions inside Freyneux. The German infantry entered the village while the assault guns closed in to give support; this was what the short-barreled Shermans needed. They destroyed or crippled over half the guns, an American tank destroyer shelled the enemy infantry out of the houses, and the skirmish abruptly ended.

A second German force meanwhile had made a pass at the third of Kane's roadblock positions here in the valley, Lamorménil, just west of Freyneux. In this case the enemy first perched up on the heights, trying to soften the American detachment with long-range assault gun fire, but when the guns moved down into the village for the kill the American tankers promptly knocked out the leaders. At twilight further enemy adventures in this sector were abandoned since the possession of Odeigne opened the way for a flanking thrust at the Manhay crossroads and the seizure of Grandménil on the road to Hotton and the Ourthe. In any case the 1130th had sustained such severe losses during the day that it was temporarily out of action. Kane's task force was not hit again and withdrew to the north under cover of fog and artificial smoke on the 26th.

It will be recalled that Task Force Brewster had established a roadblock position athwart the Manhay road late on the 23d. During the night German infantry had filtered into and through the surrounding woods, taking possession of Odeigne—only 1,200 yards to the west—in the process, but Brewster's tanks and guns were deployed with enough infantry to hold the enemy riflemen at arm's length. For any one of a number of reasons General Lammerding did not essay a tank assault in force to oust Brewster from the highway. The Americans in part were masked from direct observation, the ground was poor, the German main force needed a wider corridor than possession of twenty-two feet of pavement would provide, the American fighter-bombers were exceedingly busy—whatever his reason Lammerding did no more during the morning than to probe at Brewster's position while waiting for elbow room to be won a mile or two on either side of the highway.

Remer's Fuehrer Begleit Brigade, which had the task of driving the Americans back and giving free play to the east wing of the 2d SS Panzer, moved up past Salmchâteau in the early morning and struck through the village of Regné, where a platoon of paratroopers and three 57-mm. antitank guns proved no match for the panzers. Possession of Regné opened the way into the Lienne River valley, thus endangering the 82d Airborne flank and line of supply. More immediately, the German coup de main at Regné opened the way for the 4th Panzer Grenadier to initiate a pincers attack against the 2d Battalion of the 325th Glider Infantry at Fraiture, the western corner post of the 82d Airborne defenses. Hard on the heels of the German infantry, the point of the Fuehrer Begleit swung to take a hand against Fraiture. Here the 2d Battalion, "tired of attempting to stop armor with tired men and thin air," received permission about noon to withdraw a half-mile to the northeast. The battalion fell back with almost no loss, although it had to take on one of the flanking detachments from the 4th Panzer Grenadier en route.

While this rear guard action was in progress, the reserve company of the 325th and a medium tank company from the 14th Tank Battalion counterattacked at Regné and wrested it from the tank detachment left there by Remer. This village no longer had a place in the Fuehrer Begleit scheme. The brigade was shifting to Fraiture, and even before its columns could close new orders arrived from Marshal Model which would send Remer and his panzers hurrying posthaste to join the Fifth Panzer Army farther west.

During the morning of the 24th a series of somewhat un-coordinated and disconnected steps had been taken by the American commanders facing the threat posed by the II SS Panzer Corps. General Ridgway had no direct authority over the 3d Armored Division troops, who belonged to the VII Corps, and the units which had just come out of the St. Vith salient were scattered hither and yon without much regard to tactical unity or proper integration in the wire and radio command net earlier established for the XVIII Corps formations west of the Salm. On the night of the 23d Ridgway had ordered Hasbrouck to collect a force from the 7th Armored sufficient to hold the Manhay junction and to tie this force to the 82d Airborne positions. Hasbrouck selected Colonel Rosebaum's CCA, which had come through the withdrawal from St. Vith in fair shape. The first part of the 7th Armored mission was carried out in the early morning of the 24th when a task force outposted Manhay and its radial roads, but a reconnaissance detachment sent southeast to contact the 82d Airborne was halted by a blown bridge. There remained a gap, therefore, between the 7th Armored advance task force, which was assembling at noon in the vicinity of Malempré, southeast of Manhay, and the new 82d Airborne flank being formed north of Fraiture.

On the west wing coordination between the 7th Armored and the 3d Armored task forces would prove to be very complicated indeed. That portion of General Rose's division east of the Ourthe River by now was fighting two separate battles, one in the Hotton-Soy sector where the 560th Volks Grenadier penetration had occurred, and the other along the series of blocking positions that reached from Task Force Brewster's handhold on the Manhay road, through Freyneux and Lamorménil, and northwest to Orr's position at Amonines on the Aisne River. To give cohesion to the 3d Armored defensive battle east of the Aisne, General Rose recalled Brig. Gen. Doyle Hickey, his CCA commander, from the 84th Division sector and placed him in command there. Early in the afternoon Hickey met Colonel Rosebaum, who had just brought the main force of CCA, 7th Armored Division, into Manhay, and the two worked out a plan to coordinate the efforts of their respective commands. The 7th Armored troops would deploy on the high ground south of Manhay and extend their line across the highway and along the ridge leading east to Malempré. Thereafter Task Force Brewster would attempt to withdraw from its beleaguered roadblock position, retire through the 7th Armored line, and swing westward to bolster the 3d Armored outposts in the Lamorménil-Freyneux sector.

Colonel Rosebaum's command took the rest of the daylight hours to carry out the planned deployment, but before Task Force Brewster could begin its retirement new orders arrived from the XVIII Airborne Corps. Field Marshal Montgomery had visited Ridgway's headquarters in midmorning and had decided at once that the American front between the Ourthe and the Salm was too full of holes and overextended. 3 Furthermore he was concerned with the increasing German pressure on the western flank of the First Army as this was represented by movement against the VII Corps flank at Ciney. He told the First Army commander, therefore, that the XVIII Airborne Corps must be withdrawn to a shorter, straighter line and that the VII Corps could be released from "all offensive missions." General Collins might, on his own volition, draw the left wing of the VII Corps back on the line Hotton-manhay, conforming to Ridgway's regroupment.

The American line to be formed during the night of 24 December was intended to have a new look. The 82d Airborne would pull back to a much shorter front extending diagonally from Trois Ponts southwest to Vaux Chavanne, just short of Manhay. CCA of the 7th Armored would withdraw to the low hills north of Manhay and Grandménil (although Colonel Rosebaum protested that the high ground now occupied by his command south and southeast of Manhay was tactically superior) and retain a combat outpost in the valley at Manhay itself. The 3d Armored task forces had been promised support in the form of the 289th Infantry, due to arrive on Christmas Eve; so Hickey mapped his new position to rest on the Aisne River with its east flank tied to Grandménil and its west resting on Amonines. Since the 289th, a green regiment, would be put into an attack on the morning of the 25th to clear the Germans out of the woods near Grandménil, Hickey decided that Task Force Kane would have to remain in its covering position at Freyneux and Lamorménil while the 289th assembled, and that Task Force Brewster—thus far exposed only to desultory attack—would have to hold on at the Manhay road until the 7th Armored had redressed its lines.

A glance at the map will show how difficult the series of American maneuvers begun on Christmas Eve would be and how tricky to coordinate, particularly in the Manhay sector. Yet it was precisely in this part of the front that communications had not been thoroughly established and that tactical cohesion had not as yet been secured. As shown by later events, communication between the 3d Armored and the 7th Armored commanders and staffs failed miserably. There had been so many revisions of plans, orders, and counterorders during the 24th that Colonel Rosebaum did not receive word of his new retrograde mission until 1800. The withdrawal of CCA, 7th Armored, and the elements of CCB, 9th Armored, south and southeast of Manhay was scheduled to begin at 2230 and most of these troops and parts of the 3d Armored would have to pass through Manhay.

Toward Manhay, on the night of 24 December, the main body of the 2d SS Panzer Division was moving. The seizure of Odeigne the night before had opened a narrow sally port facing Grandménil and Manhay, but there was no road capable of handling a large armored column between Odeigne and the 2d SS Panzer assembly areas south of the Baraque de Fraiture. On the 24th the commander of the 3d Panzer Grenadier Regiment secured General Lammerding's approval to postpone a further advance until the German engineers could build a road through the woods to Odeigne. By nightfall on Christmas Eve this road was ready—and the Allied fighter-bombers had returned to their bases. The 3d Panzer Grenadier now gathered in attack formation in the woods around Odeigne, while tanks of the 2d Panzer Regiment formed in column along the new road. To the east the 4th Panzer Grenadier sent a rifle battalion moving quietly from Fraiture through the woods toward Malempré. By 2100, the hour set for the German attack, the column at Odeigne was ready. Christmas Eve had brought a beautifully clear moonlit night, the glistening snow was hard-packed, tank-going good.

About the time the German column started forward, the subordinate commanders of CCA, 7th Armored, received word by radio to report in Manhay, there to be given new orders—the orders, that is, for the general withdrawal north. The commander of the 7th Armored position north of Odeigne (held by a company of the 40th Tank Battalion and a company of the 48th Armored Infantry Battalion) had just started for Manhay when he saw a tank column coming up the road toward his position. A call to battalion headquarters failed to identify these tanks, but since the leader showed the typical blue exhaust of the Sherman, it was decided that this must be a detachment from the 3d Armored. Suddenly a German bazooka blasted from the woods where the Americans were deployed; German infantry had crept in close to the American tanks and their covering infantry. Four of the Shermans fell to the enemy bazooka men in short order and two were crippled, but the crippled tanks and one still intact managed to wheel about and head for Manhay. The armored infantry company asked for permission to withdraw, got no answer, and finally broke—the survivors turning toward Manhay.

A thousand yards or so farther north stood another 7th Armored roadblock, defended by an understrength rifle company and ten medium tanks which had been dug in to give hull defilade. Again the Americans were deceived by the Judas Goat Sherman leading the enemy column. When almost upon the immobile American tanks the Germans cut loose with flares. Blinded and unable to move, the ten Shermans were so many sitting ducks; most were hit by tank fire and all were evacuated by their crews. The American infantry in turn fell prey to the grenadiers moving through the woods bordering the road and fell back in small groups toward Manhay.

It was now a little after 2230, the hour set for the 7th Armored move to the new position north of Manhay. The covering elements of the 3d Armored had already withdrawn, but without notifying CCA of the 7th. The light tank detachment from Malempré had left that village (the grenadier battalion from the 4th Regiment moving in on the tankers' heels), the support echelon of CCB, 9th Armored, already had passed through Manhay, and the headquarters column of CCA, 7th Armored, was just on its way out of Manhay when the American tanks that had escaped from the first roadblock position burst into the latter village. Thus far the headquarters in Manhay knew nothing of the German advance—although a quarter of an hour earlier the enemy gunners had shelled the village. A platoon commander attempted to get two of his medium tanks into firing position at the crossroads itself, but the situation quickly degenerated into a sauve qui peut when the leading panzers stuck their snouts into Manhay. In a last exchange of shots the Americans accounted for two of the panzers but lost five of their own tanks at the rear of the CCA column. Thus Manhay passed into German hands.

The medium tanks and armored infantry that had started to follow the light tank detachment out of Malempré circled around Manhay when they heard the firing. Working their way north, the road-bound tanks ended up at Werbomont while the riflemen moved cross-country to reach friendly lines about two thousand yards north of Manhay. There Colonel Rhea, commanding the 23d Armored Infantry Battalion, had formed a defense on the hills bordering the highway to Werbomont and Liège. All this while Major Brewster and the task force astride the highway south of Manhay had been under fire, but the enemy had refused to close for a final assault. It soon became apparent, however, that this small American force was on its own and that the Germans were in strength to the rear. Brewster radioed for permission to pull out;

when it was granted he turned east toward Malempré, hoping to find this spot still in friendly hands. The German battalion which had come up from Fraiture met Brewster's column at Malempré and shot out his two lead tanks. Since there was no other road, Brewster ordered his vehicles abandoned and released his men to reach the American lines on their own — most of his command made it.

Although the 2d SS Panzer had preempted a piece of the new American line, General Lammerding was none too pleased by the results of the Christmas Eve attack. His tanks had bitten only a small piece from the tail of the "long American column" reported fleeing Manhay. (Their inability to do better his officers ascribed to the difficulty attendant on bringing more than one or two tanks into firing position on the narrow roads.) The accompanying infantry formations had failed to coordinate their advance with that of the armored assault from Odeigne and to seize, as planned, the wooded heights northwest of Manhay and Grandménil. Lammerding and the II SS Panzer Corps commander, General Bittrich, agreed that the 1st SS Panzer should continue the battle with shock tactics aimed at securing an enlarged maneuver space east and west of Manhay. The 9th SS Panzer (which had crossed the Salm River behind the withdrawing 82d Airborne) was to align itself as rapidly as might be with Lammerding's division in an advance up the Lienne valley toward Bras, commanding the high ground northeast of Manhay.

The fall of Manhay roused considerable apprehension in the American headquarters. General Ridgway saw that his new corps defense might be split in the center before it could properly solidify. General Hodges sent message after message to the XVIII Airborne Corps insisting that Manhay must be retaken, for it was all too clear that if the Sixth Panzer Army could reinforce the Manhay salient, Liège and the Meuse bridgehead would be in grave danger. In addition, he pressed Field Marshal Montgomery for more divisions to backstop the threatened sector between the Salm and the Ourthe.

By daylight on the 25th Colonel Rhea had amassed a sizable force on the hills north of Manhay, his own armored infantry battalion, reinforced by the 2d Battalion of the 424h Infantry, plus the tanks and stragglers that had worked their way past the enemy in Manhay. The Germans scouted this position, then broke contact — probably discouraged by twelve P-47's from the 389th Squadron who claimed ten tank kills on this mission. To the east General Gavin sent the 1st Battalion of Billingslea's glider infantry to secure his division's right flank at Tri-le-Cheslaing, a tiny collection of houses in the valley about 2,000 yards east of Manhay. For some reason, perhaps the lack of coordination which had bothered Lammerding, the 4th Panzer Grenadier had not pushed forward and the village was unoccupied. Thus far the 82d Airborne had had no physical contact with CCA of the 7th Armored, but Gavin was apprised by radio that his western neighbor was in position on the Werbomont-Liège highway.

General Bittrich had no intention of pushing the 2d SS Panzer north toward Liège. Although the time at which the II SS Panzer Corps commander received his orders is uncertain, it is known that by the small hours of 25 December Bittrich was embarked on a new mission assigned by General Kraemer, the Sixth Panzer Army chief of staff. The 2d SS Panzer now was to turn west from Manhay, drive along the lateral road to Erezée on the Aisne River, then pivot northwest to seize the Ourthe bridgehead at Durbuy, all this as a maneuver to strike the American VII Corps in the flank and break the deadly grasp Collins and Harmon had on the throat of the Fifth Panzer armored columns in the Celles-Marche sector.

For such a change of axis the Germans needed turning room, and they could best gain it by seizing the road center at Grandménil just west of the Manhay crossroads. As a result, then, the major part of the 2d SS Panzer would turn away from the 7th Armored to engage General Hickey's troops from the 3d Armored. Richardson's task force, really little more than a light tank platoon, had fallen back from Manhay to Task Force Kane's roadblock at Grandménil. Here Kane had his trains and a platoon of tank destroyers. The Panthers, followed by the German infantry, pursued the Americans into Grandménil. The American tank destroyers attempted a fight from the high ground west of the village but had no infantry in support and, as the grenadiers close in, withdrew westward along the road to Erezée. By 0300 on 25 December then, the Germans held Grandménil and were poised on the way west. It will be remembered that the new

289th Infantry (Col. Douglas B. Smith) had come into assembly areas west of Grandménil on Christmas Eve in preparation for a dawn attack to drive the enemy off the wooded hills southwest of Grandménil. The lead battalion, the 3d, actually had started forward from its bivouac in Fanzel when it encountered some 3d Armored tanks (the latter supposed to be screening the 289th deployment) hurrying to the west. About this time the battalion received orders from Hickey that it should dig in to bar the two roads running west and northwest from Grandménil. Deploying as rapidly as possible in the deep snow, the battalion outposted the main west road to Erezée. The Germans negotiated this forward roadblock without a fight, the ubiquitous and deceptive Sherman tank again providing the ticket. When the panzers, some eight of them, arrived at the main foxhole line the German tankers swiveled their gun turrets facing north and south to blast the battalion into two halves. One unknown soldier in Company K was undaunted by this fusillade: he held his ground and put a bazooka round into the spot but he had stopped the enemy column cold in its tracks, for here the road edged a high cliff and the remaining panzers could not pass their stricken mate. Apparently the Panther detachment had outrun its infantry support or was apprehensive of a close engagement in the dark, for the German tanks backed off and returned to Grandménil.

It took some time to reorganize the 3d Battalion of the 289th, but about 0800 the battalion set off on its assigned task of clearing the woods southwest of Grandménil. At the same time the rest of the regiment, on the right, moved into an attack to push the outposts of the 560th Volks Grenadier Division back from the Aisne River. General Hickey, however, needed more help than a green infantry regiment could give if the 3d Armored was to halt the 2d SS Panzer and restore the blocking position at Grandménil. His plea for assistance was carried by General Rose up the echelons of command, and finally CCB was released from attachment to the 30th Division in the La Gleize sector to give the needed armored punch.

Early in the afternoon Task Force McGeorge (a company each of armored infantry and Sherman tanks) arrived west of Grandménil. The task force was moving into the attack when disaster struck. Eleven P-38's of the 430th Squadron, which were being vectored onto their targets by the 7th Armored Division, mistook McGeorge's troops for Germans and made a bombing run over the wooded assembly area. CCB later reported that 3 officers and 36 men were killed by the American bombs. Here again the failure of communications between the 3d and 7th Armored Divisions had cost dear. A new attack was mounted at 2000, McGeorge's armored infantry and a company from the 289th preceding the American tanks in the dark. Within an hour five tanks and a small detachment of the armored infantry in half-tracks were in

Grandménil, but the enemy promptly counterattacked and restored his hold on the village.

The 2d SS Panzer had nevertheless failed on 25 December to enlarge the turning radius it needed around the Grandménil pivot. The German records show clearly what had stopped the advance. Every time that the 3d Panzer Grenadier formed an assault detachment to break out through the woods south and west of Grandménil, the American artillery observers located on the high ground to the north brought salvo after salvo crashing down. All movement along the roads seemed to be a signal for the Allied fighter-bombers to swoop down for the kill. To make matters worse, the 9th SS Panzer had failed to close up on the 2d SS Panzer Division's right. General Lammerding dared not swing his entire division into the drive westward and thus leave an open flank facing the American armor known to be north of Manhay.

Although General Ridgway had ordered the 7th Armored to recapture Manhay "by dark tonight," the means at Hasbrouck's disposal on the 25th were meager. CCA, which had been employed earlier because it had come out of the St. Vith fight with the fewest wounds, now was in poor shape indeed, having lost nearly two medium tank companies and much of its tank destroyer complement. CCB had not yet been reorganized (and in any case it was very much below strength in men and vehicles) but it could furnish two understrength tank companies and one company of armored infantry. The main road into Manhay from the north, intended as the avenue of Hasbrouck's advance, would take some hours to clear, for the retreating tankers had littered it with felled trees during the night withdrawal. To get at grips with the enemy from this direction the 2d Battalion of the 424th Infantry was added to the attack; the whole operation would, or so it was hoped, mesh with the 3d Armored advance on Grandménil from the west.

The abatis on the Manhay road effectively stopped the 7th Armored tanks. When a company of six tanks lined up for a charge into Manhay from the east, half of them were knocked out; General Hasbrouck, who was on the scene, ordered the remaining tanks to retire. The battalion from the 424th did succeed in nearing the village but paid a heavy toll for the few hundred yards crossed—later estimated as some 35 percent casualties—and at dark was ordered back to the north.

The Fight in the Aisne Valley

While the 2d SS Panzer was struggling to shake itself loose for the drive west along the Erezée-Soy road, the battle-weary and depleted 560th Volks Grenadier Division fought to gain control of the western section of the same road between Soy and Hotton. Having driven a salient north in the Aisne valley, the left wing of this division set up a night attack on Christmas Eve intended to dislodge Task Force Orr from the Aisne bridgehead at Amonines. This small American task force held a three-mile front—little more than a chain of pickets—with no support on the flanks and no troops to cover its rear. When evening came, crisp and clear, the enemy guns and rocket launchers set to work. Probably the Germans used a battalion of infantry, making twelve separate attempts to break through Orr's line. At one point they were near success: Orr said later, "If they'd have had three more riflemen they'd probably have overrun our positions." But the attacker lacked the "three more riflemen" and Task Force Orr retained control of Amonines.

While the enemy hammered futilely at Task Force Orr on the night of 24 December, Hogan's encircled task force far to the south at Marcouray finally made a break to reach the American lines. All the operable vehicles were destroyed or damaged, and the wounded were left in the charge of volunteer medical aid men. Guiding on the stars and compass, Hogan's men moved stealthily through the enemy positions. At one point a German sentry gave a challenge, but a sergeant got to him with a bayonet before he could spread the alarm. Most members of the task force reached their comrades by Christmas morning.

The appearance of the 75th Infantry Division (Maj. Gen. Fay B. Prickett) in the 3d Armored sector promised the needed rifle strength to establish a solid defense in the rugged country east of Hotton and along the bluffs of the Aisne River. To establish a homogeneous line the Americans would have to seize the high, wooded, and difficult ground south of the Soy-Hotton road, and at the same time push forward on the left to close up to the banks of the Aisne over the tortuous terrain south of the Erezée-Grandménil road. With the two regiments of the 75th attached to the 3d Armored (the 289th Infantry and the 290th Infantry), General Rose ordered a drive to cement the CCA wing in the west.

The units of the 75th had been scattered in widely separated areas after their arrival in Belgium. A smooth-running supply system had not yet been set up, and to concentrate and support the rifle battalions would prove difficult. But the 290th (Col. Carl F. Duffner), which had been moving into a defensive position around Petit Han, north of Hotton, received orders at 1600 on the 24th to assemble at Ny for an attack to begin two hours later. There ensued much confusion, with orders and counter-orders, and finally the attack was rescheduled for a half-hour before midnight. The regiment had no idea of the ground over which it was to fight but did know that the line of departure was then held by a battalion or less of the 517th Parachute Infantry Regiment deployed along the Soy-Hotton road. The 2d and 3d Battalions of the 290th were chosen for this first battle, their objective the wooded ridge south of the road.

About midnight on the 24th the battalions started their assault companies forward, crossing a small stream and ravine, then halting to reorganize at a tree line which edged a broad meadow over which the assault had to be carried. Here all was confusion and the companies were not straightened out until dawn. Finally the assault began, straight across the open, snow-covered meadow beyond which lay the ridge line objective. Losses among these green troops were severe and most of the officers were killed or wounded. Despite this harsh baptism of fire the troops reached the wood cover at the foot of the ridge and held on. In midafternoon more infantry came up (probably from the 517th), plus a platoon of tank destroyers, and a fresh assault was now organized. This carried through the woods and onto the ridge. Participants in the action later estimated that the 3d Battalion, 290th Infantry, alone suffered 250 casualties, but this figure probably is exaggerated.

Farther east the 289th Infantry also had a rough introduction to battle on rugged terrain far more difficult than any training ground in the States. On the night of 24 December the regiment moved by truck to Fanzel, north of Erezée, there receiving orders to attack at 0800 the next morning and seize the high ground north of the Aisne. Early on Christmas morning, as already related, the 3d Battalion was hastily thrown into the fight being waged by the 3d Armored troops west of Grandménil. By the hour set for the 289th to attack, however, a part of the 3d Battalion could be freed to move into the regimental advance. The 560th Volks Grenadier Division had only a thin screen facing the 289th and by dusk the 3d Battalion was on its objective, the hill mass southwest of Grandménil. On the right flank the 1st Battalion reached the line of the Aisne, but in the center the yd Battalion lost its direction in the maze of wooded hills and ravines. By midnight of the 25th it had gravitated into and around La Fosse, a village southwest of Grandménil, leaving a wide gap between itself and the 1st Battalion. The next day, under a new commander, the 2d Battalion deployed along the Aisne but still had no contact with the 1st.

The 2d SS Panzer Is Halted

Although the 2d SS Panzer Division still held Grandménil and Manhay on the morning of 26 December, it had lost much of its bite and dash. The two grenadier regiments had been whittled down considerably; the 4th Panzer Grenadier had lost heavily, particularly in officers, during the fight for the Baraque de Fraiture. Across the lines thirteen battalions of field artillery were firing into the German positions between the Aisne and the Lienne, and the II SS Panzer Corps had been unable to bring forward enough artillery and ammunition to engage in any counterbattery duels. So heavy was the traffic on the meager Sixth Panzer Army line of communications, and moving as it did by fits and starts under the watchful eyes of Allied air, that only one battalion of corps artillery and one corps Werfer battalion succeeded in crossing to the west bank of the Salm. Ammunition resupply from the rear was almost nonexistent. On Christmas Eve the corps had taken matters in its hands and dispatched its own trucks to the ammunition dumps back at Bonn, but each round trip would take three to four nights because the daylight movement of thin-skinned vehicles carrying high explosive was almost certain suicide. Finally, the 9th SS Panzer had failed to keep to schedule and probably would not come abreast of the 2d SS until the night of 26 December.

But General Lammerding could not delay his bid for a breakout until reinforcements arrived. On the morning of the 26th he ordered the 4th Panzer Grenadier to attack northward, using Manhay and the forest to the east as a line of departure. The 3d Panzer Grenadier would have to make the main effort, forcing its way out of Grandménil and along the road west to Erezée.

The enemy attempt to shake loose and break into the clear proved abortive. On the right the 4th Panzer Grenadier sent a battalion from the woods east of Manhay into an early morning attack that collided with Billingslea's glider infantry in Tri-le-Cheslaing. In the predawn darkness some of the grenadiers sneaked in on the battalion command post, only to be driven off by a reserve platoon. A move to encircle the village from the east was beaten back almost single-handedly by a stray Sherman tank which the glider infantry had commandeered during the 7th Armored withdrawal. When daylight came the enemy assault force was in full retreat, back to the woods. Plans for a second attack north from Manhay died aborning, for by that time the Americans had the initiative.

The German advance out of Grandménil was planned as a double-pronged assault: one column thrusting straight west on the Erezée road; the other heading off to the northwest along a narrow, precipitous road which would bring it to Mormont and a flanking position vis-à-vis Erezée. The westward move began at false dawn, by chance coinciding with Task Force McGeorge's renewal of its attack to enter Grandménil. Again the road limited the action to a head-on tank duel. McGeorge's Shermans were outgunned by the Panthers, and when the shooting died down the American detachment had only two medium tanks in going condition.

Sometime after this skirmish one of the American tanks which had reached the edge of the village during the attack of the previous evening suddenly came alive and roared out to join the task force. What had happened was one of the oddities born of night fighting. Captain Jordan of the 1st Battalion, 3d Armored Regiment, had led five tanks into Grandménil, but during the earlier fight four had been hit or abandoned by their crews. Jordan and his crew sat through the night in the midst of the dead tanks, unmolested by the enemy. When the captain reported to his headquarters, he told of seeing a German column, at least twelve Panthers, rumbling out of Grandménil in a northerly direction. The 3d Armored put up a liaison plane to find the enemy tanks, but to no avail. It is known that Company L of the 289th Infantry knocked out a Panther leading a vehicular column through a narrow gorge on the Mormont road and took a number of casualties during a scrambling fight between bazookas and tank weapons. The German accounts say that this road was blocked by fallen timber and that intense American artillery fire halted all movement north of Grandménil. Whatever the reason, this group of tanks made no further effort to force the Mormont road.

Task Force McGeorge received sixteen additional Shermans at noon and a couple of hours later, on the heels of a three-battalion artillery shoot, burst through to retake Grandménil. The pounding meted out by the 3d Armored gunners apparently drove most of the grenadiers in flight from the village; by dark the 3d Battalion of the 289th had occupied half of the village and held the road to Manhay.

There remains to tell of the 7th Armored's attempt to recapture Manhay. To visualize the 7th Armored as a ready combat division at this time would be to distort reality. By the 26th its three armored infantry battalions were woefully understrength, and less than 40 percent of its tanks and tank destroyers were operable. Even this very reduced capability could not be employed with full effect against the enemy. It was only a matter of hours since the 7th Armored had been driven from St. Vith, and the officers, men, and vehicles of most of its units were spread about helter-skelter from village to village just as they had arrived back in the American lines after the disorganization attendant on the withdrawal across the Salm. The problem of combat morale is more difficult for the historian, writing long after the event, to analyze. Hasbrouck's division had made a fight of it at St. Vith, more than meriting the eulogy of Field Marshal Montgomery's retreat order, "They come back in all honor"; but it was too much to expect of human flesh and blood, mind and heart, that the 7th Armored should continue, only hours after the retreat, to demonstrate the same high order of combat efficiency seen in the defense of St. Vith.

General Hasbrouck had no plans for retaking Manhay on the morning of the 26th; he counted rather on a few hours to regroup his command. But about 0900 General Collins called from the VII Corps to ask that Ridgway put the 7th Armored into an attack at Manhay as an assist for the 3d Armored drive against the twin village of Grandménil.

Within the hour the First Army Commander had General Ridgway on the telephone, insisting that the 7th Armored must attack — and that forthwith. Ridgway could do no more than tell Hasbrouck to retake Manhay "as soon as possible." The 7th Armored commander put the few tanks he could scrape together into a march toward the road linking Manhay and Grandménil, but this move was slow in starting and the 3d Armored troops entered Grandménil while the 7th Armored tanks still were several hundred yards to the north. About this time the 7th Armored detachment came under accurate direct fire from some German tanks dug in north of the connecting road and the Americans halted.

Meanwhile Allied fighter-bombers had been vectored over Manhay to soften up the defenders, and General Ridgway decided to use the fresh 3d Battalion of the 517th Parachute Infantry, which had just come down from helping the 30th Division in the

La Gleize operation, for a night assault at Manhay. This attack, made an hour or so after midnight and preceded by an eight-battalion artillery concentration fired for twenty minutes, gained quick success. By 0400 on 27 December the paratroopers had cleared the village, at a cost of ten killed and fourteen wounded. By dawn airborne engineers had cleared the fallen trees from the road back to Werbomont, and a platoon of medium tanks moved in to cover the approaches to the village. Some clue to the ease with which the paratroopers took Manhay—not forgetting, of course, the weight of metal thrown into the town by the American cannoneers—may be found in the German account of events on the 26th. It would appear that the 7th Armored tank detachment which had neared the Grandménil-manhay road had convinced the commander of the 3d Panzer Grenadier that his battalion in Manhay was in danger of being surrounded (particularly since Billingslea's paratroopers to the east had driven back the 4th Grenadiers) and that he had ordered the Manhay garrison to withdraw under cover of night, leaving its wounded behind.

The loss of Manhay ended the 2d SS Panzer battle in this sector, and the German corps and division commanders agreed that there seemed little chance of starting the attack rolling again. On the morning of the 27th orders from Sepp Dietrich told General Lammerding that his division would be relieved by the 9th SS Panzer Division and that the 2d SS Panzer would move west to join the 560th Volks Grenadier Division and the newly arrived 12th SS Panzer Division in a new Sixth Panzer Army attack directed at the Hotton-Soy-Erezée line.

The 82d Airborne Withdraws From the Salm River Line

When the XVIII Airborne Corps commander ordered the defense of St. Vith abandoned on 23 December, one of his chief concerns was the mounting enemy strength which threatened to outflank and overrun the small detachments of the 82d Airborne Division, plus the 3d Battalion, 112th Infantry, deployed to hold the bridgeheads at Salmchâteau and Vielsalm through which the St. Vith garrison had to withdraw. The 82d, it will be remembered, was forced to hurry troops from its north flank, where they had been involved in hard battle with the 1st SS Panzer Division around Trois Ponts and Cheneux, in order to reinforce the opposite flank of the division, which extended from Salmchâteau west to Fraiture, at Fraiture dangling in the air. The danger now was that the German armor already on the west side of the Salm River would speed to turn this open flank and crush the 82d Airborne back against the Salm, or at the least—make a powerful jab straight along the west bank to dislodge the American hold on the two bridgehead towns. Kampfgruppe Krag, as already recounted, did succeed in doing exactly that at Salmchâteau late on the 23d and entrapped part of Task Force Jones and the last column of the 112th Infantry on their way back from St. Vith.

The 9th SS Panzer Division, charged in the enemy scheme with breaking across the river at Salmchâteau and Vielsalm and here rolling up the 82d Airborne south wing, failed to arrive at the Salm on schedule. As a result General Gavin was faced with one major threat against his position, on the night of 23 December posed by the 2d SS Panzer and the Fuehrer Begleit Brigade at Fraiture, rather than two as the II SS Panzer Corps had hoped. By midday on the 24th, however, the Germans had patrols across the river at Vielsalm. This covering force came from the 19th Panzer Grenadier Regiment, recruited from Germans living in the Black Sea area, and it had earned a reputation as the elite regiment of the 9th SS Panzer Division. The rest of the 9th SS Panzer either had been detached on other missions or was straggling to the east—

indeed, the divisional tank regiment did not reach the Salm sector until the first days of January. American identification of this new armored division, however, added to the list of factors that resulted in the decision to withdraw the 82d Airborne and shorten the XVIII Airborne Corps line.

Early on Christmas Eve General Gavin met with some of his officers in the command post of Ekman's 505th. He knew that his division was faced by elements of at least three German divisions, his right was overextended, the support which might be expected from his right wing neighbor was problematical, and a large German force (the remnants of Kampfgruppe Peiper) was actually in his rear somewhere near Trois Ponts. Gavin now had to decide whether he should divert some of his troops to hunt out and fight the enemy in his rear or proceed with the planned withdrawal. The main problem, Gavin concluded, was to put his division in an organized position, dug in with wire and mines in place, to confront the attack of "several" panzer divisions on the morning of the 25th. He held, then, to his plan for withdrawing the 82d Airborne.

Gavin's plan was to bring back the bulk of his regiments under cover of night; he would leave small detachments from each as covering shells until the early morning. About 2100 the division moved out for the new Trois Ponts-manhay line. Christmas Eve was crystal clear and the moonlight on the snow made it easy to follow the routes assigned. (Overhead the buzzbombs could be traced on their flight to Antwerp.) At only two points did the enemy interfere with the marching columns of the 82d Airborne, and at only one of these by design. After the debacle at La Gleize, Colonel Peiper and some 800 of his kampfgruppe had taken refuge in the densely wooded and broken ground north of Trois Ponts, waiting for an opportunity to cross the Salm and rejoin their comrades of the 1st SS Panzer. The hour chosen by Peiper coincided with the move made by the 50th Parachute Infantry as it pivoted on Trois Ponts back from the river. The two forces, both attempting to withdraw, brushed against each other and one company of the 505th got into a brief but hot fire with Peiper's men. Colonel Ekman, however, had a mission to complete before day dawned and with General Gavin's permission the 505th let Peiper go.

The second action this night was no accident. It involved the covering force of the 508th, led by Lt. Col. Thomas Shanley, in what the regiment later recorded as "one of the best pieces of fighting in the 508th's history." The main body started on the seven-mile trek to its new line with no sign of the enemy and by 0415 was in position. Some time around midnight the covering platoons near the Vielsalm bridge site (one each from Companies A and B) heard much noise and hammering coming from the direction of the bridge, which the airborne engineers had partially demolished. Suddenly artillery and mortar shells erupted around the American foxhole line, a barrage followed by smoke shells. Out of the smoke rose dark figures, whooping and yelling as they charged the paratroopers. The platoon from Company B had a few moments to get set and then stopped the grenadiers with machine gun fire before they could reach the position. The Company A platoon, closer to the river's edge, had a worse time of it. Here a few of the enemy got into the American position, while others blocked the withdrawal route to the west. At one point the 508th wrote this platoon off as lost; but skillfully led by 1st Lt. George D. Lamm the paratroopers fought their way through the enemy and back to their own lines.

The 19th Regiment, which had hit the paratroopers at Vielsalm, followed the American spoor doggedly, despite the laggard pace of the rest of the division, and in the early afternoon of 25 December was observed in Odrimont, a couple of miles from the 508th outpost line. That night the 19th hit the regimental left, with perhaps two battalions making the assault, but was beaten back after a three-hour fire fight. Two nights later the 19th struck again, this time driving on a narrow front against the right wing of the 508th. Company G was driven out of the twin villages of Erria and Villettes where it was bivouacked, but this penetration came to an abrupt halt when two artillery battalions went to work. The following morning the commander of the 3d Battalion (Lt. Col. Louis G. Mendez) organized a counterattack which swept through Erria (catching a number of the tired grenadiers still asleep in captured bedrolls) and restored the line. The American gunners had done much to take the sting out of the enemy force over 100 German dead were counted around the village crossroad (the German account relates that the 1st Battalion of the 19th was "cut to pieces" here).

"The Sad Sack Affair"

As the year came to a close the Sixth Panzer Army made one last effort to breach the American defenses between the Salm and the Ourthe. This battle took place in and around the hamlet of Sadzot (so tiny that it does not appear on most of the Belgian maps). Sadzot lay on a small creek 400 yards south of Briscol, a village on the main road between Grandménil and Erezée. The engagement at Sadzot was fought by squads and platoons, and so may be appropriately called a "soldiers' battle"; with equal propriety the name coined by the GI's for this confused action is used here: "The Sad Sack Affair."

Having given up the fight for Manhay and Grandménil, the 2d SS Panzer began to parcel out its troops. Some were left to cover the deployment of the 9th SS Panzer as it extended its position in front of the 82d Airborne to take over the onetime 2d SS Panzer sector. Other units shifted west to join the incoming 12th SS Panzer in what was planned as a major attack to cross the Trois Ponts-Hotton road in the vicinity of Erezée and regain momentum for the drive to the northwest. Once again, however, the forces actually available to the II SS Panzer Corps were considerably fewer than planned. The march west by the 12th SS Panzer Division had taken much longer than reckoned, for the slow-moving 9th SS Panzer had jammed the roads in front of the 12th SS Panzer, there had been a series of fuel failures, Allied air attacks had cut most of the march to night movement, and just as the division was nearing the Aisne River OB WEST had seized the rearward columns for use at Bastogne. All that the 12th SS Panzer could employ on 27 December, the date set by the army commander for the new attack, was the 25th Panzer Grenadier Regiment, most of which was already in the line facing the 3d Armored. The 2d SS Panzer contribution perforce was limited: its reconnaissance battalion, a battalion of mobile guns, and two rifle companies, a task force commanded by the same Major Krag who had raised such havoc at Salmchâteau. The time for the attack was midnight.

During the 27th the lines of General Hickey's command had been redressed. In the process the 1st Battalion of the 289th Infantry had tied in with Task Force Orr on the Aisne River while the 2d Battalion, having finally straightened itself out, continued the 3d Armored line through the woods southwest of Grandménil. Unknown at the time, a 1,000 yard gap had developed south of Sadzot and Briscol between these two battalions.

At zero hour the German assault force started forward through the deep woods; the night was dark, the ground pathless, steep, and broken. The grenadiers made good progress, but radio failed in the thick woods and it would appear that a part of the attackers became disoriented. At least two companies from the 25th Panzer Grenadier Regiment did manage to find their way through the gap between the battalions of the 289th and followed the creek into Sadzot, where they struck about two hours after the jumP-off.

The course of battle as it developed in the early morning hours of 28 December is extremely confused. The first report of the German appearance in Sadzot was relayed to higher headquarters at 0200 by artillery observers belonging to the 24th Armored Field Artillery Battalion, whose howitzers were emplaced north of the village. The two American rifle battalions, when queried, reported no sign of the enemy. Inside Sadzot were bivouacked Company C of the 87th Chemical Battalion and a tank destroyer platoon; these troops rapidly recovered from their surprise and during the melee established a firm hold on the north side of the village. General Hickey immediately alerted the 509th Parachute Infantry Battalion near Erezée to make an envelopment of Sadzot from west and east, but no sooner had the paratroopers deployed than they ran into Krag's kampfgruppe.

This meeting engagement in the darkness seems to have been a catch-as-catch-can affair. The American radios, like the German, failed to function in this terrain (the 3d Armored communications throughout the battle were mostly by wire and runner); the Germans were confused and put mortar fire on their own neighboring platoons; and the fight on both sides was carried by squads and platoons firing at whatever moved. When daylight came the paratroopers got artillery support, which far outweighed the single battalion behind the enemy assault force, and moved forward. By 1100 the 509th had clicked the trap shut on the Germans inside Sadzot.

There remained the task of closing the gap between the two battalions of the 289th. General Hickey put in the 2d Battalion of the 112th Infantry at dark on the 28th, but this outfit, hastily summoned to the fight, lost its direction and failed to seal the gap. Early on the morning of the 29th Hickey, believing that the 112th had made the line of departure secure, sent the 509th and six light tanks to attack toward the southeast. But the enemy had reorganized in the meantime, put in what probably was a fresh battalion, and begun a new march on Sadzot. In the collision that followed, a section of German 75-mm. antitank guns destroyed three of the light tanks and the paratroopers recoiled; but so did the enemy.

During the morning the 2d Battalion, 112th Infantry, got its bearings — or so it was believed — and set out to push a bar across the corridor from the west, where contact with the 1st Battalion of the 289th was firm, to the east and the socket provided the 2d Battalion, 289th. Across the deep ravines and rugged hills American troops were sighted, and believing these to be the 2d Battalion the troops from the 112th veered toward them. What had been seen, however, proved to be the paratroopers of the 509th. After this misadventure and the jolt suffered by the paratroopers, Hickey and the battalion commanders concerned worked out a coordinated attack. First the paratroopers put in a twilight assault which forced the Germans back. Then the 2d Battalion of the 112th made a night attack with marching fire, guiding this time on 60-mm. illuminating mortar shells fired by the 2d Battalion of the 289th. Crossing through deep ravines the infantrymen of the 112th drove the enemy from their path. At dawn on the 29th the gap finally was closed.

The German failure to penetrate through the Erezée section on 28-29 December was the last serious bid by the Sixth Panzer Army in an offensive role. On that day Field Marshal Model ordered Sepp Dietrich to go over to the defensive and began stripping the Sixth of its armor. The German commanders left facing the VII and

XVIII Airborne Corps east of the Ourthe record a number of attacks ordered between 29 December and 2 January, the units involved including infantry detachments from the 9th SS Panzer Division and the 18th and 62d Volks Grenadier Divisions. But to order these weak and tired units into the attack when the German foot soldier knew that the great offensive was ended was one thing, to press the assault itself was quite another. The American divisions in this sector note only at the turn of the year: front quiet," or "routine patrolling." The initiative had clearly passed to the Americans. General Ridgway, who had been champing at the bit to go over to the offensive even when his corps was not hard pressed, sought permission to start an attack on the last day of the year with the XVIII Airborne, but Field Marshal Montgomery already had decided that the Allied offensive on the north flank would be initiated farther to the west by Collins' corps and had set the date—3 January 1945.

The Elsenborn Shoulder

The four infantry divisions of the V Corps by 24 December formed a firm barrier along the northern shoulder of the deepening German salient. This front, extending from Monschau to Waimes, relapsed into relative inactivity. The Sixth Panzer Army had tried to widen the road west by levering at the American linchpin in the Monschau area, by cutting toward the Elsenborn Ridge via Krinkelt-Rocherath, and by chopping at Butgenbach in an attempt to roll back the V Corps' west flank, but the entire effort had been fruitless and its cost dear. Having failed to free the right wing of the Sixth Panzer Army, the higher German commands gave the ball to the Fifth Panzer Army and perforce accepted the narrow zone of advance in the Sixth Panzer Army sector which gave two instead of the originally scheduled four main roads for its drive west. Be it added that the northernmost of the two remaining roads was under American artillery fire for most of its length.

It cannot be said that the Sixth Panzer Army clearly had written off the possibility of overrunning the Elsenborn Ridge. The attacks by the German right wing had dwindled away by 24 December because of sheer fatigue, heavy losses, the withdrawal of most of the German armor, the feeling on the part of the army staff that it would be best to wait for further successes in the south before going out on a limb, and the desire to withhold sufficient strength to meet any American counterattack directed from the Elsenborn area against the shoulder of the salient. Furthermore, on 24 or 25 December, Hitler dropped the plan for the secondary attack by the Fifteenth Army toward Maastricht and Heerlen, which had been intended to assist the Sixth Panzer drive after the latter got rolling.

But there still were five German divisions in this sector under Hitzfeld's LXVII Corps, the corps maintaining a front whose boundaries coincided almost exactly with those of the American V Corps. These could be no further thought of a drive to Eupen and the establishment of a blocking cordon west of that point; this mission had been scrubbed when the last attacks at Monschau collapsed. Nor was there hope that the right wing of the Sixth Panzer Army could be set in motion at this date, the armor already having been shifted to beef up the advance on the left. Hitzfeld's task was to defend, to hold the shoulder; but his line, bent in a sharp right angle near Wirtzfeld, was expensive in manpower and tactically poor. On Model's order Hitzfeld and his division commanders ran a map exercise on 26 December whose solution was this; the angle at Wirtzfeld must be straightened and the line shortened. The powerful groupment of American artillery on Elsenborn Ridge constituted an ever-present threat; therefore this ground should be taken. Four divisions, it was planned, would attack to achieve this solution.

Meanwhile the main German advance was having trouble. The Bastogne road center continued in American hands, greatly hampering the development of the Fifth Panzer Army attack. The forward wing of the Sixth Panzer Army had collided with the American defenses along the line of the Amblève and Salm Rivers but had failed to gain maneuver room and was proceeding on a dangerously narrow front. Every mobile or semimobile unit which could be found would have to be thrown into the main advance. The Army Group B commander, acting on Hitler's order, took the 3d Panzer Grenadier Division out of the LXVII Corps and told Hitzfeld to abandon his planned attack against the strong Elsenborn Ridge position. The corps was left a limited task, to iron out the Wirtzfeld angle.

Finally, on 28 December, Hitzfeld was ready, but his assault force now represented only parts of two divisions, the 12th Volks Grenadier Division and the 246th. Early that morning two battalions of the 352d Regiment (246th Volks Grenadier Division) moved out of the woods near Rocherath against the forward lines of the 99th Infantry Division on the Elsenborn Ridge. This attack was blown to pieces by accurate shelling from the batteries on the ridge. A battalion of the 48th Regiment (12th Volks Grenadier Division) met an identical fate when it started toward the 2d Infantry Division position northwest of Wirtzfeld. Two battalions from the 27th Regiment (12th Volks Grenadier Division) took a crack at the 1st Infantry Division front in the Butgenbach sector, but intense rocket fire and shellfire failed to shake the defenders and left their supporting artillery unscathed. The German assault battalions had not even deployed from approach march formation when a rain of bursting shells scattered them in every direction. A handful of riflemen and engineers reached a draw leading to the American foxhole line only to be captured or driven off. This was the last attack against the American forces arrayed on the north shoulder. Hitzfeld was left to hold what he could of his lengthy front with a force which by the close of December had dwindled to three understrength divisions.

The German High Command and the troops of the Sixth Panzer Army now waited apprehensively and hopelessly for the retaliatory blow to fall. That the American attack would come in a matter of hours or a very few days was clear to all. Where it would be delivered along the length of the north flank of the Ardennes salient was a good deal less certain. A few of the German leaders seem to have anticipated originally that the Allied counterattack would come from north and south against the base of the salient, but by the end of December intelligence reports definitely ruled out any Allied build-up at the shoulders of the salient. The Sixth Panzer Army staff, acutely aware of the weakened condition of the German troops in the Malmédy sector, was apprehensive that the Allied effort would be made there in a drive through to St. Vith, and set two ordnance companies scrambling to recreate a single operational tank company from the armored debris the 1st SS Panzer Division had brought out of the La Gleize debacle. What Rundstedt and Model expected of their adversary can never be known, although their respective staffs seem to have read into Patton's battle around Bastogne a strong indication that the poised Allied pincers would close somewhere in the vicinity of Houffalize. It is known, however, how Rundstedt regarded the Allied strategy which on 3 January sent the American divisions attacking from north and south to snip off the tip of the salient at Houffalize: this was, says the OB WEST War Diary, "the small solution."

Chapter XXIV. The Third Army Offensive

Widening the Bastogne Corridor

When the 4th Armored tanks reached the Bastogne perimeter on 26 December, the contact between McAuliffe's command and the Third Army was dramatic and satisfying but none too secure. The road now opened from Assenois to Bastogne could be traversed under armed convoy, and for the moment the Germans in this sector were too demoralized by the speed and sharpness of the blow to react in any aggressive manner. The two main highways east and west of the Assenois corridor, however, still were barred by the Seventh Army and such small detachments as could be hurriedly stripped from the German circle around Bastogne. Continued access to Bastogne would have to be insured by widening the breach and securing the Arlon highway—and perhaps that from Neufchâteau as well-before the enemy could react to seal the puncture with his armor.

The main weight of Gaffey's 4th Armored, it will be recalled, lay to the east of Assenois on the Arlon-Bastogne axis. On the right of the 4th Armored the 26th Infantry Division was echeloned to the southeast and on 26 December had put troops over the Sure River, but the only direct tactical effect this division could have on the fight south of Bastogne would be to threaten the Seventh Army line of communications and divert German reserves. The gap between the 26th Infantry and the 4h Armored Divisions, rather tenuously screened by the 6th Cavalry Squadron, would be filled by the 35th Infantry Division (Maj. Gen. Paul Baade), which had just come up from Metz and had orders to attack across the Sure on 27 December. If all went well this attack would break out to the Lutrebois-Harlange road, which fed into the Arlon highway, and proceed thence abreast of the 4th Armored.

West of the Assenois corridor the left wing of Gaffey's command was screened, but rather lightly, by scratch forces that General Middleton had gathered from his VIII Corps troops and what remained of Cota's 28th Division. On the afternoon of 26 December General Patton assigned CCA, 9th Armored, which was near Luxembourg City, to the III Corps with orders that it be attached to the 4th Armored and attack on the left to open the Neufchâteau-Bastogne highway. The 9th Armored Division's CCA was relieved that same afternoon by CCA of Maj. Gen. Robert W. Grow's 6th Armored Division.

Although the enemy troops around Assenois had been broken and scattered by the lightning thrust on the 26th, the III Corps' attack on the following day met some opposition. The 35th Division, its ultimate objective the Longvilly-Bastogne road, had more trouble with terrain and weather than with Germans, for the enemy had elected to make a stand on a series of hills some five thousand yards beyond the Sure. On the left the 137th Infantry (Col. William S. Murray) trucked through the 4th Armored, crossed the tankers' bridge at Tintange, and moved out cross-country in snow six inches deep. The 2d Battalion drove off the German outpost at the crossroads village of Surré, but to the west the 3d Battalion, defiling along a draw near Livarchamps, came suddenly under fire from a pillbox which checked further movement. The 320th Infantry (Col. Bernard A. Byrne) had to make its own crossings at the Sure, one company wading the icy river, but Boulaide and Baschleiden, on the single road in the regimental zone, were occupied without a casualty. Thence the Battalion pushed on toward the north.

In the 4th Armored zone CCR shepherded trucks on the Assenois road while CCB and CCA continued the foot-slogging pace north toward Bastogne. The armored infantry and the two rifle battalions of the 318th marched through the snow, fighting in those woods and hamlets where the German grenadiers and paratroopers—now with virtually no artillery to back them up—decided to make a stand. CCB made its attack from west of Hompré against troops of the 15th Panzer Grenadier Division, here faced about from Bastogne; by nightfall its patrols had reached the 101st Airborne perimeter. CCA, farther from the point of impact on 26 December, had a rougher time although the commanders of the two battalions from the 15th Parachute Regiment confronting the Americans had been captured in battle the previous day. When the 51st Armored Infantry Battalion moved toward the village of Sainlez, perched on a hill to the front, the enemy paratroopers made such good use of their commanding position that the Shermans had to enter the action and partially destroy the village before the German hold was broken. The defenders flushed from Sainlez moved east and struck the 1st Battalion of the 318th, which had cleared Livarchamps, in the rear, starting a fire fight that lasted into the night. American battle casualties in this sector were high on the 27th, and about an equal number of frost bite cases plagued the infantrymen who had now spent six days in the snow and wet.

While the 4th Armored and its attached troops pressed forward to touch hands with the Bastogne garrison, the perimeter itself remained in unwonted quiet. General Taylor went into the city to congratulate McAuliffe and resume command of his division. Supply trucks and replacements for the 101st rolled through the shell-torn streets. A medical collecting company arrived to move the casualties back to corps hospitals and by noon of the 28th the last stretcher case had left the city. Perhaps the most depressing burden the defense had had to bear during the siege was the large number of seriously wounded and the lack of medical facilities for their care. As early as 21 December the division surgeon had estimated the 101st casualty list as about thirteen hundred, of whom a hundred and fifty were seriously wounded and required surgery. As this situation worsened the Third Army chief of staff, General Gay, made plans on his own responsibility to move surgeons into Bastogne under a white flag, but the successful flight of the Third Army surgeons sent in by liaison plane on the 25th and by glider on the 26th changed the plans and did much to alleviate the suffering in the cellar hospitals of Bastogne. The casualties finally evacuated numbered 964; about 700 German prisoners were also sent out of the city.

Uncertainty as to the tenure of the ground corridor resulted in a continuation of the airlift on the 27th. This time 130 cargo planes and 32 gliders essayed the mission, but by now the German ack-ack was alert and zeroed in on the paths of approach. Most of the gliders landed safely, but the cargo planes carrying parapacks suffered heavily on the turnaround over the perimeter; of thirteen C-47's sent out by the 440th Troop Carrier Group only four returned to their base.

During the morning of 28 December it became apparent that the German units in front of the III Corps were stiffening. The 35th Division gained very little ground, particularly on the right. On the left the 137th Infantry made slow going over broken ground and through underbrush, the bushes and scrub trees detonating percussion missiles before they could land on the German positions. The 3d Battalion, pinned down in the ravine in column of companies, took nearly all day to work around the irritating pillbox, which finally was destroyed. Thus far the 35th Division, filled with untrained replacements, was attacking without its usual supporting battalion of tanks, for these had been taken away while the division was refitting at Metz.

Meanwhile General Earnest, commanding CCA of the 4th Armored, had become concerned with the failure of the 35th to draw abreast on his open east flank, particularly since the rifle battalion borrowed from the 80th Division was under orders to rejoin its parent formation. He therefore asked that the reserve regiment of the 35th (134th Infantry) be put into the attack on his right, with the object of taking Lutrebois, a village east of the Arlon highway. During the night of the 28th the 134th Infantry (Col. Butler B. Miltonberger) relieved the tired troops from the 80th, taking attack positions east of Hompré. The orders were to push any German resistance to the right (that is, away from the Arlon road); thus insensibly the 35th Division was turning to face northeast instead of north with the 320th behind the 137th and the 137th falling into position behind the 134th. This columnar array would have considerable effect on the conduct of the ensuing battle.

The Opposing Grand Tactics

By Christmas Day it was apparent in both the Allied and German headquarters that the Ardennes battle had entered a new phase and that events now afoot required a fresh look at the grand tactics to be applied as the year drew to its close.

The Allied commanders had from the very first agreed in principle that the ultimate objective was to seize the initiative, erase the German salient, and set an offensive in motion to cross the Rhine. There was division in the Allied camp, however, as to when a counteroffensive should be launched and where it should strike into the salient. Beyond this, of course, lay the old argument as to whether the final attack across the Rhine should be on a wide or narrow front, in the British or in the American sector.

On 25 December the commanders of the two army groups whose troops faced the Germans in the Ardennes met at Montgomery's Belgian headquarters. General Bradley, whose divisions already were counterattacking, felt that the German drive had lost its momentum and that now was the moment to lash back at the attackers, from the north as well as the south. Field Marshal Montgomery was a good deal less optimistic. In his view the enemy still retained the capability to breach the First Army front (a view shared by the First Army G-2, who was concerned with two fresh German armored divisions believed to be moving into the Malmédy sector); the American infantry divisions were woefully understrength; tank losses had been very high; in sum, as Montgomery saw it, the First Army was very tired and incapable of offensive action. Bradley was distressed by Montgomery's attitude and the very next day wrote a personal letter to his old friend, the First Army commander, carefully underscoring the field marshal's authority over Hodges' army but making crystal clear that he, Bradley, did not view the situation "in as grave a light as Marshal Montgomery." As Bradley saw it the German losses had been very high and "if we could seize the initiative, I believe he would have to get out in a hurry." The advice to Hodges, then, was to study the battle with an eye to pushing the enemy back "as soon as the situation seems to warrant."

Perhaps, after Bradley's visit, the field marshal felt that he should set the record straight at SHAEF. After a long visit with Hodges on the 26th, he sent a message to Eisenhower saying that "at present" he could not pass to the offensive, that the west flank of the First Army continued under pressure, and that more troops would be needed to wrest the initiative from the Germans. At the moment, however, the Supreme Commander was concerned more with the slowness of the Third Army drive (earlier General Patton had called twice to apologize for the delay in reaching

Bastogne) than with an enlargement of the Allied counterattack. In the daily SHAEF staff meeting on the morning of the 26th Eisenhower ruled that General Devers would have to redress the lines of his 6th Army Group by a general withdrawal to the Vosges, thereafter joining his flank to the French north of Colmar. Such regrouping, distasteful as it was, would free two or three American divisions for use in the Ardennes. (It would seem that the SHAEF staff approved the withdrawal of Devers' forces—all save Air Marshal Tedder who did not think the withdrawal justified and argued that Montgomery had British and Canadian divisions which could be freed to provide the needed SHAEF reserve.)

The lower echelon of Allied commanders was meanwhile stirring restively. Having reached Bastogne late on the 26th, Patton set his staff to work on plans for a prompt redirection of the Third Army attack. On the 27th General Collins arrived at the First Army command post with three plans for an attack led by the VII Corps, two aimed at a junction with Patton in the Bastogne sector, one with St. Vith, deeper in the salient, as the objective.

Collins' proposals posed the problem of grand tactics now at issue—should the German salient be pushed back from the tip or should it be cut off close to the shoulders—but it remained for Patton, the diligent student of military history, to state in forthright terms the classic but venturesome solution. Arguing from the experiences of World War I, the Third Army commander held that the Ardennes salient should be cut off and the German armies engulfed therein by a vise closing from north and south against the shoulders of the Bulge. Thus the Third Army would move northeast from Luxembourg City toward Bitburg and Prüm along what the Third Army staff called the "Honeymoon Trail." General Smith, the SHAEF chief of staff, was in agreement with this solution, as were Hodges, Gerow, and Collins—in principle. The salient at its shoulders was forty miles across, however, and a successful amputation would necessitate rapid action by strong armored forces moving fast along a good road net. The First Army commanders, as a result, had to give over this solution because the road complex southeast of the Elsenborn Ridge, which would be the natural First Army axis for a cleaving blow at the German shoulder, could not sustain a large attack force heavy in armor—hence Collins' compromise suggestion for an attack from a point north of Malmédy toward St. Vith.

How would the two army group commanders react to the pressures being brought to bear by their subordinates? Bradley was concerned with the vagaries of the winter weather, which could slow any counterattack to a walk, and by the lack of reserves. He may also have been uncertain of his air support. Bad flying weather was a distinct possibility, and the Eighth Air Force—a rather independent command— was increasingly disenchanted with its battlefield missions over the Ardennes (indeed, on 27 December the Eighth Air Force had stated its intention of scrubbing the battle zone targets and going after the Leipzig oil depots, weather permitting). Bradley decided therefore to settle for half a loaf and on the 27th briefed the Supreme Commander on a new Third Army attack to be mounted from the Bastogne area and to drive northeast toward St. Vith. Bradley was careful to add that this plan was not Patton's concept of a drive against the south shoulder.

There remained Montgomery's decision. By the 27th he was ready to consider definite counterattack plans. When this word was relayed to Eisenhower at his daily staff meeting it elicited from him a heartfelt "Praise God from Whom all blessings flow!" and the Supreme Commander set off at once to meet the field marshal in Brussels. Hodges, Collins, and Ridgway did their best in the meantime to convince

Montgomery that the First Army attack should be initiated not around Celles, as the field marshal had first proposed, but farther to the east. On the evening of 28 December Eisenhower phoned General Smith from Brussels and told him that he saw great possibilities in a thrust through the Bastogne-Houffalize area. As it turned out, this would be the maneuver ultimately adopted. Perhaps the field marshal had given Eisenhower reason to think that the First Army would make its play in a drive on Houffalize; perhaps—and this seems more likely—Montgomery still had not made any final decision as to the place where the counterattack would be delivered. Certainly no time had been set although 4 and 5 January had been discussed as possible target dates. Hodges and Collins continued to press for a decision to get the attack from the north flank rolling—the prospects for which brightened when the British offered the loan of two hundred medium tanks. Meanwhile the new Third Army attack against the south flank commenced. On the last day of December, the serious prospect of bad weather outweighed by the fact that the Germans were thinning the First Army front to face the Third, Montgomery gave his decision and Hodges consented: the VII Corps, followed by the XVIII Airborne Corps, would attack toward Houffalize and St. Vith respectively on 3 January.

Eisenhower's telephone call from Brussels on the 28th released the 11th Armored and 87th Infantry Divisions from the SHAEF reserve for use by Bradley. That night Patton met with the VIII and III Corps commanders to lay out the new plan for continuation of the Third Army attack. Middleton's VIII Corps would jump off from the Bastogne area on the morning of 30 December, its objective the high ground and road nexus just south of Houffalize. Millikin's III Corps would move into the attack on 31 December, driving in the direction of St. Vith. The initial pressure on the salient would be exerted much farther to the west than Patton wished. Bradley made doubly sure that the Third Army would indeed place its weight as planned by telling Patton that the two fresh divisions could be employed only by the VIII Corps. But the Third Army commander put his cherished concept into the army operations order by means of a paragraph which called for the XII Corps to be prepared for an attack across the Sauer River and northeast through the Prüm valley—ultimate objective the Rhine River crossings at Bonn as the entire Third Army swung northeast.

On Christmas Day the German commanders sensed, as their opponents across the line had done, that they were at a turning point in the Ardennes battle. How should the higher commanders now intervene to influence the course of battle, or, more accurately, could they intervene? Manteuffel's plan was to make the suit fit the cloth: put enough new troops in to take Bastogne, then swing the left flank of the Fifth Panzer Army toward the Meuse and fight the Allies east of the river—the old Small Solution. Field Marshal Model agreed that Bastogne must be taken and that additional troops would be needed for the task, but the only armor immediately available was the Fuehrer Begleit Brigade and he had just extricated this unit from the Manhay fight to give added weight to the Fifth Panzer Army drive against the American line on the Ourthe River. As it turned out, Remer's brigade arrived in the Ourthe sector only a few hours before the Americans broke through to Bastogne. It had time to put in only one probing assault when Model, on the late afternoon of the 26th, sent the Fuehrer Begleit again on its travels, this time countermarching to seal the gap in the Bastogne ring with a riposte between Sibret and Hompré.

Model and Rundstedt seem to have agreed on a plan of action which may or may not have had the Fuehrer's approval (there is no record). The Fifth and Sixth would seek to destroy the Allied forces east of the Meuse while the Seventh held on as best it could; as a first step an attack would be made to eradicate the Americans in the Bastogne area. Obviously the German lines would have to be shortened somewhere, and Model, directly under Hitler's baleful eye, dare not surrender ground. This responsibility fell to the Fifth Panzer Army commander, who on 26 December (with tacit approval from Model at every step) set about creating a defensive front in the west roughly following the triangular outline Bastogne-Rochefort-Amonines. The battered 2d Panzer Division was brought back through the Rochefort bridgehead and troops from the 9th Panzer took over from Panzer Lehr in the Rochefort area, the latter sidestepping toward the southeast so that one flank finally would lie on the Lesse River with the other fixed at Remagne, five miles west of the Neufchâteau-Bastogne highway. The LVIII Panzer Corps, possibly as a sop to Hitler, was allowed to continue its fruitless attacks in the Ourthe sector, but with the Fuehrer Begleit out of the picture these quickly dwindled away. Manteuffel made his old comrade Luettwitz responsible for the defensive western front and took a new corps headquarters, which had been sent up from the OKW reserve, to handle the Bastogne operation. This, the XXXIX Panzer Corps, was commanded by Generalleutnant Karl Decker, a very experienced officer with a reputation for prudence combined with determination. Decker, despite protests by Luettwitz, was placed under the latter, and for a few days the German order of battle would show an "Army Group Luettwitz."

Manteuffel counted on the Fuehrer Begleit to carry the main burden of the counterattack south of Bastogne. The brigade had about forty Mark IV tanks plus an assault gun brigade of thirty tubes, and its infantry had not been bled white as in the rest of the armored formations. In addition, Manteuffel had been promised the beat-up 1st SS Panzer Division, the 3d Panzer Grenadier Division, and the Fuehrer Grenadier Brigade, parts of these formations being scheduled to reach Decker on 28 December. Advance elements of the Fuehrer Begleit did arrive that morning, taking station in the Bois de Herbaimont north of the Marche-Bastogne road, but the Allied Jabos were in full cry over the battlefield and Remer could not bring all his troops forward or issue from the forest cover. Time was running out for the Germans. As early as the night of the 27th Rundstedt's staff believed that unless Remer could make a successful attack at once it was "questionable" whether the Bastogne gap could be sealed. Manteuffel later would say that this job could have been done only by counterattacking within forty-eight hours.

On both sides of the hill, then, the troops were being moved for a set piece attack on 30 December. Would either opponent anticipate the ensuing collision? German intelligence officers did predict that the 6th Armored Division soon would appear between the III and XII Corps. The OB WEST report of 27 December reads: "It is expected that the units of the Third Army under the energetic leadership of General Patton will make strong attacks against our south flank." Within twenty-four hours this view altered: The First Army was said to be having difficulty regrouping and still showed defensive tendencies; therefore, even though the Third Army was in position to attack, it probably would not attack alone. The American intelligence agencies had practically no knowledge of any German units except those immediately in contact. Of course some kind of counterattack was expected, but this, it was believed, would come when bad weather cut down friendly air activity. The weather did turn foul late on the 28th and the word went out in the American camp: Prepare for an armored counterattack, enemy tanks are in movement around Bastogne.

The Sibret-Villeroux Actions

While the Fuehrer Begleit Brigade was assembling, General Kokott did what he could to gather troops and guns in the sector west of Assenois and there make some kind of a stand to prevent the tear in the Bastogne noose from unraveling further. The key villages in his original defense plans were Sibret and Villeroux, overwatching as they did the Neufchâteau-Bastogne highway. Kokott could expect no help from the 5th Parachute Division, originally entrusted with the blocking line in this area, for on the night of 26 December an officer patrol reported that not a single paratrooper could be found between Sibret and Assenois. Kokott's own division, the 26th Volks Grenadier, and its attached battalions from the 15th Panzer Grenadier had taken very heavy losses during the western attack against the 101st Airborne on Christmas Day. The rifle companies were down to twenty or thirty men; most of the regimental and battalion commanders and executive officers were dead or wounded; a number of heavy mortars and antitank guns had been sent back to the divisional trains because there was no more ammunition; and the only rifle replacements now consisted of what Kokott called "lost clumps" of wandering infantry.

When CCA of the 9th Armored Division (Col. Thomas L. Harrold) got its orders on the 26th to come forward on the left flank of the 4th Armored and attack toward Sibret, there was more at stake than defending the corridor just opened through the German lines. General Middleton was already busy with plans for his VIII Corps to join the Third Army attack beyond Bastogne and, with the memories of the traffic congestion there early in the fight still fresh in mind, was most unwilling to drag the VIII Corps through the Bastogne knothole in the forthcoming advance. Middleton convinced Bradley and Patton that the VIII Corps should make its drive from a line of departure west of Bastogne, and for this the Neufchâteau road first had to be opened and the enemy driven back to the northwest.

When CCA started down the Neufchâteau road on the morning of the 27th, it faced a catch-as-catch-can fight; no one knew where the enemy might be found or in what strength. Task Force Collins (Lt. Col. Kenneth W. Collins), in the lead, was held up some hours by mines which had been laid north of Vaux-lez-Rosières during the VIII Corps' withdrawal; so Task Force Karsteter (Lt. Col. Burton W. Karsteter) circled to head for Villeroux, leaving Task Force Collins to take Sibret. Karsteter, who had two medium tank companies, got into Villeroux, but night was coming and the tanks were not risked inside the village. Collins sent his single company of Shermans into Sibret, firing at everything in sight. The Americans could not be said to hold the village, however, for a small detachment of the 104th Panzer Grenadier Regiment was determined to make a fight of it and did. It took all night to drive the German grenadiers out of the cellars and ruined houses.

During the night of 27 December the Germans put more men into Villeroux (the 39th Regiment was slowly building up a semblance of a front) but to no avail. American artillery and Allied fighter-bombers shattered the village, and Karsteter finished the job with his tanks. Task Force Collins was delayed on the 8th by a formidable ground haze which lingered around Sibret all morning. Halfway to its next objective, the crossroads at Chenogne north of Sibret, the American column came under enfilading fire from a small wood lot close to the road. The tank company turned to deal with this menace and finally suppressed the German fire, but light was fading and the column laagered where it was.

In the meantime General Kokott had gathered a counterattack force, a company of the division Pioneers, to retake Sibret. While at breakfast on the 29th eating K rations on the tank decks and in foxholes beside the road, Collins' troops suddenly saw a body of men march out of the nearby woods. An American captain shouted out and the leading figure replied, "Good morning"—in German. The Americans cut loose with every weapon, to such effect that some fifty dead Germans were counted, lying in column formation as they had fallen. Late in the day, however, the fortunes of war turned against the Americans. Collins' tanks had moved through the village square in Chenogne and were approaching a road junction when high velocity shells knocked out the two lead tanks. Then, in a sharp exchange of shots, the enemy gunners accounted for two more of the Shermans, and the Americans withdrew. They could not discover the exact enemy locations in the twilight but were sure they were facing tanks. That night, the VIII Corps artillery reported, it "blew Chenogne apart."

While Task Force Collins was engaged on the road to Chenogne, Task Force Karsteter also was moving north, its objective Senonchamps, the scene of hard fighting in previous days and a sally port onto the main road running west from Bastogne to Marche. Here Task Force Karsteter was unwittingly threatening the assembly area of the Fuehrer Begleit which lay in the woods north of the highway, none too securely screened by remnants of the 3d Battalion of the 104th Panzer Grenadier around Chenogne. Remer's brigade already had taken some share in the action against CCA and one of his 105-mm. flak pieces was responsible for holding up Task Force Collins in the fight at the roadside woods, continuing in action until it was rammed by a Sherman tank.

Not far out of Villeroux, Task Force Karsteter came under hot and heavy fire from the Bois de Fragotte, lying over to the northwest. What the Americans had run into was the main body of the 3d Panzer Grenadier Division. Losses among the armored infantry were very high, and that night a liaison officer reported that the task force front was "disorganized." Four of Karsteter's tanks ran the gauntlet of fire from the woods and entered Senonchamps, but the infantry failed to follow. The cumulative losses sustained by CCA in the three-day operation had been severe and it was down to a company and a half of infantry, although 21 medium and 17 light tanks still were operable.

The Two Attacks Collide

The grand tactics of the two opponents had been solved—at least on the planning maps—by set-piece attacks in the Bastogne sector which were scheduled to commence on or about 30 December. This date was firm insofar as the American Third Army was concerned. In the German camp the date was contingent on the caprices of the weather, traffic congestion on the roads running into the area, the damage which might be inflicted by the Allied fighter-bombers, and the uncertainty attached to the arrival of fuel trucks coming forward from the Rhine dumps. The two attacks nevertheless would be launched on 30 December.

Middleton's VIII Corps, scheduled to provide the American curtain-raiser thrust on the left wing of Patton's army, took control of the 101st Airborne Division and the 9th Armored Division the evening before the attack began. Although General Taylor's paratroopers and glider infantry would play no offensive role in the first stages of the Third Army operation, they had to hold the pivot position at Bastogne and provide couverture as the scheme of maneuver unfolded. Of the 9th Armored commands only CCA, already committed, could be used at the onset of the VIII Corps advance toward Houffalize. On the morning of the 30th, then, the corps order of battle (east to west) would be the 101st, CCA of the 9th Armored, the 11th Armored Division, and the 87th Infantry Division, with these last two divisions designated to make the main effort.

The 11th Armored (General Kilburn) had been hurried from training in the United Kingdom to shore up the Meuse River line if needed and had some cavalry patrolling on the east bank when Eisenhower turned the division over to Bradley. Late on the evening of the 28th General Kilburn received orders from Middleton to move his division to the Neufchâteau area, and two hours after midnight the 11th Armored began a forced march, the distance about eighty-five miles. The heavy columns were slowed by snow, ice, and the limited-capacity bridge used to cross the Meuse, but CCA, in the van, reached the new assembly area a couple of hours before receiving the corps attack order issued at 1800. CCB and the remainder of the division were still on the road. Some units of this green division would have to go directly from the march column into the attack, set for 0730 the next morning. There was no time for reconnaissance and the division assault plan had to be blocked out with only the hastily issued maps as guidance.

The general mission given the 11th Armored — and the 87th as well — was to swing west around Bastogne, capture the heights south of Houffalize, and secure the Ourthe River line. The first phase, however, was a power play to drive the enemy back to the north in an assault, set in motion from the Neufchâteau-Bastogne road, which would sweep forward on the left of CCA, 9th Armored. General Kilburn wanted to attack with combat commands solidly abreast, but the VIII Corps commander, concerned by the thought of exposing the relatively untested 87th without tank support, ordered Kilburn to divide his force so as to place one combat command close to the new infantry division. Thus the 11th Armored would make its initial drive with CCB (Col. Wesley W. Yale) passing east of a large woods — the Bois des Haies de Magery — and CCA Brig. Gen. Willard A. Holbrook, Jr.) circling west of the same. The 87th Infantry Division (Brig. Gen. Frank L. Culin, Jr.) had arrived on the Continent in early December and been briefly employed as part of the Third Army in the Saar offensive. Ordered into the SHAEF reserve at Reims on 24 December, the division was at full combat strength when, five days later, the order came to entruck for the 100-mile move to the VIII Corps. There the 87th assembled between Bertrix and Libramont in preparation for an advance on the following morning to carry the corps left wing north, cut the Bastogne-St. Hubert road, and seize the high ground beyond. Middleton's two division attack would be well stiffened by ten battalions of corps artillery.

Across the lines, on the afternoon of 29 December, General Manteuffel called his commanders together. Here were the generals who had carried the Bastogne fight thus far and generals of the divisions moving into the area, now including three SS commanders. Manteuffel, it is related, began the conference with some critical remarks about the original failure to apprehend the importance of Bastogne. He then proceeded to tell the assemblage that the Ardennes offensive, as planned, was at an end, that Bastogne had become the "central problem," and that the German High Command viewed the forthcoming battle as an "opportunity," an opportunity to win a striking victory or at the least to chew up the enemy divisions which would be poured into the fight. The operation would be in three phases: first, close the ring once again around Bastogne; second, push the Americans back to the south; third, with reinforcements now on the way, take Bastogne in a final assault.

Army Group Luettwitz would conduct the fight to restore the German circle with the XXXIX and XLVII Panzer Corps, the first attacking east to west, the second striking west to east. A number of the divisions en route to Bastogne had not yet arrived and the attack set for the 30th would be neither as strong nor as coordinated as Manteuffel would wish, but he was under pressure from his superiors and could entertain no further delay. The eastern assault force comprised the much understrength and crippled 1st SS Panzer and the 167th Volks Grenadier Divisions; its drive was to be made via Lutrebois toward Assenois. The attack from the west would be spearheaded by the Fuehrer Begleit advancing over Sibret and hammering the ring closed. The 3d Panzer Grenadier Division was to advance in echelon to the left of Remer's brigade while the remnants of the 26th Volks Grenadier Division and 15th Panzer Grenadier Division screened to the west and north of Bastogne. The timing for the arrival of the incoming reinforcements — the 12th SS Panzer, the 9th SS Panzer, and the 340th Volks Grenadier Divisions — was problematical.

The Contact

Generalmajor Walter Denkert, commanding the 3d Panzer Grenadier Division, planned to attack at 0730 on 30 December because of the predisposition the Germans had noted (and on which they had capitalized many times) for the Americans to delay the start of the day's operations until about eight or nine o'clock in the morning. His division expected to move south through the Bois de Fragotte (between Chenogne and Senonchamps), then swing southeast to retake Villeroux. The attack plan was intended to pave the way for Remer's brigade (attached to the 3d Panzer Grenadier Division since Denkert was the senior commander) to seize Sibret and permit the combined force to debouch against Assenois and Hompré. The Americans, as it turned out, were not as dilatory as had been anticipated — both their attack divisions were moving north by 0730. Remer also kept to his time schedule.

The Fuehrer Begleit advance was geared for a one-two punch at Sibret. The battalion of Remer's panzer grenadiers, which had clashed briefly with Task Force Collins in Chenogne the previous evening, moved out over the snow-covered fields to pry an opening on the north edge of Sibret, while the Fuehrer Begleit tank grouP-carrying a battalion of grenadiers — waited in Chenogne to move forward on a parallel trail which passed through Flohimont and entered Sibret from the west. A dense ground fog covered the area for a few hours, masking the opposing forces from one another. The grenadier battalion made some progress and drove Task Force Collins back toward Sibret, but the battalion commander was killed and the advance slowed down. Remer's tank group was nearing Flohimont when the fog curtain raised abruptly to reveal about thirty American tanks.

Colonel Yale had divided CCB of the 11th Armored into a tank force (Task Force Poker) and an infantry task force (Task Force Pat). Task Force Pat, essentially the 21st Armored Infantry Battalion, had marked Flohimont on the map as its line of departure but in the approach march became confused. Communications failed, and the reconnaissance troops in the van of CCB got lost and fell back on Task Force Pat. Adding menace to confusion the German artillery began to pound the Jodenville-Flohimont road along which the attack was directed. Meanwhile the reinforced 41st Tank Battalion (Task Force Poker), which had picked Lavaselle from the map as its goal, rolled north with little opposition and reached its objective about a mile and a half west of Chenogne. These were the American tanks seen by Remer.

Lavaselle turned out to be located in a hollow, hardly a place for armor, and the task force commander (Maj. Wray F. Sagaser) decided to move on to the villages of Brul and Houmont which occupied some high ground just to the north. There was a creek to cross with a single rickety bridge, but the tanks made it. The twin hamlets were defended only by a few infantry and fell easily — then intense rocket and mortar fire set in. Task Force Poker was on its own, well in front of the rest of the 11th Armored, uncertain that its sister task force would succeed in forging abreast at Chenogne, and with night coming on.

Remer apparently decided to forgo a test of strength with the American armor moving past in the west, his mission being to attack eastward, but when word reached him that the Americans had hit the outpost at Lavaselle he hurried in person to check the security screen covering the western flank. Here one of Remer's panzer grenadier battalions had thrown forward an outpost line extending as far west as Gerimont and backed by a concentration of flak, assault guns, and mortars in the Bois Des Valets to the north of and about equidistant from Houmont and Chenogne. Satisfied that this groupment could hold the enemy, Remer returned to Chenogne. He found that the village had been bombarded by planes and guns till it was only a heap of stones with a handful of grenadiers garrisoning the rubble. Remer instantly sent a radio SOS to the commander of the 3d Panzer Grenadier, then set out to find his tank group.

When the bombardment started at Chenogne, the German tanks still there simply had pulled out of the village. About the same time, Task Force Pat resumed its march on Chenogne, Company B of the 22d Tank Battalion leading and the armored infantry following in their half-tracks. Near the village, in a lowering fog, the German armor surprised the company of Shermans and shot out seven of them. The enemy allowed the American aid men to carry away the surviving tankers and both sides fell back. As dusk came Remer set about pulling his command together, and the 3d Panzer Grenadier — heeding his call for assistance — moved troops into the ruins of Chenogne. This division had taken little part in the day's activity, probably because of the intense shelling directed on its assembly area in the Bois de Fragotte by the 4th Armored and corps artillery, the cross fire laid down from Villeroux by the tanks of Task Force Karsteter, and the uncertainty of Remer's situation.

The western advance on 30 December by CCA of the 11th Armored met almost no resistance during the first few hours, in part because the 28th Cavalry Squadron had driven the German outpost line back on Remagne. The immediate objective, Remagne, was the anchor position for the left wing of the new and attenuated Panzer Lehr position, but this division had just completed its shift eastward and had only small foreposts here. One of these, in the hamlet of Rondu about a mile and a half south of Remagne, seems to have flashed back warning of the American approach. In any case the 63d Armored Infantry Battalion, leading the march as Task Force White, had just come onto the crest of the ridge beyond Rondu when, as the men on the receiving end vividly recall, "All hell broke loose." The two tanks at the point of the column were hit in one, two order. The armored infantry took a hundred casualties in thirty minutes while digging madly in the frozen ground. Task Force Blue (the 42d Tank Battalion) was shielded by the ridge and received little fire. Since the 87th Division had not yet come up on the left, the 41st Cavalry Reconnaissance Squadron moved around to the west flank in anticipation of a German counterthrust.

It was midafternoon. German high velocity guns were sweeping the ridge, and there was no room for maneuver: the Ourthe lay to the west and the Bois Des Haies de Magery spread to the east, separating CCA and CCB. General Kilburn asked the corps commander to assign Remagne to the 87th and let CCA sideslip to rejoin CCB east of the woods. Middleton agreed and a new maneuver was evolved for 31 December in which all three combat commands of the 11th Armored would attack to concentrate at the head of the Rechrival valley, thus following up the drive made by Task Force Poker. An hour before midnight CCA began its withdrawal.

On the left wing of the VIII Corps the assault units of the 87th Division were trucked northward on the morning of 30 December to the line of departure in the neighborhood of Bras, held by the 109th Infantry. Since the first major objective was to sever the German supply route along the St. Hubert-Bastogne road the attack was weighted on the right, with the 345th Infantry (Col. Douglas Sugg) aiming for a sharp jog in the road where stood the village of Pironpré. On the left the 346th Infantry (Col. Richard B. Wheeler) had a more restricted task, that is, to block the roads coming into St. Hubert from the south.

Earlier the Panzer Lehr had outposted Highway N26, the 345th route of advance, but apparently these roadblock detachments had been called in and Sugg's combat team marched the first five miles without meeting the enemy. The advance guard, formed by the 1st Battalion (Lt. Col. Frank L. Bock), was within sight of the crossroads village of Moircy and less than two miles from the objective when a pair of enemy burp guns began to chatter. This was only outpost fire, and the leading rifle company moved on until, some five hundred yards short of Moircy, the enemy fire suddenly thickened across the open, snow-covered fields, causing many casualties and halting the Americans. The accompanying cannoneers (the 334th Field Artillery) went into action, the mortar crews started to work, and both Companies A and B deployed for the assault. Short rushes brought the rifle line forward, though very slowly. By 1400 the Americans were on the edge of Moircy, but the two companies had lost most of their officers and their ranks were riddled.

Colonel Bock ordered his reserve company to circle west of the village and take the next hamlet, Jenneville. While moving over a little rise outside Jenneville, the leading platoon met a fusillade of bullets that claimed twenty casualties in two minutes. Nevertheless the 2d Platoon of Company C reached the edge of the village. At this moment two enemy tanks appeared, stopped as if to survey the scene, then began to work their machine guns. The artillery forward observer crawled toward the panzers to take a look, and was shot. The Company C commander then called for the artillery, bringing the exploding shells within fifty yards of his own men. The German tanks still refused to budge. Two men crept forward with bazookas, only to be killed by the tank machine guns, but this episode apparently shook the tank crews, who now pulled out of range. Meanwhile Moircy had been taken and the battalion commander told Company C to fall back.

The expected German counterattack at Moircy came about three hours before midnight. Tanks pacing the assault set fire to the houses with tracer bullets, and the two battalion antitank guns were abandoned. Although Colonel Sugg ordered the battalion out, the company radios failed and in the confusion only Companies A and B left the village. Some of the machine gunners, a platoon of Company B, and most of Company C stayed on, taking to the cellars when the American artillery—including a battery of 240-mm. howitzers—started to shell Moircy. By midnight the Germans had had enough and evacuated the village. Bock then ordered the remaining defenders out. This day of sharp fighting cost the 1st Battalion seven officers and 125 men. Most of the wounded were evacuated, however; during the night battle in Moircy one aid man had twice moved the twelve wounded in his charge from burning buildings.

The much touted Fuehrer Begleit attack failed on the 30th to dent the Bastogne corridor — indeed it can be said that it never started. What of the eastern jaw of the hastily constructed German vise — the 1st SS Panzer attack?

The 1st SS Panzer was still licking its wounds after the disastrous fight as advance guard of the Sixth Panzer Army, when Model ordered the division to move south, beginning 26 December. Most of its tanks were in the repair shops, fuel was short, and some units did not leave for Bastogne until the afternoon of the 29th. This march was across the grain of the German communications net and became badly snarled in the streets of Houffalize, where Allied air attacks had caused a major traffic jam, that forced tank units to move only in small groups. It is probable that fewer than fifty tanks reached the Bastogne area in time to take part in the 30 December attack.

The appearance of this SS unit was greeted by something less than popular acclaim. The regular Army troops disliked the publicity Goebbels had lavished on the feats of the SS divisions and the old line commanders considered them insubordinate. Worse still, the 1st SS Panzer Division came into the sector next to the 14th Parachute Regiment: the SS regarded themselves — or at least were regarded — as Himmler's troops, whereas the parachute divisions were the personal creation of Goering. (It is not surprising that after the attack on the 30th the 1st SS Panzer tried to bring the officers of the 14th before a Nazi field court.)

The 167th Volks Grenadier Division (Generalleutnant Hans-Kurt Hoecker), ordered to join the 1st SS Panzer in the attack, was looked upon by Manteuffel and others with more favor. This was a veteran division which had distinguished itself on the Soviet front. The 167th had been refitting and training replacements from the 17th Luftwaffe Feld Division when orders reached its Hungarian casernes to entrain for the west. On 24 December the division arrived at Gerolstein on the Rhine; though some units had to detrain east of the river, Hoecker's command was at full strength when it began the march to Bastogne. A third of the division were veterans of the Russian battles, and in addition there were two hundred picked men who had been officer candidates before the December comb-out. Hoecker had no mechanized heavy weapons, however, and the division transport consisted of worn-out Italian trucks for which there were no spare parts.

The 167th and the kampfgruppe from the 1st SS Panzer (be it remembered the entire division was not present on the 30th) were supposed to be reinforced by the 14th Parachute Regiment and the 901st of the Panzer Lehr. Both of these regiments were already in the line southeast of Bastogne, but were fought-out and woefully understrength. The first plan of attack had been based on a concerted effort to drive straight through the American lines and cut the corridor between Assenois and Hompré. Just before the attack this plan was modified to make the Martelange-Bastogne highway the initial objective. The line of contact on the 30th extended from Neffe south into the woods east of Marvie, then followed the forest line and the Lutrebois-Lutremange road south to Villers-la-Bonne-Eau. The boundary between the 167th and the 1st SS Panzer ran through Lutrebois. The 167th, lined up in the north along the Bras-Bastogne road, would aim its assault at the Remonfosse sector of the highway. The 1st SS Panzer, supported on the left by the 14th Parachute Regiment, intended to sally out of Lutrebois and Villers-la-Bonne-Eau. Lutrebois, however, was captured late in the evening of the 29th by the 3d Battalion of the 134th Infantry. A map picked up there by the Americans showed the boundaries and dispositions of the German assault forces, but either the map legend was unspecific or the word failed to get back to higher authority for the German blow on the morning of 30 December did achieve a marked measure of tactical surprise.

The 35th Infantry Division stood directly in the path of the German attack, having gradually turned from a column of regiments to face northeast. The northernmost regiment, the 134th Infantry, had come in from reserve to capture Lutrebois at the request of CCA, 4th Armored, but it had only two battalions in the line. The 137th Infantry was deployed near Villers-la-Bonne-Eau, and on the night of the 29th Companies K and L forced their way into the village, radioing back that they needed bazooka ammunition. (It seems likely that the Americans shared Villers with a company of German Pioneers.) In the south the 320th Infantry had become involved in a bitter fight around a farmstead outside of Harlange — the German attack would pass obliquely across its front but without impact.

During the night of 29 December the tank column of the 1st SS Panzer moved up along the road linking Tarchamps and Lutremange. The usable road net was very sparse in this sector. Once through Lutremange, however, the German column could deploy in two armored assault forces, one moving through Villers-la-Bonne-Eau, the other angling northwest through Lutrebois. Before dawn the leading tank companies rumbled toward these two villages. At Villers-la-Bonne-Eau Companies K and L, 137th Infantry, came under attack by seven tanks heavily supported by infantry. The panzers moved in close, blasting the stone houses and setting the village ablaze. At 0845 a radio message reached the command post of the 137th asking for the artillery to lay down a barrage of smoke and high explosive, but before the gunners could get a sensing the radio went dead. Only one of the 169 men inside the village got out, Sgt. Webster Phillips, who earlier had run through the rifle fire to warn the reserve company of the battalion west of Villers.

The battle in and around Lutrebois was then and remains to this day jumbled and confused. There is no coherent account from the German side and it is quite possible that the formations involved in the fight did not, for the reasons discussed earlier, cooperate as planned. The American troops who were drawn into the action found themselves in a melee which defied exact description and in which platoons and companies engaged enemy units without being aware that other American soldiers and weapons had taken the same German unit under fire. It is not surprising, then, that two or three units would claim to have destroyed what on later examination proves to have been the same enemy tank detachment and that a cumulative listing of these claims — some fifty-odd German tanks destroyed — probably gives more panzers put out of action than the 1st SS Panzer brought into the field.

It is unfortunate that the historical reproduction of the Lutrebois fight in the von Rankian sense ("exactly as it was") is impossible, for the American use of the combined arms in this action was so outstanding as to merit careful analysis by the professional soldier and student. The 4th Armored Division artillery, for example, simultaneously engaged the 1st SS Panzer in the east and the 3d Panzer Grenadier in the west. Weyland's fighter-bombers from the XIX Tactical Air Command intervened at precisely the right time to blunt the main German armored thrust and set up better targets for engagement by the ground forces. American tanks and tank destroyers cooperated to whipsaw the enemy assault units. The infantry action, as will be seen, had a decisive effect at numerous points in the battle. Two circumstances in particular would color the events of 30 December: because of CCA's earlier interest in Lutrebois, radio and wire communications between the 4th Armored and the 35th Division were unusually good in this sector; although the 35th had started the drive north without the normal attachment of a separate tank battalion, the close proximity of the veteran 4th Armored more than compensated for this lack of an organic tank-killing capability.

Lutrebois, two and a half miles east of the German objective at Assenois, had most of its houses built along a 1,000-yard stretch of road which runs more or less east and west across an open plain and is bordered at either end by an extensive wooded rise. On the morning of the 30th the 3d Battalion of the 134th Infantry (Lt. Col. W. C. Wood) was deployed in and around the village: Company L was inside Lutrebois; Companies I and K had dug in during the previous evening along the road east of the village; the battalion heavy machine guns covered the road west of the village. To the right, disposed in a thin line fronting on the valley, was the d Battalion (Maj. C. F. McDannel).

About 0445—the hour is uncertain—the enemy started his move toward Lutrebois with tanks and infantry, and at the same time more infantry crossed the valley and slipped through the lines of the 2d Battalion. As the first assault force crossed the opening east of Lutrebois, the American cannoneers went into action with such effect as to stop this detachment in its tracks. The next German sortie came in a hook around the north side of Lutrebois. Company L used up all of its bazooka rounds, then was engulfed. The German grenadiers moved on along the western road but were checked there for at least an hour by the heavy machine guns. During this midmorning phase seven enemy tanks were spotted north of Lutrebois. A platoon of the 654th Tank Destroyer Battalion accounted for four, two were put out of action by artillery high explosive, and one was immobilized by a mine.

News of the attack reached CCA of the 4th Armored at 0635, and General Earnest promptly turned his command to face east in support of the 35th Division. By 1000 General Dager was reshuffling CCB to take over the CCA positions. The first reinforcement dispatched by CCA was the 51st Armored Infantry Battalion, which hurried in its half-tracks to back up the thin line of the 2d Battalion. Here the combination of fog and woods resulted in a very confused fight, but the 2d Battalion continued to hold in its position while the enemy panzer grenadiers, probably from the 2d Regiment of the 1st SS Panzer, seeped into the woods to its rear. The headquarters and heavy weapons crews of the 3d Battalion had meanwhile fallen back to the battalion command post in the Losange château southwest of Lutrebois. There the 51st Armored Infantry Battalion gave a hand, fighting from half-tracks and spraying the clearing around the château with .50-caliber slugs. After a little of this treatment the German infantry gave up and retired into the woods.

During the morning the advance guard of the 167th Volks Grenadiers, attacking in a column of battalions because of the constricted road net, crossed the Martelange-Bastogne road and reached the edge of the woods southeast of Assenois. Here the grenadiers encountered the 51st. Each German attempt to break into the open was stopped with heavy losses. General Hoecker says the lead battalion was "cut to pieces" and that the attack by the 167th was brought to nought by the Jabos and the "tree smasher" shells crashing in from the American batteries. (Hoecker could not know that the 35th Division artillery was trying out the new POZIT fuze and that his division was providing the target for one of the most lethal of World War II weapons.)

The main body of the 1st SS Panzer kampfgruppe appeared an hour or so before noon moving along the Lutremange-Lutrebois road; some twenty-five tanks were counted in all. It took two hours to bring the fighter-bombers into the fray, but they arrived just in time to cripple or destroy seven tanks and turn back the bulk of the panzers. Companies I and K still were in their foxholes along the road during the air bombing and would recall that, lacking bazookas, the green soldiers "popped off" at the tanks with their rifles and that some of the German tanks turned aside into the woods. Later the two companies came back across the valley, on orders, and jointed the defense line forming near the château.

Thirteen German tanks, which may have debouched from the road before the air attack, reached the woods southwest of Lutrebois, but a 4th Armored artillery observer in a cub plane spotted them and dropped a message to Company B of the 35th Tank Battalion. Lt. John A. Kingsley, the company commander, who had six Sherman tanks and a platoon from the 701st Tank Destroyer Battalion, formed an ambush near a slight ridge that provided his own tanks with hull defilade and waited. The leading German company (or platoon), which had six panzers, happened to see Company A of the 35th as the fog briefly lifted, and turned, with flank exposed, in that direction. The first shot from Kingsley's covert put away the German commander's tank and the other tanks milled about until all had been knocked out. Six more German tanks came along and all were destroyed or disabled. In the meantime the American tank destroyers took on some accompanying assault guns, shot up three of them, and dispersed the neighboring grenadiers.

At the close of day the enemy had taken Lutrebois and Villers-la-Bonne-Eau plus the bag of three American rifle companies, but the eastern counterattack, like that in the west, had failed. Any future attempts to break through to Assenois and Hompré in this sector would face an alert and coordinated American defense.

The III Corps Joins the Attack

Despite the events of the 30th there was no thought in the mind of General Patton that Millikin's III Corps—would give over its attack toward St. Vith, scheduled to flesh out the Third Army offensive begun by Middleton. General Millikin would nonetheless have to alter his plans somewhat. It had been intended that the 6th Armored Division, coming in from the XII Corps, would pass through the 4th Armored (which now had only forty-two operable tanks) and set off the attack on 31 December with a drive northeast from the Bastogne perimeter. The 35th Division was to parallel this drive by advancing in the center on a northeast axis, while the 26th Division, on the corps' right wing, would turn its attack in a northwesterly direction. The 4th Armored expected to pass to Middleton's corps, but the latter agreed on the night of the 30th that Gaffey's command should continue its support of the 35th Division. Whether the 35th could shake itself free and take the offensive was questionable, but General Baade had orders to try. The 26th Division was now deployed in its entirety on the north side of the Sure River and its center regiment was almost in sight of the highway linking Wiltz and Bastogne (the next phase line). Both flanks of the division were uncovered, however, and German tanks were observed moving into the area on the 30th.

One thing the III Corps commander sought to impress on his infantry divisions as H-hour loomed—they must keep out of time—consuming and indecisive village fights. This, after all, was an order which had echoed up and down the chain of command on both sides of the line, but neither German nor American commanders could alter the tactical necessities imposed by the Ardennes geography or prevent freezing troops from gravitating toward the shelter, no matter how miserable, promised by some wrecked crossroads hamlet.

Admittedly the battle which had flared up on the left wing of the III Corps was serious, but General Millikin expected (or at least hoped) that the 6th Armored Division attack would improve the situation. While deployed on the Ettelbruck front with the XII Corps, General Grow's troops had not been closely engaged, and the division would enter the Bastogne fight with only a single tank less than prescribed by the T/O&E. Its orders to move west were given the division at 0230 on the 29th.

Although the distance involved was not too great, the movement would be complicated by the necessity of using a road net already saturated in the support of two corps. The push planned for 31 December turned on the employment of two combat commands abreast and for this reason the march north to Bastogne was organized so that CCA, ordered to attack on the right, would use the Arlon-Bastogne highway while CCB, ticketed for the left wing, would pass through the VIII Corps zone by way of the Neufchâteau-Bastogne road.

During the night of 30 December CCA (Col. John L. Hines, Jr.) rolled along the icy highway, where the 4th Armored had accorded running rights to the newcomers, and through the city; the advance guard, however, took the secondary road through Assenois because of the German threat to the main route. By daylight CCA was in forward assembly positions behind the 101st Airborne line southeast of Bastogne.

CCB failed to make its appearance as scheduled. What had happened was a fouling of the military machine which is common in all large-scale operations and which may leave bitterness and recrimination long after the event. The 6th Armored commander believed he had cleared CCB's use of the Neufchâteau road with both the VIII Corps and the 11th Armored, but when Col. George Read moved out with his column he found the highway not only treacherously iced but encumbered with 11th Armored tanks and vehicles. What Read had encountered was the switch bringing the 11th Armored force from the west around to the right wing. The 11th Armored had not expected the 6th Armored column to appear before midnight of the 31st. An attempt to run the two columns abreast failed because the tanks were slipping all over the road.

CCB later reported that the 11th Armored blocked the highway for six hours, that is, until ten o'clock on the morning of the 31st. Finally General Grow ordered Read's force to branch off and go into assembly at Clochimont on the Assenois road.

Colonel Hines intended to postpone the CCA attack until the running mate arrived. There was no cover where his troops were waiting, however, and as the morning wore on intense enemy fire began to take serious toll. He and Grow decided, therefore, to launch a limited objective attack in which the two CCA task forces would start from near the Bastogne-Bras road and thrust northeast. The armored task force, organized around the 69th Tank Battalion (Lt. Col. Chester E. Kennedy), had the task of capturing Neffe and clearing the enemy from the woods to the east; the infantry task force, basically the 44th Armored Infantry Battalion (Lt. Col. Charles E. Brown), was to move abreast of Kennedy, scour the woods south of Neffe, and seize the nose of high ground which overlooked Wardin on the northeast. The assault, begun shortly after noon, rolled through Neffe with little opposition. But snow squalls clouded the landscape, the fighter-bombers sent to blast targets in front of CCA could not get through the overcast, and the armored infantry made little progress. CCA's expectation that the 35th Division would come abreast on the right was dashed, for the 35th had its hands full. Just before dusk small enemy forces struck at Hines's exposed flanks, and CCA halted, leaving the artillery to maintain a protective barrage through the night.

The role of the artillery would be of prime importance in all the fighting done by the 6th Armored in what now had come to be called "the Bastogne pocket." Not only the three organic battalions of the division, but an additional four battalions belonging to the 193d Field Artillery Group were moved into the pocket on the 31st, and the firing batteries were employed almost on the perimeter itself. A feature of the battle would be a counterbattery duel—quite uncommon at this stage of the Ardennes Campaign—for the I SS Panzer Corps had introduced an artillery corps, including some long-range 170-mm. batteries, and a Werfer brigade southeast of Bastogne. Now and later the American gunners would find it necessary to move quickly from one alternate position to another, none too easy a task, for the gun carriages froze fast and even to turn a piece required blow torches and pinch bars.

On the morning of New Year's Day CCB finally was in place on the left of Hines's combat command. The immediate task in hand was to knife through the German supply routes, feeding into and across the Longvilly road, which; permitted north-south movement along the eastern face of the Bastogne pocket and were being used to build up the forces in the Lutrebois sector. CCA would attempt a further advance to clear the woods and ridges beyond Neffe. CCB, working in two task forces, aimed its attack on Bourcy and Arloncourt with an eye to the high ground dominating the German road net. The 6th Armored Division expected that troops of the 101st Airborne would extend the push on the left of CCB and drive the enemy out of the Bois Jacques north of Bizory, the latter the first objective for CCB's tank force. The previous afternoon the VIII Corps commander had ordered General Taylor to use the reserve battalion of the 506th Parachute Infantry for this purpose, then had countermanded his order. Apparently General Grow and his division knew nothing of the change. Communication between divisions subordinate to two different corps always is difficult, but in this case, with an armored and an airborne division involved, the situation was even worse. At this time the only radio contact between Taylor and Grow was by relay through an army supply point several miles south of Bastogne, but the two generals did meet on 31 December and the day following.

The morning of the attack, 1 January 1945, was dark with cloud banks and squalls as the 68th Tank Battalion (Lt. Col. Harold C. Davall) moved rapidly along the narrow road to Bizory. The 78th Grenadier Regiment, in this sector since the first days of the Bastogne siege, had erected its main line of resistance farther to the east and Bizory fell easily. At the same time Davall's force seized Hill 510, which earlier had caused the 101st Airborne so much trouble. About noon the Americans began to receive heavy fire, including high velocity shells, from around Mageret on their right flank. Although doing so involved a detour, the 68th wheeled to deal with Mageret, its tanks crashing into the village while the assault gun platoon engaged the enemy antitank guns firing from wood cover nearby. The grenadiers fought for Mageret and it was midafternoon before resistance collapsed. Then the 69th Tank Battalion from CCA, which was on call, took over the fight to drive east from Mageret while its sister battalion turned back for the planned thrust at Arloncourt.

By this time the sun had come out, visibility was good, and the CCB tanks were making such rapid progress that the division artillery commander (Col. Lowell M. Riley) brought his three battalions right up on Davall's heels. Within an hour the 68th was fighting at Arloncourt, but here it had hit the main German position. Briefly the

Americans held a piece of Arloncourt, withdrawing at dark when it became apparent that the 50th Armored Infantry Battalion (Lt. Col. Arnold R. Wall), fighting through the woods to the northwest, could not come abreast. As it turned out, the 50th was forced to fall back to the morning line of departure. It too had collided with the main enemy defenses and was hit by a German counterattack—abruptly checked when the 212th Field Artillery laid in 500 rounds in twenty minutes.

The brunt of the battle in the CCA zone was borne by the 44th Armored Infantry, continuing doggedly through the woods southeast of Neffe against determined and well entrenched German infantry. Whenever the assault came within fifty yards of the foxhole line, the grenadiers climbed out with rifle and machine gun to counterattack. Two or three times Brown's battalion was ejected from the woods, but at close of day the Americans were deployed perhaps halfway inside the forest. The 6th Armored had gotten no assistance from the 35th Division during the day, and it was apparent to General Millikin that Grow's division would probably have to continue its attack alone. He therefore extended the 6th Armored front to the right so that on the evening of 1 January it reached from Bourcy on the north to Bras in the south. General Grow immediately brought his extra tank battalion and armored infantry battalion forward from CCR to beef up the combat commands on the line. Every tank, gun, and man would be needed.

The new and wider front would bring the 167th Volks Grenadier Division into action against the 6th Armored south of Neffe. But this was not all. At the Fifth Panzer Army conference on the 29th one of the SS officers present was General Priess, commander of the I SS Panzer Corps. He was there because Manteuffel expected to re-create this corps, as it had existed in the first days of the offensive, by bringing the 12th SS Panzer Division in from the Sixth Panzer Army and joining to it the 1st SS Panzer Division, at the moment moving toward Lutrebois. The subsequent failure at Lutrebois was overshadowed by the American threat to the Panzer Lehr and Fuehrer Begleit west of Bastogne, and on the last day of December Manteuffel ordered Priess to take over in this sector, promising that the 12th SS Panzer shortly would arrive to flesh out the new I SS Panzer Corps.

On the afternoon of New Year's Day Priess had just finished briefing his three subordinate commanders for a counterattack to be started in the next few hours when a message arrived from Manteuffel: the 12th SS Panzer was detached from his command and Priess himself was to report to the army headquarters pronto. The two generals met about 1800. By this hour the full account of the 6th Armored attack was available and the threat to the weakened 26th Volks Grenadier Division could be assessed. Manteuffel ordered Priess to take over the fight in the 26th sector at noon on 2 January, and told him that his corps would be given the 12th SS Panzer, the 26th Volks Grenadier Division, and the 340th Volks Grenadier Division, which was en route from Aachen.

The 6th Armored Division would be given some respite, however. When Field Marshal Model arrived to look over the plans for the counterattack, on the afternoon of the 2d, only a small tank force had come in from the 12th SS Panzer, and the main body of the 340th was progressing so slowly that Model set the attack date as 4 January. He promised also to give Priess the 9th SS Panzer Division for added punch. It must be said that Manteuffel's part in these optimistic plans was much against his own professional judgment.

Faced with a front normally considered too wide for a linear advance by armor, General Grow put five task forces into the attack on 2 January, holding only one in reserve. The boundary between CCA and CCB was defined by the railroad line which once had linked Bastogne, Benonchamps, and Wiltz. CCB now had two tank battalions (the 68th and 69th) plus the 50th Armored Infantry Battalion to throw in on the north wing; CCA got the two fresh battalions from CCR.

About one o'clock on the morning of the 2d the Luftwaffe began bombing the 6th Armored area. Although the German planes had been more conspicuous by their absence than their presence during the past days, it seemed that a few could always be gotten up as a token gesture when a large German ground attack was forming. (For example, on 30 December the Luftwaffe had supported the eastern and western attacks with great impartiality by dropping its bombs on Bastogne, the most concentrated air punishment the town received during the entire battle. CCB, 10th Armored, was bombed out of its headquarters, and a large portion of the Belgian population sought safety in flight.) While the German planes were droning overhead, dark shapes, increasing in number, were observed against the snow near Wardin. These were a battalion of the 167th Volks Grenadier forming for a counterattack Nine battalions of field artillery began TOT fire over Wardin, and the enemy force melted away. Just to the north, but in the CCB sector, the advance guard of the 340th Volks Grenadier Division made its initial appearance about 0200 on the 2d, penetrated the American outpost line, and broke into Mageret. The skirmish lasted for a couple of hours, but the Luftwaffe gave the defenders a hand by bombing its own German troops.

In midmorning the 68th Tank Battalion sortied from Mageret to climb the road toward Arloncourt, the objective of the previous day. The paving was covered with ice and the slopes were too slippery and steep for the steel tank treads; so the armored engineers went to work scattering straw on all the inclines. Finally, Company B came within sight of the village, but the Germans were ready— Nebelwerfers and assault guns gave the quietus to eight Shermans. The enemy guns were camouflaged with white paint and the snow capes worn by the gunners, and the supporting infantry blended discreetly with the landscape. So successful was the deception that when a company of Shermans and a company of light tanks hurried forward to assist Company B, they were taken under fire on an arc of 220 degrees. Colonel Davall radioed for a box barrage and smoke screen; Riley's gunners met the request in a matter of seconds and the 68th got out of the trap.

Farther north, and advancing on a route almost at a right angle to that followed by the 68th, the 50th Armored Infantry Battalion pried a few grenadiers out of the cellars in Oubourcy and marched on to Michamps. The reception was quite different here. As Wall's infantry entered Michamps the enemy countered with machine gun bursts thickened by howitzer and Werfer fire coming in from the higher ground around Bourcy. This time twelve artillery battalions joined in to support the 50th. At sunset German tanks could be seen moving about in Bourcy and Colonel Wall, whose force was out alone on a limb, abandoned both Michamps and Oubourcy. (Wall himself was partially blinded by a Nebelwerfer shell and was evacuated.) The German tanks, two companies of the 12th SS Panzer which had just arrived from west of Bastogne, followed as far as Oubourcy.

South of the rail line the 15th Tank Battalion (Lt. Col. Embrey D. Lagrew) came forward in the morning to pass through Brown's 44th Armored Infantry Battalion, but this march was a long one from Remichampagne and it was nearly noon before the 15th attack got under way. On the right the 9th Armored Infantry Battalion (Lt. Col. Frank K. Britton) came in to take over the fight the 44th had been waging in the woods near Wardin. It was planned that the armored infantry would sweep the enemy out of the wooded ridges which overlooked Wardin from the southwest and south, whereupon the tank force would storm the village from the north.

Britton's battalion was caught in an artillery barrage during the passage of lines with Brown, became disorganized, and did not resume the advance until noon. Shortly thereafter the 9th was mistakenly brought under fire by the 134th Infantry. There was no radio communication between Lagrew and Britton, probably because of the broken terrain, and Lagrew reasoned that because of his own delay the infantry attack must have reached its objective. The tanks of the 15th Tank Battalion gathered in the woods northwest of Wardin, then struck for the village, but the German antitank guns on the surrounding ridges did some expert shooting and destroyed seven of Lagrew's tanks. Nonetheless a platoon from Company C of the 9th, attached to Lagrew's battalion, made its way into Wardin and remained there most of the night. All this while the 9th Armored Infantry Battalion was engaged in a heartbreaking series of assaults to breast the machine gun fire sweeping the barren banks of a small stream bed that separated the wood lot southwest of Wardin from another due south. This indecisive affair cost the 9th one-quarter of its officers and many men. .

Despite the heavy losses incurred, the 6th Armored had gained much ground on 2 January, but it would be another eight days and the enemy would be in retreat before these gains would be duplicated. The tanks and infantry had been ably supported by the artillery, but the division official record is instant in giving full marks to the fighter-bombers of the XIX Tactical Air Command, that old and valued friend which together with the 6th Armored had patrolled the long, open flank of the Third Army weeks before on the Loire.

That night, when it was clear that Task Force Brown must be thrust back into the line to assist the 9th, General Grow reported to the III Corps commander that his entire division was committed and that his only reserve was the single company held out by each of the two combat commands.

By the close of 2 January it could be said that the III Corps' attack had been carried solely by the 6th Armored Division. Even though the German effort to open a path through the left wing of the 35th Infantry Division at Lutrebois had failed in its intended purpose, it had achieved an important secondary effect, becoming, as it did, a true spoiling attack that put the 35th out of the running from 31 December on. The main battle positions held by Baade's division (which had nowhere been broken by the 1st SS Panzer) followed the trace of a wide, lopsided V, reaching from Marvie in the northeast to a point west of Villers-la-Bonne-Eau, then back southeast to Bavigne. Before the 35th could regain its stride, it would be necessary to reduce the opposition that had flared up at three points: Lutrebois, Villers-la-Bonne-Eau (where the two companies from the 137th Infantry had been entrapped), and Harlange.

On the left wing the 2d and 3d Battalions of the 134th watched through the morning hours of 31 December while the corps artillery fired TOT's on Lutrebois, then rose from the foxhole line to renew the assault eastward. As the 2d Battalion tried to move out across the valley, it made a perfect target for the small arms fire sweeping in from the opposing wooded crest, took ninety casualties, and fell back. The 3d Battalion made a pass at Lutrebois, but the fire from the woods covering the high ground to the northeast barred entrance to the village.

The entire regiment joined the attack on 1 January. Now it was going up against the 167th Volks Grenadier Division, which finally had entered the line in its entirety (relieving the 1st SS Panzer) and was deployed on the right wing of the LIII Corps opposite Marvie and Lutremange. On the left the 1st Battalion, separated by three thousand yards from the neighboring 3d, set out from Marvie to bring the division flank forward and neutralize the German hold on the ridges overlooking Lutrebois. The veteran 167th, however, quickly sensed the gap in the American line and cut through to the rear of the 1st; nor did the 2d have any better luck at Lutrebois. In the afternoon the 2d Battalion assault had put Companies E and G across the valley and into the woods, when a sharp German riposte struck the two companies, isolating them completely by nightfall. Next morning the two American companies broke loose, and the 3d Battalion again attacked across the open space west of the village to seize a few buildings from which to build up the assault. Finally coming within yards of the first house, Company K was pinned down by a machine gun firing from one of the windows. A platoon leader left his men, climbed to the roof, and tossed down a hand grenade. With this building in hand the American infantry began methodically to clear Lutrebois (a two-day task as it turned out) while corps artillery put more TOT fire on the sections of the village still occupied by the enemy.

East of Marvie the 1st Battalion had to delay its advance in order to dig out the grenadiers who had settled themselves in the woods to the rear. Eventually the battalion started forward and, for the first time, made physical contact with the 6th Armored—after mistakenly starting a firefight with Britton's armored infantry. By the end of 2 January the left wing of the 35th Division was beginning to inch forward, but the terrain features set for seizure by the III Corps commander—two 510 meter hills on a thrust line bearing generally northeast from Lutrebois—would prove to be days away.

The 137th Infantry had hopes on 31 December that its two rifle companies still were in Villers-la-Bonne-Eau, but all attempts at relief were thwarted by the 14th Parachute Regiment, decimated though it was, in the surrounding woods. (Actually Companies K and L already had surrendered to flame throwers and tanks.) That night Colonel Murray wrote off the two companies, but no matter what the case Villers-la-Bonne-Eau had to be taken before the road net to the east could be opened. So it was that on 1 January the 137th Infantry commenced what its official history would call the roughest battle ever fought by the regiment—ten days of bloodletting and frustration In this the 137th would have yeoman help from the troopers of the 6th Cavalry Squadron, fighting dismounted and the GI's accolade "like infantry." The understrength 14th Parachute Regiment had recovered sufficiently from its disastrous experience at the hands of the 4th Armored to fight a tenacious defensive action through the woods and the deep snow in the fields.

After crossing the Sure River and taking Baschleiden, the 320th Infantry had continued the march north along the road to Harlange, the only negotiable avenue of advance here on the right flank of the 35th Division. On 29 December the 2d Battalion was hit hard by fire coming from a collection of farm buildings (Fuhrman Farm) at a jog in the road where it ascended a ridge a thousand yards southeast of Harlange. That night the 320th reported that it was "locked in a bitter battle" at the farmstead and in the neighboring woods.

Here stood the 15th Parachute Regiment, which had come through the debacle south of Bastogne in good shape and was, in the opinion of the higher command, "well in hand." The German counterattack leveled against the rest of the division on 30 December did not extend to the 320th Infantry, but did result in delaying a full-bodied American attempt to break through at Harlange until the first day of January.

At that time the division commander turned the reserve battalion of the 320th over to the 137th, leaving Colonel Byrne to fight the battle with only the 2d and 3d Battalions.

Neither the 320th nor the 15th Parachute had tank support; this would be an infantry battle with infantry weapons—principally the rifle and the machine gun. In the afternoon the battle flared up around Fuhrman Farm but left the attackers with nothing but their losses. Another series of assaults the following day was equally unsuccessful. That night the 320th got some pleasant news—nine tanks were on their way to join the attack. Across the lines the German corps commander, General von Rothkirch, was doing his best to find a few tanks for the paratroopers. The two opposing regimental commanders must have wondered which would be first to break the infantry deadlock.

The Lone Battle of the 26th Division

The right wing of the III Corps had been brought forward on 27 December when General Paul's 26th Division put its leading battalions across the Sure River. Wiltz, the division objective, was only a little more than four air-line miles to the north. The immediate objective remained the Wiltz-Bastogne highway, which meandered at distances of two and three miles from the Sure crossings. The approach to the target sector of the highway south of Wiltz was constricted to three poor, narrow roads that near their entrance were dominated by the villages of Bavigne, Liefrange, and Kaundorf respectively—this array west to east—and which converged in an apex touching the main highway at Nothum and a crossroads farmstead known as Mont Schumann. The battle commencing on 27 December would evolve, as the division neared Wiltz, into a series of pitched fights for blocks of high ground, which were so sharply etched by interlacing deep draws and ravines that a sweep forward on a solid division front was impossible. Tactically the 26th Division faced a lone battle, for its western neighbor, the 35th, had fed into the III Corps front in a column of regiments, turning under German pressure from column into line on a northwest-southeast axis instead of forming on the left flank of Paul's division. The tie with the XII Corps on the right was equally tenuous, for the 80th Division was forging due north while the 26th would gravitate toward the northwest. General Paul's problem, then, was to flesh out the III Corps attack while at the same time guarding both of his exposed flanks.

The leading companies of the 101st Infantry scaled the steep slopes on the north bank of the Sure during the night of 26 December, and a couple of hours after midnight Company I reported that it held Liefrange, the sally port onto the center of the three cart roads leading northward. Apparently the German Seventh Army had not yet been apprised of the crossings at the Sure, for in the early hours of the 27th Major von Courbiere, acting commander of the Fuehrer Grenadier Brigade, was dispatched with two rifle battalions and a few tanks to bar a crossing at Liefrange. This German foray struck Liefrange at about 0720 and momentarily ruled the field. But any hope of sweeping the north bank clear of the Americans evaporated when a dozen artillery battalions took the grenadiers under fire, followed less than two hours later by the Allied fighter-bombers.

In the meantime the 26th Division engineers rushed the last sections of a vehicular bridge into position north of Bonnal. By 0900 the bridge was ready and tanks and tank destroyers rumbled across to support the riflemen. Northeast of Liefrange two companies of the 3d Battalion, 101st, climbed the hill at Kaundorf, the highest ground in the area, but were repelled when von Courbiere turned his tanks into Kaundorf and knocked out half the platoon of Shermans accompanying the

Americans. At best, however, the understrength battalions of the Fuehrer Grenadier Brigade could only inflict delay now that the American bridges were in operation.

By early afternoon the entire 101st Infantry was across the river, and when night fell the bulk of the 104th was on the north bank taking position to the right of the 101st on the hills east of Kaundorf. To make his left wing secure, General Paul ordered the 101st to take Bavigne during the night of the 27th and told the commanders of the two regiments on the north bank to begin a coordinated attack at 0800 on the 28th. Company C of the 101st did shoot its way into Bavigne before midnight but took most of the next morning to root out the last of the German grenadiers.

Late on the 27th the 2d Battalion of the 101st Infantry had forged well ahead of the other American units, halting for the night outside Nothum near the apex of the secondary road net in the division zone. At this point the battalion encountered tank fire, and when it moved forward for the attack on the 28th it became clear that the German tanks would have to be destroyed or driven off before Nothum could be taken. Some hours passed here while the American tanks and tank destroyers maneuvered and dueled with the Germans, but in the late afternoon the way was clear and the infantry fought their way into and through the village. Earlier in the day the 3d Battalion of the 101st had retaken Kaundorf and started a drive with its companies abreast to clear the woods along the road to Nothum. During the morning the leading companies of the 104th Infantry set out to seize Buderscheid but came under extremely heavy fire from enemy dug in on some wooded heights east of the village. The capture of Kaundorf, however, permitted a flanking move against this German pocket, so Companies F and G, accompanied by tanks, swung west and north, the enemy decamping as the envelopment of Buderscheid became apparent. On the whole the progress made during the day was satisfying, but the division came to an abrupt halt just before midnight with the word from corps headquarters that the enemy would launch a counterattack from the northeast on the morning of the 29th.

The anticipated counterattack, probably conjured up by the inability of Allied air reconnaissance to function during bad flying weather late on the 28th, failed to appear. Paul waited until 1015, then telephoned the two regimental commanders to resume the advance. There was no longer any possibility of a full-bodied division attack. With both division flanks exposed the 328th Infantry had to be kept in the division commander's hand as reserve, and the 101st and 104th would have to move with battalions echeloned rearward out to the wings. Furthermore, visibility on the ground had dwindled so that visual contact between companies was almost nonexistent.

But the Wiltz River crossing—and the town itself—were not so far away. (At midnight on the 28th the corps and division artillery commenced to fire Tot's against Wiltz.) Paul ordered the two regiments to get patrols to the river but not to descend in strength into the Wiltz valley. The initial task at hand would be to clear the enemy pockets from the wooded high ground to the division front and cut the highway to Bastogne. This fight on the hills would be one at close range with opposing rifle companies and platoons gone to ground and entrenched only 75 to 150 yards apart.

The 101st began its advance at noon on the 29th, the immediate goal being to take the high ground north of Berle and the Schumann crossroads which commanded the highway. Here, as elsewhere along the division front, the enemy made up for his lack of riflemen with constant and accurate fire from dug-in tanks and Nebelwerfers, reinforced at likely points by a few 88's. Despite the presence of the division 105-mm. howitzers, which had been pushed to within fifteen hundred yards of the rifle line, the 101st made little headway. At nightfall Company A had reached a point five hundred yards south of Berle, but Company B had run into serious trouble and the 2d Battalion had been pinned down by direct fire not far from Nothum. The 1st and 2d Battalions of the 104th Infantry, faced with direct tank fire, made no substantial progress, although patrols in front of the attack wave did reach the woods southwest of Nocher and elements of the 1st reached a ridge overlooking the town of Wiltz.

The two-regiment attack on the morning of 30 December got off to a fast start, the orders now to "secure Wiltz." On the left the 101st Infantry met little but small arms fire and the 3d Battalion set up a roadblock on the Wiltz highway. The regiment gathered 140 prisoners from the 9th Volks Grenadier Division in its sweep through the woods north and west of the highway. The enemy, however, had no intention of allowing a parade march down into the Wiltz valley. An hour before dusk a German counterattack drove Companies I and K, the leaders, back onto the hill rising at the junction of the Wiltz and Roullingen roads. There followed a period of quiet, and then in the dark the grenadiers struck again. This time they were in battalion strength and had three or four tanks to harden the blow. Companies I and K took a substantial number of casualties and were left so disorganized that the regimental commander asked Paul to delay the attack scheduled for the next morning in order to get the 3d Battalion straightened out.

The 104th Infantry ran into trouble in the first minutes of its advance on the 30th. Both assault battalions were moving against enemy troops well established on the wooded high ground north of Buderscheid, and both came under an unusually heavy amount of tank and Nebelwerfer fire. Clearly enemy resistance in this sector was stiffening. Lt. Col. Calvin A. Heath's 2d Battalion was pinned down almost at once at a crossroad and, under direct tank fire, could not work its way around the German pocket. The 1st Battalion briefly gained control of a crest to its front but then was driven off by a savage attack which engulfed parts of Companies A and C. Paul ordered the 3d Battalion of the 328th Infantry up from reserve to back the 104th, and the Americans regained some of the ground lost north of Buderscheid. When the day ended, however, the enemy intention to hold this part of the line was underscored by a sudden and considerable increase in artillery fire.

The exposed condition of the 26th Division salient, as the year ended, is accurately described in the regimental orders issued to the 101st Infantry: "Each Battalion will be prepared to meet counterattacks from the north, northwest and northeast." The first of these anticipated thrusts came at the 101st roadblock about 0530 on 31 December, commencing a battle which embroiled both the 1st and 3d Battalions and lasted all day long. The main German effort seems to have been directed at the 3d Battalion roadblock southwest of Roullingen, and as a result Companies I and K, much weakened by the mauling received the previous day, took the first blows. As the German attack gained momentum, Colonel Scott ordered the two companies to fall back on the foxhole line dug earlier south of the Roullingen road. Light tanks and tank destroyers sent forward to help the 101st could made no headway, nor could they maneuver, on the icy roads. The enemy, however, had no tanks in action, and by noon the 2d Battalion line was stabilized. Now the 2d Battalion took over the fight on the left wing of the 101st, moving forward behind a rolling barrage to clear the woods north of Nothum. This attack made progress, but once again as dusk came on the enemy counterattacked. Company G, which had entered the woods to support the two assault companies there, either ran into the German advance or lost its way and was encircled; only half the company escaped.

The 104th Infantry lay on 31 December with its right facing along the Buderscheid-Wiltz road and its left facing north along and overlooking the Roullingen sector of the Bavigne-Wiltz road. Much of its strength had been diverted for the long north-south blocking line which guarded the division—and corps—east flank, but a battalion of the 328th Infantry was moving by truck and on foot to take over this task. Although the 104th Infantry had an attack mission and did push out a little through the woods to the north, most of the day was spent in an inconclusive firefight.

At the close of the year the 26th Division lay in a wedge, the 101st Infantry at the point around Nothum, the 104th on the right facing the diagonal formed by the Buderscheid section of the highway, and the 328th on the division left in the neighborhood of Bavigne. Both flanks of the division still were exposed and the troops were deployed on a very wide front, considering the broken character of the ground.

The old enemy—the Fuehrer Grenadier—had withdrawn during the last nights of December to go into the Seventh Army reserve at Wiltz, its place being taken by the 9th Volks Grenadier Division (Colonel Kolb). The 9th had been formed as one of the first German Army divisions in 1935 but no longer bore much resemblance to the formation that had fought in France and Russia. Almost completely destroyed during the withdrawal from Rumania, the 9th Volks Grenadier was reorganized and trained in Denmark, whence it was transferred to the Seventh Army. The very first battalion to arrive in the Sure area had been put into action to help the Fuehrer Grenadier and had been wiped out, a traumatic experience from which the rest of the division never seems to have fully recovered.

With the 6th Armored advance just getting under way on 1 January and the 35th Division grappled by the enemy in a seesaw battle, General Millikin gave orders for the 26th Division to attack on the 2d and cut the Wiltz-Bastogne highway, which was supporting not only the German Seventh Army but a portion of the enemy build-up east of Bastogne. General Paul determined to use his entire division in this operation. The two flank regiments were intended to make holding attacks only, leaving it to the 101st—in the center—to thrust northeast from Nothum and seize Hill 490, the latter just beyond the wooded junction where a secondary road from Roullingen met the main highway winding up from the Wiltz valley. By this time the 26th Division had learned the hard way what an attack over hills and ravines, through underbrush, tangled woods, and snowdrifts—with little room for maneuver—was like. General Paul arranged for the corps and division artillery to curtain the advance with a "rolling barrage of high intensity." This tactic was made easier because only one rifle battalion (the 2d, 101st Infantry) would make the assault—and in column of companies—into the triangle where Hill 490 lay.

The 2d Battalion jumped off in the attack at daybreak and hit the German outpost line just north of Mont Schumann. Toward the hill objective, less than a thousand yards ahead, the advance could move only at a crawl, for there was little space for maneuver on either side of the road. Roadblock followed roadblock, and the rifle companies had to squeeze past each other as the leader was pinned down by enemy tank and machine gun fire. A few of the American tank destroyers were able to find firing positions from which to engage the forward German tanks but could not get close enough to blast the panzers, which had been hidden in "trench garages" around the crown of Hill 490. By noon the 2d Battalion had come to a standstill and was completely fought out. General Paul ordered up his division reserve, the 3d Battalion of the 328th, to take a crack at the enemy in the tough triangle.

This abrupt renewal of activity in front of Wiltz had a much greater impact on the Seventh Army than a battalion attack normally would occasion. General Brandenberger and his chief of staff, General von Gersdorff, had become gravely concerned lest the American attacks around Marvie and Harlange should suddenly break through and trap the 5th Parachute Division in what the Germans now were calling "the Harlange pocket." The renewal of the 26th Division attack on 2 January and the threat to the Bastogne-Wiltz road increased this apprehension about the possibly precarious position of the 5th Parachute and the link it furnished between the Seventh and Fifth Panzer Armies. As a result General Brandenberger asked Model's permission to pull his troops back from Villers-la-Bonne-Eau and Harlange, but Model gave a nay, reminding the importunate army commander that Germany now was in a battle of attrition by which the Allies would become enmeshed and round down.

The VIII Corps' Attack Continues

The pitched battle with the 87th Division's 345th Infantry at Moircy on the night of 30 December had involved the reserve tanks and infantry supporting the thin-spread 902d, which was holding the Panzer Lehr left flank, and during the next afternoon the 345th captured Remagne without sustaining the usual counterattack. For a relatively untried outfit that had ridden a hundred miles, crowded in jolting trucks, and had gone into an attack over unfamiliar terrain all in the space of less than twenty hours, the 345th had done well. But it had taken many casualties, and now that the fresh 347th Infantry (Col. Sevier R. Tupper) had come up General Culin turned the advance on the division right wing over to the latter. The 346th continued its blocking mission at St. Hubert and Vesqueville. (Even the move into reserve cost the 345th lives and equipment, for the constant traffic uncovered and exploded German mines which earlier had lain harmless under the deep snow.)

The morning of 1 January came with snow, sleet, and bitter cold. The 347th set out from Moircy and Remagne, plowing through the drifts, its objective to cut the Bastogne-St. Hubert road al Amberloup. The 1st Battalion (Maj. Cecil Chapman) managed to put patrols across the highway north of Remagne. It had been advancing with two tanks in front of each company and the enemy reaction through the daylight hours was confined to small arms fire and occasional bursts of artillery. The 347th, however, was moving against that part of the 902d line which was backed with armor, for Bayerlein had put his assault guns in to stiffen the Panzer Lehr western terminus at St. Hubert and placed his few remaining tanks as backstop for the eastern flank. At dusk, when the sky was empty of the fighter-bombers, the enemy tanks struck and drove the 1st Battalion back toward Remagne.

The 3d Battalion (Lt. Col. Richard D. Sutton) moved north from Moircy along the road to Pironpré and at noon took the intermediate village of Jenneville, where Company C of the 345th had suffered a bloody head two days before. When the battalion defiled from Jenneville the German fire stepped up its cadence, and now the sharp bark of tank guns could be heard from Pironpré. The road junction at the latter point was of considerable concern to General Bayerlein. He could spare only a small detachment of grenadiers (probably no more than thirty were inside Pironpré), but he did put a half dozen tanks into the defense. These tanks were carefully sited to give maximum fire and were masked from the road by the piles of lumber surrounding the local sawmill. The Americans could not locate this opposition and halted for the night.

Before daybreak the two battalions went into attack positions close to the road which ran diagonally from St. Hubert to Morhet, set as the regimental line of departure. They left the hornet's nest at Pironpré undisturbed, moving around it on the right and left. This second day of the new year the 347th made progress. The 1st Battalion captured Gerimont and the 3d Battalion took Bonnerue, in the process losing four of its attached tanks to armor-piercing fire (probably from the panzers hidden in Pironpré). But by nightfall it was apparent that a dangerous gap had been created between the two battalions, and Colonel Tupper ordered his reserve battalion to clean out Pironpré and the thick woods beyond. The 87th Division now could claim that the Bastogne-St. Hubert road had been pierced because the seizure of Bonnerue had put a part of the 347th athwart this highway.

The 11th Armored Division had regrouped during the night of 30 December with the object of consolidating the entire division for a drive north along the Rechrival valley. CCA moved over the icy roads south of the Bois Des Haies de Magery, which had separated it from the rest of the division, and onto the Neufchâteau-Bastogne road, where the columns ran afoul of those of CCB, 6th Armored. In the morning CCA turned off the highway and assembled around Morhet. The new scheme of maneuver called for CCA to attack in the center of the valley, erupt from it at Rechrival and Hubermont, then capture Flamierge. CCR (Col. Virgil Bell) had been brought up from reserve to cover the CCA left flank in a sequence of blocking positions at Magerotte and Pinsamont where branch roads gave entrance to the Hubermont road. CCB, still entangled in the Chenogne fight, had orders to take that village and proceed along the east side of the valley—which would involve clearing the troublesome Bois Des Valets—until it reached its objective at Mande-St. Etienne. With Flamierge and Mande-St. Etienne held in force, the German line of communications west of Bastogne would be effectively blocked.

Now that General Kilburn had his whole division in hand, he took an optimistic view of the power play to be made on the 31st. Indeed his staff informed the 101st Airborne Division, with what was pardonable presumption when a green division was seeking to impress the veteran and haughty paratroopers, that Mande-St. Etienne would be taken by noon. In midmorning CCA passed CCB's Task Force Poker, which had laagered at Brul and Houmont the evening before and was waiting for Task Force Pat to get through Chenogne. Near Rechrival the march was interrupted by an enemy screening force that had been deployed by the 3d Panzer Grenadier to protect its western flank. This detachment, equipped with antitank and assault guns, was promptly reinforced by the 115th Regiment of the 15th Panzer Grenadier (reduced by the bloody attack west of Bastogne to battalion strength). Loosing a series of jabs at the head of the American column, the 115th used the Panzerfaust to put a number of tanks hors de combat. The ever-ready fighter-bombers intervened to help CCA with a strike on Rechrival, but in any case the American armor carried the weight necessary to push back the grenadiers, and after considerable reorganization the march resumed. Rechrival was found empty—apparently the Jabos had done their work well-and the command outposted for the night. Task Force Pat turned again to assault Chenogne at noon on the 31st, the armored infantry walking through knee-deep snow. The Sherman tanks mired in while attempting to cross a small creek, but the light tanks and a platoon of antiaircraft half-tracks wielding the dreaded .50-caliber quads gave sufficient fire power to force entry at the edge of the village. Inside was a scratch garrison recruited from the 39th Fuesilier Regiment (26th Volks Grenadier Division), the 3d Panzer Grenadier, and Remer's brigade. The mainstay of the defense in this sector, however, was a group of twelve to fifteen tank destroyers which had Mark IV carriages mounting the high-velocity, long-tube L70 guns. These were brought into action late in the day and drove the Americans out of Chenogne.

CCR carried out the first phase of its blocking mission with no opposition, scoured the woods northwest of Magerotte, and gained the ridge there. On the reverse slope some of Remer's grenadiers were entrenched, but the Shermans machine-gunned the way clear and the attack moved on to put in the next block at Pinsamont. German mortar and artillery fire was so intense here (this was a special groupment of weapons which Remer had positioned to protect his brigade's flank) that CCR withdrew to the Magerotte crest line. That night Remer's 3d Grenadier Battalion essayed two fruitless counter-attacks. This rather minor series of skirmishes on the 31st cost the 55th Armored Infantry Battalion over eighty casualties.

German action on this date was not solely directed against the 11th Armored. There was some fighting at Sibret, although by noontime Field Marshal von Rundstedt's headquarters had agreed that any further attempt to break through the Bastogne corridor via Sibret would have to await success by the eastern counterattack force. Surprisingly the enemy broke the quiet on the 502d Parachute Infantry front with a foray directed against Champs. Actually the attackers were trying to get a foothold in three houses just outside the village. The paratroopers reported two hours of "bitter fighting" before quiet was restored, for the enemy had been ably supported by artillery fire. Thirty prisoners were taken from what the 502d reported as an "assault wave" of three officers and fifty men. This minor affair is mentioned here only because it furnishes a very revealing commentary on the state of the German formations which had been in the Bastogne fight through all the recent days: the "assault wave" was the total strength of two rifle companies from the 77th Grenadier Regiment of the 26th Volks Grenadier Division.

If the 11th Armored attack was to click, the trailing right wing would have to break through at Chenogne. General Kilburn ruled that the main effort by the division on 1 January would be made by and in support of CCB. This attack would be coordinated with that of CCA, 9th Armored, which thus far was making no headway at Senonchamps to the east. At Chenogne, on the morning of the 1st, two medium tank companies made the assault after all the division artillery had cooperated in working the village over. This time the village was occupied with ease, although a few of the Mark IV tank destroyers had lingered long enough to stick their long barrels out of hayricks and destroy four Shermans. During the night the commander of the 3d Panzer Grenadier, apprehensive lest the American thrust in the valley crumple his supply lines, had withdrawn his right, leaving most of the large woods between Chenogne and Senonchamps unoccupied and reducing the garrisons in the two villages to covering shells.

Now for the first time Task Force Pat and Task Force Poker could make a coordinated effort and employ a force which was balanced tactically. The CCB fusion was aided in its sweep north through the Bois Des Valets by thirteen battalions of artillery whose sustained fire left a great number of the enemy dead in the woods. Colonel Yale believed that his combat command might achieve a quick stroke out of the woods and seize Mande-St. Etienne or at least its suburb, Monty. A short distance north of the Bois Des Valets the trail—for it was little more—ran between two wood lots. While passing between the two woods the leading platoon of Shermans bogged down. Just such a lapse was what the German bazooka men had been waiting for—they wiped out the platoon. CCB withdrew into a semicircle following the edge of the Bois Des Valets, and there the armored infantry, with no cover overhead, sweated out the night while the German shells burst in the trees.

Slow in getting started on 1 January, CCA had just begun to assemble on the road when it was surprised by a counterattack led by Remer. Most of the infantry belonging to the Fuehrer Begleit and its attached assault gun brigade were in the line screening the western flank of Denkert's 3d Panzer Grenadier Division, but on the 31st Remer's tank group and one of his grenadier battalions had been relieved for a little rest in the village of Fosset, northwest of Hubermont, there becoming the XLVII Panzer Corps reserve. Whether Remer or Luettwitz saw this glittering opportunity to take the American columns at Rechrival by surprise is uncertain. In any case Remer did achieve surprise by circling into the Bois Des Valets, then bursting onto his enemy.

Remer's tanks and assault guns knocked out a considerable number of American tanks, and the battle went on for three hours before CCA, the 11th Armored artillery, and the fighter-bombers succeeded in crushing the counterattack. At 1530 CCA was moving again. The fight had removed the sting from the German defense and the American tanks forged ahead rapidly, reaching Hubermont at twilight. Because the armored infantry had not kept pace with the tanks and, for all the Americans knew, another counterattack might be brewing, CCA retired and set up its lines around Rechrival and Brul.

That night the VIII Corps commander visited the 11th Armored command post at Morhet and ordered the division to consolidate its positions on the following day before it was relieved by the 17th Airborne Division. This word was relayed to the combat commands, but Colonel Yale, whose CCB was only mile or so from its original objective, Mande-St. Etienne, asked for and was given permission to take that town on 2 January. Ample artillery was wired in to support the attack—twelve battalions fired 3,800 rounds on 120 targets in and around Monty and Mande-St. Etienne. For some reason the attack started in midafternoon, probably too late to have made a quick and thorough purge of the German defenders. Both infantry and armored task forces got into the town but were forced to fight street to street and cellar to cellar all through the night before securing full possession.

When the 17th Airborne moved in on 3 January to take over from the 11th Armored Division, the 11th could look back at a bitterly contested advance of six miles in four days. The human cost had been 220 killed and missing and 441 wounded; the cost in matériel, 42 medium and 12 light tanks.

The failure of the Fifth Panzer Army to close the gap opened by Patton's troops at Bastogne convinced General Manteuffel that the time had arrived for the German forces in the Ardennes to relinquish all thought of continuing the offensive. Withdrawal in the west and south to a shortened line was more in keeping with the true combat capability of the gravely weakened divisions. At the end of the year Manteuffel had advised pulling back to the line Odeigne-La Roche-St. Hubert. By 2 January the VIII Corps' capture of Mande-St. Etienne so endangered the three weak divisions in the Rochefort sector at the tip of the salient that the Fifth Panzer Army commander went to Model with a plea for a general withdrawal by the two panzer armies to the line Vielsalm-Houffalize-Noville. This pessimistic but realistic view of the German situation was supported by Luettwitz, commanding in the west, who had expected as early as 28 December that the British would mount an attack in the

Rochefort area. His suspicions were confirmed on New Year's Day by the identification of the British 50th Infantry Division in the Allied line.

Model apparently gave tacit professional agreement to Manteuffel's views. But he was, quite literally, the prisoner of Hitler and the Nazi machine—it may be said that Model's life depended on continuing the fiction that the Wehrmacht would give no ground. So the staff at Army Group B continued to pore over maps and march tables for still another attack on 4 January to "erase" Bastogne. One may wonder what were the private thoughts of the old soldier Rundstedt as he watched the Allied divisions coming into array on the OB WEST situation map, readying for the kill. Whatever these thoughts, they remained his own for he no longer had the power or the prestige to influence Hitler or the course of the Ardennes battle. The last entry for the year 1944 in the OB WEST War Diary simply expresses the hope that the German initiative now lost in the Ardennes may be regained in the new offensive being unleashed that very moment against the American and French forces in Alsace. This new battle, however, would have little effect on the German forces which, on 3 January, faced the great Allied counteroffensive as it moved into high gear to flatten the Bulge and steamroller a path to and over the Rhine.

Chapter XXV. Epilogue

The Weather

There is an axiom that weather on the battlefield is divided equally between the combatants—but its impact on military operations is not equal in amount or direction. The German selection of a target date for the commencement of the Ardennes offensive turned on the prediction of poor flying weather. This type of weather had a useful side effect during the rupture of the American lines since it veiled the attacker with fog and mist, a very important feature of the initial German successes just as it had been in the great offensives of 1918. The high pressure system which came in from the Atlantic on 18 December, however, worked momentarily against the attacker. A thaw set in which slowed his tanks and the erstwhile heavy ground fog began to show sudden openings, such as those which exposed the German tanks and infantry during the fight at Noville. On the 20th and 21st the higher ground began to freeze in patches, leaving stretches of the Ardennes roads slippery and muddy. By the 22d competing weather systems from Russia and the Atlantic had brought on a hodgepodge of snow, blizzards, fog, and rain. In the north the Sixth Panzer Army was bogged by rain and mud, in the south the Fifth Panzer Army was hampered in its swing around Bastogne by fog and snow, and along the German supply roads back over the Eifel snow fell continuously.

The dramatic change of the 23d, brought by cold, dry winds from the east, stripped the German armies of their immunity to air attack. But this was not the whole story. Snow began to drift in the Eifel hills, bringing traffic on the main supply roads west of the Rhine almost to a standstill. Horse-drawn snowplows were few and ineffective, hastily erected snow fences were torn down by troops scrounging for firewood, there was no gravel available, and a large number of the engineer construction battalions had been taken west for employment as infantry. By the time power snowplows reached the Eifel the American fighter-bombers were strafing and bombing every large vehicle that moved. Engineers were brought into the Eifel, but their very efforts delayed the German truck columns so urgently needed farther west.

For five days the weather favored the Americans, in the air and on the ground. Superior numerically in tanks, the Americans benefited more than the Germans from the sure footing the big freeze provided for armor. Then, on 28 December, came clouds and overcast followed, a day later, by arctic air from Scandinavia, heavy snows, blizzards, and greatly reduced visibility at ground level. Vehicular movement was slow, the riflemen exhausted themselves wading through the drifts, and the wounded—those in a state of shock—died if left in the snow for more than half an hour or more. This was the state of the weather when, on 3 January, the Allies began their final counterattack.

The Opposing Troop Strengths

On the morning of 16 December the American forces in the path of the German counteroffensive comprised four and two-thirds divisions with an effective strength of about 83,000 men. The heavy weapons then available numbered 242 Sherman tanks, 182 tank destroyers, and 394 pieces of corps and divisional artillery. These troops and weapons were deployed on a meandering front of 104 miles.

The enemy assault divisions posed to the east had concentrated behind some ninety miles of the front manned by Army Group B, and during the night of 16 December over 200,000 combat troops gathered in the forward assembly area, about three miles in depth. The German attack, as it developed during the course of 16 December, was made on an assault front of sixty miles and included 5 armored divisions, 12 2/3 infantry divisions, and about 500 medium tanks, the whole supported by the fire of 1,900 guns and Wefers.

Although it is impossible to measure the exact number of rifle battalions and tank battalions committed by the Germans during the initial breakthrough attack, it is probable that the over-all ratio of German infantry to American was three to one, with a ratio of six to one at points of concentration. German armored superiority was somewhat less pronounced during the first-day assault, only about two to one in medium tanks. If the self-propelled guns employed in a tank role are considered, the superiority enjoyed by the attacker was about four to one.

By 2 January 1945, the eve of the Allied attack to destroy the Ardennes salient, the Germans had thrown 8 armored divisions, 20 infantry divisions, and 2 mechanized brigades into the Battle of the Bulge. During these eighteen days the Americans had employed 8 armored, 16 infantry, and 2 airborne division in the line. This tabulation of the opposing divisions, however, does not give a true measure of the relative combat strength deployed in what may be called the German phase of the winter battle in the Ardennes.

The American rifle division in 1944 was organized at a strength of 14,032 men, and most of the divisions engaged in this operation entered the fray at full complement. The personnel strength of the German infantry divisions varied, at the time of their commitment, between 8,000 and 17,000, the lower figure representing those divisions which had been refitted at 80 percent of the 1944 Volks Grenadier division table of organization and equipment and the upper figure, which can be applied to only three or four divisions, representing those, like the 26th Volks Grenadier Division, which retained the older, regular infantry division composition. The strength of the German infantry divisions across the board probably averaged little more than 10,000 men. The normal German rifle regiment numbered 1,868 as contrasted with the American infantry regiment of 3,207 officers and men.

The majority of the German panzer divisions had the same manpower configuration as the two U.S. square armored divisions (the 2d and 3d), that is, a little more than 14,000. The six remaining US armored divisions had the new triangular organization with a roster reduced to 10,666 officers and men. The armored weight of the opposing divisions, however, strongly favored the Americans, for the German panzer division brought an average of 90 to 100 medium tanks into the field whereas the American triangular division was equipped with 186 and the two square divisions had 232 medium tanks in their organization tables. Hitler personally attempted to compensate for this disparity by ordering the attachment of separate Army tank battalions of 40 to 50 Panther or Tigers to the regular panzer divisions.

The battle area during the period of 16 December through 3 January has to be measured as a salient in which the relation between the width of the base and the depth of the penetration represents a measure of the adequacy of the forces employed and their operational mobility. The German failure to break through on the north shoulder at Monschau had considerable impact on the width of the planned assault front, and by 18 December the base of the salient had stabilized at a width of forty-seven air-line miles, narrower than desired. The greatest depth of the German penetration, achieved on the tenth day of the attack, was about sixty airline miles. On that date, however, the average width of the salient had been reduced to thirty miles and at its tip measured no more than a five-mile front facing the Meuse. Indeed, the width of the assault front proper can be considered as the range of the 75-mm. guns of the 2d Panzer tanks. By this time the Americans had something approaching a coordinated and homogenous line as a retaining wall north and south of the salient, with a frontage of nearly seven miles per division on the north flank and a little more than thirteen miles on the southern flank.

The Opposing Weapons

Although winter in the Ardennes placed severe limitations on the use of armor, the tank was a major weapon in the hands of both antagonists. The Sherman tank, a medium of the thirty-ton class, bore the brunt of all American armored action, while the light tank was relegated to minor tactical tasks. The Sherman (M4) was battle tested, and most of the mechanical bugs had been removed. Its major weakness—tank gun and armor—by this time were well appreciated by the user. A new model, the M4A3, had been equipped with a to replace the old, short-barreled 75-mm., but not many of these were in the European Theater of Operations. Also, a very few Shermans had been modified to carry a heavier weight of armor plate—the so-called Jumbo tanks. The Jumbos, which had been tried out during the autumn fighting, proved so successful that General Patton ordered their use as lead tanks in the drive to Bastogne-but most American tankers never saw the Jumbo in December 1944.

The Germans had a family of three main battle tanks. The Mark IV, which received its first real combat test in May 1940, weighed twenty-seven tons, had somewhat less armor than the Sherman, about the same maximum road speed, and a tank gun comparable in weight of projectile and muzzle velocity to the 76-mm. American tank gun but superior to the short-barreled 75-mm.

The Panther, Mark V, had proved itself during 1944 but still was subject to mechanical failures which were well recognized but which seemingly could not be corrected in the hasty German production schedules. This tank had a weight of fifty tons, a superiority in base armor of one-half to one inch over the Sherman, good mobility and flotation, greater speed, and a high-velocity gun superior even to the new American 76-mm. tank gun.

The Tiger, Mark VI, had been developed as an answer to the heavy Russian tank but had encountered numerous production difficulties (it had over 26,000 parts) and never reached the field in the numbers Hitler desired. The original model weighed fifty-four tons, had thicker armor than the Panther, including heavy top armor as protection against air attack, was capable of a speed comparable to the Sherman, and mounted a high-velocity 88-mm. cannon. A still heavier Mark VI, the King Tiger, had an added two to four inches of armor plate. Few of this model ever reached the Ardennes, although it was commonly reported by American troops.

Exact figures on German tank strength are not available, but it would appear that of the estimated 1,800 panzers in the Ardennes battle some 250 were Tigers and the balance was divided equally between the Mark IV and the Panther. Battle experience in France, which was confirmed in the Ardennes, gave the Sherman the edge over the Mark IV in frontal, flank, and rear attack. The Panther often had been beaten by the Sherman during the campaign in France, and would be defeated on the Ardennes battleground, but in nearly all cases of a forthright tank engagement the Panther lost only when American numerical superiority permitted an M4 to get a shot at flank or tail. Insofar as the Tiger was concerned, the Sherman had to get off a lucky round or the result would be strictly no contest.

American and German divisional artillery was very similar, having followed the same developmental pattern during the 1930'S. Differences in corps artillery were slight, although the Germans placed more emphasis on long-range guns in the heavy calibers, 170-mm. and above. The German Army, as the result of its battles on the Eastern Front and experiences with the Soviet rocket artillery, placed great faith in the Wefer, a multiple-tube rocket launcher. This weapon was easy to produce and could be easily transported, a major design feature when the production of heavy trucks and artillery prime movers began to fall off in the Reich. The 150-mm. version weighed only 1,200 pounds and could fire a quarter-ton of high explosives in ten seconds; the 210-mm. model weighed about a ton and a half and could discharge over half a ton of high explosives per salvo. These weapons lacked the accuracy and fire control features of conventional artillery, and because of the blast could be readily spotted, but their mobility seems to have been a major feature in carrying German firepower forward during the Ardennes offensive.

American and German doctrine and organization for the employment of infantry-support weapons had followed different paths during the development cycle between the two World Wars when the problem of the "infantry—accompanying gun" had plagued all armies. The German Army ultimately opted for a self-propelled 75-mm. assault gun designed to help the infantry platoon forward in the assault and, at the same time, to provide a real antitank capability. The concept and the weapon had proved themselves on the Eastern Front, but the battle wastage of this weapon, like that of the assault infantry it supported, was extraordinarily high. In December 1944, the German infantry used a battle drill and tactics "leaning" on an accompanying weapon which no longer could be issued in proper numbers to even the most favored divisions. German battle commanders invariably point to the lack of this weapon in explaining particular failures of their infantry in battle.

The American approach to this problem reflected the opposition of the US Army to dual-purpose weapons, and as a result the US rifle regiment carried both a cannon company and an antitank company. On the whole neither of these units performed as desired during the Ardennes battle. The howitzers of the cannon company seemed to fire effectively only when tied with the divisional artillery, the 57-mm. antitank gun lacked the punch to meet German tanks, and, what was worse, most division commanders looked upon these weapons companies as providing additional riflemen to put into the foxhole line. So it was on the thinly held American front of 16 December.

The American self-propelled 90-mm. tank destroyer and the 88-mm. German equivalent were much feared, or at the least highly respected, for they had the power to penetrate the armor they faced, they could jockey for position along the winding Ardennes roads and defiles, and they were hard to destroy. Both antagonists used 75-mm. towed antitank weapons and both lost these towed weapons and other towed artillery in large numbers. In the mud and snow, and under direct fire and infantry assault, the task of limbering gun to truck or tractor was difficult and hazardous. Furthermore, in heavy and close combat the tow vehicle often was shot up or immobilized while the gun, dug in, remained intact. The mobile, tactically agile, self-propelled, armored field artillery and tank destroyers are clearly traceable in the Ardennes fighting as over and over again influencing the course of battle. Their record should be pondered in the design of tactics and missiles.

The difficult terrain on which the winter campaign was fought, the prevalence of pitched battles at night and in fog, the tactical failure of the American 57-mm. antitank gun, and the paucity of German assault guns and self-propelled tank destroyers brought the bazooka into a place of prominence on both sides of the line. Admittedly the bazooka was a suicide weapon, but there were always brave men—mostly platoon and squad leaders—to risk its use against an enemy tank. In the autumn of 1944 the German Army recognized that it was too late for building tank destroyers in the numbers required and that in any case fuel was lacking for their transport into battle. Therefore the decision was made to build hand rocket weapons and rely on the courage of the "single fighter"—a decision like that made in 1917–1918 when the Kaiser's army turned to armor-piercing rifles in the hands of the single fighter to stop Allied tanks. In December 1944 both sides learned that infantry companies armed with bazookas could not do the work of tank destroyers.

The success of field artillery as an antidote to the tank is difficult to assess quantitatively. American and German doctrine taught that long-range artillery could be used to break up tank concentrations before these reached the infantry zone. In the Ardennes, however, American artillery groupments not only performed this interdiction role but on numerous occasions stopped the tank assault right at the rifle line. Surprisingly enough, in several of those battles where causative agents in tank kills could be determined by postmortem possession of the battle area, the high explosives fired by American field artillery accounted for a large share of the kills made, although the actual damage inflicted may have been no more than a broken track or sprocket wheel.

Mortars, machine guns, and rifles functioned in a comparable manner on both sides of the line. Here the design of the infantry weapon proved less important in the bloody competition of the firefight than the supply of ammunition, the numbers employed, and the small unit tactics. The single exception is the machine pistol, which had been issued in large numbers to the new Volks Grenadier divisions and was very successfully employed by the German special assault companies formed in each infantry regiment.

Weapons and fire control turned mainly on wire communications, laid forward to observation posts and back to command posts. The vulnerability of telephone wire was adequately demonstrated on the morning of 16 December and throughout the campaign—yet it continued to be the primary means of tactical communication. Radio, of the type used in late 1944, lacked the necessary range and constantly failed in the woods and defiles. Both sides engaged in jamming, but for the most part the really damaging interference came from friendly transmitters.

Three additional items of equipment deserve attention in the history of the December battle: the V-weapon, the searchlight, and the proximity fuze. The V-weapon turned out to have no tactical significance, although the German high command stepped up the attack on the Allied depots at Antwerp and Liège during the Ardennes offensive, averaging at least 121 firings a week against Liège and 235 against Antwerp. These mostly were the pilotless aircraft or V-1 type, bearing 2,240 pounds of explosive. The military casualties inflicted by this V-weapons attack were slight, except for one strike on 16 December which destroyed an Antwerp cinema, killing 296 British soldiers and wounding 194.

Searchlights had been used by the Allies to illuminate the battlefield during the North African and Italian campaigns. However, the six battalions of tank-mounted searchlights (Canal Defense Lights) which the Americans brought into Normandy had been reconverted in November for normal armored use on the grounds that no "operational requirement" for the Canal Defense Light existed. The Germans had produced a large number of searchlights for use with flak batteries in the defense of major target centers in the Reich. In early December OB WEST ran two tests of searchlights in a ground role, with and without troops. These tests showed that an accidented battlefield could be extensively illuminated in front of attacking infantry. As a result some two hundred searchlights were gathered immediately behind the assault front and, on the morning of 16 December, flicked on to guide the first waves of infantry and to point targets, by cloud reflection, during the artillery preparation. Although very successful in assisting the assault companies over the first one or two thousand yards, the 60-cm. lights (with a ground range of little more than three thousand yards) could not keep up with the attack, and a number of German detachments, supposed to guide on the searchlight beams, wandered away from their objectives. Some of these smaller lights were brought forward and appeared in attacks as late as 18 December, but the ponderous 150- and 200-cm. lights seem to have been left behind at the original line of departure.

The proximity fuze, a tightly guarded American secret design for detonating projectiles by external influence in the close vicinity of a target, without explosion by contact, got its first battle test in a ground role during the Ardennes. This fuze, also known as the VT or POZIT fuze, had been prepared for some 210,000 rounds of artillery ammunition on the Continent in December. Most of this stock was antiaircraft artillery ammunition, and the 12th Army Group had proposed to try it out in the so-called Liège River Belt, the cordon of antiaircraft gun battalions which was organized to shoot down the V-weapons in flight to Liège. On 16 December a few field artillery battalions in the First Army had small stocks of the new ammunition, a few had witnessed demonstrations, and a very few had fired it. Two battalions in the VIII Corps artillery had been issued some rounds of VT ammunition, but so far as can be determined none were fired on the first day of the German attack. Actually this highly secret ammunition was employed on only a few occasions prior to the Allied counterattack in early January, and then usually at night or in poor weather when the

American gunners could not get sensing for normal time fire missions. The postwar claims as to the value of the much touted VT fuze in halting the German advance are grossly exaggerated.

American records on the causes of combat wounds and deaths are woefully inadequate and German records for this period do not exist. In the Third Army it is reckoned—in a very broad manner—that during the period 1 August-31 November 1944 the causative agent for between 27 and 30 percent of the total wounded admitted to Army hospitals was the gunshot wound, while high explosive agents (artillery shell, mortar shell, bombs, mines, and the like) accounted for between 50 and 60 percent of the monthly rosters of wounded. During December these two causative agents respectively accounted for 25 percent and 60 percent of the wounded. There is no accurate accounting for the causative agent in the case of men killed in action.

The Artillery Arm in the Ardennes

The dramatic and successful offensive operations of the German Army in the early years of World War II had featured the extensive employment of assault aircraft to punch the holes through which the panzers poured. At the close of 1944 the Third Reich lacked the planes which once had provided the airborne "artillery" of blitzkrieg. So Hitler, the infantryman of World War I, turned to the time-tested tactic he knew, massive artillery preparation for the ground assault. In many ways the German use of the artillery arm on 16 December was a carbon copy of the artillery preparations for the great offensives in 1918. But there were some major differences. Intense counterbattery fire, a necessary feature of the artillery preparations in 1918, no longer was possible; Germany lacked the huge ammunition stocks required. Captive balloons and observation planes had directed the movement of artillery fire in 1918. These auxiliaries were missing in the Ardennes, and ground observation there normally favored the Americans. Ludendorff had been able to mass ninety heavy caliber guns per kilometer for the March offensive. Model would have fewer than twenty tubes for each kilometer of the assault front.

Hitler, looking back to 1918, had demanded a massive artillery preparation lasting for two or three hours, and this in full daylight. Probably at Manteuffel's instigation, he finally agreed that a short, sharp, predawn artillery preparation—of the sort conventionally practiced on the Eastern Front—would be used in the Ardennes. There seems to have been no gigantic, homogeneous artillery fire plan on 16 December, as had been the practice in 1918. In the Sixth Panzer Army a 30-minute preparation was fired on villages and deep assembly positions to the rear of the American line, and followed by unobserved area fire along the main line of resistance. The guns and Wefers in the Fifth Panzer Army fired forty rounds per tube in the first twenty minutes against predesignated targets, then commenced a rolling barrage, the old World War I Feuerwalze, with sixty rounds at each piece.

There were deviations from this pattern in accordance with the ground and estimated American strength. The 26th Volks Grenadier Division, for example, advanced behind a preparation fired by three hundred tubes which, for seventeen minutes, worked over targets illuminated by searchlights. The Seventh Army, which had a relatively small number of artillery and Wefer battalions, was forced to concentrate its fire on a few selected target areas. The most intensive preparation fired here was in support of the two assault regiments of the 5th Parachute Division: to smooth its advance seventy-two guns fired ninety rounds each as fast as the cannoneers could work their pieces. All three of the armies relied upon the speed and shock of the initial assault to overrun any deep American artillery groupments which might be in position to menace the infantry and armored advance.

There is no doubt that the German artillery helped the assault waves forward during the rupture of the American forward defensive positions. It is equally clear that the German artillery failed to keep pace with the subsequent advance, nor did it come forward rapidly enough to assist substantially in the reduction of those American points of resistance which had been left in the rear of attacking echelons. The relative immobility of corps and army artillery may be ascribed to bad roads, the lack of heavy, fully tracked artillery prime movers, and traffic congestion. The road jam at the Our bridges delayed the forward displacement of the LVIII Panzer Corps artillery until 19 December, and then only a few batteries crossed the river. The switch southward of the Sixth Panzer Army's main effort on 17 December blocked the roads on which Manteuffel was moving the Fifth Panzer artillery. The artillery corps attached to the II SS Panzer Corps took five days to reach firing positions east of Butgenbach, just to the rear of the original American line.

All these delays had a mirror-image in the transport of ammunition. This resulted in an early decision by the artillery officers of the three armies to leave about half of the guns and Wefers behind. Wefer battalions and brigades were not moved up to share in the battle until the end of December, and only a few reached the front lines. In the main the German assault infantry were forced to rely on the fire support given by tanks and assault guns, rather than massed artillery fire. There were exceptions, however, and by dint of great effort the Germans occasionally were able to create artillery groupments which, following the practice learned on the Eastern Front, became artillery "centers of gravity." This was done by the Seventh Army commander in an attempt to get his flank moving on 19 and 20 December, and a similar groupment was prepared by Model and Manteuffel to pave the way for the Bastogne counterattacks at the close of December.

Throughout the exploitation and stabilization phase of the German offensive the Americans enjoyed an immense superiority in the artillery arm. This was not true, however, during the first hours of the German attack to rupture the American defenses. On 16 December the VIII Corps artillery was caught off balance, since eight of its nine battalions were positioned to support the untried 106th Division. The 99th Division, on the north flank, had only one battalion of corps artillery in support. And the records show only 2,500 rounds shot by American corps artillery in planned defensive and counterpreparation fires on the first day of the battle.

There are a number of reasons for the American failure to apply the full weight of the artillery arm on 16 December. The initial enemy shellfire did severe damage to the US artillery communications net. Even after repairs were made, intelligence as to the German locations and intentions moved very slowly from command post to command post (the 559th Field Artillery Battalion, for example, received no warning of the German force to its front until 1215). The firing battalions supporting the 106th Division were hampered by "no-fire" lines earlier established by the division, and there seems to have been little or no attempt to lift these restrictions as the enemy assault waves swept forward to grapple the American infantry. Corps artillery proved quite as vulnerable to a fast-moving ground attack as the divisional gunners, and as early as 1035 the VIII Corps artillery was displacing rearward on orders. The towed battalions, particularly the 155-mm. and 8-in. artillery, took long to limber and even longer to find a place on the crowded roads leading west; it is not surprising that they fell prey quite as often to German infantry as to panzers. A large portion of the VIII Corps artillery was forced to displace so often that two to four days would elapse before the battalions finally settled long enough to engage the enemy. Other battalions simply were whittled away by enemy action every time they went into firing position (the 687th Field Artillery Battalion was overrun in front of Wiltz, in Wiltz, and west of Wiltz). Observation was very poor until midafternoon on the 16th, no artillery planes got up, and unobserved fire on the German West Wall positions pounded assembly areas long since left behind by the enemy moving west.

The artillery fire fight on the first day of the attack and for most of the second was carried by the divisional howitzer battalions, which began to engage observed targets two and a half to three hours after the start of the German preparation. Many of these battalions were firing with only one eye, since wire to a number of observations posts went out by 0630, others were systematically engulfed during the morning by the German assault companies, all microphones for sound-ranging were out of operation by the evening of the 16th, and several of those batteries which were firing lost their ammunition trucks in the melee along the roads to the rear. Many of the forward batteries were put out of action as soon as the infantry line to their front broke; others fired until the evening of the 17th and still were able to withdraw successfully.

Did the American gunners blunt or delay the first German thrust? At Monschau the artillery stopped the attack cold, effectively narrowing the German assault front. In the 99th Division sector the division artillery held its ground until the close of the 17th when the V Corps artillery groupment at Elsenborn took over the fight with such a weight of metal that one infantry battalion was covered by a defensive barrage of 11,500 rounds during the night of 17 December. The Fifth Panzer Army, on the contrary, was little impeded by the scant collection of American artillery to its front. On the German left wing the Seventh Army advance was damaged considerably by the American howitzers, for the batteries here retained their link to the observation posts on the heights overlooking the Sure River and succeeded in delaying the German bridging efforts for many hours.

As the American defense solidified along the shoulders of the salient or at strong points, such as St. Vith and Bastogne, the artillery arm really commenced to make its weight felt. Experienced German artillery officers estimate that their American opponents finally had a superiority in guns and ammunition of ten to one. This estimate is far too high: the Americans fired about 1,255,000 artillery rounds during the fighting covered in this account and by 23 December had brought a total of 4,155 artillery pieces into action. Just as in 1918, however, the attacker had driven the defense back upon its artillery base of fire, meanwhile progressively losing his own firepower. The Germans tend to characterize the American artillery fire as methodical, schematic, and wasteful. There is considerable indication that the German commanders quickly recognized and made gainful tactical use of the gaps at division and corps boundaries where the defenders conventionally failed to provide overlapping fire between zones. Also, it is probable, as the enemy alleges, that the American gunners fired a very considerable weight of ammunition for each German killed. On the other hand the record is replete with instances in which the attacker was diverted from his axis of advance and his scheme of maneuver was destroyed by American artillery fire, even when he suffered little physical damage. This phenomenon became even more apparent after the American spotter planes took to the air.

The German offensive phase of the Ardennes operation, with its high degree of fluidity and dispersion, may offer profitable suggestions for the future fluid battlefield. The experience of the First Army, which generously sent its medium artillery reserves south to stiffen the defense, showed the hazard in moving isolated and road-bound units with heavy equipment across the grain of the enemy advance, even when the attack was believed to be miles away. Medium and heavy corps artillery units were quite as vulnerable to enemy ground attack as the forward divisional artillery, particularly when the attacker was moving cross-country and the artillery equipment was difficult to displace and bound to the road. Displacing single batteries by leapfrog tactics in order to maintain unbroken defensive fires failed repeatedly during the first days of the Ardennes, largely because of the splitting effect of the German ground assault that isolated firing batteries and crippled control or resupply by the headquarters battery. Those forward American batteries which worked their guns, brought them off, and lived to fire another day, normally owed their tactical survival to other arms and weapons. The artillery battalion of 1944 was not organically constructed or equipped to beat off close-in infantry or armored assault, but the fortuitous attachment of antiaircraft weapons sections, although these no longer did much service in their primary role, gave the gunners an antipersonnel weapon which proved to be murderously effective. The attachment of tank destroyers to the artillery battalions also paid substantial dividends in the early days of the campaign. The most effective defense of beleaguered field artillery units, however, was that provided by prompt counterattack delivered by neighboring infantry or tanks, a tactic which turned on accurate local intelligence, unbroken communications, and the enemy inability to deflect the counterattack force with heavy supporting weapons or mines.

The Air Weapon

Postwar estimates of the Luftwaffe operational strength assigned to support the ground attack on 16 December set the number of first-line planes at about fifteen hundred. But German planes never, in the course of the campaign, appeared over the battle area in any such number. OB WEST records 849 sorties dispatched to assist the ground attack on 18 December, the largest Luftwaffe attempt to intervene directly in the Ardennes battle. The tabulation of German sorties is somewhat misleading, however, because a relatively small proportion of these sorties ever reached the battlefield in a ground support role and most were engaged by the Allied air forces far to the east of the ground combat zone. On 24 December, for example, a day characterized by the IX Tactical Air Command as the heaviest Luftwaffe effort since D-day, the Third Army — whose counterattack obviously invited retaliation from the air — reported the sighting of only one enemy squadron.

During the first ten days of the campaign the Luftwaffe sorties sent into the air varied between six and eight hundred per day. In the last six days of December the Luftwaffe was driven back to the air space over the Third Reich and the number of planes actually reaching the battlefield numbered between sixty and eighty a day, most of which struck under cover of darkness, as in the case of the 73-plane raid over Bastogne on 30 December.

At no point in the story of the ground battle can any crippling impact of German air attack be discerned. Nor was the Luftwaffe notably successful in defending the supply lines west of the Rhine. The German fighters did exact a heavy toll from the Allied planes hammering at rail yards, bridges, and supply installations. Thus the

391st Bombardment Group, flying Marauders without escort to attack the Ahrweiler railroad bridge, was jumped by about seventy-five German fighters, and lost one-half of its thirty-six planes, though it did knock out the bridge.

In the first week of the German advance the well-established Allied superiority in the air hardly made itself felt in the battle area, although two fighter-bomber groups from IX Tactical Air Command did intervene in the fighting around Stavelot and Malmédy on 18 December. But the adverse weather which denied the tactical air forces access to the fight on the ground did not halt the bombers and on 18 December bombers from the RAF, began an interdiction attack seventy-five miles or more to the east of the battle line. It is difficult to measure the damage done the German rail system west of the Rhine by Allied bombing during this early phase because the exorbitant amount of military traffic moving to support the attack resulted in severe congestion which, on a number of feeder lines, forced troops and equipment to detrain far to the east of their planned destination.

When the weather altered on the 23d, battlefield operations started to take precedence over the Allied interdiction effort. The IX, XIX, and XXIX Tactical Air Commands flew 294 sorties against targets in the forward edge of the battlefield, but this effort still represented only a minor fraction of the Allied air operations designed to stall the German advance. The Eighth Air Force and 9th Bombardment Division dropped 1,300 tons of bombs on the enemy supply lines west of the Rhine, while the Royal Air Force Bomber Command hit the Seventh Army railhead at Trier with 150 planes.

On 24 December The Allied air forces threw into action the greatest number of planes employed during the Ardennes. The Americans flew 1,138 tactical sorties (of which 734 were ground support missions in the battle zone) and 2,442 bomber sorties. Most of the latter were aimed at German airfields, but 1,521 tons of bombs were laid on rail centers and bridges. The 2d Tactical Air Force (British) flew 1,243 sorties during the day. There followed three days of good flying weather which gave the American and British fighter-bombers opportunity for a sustained attack against German supply movement, road centers, and armored vehicles. Commencing on 28 December very poor flying weather intervened to give the German divisions some respite from air attack. The Allies put up less than a hundred battlefield sorties on this and succeeding days, but even such a limited effort had an important effect on the ground battle, as witness the intervention of the 406th Bombardment Group in the Bastogne fight on the 30th.

The direct damage inflicted on the German ground formations by the Allied fighter-bombers is difficult to gauge and, of course, varied greatly. A regimental attack set by the 26th Volks Grenadier Division on 23 December had to be postponed until the Jabos quit for the day; on that same date the entire 116th Panzer Division marched in broad daylight from Hotton to Marche without difficulty. Yet there was a very appreciable increase in night attacks by the German ground forces as the Jabos' killing power mounted, beginning on Christmas Day and culminating in Model's order on the 26th forbidding major march movements in daylight.

The Allied tactical air operations in the main were directed against armored fighting vehicles, motor transport, and large troop concentrations. The thin-skinned supply vehicles which lacked tracks to carry them off the narrow, winding roads presented an easy target. German tanks were another matter. The IX, XIX, and XXIX Tactical Air Commands and 2d Tactical Air Force (British) claimed the destruction of 413 enemy armored vehicles. But a sample ground count of stricken German armor sets the number of kills inflicted by air attack at about a tenth the number claimed by the fighter-bomber pilots.

Air attack against the choke points that developed along the main and subsidiary German supply roads seriously impeded both tactical and logistic movement, but much of the over-all delay should be charged to poor German traffic control and road maintenance. Here again the record of achievement by the air is uneven. Movement on the Koblenz-Trier autobahn, a major supply artery for the two southern armies, never was seriously restricted by Allied air attack. As might be expected, the overall effectiveness of air attacks along the roads turned on the configuration of the ground. The 9th Bombardment Division put 136 tons of high explosive on St. Vith, which stood in the open with a wealth of bypass routes around it on relatively level ground, and stopped the German traffic not at all. Even when the RAF dropped 1,140 tons in a carpet bombing attack at St. Vith, the road center was out of commission for only a day. Yet a mere 150 tons put on La Roche over a period of two days stopped all major movement in this sector of the Ardennes road net. La Roche, be it noted, lay at the bottom of a gorge with access only through deep defiles.

The damaging effect of the Allied air attacks against rail lines, bridges, and marshaling yards at and west of the Rhine is quite clear in the history of the Ardennes campaign, but the time sequence between specific rail failures and the resulting impact on German frontline operations is difficult to trace. From 2 December to 2 January the Eighth Air Force, 9th Bombardment Division, and Royal Air Force Bomber Command made daily attacks against selected railway bridges and marshaling yards using an average of 1,800 tons of bombs per day. Yet the day before this bombing campaign began, feeder rail lines in the Eifel had been so crippled by air attack that through movement from the Rhine to the army railheads was no longer possible and supplies were being moved by truck and wagon between the "traffic islands" where rail movement remained in effect. German reports indicate that this transshipment from one mode of transport to another — and back again — cost at least forty-eight hours' delay. By the 26th railway bridges were out on the vital Ahr and Moselle lines, supporting the two southern armies, and the Seventh Army railhead had been pushed back to Wengerohr, near Wittlich. On the 28th the rail center at Koblenz, supporting the German left wing, was put out of operation. And by the close of the year German repair organizations could do no more than attempt to keep some of the railroad island traffic moving.

In retrospect the German effort to keep the railroads operating in support of Army Group B was phenomenal. Five of the eight railroad bridges across the Rhine were put out of service temporarily, generally by bomb damage to the bridge approaches, but all came back into service. Allied air inflicted eighty-five breaks on the Army Group B rail lines west of the Rhine and fifty-four of these were repaired. But in the last week before the Allied ground counteroffensive any hope of maintaining a satisfactory ratio between damage and repair had vanished. Of nine railroad bridges over the Ahr, Moselle, and Nette Rivers, which were designated as high priority targets for air attack, eight were put out of operation on one or more occasions, while for the six restored the average repair time was five days per bridge. The cumulative effect of this kind of damage simply saturated the German capabilities for rail repair.

Despite Allied domination of the air over the Ardennes, the Eifel, and the Rhine plain, the battlefield itself and the German armies therein never were isolated. Could the isolation of the battlefield have been accomplished? The terrain, with its sequence of river barriers and multitude of winding, steep gradients, was favorable to air interdiction. But the tactical ingredients and formula to achieve complete success were missing in late 1944. Sturdy rail bridges, particularly when defended by ground to air fire, proved hard to damage and even harder to destroy. Even the smaller bridges, such as those attacked in the Ahr River campaign, took some 250 tons of high explosive to cripple. Rail cutting attacks caused traffic islands but never succeeded in rooting out these islands or the movement between them. Movement by thin-skinned vehicles on trails, roads, and highways seemed particularly vulnerable but the physical blockage of the roads, as distinct from vehicular destruction, could be achieved only at particularly favorable points and for relatively short intervals of time. Finally, the Allied inability to operate aircraft in a ground assault role during the night and the long stretches of bad flying weather provided a built-in guarantee that the minimum supply and reinforcement requirements of the German armies would be met.

Although the Allied air forces failed to isolate the Ardennes battlefield, they did succeed in these days in dealing the Luftwaffe a mortal blow, thus making the task of their comrades on the ground much easier in 1945, on both the Western and the Eastern Fronts. Generalleutnant Adolf Galland, commander of the Luftwaffe fighter arm, has written the Luftwaffe epitaph in this manner: "The Luftwaffe received its death blow at the Ardennes offensive. In unfamiliar conditions and with insufficient training and combat experience, our numerical strength had no effect. It was decimated while in transfer, on the ground, in large air battles, especially during Christmas, and was finally destroyed."

Logistics

During the years following the invasion of Poland the German munitions of war had wasted away, so much so that in December 1944 the German armies in the Ardennes were fighting a poor man's battle. The total stock of 105-mm. gun-howitzer ammunition at the beginning of November 1944 was only half the size of the stock available on 1 September 1939 and the number of 105-mm. rounds was less than a third the number stocked in Germany at the beginning of the Polish campaign. It was still possible even so to gather a substantial ammunition reserve for the Ardennes offensive, and after the war the supply officers at OKW were able to say that before the US counterattack on 3 January 1945 there was no shortage of artillery ammunition in the field. This statement merely reflects the rarefied and isolated view of the high headquarters, for despite the 100 ammunition trains of the special Fuehrer Reserve the troops in the Ardennes operation did suffer from a shortage of ammunition. This shortage was reported as early as 21 December by the divisions attacking at Bastogne. Thereafter, as the American front solidified, the Germans consumed ammunition at a rate of 1,200 tons per day, a rate much higher than predicted by the OKW planning staffs but less than the tactical requirements of the battle. The lack of ammunition should be charged to transport failure rather than to paucity of artillery shells at the Rhine dumps. The Panzer Lehr Division, for example, first reported that it had run out of gas, then on 28 December reported a shortage of ammunition because of the "lack of transport."

The American troops, by contrast, never suffered any notable failure of ammunition at the guns. In fact, the only munitions which appear to have been in short supply during the German offensive were antitank mines and bazooka rounds. The demand for these items and rifle and machine gun ammunition was constant, but the supply line was kept full by calling forward bazooka rockets and small arms ammunition from ships in the English Channel and North Sea. Also, the 12th Army Group had built up a very sizable reserve of artillery ammunition during the first half of December in preparation for the Roer River attacks. Most of the American ammunition stocks were put on wheels (trucks or railroad cars) after 19 December. The Third Army, for example, was able to move an average of 4,500 tons of ammunition per day during the last half of December and consumed, on the average, only 3,500 tons per day.

German tank losses during the operation are unknown but appear to have been very high, probably as much from mechanical failure as from battle damage. For the 1,700 to 1,800 tanks and assault guns in Army Group B, there were only six tank repair companies. Even worse was the shortage of tank retrievers, and, after 23 December, the few available were extremely hard hit by air attack. The spare parts situation was so bad that new German tanks were cannibalized at a depot west of Koblenz. Three hundred and forty new tanks were assigned to the Western Front during the campaign, but only 125 can be traced as actually reaching the armored divisions.

The First and Third US Armies had a full complement of medium tanks when the Germans struck, that is, 1,882 between them. During the last half of December the two armies lost a total of 471 medium tanks. These losses were partially made up when 21 Army Group released 351 Shermans which had been allocated for British use. A few American ordnance companies were overrun in the first hours of the battle, but most of the tank maintenance personnel and equipment were moved out of enemy reach and continued to function effectively. The losses in divisional artillery pieces were replaced in part by a British loan of 100 25-pounders plus 300,000 rounds of ammunition for them. The 2,500 machine guns lost during the German attack were promptly replaced from American ordnance depots.

The problem of transport for supply and evacuation was one which the Germans failed to solve in December 1944. Perhaps the German staffs and commanders had been so long on the defensive that they had forgotten the special transport requirements engendered by offensive operations. In this respect Hitler and Jodl, in their borrowing from 1918, failed to remember Ludendorff who, when preparing to construct the mobile attack divisions for the German offensives, stated that the shortage of horses was the single most important problem in mounting the German attacks. Truck wastage through mechanical failure and combat attrition had been extremely heavy all through 1944, and it is estimated that the new trucks coming off the production lines numbered less than half those destroyed in the field during the same period. Not only were there too few trucks but many divisions were equipped with poor, worn-out booty vehicles that simply fell by the wayside along the bad roads of the Ardennes and had to be abandoned because there were no repair parts. At one time the German armies had been able to rely on the railroad system as the backbone of army transport. From the beginning of good flying weather on 23 December this was no loner possible and by 27 December it may be concluded that the offensive in the main was fed and armed by a road transport system quite unequal to the load forced upon it.

When it is remembered that some of the German divisions in the Ardennes had more horses than the German infantry division of 1918, one has a clearer picture of the supply problem. Resupply was accomplished over very long distances, often clear back to the Rhine, over bad roads which could not be kept in repair, and with much transport geared to horsepower which sickened and died. The heavy snowfalls on the supply roads over the Eifel, particularly after 24 December, coupled with the damage done by Allied air attack at road centers and against moving supply columns are reflected in German estimates that rated road capacities were reduced in fact by at least a third. From Christmas on, some of the supply trains from forward combat units were going back as far as Bonn for ammunition and supplies. On the last day of the year the Panzer Lehr commander ruefully noted that a supply train he had sent to Merlscheid near St. Vith, on 25 December had not yet returned.

In some respects the American transport system opposed an enemy system which had many of the outdated characteristics of 1918. Not only did the American divisions have a very large number of vehicles and trailers organic to the unit, but the number of line of communications trucks and trains available in the forward area was enormous. Perhaps even more important, the movement of American ground transport was unaffected by harassment and attack from the air. The First Army moved more than 48,000 vehicles to the battle zone during the period 17-26 December, and the XII Corps used only two roads to move 11,000 vehicles in four days over a distance of 100 miles. In contrast to the bitter German experience, the American tactical and supply moves seldom were beset by road stoppages and traffic jams, except, of course, in the initial hours of the German penetration. Although it is manifestly true that the Germans made good intelligence usage of the American radio traffic control net, this was balanced by the speed and certainty with which American transport moved.

One may also contrast the tactical availability of the great American supply complex which had been built up east of the Meuse with that prepared by the Germans east of the Rhine River. The German offensive forced the Americans away from the forward truck-heads, with their limited capacity, back on the almost unlimited resources available at railheads. Certainly there was some danger involved in the maintenance of the great supply depots so close to the uncertain battle line. Brig. Gen. Robert M. Littlejohn was ordered on three occasions to evacuate the big depots at Liège, but instead simply brought in more supplies. American supply officers seem to have learned something about logistic flexibility as a result of the pursuit operations across France in the summer of 1944. Finally, the much criticized weight of the American logistic "tail" paid off during the Ardennes, for there always was enough extra transport to meet unusual demands for supply and troop movement.

Despite the decline in the production of liquid fuel during 1944, Hitler was able to amass a POL reserve for the Ardennes offensive which equaled that available to the German armies on the eve of the Allied invasion, and the final figure of the POL allocated to Army Group B was over four million gallons. Using the German measure of one "consumption unit" as the amount of fuel required to move all the vehicles in a formation a distance of sixty-three miles, it may be reckoned that of the five consumption units requested by Model only one and one-half to two were at corps dumps on 16 December; yet there may have been as much as nine or ten consumption units available at railheads near the Rhine River.

The course of the campaign showed at least three errors in German planning. POL distribution failed to move with the same speed as the armored advance. The bad terrain and weather encountered in the Ardennes reduced the mileage gained from a tankful of fuel by one-half. And, finally, the expectation that the spearheads would move in part on captured gasoline was mistakenly optimistic. Army Group B

POL consumption reached a peak of close to 2,000 cubic meters on 18 December, but by 23 December the daily usage rate was about half that figure. In other words, the supply of liquid fuel failed to keep pace with the tactical demand.

There are two phases in the history of German liquid fuel supply during the Ardennes campaign—the one before and the one after 23 December when the Allies took to the air over the battle zone. During the first phase the movement of POL was impeded by bad roads and traffic congestion. Vehicles failed or ran out of fuel and were abandoned by the roadside, thus reducing the total transport tonnage for bringing POL forward. The attempts to introduce horse-drawn supply or artillery columns into the stream of motorized traffic during the first days of the offensive greatly slowed the distribution system. As early as 20 December the 12th SS Panzer Division, scheduled as one of the leading formations in the Sixth Panzer Army advance, was brought to a halt because there was no fuel except a few gallons for the mechanized reconnaissance battalion. On 21 December the 2d SS Panzer Division was ordered to relieve the 560th Volks Grenadier Division in the battle at Fraiture but was unable to move for thirty-six hours because there was no POL. In the Fifth Panzer Army there were reports as early as 19 December of a "badly strained" fuel situation. Three days later Luettwitz, the XLVII Panzer Corps commander, told Manteuffel that the advance of his armor was "gravely endangered" because of the failure of fuel supply. During this phase there seems to have been considerable pirating, in a disorderly manner, from the forward POL dumps. Eventually German commanders learned to send a reconnaissance detail to the fuel dumps before they committed their supply trains in a fuel-consuming trip to what might be a dry supply point. It can be concluded that the German offensive already was seriously crippled by the failure of transport and the POL distributing system before the Allied Jabos entered the fight.

The supply phase after 23 December is characterized by Allied fighter-bombers pounding roads and supply points while snowdrifts stopped the movement of traffic through the Eifel. The POL shortage in the Sixth Panzer Army seems to have assumed drastic proportions in the period 23 to 25 December. The Fifth Panzer Army was in dire straits by 24 December, in part because of the arrival of armored and mechanized formations which had come into the army area without reserve fuel. Even when bad flying weather blunted the edge of the Allied air attack, the sporadic stoppage of supply movement at the ground level continued. By the end of December three of the five divisions in the XLVII Panzer Corps were practically immobile. All this while, however, the 10th SS Panzer Division of the OKW Reserve sat in an assembly area just west of Bonn with a total POL load of eight consumption units in its train. Quite obviously the German problem had been transport rather than an overall shortage of fuel.

There is no indication that American units suffered seriously from the lack of POL, although, of course, there was always the tactical difficulty of withdrawing from contact with the enemy at night for fuel resupply, particularly in the more mobile phases of the campaign. Some American gasoline was lost to Peiper, but the total amounted to probably no more than 100,000 gallons. It is known that Peiper's supply officer had a map of American POL installations, but this did Peiper little good. Between 17 and 19 December American supply troops successfully evacuated over three million gallons of POL from the Spa-Stavelot area. The biggest Allied loss to the enemy was 400,000 gallons of gasoline, destroyed on 17 December by a V-1 strike at Liège.

The Germans "fueled" their horses with greater ease than their motor vehicles. Straw and hay were plentiful in the area, although an order had to be put out forbidding the use of straw as bedding material for the troops, and those units which came late into an area found foraging sparse. Potatoes and livestock were taken from the local population in large quantities, but the supply of breadstuff was barely adequate, chiefly because of troubles in transporting bulk flour to the field bakery units. It was necessary therefore to reduce the bread ration to all but frontline troops. The Americans, as usual, were well fed during this operation. The only notable change was the new demand for the compact K ration in place of the augmented ration, with its fresh meat and coffee beans, which had been issued during the slow-moving fighting in the autumn.

In transporting their wounded, the Germans experienced grave difficulty. By the close of December the Fifth Panzer Army was having to haul its casualties clear back to Andernach on the Rhine at the expense of those freshly wounded in the firing line. The Americans lost a number of hospitals, medics, and wounded to the German spearhead formations, but on the whole were able to maintain a high standard of medical care, even in this fluid battle. In accordance with accepted Army practice both the First and Third Armies were equipped with hospitals to take a peak casualty load. On 1 January 1945, there were a total of nearly 9,000 vacant beds in the hospitals of the two armies.

Despite the fame of the German Army staff corps as masters of supply and logistics, a reputation which dated as far back as the Franco-Prussian War, the Ardennes Campaign showed little evidence of this earlier prowess except in the management of military rail transport and its rapid rehabilitation under attack. Perhaps the German staff work in the field was as good as ever, although there is evidence that it had deteriorated in the SS formations. But quite clearly the wishful thinking in which Hitler and the OKW staff indulged was no substitute for rigorous logistical analysis and planning, and these higher personalities, not the field commanders, dictated the control and management of the logistic support for the German armies in the Ardennes. One must conclude that the German offensive of December 1944 lacked the matériel and service support necessary to achieve any real measure of success and, furthermore, that Hitler and the OKW staff understood neither the importance of supply nor its effective organization.

The Turning Point in the Ardennes

When did the attacking German armies lose the initiative in their drive to cross the Meuse, and why? Surprise, the first element in successful offensive operations, had been attained by the attacker on 16 December. The defense had been surprised by the speed of the initial assault, by the weight of the attack, and, later protestations to the contrary, the American commands—both high and low—had been deceived as to the point of the attack. The German assault forces ruptured the American defenses on the first day of the advance. but not quite as planned. In the Sixth Panzer Army sector the German staffs had expected that the infantry assault would penetrate to a depth of three to five miles by noon, thus assuring a complete breakthrough within the first twenty-four hours of the offensive. This objective was not achieved. On the extreme north flank the LXVII Corps made no progress in its drive to reach the Vesdre River in front of Eupen, never succeeded in penetrating the Monschau position, and eventually gave over this attack to bring the German north flank infantry screen forward. The assault to punch a hole at Losheim went so slowly that the spearhead armor of the 1st SS Panzer Division was delayed at its line of departure for at least six hours longer than anticipated.

The first-day attack by the German center had been predicated on minimal initial delays for bridge crossings within three or four hours; the minimum actual time of construction proved to be seven to eight hours. Furthermore, no account had been taken of delays which might be incurred on the west banks as the result of American demolitions, bomb cratering, and the like. On top of this the German motorized assault as it left the river line, was forced onto exit roads which brought the Germans squarely against organized American strongpoints. The adverse impact of this collection of terrain and tactical factors is best attested by the experience of the armored reconnaissance battalions leading the 26th Volks Grenadier assault: these formations were delayed at the river by ineffectual bridge builders, they were slowed on the Gemünd-Hosingen road by bomb craters and abatis, and, when they reached the western ridge, the American defense of Hosingen forced a long halt and ultimate detour. This episode proved to be only one of numerous delays on the Fifth Panzer assault front, and that army, as a result, did not reach its first-day objectives until after midnight of 17 December.

On the German south wing the Seventh Army had even more trouble with its bridges than the northern neighbor. The green and ill-equipped 212th Volks Grenadier Division took forty-eight hours to throw a 16-ton bridge over the Sure, and along the entire army front the infantry elements were forced to carry the assault for the first three days without direct heavy weapon support. The LXXX Corps, fighting to bring the left wing of the Seventh Army into a favorable blocking position, did not reach its first-day objectives until the evening of 19 December, At the close of the first day, then, it can be said that the German attack had ruptured the American positions at a number of points but had not done much to widen the gaps so created and had failed signally to destroy the tactical continuity of the defensive positions at the shoulders of the assault zone.

The exploitation phase of the offensive may be timed from the hour at which Peiper's armor shook itself loose from the melee at Losheim and broke into the open, that is, 0400 on 17 December. Peiper's progress, therefore, is a good measure of the speed, planned and actual, of the German advance. The 1st SS Panzer Division and at least one other armored division of the Sixth Panzer Army were supposed to be across the rugged plateau of the Hohes Venn by the close of the second day, with their leading elements along a north-south line through Spa and Stavelot. In 1940 a German armored column had covered this distance in nine hours, albeit with very slight resistance, and a second column, following the more circuitous route now taken by Peiper, consumed only a day and a half on the road. Despite all the delays on the 16th, Peiper did reach Stavelot on the night of 17 December, but at Stavelot he was forced to halt—a marked departure from the German experience of 1940. Recall as well that the second of the Sixth Panzer Army's breakthrough armored divisions, the 12th SS Panzer still was involved in a bitter fight back on the line of scrimmage at the end of this second day. The Fifth Panzer Army was in even worse case: no armored exploitation was yet in progress by the night of 17 December.

If Hitler and OKW expected the armored columns to reach the Meuse in forty-eight hours, as has been reported, the German offensive was seriously behind schedule at the close of the second day of combat. If, as the German Army commanders agree, Model's own plan called for the Meuse to be reached and crossed on the fourth day of the offensive, then it seems reasonable to assume—as the Army commanders did assume—that the lost time could be regained. The immediate problem was to get armored columns into the open and into the lead—thus Rundstedt's order on the late evening of 17 December that the armor must at least keep up with the foot elements.

On the third day of the attack the German armor began to acquire momentum; the greatest gains made by the armored spearhead columns actually were achieved during the night of 18 December. With the way west thus clearing, the German mass maneuver behind the armored columns picked up speed on 19 December, this day representing the most rapid movement of the entire offensive. Yet even now the bulk of German armored weight was not forward nor operating with the speed and mobility expected of armor. For this reason the Fifth Panzer Army was assigned the task of exploitation, in place of the Sixth, on 20 December.

The offensive had gone out of control, and now would follow a series of haphazard improvisations. Why had the German armored mass failed to come forward as planned? These reasons seem paramount:

The initial American defense had been more tenacious than anticipated; complete and rapid rupture of the defensive positions had not been achieved. Tactical support and logistic transport had not kept pace with the advance of the combat formations. Close operational control and fluidity of movement for the mass of maneuver required free use of the road net in the salient. This had been denied the attacker, most notably at Bastogne and St. Vith but at other points as well. The flanks of the salient had not been brought forward to keep pace with the drive in the center; the shoulders of the salient had jammed. The operational build-up of the forces in the salient had taken place so slowly as to deny real depth to the attack. The tactical reaction of the American forces and their commitment of reserves had been more rapid than anticipated.

The German failure to build up the attacking forces in the salient must be attributed to Hitler and the OKW staff since they controlled the operational reserves set aside for the Ardennes offensive. Nonetheless, there is some reason to believe that the German High Command held back the OKW Reserve divisions because of the physical difficulties attendant on feeding more troops and vehicles onto the crowded, tortuous, muddy roads during the breakdown of the German transport system in the first days of the attack.

Rundstedt made his first request for troops from the OKW Reserve on 17 December, asking for the Fuehrer Begleit Brigade, which was in readiness only thirty-five miles to the rear. He was given the 9th SS Panzer Division, which was seventy miles from the battlefield, and it required three separate petitions from Rundstedt to change the Fuehrer's mind. Subsequent requests by OB WEST for the release of two armored divisions scheduled for early commitment, the 10th SS Panzer and 11th Panzer, produced no result until 23 December when two Volks Grenadier divisions were brought west in their place. Even these Volks Grenadier formations had a string attached by OKW. When, on 26 December, Model asked for a free hand with all OKW reserves, specifically mentioning the 10th SS Panzer and 11th Panzer plus three or four armored divisions from other theaters, he was given a stone—the two Volks Grenadier divisions brought up on the 23d.

The one thing that a high command can do in modern war to influence the battle once it is joined is to allocate reserves. Hitler and Jodl repeated in 1944 the mistake made by Ludendorff during the Amiens battle of 1918 when the latter failed to throw in the reserves needed to exploit the unexpected success of the Eighteenth Army.

Specifically, Hitler and the OKW staff failed to recognize that the only real hope of success, after the Sixth Panzer Army failure, was to reinforce Manteuffel and the Fifth.

The story on the American side was quite different, surprisingly so to Hitler and his entourage who held as an article of faith that the American commanders, for political reasons, would make no major troop movements, particularly if these involved the British, without prior reference to the White House and Downing Street. This attitude probably explains the German estimate that no major units would be committed by the defense until the third day and that the Allied buildup of a counterattack force would be made west of the Meuse. Not only did the German planners fail to comprehend the degree of initiative that training and tradition have placed in the hands of American corps and army commanders, they also misunderstood the American doctrine, largely unwritten but universally accepted, that major formations having no prebattle relationship may, under fluid conditions, unite on the field after the battle is joined. Hitler seems to have made another and important personal miscalculation, namely that the weak German forces holding the sectors of the Western Front north and south of the Ardennes still retained sufficient strength to grapple the American divisions opposite them, and that the Allied commanders would therefore hesitate to weaken their forces in these sectors by stripping away divisions to meet the German attack.

When did the German armies lose the initiative in the Ardennes? As early as 20 December there are indications that small clouds of niggling doubt were present in the minds of some of the German field commanders, this because of the Sixth Panzer Army's failure to adhere to the offensive timetable. By 24 December the crippling impact of Allied air attack, resumed the previous day as the weather broke, was clearly discernible. Then, too, the course of the ground battle on that date was equally adverse. The counterattack by the Third Army menaced the whole southern flank of the German salient, while the XLVII Panzer Corps, now leading the Fifth Panzer drive, was so lone and exposed that the corps commander recommended a withdrawal of his forward elements until such time as the German flanks at the tip of the salient could be covered. This combination of threats in the air and on the ground led the Fifth Panzer Army commander to conclude on 24 December that "the objective could no longer be attained."

It is a truism that morale is a governing factor in war. Christmas in the Ardennes, 1944, very clearly is a case in point. Brig. Gen. S. L. A. Marshall has graphically described the mood of the American troops in Bastogne on the Holy Evening and shown the somber aspect of nostalgia on the part of men engaged in the grim business of war, far from home and loved ones. But in the German camp the sixth Christmas of the war seems to have made a truly indelible impression. The field postmaster for Luettwitz" corps remarks on the decline in the amount of Christmas mail reaching the front—particularly gift parcels. The German Army newspaper bitterly features a story on the Christmas gift presented by a Spanish restaurateur to Goering—a large supply of caviar. And the commander of the 276th Volks Grenadier Division, whose unit fought its hardest battle on Christmas Day, expresses the hope that in the ultimate withdrawal to the cover of the West Wall his troops will be able to re-capture the Christmas spirit.

The German Christmas traditionally was celebrated on two days, the 25th and 26th, and at this emotional nadir of war-weary soldiery the German armies in the Ardennes sustained a series of crushing reverses: the left wing of the Seventh Army was driven back to the Sauer River, over which it had crossed ten days before; the German ring around Bastogne was broken by Patton's troops; the 2d Panzer Division received orders to escape from the Celles pocket; and throughout the day of the 26th a developing "crisis" in supply and communications was noted in the journal at the headquarters of OB WEST. At 1915 on 26 December General Krebs, Model's chief of staff, made an appraisal of the German situation, "Today a certain culminating point [has been reached]."

It may be concluded that by the evening of 26 December the initiative had passed from German to American hands. Before this time the American and Allied forces had reacted to German designs and had abandoned their own. From this point in time the German attacker would be off balance and would take a series of false steps (notably at Bastogne) which were elicited by the operations of his opponent and divergent from the assigned larger objective.

Even at the time there was recognition in both camps that 26 December had been the day of decision. On the 27th the German press and radio abandoned the headline treatment of the Ardennes to feature news from Greece and Budapest. This same day the SHAEF propaganda bureau issued instructions that Liège, obviously no longer in danger, should be shown as the goal of the German offensive.

There seems to have been a slight resurgence of forced optimism in the higher German field headquarters toward the end of December when the appearance of more troops and guns gave some flicker of hope that Bastogne finally might be captured. But this optimism, if it was anything more than a disciplined and soldierly facade, quickly faded. On the last day of December the OB WEST journal notes that if Bastogne cannot be taken "that is the end of the offensive operation." Hitler, no matter what exhortations he may have dispatched to Model and Rundstedt, had turned his attention away from the Ardennes. On 29 December Rundstedt received a message that sixty-three new tanks had come off the assembly line but that OKW (for which read Hitler) would decide whether personnel replacements and artillery should be sent OB WEST in their stead—precisely the first step always taken by the Fuehrer when abandoning a military venture and denuding one fighting front to reinforce another.

The Place of the Ardennes Offensive in World War II

The German attack in the Ardennes was to be the last in the long series of great offensives and military adventures initiated by Hitler's Third Reich in September 1939. The subsequent attempts at counterattacks in Alsace and on the Lake Balaton front were bloody military divertissements occasioned by Hitler, nothing more. There would be days of stubborn fighting in the Ardennes during January 1945, but the roads back over the Eifel led straight to the decimation and collapse of the German armies on the banks of the Oder River, along the Danube, in the Ruhr pocket, and, at last, to the bunkers of Berlin.

What was the true military purpose of the Ardennes offensive? It has been alleged by survivors of the German High Command that this operation was intended to re-establish the military prestige of the Third Reich, carry its people through the grueling sixth winter of war, and win a favorable bargaining position for a suitable and acceptable peace. It seems more probable, from all that is known of Hitler's thought processes in these last months of his life, that, as in February 1918, the German decision was not between war and peace but between defense and attack. Are the military and political reasons set forth by Hitler for his choice of an offensive on the Western Front, and in the Ardennes sector, to be accepted at face value? History will never know. But there is the strong possibility that Hitler and his top generals were motivated by the same impulse which triggered so many of the bloody and useless offensives of World War I—to seize the initiative for its own sake without a viable strategic objective in view.

In late December German propagandists claimed that the object of the Ardennes offensive had been to cripple the attack capabilities of the Allied armies and chew up their divisions east of the Meuse. There also is considerable evidence that Model, and perhaps Rundstedt, accepted this as a reasonable tactical objective in the operations from Christmas onward. The attainment of this goal, to chew up Allied divisions and dull the cutting edge of the American armies, was achieved in only limited fashion. The attack of twenty-nine German divisions and brigades destroyed one American infantry division as a unit, badly crippled two infantry divisions, and cut one armored combat command to pieces. The total of American battle casualties reported for the period 16 December through 2 January (although these probably were incomplete returns) numbered 41,315 officers and men, of which 4,138 were known to be killed in action, 20,231 were wounded in action, and 16,946 were reported missing. During the same period the American formations in the Ardennes received 31,505 replacements, or "reinforcements" as these individual soldiers now were named. The matériel losses inflicted by German action represented only a temporary diminution in the fighting strength of a few of the American divisions and normally were replaced within a fortnight.

What all this cost the Wehrmacht is impossible to say. It is known that losses in matériel were very high—and these no longer could be made good. The only general indication of German casualties is found in railroad reports which show that about 67,000 troops were evacuated from the Army Group B area by rail during December. This figure, of course, would include some of the battle casualties from the earlier fighting east of Aachen, as well as disease cases. A number of German division commanders have made personal estimates of the casualties suffered by their own divisions during the last half of December, and in the cases of those formations continually in the line from 16 or 17 December the average is between two and three thousand "combat effectives" lost per division. Whatever the true number of casualties may have been on both sides, it is a fair assessment that over-all, in this particular instance, the troops on the offensive sustained heavier losses than those on the defensive.

Detailed analysis of the ebb and flow of battle shows that the German armies in the Ardennes never came close to the narrow margin between success and failure. The fortunes of war never were put in precarious balance as they had been in the spring of 1918, and it is not surprising that General Eisenhower refused to issue a "Backs to the Wall" order of the day like that wrung from Haig on April 1918.

Nevertheless, in December 1944 there was an early, emotional Allied reaction to the first speedy triumphs of the German armies which conceived of the attack as being another, albeit late, irruption of the military might which had reached out to the Atlantic and the Caucasus, the Sahara, and the Arctic Circle. On the other hand, a decade after the close of World War II, still living members of the higher German commands would classify the Wehrmacht of late 1944 as a "paper tiger." The history of the Ardennes Campaign, as recounted in the present volume, shows that neither one of these extremes was true. Probably the American war correspondent, Drew Middleton, most closely approximated the truth when, in the first days of the

Ardennes battle, he characterized the offensive as "the Indian summer" of German military might.

In the long view of history the decision to attack in the Ardennes represents only another—and risky—attempt to solve the old German dilemma of fighting a major war on two fronts. Hitler deliberately assumed the risk involved in weakening the Eastern Front so that a powerful blow could be struck in the west. When, on 14 December, he told his generals that German industry had been preparing for the Ardennes offensive for months, he meant this quite literally. Of the total production of armored fighting vehicles which came out of German assembly plants in November and December 1944, the Western Front received 2,277 while only 919 went to the East. As late as 5 January 1945 all the German armies on the Eastern Front possessed only two-thirds the number of panzers employed in the Ardennes. Equally important, of course, was Hitler's decision on 20 November to shift the Luftwaffe fighter strength to the Western Front. This diversion of matériel to the west (which began as early as September and included artillery, Wefers, tractors, machine guns, and many other items) was accompanied by a reallocation of military manpower. On 1 December 1944, the total number of combat effectives under OB WEST command was 416,713, and one month later 1,322,561 effectives were carried on the OB WEST rosters.

There seems to have been an early recognition on the part of the higher German theater commanders that Hitler's "intuition" had led to a mistaken choice between operations on the two major fronts. General Westphal later alleged that Rundstedt personally addressed himself to the Fuehrer on 22 December with a plea that the Ardennes offensive be brought to a halt in order to reinforce the Eastern Front.

Guderian, directly charged with operations against the Russians, used the occasion of official visits on Christmas Eve and New Year's Day to petition Hitler for the movement of troops from the west to the east. It is said that at the end of December, in the Ardennes headquarters, "everybody looked with dismay to the east where the big Russian offensive was about to begin any day." Hitler stubbornly refused to accede to all these requests, even after the Allied counterattack on 3 January began to collapse the German salient. Inexplicably he waited until 8 January to start the Sixth Panzer Army moving for the east—this only four days before the commencement of the Russian winter offensive.

The proximity in time of the German Ardennes offensive and the wholesale offensive of the Red Armies on 12 January would have untoward results, not only for the Third Reich, but for the relations between east and west in the postwar era. In February 1945, Stalin issued an order of the day acclaiming the recent victories on the Oder front and boasting that "The success of this [Soviet] drive resulted in breaking the German attack in the West." Unfortunately, and unwisely, Winston Churchill opened the door to this and a flood of similar Russian propaganda claims by addressing a telegram to Stalin on 6 January 1945, in which he personally asked for Soviet help by the prompt beginning of a major offensive. Only a few years later, representatives of the USSR engaged in negotiations on American claims for the repayment of wartime shipping loans would allege that these debts had been canceled when the Russian armies "saved" the American forces in the Ardennes. Postwar Russian propaganda in this same vein reached a peak in a series of articles by Col. N. Nikiforov alleging that the Soviet attack in January 1945 "averted the danger of the rout of the Anglo-American armies."

Was the risk assumed by Hitler and his senior military advisers in the Ardennes offensive a valid one? Field Marshals Jodl and Keitel, the artisans but not the architects of this venture, gave a joint answer shortly before their execution: "The criticism whether it would have been better to have employed our available reserves in the East rather than in the West, we submit to the judgment of history."

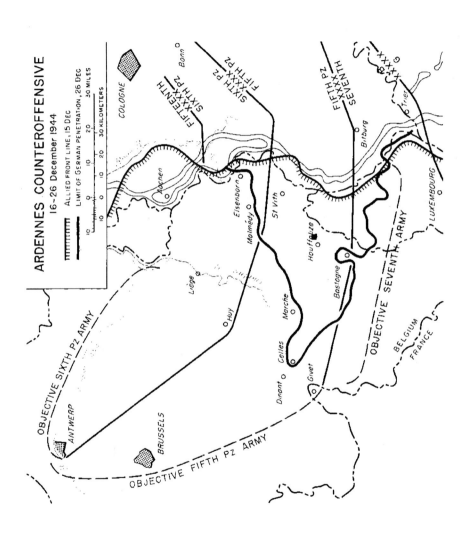

ARDENNES COUNTEROFFENSIVE
16–26 December 1944

|||||| ALLIED FRONT LINE, 15 DEC
——— LIMIT OF GERMAN PENETRATION, 26 DEC

0   10   20   30 MILES
0 10 20 30 KILOMETERS

COLOGNE

Bonn

FIFTEENTH PZ
SIXTH PZ

SIXTH PZ
FIFTH PZ

Aachen

FIFTH PZ
SEVENTH

Eisenborn

Bitburg

Malmédy

St Vith

Trier

Houffalize

LUXEMBOURG

Liège

Bastogne

OBJECTIVE SEVENTH ARMY

Huy

Marche

BELGIUM

FRANCE

OBJECTIVE SIXTH PZ ARMY

Dinant Celles

Givet

ANTWERP

BRUSSELS

OBJECTIVE FIFTH PZ ARMY

CPSIA information can be obtained at www.ICGtesting.com
Printed in the USA
LVOW030921301111

257143LV00006B/179/P